human resources and labor markets

labor and manpower in the american economy

human resources and labor markets

SECOND EDITION

SAR A. LEVITAN
George Washington University
GARTH L. MANGUM
University of Utah
RAY MARSHALL
University of Texas

Harper & Row, Publishers
New York, Evanston, San Francisco, London

Sponsoring Editor: John Greenman
Project Editor: Eleanor Castellano
Designer: Michel Craig
Production Supervisor: Francis X. Giordano
Compositor: V & M Typographical, Inc.
Printer and Binder: Halliday Lithograph Corporation
Art Studio: Vantage Art Inc.

HUMAN RESOURCES AND LABOR MARKETS: Labor and Manpower in
the American Economy, Second Edition

Library of Congress Cataloging in Publication Data
Levitan, Sar A
  Human resources and labor markets.

  Bibliography: p.
  Includes index.
  1. Labor supply—United States. 2. Manpower policy
—United States. 3. Labor economics. I. Mangum,
Garth L., joint author. II. Marshall, Ray, joint
author. III. Title.
HD5724.L4228 1976   331.1'0973   75-22175
ISBN 0-06-043999-8

To Brita, Marion, and Pat

contents

PREFACE   xix

1

HUMAN RESOURCE DEVELOPMENT IN PERSPECTIVE   1
THE SCOPE   2
THE SETTING   3
HUMAN RESOURCES IN FLUX   5
NOTES   6

part one
LABOR MARKET DYNAMICS   7

WORK LIFE, WORK TIME, AND MOBILITY   9
THE MEANING OF WORK   10
WORK LIFE: START LATER, RETIRE EARLIER   14
Men: Shorter Work Life Despite Longer Life   14
Women: More Work and Longer Life Expectancy   15
WORK TIME: FEWER HOURS, MORE LEISURE TIME   17
Workers Bypassed by Shorter Workweek   19
Leisure That Is Productive Work: Unpaid Volunteers   20
WORKERS' MOBILITY: THE AMERICAN DREAM OF
MOVING UP THE JOB LADDER   20
Upward Occupational Mobility   21
Upward Mobility for Blacks   23
Geographical Mobility   24
Removing Impediments to Mobility   24
NOTES   25

3

LABOR FORCE PARTICIPATION AND UNEMPLOYMENT   27
OVERALL SHIFTS IN LABOR FORCE   28
EDUCATION AND LABOR FORCE ACTIVITY   32
RISING EXPECTATIONS AND MULTIWORKER FAMILIES   33
"ADDITIONAL" WORKERS AND THE BUSINESS CYCLE   34
LABOR MARKET PATHOLOGIES: UNEMPLOYMENT,
UNDEREMPLOYMENT, AND SHORTAGES   35
The Historical Perspective   35
Unemployment and Underemployment   38
The Causes of Unemployment   38
Cyclical Unemployment   38
Other Types of Unemployment   39
Characteristics of the Unemployed   42
Labor Shortages and Surpluses   46
UNEMPLOYMENT IS ONLY ONE DIMENSION
OF INADEQUACY   47
NOTES   49

4

SHIFTING COMPOSITION OF EMPLOYMENT   52
PERIPHERAL WORKERS   52
Voluntary Part-Time or Part-Year Work   53
The Secondary Labor Market   55
YOUTH   56
THE GOLDEN YEARS?   59
INDUSTRIAL AND OCCUPATIONAL SHIFTS   61
Shift to Service-Producing, White-Collar Employment   61
Industrial Distribution   63
Occupational Distribution   64
THE GROWTH OF PRODUCTIVITY   69
NOTES   75

WOMEN AT WORK   77
FACTORS AFFECTING FEMALE WORK   78
Husbands' Earnings   78
Female Family Heads   79
Day-Care Facilities   80
Education and Race   82
PATTERNS AND AGES OF WORK FOR WOMEN   83
DISCRIMINATION   85

IMPROVING THE EMPLOYMENT STATUS OF WOMEN   88
NOTES   89

MEASUREMENT AND FORECASTING   91
MEASUREMENT OF THE LABOR FORCE—
MANPOWER STATISTICS   91
Major Data Sources   92
Manpower Statistics Before World War II   92
SOCIAL PROBLEMS AND STATISTICAL DEVELOPMENT   93
The Gordon Committee   94
Concepts and Sources: Their Current Status   94
Program Needs   98
FORECASTING MANPOWER SUPPLIES AND
REQUIREMENTS   99
The Nature of Manpower Projections   99
Projecting Manpower Supplies and Requirements   100
Uses of Manpower Projections   101
Labor Supplies in 1980–1985   103
Some Implications   105
Occupational Projections   106
The State of the Art   109
NOTES   110

THE STRUCTURE OF LABOR MARKETS   112
ROLE OF THEORY   112
DEFINITIONS OF LABOR MARKETS   114
THE NEOCLASSICAL THEORY   115
THE MODEL   116
THEORY OF LABOR SUPPLY   117
HUMAN CAPITAL AND BENEFIT-COST ANALYSIS   120
EXTERNAL AND INTERNAL LABOR MARKETS   120
MANPOWER IMPLICATIONS OF INTERNAL
LABOR MARKETS   125
DUAL LABOR MARKETS   126
RADICALS   128
MULTIPLE LABOR MARKETS   130
The Professional Labor Market   131
Mainstream Labor Markets   131
The Marginal Labor Market   132
The Submarginal Labor Market   132
OTHER LABOR MARKET IMPERFECTIONS   136

SUMMARY AND CONCLUSIONS   138
NOTES   139

part two
PREPARATION FOR EMPLOYMENT   141

EDUCATION IN HUMAN RESOURCE DEVELOPMENT   143
THE EMERGENCE OF EDUCATION AS A
WORK PREREQUISITE   144
EDUCATION OF THE LABOR FORCES: FUTURE PROSPECTS   148
EDUCATION AND EMPLOYABILITY   151
EDUCATION AND THE TRANSITION FROM
SCHOOL TO WORK   153
THE CONSPICUOUS CONSUMPTION OF EDUCATION   157
THE EDUCATIONAL INSTITUTIONS FOR
MANPOWER DEVELOPMENT   158
RETURNS TO INVESTMENT IN EDUCATION   162
Measuring the Returns   163
Critiquing the Concept   164
Usefulness of the Theory   166
NOTES   168

THE ROLE OF HIGHER EDUCATION   170
COSTS AND RETURNS ON INVESTMENT IN
HIGHER EDUCATION   171
ENROLLMENT IN HIGHER-EDUCATION INSTITUTIONS   175
OUTLOOK FOR COLLEGE GRADUATES   177
The Supply of College Graduates   177
Supply and Demand Relationships   178
Teachers   178
Health Manpower   179
Natural Scientists and Engineers   179
Technicians   180
Women   180
Workers with Postgraduate Degrees   181
Conclusions on the Outlook for College Graduates   185
THE CHARACTER OF THE MARKET FOR
EDUCATED MANPOWER   186

Labor Market Experience of Recent College Graduates   191
Conclusions on the Market for Educated Manpower   193
THE SOCIOECONOMIC STATUS OF COLLEGE STUDENTS   193
The Higher Education of Black Americans   195
CONCLUSION   197
NOTES   197

APPRENTICESHIP AND ON-THE-JOB TRAINING   200
PUBLIC POLICY   200
APPRENTICESHIP ISSUES   204
Limited Understanding of Apprenticeship   204
Adequacy of Apprenticeship   205
Racial Discrimination   207
Union and Employer Attitudes Toward Apprenticeship   209
Standards, Qualifications, and Procedures   211
Characteristics of Apprenticeship Programs   211
ON-THE-JOB TRAINING   213
CONCLUSIONS   216
NOTES   217

THE GOALS OF CAREER EDUCATION   219
A THUMBNAIL DESCRIPTION   219
The Components   220
The Phases   223
CAREER EDUCATION ISSUES   224
Changing Significance of Work   225
Timing of Career Choice   225
Need for Skills Training   226
Need for Change in Traditional School Practice   226
Scope of Career Education   227
The Crowded Curriculum   227
Relationship to Postsecondary Education   228
Relationship to Vocational Education   230
VOCATIONAL EDUCATION   230
Federal Legislation   231
Enrollments   234
Results of Vocational Education   238
Summarizing Current Status   240
CAREER EDUCATION'S PROMISE   240
NOTES   243

part three
REMEDIAL MANPOWER PROGRAMS   245

12

THE EMERGENCE OF MANPOWER PROGRAMS   247
THE FORCES INVOLVED   247
The Long Run   247
The Intermediate Run   248
The Short Run   250
THE PROGRAMS   250
Training the Unemployed   251
Modernizing Vocational Education   253
Declaring War on Poverty   253
Equalizing Employment Opportunity   254
Whence the Jobs?   254
Education for Equality   255
The Job Creation Issue   256
REJECTION OF THE GREAT SOCIETY   260
THE EMERGENCE OF STATE AND LOCAL MANPOWER
EXPERTISE   261
The Concentrated Employment Program   262
The Cooperative Area Manpower Planning System   263
Decentralizing Manpower Programs   264
Comprehensive Manpower Programs   266
The Comprehensive Employment and Training Act of 1973   267
A NEW ERA?   269
NOTES   270

13

THE TECHNIQUES OF PUBLIC MANPOWER PLANNING   271
WHY MANPOWER PLANNING?   271
A TYPOLOGY FOR MANPOWER PLANNING   275
Macromanpower Planning   275
Micromanpower Planning   277
Manpower Program Planning   277
Labor Market Manpower Planning   278
THE STEPS TO PLANNING   280
Establishing Manpower Policy Goals   280
Identifying Barriers   281
Examining Alternatives   281
Setting Objectives   281
Designing and Implementing a Program   282

The Evaluation Step   282
Feedback and Modification   283
APPLICATION TO MANPOWER PROGRAMMING   283
Universe-of-Need Methodology   284
Accessible Job Openings   286
Barriers Assessment   288
The Mix of Services   289
Choosing Among Alternative Service Deliverers   291
Monitoring and Evaluation   291
THE POLITICAL ENVIRONMENT   292
Sources of Influence   292
Potential Contributions   295
The Dangers   297
NOTES   299

14

THE ROLE OF THE PUBLIC EMPLOYMENT SERVICE   301
CHANGING OBJECTIVES AND FUNCTIONS   301
NEW TOOLS FOR THE EMPLOYMENT SERVICE   305
NEW OBJECTIVES AND NEW DIRECTIONS   306
The Employment Service and the Disadvantaged   307
An Electronic Employment Service   309
Labor Exchange Experimentation   312
Closing the Circle   314
LESSONS FROM THE EXPERIENCE   315
The Employment Service as Labor Market Intermediary   316
Service to the Disadvantaged   318
The Computer in Job Matching   319
SUMMARY   320
NOTES   320

15

WORK AND WELFARE   321
THE GROWTH OF WELFARE   321
THE REVOLVING DOOR   325
THE EMPLOYABILITY OF WELFARE MOTHERS   327
WORK AND TRAINING FOR RELIEF RECIPIENTS   329
"Working-off" Public Assistance   329
Antipoverty Work and Training   330
The Work Incentive Program   332
An Assessment   337
ALTERNATIVES FOR THE FUTURE   338
Income-Maintenance Strategies   339

Combining Work and Welfare   340
NOTES   341

LESSONS FROM MANPOWER PROGRAMS   343
PROBING THE LABOR MARKET'S LOWER MARGINS   344
The Structure of Unemployment   344
The Need for Manpower Services   346
The Great Dichotomy   346
The Dual Labor Market   347
THE USEFULNESS OF THE MANPOWER TOOLS   347
Outreach and Assessment   348
Classroom Education and Training   348
OJT and Apprenticeship   350
Work-Experience Training   351
Subsidized Private and Public Employment   351
Supportive Services   352
Placement Services   353
Equal Employment Opportunity   353
Welfare Recipients   354
Research, Demonstration, and Staff Development   354
State and Local Manpower Planning   355
QUERY   361
NOTES   361

part four
MINORITY INCOME AND EMPLOYMENT   363

ECONOMIC THEORY OF RACIAL DISCRIMINATION   365
NEOCLASSICAL THEORY OF DISCRIMINATION   366
CRITIQUE OF THE NEOCLASSICAL THEORY   368
Conception of Discrimination   368
Motives of the Economic Agents   369
Power Relations Among the Agents   370
Institutional Discrimination   371
Wages and Competition   372
AN ALTERNATIVE FORMULATION   376
The Actors   377
Employers   377
White Workers   378

Unions   379
Blacks   380
Environmental Factors   380
CONCLUSIONS   382
NOTES   383

BLACK EMPLOYMENT AND INCOME   385

POPULATION SHIFTS   385
EMPLOYMENT CHANGES   389
UNEMPLOYMENT   391
PROBLEMS OF THE CENTRAL CITIES   394
CAUSES OF BLACK EMPLOYMENT DISADVANTAGES   397
Discrimination   397
Labor Market Conditions   398
Transportation   399
Labor Market Procedures   399
Industry Structure and Skill Requirements   400
MANPOWER PROGRAMS   401
INCOME AND OCCUPATIONAL STRUCTURES   401
CONCLUSIONS   405
NOTES   405

AMERICANS OF SPANISH ORIGIN   406

DEMOGRAPHY, INCOME, AND EDUCATION   407
CHICANOS   412
CHICANO LABOR MARKETS   415
The Southwestern Economy   415
The Border   418
Commuters   420
Agricultural Employment and Public Policy   422
CHICANOS AND MANPOWER POLICY   423
CONCLUSION   424
NOTES   426

THE ISOLATED INDIANS   428

POPULATION AND DEMOGRAPHY   428
SOCIOECONOMIC CONDITIONS   430
EDUCATION   435
LABOR FORCE PARTICIPATION AND EMPLOYMENT   437

OBSTACLES TO ECONOMIC DEVELOPMENT   439
FEDERAL MANPOWER PROGRAMS   441
BIA Manpower Programs   442
Labor Department Efforts   446
TREATING CAUSES RATHER THAN SYMPTOMS   449
NOTES   450

21

COMBATING DISCRIMINATION IN EMPLOYMENT   451
LEGAL AND ADMINISTRATIVE REMEDIES   451
The Civil Rights Act   452
Exerting Leverage in the Marketplace   455
THE CONSTRUCTION INDUSTRY   458
The Apprenticeship Problem   458
Model Cities   460
Patterns of Discrimination   461
QUOTAS AND PREFERENTIAL TREATMENT   462
Affirmative Action Plans   462
Conclusions on Hometown Plans   466
SEGREGATED SENIORITY ROSTERS   469
CONCLUSIONS ON LEGAL REMEDIES   472
CONCLUSIONS ON MINORITY EMPLOYMENT   475
NOTES   476

part five
LABOR MARKETS AND ECONOMIC POLICY   479

22

MANPOWER AND ECONOMIC POLICIES   481
MONETARY AND FISCAL POLICIES   482
Structural Versus Demand-Deficient Unemployment   483
MANPOWER PROGRAMS AS A COUNTERCYCLICAL TOOL   485
THE TRADE-OFF BETWEEN INFLATION
AND UNEMPLOYMENT   489
Shifting the Phillips Curve   491
The Policy Mix   492
INCOMES POLICIES   493
Wartime Controls   494
The Guideposts   496

Peacetime Wage and Price Controls   497
NOTES   500

23

THE ROLE OF UNIONS AND COLLECTIVE BARGAINING   501
THE NATURE OF LABOR MOVEMENTS   501
The Origin of Labor Movements   505
Labor Movements in the Developing Countries   506
FACTORS SHAPING THE AMERICAN LABOR
MOVEMENT   507
Public Support of Collective Bargaining   511
Problems of Collective Bargaining   513
Union Structure   514
THE IMPACT OF UNIONS ON WAGES   516
Conclusion on Unions' Impact on Wages   521
UNIONS, EDUCATION, AND MANPOWER   522
Union Concerns: Manpower and Education   523
Union Training Programs   525
UNIONS AND MANPOWER PROGRAMS   527
Conclusions on Unions and Labor Markets   531
NOTES   533

24

INDUSTRIALIZATION AND RURAL DEVELOPMENT   535
AN OVERVIEW   535
INSTITUTIONS, HUMAN RESOURCE DEVELOPMENT ·
AND INDUSTRIALIZATION   537
Attitudes of Political Leaders   539
Building an Industrial Labor Force   540
THE RELATIONSHIP OF EDUCATION AND
TRAINING TO ECONOMIC GROWTH   543
MANPOWER PROGRAMS AND REGIONAL DEVELOPMENT   544
Regional Development Policy in the United States   545
Marginal Economic Activities   547
RURAL DEVELOPMENT   548
Changes in Rural America   549
Rural Problems   550
Rural Manpower Programs   551
The Adequacy of Manpower Outlays in Rural Areas   552
The Role of Manpower Programs for Rural Development   553
Migration and Relocation   553
CONCLUSION   555
NOTES   556

25

COMPARATIVE MANPOWER POLICIES   557
UNITED KINGDOM   558
Manpower Problems   558
Manpower Programs and Policy   559
NORWAY   562
Manpower Problems   562
Manpower Policy and Programs   563
JAPAN   566
Manpower Problems   568
Manpower Policy and Programs   569
SOVIET UNION   571
Manpower Problems   572
Manpower Policy and Programs   573
SELECTED DEVELOPING COUNTRIES   577
Manpower Characteristics   577
Manpower Problems   579
Manpower Policies for Developing Countries   580
CONCLUSION   581
NOTES   584

EPILOGUE   585

26

ISSUES FOR THE NEXT DECADE   587
SCARCITY AND THE MALTHUSIAN SPECTER   587
PREPARING FOR WORK   588
WORK ATTITUDES   590
ADEQUACY OF EMPLOYMENT   591
WORK AND WELFARE   591
MANPOWER PROGRAMS   592
EQUAL EMPLOYMENT OPPORTUNITY   592
THE ROLE OF GOVERNMENT   593
THE EMERGENCE OF HUMAN RESOURCE POLICY   594
RESPONDING TO CHANGE   597

MANPOWER BIBLIOGRAPHY   599

INDEXES   611

preface

A dozen years of labor in the "vineyards" of manpower policy convinced us that the integration of human resource development, labor market economics, and economic theory had been too long neglected. This second edition of the volume is an early step in that direction.

The days when textbook authors needed only a quill and parchment to prepare a manuscript are long gone. Scholarship does not flow without logistical support from research assistants, administrators, and secretaries. Financial support is vital. Our debts are many. Karen Alderman, Vernon M. Briggs, Jr., Robert Glover, Salem Ghawi, William Johnston, Malcolm Liggett, David Marwick, Robert Murphy, and Joyce Zickler made major contributions. Beverly Anderson, Louise Bond, Sandra Illig, Illa Rowley, Jane Tonn, and Susie Turner moved the words from dictating machine or foolscap to manuscript, improving them in the process. Barbara Pease prepared the volume for publication. Recognition is given to all who have advised us or from whom we have adapted ideas and to the government administrators who have borne our constant probing and querying, but their names are too many to list.

The Ford Foundation has been the major source of support for the activities of two of us over several years and a substantial supporter of the third. Most of the materials herein were prepared during the course of foundation-funded evaluations of federal manpower programs. Much was gathered in projects funded by the Office of Research and Development and the Office of Evaluation of the U.S. Department of Labor, Manpower Administration. Though none of these institutions is in the business of subsidizing textbook writers, their support of other activities made this textbook possible. We offer our gratitude and absolve them of blame.

Ultimately, our greatest debt is to you, the reader, who will use the book. We trust that the experience will be beneficial to you.

The Authors
Labor Day, 1975

human resources
and
labor markets

1
human resource development in perspective

Economists traditionally have identified three factors of production: land, capital, and labor. In the preindustrial society agriculture was the major source of wealth. Production was based on rudimentary skills passed from father to son, crude farming tools, and incremental improvements made by each generation on the "original and indestructable powers of the soil." Capital and labor were wedded to the land, and economic power belonged to those who could control its use.

With the Industrial Revolution, capital became the critical economic factor. It was capital that bought the machinery that, more than skill, accounted for rising productivity. The labor that operated the machines was relatively untrained and easily replaceable. Skill requirements increased as technology became more sophisticated, and workers gained more power by organizing, but capital remained the central factor in the mass-production economy. Government was concerned primarily with ensuring tranquil labor-management relations, and employers with maintaining a dependable labor force; neither displayed much concern with skill development.

In modern society the role of labor as a factor of production is becoming increasingly important. The world in which the bulk of the labor force was devoted to the production of goods is fading, just as did the world in which agriculture dominated the economic scene. The shift from manufacturing to service and information-processing activities and the increasing pace of technological change are making manpower the key ingredient to the nation's well-being and growth. In a service-oriented era the quality, quantity, and utilization of human resources are of central importance. Capital and natural resource endowments are vital

1

factors in advanced countries, but it is the laborer—the human resource—who contributes most to the contemporary "wealth of nations." Human beings, according to Frederick Harbison, "are the active agents who accumulate capital, exploit natural resources, build social, economic, and political organizations, and carry forward national development."[1] Thus expansion and improvement of the work force are the *sine qua non* of continued increases in this output. Labor is the major beneficiary of, as well as the chief contributor to, prosperity and growth: The bulk of the national product is distributed in wages and salaries to individual workers, and expansion of the total product has improved the welfare of these workers.

The scope

Manpower development is the process of preparing people for a productive employment role, contributing to their maximum potential in producing the combination of goods and services preferred by the society. Manpower development is, therefore, central to modern society. It embraces a broad range of areas that are of vital concern to all citizens, not only social scientists and policy formulators. Five main categories of interest can be identified.

Factors affecting the supply of and demand for labor. Demographic forces determine the total pool of available workers, as well as their ages and, to a large extent, their distribution in the labor force. Cultural and economic as well as demographic factors affect the rates of labor force participation—that is, the proportion of able-bodied persons working or looking for work. Even broader social factors affect the worker's level of commitment and the willingness of those outside the labor force to enter the world of work.

Allocation of workers among jobs and jobs among workers. Changes in the industrial and occupational distribution of employment such as the massive decline in the agricultural sector have important implications for the welfare of individuals and for public policy. In geographic areas or occupational categories where workers are in short supply, measures have to be taken to overcome shortages, and in areas or jobs characterized by an oversupply of workers, alternative opportunities may be needed. To the extent that any worker is "underemployed" in a job that does not fully utilize or develop his abilities, measures that would tap his potential would benefit not only the individual but also the whole economy.

Productivity of the work force in its various economic applications. The level of total output and the standard of living it will support depend on the skills and abilities of the labor force. In order to realize the full potential of our nation's human resources and to ensure that each worker reaps a just reward for his labors, it is vital to understand the impact of education, vocational training, work experience, and related factors on the productivity of workers.

Efficiency of labor market institutions in utilizing available human resources. Many workers may be trapped in jobs for which they are overqualified as the result of discrimination or arbitrary credentialing that qualifies workers for jobs on the basis of educational attainment that may be unrelated to performance. Other institutional imperfections may also limit the best match of supply and demand.

Public policy. Government plays an important role in the labor market. Federal manpower programs aimed at increasing the skills and employment opportunities of individuals disadvantaged by discrimination or lack of vocational preparation are one policy tool. Others include labor-management relations, educational programs, and monetary and fiscal policies. The goal of studying human resource development is to provide guidelines for public and private policy that will help develop and utilize the labor force as well as solve related problems such as poverty and racial discrimination.

The setting

Because human resource development deals with such a broad range of subjects, its study requires an understanding of the massive tides of change that are transforming our society and economy. Among the most important of these, at least in terms of their impact on the availability and use of human resources, are the following.

First, continued gains in productivity have led to rising earnings and income, which have been shared in some measure by almost all segments of the population. Affluence has significant implications for the utilization of human resources. For one thing, it means that monetary incentives are less powerful. The law of diminishing returns applies here as elsewhere, so that affluent workers can be expected to opt for leisure over work, to be less satisfied with wage gains alone, and to be unwilling to work in demeaning jobs. Affluence also means that society has greater opportunity and obligation to help those with special needs—to become concerned with the qualitative as well as quantitative aspects of life. As most people improve their incomes, poverty becomes less tolerable and increased welfare efforts more feasible. In turn, as the welfare floor is raised, the boundaries between work and dependence grow hazy, and low-wage earners may drop out of the work force if they can qualify for a more attractive income maintenance program.

A second major development is the accelerated pace of technological change. Many thousands of jobs are being eliminated annually as new techniques of production or new patterns of demand emerge and even more jobs are created. But such new jobs usually require a higher level of skill, so that workers displaced by technological change rarely qualify for the opportunities it creates. Overall, workers are increasingly pressed to demonstrate educational competence and flexibility in adapting to the job situation. But there persists a vast and probably growing number of repetitive and dull, though physically undemanding, jobs that have resulted from mechanization. Manpower policies can cushion the transitions of displaced workers and help provide the skills to meet new needs. Efforts can also be made to increase the attractiveness of employment or at least widen the opportunities for upward mobility.

A third significant development is the drastic redistribution of population and industry. Urbanization has proceeded at a rapid pace, so that over two-thirds of the U.S. population now reside in metropolitan areas. Rural outmigration continues as agricultural employment declines, and this adds relatively untrained workers to the urban labor forces. Racial and ethnic minorities tend to concentrate in the central cities, while the majority of people who have greater opportunities flee to the suburbs. Those who are locked in the central city by low income or racial discrimination face sustained job shortages. Manpower policy can recognize and deal with these locational changes, so that workers can be matched with available jobs as effectively as possible.

Fourth, the progress of racial minorities toward equal employment opportunity has been significant over the past decade, but continued pressure will be needed to finish the task. Blacks, Chicanos, Indians, and others are still denied the full measure of opportunities to develop their abilities and to compete freely in the labor market. Manpower programs and policies have played and can continue to play an important role in analyzing the problems of minorities and in implementing measures to assist them.

A final significant development is the rapid growth of government functions. Though questions may be raised about big government's accountability to the governed, its responsibilities continue to grow. Governmental support of programs designed to improve the employability and job opportunities of disadvantaged workers increased tenfold during the 1960s. The expansion of these governmental efforts has been halted during the 1970s, however. These changes were accompanied by the decentralization of responsibility from national to state and local governments. But the millions left out of the economic mainstream continue to demand society's attention, and inflationary pressures only worsen their plight. Manpower policies must necessarily be integrated with other economic policies. Human resources measures may become an increasingly significant factor alongside monetary and fiscal measures in determining economic policy.

Human resources in flux

These important transformations obviously affect the content and application of human resource development. Despite cutbacks in some areas, it is likely that this will continue to be a growth area affecting economic policy and resource allocation, both private and public. Theory and evaluation must adjust as new needs are perceived and new manpower efforts initiated.

Experiences with the educational and manpower programs of the past decade and with broader human resource questions have provided practical and theoretical lessons. We know a great deal about the factors determining the supply of labor and the institutions affecting its quality. Theories of labor markets, including an increased focus on the operations of secondary markets, explain the allocation of labor among industries, occupations, and individuals. The productivity of labor has been estimated in a number of ways, and efforts have been made to measure the gains from remedial education and training. Special efforts have been made to provide compensatory aid to victims of discrimination in order to expand their opportunities and raise their productivity. The broader implications of human resource development not only touch on discrimination, economic development, and the persistence of poverty in an affluent society but also affect the determination of national priorities and economic policies.

What further changes are likely in the nature of work, and what do they imply for human resource development and the labor market? Despite some increases in leisure time and some decline in labor force participation for marginal groups, most Americans will continue to work for a living. Perhaps with rising female participation, the proportion of working Americans will rise. Goods are not free. The age of abundance has not arrived, and he who does not work, therefore, is considered a "free rider." Ours remains a work-achievement-oriented society. Even those who can afford to do otherwise are expected to contribute to the social welfare and to fulfill their own needs. The dropouts from society are few, although their number may be increasing. The challenge we face is not a redundancy of manpower but the "human use of human beings to fulfill national goals."

The most important task at present is to draw together these diverse experiences and insights, blending theory with practical wisdom. The foundations must be strengthened so that manpower economists can learn from the past in dealing with the future.

Notes

1. Frederick H. Harbison, *Human Resources as the Wealth of Nations* (New York: Oxford University Press, 1973), p. 3.

one

---

labor
market
dynamics

2
work life, work time, and mobility

There is a myth about the nature and work life of the American worker. It projects the picture of a male family breadwinner working at his bench or desk 40 hours a week, year round from the time he leaves school until he retires. But the male, year-round, full-time workers, though still the largest group in the American work force, are no longer in the majority.

For one thing, Americans are moving toward a shorter work life. They stay in school longer, retire earlier, and live longer after they retire—somewhat over seven years, or double what it was at the turn of the century.

During the work life, leisure is assuming a greater role. Americans have decreased the number of hours they work weekly and annually, while real earnings continue to rise because of increased productivity (though inflation and rising taxes may take their toll). From one-third to two-fifths of the total rise in productivity during the present century has taken the form of increased leisure time rather than higher wages.

Mobility has also been a characteristic of American working life. Part of the American dream is that, regardless of a person's origins, he can move up to jobs requiring more skill and responsibility and offering more prestige and income than the one he started with—or his father held. More than other industrialized nations, the United States has been, and continues to be, a land of much upward social and occupational mobility of both an intergenerational and an intragenerational nature. Americans are also the most geographically mobile of industrial peoples.

These changes in work time, work life, and mobility have contributed to changes in how Americans view their jobs. For many workers the meaning of work and the work ethic has become less important as leisure time has increased and as individuals have realized greater freedom to choose where, when, and how much to

9

work. The old images of the necessity of lifelong toil to support a family have been altered in modern society.

The meaning of work

According to conventional wisdom, the work ethic was adopted by society at the beginning of the era of mass production. Because developing industries required willing and diligent labor, every agent of authority and education extolled the values of work. Wise men ranging from Luther to Ben Franklin and Horatio Alger fed workers a steady diet of exhortation and incantation from press, pulpit, and primer. All work was laudable; work well done would inevitably bring reward; work shirked led to degradation and ruin. Presumably, the naïve and malleable minds of eighteenth-century peasants were soon converted completely to this creed.

From this first flowering of the work ethic the path to the present has apparently been marked by the decay of the religious and secular props that supported the morality of work. Industrialization and urbanization, the church's loss of authority, and a gradual recognition that much of the work required by society was indeed tedious and unrewarding slowly buried the notion that work was a good in itself. Stripped of its pious veneer, work once more became the accursed obstacle standing between men and the realization of a freer, leisured paradise.

Obviously, this abstract concept of the work ethic oversimplifies complex developments. It does not explain why men worked or worked hard or what they thought of their jobs. It is not clear whether the moralists' praise of work was ever accepted by the workingman or that it actually motivated his efforts much. Nor is it necessarily true that work before the Reformation was no more than unredeemed toil. Surely, many artisans had always taken pride in their crafts and had no need of a church-sanctioned morality to shore up the self-esteem they derived from their work. Similarly, it is questionable that men in the industrial era were much motivated by the morality that revered work, no matter what the attempts at indoctrination. Andrew Carnegie may have dedicated his empire to the glory of God, but the men in his employ more likely worked for gold rather than grace.

The doubtful logic of tracing the history of the work ethic has shifted explanations of the changing meaning of work from philosophical to sociological or psychological models. These compare the kinds of work that men have performed in history and argue the effect of this work on attitudes and values.

Two classic idealized models are usually compared to work in modern society: life on the farm and the craft method of manufacture. Work on a pioneer homestead, it is argued, differed from industrial labor mostly in the relation of man to his environment, his needs, and his tools. The early farmer's work corresponded directly to the provision of the essentials for his survival. He ate from fields he sowed, wore clothes of homespun fabric, and slept in a house he built. He understood the tools he used and could usually repair them himself. He actually harnessed or dammed most of his power. Because of this close correspondence with work, its rewards, and the fabric of his life, the pioneer probably lacked equivalent concepts of work, opposed to leisure and recreation.

Similarly, the craftsman's work is imagined to have involved him more integrally than that of his industrial successors. Though he was removed from the direct production of all his necessities, he was still closely identified with his work. He set his own pace, owned his tools, and probably sold or bartered his product. He could take direct pride in his skill and gain satisfaction from his completed products. The job still closely matched the abilities and psychological needs of its performer. His survival and prosperity were constant testimony of his skill. Again, work rather than leisure was the focus of his life and his chief satisfaction.

Industrialization, according to this reasoning, conflicted severely with the close correspondence between man and work in several ways. First, the urbanization attendant upon the Industrial Revolution removed most people from the direct production of the objects they needed for living. Though a village craftsman might not make his own shoes or grow his food, he was never far removed from these activities. The rapid expansion of transportation led to the production of many essential goods far from the site of their consumption and created a society that used commodities disembodied from the knowledge of how they were made.

Second, the rewards of work became less clearly attached to work itself by the introduction of objects of universal value and complex exchanges of goods and services. Silver coins, paper money, checks, and finally unseen credit balances became the goals of work rather than the goods that these objects represented.

Third, tools and processes of production became far more important, complex, alien, and powerful. Not only did the industrial worker not own the tools of his trade, but he also understood them imperfectly, could not repair them, and usually did not control their pace.

Fourth, the development of methods and scales of production

that required the coordinated efforts of tens or hundreds or thousands of men meant that individual desires and rhythms were subordinated to imposed schedules. Labor began to be defined by time on the clock. At the same time, huge organizations removed most individuals many levels away from the center of responsibility and control. Men lost the clearly recognizable stake in production that they enjoyed as individuals or within small companies.

Fifth, and most important, the industrial process in its search for efficiency compressed the scope of individual jobs to the point that almost no production-line job required more than a tiny fraction of an individual's capabilities. Men became, in Georges Friedmann's words, "bigger than their jobs."[1] Likewise, the results of an individual's efforts became less obvious. The satisfaction of the struggle, the outlet for creative energy in bending inert matter to human will were all but lost in many occupations.

These developments in purely industrial situations created the concepts of work that most of society came to accept. To some extent they were applicable to many nonindustrial enterprises in which size and complexity created similar conditions. But, legitimately, the critique applied most to the industrial mass manufacture of goods because only in this case did the requirements of efficiency mandate great size and organization and develop the minute specialization that created the conditions deplored by critical humanists.

According to the logic of the critics, these factors led to the radical separation of work and leisure and the decline of the belief in work for "work's" sake. Men lacking outlets for their capacities in the workplace sharply divided their lives into periods of work and leisure and sought self-realization solely in their leisure time, giving rise to the goal of working to escape from work. Unsatisfying jobs reinforced the idea that work consisted of anything that was unpleasant or undesirable but necessary and continuing. And as production became less a function of labor and leisure became an increasingly available fact, consumption took on a life of its own.

Shopworn as this version of the industrial transition is, it certainly reflects the changing status of some workers through the machine age. Obviously, though, not all of industrial society falls within the scope of these influences, for factories do not employ even a fourth of society's work force.

Evidently then, philosophical and sociological history fail to supply an adequate definition of work today. Work seems to include a host of things: Artists work on paintings; pensioners work in their gardens during the "leisure" years; volunteers work without pay. Identical activities are called work or recreation, depending upon who performs them. But though no useful definition is likely to include all the exceptions, some of the elements of our notion of work may be established.

From society's standpoint work is usually thought of as a person's job, an individual's productive activity and contribution to the economy. From this standpoint the opposite of work, which produces a good or a service, is consumption or any nonproductive or nonpaid activity. Conversely, from the individual's view work is the effort society exacts in return for the goods and services placed at the individual's disposal. Work is what society charges should or must be done, contrasted to voluntary activity. In this context the opposite of work is not consumption, but free time or leisure—time to do exactly as one chooses. But the cases of individuals whose work produces no good or service for exchange or the cases of volunteers who work because they wish to suggest that the traditional definitions of work may be outmoded. Work, redefined to account for these situations, is simply sustained and purposeful activity to accomplish goals. Work is the continuing struggle to bend the world to man's will and imagination, the natural urge to triumph over the limitations of the present.

The old notion of work—the drudgery required by society in order for it to function—is possibly becoming too narrow to be useful today. Work that is productive activity exchanged in the economy may be reduced to a mechanical concept in a future society in which all can be fed, clothed, and sheltered with barely any human effort. And work that is required "slavery" may vanish in a society in which affluence and leisure are widespread.

But would work disappear in such a world; would men cease to struggle against their limitations? Released from the burdens of producing goods and services to stay alive, would the human inclination to work atrophy and be replaced by a play ethic seeking no further development? Moreover, would a society that recognized that it no longer needed the work of most individuals in order to continue to exist release its people to allow them to choose what they wish to do? Would the requirement to work give way to freedom in leisure?

These questions are not nearly so vague and speculative as they might seem. To some extent the answers are already visible in the diversity of the present. Already less than half the working population supplies all the food, power, clothing, shelter, and other goods by which society lives. Already great segments of the population enjoy amounts of leisure time that were formerly the sole prerogative of the few idle rich. And already there is argument over whether society is accepting the dead-end roles of the easy life in either work or leisure. Analysis of changes that are already taking place in work and workers can shed new light on these issues.

Work life: start later, retire earlier

Men: Shorter work life despite longer life

Men and women differ not only in the number of years they can expect to live, or life expectancy, but also, and much more significantly, in the length and pattern of their work lives.

Later entrance into the labor force and earlier retirement have arrested and reversed the long-term rise in the length of work life. The work-life expectancy of a man born at the turn of this century lengthened by about six years during the following five decades largely because average life expectancy rose. The best measure of long-term, work-life expectancy is gained by computing the average number of years spent in the labor force by males reaching adulthood. The average work-life expectancy for males age 14 rose from 39 years in 1900 to 45 years by 1950 (Table 2-1). Since 1950, however, work-life expectancy has declined to 43 years.

Many factors have contributed to later entry into the labor force. One is the great decline in farming: farmers' children were put to work at any early age. Another is the impact of child labor laws and compulsory school attendance. In 1900, when about two-fifths of the work force were employed on farms, the average age of entry into the labor force was about 15. By midcentury the average age of young men entering the labor force had risen to about 17.5 years, and currently it is almost 18.

Income support from Social Security and private pension plans and compulsory retirement programs have dramatically increased the tendency to retire at age 65 or even earlier. Almost one-fourth of the men in the labor force at age 64 retire during the next year. Retirement continues to be a more important reason than death for separation from the labor force for several years after age 65, although the tendency to retire declines very sharply after age 65. Often, those who continue to work do so part time; in 1968 over half of the 65-to-69-year-old male jobholders worked less than 50 weeks. This part-time and part-year employment may reflect the greater incidence of health problems, reduced opportunities because of discrimination, and the ceiling that Social Security puts on the retirees' earnings if they are to qualify for full-benefit payments.

The number of years males spend outside the labor force has

Table 2-1   Average Work-Life Expectancy for Men in the Labor Force, 1900–1969

| | Average Number of Years Remaining at Age 14 | | |
Year	Life Expectancy	Work-Life Expectancy	Out of the Labor Force
1900	44.0	39.3	4.7
1920	48.8	43.0	5.8
1950	54.6	45.4	9.2
1969	55.4	42.6	12.8

Source: Sar A. Levitan and William B. Johnston, *Work Is Here to Stay, Alas* (Salt Lake City, Utah: Olympus Publishing Co., 1973), p. 45.

increased nearly 50 percent during this century. A man born in 1900 spent, on the average, 19 years outside the labor force, compared with the projected 27 years for a man born in 1969. Despite later entry into the work force, the additional 8 years spent outside the labor force were added mostly at the end of life. Few could afford to retire at the turn of the century. In 1900 a man of age 20 had a life expectancy of 42 more years, of which he worked 39 years and spent 3 in retirement. In 1969 the 20-year-old could look forward to 50 more years, of which the last 9 would be spent in retirement.

Women: More work and longer life expectancy

Women have accounted for three of every five additions to the labor force in the past 25 years. Unlike men, women have quite varied work-life expectancies, depending on whether they stay single, marry, give birth to children, or become the heads of households because of separation, divorce, or the death of their husbands (Table 2-2). Most women (95 out of 100) marry—and marry young. Half are married before they are 21, and more marry at age 18 than at any other age. Whether or not they marry, about nine of ten women work outside the home at some time. Marriage and the presence of children tend to curtail employment, while widowhood, divorce, and the decrease of family responsibilities tend to bring women back into the labor force. Women begin their careers at about the same age as men, usually after finishing high school. Frequently, they leave the work force a few years after they marry to have childen; a growing proportion resume work before the children reach school age.

The small minority of women who never marry have the most

Table 2-2 Average Work-Life Expectancy for Women in the Labor Force, by Marital Status and Age, 1960

Marital Status	Age			
	20	35	50	60
Single	45.3	31.2	17.1	10.0
Married, husband present, no children	34.9	24.4	13.7	8.7
Married, husband present, in labor force after birth of last child	a	23.8	11.9	6.9
Widowed	41.8	27.3	13.4	7.1
Divorced	43.3	28.8	15.5	8.4

aAmounts not significant.

Source: Stuart H. Garfinkle, Work Life Expectancy of Females, U.S. Department of Labor, Manpower Administration, Manpower Report No. 12 (Washington, D.C.: GPO, 1967), p. 4.

continuous and longest attachment to the labor force; their work-life pattern closely resembles that of men. The 20-year-old woman who remains single will probably continue to work for about 45 years—slightly more than the average of 43 years for men. In general, however, women—especially those who can depend on their husband's income—tend to work fewer years and to retire earlier than men. The Social Security option of retirement at age 62 may also play a part in encouraging women to leave the work force.

The one married woman in ten who does not have children has a work-life expectancy of 35 years—10 years less than single women—if she enters the labor force by age 20. The working life of married women with children is less predictable because of the intermittent nature of their careers. The average woman has borne her last child by age 30; by her mid-30s all her children are in school and her family responsibilities are considerably diminished. If she returns under these conditions (usually after having been out of the labor force for about 8 to 10 years), her work-life expectancy is essentially the same as for a newly married 20-year-old woman—24 more years. This means that a far greater portion of a woman's work life occurs *after* she has reared her children to school age and has reentered the labor force.

Because the care of young children is a major factor preventing women from working, the decline in birth rates since 1958 has made it possible for larger numbers of younger women to enter or remain in the labor force. The more children a married woman has, the shorter her work-life expectancy. It is estimated that the first child reduces work-life expectancy by about ten years; each additional child reduces it by about two to three years. A relatively large percentage of widowed, separated, and divorced women return to the labor force, their work patterns often resembling those of men and single women.

Work time: fewer hours, more leisure time

During his work life, today's worker has about 800 more hours of free time each year, or 2.2 hours each day, than did the worker at the turn of the century. This is in addition to the extra eight years of nonwork time the male has gained because he starts work later, retires earlier, and lives longer.[2]

Shorter working hours do not necessarily improve the quality of a person's life or necessarily enlarge the amount of leisure time. Part of the increase in nonworking time is used up in longer hours of commuting. Household appliances, convenience foods, ready-made clothes, and smaller families made possible by birth-control technology have given housewives free time to take on paid jobs—and thus end up with the double load of work plus running the home and family.

The intrinsic value of leisure to a worker should, however, not be overlooked. Workers have not lost their zeal to reduce working hours. They wish to minimize the hours spent under supervision "to be masters of their own souls for as much of the day as possible."[3] A recent study of assembly-line workers in the automobile industry supports this view. Younger workers, especially, expressed preference for free time (away from the rigid discipline of the production line, which leaves no opportunity for personal business) rather than overtime work.[4] Nevertheless, during the 1960s, there was a stronger emphasis on raising income; only 8 percent of the rise in productivity was allocated to reducing work time, with the balance being used to boost income.[5]

Whether future productivity increases will be adequate to provide a continuation of large increases in both leisure time and standard of living remains questionable. The goods-producing sector of our economy is not now growing as rapidly as the service-producing sector, in which productivity gains are smaller. Thus past increases in leisure time and standard of living cannot be sustained without technological breakthroughs in the service sector. The three- or four-day workweek and a carefree abundance of goods are much further away than the prophets of cybernetics like to anticipate.[6]

The distribution of additional leisure time has taken several forms, and the emphasis has changed over the years from reduction in weekly hours of work to allocation of leisure time in blocks of days or weeks. Between 1900 and 1970 nonworking hours per year increased by nearly 800, distributed as follows:

> Reduction in workweek—707 hours (13.6 hours per week: from 53.2 to 39.6)
> Increase in paid holidays—32 hours (4 days: from 2 to about 6 per year)
> Increase in paid vacations—48 hours (6 days: from less than $\frac{1}{2}$ to $1\frac{1}{2}$ weeks per year)[7]

Much of the drop in workweek hours came in the first two decades of this century as social reformers citing health and fatigue factors crusaded for shorter daily hours of work. Another sharp decline toward a statutory 40-hour workweek took place in the Great Depression of the 1930s under the National Industrial Recovery and Fair Labor Standards Acts. Overtime pay was required for longer workweeks to encourage the sharing of work opportunities and to reduce unemployment. During World War II, of course, longer hours were worked, but in the postwar period the average declined slowly from the 40-hour norm to 39.3 by 1973. In recent years the decline in hours has averaged about 4 percent per decade—more because of increased part-time employment rather than a cutback in hours. The Bureau of Labor Statistics (BLS) projects that the rate of decline in average hours paid for in all private industry will be cut in half during the 1970s.[8] The BLS projections assume nearly full employment; higher unemployment would intensify pressures for reductions in hours and other work-sharing devices.

Although interest in the shorter workweek has continued, preferences for leisure shifted after World War II to increasing blocks of time off—vacations and holidays. Not only are more workers receiving vacations, but also the vacations are longer—4 weeks for workers with 20 years' service is not unusual. The United Steelworkers' sabbatical plan, which was negotiated in 1963 and was originally conceived of as a means of spreading work, allowed an extended vacation of 13 weeks, but the idea was not picked up by other industries. Paid holidays for wage earners were also a development of World War II and the postwar period: The average is about six paid holidays a year for all workers (including farmers), with workers in metropolitan areas getting more (seven for plant workers, about eight for office workers). In the quest for more blocks of free time even legal holidays were rescheduled.

More three-day weekends became a reality in 1971, when Congress decreed that Washington's Birthday, Memorial Day, Veterans Day, and Columbus Day were to be celebrated on Mondays.

Possibly a large share of future growth in productivity will be allocated to blocks of leisure time at the beginning and end of work life (especially the latter), in contrast to the earlier pattern of its absorption into shorter workweeks.[9] However, older workers might want to distribute their work and leisure differently, rearranging their total pool of work years so that they would not be forced to retire at a time when they might prefer to continue useful work. Whatever the individual preference, however, institutional arrangements and business conditions dictate the terms of nonwork time at both the beginning and end of work life. Part-time and part-year work opportunities for older and younger workers depend on the need for their services. Higher retirement benefits, though, would raise workers' options in choosing between work and leisure.

If given the choice, do workers prefer extra leisure or added income? It is difficult to generalize about this. Evidence seems to indicate that shorter hours are preferred by very young and very old workers, and by women, particularly if they are married and have household responsibilities. The bulk of part-time workers belong to these groups. More than four-fifths of the 13.4 million people in the part-time labor force in 1973 did not want full-time employment or were not available for it. In fact, some might have not worked at all if required to work regular hours.[10]

However, men with growing family responsibilities tend to maximize income instead of leisure, and many moonlight to supplement their income.[11] Almost half of all moonlighters were men between 25 and 44, though this age group comprised only about two-fifths of all employed men. The primary motivation of all moonlighters appeared to be financial pressure, with four of ten working to meet regular expenses and one of ten working to pay off debts. Further, there was no significant inverse relationship between moonlighting and length of workweek; thus among full-time workers factors other than length of workweek determined whether they were moonlighting. While women represented more than one-third of all employed persons in 1971, they accounted for only about one-fifth of the total moonlighters.[12]

Workers bypassed by shorter workweek

Despite the trend to shorter average working hours, a significant number of people—about one-sixth of all workers in 1973—are still working 49 or more hours a week. The bulk of these were persons with single jobs, not moonlighters with multiple jobs. Many of the long-hour workers genuinely enjoy their work or hold responsible positions and are either required or expected to work long hours; others who work long hours are paid low wages and frequently are not covered by minimum wage legislation requiring overtime pay after 40 hours.[13] Almost three-fifths of those who worked 49 or more hours a week were professionals, managers, or craftsmen, though these groups make up less than two-fifths of the labor force. By contrast, operatives, laborers, service workers, and clerical workers, who made up 55 percent of the work force, were only a third of those who toiled such long hours.

Leisure that is productive work: unpaid volunteers

Free time is not synonymous with leisure. While much of the extra free time is consumed by coping with the more complicated mechanics of contemporary life, some is utilized in productive work that does not show up in national accounts. This is the contribution of volunteers doing good works for diverse social causes. Almost 22 million Americans—1 out of every 6 adults—contribute free labor to some health, educational, religious, or welfare service. Their contribution is equivalent to the work performed by a full-time regular work force of over 900,000. Voluntarism is apparently a function of being part of the Establishment. For example, married people between the ages of 25 and 44—those with the most demanding responsibilities for raising families—accounted for half the volunteers. Three-fifths of the volunteers were women, and more than half also had paid jobs. The more schooling (and income) a person had, the more likely he was to do volunteer work.[14]

Workers' mobility: the American dream of moving up the job ladder

Mobility has always been a characteristic of American working life, and few people hold just one job over a working lifetime. They change employers, though not necessarily the types of work they perform; or they may change jobs while staying with the same employer (sometimes by transferring to a different branch or plant). They move to new locations, though most employment shifts are within the same community or labor market area. They shift in and out of the labor force in response to changing economic or personal conditions.[15]

Perhaps most important is workers' mobility up the occupational ladder. Quite properly, Americans persist in the belief that, regardless of one's origins, economic and social opportunity should be open to all. Social mobility is of importance not only to individuals but also to the efficiency and well-being of society as a whole. As Lloyd G. Reynolds has pointed out:

> Geographic movement is apt to be a painful necessity, costly to individuals and the community. Movement from employer to employer may be simply an aimless wandering from one mediocre job to another. Real progress comes only through movement to a new job involving more in the way of skill, responsibility, independence, and income.[16]

Upward occupational mobility

Occupational and social mobility may be analyzed either in terms of changes that occur within a worker's own lifetime (intragenerational) or in terms of changes from parent to offspring (intergenerational).[17] More than most other industrialized nations, the United States is predominantly open and upwardly mobile. Extensive studies have documented that intergenerational and intragenerational upward occupational mobility have been and remain a fact of American economic life. In longitudinal studies of men between 45 and 59 years of age, Herbert Parnes discovered that almost three-fifths had moved into occupations with higher socioeconomic status than those in which they began their work careers.[18]

Most of the upward mobility involves relatively short social distances rather than dramatic, long-distance, Horatio-Alger-type leaps. Peter M. Blau and Otis Dudley Duncan found the usual move to be only 2 or 3 steps upward in their hierarchy of 17 occupational levels (ranging from farm laborers up to self-employed professionals).[19] Nonetheless, more of America's current business leaders have emerged from lower-class and middle-class origins than at the turn of the century (Table 2-3). Higher education appears to provide the ladder for upward mobility. But, at the same time, a college education remains largely a function of family income. In 1971 it was twice as likely that a young person would attend college if his family's annual income exceeded $15,000 than if the income were between $5,000 and $7,500. The number of children who must share a family's income also is a significant factor, and the steady trend toward family limitation should promote the chances of obtaining a college education.

Immigration and westward migration, and the continued growth of economic opportunities, have prevented locked-in social stratification in the United States. More American professionals have risen from the lower classes than in other nations. Blau and

Table 2-3   Distribution of Business Executives by Family Status, 1900–
1964

Economic Status of Father	1900	1925	1950	1964	1900–1964 Difference
Wealthy	45.6%	36.6%	36.1%	10.5%	−35.1%
Medium	42.1	47.8	51.8	66.2	24.1
Poor	12.3	15.8	12.1	23.2	10.9

Source: Joseph W. McGuire and Joseph A. Pichler, *Inequality: The Poor and Rich in America* (Belmont, Calif.: Wadsworth, 1969), p. 57.

Duncan point out that about 10 percent of the sons of American manual workers moved into professional and technical occupations, compared with 7 percent for Japan and the Netherlands, 3.5 for Sweden, and 2.2 for Great Britain.[20] Comparing the United States, Great Britain, the Netherlands, and Japan, Joseph W. McGuire and Joseph A. Pichler concluded that there is more upward mobility into the middle class by craftsmen in the United States than in other industrial nations. They also found a lower rate of intergenerational downward mobility—from professional to skilled occupations—in America than in Great Britain and the Netherlands.[21]

The frustrations of blue-collar workers have received much public attention. One of their complaints is that men who start their careers as blue-collar workers have poorer chances of reaching a higher occupational status than those who start out in white-collar occupations (they already have achieved some status) or farm occupations (they are likely to benefit from mobility because of a low starting point).

But blue-collar workers may not be as hopelessly trapped in lower-rung occupations as has been assumed. As a group these workers are relatively better off than their fathers—whether they be native-born whites from low-income farm families, of foreign extraction, or blacks. Some advance to managerial or entrepreneurial ranks—as the carpenter who becomes a contractor or the truck driver who acquires a small fleet. Intergenerational upward mobility is enhanced by their children's greater access to a higher education at the rapidly growing numbers of junior and community colleges.

Upward mobility among blue-collar workers is not universal, however, and there are large groups of immobile and vulnerable workers in their ranks. Included in these sizable groups are men who hold blue-collar jobs similar to those held by their fathers or men who have even moved down the occupational scale; female heads of families who tend to be in low-paying, low-skill jobs; male heads unable to earn enough to allow their families to live much above the poverty level; and families whose children are unlikely to have access to college or other paths upward.

Just as blue-collar workers have difficulty moving up, so white-collar workers tend not to cross class boundaries into blue-collar jobs. White-collar workers who are unsuccessful in their occupations often move into retail trade, which, according to Blau and Duncan, still allows them to maintain white-collar status and to remain within the higher social scale, even though with relatively unskilled jobs.[22] Evidently, they prefer the status of a white-collar job, even though a job in coveralls or a hard hat may pay better, have shorter hours, and require more skills.

On the other hand, some blue-collar workers do shift to white-collar jobs. David B. Johnson and James L. Stern found that in the early 1960s one-fifth of the white-collar jobs in Milwaukee were filled by workers with at least a year's blue-collar experience. Though nearly two-thirds of the moves were into managerial, professional, and technical occupations, the upward mobility did not always involve an immediate financial gain and, indeed, sometimes meant reduced take-home pay because of lost overtime.[23] Most of the upward movement analyzed by Johnson and Stern involved job shifts within the same firm, and the initiative came primarily from the employers.

Government manpower programs have devoted few resources to upgrading workers, though much rhetoric has been devoted to developing new careers to help the disadvantaged. Given the limitations of the job market, it may be unrealistic to hope that large numbers of workers can be simply upgraded from dead-end to upwardly mobile jobs.

Upward mobility for blacks

The upward mobility of blacks was a central issue of the 1960s and early 1970s. Past discrimination and hurdles built into our institutional structure have prevented blacks from utilizing opportunities that lead other minority or ethnic groups such as immigrants and their children to upward mobility.

During the past decade, however, extensive civil rights legislation and the widespread rejection by American society of discrimination in employment, at least in principle, boosted the status of American blacks, though the gaps between whites and blacks were not eliminated. The mean annual earnings of black males increased from 53 to 66 percent of those for whites between 1959 and 1971, and average black female earnings leaped from 62 to 90 percent of equality with those of white females. In part, this was attributable to the fact that there was a steady movement of blacks out of the lower occupational groups (especially marginal farmers and farm laborers) into the categories of craftsmen and operatives, so that by 1973 three out of every four black blue-collar workers were in these latter categories. More striking was the fact that during the 1960s more than 300,000 blacks also gained entry into the preferred craftsmen category, although they remained under-represented. More than seven-tenths of the increase in black employment between 1960 and 1970 was in professional, white-collar, and skilled occupations, while the lowest paid occupations—private household work and farm work—registered declines. Herbert Parnes and others have questioned the significance of these increases in black family income and occupational mobility. Parnes expected blacks to show upward occupational mobility because of their low starting position. His longitudinal studies, however, convinced him that the contrary occurred and that the relative disadvantages of black men when they begin "their working lives have become more pronounced during their work careers."[24]

Geographical mobility

About 1 out of 15 Americans moves across county lines each year, with about half of these migrating into another state. Counting also those who move within a county, the ratio goes up to about one in six. The ratios show very little variation over the 25 years in which the Bureau of the Census has been measuring these changes.[25]

The character of geographic migration affecting labor mobility has changed. The flood of European immigrants has been curtailed, and western migration and the movement from the farm to the city have leveled off. A newer and more significant development is the movement from the inner cities to the suburbs. There are now more people in the suburbs than in the inner cities. This flight, primarily of white residents to the suburban rings, has been coupled with a relocation of plants and, particularly, retail and service establishments. Unemployment and transportation problems thus are compounded for those left in the inner city, as well as for suburbanites who still work in the cities.

Removing impediments to mobility

Society's challenge is to create conditions that will both optimize upward mobility and facilitate the process of matching workers and jobs. This suggests policies that open opportunities for upward movement, have sufficient clout to discourage wasteful or misdirected mobility, and maintain freedom of individual choice.

Socially beneficial occupational mobility can be achieved by providing better opportunities for education, training, retraining, and upgrading, while placing less emphasis on formal credentials such as high school diploma.[26] Continued attacks on discrimination, and efforts to sustain and solidify the advances made in the past generation must be essential ingredients of any occupational mobility policy. In promoting occupational mobility, special provisions must be made for those left behind either because they are in depressed areas, are otherwise not mobile, or have been denied opportunities for upward mobility.

Discouraging wasteful mobility certainly involves a reexamination of social values and the status of various occupations. The quality of American life is not enhanced by worship of the diploma certifying that the recipient has completed a course in higher education, while public and private services are deteriorating because society considers the providers of these services to be inferior.

Notes

1. Georges Friedmann, *The Anatomy of Work: Labor, Leisure, and the Implications of Automation* (New York: Free Press, 1961).
2. Sar A. Levitan and William B. Johnston, *Work Is Here to Stay, Alas* (Salt Lake City, Utah: Olympus Publishing Co., 1973), p. 49.
3. U.S. Congress, House Committee on Education and Labor, *Hearings on Hours of Work* (Washington, D.C.: GPO, 1963), p. 220.
4. Judson Gooding, "Blue-Collar Blues on the Assembly Line," *Fortune* (July 1970), pp. 69 ff.
5. Geoffrey H. Moore and Janice Neipert Hedges, "Trends in Labor and Leisure," *Monthly Labor Review* (February 1971), pp. 3–11.
6. Victor R. Fuchs, ed., *Production and Productivity in Service Industries* (New York: National Bureau of Economic Research and Columbia University Press, 1969), p. 10.
7. Levitan and Johnston, op. cit., p. 43.
8. U.S. Bureau of Labor Statistics, *The U.S. Economy in 1980: A Summary of BLS Projections*, Bulletin 1673 (Washington, D.C.: GPO, 1970), p. 4.
9. Juanita M. Kreps, "Time for Leisure, Time for Work," *Monthly Labor Review* (April 1969), pp. 60–61.
10. Curtis L. Gilroy and Thomas F. Bradshaw, "Employment and Unemployment—A Report on 1973," *Monthly Labor Review* (February 1973), p. 6.

11. Vera C. Perrella, "Moonlighters: Their Motivation and Characteristics," *Monthly Labor Review* (August 1970), pp. 57–64.
12. Howard V. Hayghe and Kopp Michelotti, "Multiple Jobholding in 1970 and 1971," *Monthly Labor Review* (October 1971), pp. 38–45.
13. Peter Henle, "Leisure and the Long Work Week," *Monthly Labor Review* (July 1966), p. 721.
14. *Americans Volunteer*, U.S. Department of Labor, Manpower Administration, Manpower/Automation Research Monograph No. 10 (Washington, D.C.: GPO, April 1969).
15. Major research on labor mobility in the 1960s is summarized by Herbert S. Parnes, "Labor Force Participation and Labor Mobility," in *A Review of Industrial Relations Research,* Industrial Relations Research Association Series, Vol. 1 (Madison, Wis.: The Association, 1970), pp. 33–78.
16. Lloyd G. Reynolds, *Labor Economics and Labor Relations,* 4th ed., (Englewood Cliffs, N.J.: Prentice-Hall, 1964), p. 390.
17. Joseph W. McGuire and Joseph A. Pichler, *Inequality: The Poor and Rich in America* (Belmont, Calif.: Wadsworth, 1969), pp. 48 ff.
18. Herbert Parnes et al., *The Pre-Retirement Years,* Vol. 1, U.S. Department of Labor, Manpower Administration, Manpower Research Monograph No. 15 (Washington, D.C.: GPO, 1970), p. 127.
19. Peter M. Blau and Otis Dudley Duncan, *The American Occupational Structure* (New York: Wiley, 1964), p. 420.
20. *Ibid.,* p. 435.
21. McGuire and Pichler, op. cit., p. 52.
22. Blau and Duncan, op. cit., p. 421.
23. David B. Johnson and James L. Stern, "Why and How Workers Shift from Blue-Collar to White-Collar Jobs," *Monthly Labor Review* (October 1969), pp. 7–13.
24. Parnes et al., op. cit., p. 128.
25. U.S. Bureau of the Census, *Current Population Reports,* "Mobility of the Population of the United States, March 1970 to March 1971," Series P-20, No. 235 (Washington, D.C.: GPO, 1969), p. 1.
26. S. M. Miller, *Breaking the Credentials Barrier* (New York: The Ford Foundation, 1968).

3

labor force participation and unemployment

Changing patterns of work life have been accompanied by dramatic shifts in labor force participation rates (the proportion of the working-age population employed or looking for work as opposed to working in the home, studying at school, or enjoying leisure) and in the composition of the work force. The key long-run shifts are greater participation of women and declining roles for younger and older workers. These shifts have resulted in an increased reliance on peripheral workers, whose work-life patterns are different from those of workers who are employed full-time throughout the year.[1]

Underlying the changed composition in the work force is the rising level of expectations, which outstrips the sustained but relatively modest rises in productivity. This means that millions of families now need more than the male breadwinner can earn and that the added worker is far more likely to be the wife than a son or daughter. Moreover, the growth of consumer purchases on credit has heightened pressure on family income to meet the payments. In the quarter century after World War II consumer indebtedness grew from $6 to $158 billion, outpacing the growth of all financial assets. Thus America is increasingly a nation of multi-worker families "hooked" into working to maintain the desired standard of living.

Work, however, is no longer the only way to support a family. Income-support programs—including unemployment insurance, public and private retirement or disability benefits, and public assistance—provide money, limited as it may be. Welfare (and other income-support programs) and work are increasingly interdependent. This was reflected in the movement of the 1960s toward providing assistance for parents who are capable of working but who

are unemployed; traditionally, welfare had been aimed exclusively
at helping persons outside the labor force—mothers and dependent children, the indigent aged, and the disabled.

The labor market has its pathologies, however, and not all
persons who want jobs are successful in getting them, and many
others who are employed fail to earn an adequate income to raise
their families above poverty. Forced idleness, intermittent employment, and low-income jobs fall disproportionately to blacks, Indians, Chicanos, and younger and older workers. The American
economy has not been successful in eliminating the ups and downs
of business cycles; after nearly a decade of continued growth in
the 1960s, the economy once again experienced a contraction and
unemployment rose to over 6 percent.

Overall shifts in labor force

A key change has been the sharp increase in the number of working women—especially married women. During the 1960s women
entered the labor force three times faster than men; for the first
time, married men—the group that had previously constituted the
bulk of the labor force—dropped to less than half of all workers.
A large share of newly married women are working; an increasing
number of married women return to work after their children
have entered school or grown up, and many do not wait that long.
Since the beginning of the century, participation rates of married
women have increased fivefold, and their share of the labor force
has risen sixfold, to about one-fifth.[2]

Young people, however, have shown a long-term decline in
their participation rate, in part, perhaps, because their mothers
add to the family exchequer, but more often because they encounter economic and legal barriers to work. Thus youngsters stay
in school longer before starting their full-time work careers. In the
first half of the century the participation rate for 14-to-19-year-old
males has dropped by about a third, while their share of the labor
force was cut in half—from about 10 to about 5 percent. After the
post–World War II baby boom, however, the sheer numbers of
young people increased despite a reduced participation rate. Young
workers aged 16 to 24 accounted for more than half of the labor
force increase in the 1960s, and early 1970s, which raised their proportion in the labor force from one in five to one in four.

The early work years are characterized by much part-time
work (often combined with school) and fairly frequent job
changes. The pattern changes as persons mature. Adult men reach
a peak participation rate of about 97 percent in their mid-20s, and

this percentage remains relatively stable for about 30 years. Job stability increases as the worker matures: A 55-year-old man can be expected to stay on a job over 7 years, or about 1½ times longer than a man of 20.[3]

At the other end of the age spectrum there has been a long-term decline in the participation rate of older males; for men over 65, the rate has dropped to less than half of what it was at the turn of the century. As in the case of youngsters, however, the sheer growth in the number of those 55 and older has offset their declining participation rate; there were more of these older workers in 1970 than a decade earlier.

These shifts have left overall labor force participation rates basically unchanged during the current century; the declines in some groups canceled out the increases in others. Since the end of World War II annual labor force participation rates have ranged between 59 and 61 percent of the total noninstitutional population in the United States. During the same period, male rates declined steadily from 87 to below 80 percent, while the comparable rates for women rose from 32 to almost 45 percent (Table 3-1).

Of the 148.3 million noninstitutional Americans aged 16 or older in 1973, an average of 91 million were in the labor force. Excluding the 2.3 million in the armed forces, the civilian labor force averaged 88.7 million, of whom 84.4 million were employed. This left 57.2 million outside the labor force—including full-time students, housewives (mostly with responsibilities for raising children), retired workers, and some potential workers who stopped looking for work because jobs were not available. In addition to the unemployed, many of these who were "not in the labor force," as well as those who worked only part time, comprised part of the labor reserves, some of whom (especially nonworking wives and mothers, if day-care facilities were provided) might be induced to work in a tight labor market.

In 1954, when the civilian labor force stood at 63.6 million, the labor force participation rates of white and nonwhite males were just over 85 percent (Table 3-2). Both rates declined over the following two decades, but that for nonwhites dropped off more sharply, falling to 74 percent by 1973. At the same time, the rate at which nonwhite females entered the labor force increased only slightly while white women entered the labor force in significant numbers.

Concern has centered on the falling labor force activity among men, especially among nonwhites. On the positive side, increasing school attendance among the young and earlier retirement among those over 60 years old have drawn nonwhite males from the labor force. Nonwhites and whites alike may be changing their attitudes

Table 3-1   Participation Rates and Percentage Distribution of the Labor Force, 1947 and 1973

	1947		1973	
Age-Sex	Participation Rate	Percent of Labor Force	Participation Rate	Percent of Labor Force
Total	58.9%	100.0%	61.4%	100.0%
Male	86.8	72.6	79.5	62.0
16–17	52.2	1.9	50.5	2.3
18–19	80.5	3.1	73.2	3.2
20–24	84.9	8.4	86.8	8.8
25–34	95.8	17.4	95.9	14.8
35–44	98.0	15.8	96.3	11.6
45–54	95.5	12.9	93.0	11.5
55–64	89.6	9.3	78.3	7.7
65 & over	47.8	3.9	22.8	2.1
Female	31.8	27.4	44.7	38.0
16–17	29.5	1.0	39.1	1.7
18–19	52.3	2.0	57.0	2.4
20–24	44.9	4.5	61.2	6.2
25–34	32.0	6.2	50.2	7.9
35–44	36.3	6.0	53.3	6.8
45–54	32.7	4.5	53.7	7.2
55–64	24.3	2.5	41.1	4.6
65 & over	8.1	0.7	8.9	1.2

Note: Detail may not add to totals due to rounding.

Source: Manpower Report of the President (Washington, D.C.: GPO, 1974), pp. 253–255.

toward work and turning to other income support as an alternative to low-wage jobs. Another explanation for the lower labor force participation rates among minority workers is the fact that they constitute a proportionately larger share of discouraged workers—that is, those who have given up the search for a job because they believe they cannot find one.

As noted in Chapter 2, a host of economic, political, social, and demographic factors have contributed to the changing composition of the work force, as well as to its growth and size. These factors have been transforming the United States, first from a rural, farm-oriented society to an urban, blue-collar, goods-producing society, and now to a suburban, white-collar, service-ori-

Table 3-2   Civilian Labor Force Participation by Sex and Color, 1954 and 1973

	1954		1973	
Sex and Color	Partici-tion Rate	Percent of Labor Force	Partici-tion Rate	Percent of Labor Force
Civilian Labor Force	58.8%	100.0%	61.0%	100.0%
Males				
White	85.6	62.5	79.5	54.8
Nonwhite	85.2	6.6	73.8	6.3
Females				
White	33.3	26.8	44.1	33.9
Nonwhite	46.1	4.1	49.1	5.0

Source: Manpower Report of the President (Washington, D.C.: GPO, 1974), pp. 253, 256–257.

ented people. But labor force data do not support popular impressions that work is going out of fashion. While population nearly tripled between 1900 and 1973, the labor force grew at a slightly faster pace (from 28 million in a population of 76 million, to 91 of 210 million).

The high birth rates of the post–World War II baby boom, following as they did the low birth rates of the depression and war years, resulted not only in a greater absolute number of youngsters but also in their higher proportion in the population in the 1960s. In 1940 children under ten accounted for one-sixth of the population; by 1960 one of every five persons was in that age group. As these youngsters reached work age in the mid-1960s, they swamped the labor market even though their participation rates had been declining.

Because of lower infant mortality and better health conditions, life expectancy for male babies has risen by about 21 years since the turn of the century. The number of people 65 and over increased from 9 million (6.8 percent of total population) in 1940 to 20.1 million, or 9.9 percent, three decades later. Therefore, even though their participation rates had plummeted, the number of workers 65 and older actually increased, comprising a nearly constant proportion of the work force.

During the first 15 years of the century, immigration added 10 million workers to a domestic labor force of 27 million. The immigration quotas of the 1920s and the severe unemployment of the depression sealed off U.S. borders, but illegal migrant workers are becoming an increasingly important part of the labor force. Only the heavy flow of Puerto Ricans to New York City, Cubans to Florida, and Mexicans to the Southwest has been an important exception since World War II. Today, sons and daughters of the early immigrants are indistinguishable in the labor force, sharing with other workers rising expectations and expanded educational opportunities.

Military requirements, including the draft law between 1940 and 1973, have strongly affected labor force participation. Military needs remove large numbers of younger males as a source of civilian workers and generate demand for additional workers to produce goods to support the armed forces. At the peak of World War II over 12 million persons were in the armed forces, and about 8 million of those who were unemployed in 1940 were absorbed into jobs. Thus about 20 million more people were at work or in the armed forces in 1944 than were holding jobs four years earlier.

The Korean and Vietnam wars affected the demand for and supply of labor, though to a lesser extent than World War II. The expanded military requirements in Vietnam kept about a million young men out of the civilian labor force during the second half of the 1960s (about 900,000 18- to 25-year-olds plus an undetermined number of draft-deferred students who might not have enrolled in college in the absence of a draft). The winding down of the war brought a large number of young men back into the civilian labor force during the early 1970s. Between 1969 and 1972 these veterans were hit harder by unemployment than their nonveteran cohorts. By 1973 the reduced manpower requirements of the all-volunteer force accounted for 40 percent of the increase in the civilian labor force of 20-to-24-year-old men over the preceding year. Vietnam-related increases in defense expenditures accounted for the creation of about 1.4 million new jobs in the private sector and an additional 200,000 government jobs for civilians between 1965 and 1968. Defense needs thus reversed the secular decline of blue-collar jobs that began after the Korean War.[4] Blue-collar jobs were adversely affected by the economic decline of 1970–1971, but since late 1971 they have begun to expand again.

Education and labor force activity

Labor force activity is generally greater among those workers who have attained additional educational credentials (Table 3-3). To the extent that more education brings with it greater earning

Table 3-3 Participation Rates in the Civilian Labor Force by Level
of Education, 1973

Years of School	Labor Force Participation Rate
Total	60.2
0	22.2
1–4	35.9
5–7	42.4
8	43.6
9–11	53.8
12	66.9
13–15	65.7
16	74.7
17+	84.1

Source: William V. Deutermann, *Educational Attainment of Workers, March
1973*, U.S. Bureau of Labor Statistics, Special Labor Force Report 161
(Washington, D.C.: GPO, January 1974), p. A-9.

power, the better educated the worker, the more income the person
foregoes by remaining out of the labor force. The attraction of
additional income is especially great among married women who
have invested in career training.

In 1900 the average worker had only a grade school education,
and today's worker averages 12.5 years of school. Most of the
gains have occurred among those who formerly were the least
educated, bringing the majority of today's labor force to a level
achieved by only a few in the labor force of the early 1900s.[5] Although much of the increase in education is a response to the
demands of a service-oriented economy, a large part of the gain
has occurred among workers independent of the jobs they perform. Educational advances, while enhancing worker motivation
to strive for a better job, have been lost in many cases because
the occupational structure of the U.S. economy continues to include a large number of jobs requiring only the basic skills.

Rising expectations and multiworker families

Rising expectations have significantly affected labor market behavior. It appears that when wages are high and jobs plentiful,
leisure may be deemed too expensive, especially if a still higher
standard of living is sought. Thus many secondary workers (wives
and youngsters) are encouraged to work to enable the family to

achieve the desired standard of living. Once the multiworker families become accustomed to a higher level of living, the added earners are, in effect, obliged to continue to work in order to maintain the desired level, with inflation adding extra impetus. In 1972 more than half of U.S. families had two or more gainfully employed workers—compared with about two-fifths in 1960 and less than one-third a decade earlier.

How are multiworker family members thus "hooked"? A standard of living clearly beyond the reach of the average wage earner is urged upon them, not only by manufacturers and retailers of consumer goods but also by the government, which publicizes appealing standards of living. The BLS city worker's budget (autumn 1973) for a moderate or "intermediate" standard of living (one with few luxuries) for a family of four required $12,626. The "higher" BLS budget for the same family, one perhaps more in line with the popular conception of American affluence, carried a price tag of $18,201. The BLS budgets apply to an urban family of four, husband aged 38, wife not working, son 13 years old and daughter 8.[6] Average income for this particular type of family is estimated as adequate for the intermediate budget but not for the higher budget. However, in the average husband-wife family, the husband had a median income of $10,752 in 1973. In four of every ten cases the family attempted to make up the difference between his income and their budget expectations through the wife's work, raising the median income to $15,237 in 1973 for husband-wife families in which both were in the labor force.[7]

Additional workers and the business cycle

The ready availability of jobs and a high level of economic activity are major factors in increasing labor force participation and opening opportunities for multiworker families. The size of the labor force expands when jobs are plentiful, and persons who might otherwise not seek jobs enter the work force, a process facilitated by employers' making various accommodations to the needs of secondary workers.

Just as workers are lured into the work force by high demand, they can become discouraged and drop out of the labor force when they cannot find jobs. The hypothesis that the labor force expands in depressions, as wives and children of unemployed or underemployed workers try to find jobs to replace lost income, is not supported by evidence.[8] While some additional workers enter the labor force during recessions to bolster sagging family income, more workers withdraw in discouragement.[9] The additional worker is more likely to be a low-income person than the discouraged worker.[10]

The additional-worker hypothesis was revived in 1970, when the nation was experiencing a combination of inflation and recession. The selective decline in economic activity still left job vacancies for secondary workers, especially married women, who might have sought employment to maintain family income eroded by inflation and reduced opportunities to work overtime. The net effect was an expansion of the labor force accompanied by rising unemployment rates. However, as the recession continued, the labor force participation rate declined and the labor force expansion reflected only population growth. When the recession passed in 1972 and 1973, the labor force began to expand again. However, the expansion was concentrated among workers under 35 years old, and more than half was attributable to population growth, with most of the remainder being due to the rising labor force participation rates of women. By the end of 1974 the labor force started to contract again, as the recession deepened.

Labor market pathologies: unemployment, underemployment, and shortages

In the United States labor demand has tended to fall short of the available labor supply, except in times of war. At the same time, there have been frequent sustained shortages of highly specialized labor. Some unemployment and some shortages are to be expected in any dynamic economy, regardless of the level of labor demand. Job changes, plant shutdowns, the search for a first job, and seasonal swings all cause some temporary joblessness and underemployment; innovations (e.g., widespread use of computers) or extremely large changes in demand (e.g., rapid expansion and contraction of the space program) may result in temporary shortages or surpluses of skilled personnel. As long as labor market imbalances remain brief and moderate, they are only of passing social concern—a small price to be paid for free market operations. Above and beyond some frictional minimums, however, unemployment, underemployment, and labor shortages arising from longer-term imbalances have far-reaching implications for the well-being of individuals and for society as a whole.

The historical perspective

The levels of unemployment have varied widely over the past 40 years, encompassing long periods of massive waste of manpower

Table 3-4 Average Unemployment 1929, 1933, 1944, 1947–1973

Year	Number (in thousands)	Percent of Labor Force
1929	1,550	3.2
1933	12,830	24.9
1944	670	1.2
1947	2,311	3.9
1948	2,276	3.8
1949	3,637	5.9
1950	3,288	5.3
1951	2,055	3.3
1952	1,883	3.0
1953	1,834	2.9
1954	3,532	5.5
1955	2,852	4.4
1956	2,750	4.1
1957	2,859	4.3
1958	4,602	6.8
1959	3,740	5.5
1960	3,852	5.5
1961	4,714	6.7
1962	3,911	5.5
1963	4,070	5.7
1964	3,786	5.2
1965	3,366	4.5
1966	2,875	3.8
1967	2,975	3.8
1968	2,817	3.6
1969	2,832	3.5
1970	4,088	4.9
1971	4,993	5.9
1972	4,840	5.6
1973	4,304	4.9

Source: Employment and Earnings (January 1974), p. 24. Data include 14- and 15-year-olds prior to 1947.

and considerably shorter periods of general shortages of labor (Table 3-4). Experience has shown that most of those gyrations could have been avoided or at least minimized by responsible and compassionate public policy, though complete cures for the ailments that plague the labor market remain elusive. The disaster of the 1930s, which brought unemployment rates of 25 percent or more, was eventually diagnosed as a shortage of effective demand. The crisis apparently developed mainly because economists and politicians lacked a clear remedy for the malady and relied too long on the response of automatic market mechanisms. The

massive infusion of labor demand caused by World War II solved
the unemployment problem, but at a cost of debilitating inflation.
The jobless rate declined to just over 1 percent, a condition that
could only be characterized as minimal frictional unemployment
caused by excessive labor demand and strong social pressures
against slackers during a national emergency.

The Great Depression left deep scars, and the prevailing view
during the mid-1940s was that the high unemployment would return once the war was over. Congress responded by enacting the
Employment Act of 1946, affirming the national goal of an economic climate that would provide job opportunities to all persons
"able, willing, and seeking work." The expected high level of unemployment did not develop in the immediate postwar adjustment
period, largely because labor demand was sustained at high levels
by a big backlog of consumer spending.

In the 1950s business contractions became more frequent,
and recovery after each recession grew less and less adequate,
leaving joblessness progressively higher. Although mass unemployment was avoided in the late 1940s and 1950s, the persistent rise
of unemployment raised fears of a progressive malaise that looked
increasingly like secular stagnation. The policies of the federal
government in the 1950s, primarily designed to aid and support
normal market mechanisms, were not adequate in our increasingly complex, interdependent economy. In the 1960s they were
replaced by diverse efforts to combat unemployment—aid to depressed areas, stimulation of business investment and consumer
demand, and special manpower programs aimed at improving
the opportunities of the poor and unskilled to compete in the
job market.

Policy orientation slowly shifted to the profound and continuing problems of persons who were particularly disadvantaged in
the labor market and living in poverty. Confined to the low end
of the employment ladder by a lack of skills or special personal
problems and living largely in big-city ghettos and rural slums, a
small portion of the work force was living through a continuing
cycle of intermittent unemployment and underemployment at
low-paying jobs. Ultimately, these measures, coupled with the es-
calation of the Vietnam War, generated high employment. As the
economy moved into the 1970s on a downbeat, concern shifted to
the unemployment-inflation dilemma as unemployment remained
persistently high during times of rapidly rising prices. Also, more
careful attention was paid to the character of underemployment,
subemployment, and inadequate earnings in attempts to define
more clearly those workers who are failing in or are being failed
by the labor market.

Unemployment and underemployment

Underutilized manpower resources may be divided into four distinct groups: the unemployed; persons outside the labor force who want or need work; persons who are working fewer hours than they would prefer because of economic reasons beyond their personal control; and persons employed at jobs that are below their actual or potential skill level. No reasonable estimate of the size of the last group exists, although it must be large indeed. Data for the first three groups for the high-employment year of 1969 and during the recession of 1971 are summarized in the following tabulation:

Type of Unemployment or Underemployment	Number	
	1969	1971
Unemployed	2,831,000	4,993,000
Outside labor force, but wanted work	574,000	774,000
On reduced workweeks, economic reasons	2,056,000	2,675,000

The estimates for 1969 relate to a period of strong demand, when underutilization was at one of the low points of the previous 25 years. When labor demand was weaker in 1971, underemployment and unemployment were commensurately higher.

The causes of unemployment

Total unemployment is primarily a function of the general economic environment and is in large measure responsive to policy actions. Identification of specific forms of unemployment and their causes may be helpful in designing remedial policies for particular maladies. The causes of unemployment, in good times and bad, are reasonably clear and fall into four broad categories: cyclical, frictional, seasonal, and structural. Elements of each cause of joblessness usually can be found in each unemployment situation because they tend to reinforce and compound one another.

Cyclical unemployment

Cyclical swings in business activity are the most commonly recognized (and probably most important) cause of unemployment and underemployment. The outstanding characteristic of cyclical unemployment in a modern economy is that the individual worker has little control over his fate. Since the end of World War II, business recessions have been mild and of short duration. In each, unemployment stayed quite low until the peak of business activity passed, then rose sharply as the recession grew progressively worse. For some time after the trough had passed, unemployment tended to continue high. Policy response to cyclical unemployment has taken two forms—income-protection plans and attempts at stabilization of demand and production. In a marked downturn virtually no jobs at any pay level are available in the sore spots most affected by the turn of activity. During the downturn of 1970, for example, the unemployment rate in Seattle rose to depression proportions; aerospace workers with many years' seniority were laid off for extended periods, and few other employers were hiring.

The economy has a basic productive potential that is a function of its resources—labor, capital, and natural resources—and the state of technology. A departure from the level of output appropriate to the existing resource base may result in continuing unemployment or overemployment, with neither being necessarily responsive to automatic correction by market mechanisms. Arthur Okun estimated that for each 1 percent shortfall in the level of real output (GNP) from potential output, the overall unemployment rate would be higher by about 0.3 percentage points.[11]

Policy prescriptions growing out of Okun's gap analysis are simple; they call for the stimulation or repression of consumer and business demand by the use of tax cuts or increases, higher government spending or retrenchment, and stimulation or restraint of the credit and monetary supply. Policies designed to stabilize the labor market at a high employment level are not always consistent with other economic goals of maximum price stability or minimum inflation, long-term growth, and a favorable balance of international trade and payments. Consequently, decisions often reflect goals other than high employment.

Other types of unemployment

The three remaining causes of unemployment—seasonal changes in activity, frictions in the job market, and structural imbalances —probably vary directly with cyclical joblessness and tend to be restricted to particular classes of workers.

Seasonal swings in activity—notably in outdoor work such as construction and agriculture—tend to result in temporary joblessness and contribute significantly to total unemployment. While precise measures are difficult—especially because a seasonal slack period may be extended by cyclical weakness or the slow obsolescence of an industry—the BLS estimated that seasonal unemployment accounted for about one-fourth of total forced idleness in the late 1950s; reexamination of comparable data for the late 1960s suggests a similar conclusion. In construction and agriculture the proportion was estimated at more than 40 percent compared with 10 to 15 percent in transportation and trade.[12] If seasonal joblessness could be reduced appreciably, it would benefit all sectors of the economy.

Seasonal swings recur annually, making it possible to measure in great detail their characteristics and predict their timing, amplitude, and cause (weather, institutional factors, and custom). Because seasonality is predictable within a relatively narrow range, employment and unemployment statistics are adjusted for seasonality, permitting closer identification of cyclical and secular trends. This adjustment, however, should not obscure the very sizable economic loss associated with seasonality. Much can be done to minimize these costs.[13]

Frictional unemployment results from temporary difficulties in matching available workers with available jobs. It arises mainly from lack of knowledge of opportunities and is marked by its relatively short duration. Such unemployment is unavoidable—as when women or younger workers enter the labor force or when skilled workers voluntarily quit.

Seasonal and frictional unemployment overlap, making clearcut distinctions impossible. Each June and July, for example, thousands of young people enter the labor market in search of temporary or permanent jobs. This vast inflow is partly seasonal —arising from the institutionally determined school year—and partly frictional—reflecting the time necessary to scour the market and find employment. As time passes, some of this unemployment can become cyclical or structural—that is, demand is not strong enough to absorb all of them (as in the summer of 1970), or demand is strong enough, but they are not adequately prepared for the available jobs.

Structural unemployment is more complex than seasonal and frictional unemployment and arises from basic changes in the composition of labor demand and failure of the labor supply to accommodate to new market conditions. Recent examples include large cutbacks in the space program; the decline of the railroads, which combined with the switch to diesel locomotives to displace thousands of skilled railroad workers; the decline of coal mining in Appalachia; and the relocation of the New England textile industry in the South. These and other transformations left many skilled and unskilled workers stranded in areas with job deficits and urgently needing to learn a new skill or to relocate in expanding labor markets.

Possibly a more subtle cause of structural unemployment is

technological progress and automation. Productivity advances in agriculture displaced thousands of farmers; similar displacements have occurred in the durable-goods sector of manufacturing, where automation has reduced the need for some skills and sharply modified others. Because the structurally unemployed generally have a large investment in their skill and location, they are less likely than mobile young workers to find new jobs quickly. Thus structural unemployment tends to be of long duration and requires vigorous efforts at retraining, relocation, or infusion of new capital investment creating new jobs.

Unemployment can also be measured in terms of immediate causes that result in persons' joining the ranks of the unemployed; jobless workers can be identified as job losers, job leavers, reentrants, and new entrants.[14] In 1972 the 4.8 million unemployed workers were distributed among the four categories as follows:

Classification	Percent of Unemployment in 1972
Job losers	44.3
Job leavers	13.1
Reentrants	28.8
Entrants	13.9

Job loss, accounting for the largest single group of unemployed persons, is generally either cyclically or seasonally induced, and it is most often the reason for unemployment among adult men. On the other hand, younger workers and women are most likely to be without jobs because they have recently entered or reentered the labor force. In conventional terms their unemployment is more likely to be frictional or seasonal. As involuntary idleness persists beyond a month, the probability that it is frictional diminishes; after 15 weeks or more it can no longer be considered seasonal, and a basic structural or cyclical problem becomes probable.

Comparing the duration of unemployment in two years, it is possible to classify the causes of unemployment (Table 3-5). Assuming, for example, that there was no cyclical unemployment in 1969—a year of strong demand and low unemployment—the data suggest that joblessness in a period of strong demand is essentially frictional and of short duration, though about one-eighth of the unemployment appears to have been structural. By 1971, as the recession deepened, the relative significance of frictional unemployment declined, and long-term or cyclical unemployment became relatively much more significant.

The majority of workers, however, remain without jobs for relatively short periods—that is, a large portion of unemployment

Table 3-5 Distribution of Unemployment by Duration and Cause, 1969 and 1971

Initial Classification	Less than 5 Weeks Largely Frictional and Seasonal		5–14 Weeks More Serious Problems Emerging		15 Weeks or More Structural or Cyclical	
	1969	1971	1969	1971	1969	1971
Total (all causes)	58%	45%	29%	32%	13%	24%
Job losers	51	36	32	33	18	31
Job leavers	61	46	28	32	12	21
Reentrants	62	54	26	30	11	16
New entrants	60	52	31	32	9	16

Note: Details may not add to totals because of rounding.

Source: Derived from Curtis L. Gilroy, *Job Losers, Leavers, and Entrants: Traits and Trends*, U.S. Bureau of Labor Statistics, Special Labor Force Report 157 (Washington, D.C.: GPO, August 1973), Table G.

is frictional or possibly seasonal. In 1972 only one-fifth were unemployed over 15 weeks, and half moved back into jobs after only 5 weeks or less of joblessness. The foregoing analysis assumes frictional unemployment affects all four classes of the unemployed. Seasonality, on the other hand, is more readily identifiable in the case of new entrants—students and graduates who swell the ranks of job seekers during the summer months. To a lesser extent the change of seasons also affects the job loss rate, which rises during the winter, when outdoor work is curtailed, and dips during the summer.

Job losers are the most likely to remain unemployed for longer periods of time; in 1972 they accounted for six of every ten jobless workers unemployed over 27 weeks. Since job losers are largely men in then prime working ages with strong attachments to the labor force, their numbers among the unemployed tend to increase disproportionately when cyclical unemployment is on the rise. Entrants and reentrants, in contrast, have the alternative of dropping out of the labor force again. Other factors, such as lower levels of educational attainment and the greater sensitivity of blue-collar workers to job loss, also may explain the greater likelihood of lengthy unemployment among job losers.

Characteristics of the unemployed

Employability is a function of workers' preparedness for work, as well as employers' needs and prejudices. Thus the likelihood of being unemployed varies with workers' personal characteristics as well as with the more general economic factors that generate unemployment. Forced idleness is most likely to be visited upon those who are least able to cope with it—in general, the ill-prepared and the young. If the persons involved also happen to be black or female (or both), the likelihood of being jobless is multiplied by a factor of two or more.

There is a certain socioeconomic logic in the sequence of age-sex unemployment. Most Americans live in families in which the principal—although not only—breadwinner is an adult male with job experience and training. Most such men have a full-time, year-round commitment to the labor force, and even a short period of unemployment can be a very serious matter because of their family responsibilities. Although unemployment among male family heads is appreciably lower than the national average, it tends to be especially cyclically responsive, reflecting the heavy concentration of men in manufacturing and construction. In 1969, for example, male heads of households accounted for more than half of the labor force but for only about one-fourth of the unemployed. Wives and other relatives accounted for about two-thirds of total unemployment, while female heads of households accounted for about 8 percent.

The incidence of unemployment is higher among women and is particularly severe for young workers even when high employment prevails. Frictional unemployment is higher for women and teenagers than for men, reflecting their greater likelihood of entering or leaving the labor force and the demands of school, military service, and marriage. These frictions are not the only explanations, however. Young workers and women are often restricted to entry-level jobs that are frequently sensitive to seasonal fluctuations or offer few opportunities for upward mobility. Employees have little to lose by giving up such jobs. The structural component of unemployment may also be important for younger workers and women. Mature women reentering the labor force after raising children may find their skills outmoded. Among younger workers the steady erosion of unskilled entry-level jobs probably has been very important, especially for school dropouts whose unemployment rates may be more than twice those of their peers who graduated from high school.[15]

Unemployment and its duration vary with educational attainment. In March 1973 just slightly more than 2 percent of college graduates were unemployed. The high school diploma appeared to have a significant impact, since close to 8 percent of workers who had less than a high school education were unemployed compared to under 5 percent of high school graduates.[16]

These variations by education are also reflected in unemployment rates by occupation. Professional and technical workers—many are college graduates—averaged 2 percent or less unemployed in each year between 1958 and 1970. Only in 1971 and 1972 did their unemployment go as high as 3.5 percent. The rate for laborers —many of who did not complete high school—has never averaged less than 6.5 percent and has been as high as 15 percent. The rate for laborers has typically been about five times greater than that for professional and technical workers and about two times greater than that for craftsmen. Obviously, inadequate preparation consigns a worker to the end of the employment queue and the top of the layoff list. The program implications are clear: Improved education and training can increase the supply of relatively skilled workers and rescue some of the unskilled from the cycle of recurring unemployment and underemployment.

In part, skill differentials and educational deficiencies are the cause of substantially higher levels of joblessness among blacks than among whites. The jobless rates of blacks have been consistently about double those of whites over the past two decades. Skill differentials are not the only explanation, however. Regardless of educational attainment, work experience, and sex, blacks are more likely than whites to be unemployed, to have extended periods of joblessness, and, when employed, to have lower levels of earnings. Discrimination doubtlessly accounts for a significant part of these differences.[17]

Discrimination also plays a role in the higher jobless rates of women and teenagers. A woman or teenager is more likely to be laid off than a man, more likely to be working part time for economic reasons, and less likely to be in a high-income, high-status occupation. Of course, higher unemployment among women and younger workers should be expected, given lack of seniority, initial entry in the labor force, tendency to seek new jobs, or relative lack of experience.

Association with particular industries is often a cause of high jobless levels. Construction and agriculture are subject to seasonal swings in activity, while durable-goods manufacturing is very sensitive to cyclical changes. These industries tend to have higher unemployment rates and to be particularly responsive to changes in the growth rate of the economy.

Unemployment is also a function of geography. Industrial concentrations and occupational and racial distributions are largely responsible for this.[18] Cyclical changes, for example, are greater in areas where manufacturing abounds, such as the Northeast and the North Central states. And structural problems have been evidenced in the experiences of Appalachian soft-coal regions and former New England textile and leather towns. In the early 1970s the declines in military-aerospace production boosted unemployment rates in southern California and Washington. Where minority workers constitute a larger proportion of the work force, unemployment and underemployment continue to be more severe, but occupational differences among regions have narrowed over the past decade primarily due to the upgrading of the Southern labor force and the proscription of discriminatory practices.

A more recent phenomenon is the high unemployment in central metropolitan areas, reflecting the great migration of population from backward rural areas to big-city slums and the flight of industry from the inner city. The contribution of migration to unemployment in central-city areas has not been measured; but whatever the causes, the incidence of unemployment is greater in central cities than in their surrounding rings. In the nation's 20 largest cities—which contain about one-third of all workers—the unemployment rate of central-city residents was 7.2 percent in 1972 compared with an average rate of 5.4 percent for suburban residents.

When these data are further broken down to measure specific poverty areas, the unemployment gap and extent of employment problems grow progressively worse. In 1970, when unemployment was 4.9 percent nationally, it was 9.6 percent throughout urban poverty areas.[19] Among family heads poverty area unemployment was more than twice as great as the national average. Six out of ten of the unemployed in these poorest areas were black; one-third had been unemployed for more than 15 weeks—twice the national rate. Race and lower educational attainment are no doubt important factors in the higher rates. A majority of poverty area residents were minority group members, and their median educational level was 10.2 years.

Unemployment is a problem faced by all industrialized countries, but, the United States seems to have tolerated a higher incidence of unemployment than many others (Table 3-6). Only in Canada, Great Britain, and, more recently, Italy has unemployment been as persistent a problem as in the United States.

Averages tend to understate the actual number of people hit by unemployment at some time during the year. Monthly average unemployment for 1972 was 4.8 million, but work-experience data show that 13.2 million persons were among the unemployed for at least one week during 1972.[20] The pressures of forced idleness on economic well-being, however, are greatest when unemployment extends over a long period or is repetitive. In 1972, for example, 4.6 million persons were unemployed for 15 weeks or more, many because of repeated spells of unemployment.

Table 3-6   Unemployment Rates in the United States and Eight
Industrialized Nations, 1962 and 1972

	1962	1972
United States	5.5%	5.6%
Australia	n.a.	2.2
Canada	5.9	6.3
France	1.8	2.9
Germany	0.4	0.9
Great Britain	2.8	6.2
Italy	3.2	4.0
Japan	1.3	1.4
Sweden	1.5	2.7

Note: Rates are adjusted to U.S. concepts.

Source: Constance Sorrentino, "Unemployment in the United States and
Seven Foreign Countries," *Monthly Labor Review* (September 1970), p. 14;
and Constance Sorrentino and Joyanna Moy, "Unemployment in the United
States and Eight Foreign Countries," *Monthly Labor Review* (January 1974),
p. 48.

Labor shortages and surpluses

While unemployment has been high for selected groups of workers,
there have been continuing shortages of other kinds of workers—
mainly those in the highly skilled, highly paid professions and
those in the lowest-paid occupations. Amelioration of shortages in
these groups is an important objective because manpower bottlenecks create dislocations and obstacles to balanced economic
growth. High employment levels are often erroneously identified
by employers as shortages of general labor, largely because a tight
market increases labor turnover, may reduce the rate of productivity growth, and usually results in higher unit labor costs. These
concerns have surfaced only on rare occasions, including the latter
half of the 1960s.

A more important problem exists, however, with respect to
shortages of highly skilled workers. it may require several years
of specialized training, not to mention huge costs, to develop
skilled professional personnel. Filling these gaps should be a first-
line national priority. Shortages of most unskilled jobs can usually
be cured with a bigger dose of income and a dollop of prestige.

Some shortages result from restrictive practices designed to
provide selected groups of workers with strong bargaining power.
Some unions and professional associations engage in restrictive
practices, not always successfully, to limit the supply of labor and
raise income. Well-known examples include many construction

craft unions, medical and dental associations, and university facilities that restrict the supply of new young Ph.D.'s. These special
interest groups primarily restrict supply through arbitrary qualification standards for apprenticeship, unduly extended apprenticeships, limits on the number of apprentices per journeyman, arti-
ficially high licensing standards, and other techniques. Such practices are always defended as a means of maintaining high standards to protect the public from the "untrained" and "inept." A
reasonable distribution of employment opportunities will not be
achieved unless restrictive practices are corrected.

A major departure from the historically sustained demand for
college graduates has been projected to begin during the late
1970s. By 1980 the supply of college graduates is anticipated to
outstrip demand by 140,000 persons annually.[21] Surpluses of
college-trained manpower do not necessarily imply those persons
will be unable to find work. In fact, the slowed growth of the
economy may dampen the enthusiasm of youth to invest in college training, thereby correcting part of the imbalance in supply
and demand for highly educated workers. Moreover, an overall
surplus of college graduates masks continuing needs for workers
trained in specialized occupations, many of which require other
post–high school training, but not necessarily college.

Unemployment is only one dimension of inadequacy

Since the Great Depression labor market measures have focused
on the availability of work, and policy makers have tended to react to these highly publicized barometers of economic conditions.
The underlying assumption has been that almost any job is better
than no job and that employment is the sole means to obtain
income essential for sustenance.

However, movement in and out of the labor force today is
controlled by factors different from those in the 1930s, when the
current labor force concepts were developed. For the bulk of the
population a job remains the sole source of legitimate income, but
transfer payments now account for one-ninth of total personal
income. Large groups now have an income cushion provided by
increased affluence and accumulated assets that can be used—in
addition to transfer payments—when income is interrupted. Without in any way minimizing the individual's problems in search for
gainful employment, developments such as the increasing number
of working wives, the ability of families to support dependent

children in school, and the economic padding provided for the aged and the temporarily jobless accent the need for a measure of economic need based on an adequate standard of employment and earnings combined.

The policy makers who designed antipoverty programs during the 1960s recognized a need to measure low income among the unemployed as well as forced idleness. Seeking support for employment and training programs, then Secretary of Labor, W. Willard Wirtz, encouraged the preparation in 1967 of a subemployment rate. The measure added these groups to the number of unemployed: discouraged workers, full-time workers receiving wages insufficient to lift them above the poverty standard, and part-time workers who want to work full time.

The subemployed, however, include many whose attachment to the labor force and need may be questionable—for example, full-time students and persons aged 65 years and over who are discouraged workers, and wives and other potential secondary earners whose family incomes are above average without their labor force participation. Therefore, a measure of labor market pathologies that would confine its concern to that section of the labor force that encounters difficulties in maintaining sustained employment as well as maintaining a predetermined minimum income level would have to meet the following criteria:

1. Regardless of the employment status of the people involved, the index would exclude persons with above-average household income. Experience has shown that persons who have succeeded in raising their income above the average for the total labor force normally have sufficient resources to adjust to adversity. They frequently have assets, in addition to transfer payments, to tide them over during their periods of unemployment, which are normally of short duration.
2. Conversely, heads of households whose incomes are inadequate to raise themselves and their families out of poverty would be included even if they worked full time. Secondary family workers, including working wives, probably should not be counted in the index. If a female was the head of a family, she would be counted; but to include all low earners would clearly disregard the economic realities of treating the family as a viable economic unit.
3. An index that combines employment and earnings inadequacy would include both persons who want jobs for employment and workers who hold part-time jobs while looking for full-time positions. The income criteria applied to the unemployed would hold for the discouraged and part-time workers.

Table 3-7 Derivation of Employment and Earnings Inadequacy Index for March 1972 (thousand persons)

	Current Population Survey	Persons in Households with Above-Average Income	Employment and Earnings Inadequacy
Total population aged 16 and over	143,131	—	—
Current Population Survey labor force	85,398	—	—
Current Population Survey discouraged workers	830	—	—
Less students age 16 to 21 and persons age 65 and over	-106	—	—
Net discouraged workers	724	—	—
Adjusted labor force	—	—	86,122
1. Unemployed	5,215	—	—
Less persons age 65 and over	-102	—	—
Less students age 16 to 21	-878	—	—
Adjusted unemployed	4,235	-1,504	2,731
2. Net discouraged workers	724	-182	542
3. Family heads	2,092	—	—
Unrelated individuals	243	—	—
Fully employed household heads earning less than poverty-level income	2,335	-257	2,078
4. Family heads	2,653	—	—
Unrelated individuals	1,029	—	—
Partially employed household heads earning less than poverty-level income	3,682	-204	3,478
5. Current Population Survey	2,312	—	—
Less number included in above categories	-418	—	—
Employed part time involuntarily	1,894	-781	1,113
Total with inadequate employment and earnings	—	-2,928	9,942
Employment and Earnings Inadequacy Index	—	—	11.5%

Source: Tabulations based on Current Population Survey data.

4. Other exclusions are needed to restrict the employment and earnings inadequacy measure to groups whose needs cannot be questioned. A case can be made for not counting full-time students aged 16 to 21 and all persons over 65, since their attachment to the labor force is frequently tenuous. The exclusion of persons 65 years old and over is justified on the basis that public pensions are now nearly universal and private pensions much more widespread. Many among the elderly, then, are part-time workers or have their income supplemented from other sources.

Subtracting these from the subemployment measure, it is possible to derive an index that measures more precisely both employment and earnings problems.[22] In March 1972 the new index yielded a rate of 11.5 percent—almost twice the unemployment rate (Table 3-7).

Low earnings are clearly as much or more of a problem than unemployment, discouragement, and involuntary part-time work. Employment and earnings inadequacy is a continuing structural problem. Even when the official unemployment rate declined to 3.5 percent in March 1969, nearly one in every ten persons had inadequate employment and earnings according to this index. Policy prescriptions to combat these labor market problems must include long-run commitments to eliminate inequalities in the wage structure and employment practices as well as countercyclical measures.

Notes

1. Herbert S. Parnes, "Labor Force Participation and Labor Mobility," in *A Review of Industrial Relations Research,* Industrial Relations Research Association Series, Vol. 1 (Madison, Wis.: The Association, 1970), pp. 1–33.
2. William G. Bowen and T. Aldrich Finegan, *The Economics of Labor Force Participation* (Princeton, N.J.: Princeton University Press, 1969), pp. 559–565, especially the tables on pp. 561 and 565.
3. Stuart H. Garfinkle, *Job Changing and Manpower Training,* U.S. Department of Labor, Manpower Administration, Office of Manpower, Automation and Training, Manpower Report No. 10 (Washington, D.C.: GPO, 1964), p. 1.
4. Richard P. Oliver, "Increase in Defense-Related Employment During Vietnam Buildup," *Monthly Labor Review* (February 1970), pp. 3 ff.; and U.S. Congress, Senate Subcommittee on Employment, Manpower, and Poverty, *Hearings on Manpower Development and Training Legislation, 1970* (Washington, D.C.: GPO, 1970), Part 3, pp. 1243 ff.
5. Sar A. Levitan and William B. Johnston, *Work Is Here to Stay,*

Alas (Salt Lake City, Utah: Olympus Publishing Co., 1973), pp. 56–59.

6. Jean Brackett, "Urban Family Budgets Updated to Autumn 1973," *Monthly Labor Review* (August 1974), p. 57.

7. U.S. Bureau of Census, *Money Income in 1973 of Families and Persons in the United States*, Series P-60, No. 97 (Washington, D.C.: GPO, January 1975), Tables 25 and 39.

8. W. S. Woytinsky, *Three Aspects of Labor Dynamics* (New York: Social Science Research Council, 1942), Part III.

9. Jacob Mincer, "Labor Force Participation and Unemployment: A Review of Recent Evidence," in Robert and Margaret Gordon, eds., *Prosperity and Unemployment* (New York: Wiley, 1966), pp. 73 ff.; and Bowen and Finegan, op. cit., p. 483.

10. Glen G. Cain, *The Net Effect of Unemployment on Labor Force Participation of Secondary Workers* (Madison, Wis.: Social Systems Research Institute, University of Wisconsin, October 1964).

11. Arthur Okun, "Potential GNP: Its Measurement and Significance," *Proceedings of the Business and Economic Statistics Section of the American Statistical Association* (1962), pp. 98–104.

12. Seymour Wolfbein, *Employment and Unemployment in the United States* (Chicago: Science Research Associates, 1962), p. 293.

13. Sol Swerdloff and Robert J. Myers, "Seasonality and Construction," *Monthly Labor Review* (September 1967), pp. 1–8.

14. Curtis L. Gilroy, *Job Losers, Leavers, and Entrants: Traits and Trends*, U.S. Bureau of Labor Statistics, Special Labor Force Report 157 (Washington, D.C.: GPO, August 1973).

15. Howard V. Hayghe, "Employment of High School Graduates and Dropouts," *Monthly Labor Review* (August 1970), pp. 35 ff.

16. William V. Deutermann, *Educational Attainment of Workers, March 1973*, U.S. Bureau of Labor Statistics, Special Labor Force Report 161 (Washington, D.C.: GPO, January 1974), Table B.

17. James Gwartney, "Discrimination and Income Differentials," *American Economic Review* (June 1970), pp. 396–408.

18. Christopher G. Gellner, "Regional Differences in Employment and Unemployment, 1957–72," *Monthly Labor Review* (March 1974), pp. 15–23.

19. U.S. Bureau of the Census, *Employment Profiles of Selected Low Income Areas*, Final Report PHC (3)-1 (Washington, D.C.: GPO, 1972).

20. Anne M. Young, *Work Experience of the Population in 1972*, U.S. Bureau of Labor Statistics, Special Labor Force Report 162 (Washington, D.C.: GPO, February 1974). Table C-1.

21. Jack Altman, "An Overview of BLS Projections," *Monthly Labor Review* (December 1973), p. 4.

22. Sar A. Levitan and Robert Taggart, *Employment and Earnings Inadequacy: A New Social Indicator* (Baltimore, Md.: Johns Hopkins Press, 1974).

4
shifting
composition
of employment

The dramatic enlargement in the role of women in the work force has coincided with significant declines in the roles of older and younger males. Other changes in the economy have brought increased reliance upon peripheral workers who do not work full time year round but take intermittent or part-time jobs and tend to move in and out of the labor force. There have been important changes, too, in the types of work done—in the occupations and industries in which Americans are employed. Despite these changes, the basic efficiency and productivity of the economy has continued to improve.

Peripheral workers

While the majority of workers still hold full-time, year-round jobs and account for the bulk of all hours worked, a very substantial number work intermittently. A total of 97 million persons were in the labor force during 1972, but only 57 percent were employed more than 35 hours per week (full time) for 50 weeks or more (year round). Employment averaged 81.7 million, or 15.3 million less than the total number of persons who worked during the year. There were 19.3 million part-time workers and 22.2 million who had full-time jobs but worked 49 weeks or less (Table 4-1).

These 42 million peripheral workers include many different groups with diverse employment experiences, but they have much in common.[1] They are usually marginal workers who enter and leave the labor force as secondary earners. And, for the most part, they toil in low-paying, dead-end jobs (Figure 4-1). For some of these workers the attractions of wage jobs are balanced

Table 4-1   Work Experience of Persons 16 Years Old and Over, 1972

	Both Sexes	Men	Women
Total Who Worked During the Year	96,972	57,054	39,918
Percent	100.0	100.0	100.0
Full Timeª	80.0	87.7	69.2
50–52 weeks	57.1	67.3	42.5
48–49 weeks	2.3	2.4	2.1
40–47 weeks	4.4	4.6	4.1
27–39 weeks	5.3	4.8	5.9
14–26 weeks	5.9	4.7	7.6
13 weeks or less	5.1	3.9	6.9
Part Time	20.0	12.3	30.8
50–52 weeks	6.7	4.2	10.3
48–49 weeks	0.6	0.4	0.9
40–47 weeks	1.5	0.9	2.4
27–39 weeks	2.4	1.4	3.7
14–26 weeks	3.9	2.5	5.9
13 weeks or less	4.9	3.0	7.6

ªUsually worked 35 hours or more a week.
Source: U.S. Bureau of Labor Statistics, unpublished statistics.

against the lure of income alternatives such as welfare, unemployment compensation, crime, or "hustling" outside the regular labor market. For these groups there is a continual shifting in and out of the various activities depending upon economic conditions and the opportunities that are available.

Voluntary part-time or part-year work

Voluntary part-time workers deserve separate attention because their number has been growing at a rapid pace, from roughly one-eighth of average full-time workers in 1960 to one-sixth in 1973. This has not happened because of a shortage of full-time jobs, but rather because of a growth in part-time positions that are attractive to those who do not want to work full time.

More than two-thirds of the voluntary part-time workers are female; and three-fifths of these are married and living with their husbands. Overwhelmingly, their jobs are concentrated in the ser-

Figure 4-1   Labor force in nonagricultural industries by full-time and part-time status, 1957–1973.

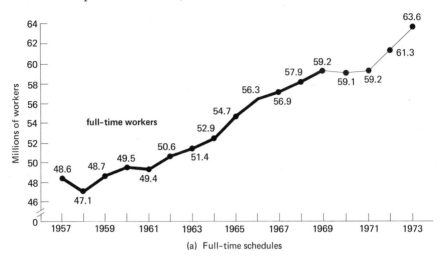

(a) Full-time schedules

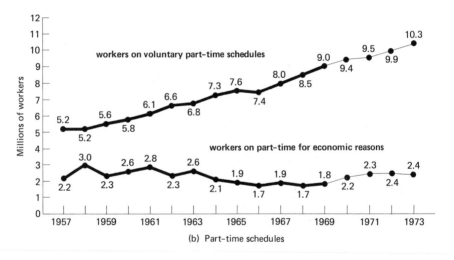

(b) Part-time schedules

Source: U.S. Department of Labor.

vice and retail sectors, which accounted for almost three-fourths of the voluntary part-time jobs in 1973. More and more employers are restructuring their operations to use part-time personnel, and married women are increasingly willing to combine part-time work with family care.

In addition to women, who often prefer part-time or part-year jobs, two other groups account for the bulk of the remaining peripheral workers: (1) Older persons in the process of leaving the labor force are often characterized by limited employability, alternative sources of income, and a desire for less demanding work; and (2) youths and college students are just entering the labor force, supplementing income while attending school, or are unable to find full-time, year-round jobs.

The secondary labor market

Peripheral workers are generally employed in low-wage, low-skill, and low-status occupations. They are likely to be agricultural laborers, textile workers, and workers concentrated in the service and retail sectors with few paying more than the minimum wage and many paying less. Even when worked full time, these jobs usually yield an income near or below poverty thresholds. Because of unattractive working conditions and low pay, they are characterized by high absenteeism and rapid turnover.

Peripheral workers and the marginal jobs for which they are hired constitute a secondary labor market, which is different in many ways from the market for full-time, year-round workers. Intermittent work patterns are built into the secondary system. Employers act on the assumption that these employees are not committed to sustained work: Fringe benefits are minimized, little investment is made in training, and opportunities for advancement are closed off. On the other hand, employees feel little attachment to their jobs and tend to quit on a moment's notice. They have little interest in retirement plans or any long-range benefits because they expect their tenure to be limited; they tend to rely on job changes rather than advancements within the firm as a route upward.

This system has different effects on different people. It may fill the need of a wife to get out of the house several afternoons a week or of a college student to earn money over Christmas or during the school year. But it is inimical to the migrant worker and his family who cannot find year-round employment or the ghetto family head who moves from one dead-end job to another.

Peripheral workers can be divided into two major groups: those who are employed at full-time jobs interrupted by periods of forced idleness and those who work at part-time jobs because full-time work is not available (discussed in the next chapter). Within these two groups are those who hold seasonal jobs in which unemployment is predictable and regular, those who are underemployed or unemployed for a comparatively short time while searching or preparing for new employment, and those who have serious problems in finding and holding jobs throughout the year.

Certain occupations and industries, especially agriculture and contract construction, have largely seasonal employment patterns. Agriculture is highly seasonal, and though migration can usually extend the working period, unemployment is still frequent. In 1972 more than half of farm laborers and foremen worked less than 50 weeks, and 40 percent held jobs less than half the year. However, agricultural employment is declining; the number of farm laborers fell from 2.3 million in 1958 to 1.4 million in 1973. Thus agriculture is becoming a less important factor affecting labor force behavior.

Many of the 43 percent of all workers who held part-year or part-time jobs during 1972 found their employment interrupted by periods of forced idleness. Many suffer from serious deficiencies and are unable to find or hold down continuous employment. A growing proportion, however, are those who seek part-time employment because of other interests or concerns.

The employment patterns of these peripheral workers are likely to continue in their recent trends. Seasonal unemployment will diminish as agricultural employment continues to decline, as construction becomes more stable through better planning and the introduction of industrialized methods, and as the number of teenagers looking for summer jobs levels off during the 1970s. Some inroads will probably be made against frictional unemployment through improved labor market services; and manpower programs may help those with the severe employment problems—though accelerating technological change could undo any gains that are made. However, part-time employment will probably continue to grow along with expansion of the service sector, not to mention increases in the number of married women seeking part-time work as birth rates remain low. It appears that employment patterns will become more flexible; and, hopefully, the impact of adverse economic factors will be reduced.

Youth

In the course of U.S. economic history the age of first entrance into the labor force has come later and later in life. Children once took jobs before reaching their teens; today, some youth may reach their mid-20s before entering the labor force permanently. Increased affluence, longer education, the steady decline of family farming, and child protection laws have contributed to this trend. These factors, in combination with technological and socioeconomic changes, also have made it much more complicated for young people to find jobs that provide an opportunity to earn an adequate income and reasonable economic security. And the transition from school to work is more difficult because young people lack work experience, having spent their lives in an educational system that seldom provides the types of skills demanded by employers. Nor do government and business expend much effort to smooth the way. As a result, some youngsters—especially dropouts —never find the bridge and are doomed to lives of intermittent unemployment in low-paying, high-risk jobs.

Young men and women show divergent trends in labor force participation. Young men's participation has declined dramatically since the turn of the century, largely because of increased school enrollment.[2] Among young women, participation rates have risen since the end of World War II, probably because of growing job opportunities for part-time workers in retail trade and services. Labor force participation rates of 16-to-24-year-old women in 1947 and 1973 were:

Participation Rates

Age	1947	1973
16–17	29.5%	39.1%
18–19	52.3	57.0
20–24	44.9	61.2

At the same time, the extremely high birth rates of the post–World War II era meant that in the 1960s the number of teenagers (aged 16 to 19) burgeoned from 10.6 million in 1960 to 16.1 million in 1973. As a result, their proportion of the total labor force rose to nearly 10 percent despite further declines in the participation rates of young men.

Pursuit of higher education to qualify for more complex jobs is the main reason for late entry into the labor force. However, some young men are simply discouraged; about 780,000 16- to 21-year-olds, many of them school dropouts, were neither in the labor force nor enrolled in school in 1972. Overrepresented in this category were young black men, many of them living in city slums, where the problems of drugs, delinquency, and crime have grown progressively worse in an atmosphere of idle hopelessness. Whatever their special job difficulties, these young people are prime candidates for lives of underemployment. Why are such youngsters outside the work force? Some believe that no one will hire them because they are too young.[3] And judging from the unemployment rates of their peers who are in the labor force, this is probably true. Others have given up entirely or are engaged in illicit pursuits but are not counted among the unemployed. Some depend upon parental support and do not need or care to work.

Among the 16-to-21-year-old males going to school, a little over one-third were in the labor force—mostly working at or seeking part-time jobs. Many young men in school and not in the labor force—over 3 million in 1973—would probably like to have some additional income but feel that work is not available.

When employed, teenagers and men in their early 20s tend to be entry-level workers such as laborers, semiskilled operatives, and service workers. A large number work only part time. Teenagers are about three times more likely than mature men to be working in agriculture. The 1972 income of young men reflected their concentration in low-paying jobs:

Type of Income	All Males	16- to 19-Year-Olds	20- to 24-Year-Olds
Total money income	$7,450	$1,007	$4,614
Year-round, full-time workers' income	10,538	4,257	7,019

Joblessness and job turnover have always been relatively high among younger workers who are adjusting to new jobs. In 1973, a year of strong demand and tight labor markets, the rate of unemployment for 16- to 24-year-olds averaged 10.5 percent, more than triple the rate for persons aged 25 and over. In fact there were more unemployed workers younger than 25 years than older. The unemployment situation for black and other minority group youngsters was much worse; their rates ranged upward to levels approximating depression conditions. Obviously, high unemployment and undesirable jobs are critical factors keeping large numbers of young men outside the labor force, regardless of their school status.

In recent years the younger workers' normal liabilities have been reinforced by the great increases in the numbers of such workers and the continuing decline in the number of unskilled, entry-level jobs.[4] The proportion of jobs in the less skilled laborer, operative, and farming occupations has dropped substantially since the late 1940s—from over 4 of every 10 jobs to less than 1 in 4 by 1973; at the same time, the more demanding white-collar positions have risen from $3\frac{1}{2}$ in 10 to nearly 5 in 10. However, this does not necessarily mean that youth employment opportunities have been adversely affected, because education has kept pace with the increased demand for higher skills. Since 1940 the proportion of workers with high school diplomas has doubled, and the proportion with college degrees has tripled; the median number of school years completed has risen from 9.1 years to 12.4.

Economists disagree over the impact upon youth employment of rising federal minimum wages and broader coverage under the Fair Labor Standards Act (FLSA). Arguments purporting to show that the FLSA contributed directly to a decline in employment opportunities for youth and that minimum wage provisions are therefore responsible for recent high youth joblessness are not persuasive; but proponents of higher minimum wages have not disproved the claims that statutory minimum wages may have exerted long-run impacts and slowed the growth of those sectors employing youth. Swayed by this argument, Congress adopted a dual minimum in 1974 with one rate for adults and a lower rate for students under the assumption that the differential would encourage youth employment but still provide meaningful protection.

The golden years?

Older Americans, men and women alike, are faced with a bewildering and growing array of socioeconomic problems. Trained and educated in the pre–World War II years, many lack the skills necessary to compete in a highly technical job market. As a result, many are employed at jobs below their potential skill levels; others have left the work force altogether. Our society takes pride in the recent increases in early retirement for what some call the golden years. This pride is partly misplaced; a large number of older Americans do not have adequate incomes to sustain a decent standard of living, and many have been forced by unemployment into premature retirement.

Older workers' employment problems spring partly from the failure of employers to recognize the vast accumulation of skill and experience currently being unutilized. Recent estimates place the number of healthy males aged 65 and over at over 2 million, and there were another half-million men 45 to 64 outside the work force. Many of these men are voluntarily retired and have adequate incomes; however, many others have been forced out of the market and are living on substandard incomes.[5]

As with younger workers, sheer population growth among older Americans has offset declining participation rates since the turn of the century, and especially in the post–World War II years. The number of older Americans (aged 55 and over) has increased by more than 50 percent since the end of World War II, rising to about 39 million. High birth and immigration rates before the Great Depression account for much of the increase, but the rise also reflects a longer life span brought about by better living, health, and work conditions. These same factors might be expected to stimulate participation by older people, and women seem to have benefited from them. However, men apparently encounter offsetting factors, for the proportion working has declined sharply—especially after age 65, though declining rates are also evident in preretirement years, especially for reasons of poor health.[6] Older men account for a steadily declining proportion of the labor force, even though their percentage of the total population has held quite steady. About 9 million men aged 55 years and over were employed in 1973. They accounted for 10.3 percent of total employment, down from 12.6 percent in 1960 and 13.7 percent in 1947. The number of older persons is expected to increase dramatically to a total of 44 million in 1980—a 70 percent jump from 1950. This increase also should be accompanied by further improvements in health care, permitting an extension of working life.

These large numbers of nonworking retirees would not constitute a serious social and economic problem if they had enough income to assure an adequate standard of living. However, many retirement incomes are inadequate: More than 3.7 million older Americans (aged 65 and over) were living in poverty in 1973.

The pivotal retirement age is 65, reflecting the rapid development and liberalization of private and public pension plans. Many workers are retiring even earlier. More than half of those eligible are electing to draw Social Security benefits before age 65. Beyond that age, only one in four older men is in the labor force, and, of those working, more than one-third hold part-time jobs. Although these older men usually work part time by choice, they are twice as likely to do so for economic reasons as men in their prime working years.

Older workers are less likely than young workers to move among jobs. The benefits that accrue to seniority (especially job security) are important to older workers, who usually have considerable training, experience, community ties, and company loyalty. In addition, age barriers limit their opportunities for changing jobs. In part because they are less mobile, older workers tend to be concentrated in declining occupations and industries. Many are farmers or self-employed. As a result of this uneven distribution of employment, there are great disparities in the earnings of older men. On the average, however, their earnings are lower than for the next youngest age cohort.[7] This difference is partly due to the tendency for some older workers to work only part time or part year; but there are also significant differences among full-time, year-round male workers, as shown in the following tabulation for 1972:

Classification	Age in Years		
	45–54	55–64	65 and over
Median total income, all persons with income	$10,771	$8,902	$3,746
Median income, full-time, year-round workers	11,840	10,763	7,757
Percent of total with incomes of less than $3,000	7.4	14.2	37.6

The unemployment problems of older workers are somewhat unique. Because they have long job tenure, they are less likely to lose their jobs through layoff.[8] But once set adrift from employment, they are apt to be shunted around among low-paying temporary jobs. Not only are there age barriers in hiring, but also older workers often lack adequate training for today's technical jobs. Older workers are thus much more likely than their middle-aged colleagues to have frequent spells of unemployment and, to spend many more weeks of fruitless searching for employment[9] (Table 4-2). Faced with this experience, many older workers simply withdraw from the labor force, often without adequate income.[10]

Industrial and occupational shifts

Shift to service-producing, white-collar employment

At the turn of the century 70 percent of all workers were in industries producing physical goods—in agriculture, forestry, fishing,

Table 4-2 Frequency and Duration of Unemployment of Persons with Work Experience by Age, 1972

Age	Percent with Unemployment in 1972	Percent Unemployment			
		2 Spells	3 or More Spells	15 to 26 Weeks	27 Weeks or More
25–34 years	16.3%	14.2%	15.9%	20.2%	12.9%
35–44 years	11.0	14.4	15.7	22.2	12.6
45–54 years	9.9	14.2	18.3	24.0	14.7
55–64 years	8.8	13.9	18.8	26.4	15.5
65 yrs. & older	6.4	13.6	15.7	26.3	22.7

Source: U.S. Bureau of Labor Statistics, unpublished statistics.

mining, manufacturing, and construction; the rest were in service-producing industries. In 1973 the relative importance of the two was reversed, with nearly seven of every ten workers employed in service-producing industries—wholesale and retail trade, personal and business services, government, transportation and public utilities, finance, insurance, and real estate.

The most notable changes have been the persistent decline in farm employment, coupled with the burgeoning of service jobs. After 1950 farm employment declined by about 200,000 annually. In 1953, for the first time, the number of service workers—including cooks, janitors, barbers, practical nurses, firemen, and policemen—equaled the agricultural work force. The gap between the two continued to widen, and by 1973 there were almost four service workers for every farm worker.

The shift from goods-producing to service-producing industries was accompanied by a shift from blue-collar to white-collar occupations. In 1900 white-collar workers accounted for only 18 percent of employment. By 1956, for the first time, white-collar workers outnumbered blue-collar workers; now they account for almost half of all employment. The rising demand for white-collar service workers reflects higher standards of living, including better health care, more government services, and more luxuries.

The occupational and industrial shifts were accompanied by pervasive changes that have broad implications for the economic and social structure of the nation. The shifts favored occupations requiring more extensive skills and educational attainment. In 1900 laborers outnumbered managers and professionals. By 1970 nearly 25 percent of all workers were managers or professionals compared to only 5 percent who were laborers. Profound occupational changes have also occurred within the goods-producing industries. Technological and organizational changes have enhanced the importance of nonproduction workers—for example, the white-collar jobs of executives, sales personnel, office workers, and engineers—as opposed to blue-collar positions. In manufacturing there were five production workers for each nonproduction worker in 1947. Today the ratio has been halved. While there may be disagreements about the net effects of technological advances—whether they have created more jobs than they have eliminated—there is little dispute that the occupational shifts have emphasized higher skills, both at the manual and intellectual level—definitely a step away from arduous, unskilled labor. The examples of coal miners displaced by automatic digging machines, stevedores by hoisting machinery, and clerks by automated billing and office machines are well-known, representative cases.

The movement of millions of workers from goods production to service production has not slackened the demand for labor. The

fears or hopes of the prophets of cybernetics have not material-
ized, and instead of vast numbers of available but unneeded workers, the problem during the last half of the 1960s was more one of
labor shortages in highly skilled occupations than surpluses.

Industrial distribution

Despite the reduced relative importance of employment in goods-
producing industries, manufacturing, remains the largest single
provider of jobs (Table 4-3). Its share of employment grew from

Table 4-3 Distribution of Employment by Industry, 1900, 1947, and
1973

Industry	1900	1947	1973
Total Employment[a]			
Thousands	26,278	51,772	79,023
Percent	100.0	100.0	100.0
Goods-producing industries	69.7	50.9	34.7
Manufacturing	20.8	30.0	25.1
Durable goods	—	16.2	14.7
Nondurable goods	—	13.8	10.4
Mining	2.4	1.8	0.8
Construction	4.4	3.8	4.6
Agriculture	42.1	15.2	4.4
Service-producing industries	30.2	49.1	65.1
Transportation and utilities	8.7	8.0	5.8
Trade	9.5	17.3	20.6
Wholesale	—	4.6	5.2
Retail	—	12.7	15.5
Finance, insurance, real estate	1.2	3.4	5.1
Services and miscellaneous	6.6	9.8	16.3
Government	4.2	10.6	17.3
Federal	—	3.7	3.3
State and local	—	6.9	14.0

Note: Detail may not add to totals due to rounding.

[a]Agriculture includes wage and salary, self-employed, and unpaid family
workers. Data for other industries exclude self-employed and unpaid family
workers.

Source: Data for 1900 are from C. G. Williams, *Labor Economics* (New
York: Wiley, 1970), p. 1617; data for 1947 and 1973 are from *Employment
and Earnings* (March 1971), pp. 21, 49, and (January 1974), pp. 154, 170.

21 percent in 1900 to 30 percent in 1947. Since then the relative importance of manufacturing as a source of jobs has declined to 25 percent of total employment. Nevertheless, manufacturing employment in 1973 stood at 20 million, not far below the all-time peak reached in 1969. The largest employers were the durable-goods industries, reflecting growing consumer demand for televisions, autos, and other consumer capital goods and, in the 1960s, the immense production of the American armaments industry.

The major growth in employment occurred in the service-producing industries, with the government sector growing faster than any other major industry since World War II. State and local governments account for the largest share of public employees (seven of eight in 1973) and most of the growth. The federal payroll increased by less than half between 1947 and 1973, while state and local employment more than tripled to almost 11 million. Two-thirds of the state and local gains made during the past decade have been in education (schools account for half of all state and local workers).

Retail and wholesale trade, providing one of every five jobs in 1973, has doubled its share of employment since 1900. This growth has been an important source of employment for women and youth entering the labor force, and it came about despite the industry's increasing reliance on self-service techniques, automatic materials-handling equipment, and vending machines.

Employment in the heterogeneous service industry group—varied personal, business, health, and private educational services—more than doubled its share of total employment between 1900 and 1973. Private medical and health services experienced the largest gain, with private hospital employment accounting for about half that expansion; this reflects higher standards of health care and extension of private medical insurance plans as well as Medicare and Medicaid programs.

Occupational distribution

Technological innovation, together with the shift from goods-producing to service-producing industries, caused significant occupational changes (Table 4-4). Among white-collar workers, professional and clerical workers have accounted for the bulk of the employment gains made during this century. Together these two categories grew from 2 million to 25 million. Managers and sales workers have grown less spectacularly; totaling 3 million in 1900, these groups accounted for 12 million in 1970. The wide variations in relative growth demonstrate that increasing white-collar employment has not been entirely an explosion of executives and ex-

Table 4-4 Distribution of Employment by Occupation, 1900, 1950, and 1973[a]

Occupation	1900	1950	1973
Total			
Thousands	29,030	58,999	84,409
Percent	100.0	100.0	100.0
White-collar workers	17.6	36.6	47.8
Professional and technical	4.3	8.6	14.0
Managers, officials and proprietors, except farm	5.8	8.7	10.2
Clerical	3.0	12.3	17.2
Sales	4.5	7.0	6.4
Blue-collar workers	35.8	41.1	35.4
Craftsmen and foremen	10.5	14.1	13.4
Operatives and kindred	12.8	20.4	16.9
Laborers, except farm and mine	12.5	6.6	5.1
Service workers	9.0	10.5	13.2
Private household	5.4	2.6	1.6
Service workers, except private household	3.6	7.9	11.6
Farm workers	37.5	11.8	3.6
Farmers and farm managers	19.9	7.4	2.0
Farm laborers and foremen	17.7	4.4	1.6

[a]Not directly comparable. Figures for 1973 are employed persons 16 years and older; for 1900, gainful workers; and for 1950, labor force figures.

Source: U.S. Department of Labor, *Manpower Report of the President* (Washington, D.C.: GPO, 1974), p. 268.

perts. Rather, it reflects the increase of a variety of information-based jobs, including numerous paper-pushing tasks.[11]

An analysis of specific occupations within these broad categories reveals more about the changing character of work. Among professionals and technicians, teachers have always been the most numerous group, and their numbers continue to increase rapidly. By 1970 there were more elementary schoolteachers than the total of all doctors, lawyers, and natural scientists in the nation. The fastest growth, though, has been among college teachers—from 7,000 to 486,000 during the century, having quadrupled in the past two decades.

Medical specialists are second in importance among professional and technical workers. Most of the employment increase in this field has come from occupations that have been added to the health-care field (for example, nurses, medical technicians, and paramedics) rather than from increases in the traditional medical professionals, such as physicians, dentists, and pharmacists. In fact, physicians and surgeons have declined as a percentage of the labor force and the population. In 1900 three of four medical professionals were either doctors or dentists. Today only one in four holds one of these titles.

Third in numbers, and one of the fastest growing of all occupations, are engineers, who numbered 1.2 million in 1970. Virtually all of these jobs have been added to the economy since 1900, when only 38,000 engineers were at work.

Except for teachers, most of the employment gains in the professional and technical fields have come in occupations that were unknown or numerically insignificant in 1900. This continues to be the pattern as technological, educational, and scientific advances determine the types of jobs created in the economy. Hundreds of thousands of accountants, computer specialists, draftsmen, social workers, and many others are employed today in professions that barely existed 70 years ago. The time-honored professional fields —doctors, lawyers, clergymen—are not only losing importance among the professions but are shrinking in proportion to the labor force as a whole. Occupations developed in the past 70 years have instead come to dominate professional employment.

In the burgeoning clerical field secretaries, stenographers, and typists are by far the most numerous, outnumbering teachers as the largest single occupational group. These occupations have grown to 3.8 million during the century, an increase of 2700 percent since 1900. This demand for secretaries shows no sign of diminishing. During the 1960s, 1.5 million secretaries were added to the labor force, a greater increase than the total number of assemblers in manufacturing. Other occupations that have gained dramatically in the past two decades are cashiers, bookkeepers, bank tellers, and office-machine operators. Each has more than doubled in the past 20 years.

The growth of clerical workers has paralleled the increase in the employment of women in the labor force. In 1900 the 212,000 women working in clerical occupations constituted 4 percent of all female workers and less than a hundredth of the total labor force. In 1970 the 10.1 million women in clerical occupations accounted for one-third of workingwomen, almost one-seventh of the labor force, and three-fourths of all clerical workers.

The category of managers, officials, and proprietors has grown more slowly than either clerical or professional employment, and the patterns of growth have not been concentrated among a few occupations as is the case with professional and clerical work. But one trend operating through the past several decades has had an important effect on these jobs. Increasingly, managers are becoming employees rather than their own bosses. Since the advent of mass production and the demise of the handcraftsman, farmers and proprietors have been the last bastions of self-employment. But, evidently, both of these strongholds are under fire. In 1957, 3.6 million, or 57 percent, of all managers, officials, and proprietors were self-employed. By 1970 the number of those working for themselves had decreased by more than a million, and the percentage of managers who were self-employed had fallen to 27. The entrepreneur and the small businessman are losing ground to bigger organizations, franchised outlets, and mass merchandising. The nation's managerial class is rapidly becoming a salaried group of employees, subordinate to larger organizational structures.

Similar factors have combined to slow the growth of sales occupations. Although the number of salesmen increased through the century, in the past two decades sales workers were a constant percentage of the labor force, despite a substantial rise in the dollar volume of products sold. The value of wholesale and retail trade grew threefold from 1950 to 1971, but sales workers grew only from 7 to 7.1 percent of the work force. Trends toward larger sales units with self-service merchandising systems held sales employment back. Insurance and real-estate salesmen advanced more rapidly, but the bulk of sales positions—those in retail trade—expanded slowly.

Obviously, the facts of employment do not support the image of a white-collar economy peopled mostly with scientists and executives. Secretaries and typists outnumber all other occupations; clerical workers are the most numerous category by far. In the professional category noncollege teachers, paraprofessional occupations—draftsmen, nurses, and medical technicians—and artists and entertainers have accounted for more than a third of all new jobs. Though these workers indeed often wear white collars, it is misleading to add their jobs to the white-collar total and generalize about the changes in the quality of work.

Blue-collar work also disguises a multitude of barely related job experiences ranging from the proverbial tightening of bolts to handcrafting scientific instruments. Among skilled workers two occupational groups have accounted for most of the employment gains. First, repairmen of all kinds have increased sharply in order to maintain the tremendous quantities of complex equipment and machinery needed in a postindustrial age. By 1970 repairmen had displaced construction workers as the most numerous skilled workers. In 1900 skilled construction workers outnumbered repairmen by nearly four to one. By 1970 repairmen had multiplied ninefold to 2.8 million, representing nearly a third of all craftworkers and surpassing the 2.7 million construction craftsmen. The vast accumulation of fixed capital, equipment, machinery, and durable goods has shifted much of the employment of skilled manual workers to maintenance rather than initial construction.

A second development among skilled workers has been the increase of foremen. From 162,000, or 5 percent, of skilled blue-collar workers in 1900, foremen have increased to 1.6 million in 1970—15 percent of manual workers. This growth has been especially rapid during the past three decades. Production units of greater size and complexity and technology of greater sophistication have apparently raised the needs for first-level supervision in production. Together, foremen and repairmen have accounted for 60 percent of the growth of skilled trades since 1900 and for 75 percent of that growth since 1940.

In contrast to craftsmen, semiskilled operatives are typically employed as machine tenders in manufacturing industries. In 1970 almost two-thirds of the 14 million operative jobs were in manufacturing industries. Two million of these workers operated various powered machines, while almost a million were assemblers. Other large groups included 834,000 sewers and stitchers, 690,000 checkers, 391,000 painters, and 380,000 packers. However, during this century the greatest growth in operative employment has occurred in jobs associated with transportation rather than manufacturing: bus, truck, and taxi drivers and parking-lot and service-station attendants. These automobile-created occupations, nonexistent at the turn of the century, now employ 2.2 million individuals, one of every six operatives.

Evidently, beneath a surface of stable employment growth some significant changes have occurred in blue-collar work. Technology and economic growth have shifted blue-collar work toward repair, supervision, and transportation. None of these types of work conforms to the stereotype of blue-collar work—that is, the routine of the factory or assembly line.

The service category is even more diverse in skill and social status than the blue- and white-collar categories. Except for those with a clearly professional skill (for example, doctors), workers who provide health care, prepare and serve food, protect property, and clean or perform valet services are classed as service workers.

Seventy years ago, most service jobs were those of servants in private homes. That is, 60 percent of service workers were in private households. Today, private servants have given way to publicly available service workers shared by a broader group. In 1970 the number of private household workers dropped to 1.1 million, only 12 percent of the expanded service sector. Instead, restaurant workers have replaced personal butlers and cooks, and charwomen have supplanted live-in maids. The luxuries of personal attention are no longer loyally reserved to the few most wealthy but more often are sold to all comers in the open market.

This trend can be clearly seen in two of the fastest-growing sectors of the service industry: food service and cleaning occupations. Food service occupations (waiters, cooks, bartenders, and associated occupations) and cleaning jobs (maids, janitors, charwomen, dishwashers, etc.) numbered almost 5 million by 1970. The unpleasant daily tasks of cleaning and fixing food have been partly eliminated by machines, prepackaged foods, and throwaway containers, but the work that remains is more and more done by paid servants who perform these duties for many "masters."

The growth of institutional health care has stimulated the increase of nonprofessional hospital service jobs. As in the food and cleaning services, this development represents a shift away from work done at home to that paid for in the market. Care of invalids, once primarily the responsibility of the household and the visiting doctor, has now been almost entirely contracted out. Emptying bedpans, changing sheets, and taking temperatures, formerly the work of friends or relatives, now are paid occupational tasks occupying more than a million people.

These sharp rises in the demand for service workers are the logical outgrowths of affluence and technological advancement. With machine-supported production able to provide goods for all and with substantial purchasing power in the hands of many, desires for personal services have grown. Accenting this evolution has been the shift of women from the house to outside jobs, and the corresponding shift of the burden of many home and personal maintenance tasks formerly done by unpaid wives to hired, outside servants. To a large extent, former domestic services have been incorporated into the public domain. Though much the same type of work is being done, it is now less the private privilege of the few or the natural duty of the wife than service contracted to specialists. Because many people no longer wish to be burdened with these tasks, new institutions have been established to provide the services.

The growth of productivity

Though both the characteristics of the labor force and the occupational and industrial mix of the labor market have shifted substantially over the past several decades, one characteristic of the economy has remained unchanged: Its productivity has risen steadily. Productivity, defined as the ratio of the inputs to production (labor, capital, energy, etc.) to its output (goods or services), has fluctuated with business cycles. Most productivty measures, which are simply shorthand notations for the overall efficiency with which industry uses natural and human resources to fulfill society's needs, have trended upward and continue to do so.[12]

There are many alternative productivity measures. One common index—output per manhour—measures the productivity of a single input—labor. The routinely cited figures concerning American productivity are such output-per-manhour measures, compiled by comparing the total value of all goods and services (in constant dollars) produced in the nation—the GNP—with the total number of hours worked. Other measures record output per unit of capital. Such estimates are important in corporate investment planning, for example, in determining how many barrels per day a new refinery must produce in order to repay its cost of construction. Other more complete indexes combine and weigh all input factors to arrive at a single figure for overall productivity. There are also narrower measures that record the efficiency and usage of a single resource, for example, the board feet of salable lumber that a sawmill can cut from a given quantity of logs or the kilowatts of electricity that a power plant can generate from a certain quantity of fuel.

Each of these productivity indexes has specific uses. Output per manhour is useful for determining how fast wages can rise, since real compensation per hour must closely parallel output per hour. The overall efficiency indexes comparing output to weighted inputs of both capital and labor may be used to compare industries or national economies with each other. The relative strength of currencies, the need for new capital investments, or the impact of substituting capital and labor may be determined from such productivity indexes.

Despite the assumed certainty of published figures such as "productivity rose 2.8 percent in 1973," there are numerous problems with the measurement of productivity. First, few of the data collected by federal or private establishments are designed specifically for measuring productivity. Thus production figures, manhour totals, or capital investment estimates may give an inaccurate picture of productivity gains because they are not detailed enough or because they only approximate actual changes in productivity.

Second, the measurement of various inputs can be difficult. For example, though the concept of manhours seems straightforward, does it include coffee breaks, "downtime," paid sick days, or vacation time? And the more complex issue is: Are hours of labor by various employees of equal value—is the company president's time at $50 per hour equal to the janitor's hour? In general, most indexes count only hours actually spent on the job in productivity indexes, and some weigh manhours by wage differentials.

The measurement of capital inputs is even more difficult. The value of plant, equipment, land inventories, and other factors is greatly affected by accounting and depreciation methods. More-over, the flow of capital—that is, the capital actually used in production is even more difficult to gauge than the value of capital stock. The only truly accurate measure of capital input would be a record of the hours of use of each type of capital, multiplied by the rental value. Obviously, such detailed and complex computations are seldom possible.

Third, the measurement of output can also be quite tricky. Though some physical inputs lend themselves to easy computation —for example, the number of bricks that a mason can lay per day —most are less clear. Issues of quality are important; for example, the production of a ton of tool steel is not equivalent to that of a ton of cast iron. Continuous changes in products and the introduction of new products make longitudinal comparisons difficult. When counting identical goods is not possible, productivity must be gauged by the dollar value of the output, which, of course, must be adjusted for price changes. Since the consumer price index tends to ignore quality improvements, long-term productivity gains may be underestimated.

The difficulties with measuring output are nearly insurmount-able in the case of service industries, particularly government, and in the construction industry. Since new buildings vary widely in purpose and value, construction output is usually approximated by the dollar value of the structures, adjusted for price changes. But structure value is largely a function of the labor and materials required in construction, so that productivity indexes for construc-tion tend to be cost indexes that show little change in output per unit of input.

In service industries, where the output is often intangible, measures of productivity are usually based on the dollar value of services, deflated for price changes. As in the case of construction, this method depends on the adequacy of the price index. Govern-ment services, which are not bought and sold, much be approxi-mated by wage rates and employment figures. These indicators, however, will reveal no change in labor productivity, since the output and input measures are identical. As a result, government is usually excluded from national productivity totals, which is un-fortunate, since government employs over a sixth of the labor force.

Figure 4-2 Output per manhour and real compensation per manhour,
total private economy, 1950–1973.

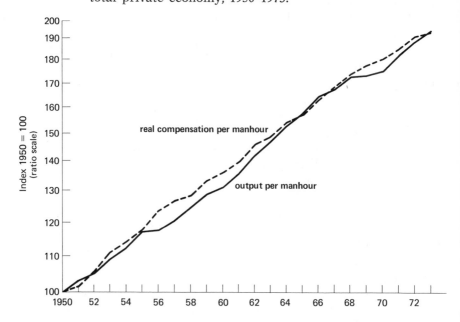

Source: *Economic Report of the President, 1974* (Washington, D.C.:
GPO, 1974), p. 286.

These limitations indicate that considerable research and data
collection must be initiated before firm conclusions regarding
changes in productivity may be drawn. Yet the most carefully constructed productivity indexes point up significant long-term trends.

Since 1900 U.S. productivity has improved steadily. From 1900
to 1950 the rate of increase averaged about 2 percent per year;
since then, it has grown at a pace nearer 3 percent (Figure 4-2).
Annual fluctuations have been quite varied depending on the business cycle and the impacts of advances in technology. There was
little improvement during the depression, for example, and quite
rapid acceleration following World War II. In recent years productivity growth has varied, averaging 2.8 percent from 1950 to
1960, jumping to 3.9 percent during 1960–1965, and receding to 2.1
percent for the next five-year period. In 1971 and 1972 the rise in
productivity rebounded to an average of 3.9 percent per year, falling back to 2.8 percent in 1973. These figures for the whole economy smooth out wide differences in industries. Generally, agriculture and the goods-producing industries have made the greatest
gains during the century, while service industries, which have been
less able to substitute capital for labor, have shown smaller in-

creases in output per manhour. Farming, in which productivity growth has averaged about 5.5 percent per year since 1950, has led the way, but other goods-producing industries have also registered sharp gains. Hosiery, radio and TV, household appliances, concrete products, and petroleum products all raised output per manhour by more than 60 percent during the 1960s. Some goods producers, however, have registered slower gains, for example, auto, steel, and iron.

Some service industries have increased output at rates that equal goods producers. Air and rail transport and utility industries benefited by rapid growth that made possible great economies of scale. Each raised productivity by an average of 6 to 8 percent per year. Most other service industries, such as trade, insurance, and banking, though they raised productivity some by applying technology, mass marketing, and self-service concepts to their enterprises, were unable to improve productivity as fast as the rest of the economy.

Compared to other countries, U.S. productivity is still considerably greater, but this advantage has narrowed in recent years (Figure 4-3). In 1960 it was estimated that U.S. workers produced about twice as much per hour of labor as most other industrialized nations, including Japan, the U.S.S.R. and Western Europe. With growth rates of about 5 percent per year in Europe and 14 percent in Japan, however, foreign nations closed this gap appreciably during the 1960s, particularly during the last half of the decade, when U.S. productivity grew slowly. In some industries, notably the manufacture of steel, West German and Japanese productivity has equaled or surpassed U.S. levels.

In the future, productivity growth in the United States should continue to improve at about the same rate that has prevailed since World War II—3 percent. Some have argued that an economy dominated by service industries may not be able to sustain past rates of growth in productivity that were characteristic of the goods-producing economy. Goods-producing industries were able to double their output between 1950 and 1970 with only a small increase in the number of workers. Based on extensive studies of the service industries, Victor Fuchs concluded that the growth in productivity per worker since World War II in the good-producing industries was twice as great as in the service industries; as the proportion of workers engaged in service industries increases, he argues, economic growth will necessarily slow.[13]

But the shift of employment to services in which productivity growth is slow will be offset by the continuing application of sophisticated technology to most industries. Though rates of ad-

Figure 4-3 Productivity gains, 1960–1970.

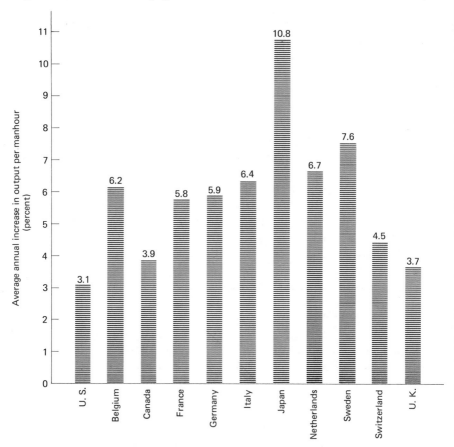

Source: Arthur Neef, "Unit Labor Costs in Eleven Countries,"
Monthly Labor Review (August 1971), p. 4.

vance will be uneven, the overall trend will continue upward. On
the other hand, it may be expected that other countries' rates of
productivity growth may be faster than that of the United States
because of the increasingly rapid diffusion of technological know-
how and the growing penetration of multinational companies in
the world markets.

The continued growth of American productivity is crucially
important if Americans are to continue to enjoy the improvements
in standards of living that they have come to expect and if they
are to sell their goods on a competitive basis abroad. Ultimately,
improvements in the quality of life and increases in leisure time
must stem from productivity gains. Unless wage gains are backed

by increased output, they merely inflate the money supply and result in no real gain. Thus productivity growth is one of the most important tools for controlling inflation. In the same way, as the productivity gap between the United States and other industrialized countries shrinks, the maintenance of foreign markets for U.S. goods will depend on productivity keeping pace with wages.

Notes

1. Dean Morse, *The Peripheral Worker* (New York: Columbia University Press, 1969).
2. Jacob Mincer, "Labor Force Participation and Unemployment: A Review of Recent Evidence," in Robert and Margaret Gordon, eds., *Prosperity and Unemployment* (New York: Wiley, 1966), pp. 73–112.
3. Robert Stein, "Reasons for Nonparticipation in the Labor Force," *Monthly Labor Review* (July 1967), p. 26.
4. Edward Kalachek, *The Youth Labor Market* (Ann Arbor, Mich.: Institute of Labor and Industrial Relations, University of Michigan, January 1969), p. 55.
5. National Council on the Aging's National Institute on Industrial Gerontology, *Employment Aspects of the Economics of Aging*, U.S. Senate Special Committee on Aging (Washington, D.C.: GPO, December 1969).
6. Herbert Parnes, et al., *The Pre-Retirement Years*, U.S. Department of Labor, Manpower Administration, Manpower Research Monograph No. 15 (Washington, D.C.: GPO, 1970) [cf. p. 21, n. 17], Vol. 2, p. 7.
7. U.S. Bureau of the Census, *Current Population Reports*, "Income in 1969 of Families and Persons in the United States," Series P-60, No. 75 (Washington, D.C.: GPO, 1970), Table 45.
8. Edward O'Boyle, "Job Tenure: How It Relates to Race and Age," *Monthly Labor Review* (September 1969), p. 18.
9. U.S. Bureau of Labor Statistics, *Work Experience of the Population in 1969*, Special Labor Force Report 127 (Washington, D.C.: GPO, 1971).
10. Lenore Bixby and Eleanor Rings, "Work Experience of Men Claiming Retirement Benefits in 1966," *Social Security Bulletin* (August 1969).
11. The discussion is based on Sar A. Levitan and William B. Johnston, *Work Is Here to Stay, Alas* (Salt Lake City, Utah: Olympus Publishing Co., 1973), pp. 88–93.
12. The discussion of productivity measurement is drawn from Leon Greenberg, "The Economics of Productivity," *Economic Topic* (New York: Joint Council on Economic Education, 1973), and Jerome A. Mark, "Concepts and Measures of Productivity,"

The Meaning and Measurement of Productivity, Bulletin 1714, U.S. Bureau of Labor Statistics, 1971.

13. Victor R. Fuchs, *The Service Economy* (New York: National Bureau of Economic Research and Columbia University Press, 1968), p. 47.

5

women at work

Women, especially wives and mothers, have played a key role in the changing composition of the labor force. Women workers are on the increase, not only in the percentage who work but also in their share of the labor force and in the variety of jobs they hold. Participation rates of women have doubled since 1900. With an average of 33.9 million women in the work force, women accounted for nearly two-fifths of the total workers in 1973. Since the end of World War II about three-fifths of the total increase in civilian employment has come from women workers. Increases in the number of working wives and mothers in this period have been most dramatic. The number of working mothers almost quadrupled since 1950, although the total number of women workers less than doubled. In March 1973, 13 million mothers with children under 18 were working or seeking work, accounting for 44 percent of mothers with children that age. In 1960 only three of ten such mothers were working, and less than one of ten in 1940.

More than four of every ten married women were employed in 1973, compared with one of every three in 1960 and only one of 20 in 1900. The 19.8 million working wives comprised slightly over one-fifth of the 1973 labor force. Between 1960 and 1973 about two-fifths of the increase in the total labor force came from married women. In addition, about one of every eight families was headed by a woman in 1973, and half of these women were in the labor force. Divorced, separated, and widowed women accounted for 14 percent of the labor force expansion since 1950. In 1973 seven of every ten divorcees worked but only one-fourth of widows. The latter were generally older, and many received public or private pensions.

Factors affecting female work

American women of all classes have entered the labor market; black women and immigrants were the pioneers, followed by young single women, then mature wives. The latest influx has been of young mothers. The husbands' occupations seem to have little impact upon wives' employment. There is little variation in labor force participation among wives of blue-collar, clerical, or professional workers. The major variables affecting women's participation are husbands' earnings, marital status, availability of child-care facilities, educational attainment, and race.

Husbands' earnings

The level of husbands' earnings affect their wives' labor force participation rates, although the relationship varies by race, age of wives, and presence and age of children. In 1973 participation of wives increased as husbands' earnings rose during the preceding year to $10,000. After that point the rate of wives' labor force participation generally declined. However, if preschool-age children are present, participation rates are highest when husbands are in the lowest earning bracket. Black wives not only have higher overall participation rates, but, they also tend to remain in the labor force as husbands' incomes rise even if young children are present (Table 5-1).

Wives' earnings are important for achieving what many Americans deem a good living—say, $15,000 or more a year. The number of families at this income level would have been cut by half in

Table 5-1 Income of Husband, 1972

	Total	Under $3,000	$3,000– 4,999	$5,000– 6,999	$7,000– 9,999	$10,000+
		Percent in the Labor Force				
All Wives	42	37	38	45	49	41
With children aged under 6 years	33	45	36	39	38	26
Black Wives	54	40	53	54	60	58
With children aged under 6 years	54	48	53	52	56	56

Source: Howard Hayghe, *Marital and Family Characteristics of the Labor Force in March 1973*, U.S. Bureau of Labor Statistics, Special Labor Force Report 164 (Washington, D.C.: GPO, 1974), Table J.

1968 if the families were to depend exclusively on the earnings of the husband alone rather than the income of the entire family.[1] An estimated 60 percent of husband-wife families with incomes above $15,000 included a working wife in 1972.[2]

However, sheer economic necessity, in the most basic meaning of the phrase, is the reason that more than half of the women in the labor force work. Of the 33.9 million women at work in 1973, about 42 percent were either single, divorced, separated, or widowed. Many of these women are the sole supporters not only of themselves but also of children or parents. In addition, 37 percent of the 10 million women married to men who earned less than $5000 annually worked. As Juanita Kreps has pointed out, these women do not have the luxury of choosing work at home over work in the marketplace.[3]

Female family heads

Women—6.6 million of them—head one of every eight families. In 1972 six of every ten female-headed families included minor children. The female head of these families reared 7.9 million children, and they provided for an additional 6 million persons in their families. In 1972, 38 percent of female family heads were widows, half were divorced or separated, and 12 percent were single women who had never married—although almost half of them had children.[4]

Female-headed families have been increasing faster since 1960 than the total number of families—47 percent compared with only 21 percent. They account, moreover, for a growing portion of the remaining poverty in the United States. In 1972 over half of poor families with children were headed by women. The growing number of female-headed families with children is one reason for the rise of welfare rolls in recent years.

The rising incidence of families headed by women is not due exclusively to increasing marital instability or illegitimacy. An estimated two-fifths of the 1.6 million additional female-headed families formed between 1940 and 1970 have been attributed to increased propensity to form separate households rather than sharing housing with other relatives. Income-support programs may also have boosted the growing ranks of female-headed families, as did declining childlessness and, of course, general population increases.[5]

The median income of female-headed families was not quite half that of husband-wife families. When children were involved, families headed by women experienced much greater income disadvantages. The median 1972 family income of families headed by a mother with children was $4,200, compared with $11,749 for two-parent families with children. Six in ten children with both parents had family incomes of $10,000 or more compared with 1 in twelve children living in female-headed families.[6]

Many female family heads are prevented from working full time, year round by the presence of children, educational disadvantages, lack of salable skills, and residence in high unemployment areas. Although 58 percent of female family heads with minor children worked in 1972, only 26 percent worked full year, full time. Nor did full-time work guarantee an exit from poverty, for 14 percent remained poor despite full-time work efforts.

The proportion of families headed by divorced women has gone up by almost half between 1968 and 1973—to about 3.1 percent (or 1.6 million) of all families. Families headed by separated and single women have also increased, but not as markedly. Our mores seem to require that the mother assume responsibility for caring for the children. Though the father is not relieved of economic responsibility, the brunt of the support usually falls on the mother. Divorced and separated women are thus more likely to be found in the labor force than are wives, widows, or even single women. The proportion of divorced women who worked in 1973 was 71 percent, compared with 42 percent for wives and 53 percent for separated women. Divorced and separated women are also more likely than wives to be employed in full-time jobs. Further, the participation rates of divorced, widowed, or separated women with children under six are markedly higher than those of mothers with husbands present.

Marital Status of Mothers with Children Under Six	Labor Force Participation Rate, March 1973
Total	34.2
Married, husband present	32.7
Divorced, separated, widowed	46.6

High participation rates, coupled with the generally lower income of female-headed families, indicate that day-care facilities at reasonable cost are particularly important to this group of women.

Day-care facilities

Although the presence of children, especially children under six, greatly reduces the chances of a woman's working, an increasing proportion of mothers with young children have remained in the labor force and others have shortened the interval of nonlabor force participation after giving birth to children. Trends of delayed marriage and first births and limiting family size resulted in a 22 percent drop between 1960 and 1973 in the under-five-year-old population despite the fact that maturation of the baby boom generation added 6.8 million women to the 18-to-44-year-old population. Between 1965 and 1973 alone the number of working mothers with preschool-age children increased by almost 2 million.

Three in ten wives with children under the age of three work, as do almost two-fifths of those whose youngest child is between three and five and one-half of those with school-age children. In 1948 only 13 percent of all mothers with children under six were in the labor force; in 1973 one-third worked. Estimates for the future show a continuing rising trend. As already indicated, a group of mothers with children under six who have particularly high participation rates are those who are divorced, widowed, or separated, and their numbers are increasing.

As the number of working mothers with young children rises, day-care facilities become increasingly important. However, the types and quality of day care used by working mothers vary widely, with child-care centers accounting only for a minute proportion of day care. Nearly half of all children under 14 whose mothers worked part or full time in 1964 were cared for in their own homes, usually by relatives; about 16 percent were maintained in someone else's home. Only 2 percent of all children, and 6 percent of children under six, were in child-care centers. The rest were provided for under other arrangements or left to shift for themselves—"latchkey" children.[7]

For the most part child-care arrangements remain informal either in the child's or caretaker's home. Licensed day-care centers, serving primarily three- to five-year-olds, almost quadrupled between 1960 and 1973. The growth, resulting from stepped up licensing of existing facilities as well as the addition of new ones, reflected federally backed efforts to ensure quality child care for low-income mothers engaged in government-sponsored job training or employment.

Day-care facilities are run by a variety of sponsors—including private, for-profit groups, unions, churches, and other nonprofit community or governmental organizations. In fiscal year 1973 federal programs contributed approximately $540 million for the purchase of close to 700,000 child-care years through programs supporting welfare clients and other near poor persons. The actual number of children whose care was subsidized was probably as high as 1.5 million.

Regulations require higher quality, more formal, and consequently more costly arrangements than those obtained by most working mothers. In practice, arrangements meeting federal standards are scarce and enforcement is lax. If the regulations were to be met, costs of day care would rise. A sample study of federally subsidized care in 1972 placed annual expenditures per child in a day-care center at $2110; services in family day-care homes cost $657, and care in the child's home cost $1180.[8]

The fact that day-care facilities remain relatively scarce and costly has led to demands for further government outlays, not only to support more facilities but also to subsidize part of the costs to enable more working mothers to provide decent facilities for their children. Since the proportion of working mothers is highest among families in which family income is below $10,000, decent day-care facilities cost more than most are willing or are able to pay unless a subsidy is available.

In addition to direct subsidies for the purchase of child care, a limited tax deduction for work-related child-care expenses has been available since 1954. The Revenue Act of 1971 and the 1975 tax cut bill liberalized the law substantially allowing increasing proportions of middle- and upper-income families to take advantage of the provision. Starting in 1976 families with $35,000 annual income qualify for the maximum annual deduction of $4800 reduced 50 cents on the dollar up to an income limit of $44,600. In 1972 an estimated 1.6 million families deducted $1.1 billion from their income taxes, amounting to an actual tax subsidy of $220 million.

Education and race

The more education a woman acquires, the more likely she is to work. Educational attainment is more a determinant of labor force participation for women than for men, who, once out of school, tend to stay in the labor force regardless of educational attainment. In 1973 the participation rate ranged from 24 percent for women with an elementary education to 61 percent for women with a college education. Except for 20- to 24-year-olds with a college education, labor force participation of men outstripped that of women, and this exception was probably due to higher proportions of men in advanced training or military service.

Job opportunities for college-educated women have increased substantially. Better-educated women are able to take advantage of rising demand in the expanding clerical and technical occupations; they may also be less satisfied with housekeeping. Women who have invested in a college education may also be reluctant to forgo the rewards from work in professional fields; their opportunity costs of staying at home are greater than for less educated women. Women with four or more years of college who worked full time, year round in 1972 earned twice as much as those with grade school education.

Race is also an important determinant of female labor participation. Black married women have had a longer history of labor force participation than white women. Their earnings, though low, have been needed to supplement the comparatively lower earnings of their husbands and to support larger families. More black married women than white work at some point during the year—60 percent of blacks had work experience in 1972, compared with 49 percent of whites. Black women are more likely to be forced into idleness, primarily because of the kinds of jobs open to them. The incidence of unemployment among white women—5.3 percent—was half as high as among blacks, and spells of joblessness were of shorter duration (almost three-fifths of unemployed black women were out of jobs five or more weeks compared with about half of the unemployed whites).

Although black women lag behind white women in educational achievement—10 and 12.1 years, respectively—the education differential among working women is minimal. Similarly, racial occupational barriers also persist, but professional and managerial opportunities available to college-educated black women have improved. In 1973 two-fifths of employed black women with at least a high school diploma worked at blue-collar and service occupations compared with one-fourth of all employed white women with the same education. On the other hand, 82 percent of college-educated black women held professional or managerial jobs compared with 80 percent of whites.[9]

A contributing factor to the black wives' higher labor force participation is that they are better educated than their husbands; the reverse is true for whites. With more education, earnings potential and attractive work opportunities increase. Black wives who had some work experience in 1972 contributed more to family income than white wives—32 percent compared with 26 percent. When family income was over $15,000, black wives contributed 35 percent of the total compared with 27 percent by whites, suggesting that black wives play a greater role in helping their families reach middle-class status.

Patterns and ages of work for women

Wives and mothers more frequently move in and out of the labor market, either on a part-time or full-time basis, in response to

Figure 5-1   Labor force participation rates, 1947 and 1973.

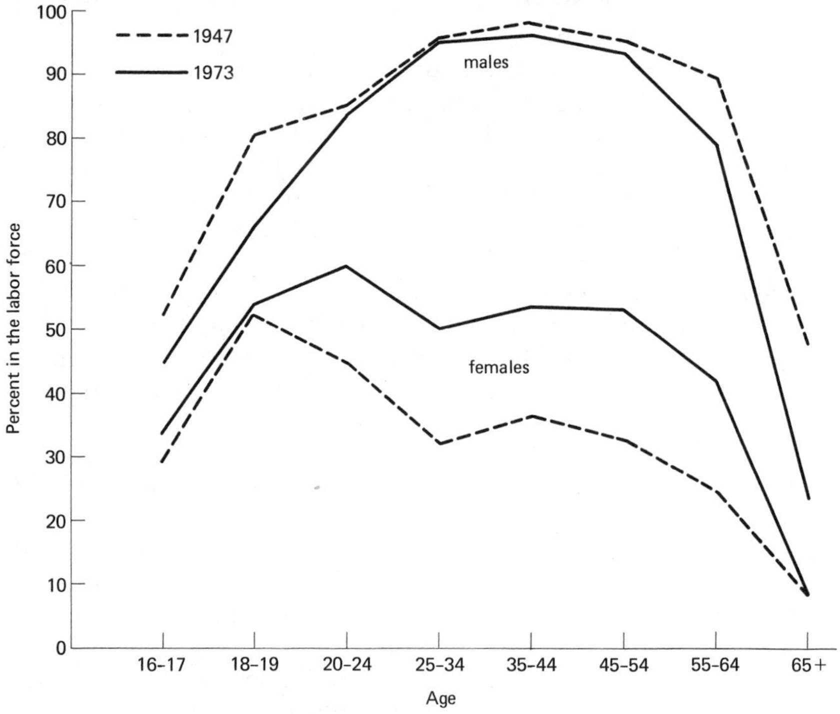

Source: *Manpower Report of the President* (Washington, D.C.: GPO, 1973), Table A-2; and Howard Hayghe, *Marital and Family Characteristics of Workers, March 1973*, U. S. Bureau of Labor Statistics, Special Labor Force Report 164 (Washington, D.C.: GPO, 1974), Table B.

their families' shifting needs, their own work desires, and labor market conditions. About half of all wives worked at some time during 1972, but only two of every ten workers were employed full time, year round. Since about three of every four employed married women work at full-time jobs, many did not work year round. Many women prefer part-time employment; they accounted for two-thirds of all voluntary part-time employment experience in 1973.

The distribution of womens' employment rates by age is bimodal. This M-shaped curve (Figure 5-1) reflects two peak participation periods: the first in early adulthood, when women are just out of school or are young wives earning money at the start of married life; and the second when mature women return to work after their children have entered school or are grown. Comparison of 1947 and 1973 data suggests men are working less and women more.

For many years 18- and 19-year-olds had the highest participation rates among women; these were premarriage and prechildren years. After World War II many mature 45-to-54-year-old women entered and stayed in the job market, and the labor force participation rate of this group surpassed the younger group. But since 1964, participation rates of 20-to-24-year-old women have been rising most rapidly. In 1973 this age group had a participation rate of 60 percent, exceeding that of every other age group. The rising participation rates of younger women reflect higher levels of education, delayed marriage, deferment of first births, and smaller family size. These trends are especially pronounced among younger women. In 1967 slightly more than one-third of 25-to-29-year-old wives expected two or fewer births. Five years later, almost two-thirds of all wives planned to limit family size to two or fewer children. Among younger wives the percentage desiring no more than two children was even higher.[10] If these expectations are realized, the bimodal labor force participation is likely to flatten further.

Discrimination

The recent interest in the women's liberation movement and the equal rights amendment has again illuminated the discrimination against women in the job market. Women earn less than men, and the gap has been widening. In 1955 the median wage for women who worked full time, year round was 64 percent of what men earned; in 1971 only 59.5 percent. However, full-time women workers average fewer hours per week than men. If one takes this factor into account, women's overall earnings ratio in 1971 was two-thirds that of men. Earnings disparities varied by occupation ranging from less than half in sales to almost three quarters for professionals (Table 5-2).

The earning comparisons give some idea of the disparity between men and women, but they do not present a prima facie case of the exploitation of women. The female labor force is heavily weighted with married women whose attachment to the work force is not as committed as that of men. Even comparison by sex of earnings of full-time, year-round workers leaves much to be desired. For example, married women have less occupational choice because they may put convenience of location or flexibility of hours above earnings. Their family ties give them less geographic mobility than males, and some, indeed, give up

Table 5-2 Women Workers' Earnings as Proportion of Men's Earnings,
1971

Occupational Group	Actual Ratio	Adjusted Ratio^a
Total	59.5	66.1
Professional and technical workers	66.4	72.4
Teachers, primary and secondary	82.0	n.a.
Managers, officials, and proprietors	53.0	56.8
Clerical workers	62.4	66.9
Sales workers	42.1	47.4
Craftsmen and foremen	56.4	60.2
Operatives	60.5	66.6
Service workers, excluding private household	58.5	63.2

^aAdjusted for differences in average full-time hours worked.
Source: Economic Report of the President (Washington, D.C.: GPO, 1973),
p. 104.

good jobs to follow husbands who decide to accept jobs elsewhere.
And there is a question about whether employers—or possibly
even women themselves—are willing to invest in their productivity
due to uncertainty about their future work patterns. Whatever
the cause, there is strong evidence that women are paid less than
men for performing the same work, laws to the contrary notwith-
standing. According to one recent study, at least half of the one-
third earnings differential between married men and women
cannot be accounted for after controlling for differentials in educational achievements or work experience and continuity.[11]

The maldistribution of occupations by sex is a better indicator
of the impact of discrimination (Table 5-3). The majority of
women are in clerical and service work (including domestic work),
retail sales, teaching, and nursing. Even though women can now
be found in virtually every occupation, most of the growth has
been in these "women's" occupations, with the result that the
bulk of women are still concentrated there. According to one
estimate, almost half of the net increase in employed women between 1950 and 1960 occurred in occupations in which at least 70
percent of the workers were women, and almost 60 percent of the
increase was registered in occupations that had a majority of
women.[12]

Women are forced to concentrate in jobs that tend to have
lower levels of responsibility and pay, while the better-paying jobs
and occupations offering opportunities for upward mobility have
frequently been foreclosed. Segregation of occupations by sex is
especially pronounced in skilled blue-collar jobs controlled by

Table 5-3 Distribution of Employed Women by Occupation, 1940 and
1973

Major Occupation Group	Percent of Women Employed		As Percent of Both Sexes Employed in Occupation	
	1973	1940	1973	1940
Total				
Thousands	31,924	11,920	—	—
Percent	100.0	100.0	38.5	25.9
White-Collar Workers				
Professional, technical workers	15.1	13.2	41.0	45.4
Managers, officials, proprietors	5.0	3.8	18.8	11.7
Clerical workers	34.0	21.2	76.1	52.6
Sales workers	6.8	7.0	40.6	27.9
Blue-Collar Workers				
Craftsmen, foremen	1.3	0.9	3.8	2.1
Operatives	13.7	18.4	31.2	25.7
Nonfarm laborers	0.8	0.8	0.7	3.2
Service Workers				
Private household workers	4.3	17.6	98.3	93.8
Service workers (except private household)	17.5	11.3	57.1	40.1
Farm Workers				
All farm occupations	1.3	5.8	15.1	8.0

Source: *Manpower Report of the President* (Washington, D.C.: GPO, 1971),
Table A-9; and William V. Deutermann, *Educational Attainment of Workers,
March 1973*, U.S. Bureau of Labor Statistics, Special Labor Force Report 161
(Washington, D.C.: GPO, 1974), Table I.

unions. Few apprenticeships, which have the promise of upward
mobility built in, are open to women. Indeed, women's share of
professional and technical occupations has actually declined during the past three decades from 45 to 39 percent, even though the
absolute numbers of professional and technical women workers
almost tripled. The relative decline, however, reflects a change in
the mix of professional jobs. For example, the increase in professionals included the spurt of engineering and related space-
age occupations, which are predominantly male. Whether this
change in mix is a function of discrimination or unavailability of
women to fill these positions is left to speculation.

As Elizabeth Waldman of the BLS has pointed out, the broad category of professional jobs is a "notorious example of a field divided along sexual lines."[13] Two-thirds of all professional women workers are either nonpractitioner health workers or teachers, and women teachers are mostly confined to primary grades while men tend to teach in high school and college.

Many factors contribute to make women seek out, and remain in, low-paying, low-status "women's" jobs. Not only does society place a low value on women's market services, but also women themselves have tended to base their job choices on short-run needs rather than on long-run career considerations. Thus they are frequently willing to take these less desirable jobs because the hours and location are convenient, enabling them to combine family and job responsibilities more easily.

During the 1960s, rapid expansion of women workers in few occupations tended to depress women's earnings. However, Victor Fuchs views this as a short-run phenomenon, and he anticipates that earnings differentials will lessen in the long run.[14] In an era of increasing childlessness, declining family size, and delayed first births, careers have gained greater importance in women's lives, and demands for greater occupational opportunities are becoming more articulated and militant.

The low value given to housewives' nonmarket homemaking duties is reflected in the fact that this productive work is not counted in the gross national product or other national accounts, although such services are counted if maids or others are paid to perform them. If, in 1964, the value of housewives' unpaid services had been counted in monetary terms—by using the wage rates of domestic workers—wives would have added about one-fourth to the GNP, or an additional $180 billion in 1971 dollars.[15]

Improving the employment status of women

For many years legislation dealing with women workers was confined to state protective laws regulating minimum wages, maximum hours, and other standards of work concerned with promoting their health and safety. In 1938 the Fair Labor Standards Act (FLSA) was adopted to provide federal standards on wages and hours for both men and women. More recently, the emphasis has shifted toward curbing sex discrimination and providing equal pay and employment opportunities. While many states adopted such laws, it was not until the 1960s that the federal government entered this field.

Among the major laws are the Equal Pay Act of 1963 and

Title VII of the Civil Rights Act of 1964, which prohibit discrimination in employment based on sex as well as on race, color, religion, and national origin. In addition, Executive Order 11246 prohibits discrimination based on sex (as well as race, color, religion, and national origin) by federal contractors and subcontractors; and the Age Discrimination in Employment Act of 1967 proscribed discrimination on the basis of age against persons between the ages of 40 and 65. The 1972 Equal Opportunity Act gave the Equal Employment Opportunity Commission the right to sue private companies for job discrimination.

The mere passage of legislation, of course, does not guarantee equal employment opportunities. The laws leave much to be desired in coverage, scope, and sanctions, and little is done to ensure compliance with existing provisions. For instance, the Equal Pay Act is an amendment to the FLSA, and its coverage is limited generally to that of the federal minimum wage law, leaving out higher-paying executive, administrative, and professional positions—the very jobs where discrimination appears most rampant and its elimination most crucial if women are to achieve an equal footing with men. The 1974 amendments to the FLSA extended coverage to low-skilled jobs that employed predominantly females, including domestic work and retail occupations.

The most publicized and controversial of the recent legislative attempts to improve the status of women is the proposed Equal Rights Amendment to the Constitution. It states that "equality of rights under the law shall not be denied or abridged by the United States or by any State on account of sex," and it would make discriminatory laws unconstitutional. If it were adopted, women would presumably acquire the same "rights" as men in all areas of economic, social, and political life. However, some groups that favor improving the employment status of women oppose the amendment on the grounds that it would erode hard-won protective legislation. Concern over drafting women for military service seems unfounded in lieu of the all-volunteer armed forces. Charges that the amendment will adversely affect alimony and child-custody arrangements have been dismissed as invalid by supporters.

Notes

1. Herman P. Miller, *Rich Man, Poor Man* (New York: T. Y. Crowell, 1971), Chap. 12.
2. U.S. Bureau of the Census, *Money Income in 1972 of Families and Persons in the United States*, Series P-60, No. 90 (Washington, D.C.: GPO, December 1973), Table 32.

3. Juanita M. Kreps, *Sex in the Market Place: American Women at Work* (Baltimore, Md.: Johns Hopkins Press, 1971).

4. U.S. Bureau of the Census, *Household and Family Characteristics: March 1972*, Series P-20, No. 246 (Washington, D.C.: GPO, February 1973), Table 4.

5. Phillips Cutright and John Sconzoni, "Income Supplements and the American Family," U.S. Congress, Joint Economic Committee, *Studies in Public Welfare*, No. 12, Part 1 (Washington, D.C.: GPO, 1973), p. 67.

6. Anne M. Young, *Children of Working Mothers, March 1972*, U.S. Bureau of Labor Statistics, Special Labor Force Report 154 (Washington, D.C.: GPO, 1973), Table A.

7. Seth Low and Pearl Spindler, *Child Care Arrangements of Working Mothers in the United States*, U.S. Department of Labor and U.S. Department of Health, Education, and Welfare (Washington, D.C.: GPO, 1968), pp. 15–16.

8. AVCO Corporation, "Cost of Day Care," *A Demonstration Child Care Review System, Final Report*, Contract HEW, SRS 71-48 (Washington, D.C.: AVCO International Services Division, 1973), p. 4.

9. William V. Deutermann, *Educational Attainment of Workers, March 1973*, U.S. Bureau of Labor Statistics, Special Labor Force Report 161 (Washington, D.C.: GPO, 1974), Table J.

10. U.S. Bureau of the Census, *Current Populations Reports*, "Birth Expectations of American Wives, June 1973," Series P-20, No. 254 (Washington, D.C.: GPO, October 1973), Table 2.

11. *Economic Report of the President, 1974* (Washington, D.C.: GPO, 1974), p. 155.

12. Valerie Kincade Oppenheimer, *The Female Labor Force in the United States*, Population Monograph Series No. 5 (Berkeley, Calif.: University of California, 1970), p. 160.

13. Elizabeth Waldman, "Women at Work: Changes in the Labor Force Activity of Women," *Monthly Labor Review* (June 1970), p. 11.

14. Victor R. Fuchs, "Short-Run and Long-Run Prospects for Female Earnings," NBER Working Paper Series, No. 20 (New York: Center for Economic Analysis of Human Behavior and Social Institutions, 1973), p. 14.

15. Ahmad Hussein Shamseddine, "GNP Imputations of the Value of Housewives' Services," *The Economic and Business Bulletin* of the School of Business Administration, Temple University (Summer 1968), pp. 53–61.

6

measurement
and forecasting

Sophisticated measurement techniques and extensive data gathered over the years by governmental and private organizations have given us a clear picture of the changing patterns of American work. As a nation we have been fortunate in having such extensive data, although there is room for improvement. The challenge is to interpret the data wisely and apply the lessons learned to achieve societal goals.

Measurement of the labor force—manpower statistics

The United States has one of the most comprehensive flows of labor market information in the world. Each month the Bureau of Labor Statistics and the Manpower Administration, working with other federal, state, and private organizations, collect and publish a detailed history of the previous month's labor market activity.[1] These analyses and statistical reports include reliable estimates of (1) the size, marital status, and demographic composition of the population aged 16 years and over; (2) the number of workers by occupation, hours worked, age, sex, and color; (3) the number of filled jobs in nonfarm industries and average weekly hours and earnings for nonsupervisory personnel; (4) the total number of persons actively seeking work and the number drawing jobless pay; the extent of strike activity, recent collective bargaining settlements, and pending negotiations; and (5) trends in wages, productivity, and unit labor costs.

    Other federal agencies provide information on (1) total income flow earned from both past and present work or resulting from other transfer payments; (2) investments in training, especially formal education; (3) employment in select sectors of the economy (e.g., manufacturing) or by profession (e.g., scientific and technical personnel); and special analytical measures such as full-time equivalent employment and income.

Special data have been developed to supplement the recurring monthly and annual data. These special studies, which are designed mainly to portray labor market interactions at more detailed levels, include surveys of the poverty population (e.g., the Urban Employment Survey) and longitudinal labor force participation and work-experience studies.

Because of the great expansion of labor market information and research in the past three decades, analysts can verify most labor market measures by comparison with an alternative, totally independent source. Until 1940 there were no reliable estimates of the current employment status of the population aside from the decennial censuses, and even that information had serious conceptual flaws for the analysis of labor market conditions.

This vast flow of manpower data, collected from thousands of homes and firms, comprises a keystone for the formulation and implementation of monetary and fiscal policies and federal, state, municipal, and private manpower programs. These same data figure prominently in business research and planning and in private research.

Major data sources

The manpower statistics now in wide use originate from three major sources: (1) *household interviews*, including decennial censuses, monthly current population surveys, and special household surveys; (2) *employer surveys*, including industry censuses, monthly payroll reports from individual firms, and special industrial studies; and (3) *documentary or administrative statistics* drawn from the operating records of the Social Security Administration, the Manpower Administration, the Commerce Department, and various regulatory organizations such as the Interstate Commerce Commission. Each source has its own strengths, weaknesses, and unique conceptual and methodological properties. Together, however, these sources provide a network of manpower information that, while different in collection technique and concept, is unmatched in its detail that satisfies quantitative requirements for macroanalysis while providing a considerable body of microanalytical data.

Manpower statistics before World War II

The decennial census, required by the Constitution to help apportion representatives among states, was not intended to provide manpower information. It did, however, furnish data on population, the human resource base from which all manpower analysis departs. By the mid-1800s tidbits of economic intelligence, notably industrial employment estimates, were beginning to be collected in the decennial censuses.[2] In each subsequent census the volume of employment information was expanded and refined as new departments and agencies sought to cope with the problems of a growing nation. Designed for other purposes (mainly political apportionment and tax assessment), the censuses became a vehicle for the collection of manpower data and are virtually the only source of national socioeconomic information for the 1800s. Because of collection and definitional weaknesses, these early employment data are of very limited value in economic analysis.[3]

Employment figures gathered in the censuses of the early 1900s were based on the so-called gainful worker concept. Individuals were recorded as gainfully employed if they reported a trade (occupation) that provided money income or its equivalent. This concept had no time reference and tended, therefore, to exclude unemployment—most of the unemployed had held a job of one kind or another—and to inflate the employment figures further because those who had retired also had a gainful occupation. During the late 1930s, the gainful worker concept—which provided a useful inventory of occupational skills—was displaced by the more precise activity-oriented concept now in use.

Social problems and statistical development

Most present-day manpower information systems were byproducts of programs designed for other needs, or else thrown together in response to large-scale socioeconomic crises. As a result, available manpower information has grown erratically—almost haphazardly —and has taken a distinctly social rather than economic orientation. Major developments and improvements of manpower statistics closely followed and largely resulted from the Great Depression of the 1930s, the cumulative recessions of the 1950s, and the overriding concern of federal officials with the nature and origins of poverty in the late 1960s.

The state of other arts also affected the evolution of the information network. Breakthroughs in communications, data processing, methods of statistical analysis, new methods of data collection, sampling techniques, and other factors played an important role in the growth of manpower data systems, as did the consolidation of the reporting and analysis of manpower information in the Department of Labor in the late 1950s.

There has always been a certain ambivalence in the collection and analysis of employment and unemployment statistics, arising from differences in the objectives of the users. Some analysts, concerned with the welfare implications that may be drawn from the statistics, focus attention on the conditions and availability of jobs, with special reference to the impact of unemployment. More recently, manpower data have been used extensively in analyzing resource use, with a special view to the elimination of labor bottlenecks and the promotion of long-term growth. Oscillations between the two views have coincided with cyclical swings in unemployment.

Based on the old practice of blaming the messenger for the bad news, it was inevitable that the collectors of manpower statistics would be criticized by some when they reported unwelcome news. As the credibility of the employment and unemployment figures came under severe analytical and political attack, President Kennedy in 1961 appointed a panel of experts to appraise the employment and unemployment statistics.

The Gordon committee

The presidential committee chaired by Professor R. A. Gordon—hence the Gordon Committee—interpreted its mandate widely. It examined and reported on the concepts, techniques, prospects, and problems involved in all major manpower data series then in existence.[4] The committee's report was significant mainly because it synthesized past statistical experience and clarified certain conceptual and methodological problems and recommendations for the future development of manpower information systems along resource-use lines. The report set the tone for the further development of labor markets statistics in the 1960s and 1970s. Aside from its substantive contributions, the committee gave the collectors of manpower data a clean bill of health and made special efforts to remove manpower data collection from the political arena.

Concepts and sources: their current status

The concept of employment used in manpower statistics is based essentially on remuneration, not work. The labor force statistics, therefore, exclude the work of housewives, students, and volunteers. Also excluded from the manpower statistics are groups engaged in illicit occupations. The latter exclusions are based not on conceptual or moral objections, but rather on the difficulties in obtaining such data. Nonetheless, the unmeasured activities are important and result in serious gaps. The annual gross revenue accruing to organized crime is variously estimated at $10 to $60 billion, and more states are now moving to capture some of this income by legalizing and regulating lotteries and horseracing. The services of housewives are more vital, providing the minimum equivalent of about one-fourth of the total GNP in unpaid domestic service annually. Volunteer work is also very important, involving during a typical period the equivalent of about 900,000 full-time, year-round workers. Because of the large outputs generated by these nonemployment activities, it is important to remember that employment figures used in manpower analysis are based on a definition that embraces mainly *reported* pay or profits.

Employment. The oldest continuous employment series is the *payroll employment* data, which date back to 1919. These data, which include all forms of wage and salary employment in private firms, government units, and nonprofit organizations, are relatively easy and inexpensive to collect. It is a highly reliable count of all filled jobs—the numbers are taken directly from payroll records— and provides consistent national, regional, state, and city figures on the number of jobs in a wide variety of industries. This monthly series is the best source of information on trends in wage and salary employment and a major source of information on hours of work paid for, average hourly and weekly wages of production and nonsupervisory workers, and labor turnover (total hiring and total separations) in manufacturing. Compiled from mail questionnaires, the series covers a sample of firms employing about 30 million workers.

Some kinds of work do not fit in the establishment employment definitions because they do not appear on a normal payroll record. Included are the self-employed, domestics working in private homes, unpaid family workers, and agricultural workers. Employment estimates for these groups are drawn largely from household surveys and administrative statistics.

Wage and salary employment is also measured in the *monthly household survey* (Current Population Survey, or CPS). Because of conceptual and methodological differences the count of persons with wage and salary *employment* differs from the number of jobs counted on payroll records.[5] The most important difference is multiple jobholding—a person may hold two jobs but is only counted once in the household survey. There are also differences attributable to unpaid absences from work. If no payroll entry occurs for a person, then no payroll job is recorded in the survey of firms. However, he is counted as employed in the household survey if he is away on an unpaid vacation, personal business, on strike, or for similar reasons.

The household survey is wider in scope than the establishment data. It covers all forms of employment, including self-employment, unpaid family workers, private household workers, and agriculture—all of which are excluded from the industry employment estimates based on employer reports. Each of these sets of data makes a unique contribution to the understanding of employment trends. The industry survey concentrates on industry and geographic detail, while the household data focus on characteristics of the employed, including age, sex, education, and occupation.

Unemployment. The unemployment rate has an enormous impact on government policy and public opinion, but it is one of the least understood and most controversial statistics issued by the government. No single definition of what constitutes unemployment has ever been devised that is acceptable to all political and economic groups. The unemployment statistic used today is rooted in the Great Depression. When mass unemployment in the 1930s underscored the need for reliable current statistics, experiments with household (or population) surveys were begun. These efforts were sound in design but lacked the necessary objectivity because the definition of unemployment was based on a person's reported willingness and ability to work. The concept was dependent on the interpretation and attitudes of both the interviewer and interviewee. A more objective and rigorous standard had to be devised. A small group of economists, statisticians, and sociologists in the Works Progress Administration developed a more objective measure based on actual activity during a specified week. Responsibility for the national sample survey (begun in 1940) was ultimately passed to the Bureau of the Census, and the survey (now the CPS) continues to utilize essentially the same concepts and methods today.

Although technical in detail, the concepts and definitions used in the CPS are very simple. The labor force consists of all employed and unemployed persons who are at least 16 years old. For purposes of the survey, people are counted as employed if they worked a single hour during the survey week for pay or profit or worked 15 hours or more in a family enterprise. People who had regular jobs but were temporarily absent during the survey week for such reasons as vacation, illness, strikes, or bad weather are also counted as employed. Specifically excluded are those whose activity was confined to work around the house (mainly housewives) or to unpaid volunteer work for charitable organizations. Unemployed persons are those who were not working during the reference period, were available for work and had engaged in specific work-seeking activity within the prior 4 weeks, were waiting to be called back from layoff, or were waiting to report to a new job beginning within 30 days.

The CPS is limited to a very definite group composed of working-age (16 years and over) civilians who are not in institutions. Because it is useful to know the importance of defense demands on the manpower supply, official figures from the Department of Defense on the size of the armed forces are added to the civilian work force to provide an estimate of the total labor force. Persons who are neither employed nor unemployed—mostly housewives, students, disabled, and retired workers—are considered "not in the labor force."

Monthly employment and unemployment data are obtained by skilled interviewers from a sample survey of about 47,000 households. At the Bureau of the Census, data from the sample households (for the calendar week including the 12th of the month) are then "blown up" to national totals. Most data from this CPS are cross-classified by demographic characteristics such as age, sex, color, marital status, occupation, hours of work, and duration of and reasons for unemployment. The survey also provides data on the characteristics and past work experience of those not in the labor force.

The CPS also yields information on topics of special interest through supplemental questions each month. In the various months, questions dealing with matters such as work experience in the prior year, income, marital and family status, and multiple jobholding are explored. Most contemporary labor market analysis is based on material drawn from CPSs or the decennial census.[6]

Administrative statistics. Administrative statistics tend to reflect the peculiarities of the program for which they are collected and, therefore, cannot be conveniently lumped into a simple classification scheme. Important labor market data are derived from Social Security files and from insured unemployment coverage and claims records. Both programs are limited in coverage but provide detailed data of considerable analytical significance. The Social Security figures cover employment by size of firm, geographic location of employment, and some earnings data. Insured unemployment claims—persons reporting a week of unemployment under an unemployment insurance program—comprise a cyclically sensitive cross-check of the total unemployment estimates and are available in considerable geographic detail. However, unemployment insurance data do not measure total unemployment because they exclude persons who have exhausted their benefit rights, who have not earned rights to unemployment insurance, and who have lost jobs not covered by unemployment insurance.

Program needs

Despite improvements brought about by the Gordon Committee report and the recent introduction of new data series growing out of the concern with poverty, important gaps remain in our knowledge of labor market interactions. Possibly the most significant omissions are data on underemployment—which would provide insights on short workweeks, productivity and low earnings, the extent of employment below capabilities and, most important of all, some reasonable assessment of the real social and economic costs of underemployment. (Several attempts to measure underemployment and subemployment are discussed in Chapter 3.) Such efforts, of course, involve difficult statistical and definitional problems, and the potential use of the data to affect social policy is bound to raise controversy. Yet the costs of not fully assessing underutilized labor supplies may well be greater than currently supposed. The social disruptions that occurred in the 1960s strongly suggest that society cannot continue to ignore the inequities implicit in the highly unequal pattern of economic opportunity. Low national unemployment rates are no reason for complacency if that low rate coexists with substantial involuntary nonparticipation or underutilization of women, younger workers, older workers, and minority groups.

Data on worker motivation, while important, are largely absent from governmental labor market information. Attitudinal data directed at assessing the determinants of work-seeking activity, development of job skills, and the desire to achieve are increasingly important to adequate decision making and policy planning in our complex yet fragmented society. It may prove dangerous to ignore the ghettos and campuses, which are promoting attitudes and actions that seemingly divert sectors of the population from the mainstream of American life. Attitudinal studies should also recognize the pervading significance of industrial peace and provide employers and unions with a notion of the kinds of job restructuring, administrative changes, and reward systems necessary to give the worker a greater stake in his job and company. Obviously, such a departure from the traditional modes of labor market analysis and data collection would require fuller development of interdisciplinary research, drawing heavily on the training and techniques of psychologists, sociologists, and political scientists.

Forecasting manpower supplies and requirements[7]

The Employment Act of 1946 stimulated interest in the size of the labor force for which jobs were to be provided "for all of those able, willing and seeking to work." In the 1950s creeping unemployment, often attributed to a mismatch between available and demanded skills, intensified the need to foresee changes in manpower supply and demand. The development of new manpower programs in the mid-1960s increased demands for advance information about manpower changes. At its best, forecasting is a critical ingredient in advance planning, encouraging the realistic appraisal of the likely costs and benefits of differing programs to facilitate a reasonable distribution of scarce resources. It is also used for individual career planning, market research, policy evaluation, and analysis of socioeconomic objectives.

The nature of manpower projections

Projections and forecasts are often differentiated, but in reality the difference lies in the confidence of the forecaster. After examining past trends, the projector develops a working model of the system. Assumptions about how the important variables are likely to behave in the future are developed and then applied to extend the past performance of relevant variables. Accuracy in projections is largely a function of the realism of the assumptions and the identification of all relevant variables; consequently, the cardinal sin of the projector is failure to make his assumptions explicit. Confusion also stems from failure to differentiate between descriptive projections (what is likely to be) and normative projections (what ought to be). Users of projections must take note of the underlying assumptions and appraise their validity; they should avoid reading into long-range forecasts an implied commitment to an imputed straight-line trend at intermediate points.

In the United States projectors generally emphasize descriptions that may enable decision makers to make more rational decisions. As various forms of public planning become more accepted in the United States, policy makers will be forced into more serious consideration of the manpower implications of their decisions.

In summary, forecasts are based on implicit and explicit assumptions concerning the nature and direction of future trends. Because anticipated expectations are rarely met, forecasts should be regarded as "most likely" approximations. With all these caveats competent long-range manpower supply and demand forecasts can, nonetheless, influence decision making because they (1) illuminate likely bottlenecks and imbalances in particular segments of the labor market, (2) indicate the likely consequences of instituting changes in existing programs or introducing new programs, and (3) provide an estimate of the total manpower resource pie by helping to price out societal goals in manpower terms, to choose among these goals when necessary, and to move them along the least-cost path.

Projecting manpower supplies and requirements

Forecasts may be calculated in a wide variety of ways, ranging in complexity from simple linear extrapolation of past trends to complex econometric models. Each technique has its own special properties of detail, conditional restraints, and applicability to reality.[8] Because they are based on known population levels and longstanding trends in labor force participation, projections of the potential total labor supply are quite reliable. Unfortunately, no reliable base exists from which to project labor supplies by skill level or any qualitative element other than educational attainment. Thus few attempts are made to project the supply of skills. However, this is not a serious loss, since few jobs have fixed skill requirements. Most employers vary their requirements to suit the state of the labor market, while the workers' mobility renders projections of supply by occupation and industry of little value.

Because employment levels in modern economics are in large part the consequence of public policy, levels of labor demand are subject to guess. Projectors have resorted to two major approaches with little practical difference between them. One is to assume a level of unemployment based either on a normative or descriptive judgment. The other is to project GNP on the basis of assumed future growth rates and estimate the consequent employment. Neither method is very reliable, but in any event the purposes of the manpower analyst are usually best served by projections of the *structure* of labor demand rather than the *level* of total demand.

When the structure of manpower requirements is projected, total assumed GNP is distributed among industries on the basis of further assumptions regarding national economic goals. These are translated into anticipated patterns of consumption, investment, and government spending. Projecting requirements is especially difficult because the priorities assigned to national goals may change radically. The unexpected appearance of Sputnik and the resulting massive mobilization of scientific and technical personnel in the space program in the 1960s illustrates a radical alteration of national priorities that affected the composition of manpower demand. In addition, goals are heavily determined by private units, which may sharply and quickly change their demand patterns. Finally, innovations may alter the composition of labor demand and also modify the relative significance of different goals. Despite these difficulties, analysts are increasingly engaged in assessing the likely patterns of demand, relating these demands to manpower requirements, and measuring the requirements against the anticipated supply.

Overall manpower forecasts, therefore, usually involve a two-pronged effort. On one side, technicians—demographers, statisticians, and economists—develop detailed projections of the probable labor supply in its quantitative and even qualitative aspects. On the other side, policy makers articulate needs, specify goals, and establish a scheme of priorities. The broad estimates are then brought together, yielding a view of the likely future interaction of labor supply and demand.

Uses of manpower projections

A major concern of government is to avoid mismatches between manpower demands and supplies. Clearly, the minimum level of unemployment attainable with tolerable inflation and the speed with which it can be achieved are affected by the degree to which open jobs match the qualifications of available workers. This requires more detailed and reliable short-term and medium-term projections of the labor supply by age, sex, race, and skill than are currently available. In fact, usable projections are largely limited to long-term forecasts of the total supply of labor. These projections may also provide warning, however. For example, projected age, race, and sex characteristics of the labor force portend growing imbalances between manpower demand and supply unless traditional employment patterns are substantially altered.[9] If the rates at which younger workers and blacks are penetrating certain occupations fail to increase substantially, unemployment of these groups will be significantly worsened in the years ahead. Providing warnings of projected shortages (or surpluses) of teachers, medical personnel, or scientists and engineers also is a familiar use of these long-term projections.

Less familiar is the increasing demand for manpower projections created by three policy developments. First, welfare- and education-oriented programs require assessment of manpower requirements as well as dollar costs so that potential manpower bottlenecks can be noted and efforts made to avoid them. Second, the expanded role of government in the economy has increased the need to foresee the impact on manpower of government decisions, especially those involving defense and space efforts. Changes in manpower demand resulting from evolving governmental policies accentuated the need for contingency plans to generate jobs for the diverse groups that are victimized by federal policies. Third, the threat of major technological change has aroused some interest in projections of regional, industrial, and occupational employment fluctuations. Such early warning signals might stimulate advance planning to ease the adjustment to change. Recent recessions indicate that little progress has been made in this area.

Educational planners, involved in decisions concerning physical facilities, finances, and curricula, are among those most persistently demanding projections of the manpower future. Fortunately, the required projections are not as difficult as might be assumed. Buildings have a long life, but they exercise little constraint on curriculum choices, and financial needs depend primarily on the number of students. Curriculum planning requires relatively little lead time or detail because curricula are relatively uniform in elementary schools and high schools and, even at the college levels, concentrations are sufficiently broad to require comparatively little detailed anticipation of occupational choices.

Vocational education and apprenticeship are oriented to specific occupations and thus require detailed projections of the employment outlook. But the number needed for replacement and industry expansion almost always exceeds the number trained, and the gap is flexibly filled by those who pick up the trade outside the formal channels. The more specific the occupational training required, of course, the greater the need for projections. But lack of projections is probably less of a barrier to planning than structural and institutional difficulties: (1) Budgetary constraints are more to blame than is lack of information for the oft-noted (but probably exaggerated) obsolescence of vocational school equipment and curricula; (2) more information is available than is used; (3) there are no overwhelming obstacles to reasonably accurate two-to-five-year projections of local manpower requirements; and (4) planning should not be based entirely on local projections—from a national viewpoint, for example, it would make sense to allocate expenditures in declining regions for vocational education deliberately aimed at providing training for future outmigrants.

Projection needs for counseling and guidance parallel those of educational planning. Persistent youth unemployment has caused dissatisfaction with the information available for counseling and making vocational choices. The standard source is the *Occupational Outlook Handbook,*[10] a BLS publication that projects, in terms of general trends, employment in nearly 850 specific occupations for roughly a decade ahead. The *Handbook* has gained wide acceptance by educational counselors.

Interest in improving the occupational projections of manpower planners, counselors, and educators spurred several new efforts by the BLS and the Manpower Administration to collect additional labor market information. Based on census data, a national industry-occupational employment matrix was developed by BLS, covering 200 industries and 400 occupations. Similar state matrices are being developed by state employment service analysts. To help the states expand their matrices and improve their capabilities in occupational projections, the Manpower Administration is supporting the collection, currently in 26 states, of more detailed occupational employment statistics by employer surveys. Another potentially helpful experiment to canvass employers in selected metropolitan areas in order to project related information on job vacancies and labor turnover was abandoned in 1973.

Labor Supplies in 1980–1985

The working-age population (aged 16 years and over) will total about 167 million in 1980 and about 176 million in 1985. The projection that the labor force will reach 102 million in 1980 may be made with considerable confidence. This means an average annual increase in the labor force of 1.6 million between 1972 and 1980, compared with average annual increases of about 1.4 million between 1960 and 1972.[11]

Labor force growth is expected to slow down after 1980 because the working-age population will increase by only 1.7 million annually between 1980 and 1985, compared with about 2.4 million annually between 1972 and 1980. This slowing of population growth is definite because all the people who will reach working age between 1980 and 1985 have already been born. However, this anticipated growth in the work force must also include changes in participation rates, which tend to evolve relatively slowly, while population changes generally are more important over the longer run.[12] Between 1960 and 1972 the labor force participation rate of men declined by 3.8 percentage points and is expected to decline by only 0.1 percentage point between 1972 and 1985 due to the increased number of prime working-age men. In contrast, the more rapidly growing labor force participation rate among women accounts for more of the projected growth in the labor force. The labor force participation rate of women increased 6 percentage points between 1960 and 1972 and is expected to increase by another 2.3 percentage points by 1985. However, continuing declines in birth rates during the next decade could induce more women to enter the labor force.

The labor force changes constantly, renewing itself as older workers retire and are replaced by younger workers and reentrants. These gross flows resulted in very large labor force increases between 1960 and 1970 when 2.4 million 16- to 19-year-olds joined the labor force. The growth slowed in the 1970s, and in the 1980s the teenage labor force will actually decline, reflecting the reduced birth rates of the 1960s.[13] In the late 1950s the BLS correctly projected rapid expansion in the teenage work force and suggested a probable deterioration of their employment situation. The slow growth and ultimate decline in their labor force in the 1970s and 1980s may improve the job opportunities for teenagers. While one major labor market concern of the 1960s was the mounting of efforts to bring youngsters into the mainstream of economic activity, the 1970s and 1980s may bring greater concern for offering career opportunities to older workers.

Labor force increases for persons just over 25 years of age are going to be one of the dramatic and productive labor force changes of the 1970s. The same persons who flooded labor markets as teenagers and young adults in the 1960s—and in many instances were not absorbed for a long time—will now appear as highly educated, full-time, year-round workers. In particular, the number of 25-to-34-year-old workers will increase enormously between 1970 and 1980—by over 900,000 a year, or nearly 60 percent, to more than 26 million in 1980. By 1980 one of every four workers will be in this age group in comparison with about one in every five in 1970.

The number of workers aged 35 to 44 will show only a fractional increase prior to 1980 and then, reflecting the same World War II baby boom, will surge dramatically by over 80 percent. During the 1970s, the supply of these workers will increase only moderately. The number of workers aged 45 years and over is expected to increase by only 1 million in the 1970s, compared to 3 million in the 1960s. This smaller rise reflects the comparatively few people born in the depths of the Great Depression. There is a problem here, of course, in the form of a potential large shortage of skilled senior managers and professionals. Younger workers will have to be advanced rapidly during the 1970s and groomed to take on greater responsibility earlier than their fathers and grandfathers—a development the younger workers are likely to welcome.

Dramatic changes are forecast in the average educational attainment of the labor force. The entrance of better-educated young workers at the same time that older, less-educated workers are retiring continues to tip the balance toward a higher and higher average educational attainment for the nation's working force. By 1990 more than four of every five persons in the adult labor force (aged 25 years and over) will have graduated at least from high school, and almost one in four (about 22 million) will have completed four years or more of college work—compared with 64 percent high school graduates and 15 percent college graduates or higher of the early 1970s. The decline in the number of workers at the lower end of the educational scale is perhaps more dramatic. In the late 1950s one-third of the labor force had only an eighth-grade education or less; by 1990 only 1 of every 16 workers will be in that group.[14]

Labor force increases for blacks will probably continue to be relatively larger than for whites in the 1970s, especially among younger workers and adult males. The black labor force is expected to rise by more than one-fourth by 1980, compared with an increase of about one-sixth in the white labor force. The rapid rate of growth—which reflects a sharp population increase—raises the possibility of exacerbating the already high unemployment rates for nonwhite workers. However, higher levels of educational attainment and progress toward equal employment opportunities may combine to produce further improvements in the employment status of blacks.

Some Implications

The major conclusions of the new labor force projections are that (1) the rate of growth of the labor force in the 1970s will be only slightly less than during the preceding decade, but will slow markedly during the following decade; (2) the teenage labor force, with its myriad of special problems, will grow much more slowly in the current decade and will begin to contract during the 1980s; and (3) the number of young adult workers, ages 25 to 34, will grow at a rapid rate during the 1970s, while the increase of workers 35 and over will be very small.

The expected overall growth of the labor force should provide more than an adequate base for sustaining the economic growth of the 1970s. Even the slower growth of the labor force during the 1980s may not necessarily induce lower rates of economic growth because the long-term rise in the educational attainment of workers offers potential for increases in productivity, work hours are declining, and women and young people may be attracted to the work force in even greater numbers than are projected. The increased supply of educated workers should help relieve skilled-worker and white-collar bottlenecks caused by a shortage of mature workers. Unemployment problems for the young should be reduced because fewer youths will compete for jobs, while opportunities for advancement by younger workers to higher levels may improve because the supply of mature workers is likely to be stretched thin. However, increased education and training do not automatically mean the end of skilled manpower shortages or of youth unemployment. Sending more youngsters to college will not train the plumbers, electricians, or other skilled workers who are in short supply; overemphasis on college education for white-collar jobs—which may pay less, have longer hours, and require little preparation—presents the real possibility that some young people are being overeducated. As a result, they may lack jobs commensurate with their education at the same time that skilled jobs go unfilled.

With concern focusing on the potential surplus of highly educated workers, the plight of workers at the opposite end of the educational spectrum should not be overlooked. Although their numbers are declining, their relative disadvantage compared to the average worker is increasing as the average worker becomes better educated. Entry-level job requirements may be adjusted up as employers perceive the rise of the educational endowment of the work force. Thus, despite their dwindling number, the nation cannot be complacent about the undereducated and untrained; manpower and retraining programs will need to be expanded to correct these serious deficiencies.

Occupational projections

Projections of manpower requirements by occupation depend largely on differences in the rate of growth of segments of the economy. One way the growth and decline of industries has been forecast is by analyzing national priorities. Although national goals are not exclusively set by the federal government, legislation and federal budgets have a great deal of influence throughout the economy. For example, more than nine of every ten dollars that will be spent on air-pollution control during the 1970s are estimated to be private-sector outlays.

Relative price tags are usually the first consideration in deciding whether goals and priorities are feasible. The employment and skill requirements demanded, however, do not necessarily follow. Analysts at the National Planning Association converted the national goals for individual and social welfare set by a presidential commission in 1960 (plus space exploration) into man-

power costs and related them to the likely configuration of manpower supply in the 1970s.[15] They concluded that full achievement
of the goals would require about 12 percent more workers than
were expected to be in the labor force by the mid-1970s.[16]

An example of translating a national goal into the demand
for certain types of manpower is the demand that is expected to
be generated for scientists and engineers by the establishment of
pollution abatement standards. The National Planning Association projects the need for scientists and engineers will be increased by 91,300 by 1980.[17] The estimate takes into account not
only the direct requirements for specialists in antipollution activities but also the indirect demand for scientists and engineers
that will result from the growth in plant and equipment purchases
needed for pollution control. To the extent that the environmental
field will grow during the 1970s, its skill demands will have an
impact on the occupational structure of the 1980s. In an opposite
case, due to the rapid drop in the birth rate, the demand for
elementary and secondary teachers will decline during the 1980s
and will have a noticeable effect on the slower growth of professional and technical workers.

Other factors affecting occupational projections is the changing technology within industries and the productivity of workers.
Patterns of employment in American industries are altered in
response to innovations, and since the turn of the century U.S.
employment has changed from agrarian to industrial to white
collar. New jobs are created, and some skills become obsolete.
For example, since 1950 the computer has resulted in a variety of
new technical specialists. Occupational projections for the 1970s
and 1980s indicate that the demand for professional workers to
develop and use the computer will continue to grow while some
clerical occupations—payroll and inventory clerks, for example—
will contract.[18]

While the occupational mix will be determined by the choices
made among national priorities, industrial growth, and technological changes, the direction of long-term trends in the broad
categories of workers—white collar, blue collar, and farm employment—is not expected to be reversed (Table 6-1). Manpower
requirements for professional and technical workers will increase
faster than total employment—by 31 percent between 1972 and
1980 and more slowly, by 13 percent, between 1980 and 1985. The
strongest demands for professional manpower will be in the computer and health fields. The growth in clerical employment is anticipated to remain strong through 1985.

The rate of growth of blue-collar occupations will fall short
of the overall increase in employment, and as with white-collar

Table 6-1   Projected Occupational Employment, 1980 and 1985
(in thousands)

Occupation	1972	1980	1985
Total	81,703	95,800	101,500
White Collar	39,092	49,400	53,700
Professional and technical	11,459	15,000	17,000
Managers and administrators	8,032	10,100	10,500
Clerical workers	14,247	17,900	19,700
Sales workers	5,354	6,300	6,500
Blue Collar	28,576	31,700	32,800
Craftsmen and kindred	10,810	12,200	13,000
Operatives	13,549	15,000	15,300
Nonfarm laborers	4,217	4,500	4,500
Service Workers	10,966	12,700	13,400
Farm Workers	3,069	2,000	1,600

Source: Neal H. Rosenthal, "The United States Economy in 1985: Projected Changes in Occupations," *Monthly Labor Review* (December 1973), Table 1.

occupations growth will be uneven. The largest increases will be in the skilled crafts that depend heavily on construction and manufacturing activity. During the early 1970s, the number of skilled mechanics and construction workers grew rapidly and began to balance the shortage in construction and mechanical skills noted in some areas during the 1960s. The demand for semiskilled and unskilled workers is expected to increase very slowly during the next decade, reflecting the continued replacement of repetitive mechanical and manual chores with automated techniques. Due to rising productivity on farms, the number of farm laborers will continue to decline into the 1980s.

Demand for manpower in the latter half of the 1970s should be strong, with the most significant barrier to attaining our national goals being the potential mismatches of manpower supply and demand. If one looks ahead to the 1980s and a dampening of economic growth, it appears that the mismatches are likely to continue. These projections illustrate the need to intensify human resource efforts, developing the capabilities to respond to shortages and surpluses in manpower with education and manpower training programs that will facilitate economic growth.

The state of the art

National projections do not provide a blueprint of the future, but they do signal the warnings necessary for sound fiscal, monetary, and manpower policies. It was not for lack of knowledge that inadequate provisions were made for teachers and classrooms to serve the postwar baby boom or that insufficient jobs were generated to absorb veterans returning from Vietnam or engineers laid off in the aerospace industry. Employment policy that takes seriously the goal of "useful jobs for all of those able, willing and seeking to work" will pay more attention to the age, sex, and racial structure of the labor force for which jobs must be provided, but here too there is no lack of reliable knowledge. Demographic projections provide adequate guidance for 10 to 15 years ahead on growth potential, employment needs, and quantitative educational requirements. It would be useful to have more advance information concerning the qualitative characteristics of the labor supply, but provision of better education and broader skills is an adequate substitute for detailed projections.

At local and regional levels, projections are more difficult because changes are less likely to be washed out by crosscurrents. The first need, of course, is a consistent national policy of full employment to maximize opportunity and provide a solid base for local projections. The second is to proceed with a program of making projections, so that experience can be gained.

Educational planners have all the enrollment projections and information about their students' employment prospects that they need for planning general education. The shortages of elementary teachers in the 1950s, of high school teachers in the early 1960s, and the excess supply of teachers emerging now were not difficult to foresee, given postwar birth rates and college enrollment figures for the 1960s. What was lacking was not forewarning but sufficiently flexible institutions.

Planners of more employment-oriented types of education and training—apprenticeship and vocational, technical, and to a lesser extent graduate education—need more detailed projections. Counseling and guidance people have less information than they need, but, all too often, more than they use.

Serious obstacles to satisfactory adjustment to manpower changes are still posed by lack of knowledge concerning job content, skill requirements, and transferability of skills. Employers tend to require excessive education and training, in part because they do not know what skills a job actually requires. And without knowledge about the transferability of skills, neither the detail required of projections nor the appropriate content of training can be satisfactorily determined. Manpower planning by individual economic factors—workers and firms—is increasingly important. In the past, firms have planned production, investment, and expansion but rarely their manpower needs. Some firms have discovered the road to high profits may lie in their ability to attract and hold good employees. Also, increasing sensitivity to human distress and to criticism for failure to avoid displacement brought some commitment to the principle of planning to adjust to reduced manpower needs through attrition.

On balance, although there is need for improvement in manpower projections, their deficiencies are not a serious limiting factor in program analysis and decision making. Methodological improvements can and should be made, but steps to improve the presentation and dissemination of available projections are probably more important. In the end, the manpower problems of the past few years cannot be blamed upon the lack of information concerning the manpower future. Action, not information, has been the absent factor.

Effort and resources might be invested in the development of manpower projections within the region, the locality, and the firm. Many organizations and individuals are involved in projecting, and all are not equally expert. The work of the BLS is the soundest available; less sophisticated agencies, usually involved in projections of specialized types of manpower, would be aided by government-wide projection guidelines. More intensive research effort needs to go into understanding skill requirements and transferability. In the end, however, the main burden is on the projection user: Accept the fact that even with the best of techniques, the future will remain opaque; use projections with patience and wisdom; and have faith in the far-from-perfect but reasonable flexibility of the labor market and the adaptability of human beings.

Notes

1. Among the more important statistical publications are the *Monthly Labor Review, Employment and Earnings, Area Trends in Employment and Unemployment, Manpower Report of the President* (annual), *Current Wage Developments*, and *Unemployment Insurance Statistics*.
2. J. E. Morton, *On the Evolution of Manpower Statistics,* Studies in Employment and Unemployment Series (Kalamazoo, Mich.: Upjohn Institute for Employment Research, December 1969), pp. 36–51.

3. Stanley Lebergott, *Manpower in Economic Growth* (New York: McGraw-Hill, 1964).
4. The President's Committee to Appraise Employment and Unemployment Statistics, *Measuring Employment and Unemployment* (Washington, D.C.: GPO, 1962).
5. Gloria P. Green, "Comparing Employment Estimates from Household and Payroll Surveys," *Monthly Labor Review* (December 1969), pp. 9–20.
6. William G. Bowen and T. Aldrich Finegan, *The Economics of the Labor Force Participation* (Princeton, N.J.: Princeton University Press, 1969).
7. This section draws heavily on Garth L. Mangum and Arnold L. Nemore, "The Nature and Functions of Manpower Projections," *Industrial Relations* (May 1966), pp. 1–16.
8. Herman Stekler, *Economic Forecasting* (New York: Praeger, 1970), pp. 3–15, 92–102.
9. National Commission on Technology, Automation, and Economic Progress, *Technology and the American Economy* (Washington, D.C.: GPO, 1966), pp. 54–55.
10. U.S. Bureau of Labor Statistics, *Occupational Outlook Handbook*, 1974–1975 ed., Bulletin No. 1785 (Washington, D.C.: GPO, 1974).
11. Denis F. Johnston, "The United States Economy in 1985: Population and Labor Force Projections," *Monthly Labor Review* (December 1973), pp. 8–17.
12. Richard Easterlin, *Population, Labor Force and Long Swings in Economic Growth* (New York: Columbia University Press, 1968), pp. 141–182.
13. Denis F. Johnston, *The U.S. Labor Force: Projections to 1990*, U.S. Bureau of Labor Statistics, Special Labor Force Report 156 (Washington, D.C.: GPO, July 1973), Table 3.
14. Denis F. Johnston, "Education of Workers: Projections to 1990," *Monthly Labor Review* (November 1973), pp. 22–31.
15. American Assembly, *Goals for Americans: The Report of the President's Commission on National Goals* (Englewood Cliffs, N.J.: Prentice-Hall, 1960).
16. Leonard Lecht, *Manpower Needs for National Goals in the 1970s* (New York: Praeger, 1969), pp. 10–11.
17. Leonard A. Lecht, *Changes in National Priorities, Manpower Projection Techniques, and Requirements for Scientists and Engineers* (Washington, D.C.: National Planning Association, April 1974), pp. 10–11.
18. Neal H. Rosenthal, "The United States Economy in 1985: Projected Changes in Occupations," *Monthly Labor Review* (December 1973), pp. 18–20.

7

the structure of
labor markets

In modern times labor, as other factors of production, is allocated
partly by labor markets and partly by institutionalized arrangements that may or may not reflect market tendencies. It is, therefore, important to separate basic market forces from these institutional arrangements. A major objective of this chapter is to
discuss the operation of labor markets, in terms of the applicability of economic theory. Before doing this, however, it will be
useful to discuss the role that theory can play in illuminating the
operation of labor markets and in prescribing remedies for market-
related problems.

Role of theory

Theory attempts to identify certain basic underlying causal relationships. As such, its usefulness derives from its ability to
simplify otherwise complex phenomena. Theory, therefore, is not
a mirror reflection of reality. Indeed, the factors discussed in
some theories might not even be observable in the real world,
where the basic factors may be obscured by others that are more
apparent than real. For example, people tend to infer that unions
"cause" inflation when wage increases are followed by rising
prices. However, rising wages and prices may, in reality, be caused
by other, more fundamental forces that are less obvious or measurable. It might even be difficult to measure the results of underlying causal forces because of timing problems. When, for example,
do we start measuring the impact of union wage pressures on
prices? The wage pressures might actually be caused by price increases that occurred *before* we started our measurements.

The fundamental generalizations or principles about causal
relationships are more important to our understanding of the

basic factors at work than a detailed description of real situations. This is true because the facts change constantly. Indeed, excessive descriptions can obscure our understanding of basic causal relationships.

Theory can also play an important role in policy formulation. Indeed, with inadequate theories or conceptual frameworks, correct policies can be formulated only by chance. For example, combating inflation or unemployment requires an adequate theoretical underpinning. Similarly, a theory of wages is necessary to an understanding of the probable impact of minimum wages on employment.

Different theories of labor markets prescribe different policies for the resolution of the problems of unemployment and unequal employment opportunities. In vogue recently has been emphasis on a dual labor market theory that assumes some secondary markets more or less separated from primary markets (traditional analysis treats the whole economy as essentially one big labor market). Those who believe in dual markets argue that the problems of disadvantaged workers, who are employed mainly in the secondary markets, cannot be solved with general monetary and fiscal measures that assume some national queue for jobs.

Although theories are very useful for simplifying basic causal relationships, they also pose certain dangers that must be guarded against. It is particularly important to remember that theories are *abstractions* and, therefore, only a starting point to understanding particular situations. Because a theory is based upon certain assumptions, the predictions that flow from it are *theoretical* predictions, which means that they will obtain only so long as the basic assumptions underlying the theory are valid in the particular situations being examined. Policy makers, however, often are not interested in theoretical predictions but in *actual* predictions; that is, they are likely to be interested in more than the economic tendencies underlying a particular situation. Policy makers must, therefore, be concerned about the various noneconomic phenomena that influence the economic variable. In the case of racial discrimination, for example, the theorists can claim quite correctly that competitive markets would tend to erode racial discrimination, and this would be an accurate theoretical prediction. However, it might not be an accurate prediction of events in the real world because social events and institutions such as institutionalized racism make it very difficult for the tendencies to work themselves out. For the policy maker, therefore, economic tendencies that are counteracted by social forces are merely *theoretical*, but not *actual*, predictions of events. It is important for the policy maker to understand the theoretical economic tendencies in order to adopt proper policies, but he must know more than that. He also needs to know the institutional setting within which a particular problem must be solved.

We must also be careful, when using theoretical constructs, to avoid letting theories lead to rigid analysis. For example, the theories designed to explain labor markets at one time might be very useful because the theoretical construct reflected the basic underlying relationships at that time. However, there is a danger that the theory will be used long after the basic underlying relationships have changed, and the theory is no longer useful in explaining the labor market. For example, a labor market theory adopted during the Middle Ages clearly would not be valid in the twentieth century, primarily because during the Middle Ages the labor market was relatively insignificant and tradition was a much more important determinant of wages. The development of the free labor market, therefore, requires modification of the theory of wage determination. As we shall see, theory also causes people to generalize and, therefore, to ignore basic differences among labor markets. And theory might cause rigidity by focusing on certain phenomena at the expense of others. Because the theories cannot always be validated in the real world and because they frequently are based on events that cannot be observed, it is very difficult to keep theories flexible enough to adapt to changing circumstances.

In conclusion, therefore, theories are very useful in helping to simplify very complex labor market phenomena, but we must be very careful to be sure that the theory has indeed focused on basic causal relationships and that it does not induce such inflexibility in thinking that important variables in a particular situation are ignored as we move from the theory to the policy level.

Definitions of labor markets

A market is ordinarily thought of as a place where exchange takes place, where demand and supply work themselves out. However, the term "market" is used in somewhat different contexts. In some cases it means a specific place where buyers and sellers physically come together to arrange exchanges. An example of this would be the longshoremen's market in a port city where workers "shape up" every morning for hiring purposes.

Markets may also refer to buyers and sellers who are not necessarily brought together physically, as, for example, the market for college graduates. Workers from many different and widely separated places might compete for the same jobs, and workers in the same local labor supply might compete for jobs widely separated from each other. (It also should be observed that the terms "labor market" and "job market" are used interchangeably.) Clearly, in this latter sense the labor market concept is an abstraction and refers merely to the area within which exchanges frequently take place. Moreover, labor markets might be worldwide for certain highly specialized workers like deep-sea divers, or purely local, as it would be for construction electricians.

The main functions of labor markets are (1) to fix wages and other terms of employment and (2) to allocate labor among occupations, jobs and employers.

The neoclassical theory

The most widely accepted theory of the labor market is the neoclassical or orthodox theory. Neoclassical theorists emphasize certain common theoretical concepts, even though there are many differences among them. Proponents of this approach emphasize the abstract nature of their formulations. They attempt to focus on the most significant causal factors determining wages and employment and abstract from all others. These abstractions make it possible to reach conclusions about many different matters—income distribution, health, wages, the allocation of labor, discrimination, and many other matters—on the basis of a few abstract and simplified concepts. With modifications neoclassical economists use the same simple mechanism to analyze entrepreneurial behavior, general equilibrium for the entire economy, and international trade.

The basic neoclassical formulation ordinarily assumes perfect competition, although the model can be used to examine less-than-perfect competition. In a perfectly competitive labor market the following factors would exist on the supply side: (1) Workers have perfect knowledge of the market, including information on wage rates and available opportunities; (2) workers are rational and respond to differences in rates of return, including wages and noncash benefits; (3) workers are perfectly mobile; and (4) workers are not organized and make their own decisions on accepting jobs and wages offered.

On the demand side, perfect competition requires (1) full and perfect knowledge of the labor market by employers; (2) that employers are rational and attempt to maximize profits; (3) that

Figure 7-1

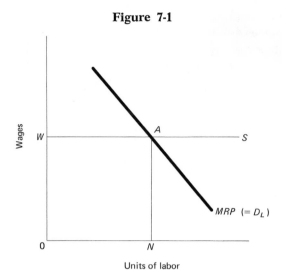

Units of labor

no employer represents a large enough part of the total demand for labor to affect wages; and (4) that employers act individually, and not in concert, in fixing wages.

The competitive assumption is important to the neoclassical model because competition helps provide a rationale for universally applicable hypotheses. In the labor market, competition expresses itself in the form of actual and potential labor mobility.

The neoclassical model also assumes individual decisions to be stronger than group or class interests. Moreover, institutional arrangements are assumed to be constant and not to change while the system is moving toward equilibrium. This assumption is necessary in order to make the model determinant.

The model

The basic neoclassical model assumes that wages and employment are determined by demand and supply. According to the theory, demand is determined by the marginal productivity of homogeneous units of labor. Marginal productivity (or marginal revenue product [MRP]) is determined by the contribution to an entrepreneur's total revenue from selling the product of an added unit of labor. This becomes the demand for labor and for the firm can be depicted as shown in Figure 7-1.

The *MRP* curve slopes downward and to the right because of diminishing returns as additional units of labor are added. Under less than perfectly competitive conditions the *MRP* curve also will decline with additional units of labor because it is assumed that the price must be lowered if these units are to be sold, whereas under competitive conditions it is assumed that the entire output can be sold at existing market prices. Under competitive conditions the supply curve of labor to the firm will be WS, as depicted in Figure 7–1, which means entrepreneurs could hire all of the labor they want at the existing wage. Equilibrium will, therefore, be where this supply curve crosses MRP, or the demand curve. At this point the firm's profits are maximized; at any lower level of labor utilization additional workers would contribute more to revenue than to cost ($W < MRP$), so that it would pay a firm to expand. At a level of labor utilization larger than the equilibrium point, costs increase more than revenue ($W > MRP$), so profits must be falling. Where $W = MRP$, employment and wages of the firm are determined.

Theory of labor supply

Because it is based on marginal productivity, the demand side of the neoclassical wage-employment determining process is theoretically more developed than the supply side. This presents some real theoretical problems, most of which are associated with the workers' inability to separate their labor from themselves. Workers might wish to work less and enjoy more leisure as wages rise (the income effect). On the other hand, there is a tendency for workers to want to work longer hours at higher wages in order to substitute the things higher wages can buy for leisure (substitution effect). If the substitution effect prevails, the individual's supply curve, showing how much labor will be supplied at different wage rates, will be shaped as shown in Figure 7-2, indicating a willingness to sell more labor at higher wages. On the other hand, if the income effect prevails, the individual labor supply curve will be as depicted in Figure 7-3, indicating a willingness to sell less labor at higher wages.

As a result of individual differences, a worker's utility function—which is determined by a combination of consumption goods purchased in the market, consumption goods purchased at home (paid for by sacrificed leisure or the amount that leisure could be sold for), and leisure—cannot be determined. In other words, we have no a priori way of telling whether the income or substitution effect predominates.

Similarly, the aggregate supply curve for the whole economy cannot be determined, although economists commonly assume it to be as depicted in Figure 7-4, indicating a positive ratio between

Figure 7-2

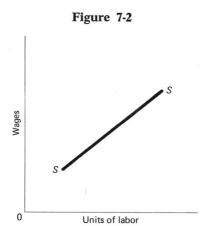

wages and labor at lower wages (the *P-S* segment of the curve in Figure 7-4) and a negative relationship between labor supplies and income at higher wages (the *S'-P* segment of the curve in Figure 7-4).

The aggregate labor supply curve is determined by labor force participation rates (LFPR), which will, in turn, be determined by the tendency for workers to enter the work force at various wage rates and labor market conditions. Unfortunately, however, there are countermovements in labor force participation rates that complicate the analysis. For instance, when unemployment rises, the involuntary loss of jobs by some family members causes others to enter the labor force; this is the so-called additional-worker hypothesis mentioned earlier. If there are many additional workers in the work force, the official unemployment

Figure 7-3

Figure 7-4

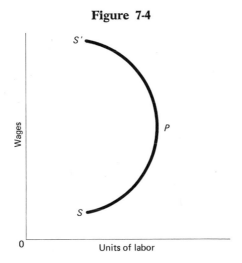

rate overstates the number of jobs needed to reach full employment because the additional workers will withdraw from the work
force as unemployment rises. The presence of these discouraged
workers causes the official unemployment rate to understate the
number of jobs needed to restore full employment because presumably many of these discouraged workers would enter the work
force in response to better job opportunities. The evidence suggests that during mild recessions, discouraged workers outnumber
additional workers.

A number of implications grow out of the neoclassical theory.
Some of these will be made clearer in Chapter 17 on the economics
of discrimination. One implication of the theory is that workers
are poor because of their low productivity. The obvious policy
implication, if this is true, would be to increase workers' productivity through increasing their human capital, discussed in
Chapter 8. Second, there is an assumption that income distribution tends to reflect differences in productivity, so that the theory
tends to justify existing income distribution.

The marginal productivity theory also leads to the queue
theory of the labor market, according to which employers are assumed to rank workers and potential workers along a single
ordinal vector according to their respective productivities. Many
manpower programs were based on the assumption that disadvantaged workers would be moved up in the employment queue
through manpower training. In order for the queue theory to be
valid it must assume fairly universal rankings throughout the
economy. If different employers had different rankings, the relationships would be upset.

Human capital and benefit-cost analysis

An extension of orthodox economic analysis into the human capital area has important implications for manpower programs. The concept of human capital, explored at greater length in Chapter 8, was adapted from physical capital investment theory by Gary S. Becker and Theodore W. Schultz during the later 1950s and early 1960s.[1] Human capital analysis was stimulated by concerns for poverty, economic development, the distribution of capital, and unemployment. Although the human capital concept had been around for some time,[2] it was not developed very much until the 1960s. It should be noted, however, that *the human capital concept depends heavily on the assumption that labor is in fact paid its marginal product* determined in factor and product markets. If labor is not paid its marginal product, human capital will not be a good measure of factor inputs. Moreover, the human capital concept forms the basis of benefit-cost analysis, which is widely used to evaluate human resource development programs. Benefit-cost analysis will, therefore, be limited by the theoretical defects in the neoclassical economic theory discussed in this and the following chapter.

External and internal labor markets

One of the first qualifications that must be made in the economists' traditional conception of a labor market is to distinguish the internal and the external labor markets. While the competitive neoclassical model concerns itself mainly with the so-called external labor market (that outside the firm or craft), the internal labor market concerns itself with the rules made within the firm or craft to fix wages and allocate labor among alternative uses. The internal labor market is controlled more by institutional rules that are not always compatible with the assumptions of the competitive labor market. For example, workers' wage rates and occupational positions within a manufacturing firm are much more likely to be determined by seniority than by relative prductivity. These rules might be highly formalized if there is a union present, and they might be more informal if there is no union and the work group sets its own rules. In a very real sense, of course, there is no such thing as an unorganized work group because each group tends to be informally organized and to establish its own code of conduct and ethics, whether or not unions are present.

Because of these internal rules that govern the relationship between workers and employers, the employer does not necessarily act (in the internal labor market) as the competitive model assumes he will. For example, the employer is not very likely to cut wages in order to reduce costs as the labor supply schedule shifts to the right because he fully realizes that a wage cut could seriously damage the morale of his workers. Nor are employers always likely to increase wages when the demand for labor increases. To some extent, then, the internal labor market is isolated, at least in the short run, from the market forces of the external labor market. The main areas where internal labor markets are connected with external labor markets are what John T. Dunlop calls the ports of entry into the company.[3] These are defined as the points within the company at which the firm hires from the outside. Because labor market adjustments are not as volatile as the traditional theory assumes they will be, if employers equate wages with productivity, as competitive theory assumes, average wages must be equated to productivity for groups of workers over time because constant adjustments clearly are not made at the margin where marginal revenue equals marginal cost at any given time.

Clark Kerr has referred to the process of establishing institutional rules that structure labor markets as balkanization.[4] In Kerr's analysis institutional rules (among other things) cause labor markets to be structured. He cites Lloyd Fisher's description of the harvest labor market in California as a good illustration of a structureless market. Fisher defines a structureless market as possessing five conditions: "(1) There are no unions with seniority or other rules, (2) the relation between the employee and the employer is a transitory impersonal one, (3) the workers are unskilled, (4) payment is by unit of product, and (5) little capital or machinery is employed." In contrast to this, Kerr conceives of other markets as possessing various degrees of structure that can be caused by other things as well as the institutional rules. For example, many workers have skills that restrict their employment to particular occupations in which they seek work. Similarly, workers and employers form attachments for each other that are not lightly broken. Therefore, these customs and attachments tend to isolate the internal labor market from the operation of external forces.

The degree of isolation, or balkanization, to use Kerr's term, is increased with the establishment of internal rules that limit entry into the market and determine the movement of workers within those markets as well as their exit from them. In Kerr's words, once these institutional rules are established, "market forces seemingly impersonal in the aggregate, but exceedingly personal in individual situations, give way to personal rules which may seem exceedingly impersonal when applied to specific workers."[5] The main purpose of these rules is, of course, to establish control over the job territory for the people who are already in the market.

Kerr distinguishes two general systems of institutional rules, each with important subtypes. The first is communal ownership. This is the type of institutionalization typical of the building, printing, trucking, and similar trades. In this kind of labor market the workers assert control over all jobs in the labor market. The workers are likely to enter the market through unions rather than through employers because unions are likely to be the most stable elements in this labor market, partly because workers change jobs frequently in these casual markets. Moreover, the unions assert control over some traditional managerial functions such as training. The unions will, therefore, establish fairly strict rules for admission into the market as well as the conditions under which people are allowed to work within the labor market. In this labor market the workers' loose tie to their employers is compensated for by a very tight tie to their occupation, and movement is, therefore, within the market and primarily horizontal rather than vertical. This is to say, workers can move about quite freely within the labor market once they gain entry into it. They have a strong identification with their craft, but they do not form strong attachments to particular employers. The significance of the union in the craft-type labor market is demonstrated by the fact that although the employer can remove workers from the job by discharging them, only the union can remove them from the market.

In the industrial situation, the second of Kerr's general systems, each worker tends to occupy his own job; when he vacates it, only one person is eligible to fill it. The group ordinarily establishes the rules, usually giving heavy weight to seniority to determine which workers will fill the job, although the workers' preference for seniority is often compromised by the employer's need to get the most productive people in particular jobs. In the industrial internal labor markets, therefore, seniority becomes much more important, and movement is largely vertical within families of jobs. The main contact of the internal and external labor markets is through the so-called ports of entry. Except for these ports of entry, competition among workers inside a labor market and those outside it tends to be very restricted.

> Competition among workers is reduced, the internal and external labor markets are joined only at restricted points, and within the

internal market, craft jobs are likely to be fairly standardized and industrial jobs filled in accordance with seniority, so that workers are not actively contesting with each other for preference. Beyond this, the distribution of work opportunities by the craft union and the rehiring rights of the industrial contract tend to hold unemployed workers in a pool attached to the craft or plant and thus keep them from competing for jobs so actively elsewhere. . . .[6]

Reduced mobility is one of the main ways in which institutional rules isolate workers in the internal labor markets from external competition. The potential mobility of workers is the main sanction that makes wage rates interrelated. Once a worker builds up a certain amount of seniority in a plant, his mobility is undoubtedly restricted, and the penalty for his withdrawal from the internal labor market becomes greater and greater. It might, therefore, be very difficult for a worker to find another job with comparable pay and status if he withdraws from a particular labor market.

Peter Doeringer and Michael Piore developed the concept of the internal labor market more completely and related it more specifically to federal manpower policy.[7] Like Kerr, their concern is primarily with the formal and informal processes governing employment relationships and the forces that influence those processes. Key factors influencing internal manpower decisions include labor supplies in the external labor markets, the type of technology in the firm or industry, the value of the internal labor market to the firm's present work force, product market conditions, and customs.

A very important theme developed by Doeringer and Piore is:

. . . that difference between the skills and abilities of the labor force are reconciled through a series of instruments which are controlled within the internal labor market. These instruments —recruitment procedures, training, compensation and the like— exist because a number of functions conventionally identified with the competitive labor market have been internalized to the enterprise. These instruments, individually and collectively, constitute a series of labor market adjustment processes by which the internal labor market adapts to changes in both production techniques and labor market conditions.[8]

As a consequence of these adaptive procedures, Doeringer and Piore tend to discount the argument that structural unemployment was a cause of rising unemployment rates during the 1960s. This, however, does not necessarily follow. Each firm can adapt labor forces of different skill levels to its own requirements and still avoid hiring large numbers of workers—like teenagers, women, and minorities—whose supplies have increased. Unless flexible wages or other benefits to entrepreneurs are assumed, there is no reason for employers to change their hiring practices to avoid hiring the workers they most prefer.

The internal labor market is generated by the specificity of skills to each firm, the prevalence of on-the-job training, and custom or unwritten rules based largely on past practices or precedent.

Doeringer and Piore challenge the neoclassical assumption that the internal labor market, which insulates workers from competitive markets, generates inefficiency. Many factors on which internal labor markets are based—the value of security and advancement to workers and savings to the employer in costs from recruitment, screening, training, and the reduction of turnover—cause efficiencies in labor utilization. However, there might be some inefficiencies resulting from attempts by workers to protect job security and ensure equitable treatment in internal labor markets. It has not been determined whether the efficiencies outweigh the inefficiencies, but there is a strong presumption that the internal labor market is, on balance, a force for efficiency.

Internal labor market analysis challenges the neoclassical assumptions that there are no fixed employment costs and that the employment relationship is temporary. Becker and Walter Y. Oi have worked out the implications of fixed recruitment, screening and training costs within the framework of neoclassical theory.[9] It can be shown that these fixed costs create incentives for employers to establish more permanent relationships, but that profit maximization no longer requires wages to be equal to marginal products at any given time; workers can be paid more than their marginal products plus training costs at first and less than their marginal products plus training costs later.

According to Doeringer and Piore, however, Becker and Oi failed to emphasize

> . . . the startling implications for neoclassical wage theory of the permanent employment relationship . . . neither employers nor workers necessarily concern themselves with the connection between wages and marginal productivity at any point in time. . . . The disruption of neoclassical equivalencies between the wage and marginal product in each pay period . . . involves the disruption of these equivalencies for a given job as well. The worker, therefore may *never* produce enough in a particular job classification to cover his wages during the period in which he is employed in that classification.[10]

This means that wages are attached to *jobs*, not to workers as the neoclassical theory assumed. In a competitive society the wage for the job would reflect the marginal productivities of workers holding those jobs, but not in the internal labor market, which tends to be insulated from competitive forces. Moreover, the wage, even at ports of entry, is more likely to reflect the expected productivities of *groups* of workers than the productivity of *individuals*. Some workers are therefore paid more than their productivity is worth, while others are paid less. "In sum, the forces which in neoclassical theory yield a determinate wage establish, in the internal market, only a series of constraints."[11]

Manpower implications of internal labor markets

The first major manpower implication of internal labor market analysis is that training should be provided by each firm utilizing it unless there are economies of scale. Most firms can do their own skill training, but they are not very well suited for general training in computational, verbal, or reading skills. Moreover, groups of firms, unions, individual workers, or governments must provide training that is not enterprise specific because particular employers are not likely to incur the costs of training if they derive only partial benefits from it.

Second, the government should provide recruitment and training procedures to accomplish social objectives, like gaining greater employment opportunities for workers likely to be screened out by the firm's recruitment and screening procedures, but, if possible, firms will normally attempt to use the least expensive devices to recruit and screen their work forces. Employers will give heavy weight, for example, to procedures that will, with a given cost, maximize the probability of acquiring the kinds of workers they desire. If the public policy makers want to have blacks, the disadvantaged, or indigenous populations employed, they might adopt preemployment screening procedures to equalize the probability that employers will be able to obtain qualified workers from among these excluded groups. Indeed, to some extent manpower development and training programs accomplished this objective for employers by recruiting and screening workers who were reliable and trainable.

Internal labor market analysis suggests considerable flexibility in the processes whereby employers match workers and jobs. However, much of this information is specific to each enterprise, even though it would be useful to other employers and public policy makers. There is, therefore, a need for a clearing mechanism to collect information on the operation of internal labor markets, analyze this information, and disseminate it to labor market participants who can profit from it.

Internal labor markets also mean that many training, promotion, and wage-determining processes have powerful appeal to incumbent employees and employers. These internal processes are relatively isolated from external wage processes and labor market conditions. Increases in labor supply and unemployment in the external market will not necessarily reduce wages in the internal market. Similarly, unemployment in the external market will not necessarily prevent internal wages from rising. The internal market also influences the ability to reduce discrimination against blacks, women, or other excluded groups. The inclusion of new groups will be resisted because of the values of the internal processes even when there are no biases against the outsiders' personal characteristics.

Dual labor markets

Another approach that has specifically challenged the neoclassical model is the "dual labor market" hypothesis. Economists have long known, that the labor market was balkanized or divided into noncompeting groups, but the dual labor market idea became more popular with scholars who were studying ghetto labor markets during the 1960s and early 1970s. These analysts at first studied ghetto labor markets in detail and then started reformulating some of the ideas of a segmented labor market developed by Kerr, Fisher, Charles Killingsworth, and others.[12] Although it is still more hypothesis than theory, the dual labor market concept is being developed more formally as a specific alternative to the neoclassical system.

Piore states the dual labor market hypothesis succinctly:

> The basic hypothesis of the dual labor market was that the labor market is divided into two essentially distinct sectors, termed the *primary* and the *secondary* sectors. The former offers jobs with relatively high wages, good working conditions, chances of advancement, equity and due process in the administration of work rules and, above all, employment stability. Jobs in the secondary sector, by contrast, tend to be low paying, with poorer working conditions, little chance of advancement; a highly personalized relationship between workers and supervisors which leaves wide latitude for favoritism and is conducive to harsh and capricious work discipline; and with considerable instability in jobs and a

high turnover among the labor force. The hypothesis was designed to explain the problems of disadvantaged, particularly black workers in urban areas, which had previously been diagnosed as one of unemployment.[13]

Piore explains the separation of markets by a number of specific arguments, which he has refined and analyzed in some detail:[14]

1. Secondary markets are distinguished from primary markets by the behavior patterns, especially unstable employment, imposed on the workers in those markets. Employers and workers adapt to unstable conditions, and labor market institutions contribute to the perpetuation of these conditions. Welfare, for example, contributes to segmentation by providing such limited support that workers are forced into the secondary market. Unions operate mainly in the primary market and, therefore, contribute to the perpetuation of better wages, hours, and job protection in that sector. Unions have more difficulty in the secondary sector because the workers have little power to win strikes. The Employment Service perpetuates secondary employment conditions by referring workers with the prescribed characteristics to secondary jobs. Workers tend to be barred from primary jobs not because of their lack of job skills but because they work intermittently and are not reliable.

2. Discrimination perpetuates segmentation by restricting certain workers to secondary markets not because of their education and skills but because they have superficial characteristics resembling most other workers in the markets. Doeringer and Piore emphasize that many workers in the secondary market have stable employment even though their jobs encourage instability.[15]

3. While technology influences the allocation of jobs between the primary and secondary sectors, many kinds of work can be performed in either sector and are where they are because of historical decisions to locate them there.

4. The behavior traits of workers in the various labor markets are reinforced by class associations. Jobs in the various sectors tend to be filled by people from particular classes. Piore defines mobility chains through which people pass. Workers enter these chains from a limited and distinct number of points that have economic and social significance.

> Thus people in a given job will tend to be drawn from a limited range of schools, neighborhoods, and types of family backgrounds; and conversely, people leaving the same school or neighborhood will move into a limited set of employment stations.[16]

5. A number of institutions and historical forces strengthen labor market segmentation. The importance of on-the-job training as a means of acquiring skills has increased the employer's incentive to hold some workers in more stable jobs, whereas other institutions have perpetuated instability. Migration of disadvantaged workers into urban areas perpetuates a supply of workers in the secondary markets. The lower-class subculture is mainly a function of the rate of migration into it by ethnic and racial groups already in a place relative to the new members.

The dual labor market approach deals with discrimination mainly as a factor in labor market segmentation, with no special theory of discrimination. Because of discrimination blacks have a high probability of being restricted to secondary labor markets. Moreover, once they get into these markets, the adaptive forces at work in that sector make it difficult for blacks to move into primary markets.

The dual labor market analysis is still in its formative stage and, therefore, it scarcely qualifies as a theory. So far, it is a classification system more than a theory. Moreover, the analysis and description apply to only parts of the economy and thus are not a complete system. Many labor markets, like those for craftsmen and independent professional and technical workers, do not fit neatly into the system. Moreover, the origin and causes of labor market segmentation are not satisfactorily formulated.

Radicals

Evaluation of radical political economists is difficult because this group is not easily identified. Radicals apparently build on the work of multiple labor market analysts, but they add twists of their own. In particular, the work of radicals

> . . . draws heavily on a precedent Marxist tradition, but it has molded and recast classical Marxism in response to modern social and historical developments; much of the classical Marxist methodology has been retained while some of the substantive generalizations of nineteenth-century Marxism have been revised to fit current realities.[17]

Like the dual labor market advocates, the radicals apparently do not have a well-developed theory of discrimination but assume, in addition to the technological and market forces producing labor market segmentation (especially the development of monopoly capitalism in the primary sector and competitive capitalism in the secondary sector), that capitalists segment labor markets in order to divide the proletariat and keep it from working as a unit in opposition to capitalism. Employers

> ... try to develop a stratified labor market in order to accomplish two complementary objectives. They were likely to seek, on the one hand, to minimize the extent to which those in jobs with less desirable working conditions could identify with those in more desirable jobs. . . . And employers were likely, on the other hand, to sharply segregate those blue-collar or secondary workers who could potentially identify with white-collar workers—and who might therefore develop class consciousness—from those blue-collar or secondary workers who were not likely to develop class consciousness, in order, obviously, to limit the potential costs of concessions to workers who made determined demands.[18]

Race enters radical analysis mainly as one means, among others, through which employers divide the working class. The radicals assume discrimination because of skin color to be mainly one form of discrimination by capitalists, who are motivated by a desire to maintain their power and increase the surplus value they can extract from workers.

The radical conception of discrimination is compatible with their overall purposes and methods. With respect to method, the radicals tend to apply global analyses, stressing the interaction of discrimination and what they consider to be the basic institutions of the capitalist system.

As a consequence of their systemic approach, radicals tend to concentrate on pervasive racism or discrimination. According to Raymond J. Franklin and Solomon Resnik, the "racist meaning of segregation in the American context derives from the fact that it is forced."[19] Moreover:

> The legacy of white supremacy, as well as the legacy underlying the modes of black adaptations to a white-dominated society, are independent neither of each other nor of the present circumstances which define black-white relations. The white and black legacies—so frequently alluded to as independent streams of history—will not disappear until the present circumstances of inequality cease to operate in ways that parallel the slave and related conditions which gave birth to them.[20]

There appear to be a number of problems with the usual radical conceptions of exploitation. In the first place, these writers probably put too much emphasis on discrimination by employers and not enough on discrimination by employees. Moreover, it is doubtful that the assumption that a basic capitalist motive is to practice segmentation in order to divide the workers can be defended in every situation. It is true that employers used black strikebreakers, but this integrated rather than *segmented* labor forces in the long run. It also seems unlikely that employers always want racial division. We think employers are motivated mainly by profit maximization, and this might require segmentation to achieve such objectives as the prevention of unionization. On the other hand, with government pressures against discrimination and in favor of collective bargaining, employers would be foolish to promote racial conflict, which might prevent them from complying with the law or provisions in government contracts. In other words, profit-maximizing employers might use racial discrimination to increase their power and profits, but it is not possible to show that they always profit by racial strife. The radicals must strain, therefore, to build a model showing how employers always gain by conscious policies to divide the races. Employers in the primary sector, according to radical theory, are the main ones who refuse to hire blacks, while employers in the secondary market extract surplus value, or exploit them.

Multiple labor markets

The traditional economic theory and the dual labor market analysis must be modified to account for broad differences among external labor markets. Within each broad classification, moreover, various submarkets could be analyzed, although we do not do so here. Public policy requires an adequate understanding of how these labor markets operate in order to avoid the mistakes that are likely to be made by assuming that the whole economy is a giant queue from which workers are hired on the basis of their productivity. If this were so, perhaps it would be possible to solve problems of unemployment and low incomes with aggregate economic policies alone. However, increasing aggregate demand by increasing the supply of money and spending through monetary-fiscal policies clearly has a differential impact on various types of labor markets. These aggregate measures might cause hyperinflation in some markets with no change in employment while leaving pockets of unemployment virtually undisturbed in other labor markets. The queue theory is, therefore, of some value *within* labor markets, but it has limited utility when applied to the whole economy.

Similarly, a dual labor market theory is deficient if it assumes that the economy can be neatly divided into two types of labor markets; one of which workers have experienced considerable progress while those in the other lag behind. Similarly, it is not very useful to divide labor markets into such simple aggregate categories as agricultural and nonagricultural. There are many labor markets, but several broad classifications might be described as ideal types for purposes of illustration. Much more work needs to be done in order to identify and define types of labor markets and their interrelationships.

The professional labor market

The first of these broad labor markets can be called the professional labor market. It comprises the various professions and is characterized by no tangible product and usually a high income elasticity of demand, which means that the demand for this kind of labor increases disproportionately with increases in incomes. Moreover, professional labor markets are characterized by very imperfect competition. Professionals often discriminate among clients according to their ability to pay, and often consider it unethical to compete either through advertising or price competition. The professional market also requires considerable formal education for entry. This market is imperfect compared with the competitive norm, not only because of the absence of competition but also because of the time lags for demand to adjust to supply and because professionals tend to control the supplies of labor in their professions through licensing and various forms of self-regulation.

The implications of this kind of labor market are clear. As national income increases, the income of professionals will increase, but there is no assurance that their productivity will go up, individually or in the aggregate. Indeed, there are very limited objective ways in which the performance of professionals can be measured by outsiders. Because of the imperfections in this market, professionals can raise their prices in accordance with their customers' ability to pay, need not be evenly distributed geographically, and are very difficult to regulate by indirect means. For example, how would a guidelines policy gearing salaries and wages to productivity operate in an industry in which there is no physical product?

Mainstream labor markets

The second market, which we shall call the mainstream, is characterized by extensive political and economic power, control of markets through product diversification and differentiation, considerable integration of production processes, the power to distribute products throughout a wide market, and ready or preferential access to credit and financial resources. Mainstream labor markets probably also have relatively high product-market concentration ratios, which means that a few firms account for large shares of total sales. The workers in this labor market usually require extensive training (either formal or on the job), have high skill requirements, are relatively well unionized, have considerable upgrading opportunities within the internal labor markets, and receive high wages. The firms in the mainstream also tend to be growth industries, with high ratios of capital to labor costs. Because of their political and economic power, the firms in the mainstream labor market are likely to have close interlocking relationships with various government agencies, particularly at the federal level but also at the state level, and account for a disproportionate amount of funds expended on government contracts. In short, the firms in the mainstream labor market are characterized by considerable power and prestige, and the workers in that labor market are likely to share that power and prestige through unions, which tend to be stronger in this labor market than in any other.

The Marginal Labor Market

A third labor market may be characterized as marginal. Firms in this labor market lack most of the advantages of those in the mainstream, are highly competitive, have low profit margins, and are characterized by a very high ratio of labor cost to total cost. Unions are weak or nonexistent, and both the unions and employers in this labor market have very limited power and prestige.

The working poor are heavily concentrated in the marginal labor market. Examples of the kinds of industries in this sector, whose employees' average hourly earnings are below the minimum wage: Southern sawmills and planing mills; nursing homes and related facilities; garment industries; laundries and cleaning services; synthetic textiles; cotton textiles; wood and household furniture; limited-price variety stores; eating and drinking places; hotels and motels; drug and proprietary stores; gasoline service stations; apparel and accessory stores; department stores; and miscellaneous retail stores.

Workers in these marginal industries have low wages and very limited upgrading possibilities. They also have relatively low levels of education and limited skills and training. Because the jobs they hold are relatively unskilled, they likewise have very limited opportunities for acquiring higher skills on the job.[21]

The submarginal labor market

A fourth type of labor market can be called submarginal. This is a much more difficult market to define: Many of the people who work in it do not show up in the income tax or Social Security accounts because often they do not pay income tax or Social Security. Moreover, this labor market may be further subdivided into those engaged in legal and those engaged in illicit activities. This market contains a very large number of teenagers, adults with poor work histories, other adults with various obstacles to employment, and those who do not participate in the work force but are involved in various illicit activities or are on welfare. Many of the jobs in this labor market are characterized by very low entry requirements, low wages, high rates of turnover, informal work patterns, and work skills and competencies specific to ghetto life, which were acquired mainly through on-the-job training rather than through formal channels.

Many of the jobs in this sector have high turnover partly because they are very low-wage, dead-end jobs. Therefore, the employment disadvantages of this sector are due more to limited high-wage opportunities than to barriers to such job opportunities as exist in this labor market. Indeed, there apparently are many low-wage jobs in the ghetto that are readily available to ghetto dwellers. The clear determinant of the character of the jobs in the submarginal labor market is that the jobs there do not provide adequate security or wages to make it possible to stabilize employment. As a consequence, both employers and workers in the market have adjusted to this unstable routine. Many of the younger people in the ghetto are underemployed for long periods and spend their time hanging around on the street. This time is punctuated occasionally by exciting events, which the people of the street tend to recall with considerable relish. Indeed, one of the attractions for the submarginal labor market is its casual and sometimes exciting character. Employers adjust to this labor market because they expect to have workers who will be absent or late, and, therefore, they do not enforce discipline. Because the jobs are not very attractive anyway, it is no great tragedy for the worker to lose one, and it is very difficult to maintain high levels of work discipline and motivation. Of course, tragedies often occur when workers are forced to rely on submarginal labor markets to support their families. The main tragedy of submarginal ghetto markets is that they tend to be associated with factors—such as racism, poverty, low levels of education—that tend to be self-reinforcing and thus difficult to escape. Not all jobs in the submarginal labor market are necessarily characterized by low wages, and many of them have high wages per unit of time. However, these tend to be mainly the illicit and dangerous activities, such as prostitution or the sale of narcotics, which have a high risk attached to them. It probably is closer to the truth to say that most of the lawful jobs in the submarginal labor market are low-wage jobs but that many illicit activities carry very high returns per unit of time worked.

These four types of labor markets have important implications for theories of labor markets. For example, the equilibrating processes of traditional labor market theory are rendered inoperative by impediments to the movement of people among these markets. The first of these impediments might be *personal*, insofar as the worker might have inadequate education, training, work history, and motivation to move from the submarginal to the marginal labor market. But because workers in the submarginal labor market frequently have higher incomes than those in the marginal labor market, they have little incentive to aspire to the jobs in the latter category. Moreover, in order to reach even some jobs in the marginal labor market, it would be necessary for the workers to overcome the disutility of geographic and occupational mobility. This is true to some extent because the jobs in marginal labor markets are located outside the central cities, where many of those who work in the submarginal market are likely to reside. Residents of the submarginal labor market who want to reach marginal jobs must expend time and money to move from the central cities to the outer ring of metropolitan areas, sometimes a distance of many miles. It is, therefore, understandable that workers who have low-wage jobs readily available to them in their immediate areas will not be too interested in traveling long distances to get jobs at the minimum wage. Clearly, however, transportation costs would be more readily borne by these workers if they could acquire jobs in the mainstream. Ironically enough, many professional and mainstream jobs are located in the central cities not too far from the places where workers attached to the submarginal labor market are likely to live.

Certain *industrial* barriers may also impede movement of people among labor markets. Employers, for example, may discriminate against people from the submarginal labor market in general and racial minorities in particular. Moreover, some workers from the submarginal labor market or the marginal labor market may be barred from the mainstream by union discrimination. Unions, like employers, can discriminate against people with the values (e.g., dress, language, or life styles) held by those who work in the submarginal labor market. Historically some union members have discriminated against blacks regardless of the blacks' personal characteristics, place of residence, or geographical origin. Moreover, during periods when the mainstream labor market is relatively loose, employers are able to recruit adequate labor supplies without dipping into marginal and submarginal labor pools. Many workers in the latter two markets might have superior qualifications for the work that actually needs to be done but still be barred from mainsream jobs because employers have unrealistically high educational requirements.

Finally, there are various *social* barriers to the movement of people between labor markets. One of these is the cost of relocating from familiar to unfamiliar areas. Workers might incur considerable personal risk in moving from familiar areas that provide some security of income (however low) and personal relationships to other areas where there is some promise of higher wages but where a worker is required to enter at the bottom of a seniority line, where he has limited opportunities for advancement, and where he might be discriminated against because of race or culture. Moreover, the lack of market information about distant places makes many workers reluctant to incur the risk of moving. In addition, the income-earning alternative of workers in the submarginal labor market might be superior to those in the marginal labor market. Indeed, the low wages in marginal and submarginal industries probably offer very limited incentives for people to even enter the labor market if they have welfare or other income alternatives.

We know much less than we should about the movement of people among these markets. The extent to which one can see movement among labor markets depends to a significant degree on his overall theory of the labor market. Traditional economic theory has been based on a queue theory that assumes that people are lined up by employers on the basis of their productivity in relation to their wage rates. In this theory workers in the submarginal labor market have lower productivities than those in the mainstream, and it is assumed, therefore, that the personal characteristics of the workers themselves account for these limited employment and income-earning opportunities. Moreover, the queue theory would recommend general economic policies to reduce the level of unemployment and give employers the incentive to move down the queue in order to hire disadvantaged workers.

The foregoing is meant to imply not that no mobility takes place among various types of labor markets, but rather that barriers among the labor markets are much more significant than those within each general labor market category. As labor markets tighten, of course, it is quite possible for firms in the mainstream to dip into the marginal and submarginal labor markets in order to meet their manpower requirements. When the labor market is slack, employers in the mainstream can use relatively inexpensive recruiting procedures and recruit internally or through referrals of outsiders by its own employees at the ports of entry into the internal labor markets. In the mainstream, employers can impose

general restrictions that yield the results desired, primarily by recruiting people who are overqualified for available jobs. This can
be done by imposing unrealistically high education and other requirements. But when the labor market tightens, employers
achieve limited results from the traditional and less expensive recruiting and screening procedures and must, therefore, adopt new
techniques that require them to recruit first from the marginal
labor market and then from the submarginal labor market. They
must also adopt more refined screening procedures and hiring
criteria, and, as a consequence, the formal qualifications of the
people hired probably tend to decline during these times. However,
companies are able to continue to meet their manpower demands
primarily through on-the-job training programs, supplemented by
hiring new workers at the ports of entry.

Many people feel that the queue theory is inadequate to explain the operation of the labor market, particularly the movement of people among the professional, mainstream, marginal, and
submarginal jobs. According to these critics, the labor market
must be conceived of as coming in two, three, or maybe more noncompeting segments; therefore, the queue theory would apply
mainly within the particular segment and not among noncompeting labor pools. The implication of this multiple labor market
theory is that expansion of aggregate demand will not necessarily
solve the problems of those in the submarginal labor market because it will simply exhaust the people in the professional or mainstream markets, bid up their wages and prices, and have relatively
less effect on the incomes and earnings of people in the submarginal or marginal labor markets. Thus those who reject the queue
theory argue for remedial labor market policies directed at the
specific characteristics of each kind of labor market.

Other labor market imperfections

Many observers have also questioned the assumptions of the neoclassical competitive theory that businessmen maximize profits,
particularly with respect to wage payments. One difficulty in testing such a theory, however, is that the observed differential wage
rates within a labor market are not necessarily incompatible with
the assumptions of traditional economic theory because the workers might really have different levels of efficiency, which would
account for some of these differentials. A company that appears to
pay more than a competitor in order to attract more efficient workers might, in reality, be paying no more for efficiency units than a

competitive market would justify. A company might believe that this wage improves its public image or helps it avoid union attempts to organize its employees. Nevertheless, there is evidence that some employers pay wages that are much more than they would have to pay in a competitive labor market. There is, for example, a very high correlation between sales margins and average hourly earnings, which Sumner Slichter argued "reinforces the view that wages, within a considerable range, reflect managerial discretion, that where management can easily pay higher wages they tend to do so, and that where managements are barely breaking even they tend to keep wages down.[22]

Lloyd Ulman has found additional evidence that the labor market does not behave in conformity with the assumptions of traditional theory. Those assumptions are that in a full-employment economy, firms in expanding industries will have to raise their relative wage rates in order to attract additional supplies of labor. However, firms not already operating on their supply schedule (which means they are paying wages above the market) can expand employment and not necessarily raise their wage rates. Ulman has called this the vacancy model of a labor market. He notes that there is little correlation between *percentage changes in wage rates* and *percentage changes in employment* for 57 industries that he studied between 1948 and 1960. Indeed, firms that already had high wages in 1948 increased their relative wages between 1948 and 1960. Ulman concludes that the wage practices of these firms during the 1948–1960 period were contrary to the assumptions of competitive theory that ". . . since the relatively high wage industries did not tend to increase employment more rapidly than the others, they did not on the average have to raise wages more rapidly, as in fact they did in order to attract additional labor."[23] However, Ulman also found some evidence that sizable changes in demand and supply relationships are associated with changes in relative wages, even though the more moderate demand and supply changes do not appear to be so related. In Ulman's study, for example, wage and employment changes were closely associated in the 10 percent of industries in which wages rose most and the 10 percent in which they rose least.

Another assumption of the competitive theory that does not appear to conform with the realities of labor markets is that the demand and supply curves are independent. In the real market there are close relationships between these curves. For example, sudden, dramatic increases in wages might tend to increase the demand schedule as well, either through the influence of wages on the demand for products or through the so-called shock effect, in which wage increases cause employers to be more efficient than they might have been in the absence of the increase.[24] The shock might come about because of an increase in minimum wages or because of an increase in union wage pressures. However, the number of times the shock effect can be used in a given situation might be limited as successive shocks reduce the efficiency slack that can be taken up.

Summary and conclusions

This chapter has emphasized the significance of theory for policy matters and has examined the traditional economic theory of labor markets. However, we have pointed out that even though the neo-classical model has some usefulness, its validity for understanding the operation of real markets is limited by a number of factors. Some of these factors—for example, the theoretical assumptions upon which the model is based—can be dealt with by refining the theory and relaxing the assumptions.

However, some of the other problems—for example, institutional rigidities that make it difficult for the market to operate, cannot be assumed away. Therefore, any realistic analysis of operational labor markets requires some understanding of these institutional forces. It is particularly important to understand the relationship between the internal and external labor markets and to know more than we presently know about the interrelationships among such broad labor market types as the professional, mainstream, marginal, and submarginal labor markets discussed in this chapter. Moreover, there is an obvious necessity to have a better theoretical explanation of the interactions of the various kinds of labor markets and the adjustment of firms and labor markets to changing general demand and supply conditions. Without an adequate theory we will be hard pressed to come up with policies that overcome the imperfections and problems discussed in this chapter. It is particularly important to try to distinguish between the so-called queue theory and theories that view the labor market as being compartmentalized. It is our feeling that the truth probably lies somewhere inbetween these positions: That is to say, the queue theory operates, albeit imperfectly, within each labor market and with less speed and precision among the labor markets, but there is a great deal to be learned from studying the characteristics of different kinds of labor markets. Unfortunately, however, we know too little theoretically and empirically about labor market operations.

Notes

1. Gary S. Becker, *Human Capital* (New York: National Bureau of Economic Research, 1964); Theodore W. Schultz, "Capital Formation by Education," *Journal of Political Economy* (December 1960) pp. 571–583 and "Investment in Human Capital," *American Economic Review* (March 1961), pp. 1–17.
2. Lester Thurow, *Investment in Human Capital* (Belmont, Calif.: Wadsworth Publishing Co., 1970), pp. 2–6.
3. John T. Dunlop, "Job Vacancies Measures and Economic Analysis," in National Bureau of Economic Research, *The Measurement and Interpretation of Job Vacancies* (New York: The Bureau, 1966), pp. 27–38.
4. Clark Kerr, "Balkanization of Labor Markets," in E. Wight Bakke et al., *Labor Mobility and Economic Opportunity* (Cambridge, Mass., and New York: M.I.T. Press and Wiley, 1954), pp. 93–109.
5. Ibid., p. 96.
6. Ibid.
7. Peter Doeringer and Michael Piore, *Internal Labor Markets and Manpower Analysis* (Lexington, Mass. Heath-Lexington Books, 1971).
8. Ibid., pp. 189–190.
9. Gary S. Becker, *Human Capital* (New York: National Bureau of Economic Research, 1964); Walter Y. Oi, "Labor as a Quasi-Fixed Factor," *Journal of Political Economy* (December 1962), pp. 538–555.
10. Doeringer and Piore, op. cit., p. 76.
11. Ibid., p. 77.
12. Kerr, op. cit., Doeringer and Piore, ibid., Charles Killingsworth, *Jobs and Incomes for Negroes* (Ann Arbor, Mich.: Institute of Labor and Industrial Relations, University of Michigan, 1968).
13. Michael Joseph Piore, "Notes for a Theory of Labor Market Stratification," *Working Paper No. 95* (Cambridge, Mass.: Massachusetts Institute of Technology, 1972), p. 2.
14. Michael Joseph Piore, "Manpower Policy," in S. Beer and R. Barringer, eds., *The State and the Poor* (Cambridge, Mass.: Winthrop Publishing Co., 1970).
15. Doeringer and Piore, op. cit.
16. Piore, "Manpower Policy," op. cit.
17. David Gordon, *Theories of Poverty and Underemployment* (Lexington, Mass.: Lexington Books, 1972), p. 53.
18. Ibid., p. 76.
19. Raymond S. Franklin and Solomon Resnik, *The Political Economy of Racism* (New York: Holt, Rinehart & Winston, 1974), p. 13.
20. Ibid., p. 14.

21. Barry Bluestone, "The Tripartite Economy: Labor Markets and the Working Poor," *Poverty and Human Resources* (July–August 1970), pp. 15–37.

22. Sumner Slichter, "Notes on the Structure of Wages," *Review of Economics and Statistics* pp. 80–91 (February 1950), quoted by Lloyd G. Reynolds, *Labor Economics and Labor Relations*, 5th ed. (Englewood Cliffs, N.J.: Prentice-Hall, 1970), p. 115.

23. Lloyd Ulman, "Labor Mobility in the Industrial Wage Structure in the Postwar United States," *Quarterly Journal of Economics* (February 1965), pp. 73–97.

24. Lloyd G. Reynolds and Peter Gregory, *Wages, Productivity and Industrialization in Puerto Rico* (Homewood, Ill.: Irwin, 1965).

two

---

prepara-
tion for
employ-
ment

8
education in human resource development

Ask what single characteristic most differentiates the steadily and well employed from those suffering sporadic or long-term unemployment or working at low wages, and the answer will generally be "Education." Ask also what single factor has had the greatest influence on the U.S. economy's record for productivity and growth; more often than not, the answer will be the same.

That consensus remains nearly universal even though education and its role in society and the economy have been the subject of increasing controversy in recent years. Given the intense interest and the tremendous investment in the years since World War II, it is too easy to forget that even the expectation of a tie between education and employability is a relatively new phenomenon. Even yet, there is no clear substantive relationship between the actual content of most jobs and most school curricula. In fact, the schools themselves seek employability for only a minority of their students. After two decades of lamenting the dropout rate and blaming lack of education for unemployment and low productivity, many are beginning to argue that the U.S. labor force is becoming overeducated in relation to job requirements.[1] It is clear that the more educated workers on the average have higher incomes and experience less unemployment than others, but this may only indicate that those who have whatever labor market success required also have what it takes to succeed in school. Education was strongly advocated during the 1960s as an instrument for lifting the poor and disadvantaged to a par with the mainstream of society. Now, in disillusion, it is argued that the schools have done little or nothing for equality and that we might be better off without them.[2] Given the controversies underlying a seeming consensus, it is worthwhile to explore the issues and examine the evidence underlying such sharply divided opinion.

The emergence of education as a work prerequisite

A hierarchy of the requirements for productivity and employability might include sound mental and physical health, a commitment to work as the most appropriate source of income, acceptance of industrial discipline, good human relations skills, basic skills of communication and computation, technological familiarity, and job skills. The list hardly seems controversial, but a generation ago the last four items would have been included for only a minority of jobs. Compared with the current 12.5 years of educational attainment by the average member of the labor force, the average worker had 8.7 years of schooling in 1940 and 10.4 years in 1952 (the rise seems to be flattening; the 1980 projections are for 12.6 years). At the turn of the century only 6 percent of the population remained in school after the 17th birthday, but it is doubtful that anyone would have blamed a person's unemployment on his lack of education.

At what point did education and formal training become a critical determinant of employability? It has not been many years since most lawyers learned their profession by "reading" law as clerks. Formal training for physicians is less than a century old. The designation of engineer gained educational connotations only in this century. Formal credentialing of schoolteachers is also of relatively recent date, and a few states still do not require a bachelor's degree. Beyond the professions, bookkeepers, accountants, stenographers, and clerks obviously were required to read, write, and cipher. Yet education had little relevance to employment for most of the labor force until about World War II.

The dramatic increase in the education of the American people surely is one of the most significant domestic developments of the past generation. In 1950, for example, 39 percent of the population 16 years of age and older had graduated from high school. By 1973 this proportion had risen to 68 percent. As we will see in Chapter 9, there have also been dramatic increases in college enrollments. There have been equally large increases in expenditures on education in the United States. The total cost of education was about $9 billion in 1950, compared with about $66 billion in 1970 and $96 billion in 1974, reflecting both increased resources and inflation.

Though the time has been too short to be certain, a reversal or at least a flattening in trend for both enrollments and expenditures appears to be occurring. A smaller proportion of high school graduates appear to be entering and graduating from college, and a re--duced proportion are entering graduate school.

The faith of Americans in education as a ladder for upward social mobility is deep seated and long term. World War II is properly designated as the event that transformed education from a minor to a major qualification for employment. The war itself imposed demands for skilled training. A 12-million-man military force was extracted from the prime labor force age group at the same time that war production multiplied the demand for technical and draft skills. In addition to those who learned new skills on the job, a vast increase in the public vocational education system allowed the training of 7.5 million persons before the war's end. Where skills could not be supplied fast enough, jobs were broken down into simpler tasks that could be performed by unskilled and inexperienced workers. Although the emphasis on vocational and skill training did not continue into the postwar period, formal education quickly emerged as a requirement for employment.

The emphasis on technology was accelerated during the war by the development of nuclear weapons and was continued with the space race in the later postwar period. Much of the increased demand for college graduates following World War II was stimulated by the federal government, in part, as a consequence of the cold war emphasis on national prestige derived from scientific and technical achievement and the rate of economic development. America's development of the atomic bomb undoubtedly "persuaded" the Russians to bridge the nuclear gap and develop their space technology, which, in turn, prompted the United States to attempt greater scientific achievements. Sputnik clearly elicited federal support for higher education—there was a space race to be won. Cold war strategy also involved economic development. A major Soviet goal was to become number one, and the competitive threat was an effective goad for the United States. Studies by economists attributing a significant part of economic growth to education therefore strengthened federal support for education.

Postwar population developments also have influenced the demand for education. The college-age population declined during the 1950s because of the low birth rates during the depression of the 1930s and World War II. But elementary and secondary enrollments were swollen by the postwar baby boom.

Why education, in the post–World War II period, became a widely accepted prerequisite for employment is a matter of controversy. Of course, as long as professional and white-collar occupations were expanding as a proportion of all employment, education was certain also to become a necessity for a growing percentage of workers. But the emphasis went far beyond that, until a high school diploma was required for most apprenticeships, many semiskilled factory jobs, and even laborers' jobs at the bottom of a seniority ladder leading into semiskilled and skilled ranks. Perhaps these jobs, or at least those a few steps up the promotion ladder, were becoming more technical—and required an ability to comprehend written instructions, to read and record from gauges and graphs, and similar activities. But why assume that instructions are to be read and workmen are to keep records? In factories throughout much of the world safety and other instructions are given on picture signs, and clerks circulate to keep records. An alternative hypothesis is that as long as educated people were available, employers preferred to hire them, and emerging jobs were structured to fit them. The post–World War II GI Bill no doubt played an important role in kicking off a spiral in which the supply of educated manpower sparked the demand for it.

It is difficult to attribute to anything but supply the fact that 33 percent of laborers had a high school education or better in 1973, compared with 14 percent two decades earlier (Table 8-1). Of course, the proportion of educated people in the labor force would of necessity expand to accompany the growth of professional, technical, and clerical jobs. But it has been estimated that this accounts for only 15 percent of the rise in educational attainment in the work force. The other 85 percent represents higher educational attainment within the same occupation. In many cases the content of the job required more education. In others the employer selected those with more education because they were available and because he assumed that education was likely to correlate positively with productivity and promotability. In still others it was simply the fact that with educational attainment rising throughout the population, anyone hired at random was likely to have more education than his predecessor.

The apparent softening of the demand for and commitment to education is probably more a short- than a long-run phenomenon, with one exception. That exception is, of course, demographic. The downturn in birth rates, which began in the late 1950s and seems to have reached a low plateau approximately equal to the depression birth rate of the 1930s, has the earmarks of a long-term trend. The consequences have already passed through the elementary schools and high schools and are just now affecting the colleges. Regardless of whether or not per capita education increases, the volume of education must inevitably decline. Since the education industry is one of the nation's largest employers, the manpower impact of this dramatic demographic shift has been a major one, with teachers in surplus supply after years of shortages.

Table 8-1 The Changing Educational Pattern of Major Occupational Groups, 1952, 1970 and 1973 (percentage distribution)

Major Occupational Group	Less than 8 Years			8-11 Years			12 Years			13-15 Years			16 Years or More			Median School Years Completed	
	1952	1970	1973	1952	1970	1973	1952	1970	1973	1952	1970	1973	1952	1970	1973	1970	1973
White Collar																	
Professional and technical	1%	a	0.5%	7%	3%	3.3%	16%	18%	17%	21%	19%	17%	55%	60%	62.4%	16.3	16.4
Managerial and officials	10	3	2.4	32	18	12.7	34	39	37.6	13	20	20.7	11	20	26.4	12.7	12.9
Clerical and sales	4	1	1.2	25	16	15.3	50	57	54.2	15	20	21.0	7	7	8.2	12.6	12.7
Blue Collar																	
Craftsmen and foremen	18	10	7.2	48	37	31.7	27	43	47.2	6	9	11.2	1	2	2.7	12.1	12.2
Operatives	25	15	11.4	50	42	40.3	21	38	40.1	3	5	6.6	1	1	1.1	11.3	11.8
Laborers	43	23	16.1	41	39	38.6	14	30	33.1	2	7	9.6	1	1	1.3	10.5	11.4
Farm	43	25	19.1	38	39	37.6	14	27	30.7	4	7	6.7	2	2	4.3	9.3	10.7
Service and Private Household	31	14	9.4	43	39	38.9	20	36	36.7	4	10	11.2	2	1	2.5	11.6	12.0

a Less than 0.5%.
Source: Derived from several U.S. Department of Labor sources.

But accompanying this seemingly longer-run trend are several short-run factors. One is the success of manpower efforts. Throughout most of the post–World War II era the nation's stocks and flows of highly trained manpower lagged behind the growth in demand. Coincidentally, demand began catching up with supply just as the shift in space race commitments, a business recession, and the consequences of the falling birth rates all struck the labor market simultaneously. The results were a short-term surplus of engineers, a longer-term redundancy in some scientific professions, and a serious surplus of teachers. Over those years of seemingly endless demand universities throughout the country had expanded their capacity at undergraduate and graduate levels enormously. That in itself was a great accomplishment. However, like the familiar inventory cycle in macroeconomics, each institution acted unilaterally, expanding without considering the expansion of others. Adding to educational capacity is a slow process involving bricks and mortar, equipment, teacher-training institutions, new faculty to train more new faculty, and so forth. Thus all the new capacity began coming "on stream" just as supply was catching up with demand.

Another result of the education explosion was the questioning of the conventional wisdom that a college diploma was a guarantee of labor market success. There was a reexamination of the relationship between education and job requirements and the discovery that only 20 percent of jobs were filled by and required college graduates. Since that was the very proportion graduating from college, there should have been no surprise in the discovery, but it clashed with the spreading myth of college for (nearly) everybody.

At the same time, education suffered from the overpromises of its enthusiasts. It had been proposed as a solution to almost every social and economic problem. It had done much to ameliorate many problems, but it could not do all that was promised—and disillusion usually brings overreaction. Later sections of this chapter explore the consequences of these developments.

Education of the labor forces: future prospects

Bureau of Labor Statistics projections promise both a younger and a better-educated labor force to 1990. While the adult labor force is expected to increase about 40 percent between 1972 and 1990, the number of high school graduates will rise 54 percent and college graduates 127 percent. In the process the labor force will become much more homogeneous in educational attainment. Most of those who entered the labor force before World War II will have retired or died. The older workers will be the postwar GI Bill generation. Those born during the postwar baby boom will rise from 24 to 34 percent of the workers 25 and older. The younger adult workers will be only slightly better educated than in 1970. But the older workers will show a marked change. Even those in the labor force 65 and over will have a median educational attainment of 12.1 years, compared with 9.6 years in 1970. The gap in educational attainment between blacks and other workers will have shrunk to 0.3 years from the 3.3 years of three decades earlier. The traditional educational advantage of female workers over male workers will have disappeared.

Of course, there will still be those having less than adequate education—20.1 million workers without high school diplomas in 1985, compared with 24.7 million in 1970. Despite black gains, this group will still include a disproportionate number of those without a high school education. If present attitudes persist, these educationally disadvantaged workers will face relatively worse job prospects. But the overwhelming fact will be the decline in the educational differentials that have persisted so long.

Does this outlook for educational attainment match the expected educational requirements of future jobs? The question may be answered differently depending upon whether the criterion is the objective requirements of job content or the preferences of employers. Occupational trends promise to continue the positive correlation between education and employment. Projections discussed in earlier chapters are repeated here to estimate the future relationship. White-collar workers increased from 20 percent of all workers at the turn of the century to 48 percent in 1972. They will comprise 51.5 percent of all workers in 1980. What links these occupations together is their reliance on intellectual and verbal rather than manual and manipulative skills. The fastest-growing occupational group in the labor market will continue to be professional and technical workers, and they, with the addition of clerical occupations, account for nearly all of the projected white-collar increase. Sales workers and managers will remain constant or decline in number. The number of farm workers will continue its rapid downward trend; blue-collar workers will decrease slowly in number.

In the blue-collar category the number of craft workers will increase though falling slightly as a proportion of all workers, with emphasis on those craft skills likely to require the most formal education. Operatives and nonfarm laborers will continue their rapid proportionate decline while remaining stable in absolute numbers. Service occupations will grow with population, but the greatest growth will be in the number of those whose jobs have

Table 8-2   Comparison of Projected Percentage Increases in Labor Force and Employment by Occupational Status Group, 1970 to 1980

Occupational Status Group	Labor Force Increase (1)	Employment Increase (2)	Difference (1)−(2)
Group I, professional, technical, and kindred	45.3	39.0	6.3
Group II, managerial, clerical, and sales[a]	24.6	21.9	2.7
Group III, craft and kindred (part of)[b]	15.1	16.5	−1.4
Group IV, operatives (part of)[c]	11.0	16.9	−5.9
Group V, laborers (part of)[d]	4.4	10.6	−6.2

[a]Includes police, fire fighters, and related occupations. Does not include shipping and receiving clerks, messengers, and office helpers.

[b]Includes farmers; operatives in selected higher wage industries, e.g., transportation equipment, chemical, and petroleum; and barbers, bartenders, and practical nurses.

[c]Includes auto mechanics; construction painters, plasterers, cement and concrete finishers, and roofers; selected service occupations, e.g., hospital attendants.

[d]Includes most farm and nonfarm laborers, cooks and kitchen workers, cleaning and building service workers, domestic workers, and laundry and dry cleaning operatives.

Source: Harold Wool, *The Labor Supply for Lower Level Occupations,* p. 252, cited in *Manpower Report of the President* (Washington, D.C.: GPO, 1974), p. 111.

some educational content—police officers, hospital attendants, cosmetologists, and practical nurses. Only the professional occupations require college degrees.

The critical message these projections convey to the educational community is that less than one out of five jobs will require a college degree. As it happens, this is about the proportion of those entering the ninth grade who now complete college. However, the labor force is growing more rapidly than employment for white-collar occupations, with the opposite being true in the blue-collar realm (Table 8-2).

As Chapter 9 suggests, college graduates probably will not experience rising unemployment relative to the less educated, but a "bumping back" process may occur, bringing the more highly educated into jobs not requiring this preparation. Many of the growth occupations have in common the need, if not the custom, of post-secondary but less than baccalaureate education. The half of all college entrants who drop out before graduation may help fill this need. The continued rapid expansion of two-year community colleges is probably a more functional approach. With 1.8 million enrollees in 1972, these institutions represent a doubling in colleges and a tripling of enrollments during the past decade.

Education and employability

The higher a person's educational attainment, the more likely he is to be in the labor force, to avoid unemployment, to be unemployed only briefly when he enters or reenters the labor force or changes jobs, and to hold a better job (Table 8-3). There is a positive and significant correlation between level of education and lifetime earnings. Studies have also shown that those nations that spend the highest proportions of their national incomes on education tend to experience the most rapid economic growth.

These should be strong testimonials to the value of education in developing the labor force and increasing the employment and earnings of people. But the relationship is far from simple. Because the educational attainment of the work force rose from 9.1 years in 1940 to 12.5 years in 1973, one might expect unemployment to have seriously diminished. But, in fact, overall unemployment has fluctuated cyclically, with no evidence of upward or downward trend over time, and for teenagers there has been an upward trend in unemployment.

Similarly, a general shift toward the upper rungs of the occupational ladder might have been expected. Those occupations, such as professional and technical, which have always attracted people with the most education, have, in fact, expanded most rapidly. Yet the major effect of the rising educational attainment has been to raise the educational level within occupations. Therefore, it is not really clear whether individuals have climbed the occupational ladder as they achieved education or whether the steps in the ladder have become farther apart as better-educated people became available for the same jobs. Too many other factors influence unemployment to make this a meaningful statement. Obviously, in the short run, education is more likely to determine who rather than how many are employed and unemployed. Whether the availability of an educated labor force sparks more rapid economic growth remains a topic of supposition and controversy.

Table 8-3 Unemployment Rates, by Age and Years of School Completed, March 1973

Years of School Completed (Both Sexes)	Percent of Labor Force Unemployed								
	Total, 16 Yrs. Old and over	16-17 Years	18-19 Years	20-24 Years	25-34 Years	35-44 Years	45-54 Years	55-64 Years	65 Yrs. and over
Total	5.2%	17.6%	12.2%	8.2%	4.6%	3.2%	3.1%	3.1%	2.5%
Elementary									
Less than 5 years[a]	4.9	b	b	b	7.3	6.7	4.1	4.3	1.6
5 to 7 years	5.8	b	b	7.6	6.8	6.1	6.3	3.7	4.4
8 years	6.7	24.4	16.4	14.4	12.1	5.7	5.3	4.9	2.0
High School									
1 to 3 years	8.9	17.2	15.3	16.5	7.3	5.0	3.8	3.4	2.3
4 years	4.6	15.6	11.1	7.8	4.3	2.6	2.7	2.8	3.4
College									
1 to 3 years	4.0	b	7.6	6.6	3.7	2.5	2.2	1.9	3.6
4 years or more	2.1	—	—	5.0	2.5	1.4	1.2	1.0	0.4

[a]Includes persons reporting no school years completed.
[b]Not computed; base too small.
Source: U.S. Bureau of Labor Statistics.

People with more education earn substantially more over a working lifetime. Does this occur because their education prepares them for better jobs, because employers value and are willing to pay for their educational attainment, or because education has been pursued by those who possess more native ability, motivation, or better labor market contacts? Do employers prefer the better educated because job content requires such workers, because they are better disciplined or more promotable, because they have demonstrated persistence, or simply because employers have unrealistic views about the value of education? Does a better-educated labor force cause an economy to grow more rapidly, or is it that a more rapidly growing economy can afford the luxury of more education? What exactly is the contribution of education to employability? None of these questions can be satisfactorily answered, but they are worth exploring. That these questions are being asked increasingly is evidence of a reaction against the sacrosanct status education has enjoyed as accepted preparation for employment over the past generation.

The independent contribution of education to employability could be measured only if certain experimental conditions were met. Youth of equal ability and socioeconomic background would have to undertake different levels of education accompanied by specified additional training before seeking jobs under prescribed circumstances from employers who are totally objective. Since the necessary studies have not been made, it is possible only to report the facts and speculate about their meaning. Whether jobs demand education or employers merely prefer it, years of educational attainment remain the best available predictor of wages and employment rates. However, recent studies controlling more carefully for other socioeconomic factors often highly correlated with educational attainment have tended to depreciate the independent influence of education on income differentials, leaving it as one among several important factors.

Education and the transition from school to work

People who attain the most education, of course, also have other advantages that would have been present without the added education. A young person's educational attainment, for example, is also highly correlated with the education and income of his parents. Low-income families produce the highest proportion of dropouts and the lowest proportion of graduates. When socioeconomic status and ability are compared, low-ability students from high-income families are more likely to attend and graduate from college than are high-ability students from poor families. Yet school-connected difficulties such as lack of interest, poor grades, and disciplinary problems are more likely to be cited than money as the immediate reason when a low-income youth drops out of school.

A Labor Department study, now a decade old but still significant, also found a relationship between amount of education and how jobs are sought and obtained. For one thing, those with higher education are more likely to have a job waiting for them when they leave school. And among those who look for employment, the better educated (particularly the college trained) find jobs sooner.[3]

Vocational training and academic education are often viewed as alternative ways of preparing for employment. However, rather than compensating for lack of education, skill training and educational attainment are positively correlated, largely because vocational training ordinarily becomes available only during the last two years of high school. By this time the compulsory school-attendance age has been reached or passed, and most who are likely to do so have dropped out.

The cooperative work-study program, though still enrolling few students throughout the nation, is potentially useful in assisting the movement of high school students into the labor force. Under this program the student's day usually is split between school and part-time employment; special efforts are made to integrate the activities into a meaningful preparation for work. Because these opportunities also become available in the last years of high school, over twice as many graduates as dropouts have participated. Even of those high school graduates who do not go on to college, three times as many undertake some form of postsecondary training as do the dropouts. The follow-up on the Department of Labor study conducted two years later found that one-fifth of the high school graduates had returned to school, compared with only one-twentieth of the dropouts. In addition, one-fourth of the graduates were participating in formal job training outside regular schools, compared with one-eighth of the dropouts.

Guidance from school or state employment service officials provides another bridge from school to job. But the Department of Labor survey of out-of-school youths noted that over half of the high school graduates and less than one-fourth of the dropouts received such help. Because most guidance is directed to students during their senior year in high school, dropouts tend to be excluded from this experience.

The effectiveness of vocational guidance is partially demonstrated by the fact that dropouts who had been counseled were again half as likely to have jobs waiting for them when they left school as those who had not been counseled. However, vocational guidance seemed to make little difference in whether or not graduates were immediately employed.

Not all students receive vocational guidance, and studies have shown that it usually is directed at those who seemingly need it least. Jacob J. Kaufman et al. found that academic students were more likely to receive guidance than vocational students.[4] Only one-half of vocational students, compared with three-fourths of academic students, recalled discussing the selection of their courses with a counselor. Actual discussion of job plans was even less frequent, with one-fifth of the vocational and one-third of the academic students receiving assistance. If academic students receive more exposure to placement services beyond high school and are generally better equipped to make decisions, then the order of priorities in high school vocational guidance activities is obviously inverted.

In contrast to those leaving school at or before high school completion, the college-to-work bridge has been a reasonably secure one. The explanation may be that college students have been a select group that has demonstrated a commitment attractive to employers or perhaps because their backgrounds gave them better labor market access. However, the first postgraduation job is rarely the first work experience. The transition from school to work is likely to have been underway for a number of years. Now with college graduation a less unusual achievement and with supply catching up with demand for most college-trained occupations, successfully crossing the bridge is less automatic. It is time for colleges to clarify their dual roles in career preparation and in educating the whole person. Concepts of career education discussed in Chapter 11 are applicable at that level as well. If college is to be a useful step in career preparation, career planning should be a part of that educational experience.

The one-half of youth who, on the average, enter but do not complete college have unknown variety of experiences. We know relatively little about the amount of schooling and training this group obtains, their reasons for failing to complete college, and their labor force experience. While those who complete a two- or three-year course probably find it a satisfactory bridge to their working career, those who fail to finish an intended four-year course are likely to be less well prepared for a specific occupation. It may be significant that those who have attended college but have not graduated experience almost as much unemployment as high school graduates.

Once most members of the labor force are high school graduates, a diploma offers little competitive advantage. At that point the quality and content of the education received becomes more significant. Chapter 11 discusses the potential of career education and the extent and role of vocational education as preparation for careers and the specific occupations of which careers are comprised. The proportion enrolled in vocational studies, the funds allocated to them, and the quality of vocational education all appear to be on the rise. No data are available concerning relative quality or results of vocational training. Overall, those who receive vocational education in high school appear to have the edge in employment and earnings during the first six to ten years beyond high school; after that point those from the general and academic curriculums catch up and begin to pass them. However, vocational enrollees tend to be of lower ability than others. When controlled for ability and socioeconomic status, high school vocational training—even at its present quality and relevance—does seem to have significant employment and earnings advantages.

The increasingly small proportion who fail to complete high school, of course, find themselves at the rear of any labor market queue. If one is looking for a simple formula for success in the transition from school to work, therefore, the statistics could be read as an endorsement for staying in school as long as possible, but observation of job content does not always explain why this is so.

Some degree of selectivity is doubtless at work, so that those who achieve the highest educational attainment tend to have the most native ability. Many with the ability to complete college successfully do not do so. We do not know whether their employability suffers compared with those of equal ability but greater educational attainment. It frequently is suggested that technological developments tend to require higher levels of education, though it is not clear whether this is attributable to change in job content or more rapid growth of higher-level jobs. The findings of the BLS appear to favor the latter explanation, with the educational upgrading within occupational classifications probably resulting more from the rising educational attainment of the labor force than from the requirements of jobs. It is to be expected, of course, that the availability of higher-quality labor would, over time, encourage development of a technology attuned to its use. Finally, it may be that employers simply consider education a meaningful screening device and select those with the highest attainment.

The conspicuous consumption of education

We have explored but not resolved the issue of whether educated people experience less unemployment because they are educated or whether those with the greatest ability and access to jobs are those who seek education. There is left the issue of employer bias. Do employers prefer better-educated people for subjective reasons and not for their potential productivity?

Ivar Berg, in an important exercise in iconoclasm (subtitled, appropriately, *The Great Training Robbery*), argued that education has little to do with productivity in many jobs and is even a negative factor in some.[5] Relying primarily on secondary sources, he identifies numerous situations in which employers have imposed educational requirements beyond the actual job needs. In these cases he finds evidence of employee unrest and high turnover, which, he asserts, occurs because workers become bored with assignments below their capabilities and expectations. He does not explore the likelihood that the employer may, in fact, be paying thrice for his conspicuous consumption of educated people. In addition to the rate he would have paid for an individual with just enough capability to do the job, the employer pays the added wage necessary to attract and meet the expectations of the over-educated employee. To this is added the cost of unrest and turnover.

There are several possible explanations of this apparently irrational bias on the part of employers. Some, concerned about promotability, may be looking ahead to the requirements of the job at the top of a promotion ladder. But relying upon past education for skills required by a future job suggests little faith in a person's ability to learn on the job. Racial bias has also been suggested as a cause of inflated educational requirements. Knowing that various minorities have lower-than-average educational attainment, employers may require education as a defensible shield for reducing the number of minority applicants. To the extent that education is a surrogate for all the advantages listed in the previous section, employers may be acting rationally and getting their money's worth.

Many employers undoubtedly share the current bias in favor of formal education. Berg's examples were primarily blue-collar and lower-level white-collar workers in repetitive jobs and life insurance salesmen, but equally well known is the restlessness of graduate engineers who find themselves doing technician-level work in production settings. Similar overqualification and underemployment can be found throughout the labor market. The use of nurses' aides who assume some of the registered nurses' responsibilities is a partial solution to one such problem. The New Careers program funded under the Economic Opportunity Act attempted to exploit such situations to provide employment for disadvantaged persons. Undereducated, disadvantaged people were trained to perform repetitive functions that require limited skills but that were being performed by professionals. Increasing the number of technicians per graduate engineer is a similar approach. This trend is opposed by many professionals who are as jurisdiction conscious as craft unionists. Various licensing and credentialing requirements, usually defended as necessary to protect the consumer, protect jurisdiction at the cost of overqualification.

There is no necessary inconsistency in arguing both that the jobs requiring formal education are growing more rapidly than any others and that overqualification is pervasive in U.S. labor markets. The less physical and the more intellectual the production processes, the greater the need for formal education. Manipulative skills, such as typing, that are generally applicable are taught more efficiently in the classroom than on the job. Given these trends, those without adequate formal education are at a technical disadvantage. Because education has purposes other than preparation for employment, the desire to consume education may lead to overqualification as a worker and overinvestment in the labor force. Yet society may profit from the nonlabor market contributions of the educated and the economy may experience greater vitality in the long run.

The educational institutions for manpower development

Since manpower is defined as the productive employment capacity of human beings, nearly every institution that affects our lives has an impact on manpower development. Consider the attributes of employability listed at the beginning of this chapter. The home is a key determinant of mental and physical health, commitment to work, acceptance of discipline, and human relations skills. The neighborhood and community are also involved. But because improvement in these basic institutions is difficult, schools and other institutions are asked to provide remedies for any deficiencies. Thus elementary and secondary schools become the focus for the development not only of a general ability to understand and function in society but also of discipline and human relations skills, as well as basic skills in communications and computation.

Manpower experts sometimes express dismay because the schools often do not accent and pursue their role as manpower developers. These experts argue that basic manpower requirements would be better met if preparation for employment were specifically included among the priority objectives of education. Rupert Evans accuses American education of concentrating on "school for schooling's sake."[6] The elementary schools prepare young people to go to high school, which concentrates on getting them into college, which is geared to meeting graduate school requirements. Only then, when the schooling potential is exhausted, is the emphasis vocational, but largely for education as a profession.

The pattern began in the days when elementary schools were assigned the job of producing literate citizens and Americanizing immigrants. Only the college bound enrolled in high school as a preparatory stage. Vocational education was established as a separate system to protect it from the disdain of the academic educator. But with the high schools providing mass education and education a growing prerequisite for employment, many feel that education needs a change of signals. One indicator is the growing interest in a career-development system; another is the growth of community colleges. Finally, dissatisfaction with the way schools fulfill their employment-preparation role is a factor in the growing political criticism of education.

Whether viewed as a vocationalization of general education or a generalization of vocational education, there is growing interest in discovering techniques for integrating the two. The basic assumption is that preparation for a working career is among the most important of education's many objectives. Thus no one without the requisites for employability, including a salable skill, can be considered educated. At the same time, skill preparation should neither supplant other general education objectives nor be so structured that the individual will not be able to realize his true potential. It is from this premise that the concepts of career education have emerged. Some of the techniques for accomplishing this goal are elementary school orientation to the world of work, information and training in occupational choice, integration of academic and vocational content so that each serves as a vehicle for the other, and a more active role for schools in the placement process.

Community colleges, as we noted earlier, have almost doubled in number in ten years, while their enrollment has tripled. The title is significant. While the term "junior college" indicates a college transfer emphasis and a desire to grow up to become a senior college, the community college is committed to serving the community's educational needs, whatever they might be. Most institutions that call themselves community colleges could have more honestly retained the "junior college" title. However, the generally recognized attributes, too often observed in the breach, are (1) a truly open door admissions policy for all persons over 18, regardless of past education, who can profit from instruction; (2) a service-oriented and student-centered philosophy that contrasts with the university's too often self-serving ambitions for a community of scholars; (3) a faculty that concentrates on teaching rather than research; (4) heavy emphasis on occupationally oriented two-year terminal programs; (5) a strong counseling and guidance program; (6) use of the campus as a community center for nonstudent activities and of the staff as a source of technical services to community institutions; and (7) an ambition to place one such institution within commuting distance of everyone in the population. A few community colleges incorporated skills centers financed by the Manpower Development and Training Act (MDTA is discussed in Chapter 12) into their facilities; these centers offer remedial training and stipends to disadvanged adults who are not stigmatized as second-class citizens by being shunted to separate and less-than-equal facilities. Many community colleges accept individual referrals or whole classes of manpower program enrollees on contract. What will happen to this movement with the replacement of MDTA by the Comprehensive Employment and Training Act (CETA) remains to be seen.

Universities are being pressured by state and local governments and community leaders to give more attention to undergraduate teaching and community service. In fact, a general reaction to the overexpectations of the 1960s seems to be subjecting the entire educational system to unfamiliar criticism. Education has long been a sacred cow, deliberately shielded from partisan politics, decentralized, and characterized by professional autonomy. The 1960s saw federal support for education rise from $2 billion to $8 billion while all U.S. expenditures on education rose from $25 billion to $66 billion. Whatever the ills of society —and many formerly unrecognized ills were uncovered during the period—more and better education was the prescription. Because the products of education are difficult to measure, education administrators tend to measure the output by the input. Getting more education was simply a question of funding: Quality was another matter.

Education reached a zenith of public support in 1965 with the Elementary and Secondary Education Act (ESEA). Since then there has been a rising crescendo of criticism. The act was designed to provide additional federal funds for school districts heavily impacted with poverty. Because of peculiarities in the distribution formula, most of the money was channeled into high-income states with high levels of public assistance. Head Start was briefly the great hope for social rehabilitation. It soon became apparent that a short preschool experience was no panacea as long as the children were then dumped into the same schools and remained in the same homes with the same problems. There was increasing concern because students emerged from the schools at various exit points without salable skills.

Manpower training programs also suffered their share of criticism. They were assailed because enrollees were trained for low-level jobs that, if available, left them in employed poverty. Too often the trained would-be worker discovered that problems of housing, transportation, isolation in a rural depressed area, or racial discrimination stood in the way of employment. Then campus unrest persuaded many that college youth, the ultimate recipients of public largess, were ungratefully biting the hand that was feeding them.

Though its implications for manpower development are peripheral as well as long term, it is worth noting, as an evidence of disillusion, the controversy over education as a route to social as well as economic equality. The major thrust of the expansion of federal support for education in the mid-1960s had been compensatory education—the hope that added inputs into those schools populated by the most deprived students could speed their rise to socioeconomic equality. This went far beyond the traditional concern for equal opportunity in pursuit of equal results. Of course, results were never equal, but then neither were the opportunities. The widely publicized Coleman Report demonstrated that family and peer group influence was a more potent force in raising the educational achievement of disadvantaged students than was either the quality of school facilities or teachers.[7] A replowing of the Coleman data by Christopher Jencks and associates concluded that all of the added expenditures had no effect on the desired equality.[8] Educational achievement seemed a largely random factor. The study has been both acclaimed and criticized. Yet the fact remains that, despite the federal investment in compensatory education, the increase in resources flowing to the education of the nondisadvantaged was much greater in absolute terms. Compensatory educational programs may or may not be a route to achieving equality in educational results. They have as yet never been tested.

Among the consequences of this disillusionment was a rising rate of rejections in school bond elections and reduced generosity among legislators. Other public needs seemed to take higher priority. For the first time a President of the United States found vetoing education appropriations less than threatening politically. There was a new demand for accountability. Granting a diploma is no evidence that education has done its job. Performance contracting in which public or private institutions are rewarded for demonstrated improvement in educational achievement aroused considerable interest and some experimentation. The failure of our educational system to prepare noncollege-bound youth (and many college graduates) for successful working careers was an important factor in this discontent. At the same time, some more radical criticism charged that the schools were merely conveyor belts designed to put people into slots in the industrial machine. Such are the penalties for the American faith in education as a key to both social change and social stability. By the mid-1970s these criticisms seemed to be moderating in crescendo. Hopefully, more balanced views may undergird a new consensus and bring about less panacea-oriented reforms.

Returns to investment in education

Within the past decade the economics of education has become a major field for professional economists. For many the subject consists of school finance. For most, however, the question has been: Does education pay? If so, how much of what kind for whom under what conditions?

The school finance approach emerged as school enrollments mushroomed following the World War II GI Bill and the postwar baby boom. Its emphasis was on how to get enough classrooms and teachers and funds to support them. The landmark in the education-as-investment approach was the American Economic Association presidential address given by Theodore W. Schultz of the University of Chicago in December 1960.[9] Titling his address "Investment in Human Capital," he noted the failure of his fellow economists to subject expenditures on education to the same rigorous analyses applied to investments in machinery, factories, and other forms of capital. The economic fathers—Adam Smith, David Ricardo, Thomas Malthus, Karl Marx, and Alfred Marshall, to name a few—had mentioned the importance of education and training in the improvement of labor as a factor of production, but none had attempted to specify a rate of return.

Schultz had been attracted to the riddle of economic growth. It had been supposed that adding greater accumulations of reproducible capital to a fixed supply of land and labor would result eventually in diminishing returns to such investments. When this did not occur in the United States, one logical explanation was that the supply of one or both of the other inputs must not be fixed. Improvements in the quality of human resources was a possible answer.

Related enigmas surrounded the persistent relatively large increases in the real earnings of workers and the unexplained residuals in economic growth. Economists involved in the postwar recovery of Europe had found economies growing more rapidly than could be explained by the aggregate inputs of manhours of labor, the stock and flows of reproducible capital, and natural resources. The residual had been explained as a product of technological change,[10] but the source had not been identified. A technological improvement could include any change in the quality of the inputs, including labor; hence education, health care, or any other investment in human beings could be a factor in that technological change.

Had the answer to the question "Does education pay?" been negative, interest among academic researchers might have died at birth. Because the preliminary results supported the predispositions of academicians and politicians, and the self-interests of the former, an immense literature emerged during the 1960s exploring and applying the concept of investment in human capital. Only the broadest outlines can be given here.

Measuring the returns

William G. Bowen has summarized the general approaches to measuring the return to investment in education.[11] One approach has been to correlate indexes of educational activity with some index of national economic activity. Examples are intercountry comparisons of the relationship between per capita educational expenditures and growth in GNP.[12] In general, among underdeveloped economies those with the highest levels of educational expenditures experience the fastest growth. But does the country grow because of its investment in human resources, or does it buy education because its favorable growth rate enables it to indulge its philosophical commitments? Or is it because well-paid workers demand better education for their children? Other studies have compared levels of educational expenditure pace to period of country growth. The indications are supportive but leave the same question: Does the country grow because it invests or invest because it is growing and can afford it? Interindustry and interfirm comparisons have the same possibilities and shortcomings.

A number of researchers have attributed to investments in human beings the residual in economic growth rates unexplained by inputs of capital and land. Such approaches rarely show a direct cause-and-effect relationship to expenditures on education, on-the-job training, health care, or any other investment in human productivity, but they give strong support to education as a major factor.

Given the difficulties of identifying the national rates of return from human resource investments, it has become the standard practice to measure the direct returns of education—that is, to compare the lifetime earnings of those with more and less education. The difference can then be expressed as an annual rate of return on the costs of the education, discounted at some appropriate interest rate to measure the present value of a future stream of incomes.

Critiquing the concept

This straightforward approach has its difficulties. First, as with any cost-benefit analysis, measurement of educational costs and benefits is not simple, and the choice of an appropriate discount rate can often predetermine the results. In calculating the returns to education or training, nonmonetary benefits, like the attractiveness of posttraining jobs, should be included, but these cannot be calculated in monetary terms. Training, education, and health increase a worker's satisfaction as a consumer of these things, but these contribute nothing to the measurable national output. These deletions would cause the internal rate of discount to underestimate the actual returns to training.

There are serious conceptual problems in determining costs as well as returns. For example, people must make expenditures for things such as food, clothing, housing, and medical care, which are maintenance costs of the human investment. But these things are needed in order for the worker to live. How much should we attribute to maintenance of the capital and how much to consumption?

There is a second difficulty with this approach. Most of the studies have looked at a cross section of people of different ages, races, education, and incomes and assumed that what was true of an age-income profile would be true of individuals over their life histories. Yet the many changes in educational costs and techniques, life expectancies, occupational structures, economic conditions, and other factors make this unlikely.

Another difficulty is that since labor cannot be separated from its owner, it cannot be sold. Therefore, it becomes more difficult than in the case of physical capital to borrow funds to make enough human investments to equalize costs and returns. The limited resources of the poor is an important constraint on their ability to make human resource investments.

A final criticism of this approach has been noted. The owners of physical capital maximize monetary returns from that capital. However, a very serious problem for human capital theorists is the fact that we cannot determine what those who make investments maximize. This is due to the fact that investors are assumed to maximize a utility function containing nonmarket factors like prestige, consumption benefits (both from the investment itself and from the nonmarket value of goods and services produced as a result of the investment), and earnings. Once we move from the assumption that all of these things (rather than only earnings) are maximized, it is not possible to tell whether or not an investor made an irrational choice. However, these are only technical difficulties. The more serious ones are conceptual. Education is only partially approached as an investment by its purchasers (investors). It may be the parent who pays and makes the judgment of usefulness and purpose. Education, being a consumption good, may change the tastes of those who receive it, radically altering other consumption and investment decisions. At the elementary and secondary levels, attendance is a matter of compulsion, not choice. Society has decided it has an interest in the education of its citizens in addition to the individual benefits. If left to their own discretion and asked to pay for their own education, people, it is assumed, would meet their individual needs, but there would be insufficient education for social purposes. Measurements of return must differentiate between private and social benefits but neglect neither. If education is left to individual investment, those who can afford it will have it while those who need it the most to rise above their present circumstances will not be able to afford it. We often are forced to infer the future by the past, which is a very hazardous procedure in a dynamic society, as we shall see in connection with the argument that education or training cannot do much to improve the conditions of blacks or the poor.

If aggregate incremental earnings are taken as a measure of the national return from investment in education, the problem of conspicuous consumption emerges. As pointed out earlier in the chapter, if the employer hires those with educational attainment greater than required for the job, he may add to employee earnings without getting a commensurate increase in productivity. The most important criticism has also been identified earlier: the assumption that there is a direct relationship between a given investment (education) and productivity. There probably is a subrelationship, but it has not been satisfactorily demonstrated. We know that incomes and education are directly correlated, but we cannot tell which is cause and which is effect. The technique of arriving at the returns to education through regression equations that account mathematically for the influence on earnings of everything other than training or education is hazardous if there are important factors like differences in natural ability that are not accounted for.

There is no question that employers demand workers with education or training, but this is not identical with demanding workers with certain productive capacities. In other words, education might be used by employers to screen workers even though there is no necessary connection between education and job performance. Human capital theory is unable to specify very precisely what it is that employers demand and what it is that workers supply, making the traditional demand-and-supply analysis much looser than many of its advocates imply. Insofar as there is a tendency for those with the greatest native ability and motivation to gain the most education, the education investment may be credited with what is really an economic rent on unusual ability.

Usefulness of the theory

For these and other reasons some economists have objected to basing human capital policy decisions on cost-benefit calculations. There is an assumption, for example, that the investment with the highest calculated rate of return would be the one decision makers should select. However, these calculations would be useful guides to action only if they were based on reasonably accurate measures of costs for achieving identical alternative objectives. Governments might decide to do nothing about the health of older people or training of any other than the brightest or youngest if decisions were made on the basis of human capital considerations alone. At best these calculations can only be used as an aid to decision making; they cannot become decision-making tools.

Even if we overcome the formidable obstacles to accurate calculation of human capital, this concept would be an imperfect guide to policy. We are still left with the problem of whose satisfaction should be maximized. Only value judgments could answer this question.

Human capital theorists have a way of meeting some of the objections to this concept by inserting new terms in their equations and proceeding as if that step solved every problem. And it is true that this procedure often helps solve theoretical problems, but it does not provide much policy guidance. For example, these analysts modify their equations for risk and uncertainty by adding probability terms. This procedure helps clarify some of the theoretical relationships involved in investment decision, but it is impossible to quantify all of these variables.

Despite its appeal, the human capital concept has many defects that limit its application to particular labor market problems. Some of these difficulties are due to ideological or political opposition to the concept. Some people oppose its use because it implies that differences in the distribution of income and wealth are due to the individuals themselves rather than to social institutions. Those who want to change social institutions will be less inclined to give weight to the human capital concept, which emphasizes marketable benefits, because it is very difficult to put a price on the value of social change. How much is it worth, for example, to eliminate or reduce racial discrimination or imperfections in labor markets? If earned incomes are due to differences in human capital, there is an implication that the poor simply were not interested enough in investing in themselves to improve their earning power, that they made bad choices relative to people who were better off, or that they simply had inferior physical and intellectual abilities. It is equally easy to argue politically that since earnings reflect productivity, taxes should not be progressive. It is not surprising, therefore, that whereas conservatives are the main champions of this concept, liberals and radicals are more likely to oppose it.

Despite all of these handicaps, however, careful scholars have appraised the contribution of a wide variety of investments in human resources, including education and training. Becker has estimated the private return on a college education and on-the-job training.[13] W. Lee Hansen has calculated the rate of return for all levels of education from the first year of grade school through college.[14] Burton A. Weisbrod has appraised the returns to lower levels of education, to health care, and to a variety of other aspects of human resource development.[15] Thomas I. Ribich has examined antipoverty efforts and manpower programs from the investment viewpoint.[16] Hansen and Weisbrod together have appraised the California educational system from the human capital viewpoint and found it guilty of an inverse redistribution of income.[17] These are only a few examples from a voluminous literature that has been summarized by Richard Perlman, Lester Thurow, and others.[18]

For the most part, the results have been favorable to education; they suggest a rate of return above that normally expected from investments in other forms of capital. In general, the prescriptive message has been "more." But, as noted, Berg has criticized possible overly favorable biases based on the factors of conspicuous consumption and native ability.[19] Neil W. Chamberlain has warned that education enthusiasts may be laying a trap for themselves in their unrestrained endorsement of the human capital approach.[20] After everyone becomes committed to justifying education by incremental earnings accounting techniques, what happens if diminishing returns set in? Will other social advantages be neglected because of overemphasis on economic values?

These considerations make the human capital approach an unsatisfactory theoretical and practical way to make manpower or other human resource decisions. Few would argue against attempting to calculate crude costs and benefits, but placing a great deal of reliance on them for decision-making purposes is another matter. In the final analysis, policy makers must make decisions on the basis of the weight of the evidence presented to them. The human capital approach might provide better evidence for or against a program, but the concept clearly should be used with great care.

There can be little question that however difficult it may be to measure precisely, trained intelligence is the main hope for solving the world's social, environmental, and economic problems. Moreover, trained intelligence clearly is an important factor in improving the production of goods and services. However, intelligence can be and is trained in places other than formal educational institutions, and various places, procedures, and institutions undoubtedly have advantages and disadvantages for various kinds of intelligence training. The task of the future is to identify the unique role of each process and to improve it.

Notes

1. Ivar Berg, *Education and Jobs: The Great Training Robbery* (New York: Praeger, 1970), pp. 4–5.
2. Ivan Illich, *DeSchooling Society* (New York: Harper & Row, 1970).
3. Garth L. Mangum, "Second Chance in the Transition from School to Work," *The Transition from School to Work*, a report based on the Princeton Manpower Symposium, May 9–10, 1968 (Princeton, N.J.: Princeton University Press, 1963).
4. Jacob J. Kaufman et al., *The Role of the Secondary Schools in the Preparation of Youth for Employment* (University Park, Pa.: Institute for Research on Human Resources, Pennsylvania State University, 1967), pp. 12:5–6.
5. Berg, op. cit.
6. Evans, op. cit., pp. 189–203.
7. James S. Coleman et al., *Equality of Educational Opportunity* (Washington, D.C.: GPO, 1966).
8. Christopher Jencks, *Inequality: An Assessment of the Effect of Family and Schooling in America* (New York: Basic Books, 1972).
9. Theodore W. Schultz, "Investment in Human Capital," in *American Economic Review* (March 1961), pp. 1–17.

10. Robert Solow, "Technical Change and the Aggregate Production Function," *Review of Economics and Statistics* (August 1957), pp. 312–320; B. F. Mossell, "Capital Formation and Technological Change in United States Manufacturing," *Review of Economics and Statistics* (May 1960), pp. 182–188.
11. William G. Bowen, *Economic Aspects of Education* (Princeton, N.J.: Industrial Relations Section, Princeton University, 1964).
12. Frederick Harbison and Charles A. Myers, *Education, Manpower and Economic Growth* (New York: McGraw-Hill, 1969).
13. Gary Becker, *Human Capital* (New York: National Bureau of Economic Research, 1964).
14. W. Lee Hansen, "Total and Private Rates of Return to Investment in Schooling," *Journal of Political Economy* (April 1963), pp. 128–137, 139–140.
15. Burton A. Weisbrod, *External Benefits of Public Education* (Princeton, N.J.: Industrial Relations Section, Princeton University, 1964), pp. 95–96.
16. Thomas I. Ribich, *Education and Poverty* (Washington, D.C.: Brookings Institution, 1968).
17. W. Lee Hansen and Burton A. Weisbrod, *Benefits, Costs and Finance of Public Higher Education* (Chicago: Markham, 1969).
18. Richard Perlman, *The Economics of Education* (New York: McGraw-Hill, 1973); Lester Thurow, *Investment in Human Capital* (Belmont, Calif.: Wadsworth Publishing Co., 1970).
19. Berg, op. cit.
20. Neil W. Chamberlain, "Some Second Thoughts on the Concept of Human Capital," in *Industrial Relations Research Association*, Proceedings of the Twentieth Annual Winter Meeting (Madison, Wis.: The IRRA, 1967), pp. 4–13.

9
the role of
higher education

Higher education, defined as all postsecondary education in colleges and universities, plays an important role in labor markets and human resource development. Postsecondary education also is a significant industry, providing employment to about 559,000 faculty members in more than 2,600 educational institutions. This system had total expenditures of $41.5 billion during the 1971–1972 academic year. About 8.5 million degree-credit students were enrolled in these schools in 1971. This represented a dramatic increase in college enrollments from the previous two decades. The number of degree-credit students increased from 2.3 million in 1947 to 6.8 million in 1968 and was projected to increase to 13.2 million in 1980.

Postsecondary schools supply a large proportion of technicians, managers, and professional workers. These institutions also advance knowledge, preserve cultural heritages, and facilitate upward social and economic mobility. The efficiency of the postsecondary educational system and the access to it by all sectors of the population are thus very important for human resource development and for political, economic, and social stability.

The importance of higher education is not vitiated by doubts about either the precise relationships between education and productivity, discussed in Chapter 8, or the fact that the higher-education system is necessary to provide the manpower to operate a society that becomes increasingly complex as it develops. It is clearly possible to exaggerate the importance of the scientific and technical requirements of an industrial economy. Although the number of scientists and technicians increased during the 1960s, this increase resulted mainly from government action and the demand for teachers rather than from a demand for highly educated manpower by the private industrial sector. Moreover, studies of output per worker and occupational skill mix do not indicate that those industries with the fastest rates of growth of output per worker increased their employment of skilled or white-collar workers faster than those whose productivity did not increase as fast.[1] Similarly, in studies of postwar developments in European countries, Edward F. Denison found no significant relationship between productivity and educational changes.[2] The experiences of countries such as Japan demonstrate the possibility of operating a sophisticated industrial economy with average educational levels much lower than those prevailing in the United States.

There can be little question, nevertheless, that postsecondary education serves to increase the incomes of individuals, whether or not there is a causal relationship between this kind of education and GNP. The evidence shows workers with college degrees to have a number of employment and income advantages, such as higher beginning salaries, lower unemployment rates, higher labor force participation rates, and higher lifetime earnings.

Costs and returns on investment in higher education

Insofar as individual workers are concerned, the net rate of return on education can be determined by calculating the discounted values of projected salaries (lifetime earnings) and deducting the costs (or investment) incurred in obtaining an education.

Allan M. Cartter, a leading authority of the economics of higher education, estimates the following cost figures of obtaining a four-year college degree and a doctoral degree at a representative private university:

Cost of Four Years of College, Beyond High School Education

Direct personal costs (tuition and fees)	$ 8,000
Personal income foregone	20,000
Subsidized direct costs	4,000
	$32,000

Cost of Doctoral Degree Over and Above College Education

Direct personal costs (tuition and fees)	$ 6,000
Personal income foregone	30,000
Subsidized direct costs	12,000
	38,000[3]

These figures thus show foregone personal earnings to be the largest cost factor for college students, although other expenses can be very significant, especially to low-income groups.

However, the expenses of going to college vary considerably

according to the type of institution. Of the total expenses incurred by colleges and universities, about 55 percent are for instructional services and 45 percent for housing and food services, organized research, extension and other public services, student aid, and other student services. In 1973–1974 the tuition per standard undergraduate student in American postsecondary schools ranged from $261 in public junior colleges to $2412 in private universities and $552 in public universities.

Because of rapidly rising costs in private higher-education institutions and a reduction in the quality gap between public and private colleges and universities, undergraduate enrollment has risen very sharply in public institutions (from 1.9 million in 1960 to 5.2 million in 1970), while enrollment in private institutions has increased relatively much less—1.3 million in 1960 to 1.8 million in 1970. In 1963 tuition and required fees were $222 for public institutions and $944 for private; by 1973 charges in private institutions had risen to $1919 as compared with $392 for public colleges and universities. In two-year institutions required charges were:

	Public	Private
1963	$97	$600
1973	242	1401

Costs of higher education influence the labor market in a variety of ways, but principally as they redistribute income among income groups and influence access to higher education. Because a much larger proportion of students from wealthy families attend college, as will be shown later in this chapter, the wealthy are subsidized more heavily by higher-education expenditure than the poor. However, once students are admitted to colleges and universities, there is very little variation in subsidy among income classes. In 1966, for example, the mean subsidy of college students was $612; students from the lowest quartile of income recipients received $660, and those from the highest received $586.

Bureau of the Census lifetime income estimates show that a college graduate earns an average of approximately $372,000 more in a lifetime than a worker who has less than eight years of formal education. According to these figures, a college education is worth $218,000 more than a high school education—a substantial return on a $32,000 investment (Table 9-1).

These calculations of return on investments in higher education do not imply causation or that educated workers are more productive than those with less education. The questions of productivity and cause are very complex. We do not know the extent to which college merely separates people with superior ability, in-

Table 9-1   Lifetime Income by Levels of Education, 1968

Education	Lifetime Income (thousands of dollars)
0–7	$196
8 years	258
1–3 years high school	294
4 years high school	350
1–3 years college	411
4 years college or more	568

Source: U.S. Bureau of the Census, *Statistical Abstract of the United States* (Washington, D.C.: GPO, 1973), p. 114.

telligence, socioeconomic status, and motivation from the less well endowed. Some writers have attempted to assess these factors and to attribute the largest part of the differential to educational experience rather than environmental factors, but there is considerable doubt about this conclusion.

In the United States higher education has been perceived by persons from low-income backgrounds as an important means of upward social mobility. To some extent this belief stems from the observation that college-educated persons have had higher incomes and less unemployment, especially during depressions such as that of the 1930s, when many of those who suffered from unemployment and loss of income acquired strong motivations to educate their children in order to make them "depression proof."[4]

There seems to have been a similar rise in aspirations to go to college by low-income groups during the 1960s, undoubtedly because these groups suffered high unemployment rates during that period and because civil rights developments raised the aspirations of many blacks and other minorities. Before the 1960s the aspirations of high school graduates from all income groups increased gradually, but during the 1960s a new trend apparently set in, and the gap between the aspirations of the poor and those of the rich began to close. Indeed, the proportion of high school graduates in the lowest income quartile who aspired to college between 1959 and 1966 increased from 23 to 46 percent. In the second income quartile the proportion desiring to go to college increased from 40 to 52 percent, and the aspirations of those in the highest two quartiles rose from 52 to 65 percent and 68 to 74 percent, respectively. Nevertheless, although there was a dramatic closing of the gap, high school graduates from the lowest quartile aspired to college much less than those in the highest quartile. Whether our system of higher education is a force for social stability clearly will depend upon the extent to which the rising expectations are matched by opportunities to acquire higher education.

Although it has clear economic significance, higher education cannot be evaluated in monetary terms alone. The higher-education system does much to preserve those cultural and intellectual traditions that influence the quality of life. In this role institutions of higher education provide benefits, such as extending the general base of technology, contributing to the advancement of knowledge and the arts, and providing support for public leadership. These benefits accrue to society as well as to individuals and, therefore, cannot be measured in benefit-cost or market terms alone.

The American emphasis on formal education undoubtedly was intensified by a number of developments during and after World War II, which strengthened the conviction that education was important for national security. The emphasis on technology during the war gave considerable impetus to higher education, an impetus accelerated by the development of the atomic bomb and the space race in the postwar period. Clearly, much of the increased demand for college graduates following World War II was stimulated by the federal government. This stimulation resulted, in part, from the cold war, which gave considerable emphasis to national prestige derived from scientific and technical achievements and the rate of economic development. Federal support for education initially concentrated mainly on the physical sciences and engineering, but it was extended to other areas as the federal government sought to strengthen educational institutions during the 1960s. In addition, as was mentioned earlier, the federal government stimulated college enrollments after World War II through the GI Bill and to some extent by granting draft deferments or exemptions to college students during the 1960s.

Postwar population developments also influenced the demand for college graduates. The college-age population declined during the 1950s because of the low birth rates during the depression of the 1930s and World War II. Indeed, there were actually fewer 15- to 24-year-olds in 1950 than there had been in 1930, even though the total population increased 45 percent during those years. As a consequence of these developments, there was only a slight increase in college enrollments in the 1950s, resulting mainly from a rising trend in the proportion of college-age people going to college rather than from an increase in the numbers of people in the college-age group. During the 1960s, the number of college graduates increased greatly because of the coming of age of those born during the postwar baby boom. The number of bachelor's or equivalent degrees increased from 187,000 in the 1940s to 287,000 in 1956 and 505,000 in 1965. The graduation of the postwar baby boom generation and the lower rate of population growth during the 1960s and 1970s are expected to cause the demand for teachers to be lower during the 1970s and 1980s relative to the supply than was the case during the 1950s and 1960s.

Enrollment in higher-education institutions

There is great diversity in the American system of higher educa-tion. There are over 8.5 million students at the postsecondary level in a great variety of institutions. About 60 percent of the class hours offered to these students are in the social sciences, humani-ties, liberal arts, and law; 17 percent are in the physical sciences; 10 percent are in fine arts and applied arts; the remainder are in computer sciences and other fields.[5] About three-fifths of the class hours offered by American postsecondary institutions are at the freshman and sophomore levels; 29 percent are in upper-division courses, and about 8 percent are graduate courses.

The number of college graduates at all degree levels has sharply accelerated since World War II and is expected to con-tinue to increase, although at not so fast a percentage rate (Table 9-2). During the decade of the 1960s, the number of new college

Table 9-2 Actual and Projected Earned Degrees, 1940–1980

Academic Year Ending June 30	Bachelor's and First Professional Degrees	Master's Degrees	Ph.D.'s
1940	186,500	26,731	3,290
1948	271,000	42,000	4,200
1958	363,000	65,000	8,900
1968	667,000	177,000	23,100
1969	755,000	189,000	26,100
1970	772,000	211,000	29,000
1971	878,000	231,000	32,107
1975ᵃ	928,000	302,000	45,600
1980ᵃ	1,074,000	382,000	59,600

ᵃProjected.

Source: Figure for 1940 from U.S. Bureau of the Census, *Statistical Abstract of the United States* (Washington, D.C.: GPO, 1969). Other figures taken from U.S. Department of Labor, *Manpower Report of the President* (Wash-ington, D.C.: GPO, 1970), p. 164. Figure for 1971 from U.S. Bureau of the Census, *Statistical Abstract of the United States* (Washington, D.C.: GPO, 1973), p. 136.

graduates more than doubled, rising to over 1 million in 1970, with two-thirds of the increase coming in the last half of the decade. The percentage increase in graduate degrees (168 percent and 205 percent for master's and doctor's degrees respectively) was much faster than the increase in bachelor's degrees (113 percent).[6]

There was considerable variation in degrees awarded according to field during the 1960s. At the bachelor's and master's levels degrees awarded in the natural sciences and engineering declined relatively (from 29 percent of all degrees in 1960–1961 to 22 percent in 1970–1971 for bachelor's and 25 and 20 percent respectively for master's), while the proportion of doctor's degrees in the natural sciences and engineering declined only slightly—from 48 percent in 1960–1961 to 46 percent in 1970–1971.

Based on the college-age population and the trends in the college-age population going to college, the U.S. Office of Education estimates that 13.6 million degrees will be awarded during the 1970s—9.8 million bachelor's, 3.4 million master's, and 0.475 million doctorates. However, only about 9.8 million college graduates are expected to enter the labor force. At the same time, demand for college graduates is expected to be as follows:

Source of Demand	Projected Demand for New College-Educated Workers 1970 to 1980, in Millions
Employment expansion	3.3
Educational upgrading	2.6
Replacement	3.7
Total	9.6

Thus these figures indicate a rough overall balance between demand and supply for college graduates, reflecting a turnabout in the demand-and-supply relations of earlier years, when the demand for college graduates exceeded the supply. For example, employment of professional and technical workers peaked at 11.1 million in 1970 and leveled off after 1971, even though the number of new graduates seeking to enter these jobs continued to increase. As a consequence, unemployment among professional and technical workers increased by 125 percent between 1969 and 1971 to 2.9 percent. However, the professional-technical unemployment rate was still considerably lower than the 5.9 percent for the entire labor force at that time.

Because of the rising demand for vocational and technically trained workers, the lower cost of education in junior colleges and community colleges, and the decline in demand relative to supply for college graduates, enrollment in two-year colleges is expected to continue to rise in the 1970s and 1980s. Between 1951 and 1969 enrollments in four-year institutions increased by 99 percent compared with 241 percent in two-year institutions. It is expected that two-year colleges will increase their proportion of college enrollments from about one-fourth in 1970 (compared with 16 percent in 1960) to 34 percent in 1980 and 43 percent in 1990.[7]

Outlook for college graduates

We should enter a word of caution about projections of the demand for and supply of college graduates. Although some aspects of these demand-and-supply conditions are fairly predictable, especially those that depend heavily on population projections, others are not as predictable, particularly those related to demand or to distant future events. In the long run, even population growth patterns change, as they did during the late 1960s and immediately following World War II. Projections also are complicated by biases in judgment, especially when those making the projections have vested interests in the outcome of those projections. For example, Cartter warns that federal agencies, such as the U.S. Office of Education, "cannot always be expected to be the frankest analysts of the needs in their own areas of concern" because "they must go to Congress each year for budget appropriations."[8] Despite these uncertainties, however, projections of probable developments in the demand for and supply of college graduates provide better individual and public planning than would be possible without these projections.

The supply of college graduates

The most important factors influencing the future supplies of college graduates are the proportions of college-age people in the population and the proportion of these who complete college. On the demographic side, college enrollments can be predicted with a fair degree of accuracy by looking at the proportion of 18-year-old high school graduates who go to college. In 1970 the tendency was for about 61 percent of 18-year-olds who graduated from high school to go to college and 12 percent to other postsecondary schools. Of those who enter college about one-half graduate.

A major factor affecting college enrollments during the 1970s and 1980s will be the low fertility rates of the late 1960s and early 1970s; there actually will be fewer high school graduates in 1986 (3,158,000) than in 1975 (3,459,000), even assuming that the proportion of 18-year-olds who graduate from high school will continue increasing at about 1 percent a year so that about 90 percent of them graduate by 1982. The number of 18-year-olds will peak at

4,344,000 in 1979 (as compared with 3,614,000 in 1969), decline to 3,509,000 in 1986, and rise gradually thereafter. The 16-to-21-year-old college-age population will peak in 1980 at 17,033,000, decline to 14,273,000 in 1988, and increase gradually thereafter. As a consequence of these developments, college enrollments in full-time equivalents will increase from 5,810,000 in 1968 to 9,834,000 in 1982 and decline thereafter to 8,541,000 in 1988.

The supply of college graduates increased sharply during the 1960s and is likely to continue rising during the 1970s, but it will decline in line with the previously mentioned enrollment trends during the 1980s. According to projections by the U.S. Office of Education, the number of bachelor's and first professional degrees probably will increase from 667,000 in 1968 to about 1.1 million in 1980, or by approximately 60 percent. These projections assume: (1) the trends in the college-age population just discussed and (2) the continuance of recent upward trends in college enrollment and graduation rates.

An even greater increase in graduate than in baccalaureate degrees is projected by the U.S. Department of Labor, based on the assumptions that past trends of those graduates obtaining higher degrees will continue and that there will be greatly expanded support of higher education. The growth in the number of M.A.'s awarded is projected at well over 100 percent between 1968 and 1980 (from 177,000 to 382,000), in Ph.D.'s at more than 150 percent (from 23,100 to 59,600). In absolute numbers, 13.3 million degrees are expected to be awarded during the period 1968–1980—10.2 million B.A.'s, 2.7 million M.A.'s, and 400,000 Ph.D.'s.

Supply and demand relationships

As noted earlier, on the basis of Department of Labor projections, it appears that there will be a rough overall balance between the supply of college-educated workers and the requirements for them in professional and other fields. Demand will total about 9.6 million over the 1970–1980 period, and 9.8 million new college graduates are expected to enter the labor force. There will still be imbalances between supply and demand in some individual occupations and specialties as well as in some areas such as small cities and rural communities.

Teachers

The outlook for teachers is important for higher education because about three-fourths of all jobs defined as requiring college education are in teaching; teachers totaled 2.7 million professionals in 1970, the largest group in that category. On the elementary and secondary levels, the aggregate supply is expected to exceed the demand significantly if recent entry patterns in the occupation continue. The number of new college graduates seeking to enter elementary school teaching during the 1970–1980 period could be nearly double the projected demand, and the number seeking secondary school positions could be nearly 75 percent above requirements. It is predicted that the supply of potential teachers holding advanced degrees will grow more rapidly than the college population. The Commission on Human Resources and Advanced Education predicts that after 1970 the demand for college teachers with less than a Ph.D. degree will decline sharply. There might be some additional opportunities for teachers without a Ph.D. in expanding nondegree programs in four-year institutions, junior and community colleges, predominantly black colleges, and in extension, mail, and TV teaching.

In spite of the projected excess supply of teachers, it still appears that shortages will remain in rural and city ghetto schools and in the fields of remedial education, specialized education for handicapped children, preschool and kindergarten teaching, and vocational education.

Health Manpower

There are and probably will still be critical shortages in health occupations in the United States in 1980. The U.S. Public Health Service estimates that the shortage of physicians is probably as high as 50,000, a shortage rate of approximately 15 percent, even though professional health workers grew by almost 450,000 between 1960 and 1970. The shortage would be even higher were it not for immigrant doctors, who comprise approximately 14 percent of all physicians in the country. The limited capacity of medical schools is a major cause of the shortage of doctors, but supply imbalances also result from the tendency of doctors to concentrate in larger cities and to avoid small towns and rural areas, many of which have grossly inadequate medical facilities. The outlook for the dentistry profession is much the same, and there already is a severe shortage of nurses and paraprofessionals in virtually all segments of the health services industry—hospitals, nursing homes, offices of medical practitioners, and medical laboratories. The passage of a national health insurance program would put considerable additional strain on the nation's limited health resources.[9]

Natural Scientists and Engineers

Regardless of short-term fluctuations in employment opportunities, which result mainly from cutbacks of federal research and development funds, the long-term employment outlook for scientists and engineers appears to be one of strong growth. Between 1960 and 1970 employment of scientists increased by over 200,000 and engineers by over 300,000. The increase in demand for engineers is projected by the Department of Labor at about 40 percent between 1968 and 1980; for natural scientists the projected growth is about 50 percent. To meet projected requirements approximately 45,000 engineering graduates and slightly under 45,000 new scientists will be needed annually. For natural scientists this would include an average of over 20,000 openings per year for physical scientists, over 15,000 for biological scientists, and close to 8,000 for mathematicians. Recent enrollment trends indicate that this need for natural scientists can be met on an overall basis. For engineers, however, U.S. Office of Education projections indicate that the supply will fall slightly short of the demand.

On the whole, the United States should be experiencing the end of a general shortage of trained scientific manpower. Naturally, supply deficits in specialties will still occur, such as in new programs in marine science and environmental control. It also appears that there will be shortages of chemists, geologists, and geophysicists. Other areas for which potential shortages of professionals are in prospect include counseling, social work, urban planning, and a variety of jobs related to the planning and administration of local government.

Technicians

Bureau of Labor Statistics Projections indicate that about 1.4 million engineering and scientific technicians will be employed in 1980. This represents an increase of over 50 percent above the 1966 total of 885,000. Physics and mathematics technicians are expected to have the fastest rates of growth. Engineering technicians are expected to grow more than 50 percent, from 300,000 total in 1966 to 450,000 in 1980. The balance between supply and demand will be improved if there is a continuation of the current trend toward expansion of enrollment in technical-training programs offered in junior colleges, technical institutes, and area vocational schools.

Women

The number of women seeking a college education is rapidly rising. In the fall of 1970 the total number of women college students was 3.1 million, about two and a half times the number ten years earlier. The number of women receiving bachelor's and first professional degrees increased from 77,000 in 1940 to 343,000 in 1970 and is expected to reach 620,000 by 1981. There has also been a steady rise in the number of women pursuing graduate studies. Between 1957 and 1968 the proportion of M.A. recipients who were women rose from 33 to 36 percent, and female recipients of doctorates rose from 11 to 13 percent of the total. In 1970 women received 83,241 M.A.'s compared with 126,146 for men; the comparable figures for Ph.D.'s were 25,892 for men and 3,980 for women.

Due to the changing supply-and-demand situation in teaching, college-educated women will have to shift their pattern of employment if they are to hold jobs matching their abilities. It is expected that more women will enter nursing, social work, nutrition, library science, and other traditional women's professions, but that the demand requirements of these fields will not be sufficient to meet the increasing supply of female college graduates.

Some limited inroads have been made by women college graduates in the traditional male fields of social sciences, psychology, health technology, physical and occupational therapy, editing and reporting, accounting, mathematics, and statistics. However, in law, medicine, dentistry, engineering, and architecture—all shortage occupations—the proportion of women remains very small. For example, in 1968 women represented only 7 percent of the nation's physicians, 2 percent of all dentists, less than 1 percent of the engineers, and only 3 percent of the craftsmen.

Changing employer attitudes, emphasis on equality of opportunity, pressure by women's groups, and better preparation of women indicate that the employment of women will adjust to manpower requirements of the 1970s better than in the past.

Workers with postgraduate degrees

There are likely to be considerable adjustments in the market for people with postgraduate degrees during the 1970s and early 1980s because graduate schools are expected to turn out 30–50 percent more degree holders than can be used in the jobs traditionally available to them. The most significant demand adjustment will be for college teachers. This relationship can be projected from college enrollments, because for each 100,000 new students, about 5,000 new teachers are required. Therefore, because of the enrollment trends discussed earlier, the demand for college teachers will decline absolutely between 1984 and 1989. The ratio of the output of Ph.D.'s to the demand for college teachers will increase from 2.5 percent in 1965–1969 to 9.5 percent in 1980–1984. Of course, all Ph.D.'s do not go into teaching. There is, however, considerable variation by fields in the extent to which Ph.D.'s enter

Table 9-3   Students with Federally Supported Predoctoral Fellowships and Traineeships, 1961–1970

Academic Year Ending June 30	Number of Students Aided (in thousands)	Percent of All Full-Time Graduate Enrollments
1961	9.4	7.5
1965	22.3	11.3
1966	28.3	12.3
1967	41.7	16.1
1968	53.6	17.8
1969	53.7	16.9
1970	45.1[a]	n.a.

[a]Preliminary.

Source: U.S. Department of Labor, *Manpower Report of the President* (Washington, D.C.: GPO, 1970), p. 165.

teaching: about 90 percent for English and anthropology and about 33 percent for chemistry and physics.

Those fields that have had a low percentage of Ph.D's in teaching are expected to experience the greatest oversupply of Ph.D.'s during the 1980s. This is largely because the fluctuations in nonacademic demand have hit this group hardest. The decline in federal aid has been particularly important (Table 9-3).

During 1956–1966, nonfederal research and development, or R & D, expenditures increased at a rate of about 7.5 percent a year in real terms (adjusted for price changes). During this period, federal R & D support to universities increased about 14 percent a year in real terms, and federal R & D support to non-

Table 9-4   Ratio of New Ph.D.'s to Faculty Needs, 1970 and 1980
[a]National Research Council.

Field	1970			1980		
	NRC[a]	OE[b]	AMC[c]	NRC	OE	AMC
Chemistry	4.1	3.9	4.1	9.0	6.6	6.1
Physics	4.7	4.6	4.7	11.2	7.9	8.1
Biology	3.1	2.7	3.1	10.0	4.5	5.4
Mathematics	3.3	3.6	3.2	6.6	8.4	5.5

[a]National Research Council.

[b]U.S. Office of Education.

[c]Allan M. Cartter.

Source: Allan M. Cartter, "Scientific Manpower for 1970–1985," *Science*, Vol. 172 (April 9, 1971), p. 136.

academic agencies increased by 10 percent a year. However, between 1963 and 1970, total federal R & D support declined about 2 percent a year in real terms, amounting to a decline of about $0.5 billion. Because the reductions hit the physical sciences hardest, the demand-supply imbalances in these fields are likely to be particularly large during the 1980s (Table 9-4).

However, not all Ph.D.'s are employed in universities, and these projections of oversupply for traditional jobs are not expected to be very serious until during the 1980s and perhaps not even then, as we shall argue later. Charles E. Falk's study of the total supply and utilization of science and engineering doctorates projected no large oversupply during the 1968–1980 period.

The approximately 147,000 Ph.D. scientists in 1968 were utilized as follows:[10]

Activity	Percent
Research and development	48
Teaching	38
Other	14
Sector Analysis	
Universities and colleges	59
Private industry	26
Government	10
Other	5

Falk notes that the labor market for this sector had moved from a situation of widespread shortages to a rough equilibrium by 1968. Although the job market had tightened considerably for science and engineering doctorates, as shown by a decline in the number of placement offers and an increase in the use of more formal placement procedures, it was estimated that less than 1 percent were unemployed and that less than 1 percent were engaged in occupations outside their area of training.

By projecting future enrollments in the science areas (at both the graduate and undergraduate levels) and by taking into account projected retirements, deaths, emigrations, and so forth, out of the sector, Falk projected a future supply of expected doctorates of 320,000 to 350,000. These figures are likely to be maximum estimates because there is some evidence of shifts of student interest away from the sciences. A 10 percent decrease in doctorate production in the last half of the 1970s would decrease the supply to 335,000; a 20 percent decrease during those years would lower the supply to 320,000.

Also assumed was a growth rate of 14 to 20 percent in the ratio of doctorates engaged in the so-called other activities (such as management, industrial operations, etc.). This basic utilization method indicated a 1980 utilization level of 277,000 to 301,000—slightly below the minimum supply projections. However, the basic utilization estimate does not provide any improvements in the utilization of scientists. An alternative projection provided for the following changes (based on the ratio of doctorates to non-doctorates): (1) graduate faculty from 85 to 95 percent; (2) other four-year faculty from 50 to 75 percent; and (3) two-year faculty from 8 to 16 percent. Other changes were that R & D spending would return to the growth rate exhibited during 1953–1966—about 10 percent per annum for federal R & D spending and about 7 percent per annum for private spending. It also was assumed that the ratio of doctorates engaged in "other" activities would increase to 25 percent.

Given these modifications, Falk derived the following projections:

Type of Modification	1980 Utilization (in thousands)
(1) Basic projection	277–301
(2) Return to previously experienced R & D funding growth rates	337–342
(3) Increase in doctorates (total faculty in postsecondary educational institutions)	300–334
(4) Increase in doctorates in "other" activities/total doctorates from 20 percent to 25 percent	296–310
(5) (2) plus (3)	365–370
(6) (2) plus (4)	349–365
(7) (3) plus (4)	320–343
(8) (2) plus (3) plus (4)	383–389

Note: The variance in utilization estimates derives from different estimating procedures—depending upon whether employment of scientists is broken down by sector or by activity.

With respect to the implications of his study, Falk concluded that significant numbers of Ph.D.'s are likely to be engaged in activities that are markedly different from those of most present doctorate holders. It is very important, therefore, that new Ph.D.'s be offered a variety of options of graduate training programs, including some that are more suitable for these new activities. Furthermore, students must not be educated with false aspirations for solely research careers. At the same time, it is very important that society transmit to graduate students an awareness that careers other than in reasearch play an important role in both national and scientific affairs.

Whether these projections are realized will depend on a number of factors, especially: (1) what happens to nonacademic demand for Ph.D.'s; (2) the ease with which supplies can adjust to demand; and (3) the validity of enrollement projections. There is little question about the enrollment projections through the last part of the 1980s because all of those who will be of college age at that time already have been born. The nonacademic demand for Ph.D.'s is the most questionable variable, but it will probably increase at least slightly. There can be some adjustment of supply to demand, but, as we shall see, the labor market for college graduates is very imperfect, and supplies are not likely to adjust to reduced demand very rapidly. The more prestigious private universities undoubtedly will cut their Ph.D output because they are in financial difficulties, which are likely to deepen during the 1970s unless they get more government support. Because graduate education is very expensive, this is one area in which to save money. Balanced against this, however, are a number of factors that tend to sustain the Ph.D. supply: (1) establishment of new Ph.D. programs in state universities; (2) the time (five to seven years) that it takes the graduate pipelines to be cleared; (3) the fixed costs many universities have in graduate education require large outputs in order to reduce the cost per student; and (4) the rising aspirations of women and minority groups to participate in the occupations requiring graduate training.

It would, however, be a mistake to conclude from these demand-and-supply relationships that many people with graduate degrees are going to be unemployed. As both Falk and Cartter emphasize, those with these degrees undoubtedly will move into jobs previously held by those with lower degrees. Moreover, as noted earlier, there will be considerable variation in demand for graduates and undergraduates in individual occupations.

Conclusions on the outlook for college graduates

The United States is thus entering a new era with respect to its highly educated manpower—an era in which the demand for and supply of people with post–high school education will tend toward equality in many areas. This is in sharp contrast to the constant shortages that have characterized this employment sector since World War II. Although it is no coincidence that teachers, physicists, and others faced difficulties in finding jobs in 1969–1970, when the economy was experiencing its first recession since 1961, there are other long-term factors at work that seem to indicate that shortages of college-educated manpower will be alleviated. The impact of ever-increasing numbers of college graduates and doctorates is now being felt in the labor market. While this surplus benefits educational institutions—because they can now hire sufficient personnel to meet their needs at salaries that are more favorable from their point of view—it also results in frustration and dissatisfaction among students who have invested a considerable amount of time and money in the hope of finding challenging, well-paying jobs in their desired fields. However, the frustration of college graduates is likely to represent a crisis of expectations rather than a problem of unemployment. An American Institute of Physics survey found that 57 percent of doctorate holders wanted to work in universities, where there were declining job opportunities; almost none wanted to work in junior colleges, and only 4 percent wanted to work in government agencies.[11]

In time, the market undoubtedly will cause highly educated workers to be more evenly dispersed throughout the work force, but the adjustment process is not very rapid, even though salary appears to be a major, although not exclusive, factor in occupational choice. Because of the long periods of training required for members of this labor market, however, such responses tend to be "lagged"—often by as much as five years. Thus while long-run adjustments move toward the desired equilibrium and allocation, short-run fluctuations remain troublesome. The operation of the market for educated manpower is discussed in the following section.

The character of the market for educated manpower

Despite widespread shortcomings, college-educated manpower labor markets do function in occupations in which much education is required and in which it takes considerable time for supply to adjust to demand. This is true not only because of the time taken for education but also because once young people do one or two semesters of work in their chosen fields in college, there apparently are very limited changes in direction possible. Moreover, the market for educated manpower is not one homogeneous market but many discrete markets with separate demand-and-supply characteristics. As a consequence of market imperfections, to be explored at greater length next, there is considerable waste of high-level manpower because of limited knowledge about the relationship between education and work requirements and over-staffing of college-educated manpower during times of manpower shortage.

The primary adjustment and allocative mechanism of college-educated manpower is its labor market. The terms "shortage" and "surplus" are essentially market related, and it is natural for the economist to use the market as an indicator of either of those manpower conditions. Critical shortages in particular occupations should reveal themselves through relative salary gains; surpluses, through relative salary declines. During the mid-1950s, for example, when private and government voices were expressing deep concern about the critical shortage of engineers, an economic study revealed that engineers' salaries were actually lagging behind those of many professional groups—a kind of market behavior that would not suggest acute scarcity. Thus while the many different definitions of scarcity as applied to the labor market and other conceptual difficulties must be overcome, the market provides a frame of reference for verifying and quantifying conflicting statements concerning the value and utilization of college-educated manpower.

The market for educated manpower is complicated by a number of factors. First, demand and supply are interrelated to the extent that the amount supplied to the market (in the form of college graduates, etc.) determines, in part, the degree of utilization by those demanding the services of educated persons. Thus it becomes very difficult to predict and quantify the demand. The supply of highly educated manpower also tends to be inelastic in the short run, causing the burden of short-run adjustment to be placed upon salary increases or substitution of less-qualified personnel.

The labor reserve of an occupation—defined as "those persons who are trained and qualified to work in an occupation and who last worked in that occupation but are not currently employed"[12] —also is a means of adjustment, especially in those occupations such as nursing, teaching, and social work that employ a high proportion of women. The labor reserve has the advantage of being a potentially rapid form of adjustment—as much as 5 to 10 percent in several years' time. Salary levels are probably not as important in influencing those in the labor reserve as opportunities for part-time work and work schedules that fit children's school schedules.

The short-run forces that operate through the labor market determine the current salary level, and this is undoubtedly related to entry on the supply side of the market for educated manpower. But the relationship between salary and long-run supply is ambiguous and hazy. There seems to be no real consensus of opinion about the factors that affect entry into a given profession, although employment does seem to expand most rapidly in those fields with the highest lifetime earnings, after allowances have been made for costs and nonpecuniary benefits.

Analysis of supply-and-demand conditions is also complicated by the fact that few labor markets are closed. Because workers cross international boundaries, it is not possible to restrict market analysis to factors influencing domestic demand-and-supply conditions. In 1969, for example, approximately 10,300 scientists and engineers migrated to the United States, and, as noted earlier, about 14 percent of medical doctors were immigrants. Although it is not known how many of these people obtained employment in their professions, in view of the past shortage situations, it is likely that most of them were able to do so. There are few data on the number of college-trained people who migrated from the United States. The number of immigrants in 1969 was 20 percent below the 1968 figures, primarily because of revisions in the immigration laws, and, in 1971, many highly trained foreigners were returning to their countries.

Shirley H. Rhine and Daniel Creamer estimate that 1800 scientists and 5100 engineers immigrated to the United States annually during the 1960s. This constituted about 9 percent of the net annual increase in scientists and 15 percent of the net annual increase in engineers.[13] If the net immigration turns to net outmigration during the 1970s, the pressure on the supply side of the U.S. market for these workers will be relieved somewhat.

Career choices are also influenced to some degree by volatile events, such as the current social issues facing the nation. This would help to explain the increase in beginning students' plans to major in social sciences during 1961–1965, when there was considerable ferment over race, manpower, and poverty problems. We might also expect the current environmental crisis to expand enrollments in biology and other ecologically related courses. However, using intentions of students entering college to predict future supply is usually not very successful because as many as 50 percent of all undergraduates change their plans between their freshman and senior years.

In the past the response to short-run problems has been focused upon expanding the educational output, and this method of adjustment can do little to relieve manpower problems in the short run. This lack of adjustment results in large measure from the considerable time lags in adjustments of supply to demand for highly educated manpower. High current salaries seem to induce many people to enter a field, but when they graduate, the large supply tends to depress wages unless something happens to increase demand. The relatively low salaries then tend to reduce the supply of people entering the field.

Another reason for the rapid changes in this labor market is found in the accelerator concept. Such change is especially prevalent in higher education, where a relatively fixed ratio is maintained between faculty and enrollment. Marginal increases in enrollment can cause a large increase in the number of teachers required, just as decreases in the rate of increase in enrollment (as was expected in the 1970s) can cause the demand for new teachers to fall rapidly.

Although the terms "shortage" and "surplus" are used to describe the demand-supply relationship in the labor market, these terms can be defined in a number of ways. Also, serious problems of interpretation of relative salary trends result from a labor market disequilibrium. In one sense, shortage means that the actual number is less than the number dictated by some social goal. However, this is a difficult concept to use because no objective measure of it is possible. A second type of shortage is the so-called wage-rise shortage, which occurs when demand increases faster than supply at the prevailing market wage, and, as a result, competitive forces increase wages. However, such an approach has its conceptual problems. If a shortage is never defined as anything other than a price rise and the analysis is always in terms of relative prices, the awkward situation is predicted in which there might be a shortage of engineers relative to teachers but not relative to medical doctors. For example, Blank and Stigler concluded that there was no shortage of engineers from 1929 to 1954 because the ratio of median engineering salaries to the average wage and salary of full-time employees had declined from 100 in 1929 to 67.9 in 1954.[14]

A third type of shortage is dynamic in nature and consists of job vacancies caused by salaries temporarily too low to clear the market. If, for example, employers do not raise salaries sufficiently fast in response to rising demand, dynamic shortages exist which ultimately would be eliminated by rising salaries. Kenneth J. Arrow and William M. Capron think that one of the causes of alleged shortages in various disciplines is caused by this reluctance (or inability to pay the necessary equilibrium rate). Using the postwar family-servant market as an example, they state:

> . . . at the price they had been paying for household help, many families found they could no longer find such people (household servants). Rather than admit that they could not pay the higher

wages necessary to keep help, many individuals found it more felicitous to speak of a "shortage." There is reason to think that at least some of the complaints of shortage in the scientist-engineer market have the same cause.[15]

Such dynamic shortages could take place readily in view of the very high skill requirements in many of the markets for workers with higher educations. In a short-run situation a drastic rise in going salary might entice only a few more entrants into the market. And the nature of. the process of career selection, while definitely having some relationship to earnings, is sufficiently vague to warrant an opinion that a salary increase, even of a large magnitude, might not affect the supply of talent in the manner predicted by traditional economic theory—namely, a shift outward.

The final type of shortage involves what is called projected, or cumulative, supply shortfalls and excesses. In this instance the supply of a particular occupation is projected, based upon certain arbitrary ratios such as enrollments and student populations, and then the supply projections are compared with utilization or demand projections. The difference between the two projections enables the forecaster to predict either a supply shortfall or a supply excess. Although this approach is useful, it presents two difficulties. First, past trends must necessarily be used to determine ratios such as employment and enrollment, and there may be no basis for assuming that such ratios will remain the same in the future. But this is a problem faced by all future predictions. Second, there is the problem of determining demand because the supply of manpower will influence the degree of utilization.

Because the demand for labor is a derived demand, some of the market imperfections for educated manpower are caused by the nature of the product market. For example, private and public benefits from research, which is a heavy user of educated manpower, are apt to diverge in a market society. First, many of the benefits of private research activity cannot be capitalized in the market. Firms, for example, have great difficulty in extracting the full economic value of knowledge that, once sold, can be resold in the market. This causes private benefits from research to be much less than the social benefits. As a consequence, the competitive market will cause inadequate basic research to be done.

Attempts to rectify this divergence by using patents or permitting royalties to be charged for private information do not solve the problem because such measures tend to impede widespread application of new and useful ideas. Moreover, R & D costs for a particular research project financed by private enterprise over a definite time period probably are subject to the law of diminishing returns, but because individual projects may complement each other, research expenditures as a whole may not be subject to that particular phenomenon. Thus the wide variety of projects undertaken yields total benefits that are greater than the sum of the individual project benefits.

The risk, uncertainty, and the length of time between project conception and fruition also may make it difficult to finance research entirely through market mechanisms. It is not always possible to anticipate the results of research. Moreover, more research might be desirable for purposes of general education and the advancement of knowledge unrelated to the *profitability* of the investments. In a sense, of course, the market might allocate research personnel after policy makers decided to expend funds for this purpose.

Labor market experience of recent college graduates

The labor market experiences of college graduates varies according to sex and field of study, as reflected in a survey of 1.1 million college graduates sponsored by the Manpower Administration of the U.S. Department of Labor.[16] Labor market experience also varies according to race, but the proportion of blacks in the survey—7 percent—was too small to provide much useful information for comparisons. This survey of those who graduated from college during 1970–1971 was undertaken in October 1971. Those surveyed were about equally divided between those who graduated in 1970 and those who graduated in 1971.

According to this study, 92.9 percent of those surveyed were employed, and 70 percent were employed in jobs directly related to their major fields of study. However, there was considerable variation among major fields in the percentages working in areas unrelated to their college majors. About 60 percent of social sciences majors were working in such unrelated jobs as compared with the following proportions of those in other fields: humanities, 50 percent; business and commerce, 8.5 percent; and all others, 8.3 percent. The all-others category includes professionals, who are very likely to be working in occupations related to their major fields. As might be expected, those who took jobs related to their majors earned considerably more than those who took unrelated jobs. Most of those who took unrelated jobs did so because this was the only employment they could find; two-thirds of the women and one-half of the men who took unrelated jobs give this reason for taking the jobs they held at the time of the survey. Many of those in the unrelated positions considered these jobs to be temporary until they could find something better.

Those who looked for jobs after graduation indicated using the following major sources to seek jobs:

	Percent
Direct application to the employer	41
Friends or relatives	21
School placement	18

The experience of men and women were similar with respect to job search methods, except that half of the women and only about a third of the men found their jobs through direct application to employers.

There was considerable variation in salaries paid the college graduates surveyed. The median annual salary was $6,633 for those with bachelor's degrees and $10,158 for all others, most of who had master's degrees. Over half of the graduates said their earnings were lower than they expected; only 11 percent of the men and 8 percent of the women graduates said they were earning more than they expected.

There also were substantial earning differences among industries and by sex. Men tended to have relatively higher earnings in private employment while women earned more working for governments. Of full-time male workers, half of those who worked in private industry, but only 23 percent of those in government work, earned $8000 a year or more. For women 48 percent of those in government employment, but only 23 percent of those who worked for private employees, earned $7000 a year or more.

Not only did women earn less than men, but they also were concentrated into fewer occupations. Although about 70 percent of both men and women graduates were professionals, 50 percent of the women and only 20 percent of the men professionals were teaching at the elementary and secondary levels. The only other area with as much as 5 percent of women professionals was health services. Five percent or more of the men professionals were college teachers, engineers, and health and medical professionals. Eighteen percent of women were in clerical occupations as compared with only 7 percent of men.

This survey thus suggests that college graduates are less likely to be unemployed than high school graduates. It also shows that graduates who take professional jobs related to their majors are likely to earn more and perceive more career potential in their jobs than graduates who take nonprofessional jobs unrelated to their major fields.

Women are concentrated in fewer occupations and tend to earn less than men, but women professionals have considerable labor market advantage over women nonprofessionals. Moreover, women are likely to earn relatively higher salaries working for the government, while men earn relatively more in the private sector.

Conclusions on the market for educated manpower

As noted in Chapter 7, labor markets are basic economic institutions, although we need to know much more than we do about how they operate. There are many kinds of interrelated labor markets. For example, there are many differences among the markets for people with postgraduate and undergraduate degrees, and, within the professional labor market, the market for medical manpower is quite different from the market for economists or attorneys, although they have certain things in common and both fall into what we define as the professional labor market in Chapter 7. We have noted, however, that labor markets for educated manpower do operate in rough conformity with economic theory and undoubtedly could be improved considerably by reducing the barriers to market adjustments, including the barriers to entry to undergraduate and professional schools.

However, even if the labor market for educated manpower were perfected, we have noted that it would not perform such functions as basic research, preservation of cultural values, and the advancement of knowledge, all of which are essential to the quality of life, very effectively. These decisions, therefore, must continue to be made by public policy or private nonprofit groups.

The socioeconomic status of college students

There is considerable evidence that the opportunity to attend college depends very heavily on socioeconomic status as well as on race. Perhaps the most important evidence of this was produced by Project TALENT, sponsored by the U.S. Office of Education, which found a very high correlation between socioeconomic status and the probability of entering college. Socioeconomic status of families is based on income, father's educational attainment, and several other factors within ability quintiles. In the top ability quintile, 95 percent of all high-socioeconomic-status high school graduates, but only 50 percent of low-socioeconomic-status high school graduates, attended college. In the bottom ability quintile, 40 percent of high-socioeconomic-status high school graduates, but only 15 percent of low-socioeconomic-status high school graduates attended college. Moreover, in 1966, 46 percent of students' families, but only 14 percent of all families, had incomes of $10,000 or more per year. At the other end of the income scale, 14 percent of all families, but only 4 percent of students' families, had income of less than $3000 per year. There also is considerable variation in the kinds of institutions of higher education that high- and low-income families are likely to attend. For example, students from high-income families are less likely to attend junior colleges but are more likely to attend larger institutions and schools where students make high grades on aptitude tests.[17] In 1970 only 34 percent of family members 18 to 24 years of age in families with incomes under $5,000 were enrolled in college, as compared with 60 percent of family members in these age groups in families with incomes of $15,000 and over.

Although the tests might have some bias in them, the general trend to use aptitude tests for admissions purposes probably has made it possible for many talented students from low-income families to attend college, especially when scholarships or fellowships are available to those with limited incomes and high abilities. According to John Gardner, former Secretary of the Department of Health, Education, and Welfare:

> Before the rise of objective tests, American teachers were susceptible—at least to some degree—to some social distortion of judgment. Against this background, modern methods of measurement hit the educational system like a breeze. The tests couldn't see whether the youngster was in rags or in tweeds, and they couldn't hear the accents of the slums. The tests heard the intellectual gifts of every level of the population.
>
> This is not to say that the tests completely eliminate unfair advantages for the young of privileged social background. They do not. But they are much more fair than any method previously used.[18]

Moreover, the tests also made it possible for teachers to identify talented youngsters who were doing poorly in school and adopt remedial programs to make it possible for them to develop. If Gardner is correct, the answer to greater educational opportunity is not to do away with tests but to perfect them and to make them more useful in predicting the college performance of youngsters from different backgrounds.

Our comments about the correlation between socioeconomic status and college attendance are not meant to imply that those who attend college have lower ability levels than those who do not. Indeed, the evidence suggests that of those going to college the number with ability is far greater than the number without. Although higher-income groups clearly have an advantage in attending college, there is a clear tendency for middle- and lower-class groups to increase their college attendance. The relative increase in the proportions of college entrants from the lower middle and lower classes were much higher than the proportionate increases of those from the upper middle class.

The higher education of black Americans

Although we do not know all of the reasons why some talented persons do not attend college, we do know that college education is not evenly distributed according to ability, social class, or race. The proportions of nonwhites who have completed at least one year of college are far below the proportion for whites in each age group.

As contrasted with other races, black college students come from families with much lower incomes. Blacks are, therefore, undoubtedly handicapped more than whites by financial barriers to education. Fifty-six percent of black students' parents had in 1968 incomes of less than $6,000 per year, while only 14.2 percent of the parents of nonblack students were in this income class. Moreover, 70.4 percent of the nonblack students' families had incomes of $8000 and above compared with only 27.5 percent for the families of black students. It is, therefore, not surprising that a survey by the American Council on Education indicated that financing education was a major concern for 20.6 percent of black freshmen compared with only 7.7 percent of nonblacks.[19]

Blacks are underrepresented in the nation's highest rated and most prestigious undergraduate schools. In 1966 they were twice as likely to be in schools rated low according to freshman aptitude scores and a third less likely to be in high-rated schools as whites. Nearly 1 in every 4 white students was enrolled in a high-rated college, but only 1 in 12 black students. In 1970 the Office of Civil Rights of the U.S. Department of Health, Education, and Welfare reported that blacks constituted 7 percent of all college students but only 4 percent of those in 63 highly prestigious schools. Even when states with few black residents were excluded from the totals, blacks accounted for only 3 percent of the enrollment on main state university campuses.[20]

Although black and white college dropout rates are similar, blacks tend to choose study areas with less certain economic payoffs. Only 7 percent of blacks major in engineering or math as compared with 13 percent of whites; 40 percent of blacks but only 28 percent of whites major in social science.[21]

Because black and white high school graduates compete in the same labor market, the relative quality of education of blacks is very important for manpower purposes. In this connection there is some concern about the relative quality of black and white education, at least as measured by aptitude test scores. One study claims, for example, that "the typical freshman (at a black college) usually performs at about ninth grade level" and that a "white student with the same aptitude as the typical Negro college entrant has only about one chance in ten of entering college and completing his freshman year in good academic standing."[22] There is considerable variation, however, in performance among predominantly black colleges and among black college students. Moreover, black colleges are not inferior because they are predominantly black but because of the cumulative effects of institutionalized discrimination.[23]

Although a number of studies, especially the Coleman Report,[24] have consistently discovered that black students fall further behind the longer they stay in school, other authorities have questioned the validity of the aptitude tests upon which these conclusions are based as predictors of success for black students. Kenneth B. Clark and Lawrence Plotkin, for example, report that blacks who generally scored low on the College Board Scholastic Aptitude Test (SAT) performed better in college than white students in the same colleges.[25] However, Berls concludes from an examination of this issue that "there is extensive and very careful evidence accumulated . . . to show that the SAT and similar tests predict Negro students' grades in Negro and integrated colleges just as well as they predict for white students."[26] Moreover, according to Berls, racial isolation causes the educational aspirations of blacks to be unrealistically high.

Equalization of the quality and quantity of black education would require considerable improvement in elementary, secondary, and college education available to blacks. However, improvement is not likely to occur at a very rapid rate, although integration of black elementary, secondary, and college students can accomplish a great deal toward equalizing educational opportunities. Most observers feel that the black colleges have an important role to play in improving the quality of black education. For one thing, many of the students attending black colleges could not gain admission to white colleges and would be denied educational improvement if the black colleges did not exist. The remedy, therefore, seems to be to improve the quality of black colleges and to attract white students to them rather than to seek admission of all black students to white colleges and universities. Moreover, it should be emphasized that improving the quality and amount of higher education alone is not likely to resolve the problem of unequal economic opportunities for blacks without improving the incomes of black families or making more scholarships available to blacks.

For those blacks who have earned college degrees, employment opportunities in both professional and managerial occupations increased greatly during the 1960s. Eighty percent of male black college graduates and 82 percent of female black college graduates were in professional and managerial occupations in 1969. These proportions were substantially higher than those for male and female whites. Effective change in industry and government hiring policy since the Civil Rights Act of 1964 have increased recruitment on predominantly black campuses, broadened curriculum offerings in traditionally black institutions, and widened opportunities for black graduates. The growing number of black enrollments in predominantly white colleges and universities, in addition to the factors listed previously, has been the major contributing factor to the opening of doors in professional and managerial occupations for blacks.

Conclusion

This chapter has demonstrated the close association between higher education and personal occupational mobility. However, the reader is reminded of the difficulties involved in establishing *causal* relations between income and education discussed in Chapter 8. Regardless of the experts' reservations about the returns to education, there is no question that higher education plays and will continue to play an important role in determining occupations. Moreover, these choices are made for many reasons other than anticipated economic returns. Improving the effectiveness of higher education for labor market considerations will require not only the basic kinds of educational reforms suggested in Chapter 8 but also the means to make it possible to equalize educational opportunities among racial and socioeconomic groups more on the basis of ability to profit by higher education than on the ability to pay for it from private family income.

Notes

1. Joseph Froomkin, *Aspirations, Enrollments, and Resources: The Challenge to Higher Education in the Seventies*, U.S. Department of Health, Education, and Welfare, Office of Education (Washington, D.C.: GPO, 1969), p. 10.

2. Edward F. Denison, *Why Growth Rates Differ* (Washington, D.C.: Brookings Institution, 1967); see also *idem, Accounting for United States Economic Growth, 1929–1969* (Washington, D.C.: Brookings Institution, 1974), pp. 207–246.
3. Allan M. Cartter, "The Economics of Higher Education," in Neil W. Chamberlain, ed., *Contemporary Economic Issues* (Homewood, Ill.: Irwin, 1969), p. 150.
4. E. Wight Bakke, *The Unemployed Worker and Citizens Without Work* (New Haven, Conn.: Yale University Press, 1940).
5. Froomkin, op. cit., Chap. 4.
6. Michael F. Crowley, "Professional Manpower: The Job Market Turnaround," *Monthly Labor Review* (October 1972), pp. 9–15.
7. Lawrence Southwick, Jr., "The Higher Education Industry: Forecasts to 1990," *Review of Social Economy* (April 1973), pp. 1–19.
8. Allan M. Cartter, "Scientific Manpower for 1970–1985," *Science,* Vol. 172 (April 9, 1971), p. 133.
9. Karen Davis, "National Health Insurance," in Barry M. Blechman et al., *Setting National Priorities,* (Washington, D.C.: Brookings Institution, 1974), pp. 243–246.
10. Charles E. Falk, *Science and Engineering Doctorate Supply and Utilization, 1968–1980,* NSF 69-37, National Science Foundation, p. 3.
11. "The Changing Job Market," *Science* (May 15, 1970), p. 781.
12. John K. Folger, Helen S. Astin, and Alan E. Bayer, *Human Resources and Higher Education,* Staff Report of the Commission on Human Resources and Advance Education (New York: Russell Sage Foundation, 1970), p. 352.
13. Shirley H. Rhine and Daniel Creamer, *The Technical Manpower Shortage: How Acute?* (New York: National Industrial Conference Board, 1969).
14. David M. Blank and George J. Stigler, *The Demand and Supply of Scientific Personnel* (New York: National Bureau of Economic Research, 1957), p. 23.
15. Kenneth J. Arrow and William M. Capron, "Dynamic Shortages and Price Rise: The Engineer-Scientist Case," *Quarterly Journal of Economics* (May 1959), p. 307.
16. Vera C. Perrella, *Employment of Recent College Graduates,* U.S. Bureau of Labor Statistics, Special Labor Force Report 151 (Washington, D.C.: GPO, 1973).
17. Roger E. Bolten, "The Economics and Financing of Higher Education: An Overview," in U.S. Congress, Joint Economic Committee, *The Economics and Financing of Higher Education in the United States,* 91st Cong., 1st Sess. (Washington, D.C.: GPO, 1969), Table 3-6, p. 64.
18. J. W. Gardner, *Excellence* (New York: Harper & Row, 1961), pp. 48–49.
19. Cited by Robert H. Berls, "Higher Education Opportunity and Achievement in the United States," in U.S. Congress, Joint

Economic Committee, *The Economics and Financing of Higher Education in the United States*, 91st Cong., 1st Sess. (Washington, D.C.: GPO, 1969), p. 183.

20. U.S. Department of Health, Education, and Welfare, *Racial and Ethnic Enrollment Data from Institutions of Higher Education, Fall 1970*, Part I (Washington, D.C.: GPO, 1972).
21. Derived from U.S. Bureau of the Census, School Enrollment, Series P-20, Annual Data.
22. Christopher Jencks and David Riesman, *The Academic Revolution* (Garden City, N.Y.: Doubleday, 1968), pp. 428–431.
23. Kenneth B. Clark, "Higher Education for Negroes: Challenges and Prospects," *Journal of Negro Education* (Summer 1967), p. 199.
24. James Coleman et al., *Equality of Educational Opportunity* (Washington, D.C.: GPO, 1966).
25. Kenneth B. Clark and Lawrence Plotkin, *The Negro Student in Integrated Colleges* (New York: National Scholarship Service and Fund for Negro Students, 1963).
26. Berls, op. cit., p. 188.

10
apprenticeship and on-the-job training

The basic idea behind apprenticeship is to have the trainee work with master workmen on the job while he acquires the necessary academic, or job-related, training in classroom situations. Ideally, apprenticeship produces well-rounded craftsmen who master the theory and practice of their trades and who, therefore, can adapt to a variety of work situations. Well-trained journeymen not only should be more productive than those with less training but also should be less vulnerable to the technological changes that might render obsolete the skills of narrow specialists.

Public policy

The basic federal law establishing apprenticeship policy is the National Apprenticeship (Fitzgerald) Act of 1937, administered by the Bureau of Apprenticeship and Training (BAT) in the U.S. Department of Labor. The BAT has a field staff and offices in every state, and its main function is to promote apprenticeship programs by giving technical assistance to unions and employers, who determine their own requirements and administer their own programs within the framework of broad standards laid down by the BAT or state apprenticeship agencies.

The administration of apprenticeship is complicated by the fact that, besides the federal programs, 30 states and Puerto Rico have programs of their own, containing over three-fourths of the nation's registered apprenticeship programs. These state programs are administered by state apprenticeship councils (SACs). The SACs take major responsibility for the registration of apprentices and the administration of apprenticeship programs in SAC states. There is, however, no clear line of jurisdiction between the functions of the SACs and BAT'S state and regional officials in SAC states.

The BAT approves state programs that meet certain minimum standards. To receive federal approval a state apprenticeship program must be administered by a state's department of labor. Other federal standards for apprenticeship programs include:

1. A starting age of not less than 16 years.
2. A schedule of work processes in which the apprentice is to receive training and experience on the job.
3. Organized instruction designed to provide the apprentice with knowledge in technical subjects related to his trade. (A minimum of 144 hours a year is normally considered necessary.)
4. A progressively increasing schedule of wages. Wages for apprentices ordinarily start at a certain proportion of the journeyman rate and progress to the journeyman levels over the period of the apprenticeship. Generally, the programs with relatively more applicants than openings (electrical, pipe trades, sheet metal workers) start apprentices at relatively lower proportions of the journeymen wages than those programs with fewer applicants relative to openings.
5. Proper supervision of on-the-job training with adequate facilities to train apprentices.
6. Periodic evaluation of the apprentice's progress, both in job performance and related instructions, and the maintenance of appropriate records.
7. Employer-employee cooperation.
8. Recognition for successful completions.
9. Selection of men and women for apprenticeship, without regard to race, creed, color, national origin, or physical handicap.[1]

If apprenticeship programs meet the standards set up by the Federal Committee on Apprenticeship and the state apprenticeship agencies, they can be registered by the BAT or the SAC, and those who successfully complete these programs are given certificates of completion either by the state agency or by the BAT.

Although some programs rely on correspondence courses for related instruction (and for keeping journeymen up to date), the public school system normally offers academic or job-related training and is financed by state, federal, and local funds. The Smith-Hughes (1917) and George-Barden (1946) Vocational Education acts provided for partial reimbursement from federal funds for salaries of teachers and vocational administrators to states with approved vocational plans. Some joint apprenticeship programs supplement the salaries of apprenticeship instructors. Moreover, an increasing number of programs seem to have their own training facilities for related instruction.

The local supervision of apprenticeship programs registered with the BAT usually is by Joint Apprenticeship Committees (JACs) representing labor and management. There are over 9000 joint apprenticeship committees; these committees may be national, state, or local in scope. Depending upon the trades, they usually are plant- or company-wide in manufacturing and nationwide in the crafts. These national committees do not impose standards usually or supervise individual training programs, although their standards usually are followed by the local committees. Local JACs might comprise a group of employers (as in the construction industry), a single employer and union, or an employer without a union. JACs sometimes merely advise employee and employer representatives who actually carry out the programs, but in a few states JACs actually direct the programs.

Table 10-1 shows the trend in registered apprentices since 1947 in selected trades. The number of apprentices peaked in 1949 and 1950 and declined thereafter partly as a result of the GI Bill, which provided stipends and costs for veterans taking apprenticeship training. An upward trend was resumed in 1962, and by 1970 enrollment surpassed the earlier peak, but it remained subject to considerable cyclical variation. One study found that more new apprentices were hired when unemployment was low, which probably reflects lenient attitudes on the part of both the employers and the unions.[2]

Apprenticeship is not only concentrated in a few industries but also varies considerably in importance within those industries. Overall, apprenticeship is not very important for some trades, viewed either in terms of the proportion of journeymen who acquire their training through apprenticeship or completion rates; but it did account for the proportions of training for the crafts indicated, according to the latest available Labor Department survey:

	Total Number Taking Formal Training (in thousands)	Percent Taking Apprenticeship Training
Compositors and typesetters	171	30.6%
Construction craftsmen	2,708	43.9
Linemen and servicemen, telegraph, telephone, and power	260	36.8
Machinists	732	34.9
Meat cutters	132	56.1

Source: U.S. Department of Labor, *Manpower Report of the President* (Washington, D.C.: GPO, 1964), Table F-9, p. 256.

Table 10-1 Registered Apprentices in Selected Trades, 1947–1972 (in thousands)

Year	All Trades[a]	Metal Trades	Tool and Die	Printing Trades	All Building Trades	Building Trades		
						Carpentry	Electricians	Plumbers and Pipefitters
1947	131[b]	—	—	—	—	—	—	—
1950	231	54	5	17	108	34	18	22
1953	159	15	6	10	77	21	14	16
1957	190	22	9	14	114	27	19	22
1962	155	22	7	13	101	22	19	20
1966	184	34	13	12	114	24	22	23
1967	208	45	17	12	122	23	25	25
1969	238	56	21	13	133	26	27	27
1970	274	57	22	14	137	27	27	28
1971[c]	274	40[b]	—	—	138[b]	—	—	—
1972[c]	264	36[b]	—	—	151[b]	—	—	—

[a]Includes trades other than those listed.
[b]Further breakdown not available.
[c]In training at the end of the year. These are not comparable with other figures, which are annual averages.
Source: U.S. Department of Labor, Bureau of Apprenticeship and Training; 1971 and 1972 figures from *Manpower Report of the President* (Washington, D.C.: GPO, 1974), p. 370.

Moreover, within a given sector of an industry—usually the part that is most heavily unionized—apprenticeship is known to account for somewhat larger proportions of journeymen than it will in the nonunion sectors.

The ratio of new registrations to completions varies considerably from trade to trade. The carpenters have by far the most new registrants but fewer completions than the electricians and the plumbers. The carpenters' programs have a high dropout rate partly because many apprentices are able to work at the trade without completing apprenticeships. The carpenters also have relatively low admissions standards as contrasted with the mechanical crafts.

Students of apprenticeship generally agree that among the construction trades, the electricians, pipe trades, and sheet-metal workers have the most extensive programs and rely more heavily on apprenticeship as a source of journeymen. This opinion is supported by studies of apprentices per thousand journeymen, completion rates, and such indicators as attendance at related instruction classes and scores on the General Classification Test for those entering the armed services in World War II.

The reasons for the size and quality of the mechanical crafts' apprenticeship programs seem to be (1) the craftsmen in these trades are employed by subcontractors and, therefore, have steadier employment than workers (carpenters, bricklayers, laborers) who work mainly for general contractors; (2) their trades require more intellectual training as contrasted with those learned primarily by on-the-job training; and (3) these are growth trades compared with the carpenters, plasterers, and painters, whose employment has been declining.

Apprenticeship issues

Limited understanding of apprenticeship

Concern over black employment, poverty, shortages of skilled workers, and inflation—each a problem touched by apprenticeship—raises questions about its practices. Nevertheless, this training system was not very well understood by those who were not a part of it.

Confusion results, in part, from considerable diversity in apprenticeship programs. Apprenticeship sometimes is a very informal system, with little attention given to providing the trainee with a variety of work experience and academic instruction related to the requirements of the particular craft. Other programs are better organized and provide all of these things. Some of the better programs are registered with either the BAT or various state apprenticeship councils, while others are not registered with any governmental agency. Registered programs vary considerably with respect to the ratio of applicants to openings, completion rates, duration of training, employer participation in training, value and nature of related instruction, ratio of apprentice to journeyman wages. This diversity makes it difficult to generalize about apprenticeship.

The ideal or expressed apprenticeship standards and requirements are often confused with the actual system. The formalized apprenticeship programs depicted in the BAT brochures are likely to conceal considerable flexibility and diversity, particularly in the construction industry where more registered apprentices are employed than in any other industry. Some apprentices, in fact, become journeymen before completing the formal apprenticeship period—depending upon such factors as the relevance of the standards and procedures to job requirements, labor market conditions, and the degree of control exercised over the program by unions and employers.

While a formal statement of the craft structure in the construction trades might suggest rigid apprentice and journeyman classifications, there are, in fact, a wide variety of actual classifications, specializations, and statuses according to type and degree of skill. Moreover, there are regular flows of people between residential jobs (which are ordinarily the least desirable and require lower skills) and the better and more highly skilled commercial and industrial jobs. In this process, depending upon craft and industry, workers learn their trades by a variety of means, including (1) completing part of an apprenticeship; (2) picking the trade up on the job or in the armed forces; (3) working in nonunion jobs and transferring into unionized programs during organizing campaigns or during periods of full employment of union craftsmen; and (4) attending vocational-technical programs.

Adequacy of apprenticeship

There is also some controversy concerning the adequacy of apprenticeship training to meet the nation's manpower needs. But because of technical difficulties in projecting manpower requirements, this is likely to remain an unresolved issue. The unions are suspicious of projection that would call forth supplies of labor beyond what the unions consider adequate to maintain steady employment. Government officials, however, often want to increase labor supplies in order to avoid labor shortages, which put upward pressure on wages and prices.

Another controversy results from a debate over the role apprenticeship plays in those trades in which it is concentrated. While the construction industry, for example, considers apprentice-trained journeymen to be all-round craftsmen with a knowledge of the theory and practice of their trade and affords such journeymen a special status, many construction workers have not served apprenticeships. Not all workers in the construction industry need to be as well trained as apprentices, but each employer must have a cadre of keymen who meet his manpower needs. These keymen, who often have served apprenticeships, supervise those who are not as well trained.

Many people question whether in every instance apprenticeship provides better training than informal means. Critics ask whether all workers need to serve apprenticeship of the same length, and some believe apprentices with the necessary academic training should not have to go back to school. Representatives of the apprenticeship establishment (unions, employers, and specialized government agencies dealing with apprenticeship) argue that workers who came into the trades through other means might be just as competent at particular tasks as apprentice-trained men, but they are less likely to have received systematic instruction. Moreover, the defenders of the system argue from the worker's point of view that apprenticeship makes it possible for trainees to become craftsmen and enter supervisory ranks faster than through other means.

Although there is not enough objective data to test the validity of all the claims made for and against apprenticeship, the available evidence suggests a number of conclusions:

1. The time required for training differs among individuals—a factor recognized by some crafts that permit apprentice dropouts to become journeymen before completing the period of apprenticeship. Moreover, other individuals take longer to complete their training than the prescribed standards because they fail one or more periodic tests and are required to repeat this phase of their training. However, many craftsmen enter their trades as "specialists" able to perform only part of the craft and are, therefore, restricted in earnings and upgrading opportunities relative to apprentice-trained journeymen.[3]
2. Little logical difference appears to exist between the methods of acquiring skills in terms of the competence of the craftsmen; the important thing is that the skills and knowledge are ac-

quired, not the method of acquisition. However, the evidence supports the conclusion that systematic training such as that provided by formal apprenticeship programs makes it possible to become an all-round craftsmen faster than informal types of training.[4]

3. The evidence also shows that men who serve apprenticeships have higher earnings and are upgraded faster than those who do not.

4. Although many craftsmen have not served apprenticeships, there was a trend in the 1950s for the construction crafts to place increasing reliance on apprenticeship.

There is no objective evidence concerning the relevance of admissions standards and procedures, and this question is not likely to be easily resolved. Because of the diversity of situations, highly specific tests would be required to clarify the issue. Moreover, to a considerable extent this judgmental question may not lend itself to precise determination. Industry representatives, who presumably have superior information, disagree among themselves. Resolution of this controversial question will, therefore, probably be in terms of agreement on the mechanism for determining qualifications and standards rather than in terms of precise determination of the standards and qualifications themselves.

Racial discrimination

The issue of racial discrimination in apprenticeship has caused considerable controversy. Civil rights leaders attacked the apprenticeship system during the 1950s and 1960s, when demand for unskilled workers was declining, because these programs led to good jobs in skilled trades in which there were very few blacks. According to the 1960s census, only 2191 apprentices, or 2.52 percent of the total, were nonwhite. The lack of black apprentices was confirmed by many other studies.[5]

The reasons for the paucity of black apprentices seem to be clear, though it is more difficult to determine the relative weights to be assigned the various factors. Most of the reasons directly or indirectly involve racial discrimination—not only through specific and overt refusal to accept black applicants but also through the more pervasive institutional segregation that discourages blacks from applying for apprenticeship programs and apprenticeship committees from including black sources in their recruitment patterns. Institutionalized discrimination also results in a lower percentage of blacks meeting the qualifications for admission to many of the apprenticeship programs.

As a result of agitation for change by civil rights groups, there have been many efforts to increase the number of black apprentices and journeymen, especially in the construction industry. In 1963 Secretary of Labor Willard Wirtz approved new federal standards requiring all registered apprenticeship programs to select participants on the basis of "qualifications alone," to use "objective standards," to keep "adequate records of the selection process," and to "provide full and fair opportunity for application." Programs established before January 17, 1964, were not required to select on the basis of qualifications alone so long as they "demonstrated equality of opportunity" in their selection procedures.[6] In 1971 these regulations were strengthened to require outreach and positive recruitment by apprenticeship sponsors with deficiencies in the use of minorities.

These regulations have had a limited impact for a variety of reasons. Basically, few blacks applied for or could meet the qualifications and testing procedures of the JACs. This was not surprising because discrimination had become institutionalized and as a rule few blacks either knew about apprenticeship or thought they could gain admission. In addition, many blacks who meet the qualifications for apprenticeship do not aspire to manual trades. Moreover, the BAT, which administered the program, had very limited enforcement powers. Deregistration, the BAT's main weapon, apparently would be more of an inconvenience than a serious deterrent to discrimination.

In addition to the federal regulations, apprenticeship programs are subject to Title VII of the Civil Rights Act of 1964, the National Labor Relations Act, government contract committees (which require observance of the BAT's apprenticeship regulations as a condition of compliance with the nondiscrimination clauses included in government contracts), and various state apprenticeship regulations and fair employment practices laws. Policies for increasing black participation in apprenticeship programs include the creation of apprenticeship information centers and the funding of specialized programs to recruit, train, and tutor blacks to get them into apprenticeship programs.[7]

A number of organizations, especially the Workers Defense League (WDL) and the National Urban League, have undertaken specific outreach programs designed to get blacks into apprenticeship programs. The WDL's approach in New York City was successful in increasing the number of black apprentices, and it has been used as a model in many other cities. It was endorsed by the AFL-CIO at its 1967 convention and by the Building and Construction Trades Department in February 1968.

By 1974 outreach programs had been established in 120 locations and had registered over 30,000 apprentices. In 1967 minorities had been less than 6 percent of all apprentices; by the beginning of 1973 they accounted for over 14 percent of all apprentices and were 17 percent of all new indentures for 1972–1973.

Although apprenticeship outreach programs have been more successful than any other approach to this problem, it remains to be seen whether they will initiate the kinds of changes throughout the country that will replace institutionalized discrimination with institutionalized equal opportunity. So far, however, they have demonstrated the importance of a comprehensive approach that recruits and prepares black youngsters for apprenticeship programs. Moreover, this approach has demonstrated its effectiveness in getting blacks into jobs outside the apprenticeable trades more effectively and at lower costs.

Union and employer attitudes toward apprenticeship

Although there are a growing number of registered nonunion apprentice programs, the U.S. apprenticeship system is mainly a product of collective bargaining. A study of Wisconsin apprenticeship programs, for example, revealed that 96 percent of the employee members of joint apprenticeship programs in the building trades belonged to unions and 79 percent of the employer members belonged to contractors' associations.[8] However, the relationship between apprenticeship and collective bargaining undoubtedly is weaker in the South, where unions are not as strong as they are in other parts of the country.

As an extension of collective bargaining, programs reflect the interests of the parties at the table. Most students and practitioners seem to agree that apprenticeship training in the United States is primarily supported by craft unions because this training system satisfies a number of their important objectives—most significantly the maintenance of wages by controlling craft competence and therefore productivity. Control of apprenticeship also provides job security by giving unions some control over the supply of labor. Apprenticeship programs exist mainly in casual occupations such as the building trades in which job opportunities are characterized by seasonal and cyclical variations and periods of unemployment. A main union objective in these situations is to gain greater job security for members and to protect the craftsman's investment in his skills. In the long run, it would be difficult for union craftsmen to maintain their wages unless their productivity made it possible for them to have unit labor costs at least as low as the alternatives available to an employer. Craft unions also see apprenticeship as a form of union security. In the absence of unions, employers have a tendency to fragment crafts by training narrow specialists in only part of the trade in order to reduce training costs and increase profits. Craft unions resist such fragmentation because it makes their members less adaptable to change and threatens the power of unions.

Unions also support apprenticeship programs in order to prevent the excessive use of low-wage workers in competition with their journeyman members, as a means of controlling the supply of labor, and as a technique for providing job opportunities to friends and relatives. The unions' interest in apprenticeship is such, according to one authority, that "although some people feel that apprenticeship is moribund, many in organized labor feel just the opposite and so strongly that if the federal government discontinued its modest programs, these unions would continue to develop apprenticeship training as they have over the years."[9]

Employers' views on apprenticeship vary considerably, from industry to industry. Construction and graphic arts employers seem to share their unions' interests in apprenticeship though they are often willing to leave the administration of these programs to the unions. Employers in industrial plants are interested in apprenticeship training when they need craftsmen in identifiable and recognized classifications. Employers in the larger high-wage industries seem willing to support apprentice programs because they are less likely than lower-wage employers to lose their skilled workers once they are trained.

Unlike their counterparts in construction, printing, and some metal crafts, many industrial employers do not seem anxious to register their apprenticeship programs with the BAT or an SAC. Although registered programs do not have to be jointly administered by unions and employers, some employers consider the federal apprenticeship program to be too closely tied to unions. Others, including some government installations, are not interested in training well-rounded craftsmen with general skills that might be transferred to other employers or labor markets; rather, they seek primarily to train workers for the specialized tasks required in their particular operations. These employers are more concerned with maintaining flexibility of manpower utilization across several craft lines and thus are not interested in the comprehensive training in a particular craft provided by the apprenticeship system. Some large employers also have no interest in registering their programs because they want to avoid government regulation and red tape.

The wage and certification advantages to be derived from registering an apprentice program, therefore, seem to be more attractive to the construction and printing industries. While apprentice rates usually are above the minimums, federal and state minimum wage regulations often permit registered apprentices to be paid less than the minimum wage. The Davis-Bacon Act of 1931 provides for the establishment of prevailing wages on federal construction projects, allows apprentices to be paid less than journeymen, and requires the maintenance of journeyman-apprentice ratios. If a program loses its registration, apprentices must be paid the journeyman rates.

Another advantage to registered apprentices is the recognition that the certificate of completion bestows on the journeyman. The graduate of a registered apprentice program knows that his training is a passport to jobs in other geographic areas because of the standards to which his certificate of completion attests.

Standards, qualifications, and procedures

Qualifications, standards, and procedures used by apprenticeship sponsors vary considerably, though registered programs must meet the minimum federal standards listed previously. The specific standards are fixed by the particular joint apprenticeship committee. The numbers of apprentices usually are controlled by prescribing eligibility standards, fixing ratios of the numbers between apprentices and journeymen for each employer, and prescribing the duration of the apprentice training period.[10]

Characteristics of apprenticeship programs

Although there is considerable diversity in apprenticeship training programs, we can make some generalizations about the usual procedures involved in becoming an apprentice. Many youngsters get information about apprenticeship programs from friends or relatives. However, the traditional father-son relationship in many skilled crafts apparently is weakening because it discriminated against minorities and because many craftsmen with higher incomes send their sons to college. Aspirants who do not have friends and relatives in a trade can now obtain information from employers, unions, the employment service, apprenticeship information centers, or other sources.

The number of apprenticeship openings varies from trade to trade and city to city. Some trades—for example, electricians, plumbers, sheet-metal workers, and printers—typically have long waiting lists, while others—for example, roofers and carpenters— are more easily entered. The number of positions with any given employer depends upon how many journeymen he has; agreements between unions and employers typically specify a so-called journeymen-apprentice ratio. These ratios apparently have considerable influence in specific cases, but, in the aggregate, employers do not train as many apprentices as their ratios would allow. An applicant who otherwise meets the requirements for entry into an apprenticeship program usually must take an oral or written examination given by the employment service, a private testing agency, the employer, the union, or a JAC. The JACs traditionally have constructed and administered their own tests, but there appears to be a trend toward reliance on professionally developed written tests. The oral interview, usually administered by the JACs, is designed to determine the applicant's interest in the trade and whether he is likely to complete it successfully.

Critics of apprenticeship procedures contend that the oral interview should be eliminated or given little weight because it offers the JACs an opportunity to discriminate against blacks or others they wish to bar. But defenders of interviews counter that it is necessary to determine the applicants' motivation, since the JAC often allots scarce positions and devotes considerable time and resources to training. Unions also are fearful of flooding the market with partially trained journeymen. Moreover, the JACs are interested in getting the "right kind" of people into their training programs, which means persons who are socially acceptable as well as productive workers. There is a certain mystique and fraternal character about apprenticeship to which the JAC expects the new apprentice to conform. Part of the ritual in many trades takes the form of hazing and menial assignments designed to initiate the apprentice into the trade.

Once the apprentice is formally registered or indentured, he is paid a progressively increasing proportion of the journeyman wage scale. He gains the journeyman's rate when he completes his apprenticeship—at least one year and typically four years after he enters a program.

In some cases, the apprentice can enter the program by passing a simple aptitude test but must find his own job. In other cases, the JACs seem to be able to assure employment to the apprentice and assume responsibility for finding him a job. Many in the apprenticeship establishment are fearful that the "hunting license" approach, whereby the apprentice finds his own job, will bring too many people into the trade.

Some apprenticeship sponsors supplement the salaries of apprentice instructors and provide apprentice coordinators to supervise the training, but overall policy and guidance is established by the JAC or other sponsors. The apprentices' wages often are paid by the employer while they attend classes during the day, but this practice varies considerably. In some cases related training classes are held in the evening.

On-the-job training

On-the-job training (OJT) is the main way in which most workers acquire their skills. In spite of its importance, very little is known about OJT for a number of reasons. For one thing, OJT takes place during the production process, often is very informal, and occurs incrementally over a long period of time. Indeed, very often little identifiable instruction takes place, and the worker undergoing the training may not even be aware of the process. As a consequence, the process cannot be described by those who are undergoing it.

Nevertheless, some generalizations can be made about OJT. Much of our knowledge derives from special studies conducted during the 1960s, when efforts to train the disadvantaged focused general attention on OJT procedures. Although we do not know much about the magnitude of this form of training—in the sense of being able to measure the changes in skills accruing to workers per unit of time—OJT probably accounts for an overwhelming proportion of the skill gains in the work force. Indeed, some of the gains in income attributed to formal education probably are due to OJT.

To some extent, the use of seniority in promotion is tacit recognition by unions and employers of the importance of OJT. In many occupations seniority districts defining lines of job progression serve training as well as production needs. It is assumed that workers who have been in closely related jobs are in the best position to learn the next higher job in terms of skill. Moreover, the fact that workers in the line of progression have some assurance that they will fill higher jobs provides a motivation for junior workers to learn the higher jobs. But OJT is not limited to jobs in the line of progression. Some workers familiarize themselves with jobs outside their immediate seniority lines by talking with workers on those jobs, observing their operations, and perhaps operating the equipment during lunch breaks or other free-time periods. Because of the importance of these informal learning procedures, incumbents sometimes have considerable influence over which outsiders learn their jobs.

Apparently, OJT is very popular with workers and employers. Workers prefer this form of training because they can see its relevance and are not as likely to consider it to be as much a "waste of time" as classroom training. Indeed, some kinds of training cannot be learned in classrooms because it is difficult to simulate the actual conditions of the work place. Also, OJT has very limited wasted training because the worker uses the skills he acquires on the job. Moreover, he is paid a regular wage and not a stipend as under institutional training.

Employers prefer OJT because there is little question of its effectiveness and because it is more flexible and less expensive for many jobs than other types of training. Its impact is readily apparent to supervisors, who can observe whether the worker is learning the job. This form of training is flexible because it can be adapted to a wide variety of work situations and can be combined with all other forms of training. In some cases, for example, workers can be given minimal instructions and left to learn the trade on their own or by observing other workers who perform the same job. But OJT also can be supplemented with (1) formal demonstrations by other workers, instructors, supervisors, or engineers; (2) basic classroom training in theoretical or academic concepts that cannot be taught on the job; (3) vestibule training for new workers to familiarize them with the job; or (4) correspondence courses.

Also, OJT is flexible because it is a means whereby employers can adjust to technological changes and shortages of skilled manpower. As Doeringer and Piore have demonstrated, minor innovations are adopted by casual learning of the new process on the job, while major changes might require more changes in the normal training patterns. Innovations that create new jobs, for example, might require a period of relatively formal instruction by engineers, factory representatives, or others who have learned to operate the new equipment. Furthermore, OJT makes it possible for employers to adapt to a variety of labor market conditions.[11] For example, if there are shortages of skilled workers, employers can, through OJT and work rearrangements, utilize less-skilled workers.

Employers also like OJT because it is economical. The training is a byproduct of production and, therefore, does not require the establishment of training staffs and procedures. The efficacy and importance of OJT undoubtedly account for the fact that very few companies have formal training programs.[12] Moreover, OJT can be carried out with craftsmen who would not be very effective in teaching formal classes but who might command considerable respect from trainees because of their demonstrated skills on the job. Similarly, OJT does not require the purchase of expensive additional training equipment.

In spite of its advantages, however, OJT is not suitable for all kinds of training, and, although less expensive than some other forms of training, it is not without its costs. Just as some skills are difficult to teach in classes, some kinds of knowledge cannot be taught very effectively on the job. For example, theoretical training is important to many kinds of jobs because it teaches the worker the basic causal relationships underlying the job. Workers who understand theoretical relationships undoubtedly are adaptable to a greater variety of work situations than those who only know how things happen but not why. Indeed, it can be argued that those who do not understand the basic theoretical aspects of their jobs probably have imperfect understandings of how things happen. Theoretical training is difficult to teach on the job because the basic causal relationships—for example, the forces conditioning the flow of current through electrical wires or causing the strength or other properties of metals—usually are invisible and thus must be demonstrated with abstract models. The noisy hustle and bustle of the job rarely is conducive to instruction in these abstractions. And supervisors and other regular production workers might not be the best instructors for such abstract academic subjects. But the effectiveness of classroom instruction is not limited to theoretical training. Although academic subjects such as reading and computation skills probably can be more effectively taught off the job, the knowledge that those skills are useful for job performance undoubtedly is a powerful motivating influence, and motivation is very important to learning.

Moreover, OJT has costs that employers must consider. Employees' learning and working at the same time are not likely to be fully productive for a period, and the productivity of supervisors and skilled craftsmen might be impaired if they spend too much time teaching trainees. At the same time, craftsmen often make poor teachers because they resent having to train "greenhorns" or because they frequently have trouble explaining what they do or are reluctant to impart trade secrets that they feel give them an advantage. And there are possible economies of size and scale in a classroom where a number of workers must acquire the same kinds of training.

Although little emphasis was given to it during the first few years of the Manpower Development and Training Act of 1962, OJT became more important after 1965. Some MDTA-OJT programs were administered by so-called national contracts, while others were administered by individual firms. Under the national contracts an organization such as a union or the National Urban League was the prime contractor and subcontracted with individual trainees. After the passage of the Comprehensive Employment and Training Act (CETA) of 1973, OJT programs were shifted mainly to local prime sponsors.

Apparently, OJT has considerable support from political leaders, and, therefore, local prime sponsors are likely to want to continue OJT arrangements under CETA. There are a number of reasons for this, including both its low federal cost per trainee compared with institutional training and the higher posttraining employment built into the system. Not only is institutional training more costly, but also there is no assurance that its graduates will be able to find jobs.

In addition to the limitations discussed previously, OJT has a number of drawbacks for training the disadvantaged. For one thing, OJT requires the worker to find an employer willing to take him, which might be difficult to do because employers are extremely reluctant to train the disadvantaged, even when compensated by the federal government.[13] During times of rising unemployment, it is difficult to place people in OJT slots because experienced workers are unemployed and there are likely to be very few job vacancies. Moreover, because employers select many of the workers to be trained under OJT, they tend to "cream" the available labor force, taking the best-qualified applicants and making it difficult for the truly disadvantaged worker to get training. However, if a disadvantaged worker acquires an OJT position, it is likely to do more to help him become and remain employed.

Conclusions

While the apprenticeship system in the United States is regarded by its supporters as a good training procedure that provides the academic and on-the-job training necessary to produce all-around craftsmen, it is criticized as being obsolete, inadequate to meet the nation's manpower requirements, and it is characterized by racial and other forms of discrimination against outsiders. The evidence suggests the following conclusions:

1. Apprenticeship in the United States is primarily an extension of collective bargaining.
2. Apprenticeship programs, while very diverse, are significant primarily in those industries and crafts in which employment is casual and in which the union is likely to be the predominant and most stable labor market institution.
3. The number of apprentices fluctuates with the business cycle, but the post-1962 trend seems to be upward. In the construction

trades, unions placed much greater reliance on apprenticeship after the 1950s than they had previously.

4. Workers who serve apprenticeships become well-rounded craftsmen in a shorter time, are upgraded faster, and have more regular employment than those trained informally.

5. Although apprenticeship outreach programs have been more successful than other efforts to increase the number of minority apprentices, these outreach programs are too new to give a clear indication of their impact on those institutional arrangements that have barred blacks and other minorities from apprenticeships. Moreover, outreach programs have been assisted by a number of other measures to reduce discrimination. In addition to outreach programs, an important determinant of entry into apprenticeship programs by blacks (and others) and their employment as journeymen craftsmen will be the nature of the qualifications required to enter these training programs and work at these crafts. Because of their significance for economic and manpower policies as well as discrimination, apprenticeship qualifications, standards, and procedures undoubtedly will remain controversial issues for some time. But the outreach programs, according to all the evidence, have greatly increased the number and proportion of minority apprentices.

On-the-job training, which is part of the apprenticeship system, is the main way most workers acquire their skills. It has many advantages over classroom instruction. However, both classroom and on-the-job training is necessary for most crafts because mathematics, science, and other academic subjects cannot be learned very effectively at work sites.

Notes

1. U.S. Department of Labor booklet, *Apprenticeship* (no date), p. 24.
2. David J. Farber, "Apprenticeship in the United States: Labor Market Forces and Social Policy," *Journal of Human Resources* (Winter 1967), p. 70; and George Strauss, "Apprenticeship: An Evaluation of the Need," in Arthur M. Ross, ed., *Employment Policy and the Labor Market* (Berkeley, Calif.: University of California Press, 1965).
3. Ray Marshall, Robert Glover, and William S. Franklin, *Training and Entry into Union Construction* (Washington, D.C.: GPO, 1974).
4. See, for example, Morris A. Horowitz and Irwin L. Hernstadt, *The Training of Tool and Die Makers* (Boston: Department of

Economics, Northeastern University, 1969). This study found that only one method of training tool and die makers, vocational high school combined with apprenticeship, uniformly rated high on such measures of effectiveness as performance ratings by supervisors, duration of training, and amount of time it took to become a competent craftsman.

5. Ray Marshall and Vernon M. Briggs, Jr., *The Negro and Apprenticeship* (Baltimore, Md.: Johns Hopkins Press, 1967), and *Equal Apprenticeship Opportunity* (Ann Arbor and Detroit, Mich.: National Manpower Policy Task Force and Institute of Labor and Industrial Relations, University of Michigan–Wayne State University, 1968); George Strauss and Sidney Ingerman, "Public Policy and Discrimination in Apprenticeship," *Hastings Law Journal* (February 1965), p. 285.

6. 29 CFR 30, 1964.

7. Marshall and Briggs, *Equal Apprenticeship Opportunity*, op. cit.

8. Alan C. Filley and Karl O. Magnusen, "A Study of Joint Apprenticeship Committees in Wisconsin Building Trades," in Center for Studies in Vocational and Technical Education, *Research in Apprenticeship Training* (Madison, Wis.: University of Wisconsin Press, 1967), p. 84.

9. Felician F. Foltman, "Public Policy in Apprenticeship Training and Skill Development," in U.S. Congress, Senate, Subcommittee on Employment and Manpower, *The Role of Apprenticeship in Manpower Development: United States and Western Europe*, Vol. 3 of *Selected Readings in Manpower* (Washington, D.C.: GPO, 1964), p. 112.

10. Marshall, Glover, and Franklin, op. cit.

11. Peter Doeringer and Michael Piore, *Internal Labor Markets and Manpower Analysis* (Lexington, Mass.: Heath, 1971).

12. John L. Iacobelli, "A Survey of Employer Attitudes Toward Training the Disadvantaged," *Monthly Labor Review* (June 1970), pp. 51–55.

13. Ibid.

■■
the goals of
career education

The term "career education" has stirred considerable ferment in educational circles in recent years, but its meaning and implications are not widely understood. Since it is perceived as encompassing all of the elements of the educational process that influence career choice, preparation, and success, it seems appropriate to explore the meaning and ramifications of this emerging concept and its relationship to more traditional academic, general, and vocational education.

A thumbnail description[1]

As noted in Chapter 8, the fundamental concept of career education is that success in a working career requires far more than merely job skills. A career is defined as the totality of work one does in a lifetime. "Job," "occupation," and "vocation" are successively broader terms, but all are narrower than, subordinate to, and components of a career. Each refers to the individual's primary economic activity at a moment in time, with vocation defined as one's primary work role and job as one's primary work role in paid employment.

Career education, then, attempts to help students understand the work ethics imposed by society, develop their own work values based on their own personal interests (but in full awareness of society's demands), become aware of the world of work and its values, explore the alternative occupations and careers available, and choose, prepare for, and, ultimately, begin and pursue a career, including the possibility of changes of occupation and of productive use of leisure during that career.

The components

The component of career education that is most clearly the responsibility of the schools is the expectation that every classroom teacher in every course at every level will emphasize, when appropriate, the career implications of the substantive content taught. This component has a twofold objective: to provide more effective job skills while giving meaning and relevance to otherwise abstract academic subject matter. It seeks to make clear the importance and contribution of such content as preparation for making a living. This emphasis is expected to provide positive educational motivations to help make school a more meaningful experience for all students. In brief, this component aims to help students see some relationships between that which they are presently studying and the possible careers they may choose to follow at some future time. As such, it represents a form of educational motivation for the teacher to use in conjunction with any other motivational devices that have worked effectively in the past.

An example would be learning to read from primers that expose the child to the community and the world of work rather than less meaningful combinations of words about the antics of pets. Math teachers, it is maintained, can use occupational examples without watering down the concepts, and the principles of physics can be taught while integrating their occupational applications. As an illustration, the importance of geometry might be driven home by showing that not only the mechanical engineer and the draftsman but also the crane operator determining the safe lifting capacity of his machine depend upon geometric principles.

This form of educational motivation is not intended to detract from the actual amount of time students spend in absorbing substantive content. Rather, the time required for providing this motivation comes from the total pool of time and effort available to every teacher for student motivation. Thus career education in no way seeks to depreciate the substantive content of the school. Instead, it seeks to assure that more such content will be meaningfully assimilated by the individual student.

A second component of career education is represented by vocational skills training to provide students with specific competencies required for successful entry (or reentry) into the occupational world. The goal of this component is to maximize the quality, appropriateness, variety, and levels of vocational skills training from which the individual can choose. This training is to be demonstrably related to existing and anticipated occupational openings and organized in ways that will allow training opportunities to change with the needs of the occupational society. This component does not require that such skills training occur in any particular institutional format. High school level vocational classes, classes not usually regarded as vocational (art for the artist, music for the musician, and so forth), postsecondary vocational or regional vocational schools, colleges, graduate schools, apprenticeship, and OJT are all routes to specific job skills.

The phrase "vocational skills training" rather than "vocational education" is used in part to emphasize the fact that any class may be vocational skills training for one or more of its students. That is, a mathematics class is vocational skills training for the prospective engineer or mathematician or skilled worker, just as a machine shop class is vocational skills training for the prospective machinist. In part, this phrase is used to emphasize the direct and substantial contributions of basic educational skills to occupational competence. In other words, both students and teachers should recognize that when students learn to read, they are acquiring skills that will be required for and useful in the work they will eventually pursue as adults.

Career education enthusiasts argue against the notion that students do not begin to ready themselves for work until after they leave the elementary school or that in the secondary school only those activities called vocational education exist to prepare students for work. They are most critical of the attitude that only students who lack the potential for successful college completion are readying themselves for work while in elementary and secondary schools. Education as preparation for work is to become an important goal of all who teach and all who learn. This emphasis is expected to add to the meaning and meaningfulness of all education without in any way detracting from any other worthy educational goal.

The third component, career development, aims to help students understand themselves in terms of their values, interests, abilities, and accomplishments. Moreover, it seeks to help students see relationships between these kinds of self-understandings and understandings of possible educational-occupational opportunities that are likely to be available to them. It also seeks to help students make some occupational or career decisions based on this knowledge. The goal of this component is to emphasize and make meaningful the inherent right of each individual to lead his own life, to control to the maximum extent his own destiny, and to see himself as a worthy and worthwhile person. It includes the provision of a variety of means, both cognitive and experimental in nature, for helping students understand and reflect upon the values of a work-oriented society. In addition, this component includes systematic and continuing assistance to students in the educational and occupational choices each must make in the process of his or her career development. This assistance must encompass helping students to understand themselves, to understand the educational and occupational alternatives available to them, and to choose wisely, based on all such understandings, in ways that fully protect individual freedom of choice. Finally, this component is to include helping students implement the choices they have made in ways that will bring personal satisfaction to the student and benefit to society.

A fourth component emerges because achieving the others requires the cooperation and positive involvement of private and public employers, labor organizations, and other institutions outside the school and the home. This component assumes that neither students nor educators can learn what they need to know about work or about the relationships between education and work by insulating themselves from the real world of work outside education.

In many ways the classroom is the most sterile of possible learning environments, useful for learning abstract concepts, but with little opportunity to demonstrate real-world applications. This component includes the provision of work observation, work experience, and work-study opportunities for students and for those who educate students in public school settings. It also involves provision of consultative and advisory services to school officials regarding the nature and needs of the occupational society. It includes training programs conducted in the business and industrial community as well as cooperative school-government-business-labor programs designed to assist students in making a successful transition from school to work. But it goes further than that. A knowledge of the economy and its workings, of production processes, of human interaction, of the role and impact of technology, and of the complex and growing problems of the physical environment can best be learned as they are experienced. The coordination of such learnings, it is argued, must be accepted as the joint responsibility of formal education and the business-labor-industrial community.

A fifth component recognizes and capitalizes upon the interrelationships among the home, the family, the community, and the occupational society—that home itself is a work setting, as well as the basic consumption unit of the products of the economy and the services of the community. Basic attitudes toward work and productivity are developed in the home, and family experiences are a major influence on occupational aspirations. The school can identify and point out the meaning of the seemingly ordinary experiences from which lifelong attitudes are formed. Perhaps, more and more parents can be brought to recognize the impact of their attitudes upon the personal value systems of their children.

A wide array of potential vocational skills as well as construction and mechanical skills can also be experienced and tried out in the home—food service, interior decorating, clothing design, and so on—if these opportunities are used constructively. Students can be helped to make wise personal decisions concerning their roles as family members, as potential parents, and as members of the outside world of careers and service.

Girls and women need particular help in preparing for and carrying out the complicated dual role of homemaker and careerist that is increasingly the lot and the choice of many of them. They need also to be made aware that homemaker and parent are admirable career roles, just as a career outside the home that involves neither is admirable. The choice is theirs. Young men need to learn that the role of homemaker and parent, except for the obvious biological specialization, is as much a male as a female challenge and responsibility.

This component sees the home as a place where work values and the dignity of all honest work can be taught. In addition, it recognizes that if we help students get ready to earn money, we must also help them get ready to spend it, and thus it assigns a consumer education role jointly to the home and the school. Finally, it recognizes the need to help parents develop and apply means of positively assisting in the career development of their children in ways that will enhance rather than detract from the goals of career education.

The phases

The five components of career education act as intervention strategies, beginning no later than kindergarten and continuing through the adult years, to provide positive assistance to persons in their career development. Thus career education, in the continuing process of making work possible, meaningful, and satisfying to the individual, gives special attention to assisting persons as they move toward vocational maturity and the choice (and likely rechoosing) of a primary work role. Thus we can speak of vocational maturation as an integral part of the total process; vocational maturation can be pictured as occurring in growth stages that, in sequential order, include:

1. Awareness of primary work roles played by persons in society.
2. Exploration of work roles that an individual might consider as important, possible, and probable for himself or herself.
3. Vocational decision making (which may go from a highly tentative to a very specific form).
4. Establishment (including preparing for and actually assuming a primary work role).
5. Maintenance (all of the ways in which one gains—or fails to gain—personal meaningfulness and satisfaction from the primary work role he or she has assumed).

The five-step process is a continuing one that most individuals will experience more than once in their lives. Indeed, it must occur whenever the individual is faced with choosing or changing his or her occupation. It is tied as intimately to why an individual chooses to work as to why he or she chooses one form of work over another. It is a concept appropriate for all students at all educational levels and in almost all kinds of educational settings. It is not a process that can be assigned to any one part of the educational establishment, but rather must involve all educators at all levels in all kinds of educational settings. Similarly, it is not a process that education, as part of the total society, can accomplish by itself. Rather, it demands the active involvement of the total community of which the school system is a part.

Career education issues

Career education has already attained widespread endorsement at the local level in many schools. At the national level the response has been a great deal of lip service and remarkably little cash. It has been argued that as a new approach to give meaning to all aspects of education—academic, general and vocational—it should not require new increments to total educational funding, but rather redirection of what is already being spent. While there is much to be said for that argument, still the best way to test society's commitment is by measuring the resources it chooses to assign to an activity. By that test the commitment seems a weak one. But at the state level career education has been made the official policy by many state legislatures and boards of education, and many local school districts have in fact made major financial commitments and curriculum shifts in the direction of career education. A number of continuing issues prevent full endorsement of the concept by many educators, though the concept seems to win almost unanimous endorsement when brought to the attention of the labor and business community and probably to the population at large.

Changing significance of work

Some find it anachronistic that education should raise the priority of employability and productivity among its objectives just when, as they perceive it, work is of declining importance in the economy and in life. They misread the signals. Leisure time has increased slowly as the fruits of productivity have been divided between higher incomes and more time off the job. But the threat is that productivity will decline, not accelerate. The 4-day week is a re-packaging of the standard 40 hours, not a decrease of work time. Much of the rising productivity that allowed the choice between income and leisure was a product of the transfer of many workers from low-productivity agriculture to high-productivity manufacturing. The transfer of labor to service industries often has the opposite effect. The nature of work and the work ethic is changing. Nevertheless, it remains true that, economically speaking, "there ain't no free lunch." Individual incomes and national strength still rest upon productivity. Some can live without work only by lowering the standard of living of all. We are wealthy enough as a society to afford to support those who cannot work for a variety of reasons. We also have the wealth to support many who contribute —that is, work—in ways not measured by wages and salaries in the labor market. Yet it remains true that no society can survive without work. Moreover, he who does not contribute in some way to society's welfare is a parasite, a situation more harmful to himself than to society. If the school prepares people for life, it must prepare them for work and help them develop their own work values.

Timing of career choice

Guidance counselors in recent years have generally advocated delay in career choice until the individual has been exposed to most of the relevant alternatives and has a well-developed self-image. The career education literature advocates early tentative choice, believing it adds to motivation and to the development of decision-making skills. Achieving these values without discouraging thorough exploration of each individual's needs and capabilities requires that choice be kept tentative, options be kept open, and experimentation and change be encouraged. Certainly, a tenth-grade view of life will be narrowly constrained, and means for constant reassessment of career choices must be built into the system both before and beyond that time.

Need for skills training

It is frequently argued that specific skills training should be an employer's responsibility, since he profits from the application of the skills. Given a choice, the employer will generally prefer the skilled to the nonskilled, but, it is alleged, he would have trained a person or persons for the skills if no skilled person was available. Therefore, it is argued, when an individual trained at public expense obtains a job, it is at the expense of one who would otherwise have been hired. Undoubtedly, work attitudes, human relations skills, the standard communications and computation ability, knowledge of alternative career choices, and other work skills that are needed in most employment should have priority in education over skills limited in application to one employer or industry. Often, the latter should be provided at the employer's expense. But there are economies of scale in skills training for employers whose businesses are too small to allow training to be conducted economically. Trained workers are also an attraction to economic development, and supply, to an extent, may create the demand. Moreover, most skills are transferable. Lack of skills training is an important contributor to the competitive disadvantages many experience in job market competition, and skills-training programs have been shown to be effective in remedying this disadvantage and offsetting others. The exact boundary between the public and private responsibility for skills acquisition should differ among locations, industries, and circumstances. But as long as employee and employer are taxpayers, they pay publicly as well as privately.

Need for change in traditional school practice

Most everyone is for change until he must make some changes himself. Career education, to realize its full potential, will require more change in educational practice than is often realized. The practice of using time in school as the primary measure of achievement must be replaced with an objective measure of performance. The philosophy that teachers and administrators know best what is good for the student and that the consumer of education usually does not know what is good for him is threatened by an open-entry/open-exit, multiple-option system. Teacher certification practices are attuned to the classroom, to lecture, to abstract subject matter, and to verbal and written learning processes, not to realistic learning environments outside the school. Teacher-training institutions will experience the greatest changes in the future in regard to career education. In fact, if career education is put into practice, nearly every teacher and administrator will have been retrained, and nearly every course prospectus and curriculum guide rewritten. New relations will exist among home, school, and work, and to reach full effectiveness even school facilities will have to take new forms. At the same time, career education has the advantage that it can be introduced in the present classroom by a committed teacher. In a time of uncertainty in educational development, it is compatible with most presently proposed innovations. It can work in open or traditional classrooms, with or without team teaching, graded or ungraded. It lends itself to accountability. It is part of the demanded change in traditional practice, but it need not wait upon all of the other needed changes for its implementations.

Scope of career education

Some who are less enthusiastic about career education judge that it is only vocational education with a new name. Others who have reacted with more alarm judge that the vocational educators are trying to take over the whole of education. However, the advocated relationship is more like that illustrated in Figure 11-1.

Career education is more than traditional vocational education, though the latter is certainly a vital part of it. Career education is one of, but only one of, education's high priorities. There is no reason to establish priorities among careers, culture, citizenship, family life, and self-awareness as educational objectives, since none is mutually exclusive, and in fact all, if correctly understood, contribute to each of the others. Careers, other than professional, have never been a significant objective of education in this country. However, adequate career preparation, along with vocational skills training, can never occur in the school system alone. It requires the contributions of other institutions of the total community of which the education system is only a part.

The crowded curriculum

Many teachers argue that the curriculum is already so full that they have little time to teach the substantive content they know students need. They are bombarded with requests to incorporate concepts of environmental education, drug education, sex education, citizenship education, and even global education into their teaching. How, they ask, can they possibly add career education to

Figure 11-1   Career education's place in education.

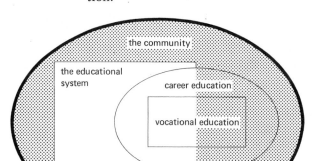

Source: Kenneth B. Hoyt, *Career Education:
What It Is and How to Do It* (Salt Lake
City, Utah: Olympus Publishing Co.,
1974), p. 35.

all these other concepts and still teach the real subject matter associated with their academic fields?

However, career education enthusiasts emphasize that, in asking that time be devoted to discussing career implications of the
subject, they are *not* urging that less time be devoted to study of
the substantive content. Rather, the time they request is a portion
of the time every good teacher devotes to motivating students
toward studying the course content. Having students learn something with respect to how they might use that knowledge in their
later vocational lives will motivate many students to try harder to
master the course content. The goal in asking teachers to emphasize the career implications of their subject matter is to help students learn more, not less, of the substantive content the teacher
is trying to convey to them. If this is done correctly, according to
career educators, students should be better prepared for college
than if this form of educational motivation was not used. The assumption is that if students are made aware of the career implications of their subjects, increased learning will take place.

Relationship to postsecondary education

Some minority group leaders have viewed with skepticism the emphasis upon career education as an intent to foreclose college at-

tendance—and, therefore, access to professional, technical, and executive jobs—to the poor, the visually different, and other groups against whom society has often discriminated in the past. Their fears arise also from the reiteration of career educationists that college is not necessarily the best career preparation for everyone. The concern is understandable. Any educational program can be used as an agent of discrimination. Career education's intent is to open options, not to close them. It does not argue against college training but only against the notion that other options and those who choose them are somehow inferior.

Career education seeks to correct this misinterpretation and help all individuals see educational opportunities as differing in *kind*, not in intrinsic worth or value. It intends to enable the individual to *choose* from among a wide variety of educational options rather than to settle for one of those remaining when he or she discovers that attainment of a college degree is unlikely or undesired. It is considered as important in helping some youth choose *not* to go to college as it is in helping others choose to go. The goal is to help in the decision-making process, not to predetermine the nature of the decisions.

Career education programs have a vital and significant role to play in serving both high school students headed toward college and in helping college and university students once they arrive on college campuses. In the case of high school students, career education seeks to help them think through the reasons why they want to go to college as well as consider how they can gain admission. Reasons for going to college, while seldom concerned exclusively with career decisions, do involve or should involve—for most high school students—these considerations. Once a student is enrolled in a four-year college or university, it is both natural and, for most, inevitable to think about how his or her college education may someday be used in the occupational society. Career education on the college and university campus seeks to help students consider career implications of their selections among courses and majors throughout their college lives rather than simply at the point when they are ready to graduate. Some seem to feel that as career education emphasizes the career implications associated with college choices, it must simultaneously be denigrating other reasons for going to college. Such conflict is not necessary. Career education merely asks those students with other goals and objectives to specify them. Students have a right to know what they can gain from any kind of educational experience, be it liberal arts or career oriented in nature. They also need to know the relationships that exist between education as preparation for making a living and education as preparation for living itself.

Relationship to vocational education

Concern of some that career education is but a subterfuge for the expansion of vocational education is based primarily on a misunderstanding. It should be clear by now that career education encompasses vocational education but goes far beyond it. However, the goals of career education can never be met until and unless vast improvement comes to the American system of vocational and occupational education. Career educationists deny that their subject is a subterfuge for the expansion of vocational education. Rather, they argue, career education demands the expansion of vocational education for both its immediate and long-run success. Career educators are concerned that this relationship to vocational education not detract from the broader conceptualization of career education nor "turn off" academic educators who see no concurrent increase in funds for expanding their programs. They argue that there is at present a great imbalance among objectives in the American educational system. If career education is to correct that imbalance, a relatively greater amount of the educator's dollar must be spent for vocational and occupational education. There is no point in emphasizing that too many high school students are enrolled in the college-preparatory curriculum unless viable alternative curricula are made available to them. There is no point in lamenting the increasing problems of midcareer changes being faced by adults today unless some means is provided for helping them cope with their problems. The most obvious need is for expansion of the variety, quality, and levels of vocational and occupational education. For that reason this chapter provides data on the current status of vocational education.

Vocational education

Vocational skills training is the vital job preparation component of career education and the only component for which there are data available to assess the amount and quality of the education and its results. Those data encompass by no means all of the vocational skills training that occurs, but they do include the direct federal, state, and local expenditures on vocational education. To assess the role of vocational-technical education on the present human resource scene, it is necessary to be aware of the sharp change of direction mandated by Congress during the 1960s. Federal support for vocational education emerged during World War I; it emphasized the limited skill needs of the labor market. Our adolescent industrial economy required comparatively few professionals and skilled workers; for most of the labor force education and formal training were unnecessary for employment. Three broad occupational categories were identified—trades and industry, vocational agriculture, and home economics—and $7 million a year was appropriated for matching grants to encourage states to train young people in those areas. Other occupational groupings—distributive education, practical nursing, fishery occupations, and technical training—were added as years passed, and federal appropriations increased to $55 million a year by 1963. But the original philosophy prevailed until that year. Then rising youth employment, one of the byproducts of the postwar baby boom, struck the labor market and provided the impetus for the first basic reconsideration of the original philosophy. The relationship between education and jobs had shifted, as explained in Chapter 8, until education and training had become prerequisites to successful labor market participation.

Federal legislation

The objective of the Vocational Education Act of 1963 was to prepare specific groups of people for employment rather than to meet the skill needs of various occupational categories. Although Congress authorized training in any nonprofessional occupation and increased federal appropriations fivefold over a three-year period, it failed to require reorientation toward the new objectives. Funds no longer had to be spent in the limited number of occupational categories, but no different distribution was mandated. Except for home economics, neither "carrots" nor "sticks" were provided to influence expenditure patterns. Ten percent of existing home economics funds and all new funds for that category were to be spent in training for gainful employment. Vocational agriculture could —but need not—include training for occupations related to, but outside of, commercial agriculture. Despite rhetorical concern for those with academic, social, and economic handicaps that interfered with their ability to profit from regular vocational education problems, no specific expenditures or programs were required for them. The definition of vocational education was broadened to allow expenditures for guidance and counseling, teacher training, and instructional materials. The act also opened the door to basic and general education where needed to facilitate skill training. Thus new objectives were declared, and funds were made available; but whether the objectives were pursued was left largely to state determination or U.S. Office of Education leadership.

Results fell far short of congressional expectations. Although expenditures tripled between 1964 and 1967, the new federal funds largely supported the old vocational categories—except for the addition of office occupations. Too little recognition had been given to new occupations, few innovative programs were undertaken, and there was little coordination between general and vocational education. It was not even certain that enrollments had increased much more than they would have in the absence of the legislation. Enrollment trends had been up prior to 1963. Office occupations, which hitherto had not been eligible for federal support, accounted for four-fifths of the enrollment increase. How much was an actual increase in enrollments, and how much was merely a transfer from state and local to federal financing? There was no way of knowing. Only 1 percent of the funds and enrollments had been specifically allocated to the disadvantaged.

Congressional dissatisfaction prompted passage of the Vocational Education Amendments of 1968. They were formulated on the basis of recommendations from an advisory council on vocational education, which conducted a thorough review of the results of the 1963 Acts to 1967. Hoping to apply leverage from outside of the system, Congress dictated the establishment of national and state advisory councils that were given independent budgets and staffs and assigned monitoring and evaluative functions. An earmarking approach was introduced to assure expenditure of grant-in-aid funds according to congressional priorities. Specific allotments were made for training the disadvantaged and the handicapped. Postsecondary education and cooperative programs—wherein students spend part of their time in the classroom and part on the job, all under school supervision—were also recipients of specific allocations. Other funds were set aside for special innovative and exemplary programs. Emphasis in home economics was redirected to give special attention to the homemaking needs of working wives and the poor. The definition of vocational education was broadened to include emerging as well as existing occupations. As part of experimental projects and programs for the disadvantaged, vocational money could be spent in elementary schools. Finally, states could receive money only upon the U.S. Commissioner of Education's specific approval of an annually updated long-range plan. In effect, the intent was to move from a grant-in-aid to a proposal-review-and-approval process.

Initial budgetary history after 1968 made it apparent that vocational education was more popular in the legislative branch than in the executive branch. In both the Johnson budget released in January 1969 and the Nixon version, which followed a few months later, the 1968 amendments were, in effect, repealed even before they came into existence by each President's failure to recommend funds for the new proposals. This decision reflected no high-level policy determination. The staff of the Office of Management and Budget (formerly Bureau of the Budget) was not as trusting as

Congress. None of the staff members had any direct experience with vocational education, and most seemed to assume without evidence that vocational education was outmoded and ineffective. Since the 1963 act had brought no significant changes in vocational education, what reason was there to think that additional moneys authorized by the 1968 legislation would be more effectively spent? Since the amendments earmarked certain proportions of the funds for special programs, the regular program would have to be cut considerably. General budgetary restraint reinforced the staff position.

Nonetheless, Congress responded to pressures from the well-organized vocational education lobby by appropriating, and re-passing after a presidential veto, somewhat over half of the authorized increases. A similar scenario of low executive request, congressional increase, and presidential veto followed for the fiscal 1971 and 1972 budgets, with overriding of the vetoes as a significant change. The result was a total federal vocational education appropriation of $498 million, nearly double that of 1968 but considerably lower than the $870 million authorized in the act for 1971. However, that was peak level for the appropriations under the 1968 authorization, and, with inflation, real resources allocated to vocational education fell in subsequent years.

Public budgets not only represent sources of funding for public programs, but they also indicate relative priorities between public and privately provided goods and services and among alternative public services. The total bill for public education in the United States is $79 billion annually, with $96 billion spent in 1973–1974 for all education. The $2.7 billion spent on publicly supported vocational education in 1972 is an indication of the relatively low priority given to employment preparation. However, the fact that state and local governments supplied 82.5 percent of that funding compared with 17.5 percent from the federal purse, whereas a 50–50 match was authorized, gives some notion of relative priorities. Average annual per capita costs for vocational education in 1972 were $266, with the federal government supplying $47. However, inflation distorts the picture. In real terms federal vocational resources increased by 51.3 percent between 1966 and 1972 rather than the 98.3 percent in current dollars. Federal expenditures failed to keep pace with the combination of price-level changes and enrollment increases so that the federal government was contributing about 20 percent less per student in real terms in 1972 than in 1966. The $266 spent per capita contrasts with $132 in 1966. Adjusting by the consumer price index on a 1966 base, the 1972 expenditure would be $203 per capita, giving some indication of qualitative improvements over the years.

The first few years following the 1968 amendments were not

unlike those following the 1963 legislation. Reorientation of an established program is always difficult to achieve. The national advisory council did prove to be an independent voice in vocational education planning, but most of the state councils were more oriented to serving as additional lobbying bodies than as reformers. Because of political reasons the U.S. Office of Education had been handicapped over substantial periods of time by an inability to fill some of its major positions, and the firing of a commissioner by President Nixon did not add to its decisiveness. Thus when a new commissioner of education made career education the watchword of his administration, vocational educators responded eagerly, even though the initial funds to be used were clearly a diversion from those allocated to vocational education. Exemplary programs funded under the 1968 vocational amendments had provided most of the experiments in and implementations of career education. All had in common three characteristics: (1) They merged "hands on" occupationally oriented training with related academic learning to demonstrate the inseparability of the two and provide motivation through demonstrated relevance; (2) they trended away from training for specific occupations in favor of entry-level competence in broadly related clusters of occupations; and (3) they tended to begin exposure earlier than the traditional 11th grade, some reaching into the elementary schools. Career education is, in part, a contribution of that fruitful decade of experiment. Vocational educators were fully aware that career education encompassed more than vocational education, and some of them were convinced that vocational education could be strengthened if it could be built on a base of career education in earlier grades.

The years since 1963 and particularly since 1968 have been the occasion for considerable progress in bridging the traditional gaps among vocational, academic, and other components of education. Vocational education has become interrelated and intermingled with industrial, practical and fine arts, business education, driver education, journalism, computer science, and other curricula. In another direction, vocational education is also more closely linked with apprenticeship, with remedial manpower training, with technical education, OJT, and work study. The cooperative work-education and work-study programs are on the increase.

Enrollments

The years following 1968 were also years of rapid expansion in vocational education. The fiscal and school year 1971–1972 provides the most recent data available for comparison. The source is

Project Baseline, a project sponsored by the U.S. Office of Education at Northern Arizona State University to compile and analyze annually the most meaningful data available concerning vocational education.[2]

Total vocational education enrollments, which were 3.9 million in 1961, 6 million in 1965, and 7.5 million in 1968, were over 10 million in 1972, an annual growth rate of 14.5 percent over a decade. Vocational education enrollments for 1000 population was up 55 percent in 1972 over 1966 and double 1961. There are arguments against including enrollments in consumer and homemaking programs in the measure of occupationally oriented education. Deleting that group, one out of four high school students was receiving vocational education in 1972. Including consumer and homemaking programs and adding industrial arts, nearly three out of four were receiving some occupationally oriented training. This does not mean that three out of four or even one out of four had made a vocational choice and was pursuing it. Boys taking auto mechanics for avocational purposes, to work on their own cars or to escape classroom regimen, for instance, would be included. The measure is not one of intent but of how many were enrolled in courses financially supportable under the requirements of the federal act. In fact, though most home economics and industrial arts education courses could be legitimately supported by those funds, most are not for a variety of reasons.

Among the major objectives of the 1968 amendments were to accentuate (1) postsecondary vocational education in response to the expansion of technician-level occupations; (2) the training of the disadvantaged, the minorities, and central-city residents; and (3) the training of the physically and mentally handicapped. Consequently, the 1968 amendments earmarked percentages of the funding for each of these areas. In 1972 postsecondary vocational education (that is, for those in full-time schooling) was 13 percent of all vocational education, enrolling 1.3 million persons. On the other hand, adult (part-time) vocational education enrolled 2.9 million in 1967 and 3.1 million in 1972, dropping from 42 percent to 31 percent of all enrollments.

The definition of disadvantaged is not precise in vocational education. However, reported proportions rose from 2.4 percent of all enrollments in 1967 to 14 percent in 1972. The physically and mentally handicapped were only 2 percent of all vocational education enrollments in 1972. Blacks are 11 percent of the population and 19 percent of vocational enrollments. American Indians are only 0.39 percent of the total U.S. population and 0.84 percent of total enrollments. Spanish-surnamed students are 6 percent of all vocational students but 4.5 percent of the total population.

Table 11-1 Percent Distribution of Enrollment in Vocational Education, 1961–1972

Fiscal Year	Total Enrollment (thousands)	Agriculture	Distributive	Health	Home Economics	Office	Technical	Trades and Industries	Other
1961	3,856	20.9	7.9	1.2	41.8	—	3.2	25.0	—
1962	4,073	20.2	7.9	1.2	42.4	—	3.7	24.7	—
1963	4,217	19.6	7.3	1.3	43.6	—	4.4	23.8	—
1964	4,566	18.8	7.3	1.3	44.3	13.5	4.8	23.4	—
1965	5,431	16.3	6.1	1.2	38.6	20.4	4.2	20.0	—
1966	6,070	14.9	6.9	1.4	31.3	22.3	4.2	20.9	—
1967	7,048	13.3	6.8	1.6	31.0	23.0	3.8	21.2	—
1968	7,534	11.3	7.6	1.9	30.3	23.0	3.6	21.6	0.7
1969	7,979	10.7	7.1	2.2	30.7	24.0	4.0	21.6	0.9
1970	8,794	9.7	6.0	2.3	29.2[a]	24.0	3.1	21.7	4.0
1971	9,161	8.9	6.3	2.9	28.9[a]	24.2	3.4	22.4	2.9
1972	10,053	8.6	6.3	3.3	28.3[a]	23.3	3.3	23.6	3.3

[a]Includes since 1970 a separate breakdown for occupational home economics as follows: 1970, 1.7 percent; 1971, 2.1 percent; 1972, 2.6 percent.

Source: Office of Education, U.S. Department of Health, Education, and Welfare.

Three out of ten vocational education enrollees are central-city residents, while rural enrollments are 45 percent of the total. Enlarging female participation was also a goal of the 1968 amendments, and the fact that 55 percent of enrollees are now women attests to both aggressive administration and changing occupational structure. Vocational education has progressed rapidly toward its objectives of expanding postsecondary training, disadvantaged, minority, and central-city enrollment. It lags behind in serving American Indians and the handicapped, but, of course, both of those groups have other programs of their own.

Cooperative education in which the student spends part of the day or week in the classroom and part on the job, both under supervision of school personnel, was singled out for praise by the 1966 study but was still only 8 percent of the total vocational education enrollment in 1972, indicating its difficulty of administration by schools and acceptance by employers. The proportion of vocational funding going to vocational agriculture and home economics was a constant source of criticism of vocational education during the 1960s. There were not more being trained for agriculture than would enter the field, but with agriculture declining so rapidly as a source of employment, it did not seem to deserve its priority. Yet in rural high schools, it was often the only male occupational field in which there was a sufficiently pervasive interest to justify facilities and instructors. The criticism of home economics was that it was primarily homemaking and, therefore, nonvocational. That homemaking was still the most universal career for young women and that relatively little money was committed despite the high enrollments were facts rarely noted. From 1961 to 1972 vocational agriculture enrollments stayed relatively stable and home economics enrollment doubled, but both declined as a proportion of the total enrollment.

Distributive education and the catchall category, trades and industries, changed little as a proportion of all vocational education. Technician enrollment fluctuated at an amazingly low level. Health enrollment more than doubled in absolute numbers and as a proportion but still enrolled only 334,000 across the entire nation, despite rapid increases in employment. Office occupations followed the labor market to rise rapidly in enrollment without changing as a proportion of all vocational education after the big jump between 1964 and 1966 (Table 11-1).

Many of the traditional vocational education categories were so broad in occupational terms as to hide internal occupational shifts. Data are available for 1971–1972 according to an occupational cluster approach developed by the state of Oregon.[3] However, this formulation is lacking in historical data.

Cluster	Proportionate Enrollment
Agriculture	6.5
Marketing	5.5
Health	3.3
Food service	3.5
Accounting	3.3
Secretarial	11.5
Other clerical	6.1
Graphics	0.7
Forest products	0.2
Miscellaneous	4.3
Industrial mechanics	7.4
Construction	4.0
Electricity & electronics	3.5
Metal trades	2.9
Child care	2.1
Clothing	4.7
Drafting	1.4
Services	5.2
Home economics	19.1

Results of vocational education

On the positive side, placement of those who complete vocational training *and* are available for placement is remarkably high, 95.5 percent in 1972 as reported in the autumn following completion. By occupational fields the rates were 99 percent in agriculture, 99 percent in distributive education, 97 percent in health, 86 percent in home economics, 92 percent in office occupations, 98 percent in education, and 98 percent in trade and industrial occupations. In 1972, 1.1 million were listed as having completed vocational education, with 112,000 leaving short of completion but judged to have attained marketable skills. With continuation to higher education (234,000), the military, marriage, and a large (211,000) group for whom data were not available, only a little over one-half (655,000) were available for placement. Of these, 482,000 were placed in training-related occupations, 143,000 in nontraining-related occupations, leaving 62,000 unemployed. Vocational education students consistently show lower unemployment rates following school than their nonvocational counterparts.

Limited data available from a few states suggests that vocational education completions represent about 36 percent of projected demand for labor in agriculture, 20 percent in distributive occupations, 24 percent in health occupations, 23 percent in home economics, 53 percent in office occupations, 41 percent in technical programs, and 27 percent in trade and industrial occupations.

Economists, however, tend to ask more questions about the results of vocational education than simply the completion and placement rates. How do vocational students compare in employment and income with those who enrolled in the general and academic curricula? What are the rates of return on investment in vocational education? Perhaps these questions are asked because vocational education has employment as an ostensible goal or because vocational education costs on the average (excluding home economics) about double the average costs of general education. Whatever the reason, vocational education is frequently asked for economic justification, whereas academic and general education rarely are.

However, the questions are more often asked than answered. Cost-benefit evaluations of vocational education have been plagued with problems in data and concept. Substantial differences exist in the socioeconomic and ability status of those who enroll in vocational, general, and academic education, and the data are inadequate to control for those differences. Few long-term longitudinal studies are available to determine what happens to the relative earnings of various groups over time. Furthermore, the occupational content of various vocational categories is so vastly different that comparisons need to be made by occupation, and few studies have done so. Relative cost data are difficult to derive.

In general, available studies support the usefulness of the additional investment necessary for vocational education. In 1966 the five-year National Longitudinal Surveys, which only partially controlled for socioeconomic status and ability, found no appreciable differences in income for those emerging from the various educational tracks, but it identified a substantial income differential in favor of the vocational students two years later.[4] Other studies have measured earning differentials in favor of vocational graduates with a return on investment in vocational education of 10 to 20 percent.[5] Income differentials between blacks and whites were less for vocationally educated than for other curricula, suggesting that blacks gained relatively more from vocational education than did blacks enrolled in other education tracks. However, earnings differentials between the graduates of secondary and postsecondary vocational-technical education did not justify added investment. Junior college graduates did better economically than graduates of postsecondary vocational-technical schools, but then they were drawn, on the average, from higher socioeconomic groupings.

Summarizing current status

A growing state and local commitment is evident as is a rise in student interest and in enrollments in absolute and relative terms.[6] Postsecondary and adult vocational education enrollments are rising more rapidly than secondary enrollments, and this is appropriate given occupational and demographic trends. Though there are no national data available, personal observations suggest that good programs in attractive occupations with high placement rates are almost always oversubscribed, particularly at the postsecondary level. There are no qualitative data other than the rising real expenditure per student, but observation suggests great improvements in facilities, equipment, and instruction. Minorities are generally overrepresented in comparison to their proportions, but this may reflect restricted opportunities for higher education as well as a desire for vocational education. Women are rising as a proportion of vocational students but primarily because of the expansion of home economics and health and office occupations rather than any inclusion in training for traditionally male occupations. Expansion is occurring across the range of traditional occupations except for the declining proportion in agriculture. Therefore, vocational education is alive, well, and expanding, but it is still having difficulty in bursting traditional bonds.

The most significant changes in vocational education are those related to the career education movement. Most of the innovations in this area grew out of vocational education experiment and research. If career education can take care of the general employment requirements—appropriate values and attitudes, a commitment to work, general knowledge of the labor market, its opportunities and requirements—then vocational education can concentrate on the skill requirements of broad occupational clusters. With this orientation its concerns can be clearly defined as choosing the demand occupations, furnishing appropriate facilities, equipment, and instructors, linking closely with employer requirements, making increased use of cooperative training, and seeing to it that there are "slots" for all those who seek job skills. These are tasks vocational educators know how to do.

Career education's promise

The term "career education" means the sum total of those experiences of the individual associated with his or her choice of, preparation for, entry into, and progress in a sequence of jobs and unpaid work throughout his or her lifetime. Career education is crucial in a society such as ours—a society that has been built and continues to operate essentially in accordance with a strong work ethic, combined with firm protection of choice for the individual.

Today the needs of all in society, both youths and adults, for individual and continuing assistance in career preparation and development are great—and they are becoming greater. Much of the current societal dissatisfaction with the schools exists because of a lack of emphasis on career education for all, an overemphasis on college degrees, which are in reality available to relatively few, and the failure to recognize that college, too, along with its other purposes, is a component of career education.

Career educators question the notion that a four-year college education is the only respectable preparation and the best route to successful employment, although college education will continue as a major path, both for career preparation and for intellectual and aesthetic satisfaction, probably for a slowly rising proportion of the total population. It must be available to all who want and can profit from it.

However career educators, in practice, claim to be the advocates of all citizens, including the four-fifths of the populace—both youths and adults, both in and out of school—who will never attain a four-year college degree. It is time, they argue, for educators to give as much concern to serving this majority of the population as they have given to the college-educated minority. Career educators do not view their contribution as being of a single variety or serving a particular small segment of American education. They argue not so much for more elementary and secondary education, more guidance, more vocational education, or more community colleges, but rather a comprehensive program of career education that covers all levels of education for all citizens. With rising longevity, changing technology, and newly emerging opportunities and challenges, adults have as much right as youth to remedial education, occupational upgrading, and preparation for new phases of their lives. Career educators advocate career education for the adult worker, the labor force reentrant, and the retired person.

Work values, they believe, can be restructured. People can find joy in achievement, in the labor market, in voluntary service, and in productive avocations. The manpower needs of industry and the society can be met while maintaining and increasing individual freedom of choice and providing challenging and well-paid employment. Dignity can be given to workers in all occupations. Meaning can be given to abstract concepts, the value of which students often do not recognize until too late. Motivation to learn can emanate from that recognition. Opportunities to learn from experience as well as from instruction can be provided. The concept of dropping out can be abolished and replaced with a variety in learning environments. New occupations can become available as old ones disappear or lose their challenge. Progress in existing careers can be speeded by upgrading.

Vocational educators have been frequently criticized for their deliberate separateness from the rest of American education. Yet their attitudes have been responses to the disinterest of other educators in preparing students for any occupation not requiring at least a bachelor's degree. To be submerged within the totality of education, they feared, would mean complete domination by academic interests. To date most of the federal funds that have been invested in the development of career education concepts have originated in vocational education appropriations. Yet vocational education commands only $2.7 billion of the total $96 billion annual 1973–74 U.S. expenditures on education. To "generalize" vocational education and "vocationalize" general education simultaneously will require either special appropriation or substantial reallocation of general education funds.

Career education emerges at a time of stringency and disillusionment with public expenditures. The traditional path to education reform by foundations and the federal government has been to supply new and additional money to be made available only when used for prescribed innovations. All too often, the new departure lasted only as long as the money. Career education has a more difficult but, it is hoped, more durable road to follow. Its growth and survival depend upon the conversion of education policy makers and the reallocation of federal, state, and local funds—primarily the latter—to the pursuit of career education concepts. Career education can be implemented without expending vast amounts of new money. The biggest single initial expense called for is that required for in-service education of teachers, counselors, and school administrators. A second sizable financial cost will arise from the need for some school systems to expand and improve their vocational education offerings, but vocational education funds are available to help defray such costs.

Nevertheless, putting career education into practice will be a long and arduous task requiring federal and state legislation and appropriation. Also needed are national leadership from the U.S. Office of Education; leadership by educational agencies at state and local levels; political pressure from national, state, and local interest groups and public officials; cooperation from employers and labor organizations; innovation and dedication from classroom teachers, counselors, and administrators; and finally, response from students. Some schools will not accept the challenge, and some students will not respond.

Only some of the frustrations of life arise and can be stilled in a work place. Deeper philosophical or theological restlessness may be untouched by career education. Economic dislocation, environmental pollution, ill health—many of the perils of personal life and society—will not disappear if career education is implemented. There will still be dull and grubby jobs that must be done. But no sensible person expects panaceas.

Marginal improvements constantly made are achievement enough, and career education's promise is one of life's basic aspects. To make work possible, meaningful, and satisfying to each individual is challenge enough. Whether career education can accomplish this remains to be seen, but it is certainly one of the most challenging—and promising—developments to emerge from human resource concerns in recent years.

Notes

1. The formulation of career education followed in this chapter is that prepared by Kenneth Hoyt, et al., *Career Education: What It Is and How to Do It*, 2nd ed. (Salt Lake City, Utah: Olympus Publishing Co., 1974).
2. Arthur M. Lee, *Learning and Living Across the Nation*, Project Baseline Second National Report (Flagstaff, Ariz.: Arizona State University, 1973).
3. Ibid.
4. *National Longitudinal Surveys, Survey of Work Experience of Males, 14–24, 1966* and *Survey of Work Experience of Young Men, 1968*, (Columbus, Ohio: U.S. Department of Commerce, Bureau of the Census, and Center for Human Resource Research, Ohio State University, 1966 and 1968).
5. Teh-Wei Hu et al., *A Cost Effectiveness Study of Vocational Education: A Comparison of Vocational Education in Secondary Schools* (University Park, Pa.: Penn State University, March 1969); and Susan Fernbach and Gerald G. Somers, *An Analysis of the Economic Benefits of Vocational Education at the Secondary, Post-Secondary and Junior College Levels*, preliminary report (Madison, Wis., May 1970); American Institutes for Research, *An Analysis of Cost and Performance Factors for the Operation and Administration of Vocational Schools for Secondary Programs* (Pittsburgh, Pa.: The Institutes, May 1967).
6. Leonard A. Lecht, *Evaluating Vocational Education—Policies and Plans for the 1970s* (New York: Praeger, 1974).

three
remedial man-
power programs

12
the emergence
of manpower
programs

Development and use of manpower resources has always been essential to economic production, but the term "manpower policy" came into use only in the 1960s.[1] Its context was the emergence of programs designed to improve the employability and to enhance the employment and earnings prospects of persons and groups suffering various disadvantages in competition for jobs. An exploration of the economic and social context in which manpower programs evolved is essential to identify their objectives and to assess their achievements.

The forces involved

The forces leading to the emergence of something approaching a manpower policy in the United States during the 1960s can usefully be examined in long, intermediate, and short-run time frames.

The long run

Economic historians often find it useful to divide economic history into an agrarian or preindustrial phase and our present industrial society, and some sociologists have begun to talk of a new stage— a postindustrial society. This formulation is especially useful for understanding the growing attention given to manpower concerns.

The primary characteristic of the economic stage before the industrial revolution was the involvement of most of the labor force directly or indirectly in agriculture. The Civil War marked the close of that period in this country. It was replaced over the following fourscore years by the industrial stage in which most of the labor force was engaged in the production and distribution of manufactured goods. In that world capital resources were the most important, and the "shakers and movers" were the owners of industrial capacity.

The term "postindustrial society" has become so intertwined with spectacular projections of wealth and technological advances that realists often reject its use.[2] Whether or not we are living through a transition to a new social stage or only the maturing of industrialization is not important for our present purposes. What is significant is that the number of white-collar workers in the U.S. labor force has exceeded those with blue collars for nearly two decades, while the number providing services, governing, and processing information far surpasses those engaged in producing and distributing foods and fibers and manufactured goods. Human resources are becoming the critical ones.[3] The wealth, power, and prestige of individuals in society are more and more determined by what these individuals know and what educational credentials they have rather than by what they own. Both the farm and the factory are controlled less and less by owners and more by professional managers. Highly trained people move freely among posts in education, government, and industry, and the boundaries between these sectors and between the private and the public sectors increasingly blur.

The intermediate run

Long-run trends often seem to accelerate during wartime, and efforts to meet the manpower requirements of World War II produced consequences that have shaped the manpower problems and policies of the entire generation that has passed since that time. To feed and arm ourselves and our allies, as well as meet the demands of our civilian population, while sending more than 11 million of our prime-age, male workers off to war, required exigencies that turned out to be irreversible. Excess rural labor was transferred to urban production, and the process of capitalization in agriculture was speeded to free still more. The rate of increase of output per manhour in agriculture leaped from 1 to 6 percent a year and has averaged around 5 percent for the past quarter-century. The pace of technological change throughout the economy was speeded, and that process continued at the new pace during the postwar period. Women entered the labor force in unprecedented numbers and never returned exclusively to the kitchen.

The postwar baby boom, referred to in Chapter 2, assured that youth unemployment would be a critical problem 16 to 18 years later. Birth rates maintained a high plateau from 1947 to 1957, then declined to 1967, from whence they have continued at roughly the same low rates that prevailed during the depression of the 1930s. With 2.5 million youth turning 16 in 1962 and 3.5 million in 1963, the policy emphasis of the years that followed was predictable.

Also, during the postwar period, the GI Bill sent unprecedented numbers to college, and an educational cycle began in which, since educated people were available, almost everyone needed education to compete. A new technology was created that assumed a well-educated labor force and, therefore, demanded it.

Important shifts occurred in the patterns of migration and the structure of cities. Throughout industrialization the movement had been from farm to city, but the cities grew largely due to the influx of European immigrants. As poor people, they sought the cheapest housing. The tenements were in the central cities, but so were the unskilled and semiskilled jobs. After World War II the migration was internal, from farm to city. By now, many of the immigrants were black and, later, of Spanish-speaking background. They still sought the oldest and cheapest housing in the central cities. However, the new technology demanded single-floor, continuous-process factories, and the necessary land at reasonable prices and acceptable taxes was in the suburbs, as were the skilled and technically trained workers. Public policy—agricultural price supports at one end and federally insured housing at the other—stimulated the trends. The new immigrants could not afford housing where the jobs were, and all too often they were denied, through prejudice, the opportunity to rent or purchase what they could afford. Transportation systems were designed to bring the white suburbanites to downtown white-collar jobs rather than distribute central-city dwellers to suburban employment opportunities. Schools that had contributed to Americanization of European immigrants did not successfully incorporate the American minority poor into the postwar society.

All these trends seemed to converge during the 1960s. A more rapidly growing labor force and rising productivity required economic growth rates 50 percent above the traditional norm. A growing proportion of teenagers and women made the labor force more volatile, leaving the labor market when jobs declined and returning with a rush as jobs became available, seeking jobs in June and abandoning them in September, and often preferring part-time jobs and those with odd hours. The combination of increasingly sophisticated technology, the growth of white-collar jobs, and the competition of rising educational attainment created a demand for remedial manpower programs. The objective was to improve the employability of those experiencing a variety of disadvantages in the competition for jobs. But the remedial emphasis was largely unaccompanied by preventive measures. The effort was to siphon off the disadvantaged from the labor market pool without staunching the flow of underprepared people into it.

The short run

The short-run forces involved in the emergence of manpower programs were unemployment and race relations. Following the Korean conflict, unemployment crept persistently upward, fluctuating over the business cycle, but climbing higher during each downturn and leaving a larger residual with each recovery until it reached over 8 percent of the labor force (unadjusted for seasonality) in February 1961. The trend had been underway for some time before public policy makers absorbed with inflation, budgetary imbalances, and balance-of-payments disequilibrium awakened to its implications. Thus it became the major domestic policy issue in the 1960 election with the challenger Senator John F. Kennedy advocating "let's get America moving again" and the defender Vice-President Richard M. Nixon proclaiming "this is just a rolling readjustment." But when the new administration took office, it was sure of neither the problem nor its solution. There were essentially three schools of thought: (1) those who blamed unemployment on the displacement effects of automation and expected the rising unemployment trend to persist ever upward; (2) the structuralists, who defined the problem as round pegs and square holes—there were allegedly enough jobs for all those seeking them, but the job seekers lacked the education or the skills or were located in the wrong places; and (3) those who attributed the problem to a deficient rate of economic growth.

The programs

Without a consensus, within as well as without the government, there was little initial action from the Kennedy administration, but Congress was better positioned to move decisively, since the leadership in the House and the Senate remained unchanged. There were bills already "in the hopper" that had been discussed in previous sessions of Congress and even passed and vetoed by the previous President. The legislators were feeling direct pressure from the voters. The fact that initiative was left to Congress predetermined the policy choice. The structural issues were readily apparent—particular people unemployed in particular places; the aggregate demand issue was pervasive and impersonal. Bill S.1 of the new Congress was the Area Redevelopment Act introduced in the relatively prosperous mid-1950s to aid depressed areas in a generally buoyant economy. All the arguments had been heard, and positions were taken. The bill had passed the Senate twice and the House once and been vetoed by President Eisenhower. In spite of the fact that this was a time of general economic slack, not the most propitious time to attract new industry to depressed areas, the act was passable, and it was passed.

Training the unemployed

A convenient beginning point for tracing the history of manpower policy developments and the growth of manpower expenditures during the 1960s was the appointment in that initial year of a special Senate committee on unemployment (Table 12-1). The work of that committee and its report had attracted the interest of some labor economists and had educated a few senators among its members. What had impressed the latter was the picture of adult male family heads with considerable labor market experience—coal miners, steelworkers, factory hands—now without jobs and complaining that machines had replaced them. A retraining program appeared to be the answer, and, as was mentioned earlier, the Manpower Development and Training Act (MDTA) became law in March 1962, though it was not funded until September of the same year.

No sooner did recruiting for the new program begin than it became apparent that the demand was less for retraining than for the training of those who had never obtained skills. In 1961, when MDTA was first proposed, the overall unemployment rate was 6.7 percent and the unemployment rate for married men was 4.6 percent; but the latter indicator dropped to an average of 3.6 percent throughout 1962 while the program was getting underway, and the tendency was to call back the experienced workers. Those left out of work were primarily new entrants to the labor force, and the recruits for the training program were primarily those who had never achieved substantial skills. Despite the abrupt fall in the unemployment rates for the adult male family head, the overall rate actually rose to 5.7 percent for 1963 after dropping to 5.5 percent for 1962. The negative offsetting factor had been youth unemployment rising to 17 percent.

The swollen 1947 birth cohort was now 16 years of age—the end of compulsory school attendance in most states—and the dropouts were striking the labor market in rapidly growing numbers. The 1963 national legislative effort was a response to those

Table 12-1 Outlays for Manpower Programs (millions)

	1961	1964	1967	1970	1973	1974
Total	$235	$450	$1775	$2596	$4952	$4666
Department of Labor						
U.S. Employment Service	126	181	276	331	431	390
MDTA-Institutional	—	93	221	260	358	1419[a]
Job Corps	—	—	321	144	188	
JOBS	—	—	—	86	104	
Jobs Optional	—	5	53	50	73	
NYC in-School	—	—	57	58	73	
NYC Summer	—	—	69	136	220	
NYC Out-of-School	—	—	127	98	118	
Operation Mainstream	—	—	9	42	82	
Public Service Careers	—	—	—	18	42	
Concentrated Employment Program	—	—	1	164	129	
Work Incentive Program	—	—	—	67	177	218
Public Employment Program	—	—	—	—	1005	598
Program Administration, Research, and Support	8	23	118	143	209	162
Department of Health, Education and Welfare						
Vocational Rehabilitation	54	84	215	441	636	755
Work Experience	—	—	120	1	—	—
Other Programs						
Veterans Programs	14	12	19	141	292	351
Other Training and Placement Programs	8	15	116	277	382	377
Employment-related Child Care	26	37	53	141	433	398

[a]Programs now authorized by CETA.

Note: Details may not add to totals due to rounding.

Source: U.S. Office of Management and Budget.

facts. A Youth Employment Act encompassing a Home Town Youth Corps and a Youth Conservation Corps, modeled after the National Youth Administration and Civilian Conservation Corps of the 1930s, passed the Senate but failed in the House. Instead, MDTA was amended to allow its youth component to expand from 5 percent to 25 percent of total enrollment.

Modernizing vocational education

In addition, in that year Congress completed the first real re-examination of the basis of vocational education legislation since 1917, based on the work of a presidentially appointed study commission, consolidating reforms in the Vocational Education Act of 1963, which was discussed briefly in Chapter 11. In essence the Smith-Hughes Act of 1917 had responded to the needs of an adolescent industrial society. The assumption was that only a few needed specialized skills, so the act had offered federal matching money to states for training in the particular occupational areas designated by Congress. Additions of other occupational areas had been made over the years, but the underlying approach had not changed. In other words, the Smith-Hughes Act focused on the skill needs of the labor market. The Vocational Education Act of 1963 assumed that nearly everyone needed specific occupational preparation. Its emphasis was the employment needs of people. It was more than coincidence, however, that it became law during the year of youth-in-manpower legislation.

Declaring war on poverty

Other emphases, gathering force over time, were to come to legislative fruition in 1964. A civil rights movement had gained momentum during the 1950s and early 1960s. That movement's demands began shifting from equal access to public facilities to the economic arena—jobs and income. Simultaneously, journalists and a few academic economists, influenced heavily by President Kennedy's experiences in Appalachia during the 1960 campaign, discovered that poverty was still extensive in affluent America.

The product was the Economic Opportunity Act (EOA) of 1964.[4] It represented a declaration by a new President, Lyndon B. Johnson, of total war on poverty. However, its weapons were neither new nor powerful. The administration's rhetoric against poverty was stronger than its will to commit resources or its knowledge of poverty's causes. The rejected Youth Employment Act of 1963 with its New Deal antecedents became the source of the Neighborhood Youth Corps and Job Corps conservation centers. The participation of the Defense Department in the internal government task force that designed the antipoverty program and the fact that a number of military bases, surplus since the Korean conflict, were slated for closing were the impetuses for the Job Corps urban centers. They were, in fact, residential vocational schools for youth whose home and neighborhood environments were considered too debilitating for successful rehabilitation. The Department of Labor recommended a large-scale work relief program modeled on the Work Projects Administration (WPA) of the 1930s, but had to settle for a small-scale Work Experience and Training Program for adults based on an even smaller program sponsored by the Department of Health, Education, and Welfare to allow public-assistance recipients to work for their benefits.

A Ford Foundation program and another aimed at juvenile delinquency were the precursors of the Community Action Program designed to pull together all public and private antipoverty agencies in communities heavily impacted by poverty to coordinate and govern them by elected boards including representatives of the poor. Other pieces of the EOA had similar antecedents. Throughout, the emphasis was on youth and on breaking the poverty cycle by preparing for and providing jobs. Underlying the effort was growing awareness that nonwhites experienced double the unemployment of the rest of the labor force, that teenagers suffered three times the average level of unemployment, and therefore, that black teenage unemployment was six times the average.

Equalizing employment opportunity

Even more direct impact of the civil rights movement was Title VII of Civil Rights Act of 1964, which forbade discrimination in employment on grounds of race or sex. Added to a previous executive order aimed at federal contractors, a strong national consensus on equal employment opportunity seemed to be emerging. Discrimination on grounds of sex was added as an obstacle by opponents of the bill to make the act more difficult to administer, but attack on that problem eventually became more potent than the original intent. Chapter 21 explores the consequences of those legislative and administrative decisions.

Whence the jobs?

The year 1964 was also the time for another important attack on unemployment. The unemployment rate had fallen from its 1961 peak of 6.7 percent but persisted at 5.5 percent and 5.7 percent respectively during 1962 and 1963. The Council of Economic Advisers (CEA) diagnosed the economy's ills as the consequences of an inadequate rate of economic growth. An accelerating pace of additions to the labor force, plus productivity rising more rapidly in the post– than the pre–World War II era, demanded a rate of growth in the Gross National Product and job creation substantially above the historical pace. Yet a war-borne tax burden and absorption with anti-inflation efforts during the 1950s was slowing the pace of the economy below its potential. An economic education for a relatively conservative President was also a prerequisite, but in 1962 and 1963 Kennedy's economic advisers first sold him and then introduced to the Congress a tax reduction package designed to get the economy moving again. President Kennedy's death intervened, but President Johnson's persuasive powers with his former colleagues and the sympathy for the unfinished program of the late President combined to spur passage of what was, at the time, a startling proposal: Cut the federal government's income without reducing expenditures at a time when the budget deficit is already large, and the result will be not a larger but a smaller deficit, plus an acceleration in the rate of job creation and a drop in unemployment.

The result, of course, was that unemployment did begin to fall—from 5.7 percent in 1963 to 3.8 percent in 1966 and 3.5 in 1969. An added discovery, important for a short period, was the so-called fiscal dividend. A growing economy with a progressive tax structure must decrease tax rates and increase public expenditure in some combination consistently or the drain on total purchasing power will be such as to force the economy to an unacceptable level of unemployment. The fact that events in Vietnam absorbed the fiscal dividend in mid-1965 did not change its validity. Unemployment had already declined from 5.7 percent to 4.5 percent before that event and was declining sedately without creating inflationary pressures. An additional gain in the public's education had little impact on the causes and cures of unemployment. Despite fears of automation and other structural changes, unemployment could be reduced by purely fiscal means. A few years more had to pass before the limitations of this approach were tested.

Education for equality

The next year, 1965, might well be called the education year. Economists were making much of discoveries concerning the returns to investment in human capital, discussed in Chapter 8. There was growing faith that education, concentrated in those schools and areas impacted by poverty and low educational achievement, could compensate for social and familial handicaps and promote equality of economic and social opportunity. This was the aim of the previously mentioned Elementary and Secondary Education Act (ESEA) of that year, the largest single input of federal aid ever made to predominately state and locally financed public education.

A less publicized but noteworthy legislative development that year was the Economic Development Act. The Area Redevelopment Act of 1961 had met with limited success; the funds had been spread too thinly over too many areas and the tools selected were not effective. The proposed remedy was to focus on a few of the most depressed areas through joint federal-state regional commissions, which are treated in Chapter 24.

The job creation issue

MDTA implied that the causes of unemployment were inherent in the unemployed. They lacked skills and, given them, could be placed in jobs. Job Corps carried the same implication, but it indicated an environmental source for the lack of skills and productivity. The Community Action Program and Civil Rights Title VII indicated an institutional source for unemployment and poverty. The issue was becoming clear, if the answer was not: When certain individuals and groups are found to suffer more than their proportionate share of unemployment and poverty, is the cause more likely to be found in their own lack of skills motivation, or in biases built into societal institutions including labor markets? Operationally, would it be more effective to concentrate on changing the people or on changing the institutions?

Training programs appeared to work well for those living in suburban areas and modest-sized cities where jobs were available to those for whom skills were provided. Those in central cities and rural depressed areas too often seemed to graduate from the training programs with only a hunting license to search for jobs that did not exist. The rural depressed areas had no jobs, and the central cities tended to require education and life styles beyond the reach of many of the inner-city residents or to offer only limited opportunities and low wages unattractive to those with any income alternatives.

The MDTA, which had operated as an act to aid all of the unemployed and was concerned with the total of the nation's manpower resources, was transformed after 1964 into primarily an additional weapon in the antipoverty war with the disadvantaged as its focus. After some years of confusing use of the term without definition, "disadvantaged" was defined in 1968 to mean those who were both poor and without satisfactory employment and either (1) under 22 years of age, (2) over 44, (3) without a high school diploma, (4) member of a minority group, or (5) physically or mentally handicapped.

Among labor economists there was emerging the hypothesis of the secondary labor market—discussed in Chapter 7—that there was a primary market of good jobs with favorable wages, fringe benefits, and opportunities for advancement separated by an impervious wall from a secondary market of low-paid, dead-end jobs of little worth and characterized by high turnover, and that most manpower programs could offer no ladder to surmount that wall. At the same time, the central cities were heating up with a growing number of riots across the country, and a search began for ways of diverting federal funds and methods of cooling the flames.

The Economic Opportunity Act was amended in 1966 and 1967 to add small-scale job creation to its offering. Operation Mainstream provided direct work-relief-type employment, mostly to older male adults in rural areas rehabilitating the physical environment. The New Careers program attempted to subsidize public agencies and private nonprofit organizations to segment from the assignments of overworked or scarce professionals tasks that did not require their full specialized training.[5] These were to be structured into new careers for the poor as subprofessional aides of various kinds. The Special Impact amendment to EOA attempted special economic development activities in urban areas heavily impacted by poverty.

There was also a growing emphasis on recruiting the cooperation of private employers in the war on poverty. After all, they had the handle on most of the jobs in the economy. The Concentrated Employment Program (CEP) of 1967 had two objectives: (1) to concentrate the efforts of federal manpower programs in those census tracts with the worst employment and income conditions; and (2) to recruit private employers to hire the disadvantaged. The second object was notable for its lack of success. However, a number of experimental efforts culminated in a dramatic major effort beginning in 1968.

In late 1967, particularly frightening riots had occurred in Detroit and Newark, following upon those in Watts, San Francisco, and elsewhere, and the nation's capital exploded upon Dr. Martin Luther King's assassination. Labor markets were tight, and general levels of unemployment were low as a result of fiscal policy and the Vietnam involvement. Yet not enough jobs seemed to be seeping into the central-city areas, and it was becoming clear that not just any job would do, particularly for the young without heavy financial responsibilities. President Johnson, in a major manpower message in January 1968, announced organization of a

National Alliance of Businessmen (NAB), under the direction of prestigious national business leaders, to administer a Job Opportunities in the Business Sector program (NAB-JOBS).[6]

The initial results were beyond expectation. The plan was for the Labor Department to supply funds from MDTA and EOA to compensate the employers for any additional costs incurred by hiring initially less competent people. Approximately one-third of those who responded accepted such compensation, but the remainder pledged to hire the disadvantaged at no cost to the government. The combination of presidential publicity, widespread labor shortage, and dramatized reality of the problem was temporarily effective.

The impact of subsidized private employment remains controversial. There was no way of checking on the actual hiring by the "freebies"—those who accepted no compensation and, therefore, were not obliged to file reports or submit to audits. It is always difficult to find out how the new situation differs from what would have happened in absence of the program. Given their manpower needs, did the employers hire people they would not have hired anyway? Were their new employees more disadvantaged than they would have otherwise been? Were additional or different employee services provided? Yet there is ample anecdotal evidence of firms that did make substantial observed changes in their recruiting, selection, training, promotion, and discipline practices in favor of the disadvantaged and minorities.

The enthusiasm soon subsided but did not disappear. A change of American Presidents reduced the personal commitment. The ashes of Detroit and Newark cooled, and unemployment began to rise. The program had been operated by business executives who, on loan from their firms, solicited pledges from their fellow executives, leaving the filling of the pledges to company personnel departments and the public employment service. They were often reluctant to continue the detour from their own careers. With seniority-holding employees on layoff, few firms could hire new personnel. Nevertheless, the program continued at a reduced pace, adding jobs for youth and veterans to its assignments and generally tending to replace the loaned executives with professional employment service personnel.

The 1968–1969 objective was jobs for the disadvantaged in the tightest labor markets that had existed in the absence of wage-and-price controls since the recording of unemployment statistics began in the 1930s. Despite levels of unemployment persisting below 4 percent from 1966 through 1969, the Labor Department estimated the "universe of need" for manpower programs at 11 million. However, the economic forces that stimulated job creation after mid-1965 were war borne and inflation prone. The plunge of unemployment during the last two quarters of 1965 and the first quarter of 1966 made labor force adjustments difficult. War is inherently inflationary, since it expands the purchasing power of the population without adding to the goods and services available for purchase—and because the military is not frugal in the pursuit of conflict. Worse yet, the existence of a major war could not be admitted politically, and no taxes were levied to pay for it. No one will ever know whether 4 percent or less unemployment could have been maintained at lesser inflationary cost under other conditions. At any rate, inflation spiraled: 1.7 percent in 1965, 2.9 percent in 1966 and 1967, 4.2 percent and 5.4 percent in 1968 and 1969, respectively, as measured by the consumer price index.

The incoming Nixon administration undertook measures to slow that spiral, and higher unemployment resulted: 3.5 percent in 1969, 4.9 percent in 1970, and 5.9 percent in 1971, though inflation continued to accelerate with relative world shortages of food and energy added to high government and consumption expenditures and political reluctance to impose the necessary taxes to bring the economy into balance. Now unemployment was not merely a problem of the disadvantaged. It struck more politically potent groups, particularly returning veterans. Congress responded with proposals for a large-scale public service employment program to offer jobs in the public sector of the economy to those not absorbed by the private sector or by existing levels of public employment. The jobs, it was hoped, would be useful and not essentially different in kind from those existing, but they would increase in number from temporary subsidization. Such an act was vetoed by President Nixon in December 1970 on the grounds that it would reintroduce the WPA of the 1930s and was not needed because the administration's economic game plan would reduce unemployment without adding to inflationary forces. When the economy failed to respond, however, and the unemployment rate rose even higher, the President, with some evident reluctance, the following August, signed into law the Emergency Employment Act of 1971.[7]

The act extended for two years and offered $2.25 billion to provide 150,000 jobs for the unemployed without restriction to the disadvantaged. It was generally conceded to be a success, providing a new increase in employment, doing so rapidly with a minimum of waste or fraud, giving jobs to those who needed them, and providing useful public services. Nevertheless, the administration again opposed its extension as its expiration neared. Despite the evidence of success, the administration's commitment to the concepts of decategorization and decentralization (discussed later in this chapter) had intensified. If public service employment was the need in a particular locality, let that locality allocate money for that purpose from the decategorized funding provided it for decentralized decision making, while those with differing needs and priorities made other choices. Nevertheless, the commitment of Congress to the public service employment approach to job creation was growing, while its trust in the administration was shrinking.

To guarantee a substantial allocation of federal funds to subsidization of public employment for the disadvantaged, a separate title was provided for that function in the Comprehensive Employment and Training Act of 1973 (CETA), which will be treated again in greater detail presently. The public motivation for job creation programs was not totally sympathetic to the poor, nor was it all oriented toward providing a kind of riot insurance.

Almost simultaneously with the initiation of the subsidized private employment concept represented by NAB-JOBS there emerged a job-oriented program with almost dramatically opposed motives. Like nearly every other manpower program, NAB-JOBS had as its underpinning some degree of sympathy with the employment and income problems of those seemingly unable to compete successfully in contemporary labor markets. The motivation of the Work Incentive Program (WIN) inaugurated by an amendment to the Social Security Act in December 1967 was primarily punitive. The experience under this effort is discussed in Chapter 15.

Rejection of the great society

Despite some 1968 campaign rhetoric rejecting concepts and programs of President Johnson's Great Society, President Nixon and his new administration in its first term made remarkably few changes in manpower policy programs. But beginning early in 1973, wholesale rejection of the Great Society and the elimination of its residue seemed suddenly to become administration policy.[8] It had become apparent as early as the 1968 election that social welfare policies that favored the disadvantaged and minorities were not endorsed by the mass of lower middle-class blue-collar, service, and white-collar workers. An effort had been made to weld together a new Republican majority, and the election returns evidenced success. A major governmental reorganization was underway, removing the previous term's appointees, who had been primarily nonpolitical experts in the various fields, and replacing them with appointees whose primary qualifications appeared to be loyalty to the White House. Manpower and other Great Society programs came under increasing attack.

Not only administration stalwarts but members of the academic community, some who had been among the architects of the same programs, recanted and joined the critical chorus, arguing that the problems had been misread and the programs misguided. Because the programs' supporters had often been unrealistic in their rhetorical advocacy and claims for the programs, it was not difficult to prove that they had not achieved all they had promised.

However, the revelations lumped together categorically under the term "Watergate" reduced administration credibility, eliminated from positions of influence some of the strongest opponents of social welfare programs, and turned public attention elsewhere. More temperate examination of evaluative data restored a consensus that, though the programs had not achieved what they had promised, their benefits had generally exceeded their costs. Reform rather than rejection became the watchword.

The emergence of state and local manpower expertise

By 1966 MDTA, EOA, and the Civil Rights Act of 1964 had introduced an institutional and an on-the-job skill training program for unemployed persons of all ages, a residential vocational skill program for youth (Job Corps), separate work-experience programs for in-school and out-of-school youth and for the adult poor, a community action program, and the beginnings of efforts to enforce equal opportunity in employment. The initiative was necessarily national. No lesser jurisdiction had the know-how or resources, and few had the interest to serve unfamiliar and often unpopular margins of the population. As illustrated, programs did not emerge from a careful exploration of problems, conduct of research, and experimentation with solutions; they were rarely based on experience. With various legislators putting their own brand on special gimmicks to serve essentially the same clientele, there were soon competing federal agencies and a proliferation of programs and service agencies at the local level. Even though more programs were to be added in 1967, 1968, and 1971, the services available among the numerous programs represented a smaller number than the programs themselves: classroom skill training, limited basic education, subsidized public and private employment, minimal work experience as an excuse for transfer payments, supportive services, placement, and enforcement of anti-discrimination measures.

The concentrated employment program

Congress, in 1966 hearings, first began lamenting the interagency competition at the national level and the proliferation of programs at the local level. The Labor Department responded to the criticism in two ways: (1) by intensifying the efforts it was already making to wrest from the Department of Health, Education, and Welfare and the Office of Economic Opportunity their hold on pieces of the manpower action and (2) by demonstrating rising concern for the increasingly restless central-city minority disadvantaged.

The Johnson administration's interest in a special employment program in ghetto neighborhoods was aroused by Labor Department surveys conducted in 1966 that showed concentrations of unemployment between 6 and 15 percent in urban neighborhoods. Therefore, in March 1967, before Congress had enacted the EOA amendments that authorized "special programs which concentrate work and training resources in urban and rural areas" of high unemployment, the Labor Department announced that $100 million in "recouped" and "unspent" EOA and MDTA funds were being set aside to establish Concentrated Employment Programs (CEPs) in 22 areas. By 1973, 82 CEPs were operating.

A byproduct, if not a major intent, of the CEP was putting the variety of programs under one roof. If it were not possible to adapt a mix of services to individual need, at least it might be possible to have a limited smorgasbord of programs with the potential for meeting diverse individual needs.

Although many CEPs have gained valuable experience in organizing comprehensive services by gathering a variety of manpower contracts, the most important lesson of the CEP experience was that mandating coordination among manpower program agents will not assure comprehensive planning and programming at the local level. It took specific legislative authority to consolidate MDTA and EOA programs, and it is not clear that the new legislative mandate will achieve more integrated and comprehensive manpower programs than the CEP or that it will even mean more efficient management.

The mandate of the CEP to include a variety of supportive services in its delivery sequences did set in motion efforts to arrange for the provision of these services to CEP clients by other agencies. Under CETA, funds to operate their own day-care centers or to hire legal or medical consultants will continue to be limited, and good relations between manpower sponsors and other agencies will be critical.

The cooperative area manpower planning system

An almost simultaneous development with the CEP was the Cooperative Area Manpower Planning System (CAMPS). The CAMPS system grew out of Labor Department efforts to introduce more consistent planning into the MDTA program. In 1967 the Manpower Administration won approval from the Department of Health, Education, and Welfare, the Office of Economic Opportunity, and the Department of Housing and Urban Development for CAMPS to consist of area, state, and regional coordinating committees. The states were to require local area CAMPS committees to formulate joint programs to be consolidated into state plans in time for regional approval. Final approval of the state and regional plans as well as individual projects would remain the prerogative of the individual federal agencies.

Initial state and local reaction to the CAMPS concept was highly favorable, but disillusionment soon set in. The planning process was impaired by the fact that no one knew how much and when Congress would appropriate for manpower programs. Appropriations were rarely forthcoming until at least three months of the fiscal year had gone by; then, in subsequent years, most and finally all of a fiscal year passed before some programs were funded for a given year. The continuing resolution of Congress was becoming a substitute for appropriations. With each program constrained by its own budget and procedures, the area and state plans were better described as individual agency plans stapled together than as comprehensive planning documents. The state and local committees complained that the Labor Department itself violated the spirit of CAMPS by superimposing major programs administratively without consulting the state and local units. The basic conflict between decentralized planning and national innovation was becoming clear.

Despite its weaknesses (natural growing pains for an innovation) CAMPS met a need for communication and sparked a desire in some areas for something more nearly approaching, at first, state autonomy. State employment services had been the initial prime movers in the CAMPS activity and usually served as the secretariat, both in the state-level CAMPS and the area CAMPS, which generally encompassed Standard Metropolitan Statistical Areas.

Soon, however, a few governors took interest and appointed their own manpower committees or appointed their own choices as CAMPS chairmen with the intention of coordinating and even bringing into subjection the usually autonomous state manpower agencies, a move that was officially endorsed by the Labor Department in 1968. Under pressure from their states, a number of senators and representatives pressed for an enlarged state role, and they appeared to view CAMPS as a potential instrument for achieving these aims.

The concept of local administration was an attractive one. A few states and cities moved to establish effective planning and administering mechanisms, and federal legislation contemplated a system that would give clout to state plans—the power to affect the flow of funds. By 1973 every state, 126 cities, 4 counties, 1 council of government, and 19 Indian tribes had grants to support manpower planning staffs.

Decentralizing manpower programs

What was happening was clear in retrospect and recognizable by 1968. Though the terms were yet to be coined, decentralization and decategorization were in the wind. Nationally uniform budget allocations among programs and services did not necessarily meet the needs of individual labor markets and communities. There were those at the state and local levels who thought themselves as well qualified to make manpower decisions as those at the federal level. Categorical programs required the applicant to meet the requirements and accept the services prescribed by the program; it was not possible to adapt the mix of services to individual need.

Within the Labor Department there was weariness and disillusionment with a system that made the department a signator of literally thousands of contracts and agreements that it could not monitor. Mayors had already been made painfully aware that the antipoverty program had bypassed them to funnel money into the central cities through ad hoc community action agencies (CAAs) that often became the focal point of anti-establishment political activity.

An amendment to EOA gave mayors and county officers power to take over the CAAs if they proved too obnoxious. Now a few governors and their staffs recognized that they too had been bypassed. Not only had funds flowed directly to the cities, which constitutionally were creatures of the state governments, but even state agencies received funding and direction from federal agencies without so much as consulting the governors.

Discussion of the pros and cons of decentralization and decategorization was widespread within the manpower fraternity in and out of government during 1968, and, following the election, a task force chaired by George P. Shultz, a prominent labor economist, recommended that policy to the incoming administration. When Shultz became the first Secretary of Labor of the Nixon administration, decentralization and decategorization became the official manpower policy.

In the next four years there were a series of manpower reform bills, all representing a growing consensus but failing to be enacted because of details or peripheral issues. All gave at least lip service to the concept of decategorization, then preserved in one form or other those categorized programs that enjoyed the personal protection of key congressional figures or were represented by well-organized interest groups. Though each legislative proposal claimed to consolidate all manpower programs, they addressed themselves only to MDTA and EOA. The Wagner-Peyser Act of 1933, Titles III and IV of the Social Security Act of 1935 (supporting among them the Employment Services, Unemployment Insurance, and WIN), and perhaps even the Vocational Rehabilitation Act should logically have been merged with an omnibus manpower bill. However, these were within the jurisdiction of other congressional committees, notably the powerful House Ways and Means Committee, and no success could be expected in attacking these bastions. All the proposals contained a laundry list of nearly every familiar manpower service to be provided at the prime sponsor's discretion.

The prime sponsor concept had been written into the EOA as early as 1967, assuming that the community action agencies would be the major manpower decision makers at local levels. In fact, that amendment had authorized decategorizing all EOA manpower programs except Job Corps, but the Department of Labor and the Office of Economic Opportunity had never been able to agree upon guidelines to implement it. The concept of a state or local unit of general government as a prime sponsor with the discretion both to plan and to administer manpower programs was widely accepted in the manpower reform proposals of 1969–1973, but there were differences over the size of those units and the relative state-city-county role. The first administration bill in 1969 was written in the Department of Labor and used the SMSA as the standard planning unit, recognizing the need for a labor-market-wide scope in manpower planning. Since then the trend has been to respond to lobbying efforts by the National League of Cities–Conference of Mayors by granting prime sponsorship to smaller and smaller governmental units and to leave the still largely disinterested states only the rural areas and small towns.

In the metamorphosis in the first Nixon term, in which the

White House staff and the Office of Management and Budget gradually replaced the cabinet departments as policy makers, administration influence upon manpower policy tended to more idealogical inputs. The decentralization notion was in accord with the extreme New Federalism that endorsed unconditional revenue sharing, providing reduced funds but giving full discretion to state and local governments with no strings attached. An administration manpower position emerged that was characterized by its opponents as "putting the money on the stump and running." Congress was unwilling to grant such a complete delegation of federal responsibility. On the other hand, most Democrats and liberal Republicans were committed to public service employment as a weapon against the unemployment that had resulted from administration anti-inflation efforts. They insisted on attaching a public service employment title to any manpower reform bill, thus courting its veto.

Comprehensive manpower programs

With federal action stymied, a number of states and then some cities established their own manpower planning councils and attempted to exercise as much discretion as possible within legislative requirements. The Labor Department's Regional Manpower Administration offices established during the later Johnson years and strengthened under the Nixon decentralization drive insisted on exercising their full prerogatives, however, and the efforts at local decision making were usually thwarted. Some of the state and city manpower planners gained the ear of the Assistant Secretary of Labor for Manpower, and the Labor Department won agreement of congressional appropriations subcommittees to a series of pilot projects called Comprehensive Manpower Programs (CMP), which were mentioned earlier, to go as far as possible in the decentralization-decategorization direction within the constraints of existing law (stretched perhaps somewhat beyond the limits of legitimate interpretation but without serious opposition).

During the two years it took to negotiate the CMP agreement, however, another election passed and further expanded the commitment to decentralization. In 1973 the administration resolved to introduce decentralization and decategorization by administrative fiat without awaiting congressional action. Manpower programs were an early target. Most of the Great Society programs had been continued, and some of them even expanded during the first Nixon term. Now the White House seemed convinced that the programs were not working and should be dismantled. Funds were frozen, budget recommendations were severely constrained, and appropriations bills exceeding them were vetoed. Decentralization and consolidation accorded with prevailing ideology, was a vehicle for reducing these federal expenditures and shifted program responsibility to state and local governments. If a few pilot CMP projects could be legitimately undertaken under existing law, why not blanket the country with them? Congress hesitated somewhat but was relatively helpless. Besides, the approach taken did not differ appreciably from what Congress had itself resolved to do. The CMP process retained a strong federal presence. The money was not on the stump.

The comprehensive employment and training act of 1973

By the time Watergate had weakened White House influence and greater authority had returned to the Labor Department (though still under close supervision of the Office of Management and Budget) for negotiation with Congress, the decentralization process had already progressed in substantial degree in all states and over 100 cities. The Comprehensive Employment and Training Act (CETA) of 1973, which was mentioned earlier, essentially endorsed, legitimized, and extended what was already in place in many areas.

The major addition in 1973 was manpower planning at the county level. The 1970 census showed that about two-thirds of the nation's poverty and unemployment was located in suburban and rural counties, *not* the central cities. New allocation formulas were devised. Plans were well underway to extend manpower planning grants to all counties having at least 100,000 population, as well as to cities of the same size, before the imminence of legislation delayed the development.

Legislation in December 1973 gave a more solid policy base to the size of prime sponsors and the relative roles and responsibilities of federal, state, and local governments. Though regulations and guidelines are new and changing and the usual number of anomalies must be worked out in practice, congressional intent was relatively clear. Any unit of general local government with a population of 100,000 or more can apply for prime sponsorship. In addition, in what he determines to be exceptional circumstances, the Secretary of Labor has discretion to grant prime sponsorship to smaller governmental units that serve major portions of the labor market or represent rural areas of high unemployment and that have demonstrated capability to carry on their own manpower programs. When two governmental units are eligible for the same area, say, a city within a county, the preference is given to the smaller unit.

There were originally five titles in CETA, but the sixth was passed by Congress in December 1974 in response to the recession to fund jobs for idle workers. Titles 1, II, and VI are locally oriented while the other three are totally federal responsibilities. A prime sponsor must submit an annual comprehensive manpower plan to the Department of Labor for approval, but federal officials may not dictate the mix of services to be provided or the target groups to be served. Indeed, funds under these titles may largely be used interchangeably.

Eighty percent of Title I funds are allocated to state and local prime sponsors by formula to provide the full gamut of manpower services: outreach, assessment, orientation, counseling, remedial education, skill training, OJT, subsidized private and public employment, supportive services, training allowances, and labor market information. Also included are services provided by community-based organizations such as the Opportunities Industrialization Centers (OIC) and SER-Jobs for Progress. Of the remaining 20 percent, 5 percent is available for incentives to combine prime sponsor jurisdictions; 5 percent is to go to governors to be used to purchase vocational education from public schools; 4 percent is to provide state services to local prime sponsors; and another 6 percent must be used to keep any prime sponsor "to the extent possible" from receiving less than 90 percent of the previous year's funding, a "hold harmless" provision. Any remainder is to be allocated among prime sponsors at the secretary's discretion.

Each state must have a state manpower services council to coordinate CETA activities throughout the state. Each state and local prime sponsor must have manpower planning councils appointed by the chief elected executive. The membership of these councils must include representatives of the client population, community-based organizations, management, labor, and general public and manpower agencies, and the state manpower service council must also have representation from local prime sponsors. Each prime sponsor must submit to the Department of Labor for approval an annual comprehensive manpower plan. Title I moneys can be used for any manpower services for the unemployed, underemployed, and disadvantaged. Title II is designated as a public service employment title but explicitly authorizes recipient prime sponsors to use the funds for other manpower services if they prefer to do so.

In addition to Title I prime sponsors, Indian tribes and areas that have experienced unemployment of 6.5 percent or more for three consecutive months are eligible to share 80 percent of Title II moneys. The Secretary of Labor distributes the remaining 20 percent at his discretion.

Title III meets the political requirements to keep intact funding for certain categorical programs and organizations that have developed potent support, and provides special assistance for groups such as Indians and migrant workers not amenable to service by state and local governmental jurisdictions. It also supports research and experimentation, evaluation, staff training and technical assistance, and provides for labor market information. The act assigns manpower responsibilities to the Secretary of Labor but requires consultation and approval by the Secretary of Health, Education, and Welfare when education and institutional skill training are involved.

Title IV supports and regulates the Job Corps; Title V calls for the establishment of a new national commission on manpower policy consisting of cabinet officers and public members, ostensibly independent of any of the federal manpower agencies and answering to the President and the Congress.

The act replaces only the MDTA and the EOA. The Wagner-Peyser Act, WIN, and other manpower aspects of the Social Security Act, the vocational rehabilitation and vocational education programs, including veterans' training, the Health Manpower Act, and others were left out of the decentralized and decategorized manpower process. This was the case because it was felt that it was politically unwise to challenge the jurisdiction of powerful congressional committees or because these programs had major components not directly related to remedying the employment handicaps of disadvantaged, out-of-school youth and adults. Accordingly, CETA encompassed only half of the manpower funding in fiscal 1975, or $3.1 billion out of $6.3 billion (Table 12-2).

A new era?

A new era in manpower policy was signaled by CETA. Federal dominance in decision making, with provision of services primarily a responsibility of state governmental agencies and private, nonprofit, community-based organizations, had given way to a system whereby state and local elected officials are responsible for choosing among the groups to be served, identifying the services to be provided, and designating the recipients of the service delivery assignment. The past is useful only to extract lessons to be passed on to the future, the subject of Chapter 16. Chapter 13 explores the techniques of state and local manpower planning.

Table 12-2   Manpower Budget Summary, 1973–1976 (millions)

Program	1973	1974	1975	1976
Comprehensive manpower assistance training	$1388	$1419	$3102	$3295
Emergency employment assistance	1005	598	58	—
Work incentive training and placement	177	218	202	198
Veterans programs	292	351	457	440
Employment service	431	390	462	452
Vocational rehabilitation	636	755	819	830
Social services training	58	30	62	50
Other training and placement programs	276	283	297	303
Employment-related child care	433	398	604	498
Program direction, research, and support	209	162	179	194
Other supportive services	48	64	52	50
Total	$4952	$4666	$6294	$6309

Note: Figures for 1975 and 1976 are estimated.

Source: U.S. Office of Management and Budget.

Notes

1. Garth L. Mangum, *The Emergence of Manpower Policy* (New York: Holt, Rinehart & Winston, 1969).
2. Daniel Bell, *The Coming of Post-Industrial Society* (New York: Basic Books, 1973).
3. Frederick H. Harbison, *Human Resources as the Wealth of Nations* (New York: Oxford University Press, 1973).
4. Sar A. Levitan, *The Great Society's Poor Law* (Baltimore, Md.: Johns Hopkins Press, 1969); Joseph Kershaw, *Government Against Poverty* (Washington, D.C.: Brookings Institution, 1970).
5. Frank Riessman and Arthur Pearl, *New Careers for the Poor* (New York: Free Press, 1965).
6. Sar A. Levitan, Garth L. Mangum, and Robert Taggart III, *Economic Opportunity in the Ghetto* (Baltimore, Md.: The Johns Hopkins University Press, 1970).
7. Sar A. Levitan and Robert Taggart III, *The Emergency Employment Act: The PEP Generation* (Salt Lake City, Utah: Olympus Publishing Co., 1973).
8. Lloyd Ulman, "The Uses and Limits of Manpower Policy" *The Public Interest*, No. 34 (Winter 1974).

13

the techniques of public manpower planning[1]

Besides endorsing state and city manpower planning, which was already in place, CETA opened it up at the county level.[2] The push for decentralization and decategorization in manpower programs is only a part of broader developments. The underlying objective is manpower planning at the labor market level, which, in turn, has a parallel development in manpower planning in the employing establishment. However, both are symptoms of some profound developments. If human resources have become preeminent among the economic factors of production while employment remains the major source of income, if the world is becoming more complex, requiring more foresight to avoid social pathologies, if computers and the spread of education and information enhance the ability to forecast the future, it is almost inevitable that there be rising concern for foreseeing and compensating for prospective labor market dislocations. In fact, manpower planning in the private sector among business firms emerged before there was a significant amount of public sector manpower planning.

This chapter supplies rationale and definitions for manpower planning in both public and private sectors of the economy but summarizes experience and practice only in state and local manpower planning as manifest in CETA and its predecessors.

Why manpower planning?

That manpower is a vital economic resource while employment is the primary source of income and status in our society are truisms. But they do not justify manpower planning. Social energy is always limited, and there is no reason to undertake planning unless

271

lack of foresight will make things worse and a successful effort to foresee future conditions and accommodate or modify them can make conditions better. Manpower has always been a vital economic resource, and employment became the primary source of income as a consequence of industrialization. What recent developments have made important what formerly was not necessary?

In the broadest context it was the transition in economic history, already alluded to in Chapter 1, that increasingly brings to human resources the primacy once held by natural and capital resources. This does not mean that natural and capital resources are no longer important. The rising productivity that has freed man to the extent he has been freed from drudgery has been primarily the result of more and better equipment to augment man's puny physical strength. Rising standards of living still depend upon increased productivity. Concern for supplies of food and energy is a sharp and belated reminder that the passengers on "Spaceship Earth" are dependent upon a fixed supply of natural resources. They can be discovered and developed but not created by man. But the failure to recognize those limitations and to plan to enjoy the good life within those constraints was a failure of human wisdom, not of natural resources. If planning is to make the best of natural and capital resource constraints, if new natural resources are to be developed and known ones conserved, it will be the wisdom and the skill of the human resource component that will achieve it.

The economic and social changes that have put a premium on the quality of the human resource contribution have had their impacts at both ends of the manpower spectrum. Those without education and training have come to be at a competitive disadvantage as their opportunities shrank relatively and the competition from better-prepared people increased. Technological, economic, and social changes isolated some in rural depressed areas and others in central-city slums. Cities developed perversely, with the well prepared often living in bedroom suburbs and working at white-collar jobs in central-city offices. While well-paid, semiskilled production jobs migrated to the suburbs, the victims of deficient education, racial prejudice, family breakup, and a variety of other social and economic ills were trapped in central cities that offered only those jobs for which they were unprepared or to which they had no access, or jobs that were unattractive and low paying.

High birth rates from 1947 to 1957 gave at least 16 years warning of swollen labor market entry rates, but public policy failed to heed the warning. School attendance multiplied and extended; labor force participation rates shifted, with those of men declining and of women rising; technological change quickened; mobility increased. All of this is an old story to any student or practitioner in the U.S. labor markets and has already been reviewed in Chapter 2.

The point is that all of these developments were foreseeable but little acted upon. That inaction brought crises that were responded to by programs ranging from those to increase the supply of educated manpower to those to improve the employability, employment, and earnings of those least able to compete successfully in labor markets. Programs with the former objectives were familiar, and they worked, perhaps even to excess in some areas of highly trained manpower. The latter programs were new, the problems to which they were addressed were unfamiliar, the techniques undeveloped, the staffs inexperienced and untrained, and the objectives complex.

When the labor market operated under crises, real or imagined, action seemed more needed than planning. At least in the public sector and at the national level, pressure of budget cycles and elections dictated a short-run focus. Since the initiatives on behalf of the disadvantaged were federal, state and local governments merely responded to administer federal resources under federal direction. At a more general level, expenditures for education and training multiplied without planning or coordination. Schools and colleges responded to perceived rising demand without wondering how their output related to that of all the other sources and to manpower requirements. Congress and federal agencies also responded piecemeal with incentives for expanding production of this or that type of specialist, with no attention to the total impact. New programs were introduced, and old policies shifted without recognition of their manpower implications or the availability of staff to carry them out.

All of this transition is occurring at a time in economic history when society is becoming incredibly complex and planning has become recognized as a vital necessity. Population growth, urbanization, and technological development have made everything related to everything else. Actions of one tend to have impact upon all. Private and social decisions are likely to bring into play long successions of unforeseen consequences. Once set in motion, such forces often seem almost irreversible. Where once planning was feared as an enemy of freedom, it is now the accepted insurance against binding strictures on future decisions. Add to all this, as the demand side of planning, the availability of massive data-processing capability augmenting the potential supply of planning capacity, put the primacy of human resources together with the demand for planning as an essential social function, and there is a recipe for the emergence of human resources and manpower planning.

Gradually, a positive response has developed out of this seeming chaos. To the extent that the availability and quality of labor have risen relative to capital and natural resources as economic considerations, one would expect to see manpower looming larger among the planning efforts of the rational business firm. Just as a firm is led by its pursuit of profit to plan ahead to obtain adequate supplies of raw materials and to invest in productive capital equipment, it should now be motivated to plan for an adequate labor supply.

Slowly, but increasingly, the larger firms in private industry are attempting to foresee critical manpower needs and prepare for them, insofar as it seems profitable to do so. Government statistical agencies provide better and better data and projections as aids to personal and institutional planning. The national government attempts to foresee total employment needs and, qualified by other goals, seeks an acceptable level of employment. Now, under CETA, a manpower planning assignment has been given to state and local governments, but planning competence and a planning format are just beginning to be developed. Nor has the planning assignment, until CETA, carried with it the discretion to relate plans to labor market needs and realities, affect operations, and achieve results. Decentralization of program responsibility from the federal to the state and local levels promises the discretion but not necessarily the competence for meaningful and effective planning. Political jurisdictions are not economic entities, whereas manpower problems occur in labor markets. Federal manpower program resources are minor in contrast to the range and size of manpower problems in any economy. Federal objectives may or may not accord with local priorities.

The sum and substance of these considerations are that:

1. Manpower planning is necessary in a world of rapid change where human resources play a vital role.
2. Manpower planning is scarce for lack of expertise and discretion, but both are growing.
3. Manpower planning should be undertaken wherever:
   a. problems can be foreseen and avoided
   b. unfavorable conditions can be ameliorated
   c. the future can be shaped in more satisfactory ways than had it just been allowed to happen
   d. looking ahead to objectives can allow measurement of progress.

4. But it cannot be done unless there are techniques, skills, and discretion.
5. When it is done effectively, the planning will be done where the problems are, that is, where people live, where jobs are created, and where the two match or fail to match.

A typology of manpower planning

As an earlier chapter defined it, manpower policy is a two-sided term encompassing all social decisions that deliberately affect (1) the use of people in labor markets as economic factors of production and (2) the ability and opportunity for people to pursue remunerative and satisfying work careers in employment.

Since the concerns of manpower policy embrace both its roles as a productive resource and as a determinant of personal welfare, it is well to think of a manpower system as those forces in society that not only use people in productive ways but also create their productivity. The system must recruit people from out of the population pool, motivate them to productiveness, prepare them for productive activity, create employment opportunities for them, match the people with the opportunities, reward them with both incomes and feelings of self-worth, and refurbish, upgrade, and replace them as economic forces or age displaces them. Planning is a systematic way of thinking through and designing a system to do these things.

Manpower planning includes every effort to foresee manpower problems, establish manpower goals, and design systematic approaches for avoiding the problems or achieving the goals. Planning activity is occurring in the public and private sectors and at the national, state, and local levels. Perspective on that assignment may be provided through a typology of manpower planning.

Macromanpower Planning

Conceptually, at least, it is useful to think of economic planning as manpower planning, as long as its primary goal is employment. The Employment Act of 1946 implied the tasks of estimating the number of persons likely to be seeking work and of devising policies for sufficient economic growth and job creation to absorb them. Though this is not a very explicit process, the Council of Economic Advisers always has available to it labor force projections made by the Bureau of Labor Statistics to forecast the number seeking jobs. The employment outlook is a key consideration in economic and political policy making, and despite the need to temper the employment goal with other goals, some action to expand or contract the pace of job creation is always recommended.

Similarly, the federal budgeting process can be considered, in part, as a manpower planning exercise. Decisions to spend various amounts on defense, aerospace, atomic energy, agriculture, education, or any of the myriads of federal budgeting allocations are also decisions for allocations of manpower resources among various sectors of the economy. Tax decisions are also decisions to allow or discourage private activities that allocate manpower within the private sector and between it and the public sector. Economic development activities such as those to aid depressed areas are in reality designed primarily to affect the spatial distribution of manpower and employment. Availability of federal aid to education influences the labor force participation of the young, just as public assistance affects the participation rates of some marginal and potential members of the labor force and just as Social Security benefits have an impact upon the participation rates of older persons. Projections of national manpower requirements both aid and influence individual choice among occupations, the planning for educational facilities and other resources, and the actions of employers.

A rational approach to manpower planning at the macrolevel would also recognize and respond to the tremendous impact on manpower policy of national decisions outside the manpower field. Just a few examples can illustrate the impact and the economic and social costs of failure to foresee and compensate for the manpower impact of national policy. Agricultural price-support programs introduced in the 1930s, for instance, were major factors in encouraging consolidation and mechanization of farms, forcing (or allowing) millions to leave the land, to migrate successfully or unsuccessfully to the cities, or to remain as the rural nonfarm poor. Medicare imposed greater burdens upon an already short supply of health manpower. Aerospace decisions encouraged large supplies of expensively trained manpower to invest their careers in that field and then abandoned them. Federal housing and high-way-building policies encouraged the demand for labor to shift to the suburbs without aiding substantial portions of the supply to follow. Availability of retirement benefits continually encourage earlier retirement in a population characterized by increasing longevity, while Social Security restrictions on continued earnings discourage second careers.

These are sufficient examples to illustrate the need and opportunities for manpower planning at the national or total economy level. The need has been discussed for some years and was most recently noted in the 1972 *Manpower Report of the President.* Recommendations have ranged over a broad number of devices including a Council of Manpower Advisers, a manpower member among the three-man Council of Economic Advisers, a special assistant to the President for manpower, an intergovernmental cabinet committee on manpower with a primary role for the Department of Labor. Yet policy responsibility still remains fragmented, with the consequence that nonmanpower decisions are made with little anticipation of their manpower consequences. Manpower considerations need not dominate, but at least there should be some focal point of recognition of manpower consequences with sufficient clout to have its voice heard.

Micromanpower planning

Though it is not the subject of this chapter, it should be noted that manpower is an increasingly important function in the individual business firm and, to a lesser degree, in the public agency as an employer.[3] Firms dependent upon sophisticated manpower look ahead, relating product and sales outlooks to manpower needs and enacting programs to get the right man at the right place at the right time. Enlightened firms also attempt to foresee declining manpower needs so that attrition can reduce otherwise excessive supplies. Most corporations at least try to look ahead at the attrition of top management and attempt to have replacements ready to take over. The number of firms undertaking such planning is relatively small but growing.

Manpower program planning

Little planning at the national level guided the variety of programs aimed at enhancing the employability and income of the poor and the competitively disadvantaged. Most were launched without clear identification of problems, explicit statement of objectives, or experimentation to see whether or not they would work. All were based on political supposition. Subsequent appropriations also have only the most casual relationship to need, being based on a variety of political judgments. At the local level, the response has been simply to accept federal funds, recruit eligible enrollees, and administer programs as directed by federal guidelines. Allocations to the state or communities from the federal level were made either by formula or by politics and grants. Allocation decisions within states were ordinarily made, without guidance, by low-level functionaries.

As Chapter 12 recorded, these were, in part, the forces that led first to CAMPS and subsequently to CETA. Disturbed at the chaotic hodgepodge of programs seeking to serve the same target groups at the local level, the federal agencies did to them what they had not been able to do to themselves. They superimposed a coordinating mechanism among program administrators at state and local levels. From a mere interagency communication system CAMPS evolved in some places toward a real effort at manpower planning. Its major weaknesses were lack of a planning format and trained staff and inadequate delegation of policy discretion so that planning could make a difference in the allocation of funds. Passage of CETA provided the needed discretion, and necessity forced the development of planning format, techniques, and staff.

Labor market manpower planning

Currently, labor market manpower planning has as its focus the employability and employment needs of those individuals finding it most difficult to compete successfully for the opportunities available in the job market. It has as its goal improvement of the employability, employment opportunities, and incomes of members of those target groups. Others, perhaps most participants, in the labor market find less than optimum fulfillment and income from their working careers and could use help as objects of manpower program planning. But resources and social energy are limited, and priorities among target groups and activities must be set.

Though labor market manpower planning seeks to enhance the ability of individuals and groups to compete successfully in labor markets, it is not the whole but only a part of the total labor market planning. A labor market is both a theoretical concept and a practical reality, but it is not a single place or event. Conceptually, it consists of all the ways in which those seeking to sell their labor and those seeking to buy labor services come into contact so that transactions—that is, hirings, promotions, and so forth—take place.

A labor market must incorporate and bring together, by definition, both the supply and demand for labor. The domain of manpower policy encompasses all supply-side concerns, but on the demand side it includes only particular employment opportunities for particular individuals. It serves as a bridge between and overlaps to some degree economic development policy on the one hand and social welfare policy on the other. The manpower planner, therefore, must limit his field so that it is manageable, but he must be familiar with and able to relate, contribute to, and use policies, programs, and resources outside of but closely related to his field of concern. Clearly, if there is no economic activity, there are no jobs, but an array of social services and amenities is necessary to make employability possible. The manpower planner must understand the economic system that creates the jobs, the employers who control them, the unions who represent the employees, the roles of the families, churches, schools, and other institutions that contribute to work values and job skills, and the institutions of the labor market that match or fail to match supply and demand.

Of course, the federally funded manpower programs for the disadvantaged are only a minor part of the moneys spent upon manpower matters. The target groups of the programs are only a small minority of the actual and potential labor force. Problems range across the entire spectrum of skills and occupations on both the demand and supply sides of the labor market. A planning process similarly dedicated to improving labor market functioning would concern itself with relationships across industries and occupations, population groups, generations, and institutions. In that exercise federal manpower program budgets would be viewed as only one important source of funding. The response would be a search for ways to fit the federal programs and funds into the pursuit of labor market objectives without violating the federal objectives.

Labor markets vary in geographic scope. Some of the most sophisticated skills are sold nationally or even internationally. For other skills and jobs the markets are regional. Only at the national level do economic boundaries coincide with political boundaries. Yet policy must be made through political instruments. For national labor markets macro-, micro-, and labor-market planning largely coincide. Occupations that are filled in national markets face demands largely determined through government policies. Both federal agencies and national employers concern themselves with the supply. The new thrust in manpower policy that raises manpower planning to the level of a major governmental effort is focused on those labor markets that are of smaller scope than state jurisdictions (though they often overlap state boundaries) but of broader scope than the cities. In general, the labor markets addressed are those over which a worker can range in search of a job or an employer in search of an employee without either having to change his residence or location. It is at that level that the challenge of manpower planning lies. There is where the problems are and where the jobs must be. Therefore, this chapter, commensurate with what is currently going on in manpower policy, addresses only one level of labor market problems—efforts to improve the employability, the employment opportunities, and the incomes of those workers experiencing difficulties in competing successfully for available jobs. This by no means covers the range of labor market manpower planning needs, but it is task enough for now.

The steps to planning

Planning itself has become an art, a science, and a recognized profession, apart from the goals of the field in which the planning occurs. There are well-recognized principles, techniques, and steps to the planning process that are worth reviewing in the manpower context before illustrating their specific application to manpower problems. The student who understands what the manpower planner (or any other planner) does should understand that planning process. Every planner has his or her own choice of the order in which planning steps are implemented, but all traverse essentially the same set of steps. If one plans only for the direction of a particular program, one begins with the goals of that program and plans for their achievement. If a wider and less specified goal is endorsed, a prior step is necessary.

Establishing manpower policy goals

Congress declared the purpose of CETA to be: "To provide job training and employment opportunities for economically disadvantaged, unemployed and underemployed persons, and to assure that training and other services lead to maximum employment opportunities and enhance self-sufficiency." The manpower services, target groups, and program objectives are rather clearly prescribed. However, unlimited scope is left for a state or community to establish its own broader manpower policy goals, subsuming CETA under it.

Social philosophy must play a preeminent role in goal setting. In general, the values placed on self-sufficiency and material standards of living in American society suggest a high priority for efforts to improve the employment status and income of those facing the most serious disadvantages in competition for jobs. However, application of that priority cannot be determined without an inventory of the major manpower and labor market pathologies that impinge upon the community. Is the most serious problem poverty, unemployment, labor shortage, skill bottlenecks standing in the way of other social priorities, loss of human resources through drugs, alcoholism, and crime, or inadequate preparation of labor force entrants, among others?

Having been presented with a list of pressing labor market pathologies, policy makers and those who advise them must choose the goals of manpower policy. For the sake of illustration assume a goal statement emanating by broad community consensus to bring out of poverty and establish self-sufficiency among all of those now with earned incomes below the poverty level.

Identifying Barriers

Having chosen a broad community manpower policy goal, man-power planning staff must then identify the specific barriers that impede its accomplishment. Why does the problem exist? Who and how many are its victims? What is the magnitude of its social costs? Who, if anyone, has a vested interest in the con-tinuance of the problem? What is the evidence that the barriers exist? What is known of their nature and magnitude? What data are required to answer these questions? To what extent do the data exist? What other data systems are required? What has been tried in the past to alleviate the barriers? What worked, and what did not? Most important of all, to what extent do the barriers ap-pear to be inherent in the shortcomings of the people themselves, and to what extent are they the shortcomings of social and labor market institutions? Must we change the people or change the institutions, and to what extent?

Examining alternatives

Nothing but frustration and waste can come of considering solu-tions that cannot work. What are all the alternative approaches that might be effective in overcoming the barriers and achieving the goals? What are the required social and technical skills for each? What are the relative resource and social costs? What are the trade-offs between money and time in the solution? What are the foreseeable byproducts and consequences of each approach? What are the likelihoods of unforeseen consequences? What is the political climate? Which solutions can win necessary political sup-port? What is the range and source of resources available to ad-dress the various alternatives? What are the probabilities of mar-shaling them? In exact dollars and numbers what will be the budget and the staff available for a specific period of time?

Setting objectives

Goals are by their nature broad and ill defined. In effect, they paint a picture of how one would like some aspects of the world and society to look. They offer little guidance for an implementable program and few measures of progress toward the goal. Objec-tives are best thought of as specific milestones on the way to a goal. To be useful they must be desirable, realistic, achievable, and measurable. Why pursue an objective that once achieved would make a situation no better or would cause ills worse than those for which cure is sought? Why pursue an unrealistic goal that cannot be achieved? As a milestone, an objective has no value unless one can measure progress toward it. How far have we come? Are our efforts moving us in the right direction? How far must we yet go? Are there ways of speeding progress? At what cost?

Having chosen as the goal elimination of that portion of poverty amenable to labor market solutions, and given the resources available, an appropriate objective might be to bring x families of y characteristics above the poverty line by z date. If persons have been identified whose poverty is labor market related, if there are jobs that can become available and services that can provide the access to those jobs, if the numbers are realistically related to the budgets available, and if the staff is sufficiently knowledgeable for planning and operation, then the objective is desirable, realistic, achievable, and measurable.

Designing and implementing a program

Having examined the alternatives and set appropriate objectives, we must now design a program and put it into effect. From the vantage point of the strategic planner this step consists of designating a target group, deciding upon an appropriate mix of services to meet these needs, and choosing and assigning one or more agencies or organizations to deliver the prescribed services. To the tactical planner at the agency level it consists of working out the logistics of facilities, staff, budgeting, administrative controls, and so forth, and for recruitment and service of the clients. To the program administrator the assignment is to do what the planners have only designed.

The evaluation step

No plan can foresee all eventualities. Estimates of relative effectiveness and costs of alternative approaches are at most judgments based on experience in never identical circumstances and are often simple best guesses. Administrators and staff, like all human beings, are rarely of the desired competence, nor do they work for long and often at peak efficiency. Performers are rarely the most objective judges of their own performance. Continuous monitoring is necessary to identify weaknesses and strengths. Only evaluation can assess the results and compare the achievements of alternative approaches. The question for evaluation is not only "how well was it done?" but also "at what costs?" Monitoring without evaluation has no measure of achievement. Evaluation without monitoring may provide knowledge of facts but no reasons for them. Monitoring and evaluation are needed at several levels in a manpower program. The program administrator monitors and evaluates his own performance for immediate reform. Strategic planners monitor and evaluate whether they have chosen the right mix of services and the most effective deliverers of service. The funding source monitors and evaluates whether effective use is made of public funds.

Feedback and modification

Manpower programming is not a one-time event. Labor market pathologies and individual barriers are usually too large in magnitude to be conquered. Individuals can be aided in overcoming the labor market barriers confronting them. But there will always be some unserved and unservable among existing clients, and new entrants will take the place of the successful.

Monitoring and evaluation make their contribution by feeding back information on relative success and failure and suggesting modifications that may make programs more effective or replace them with alternatives. The manpower task is continuous, though changing, and so must be the manpower service system.

Application to manpower programming

These standard planning steps translated into the context of public sector programs on behalf of the disadvantaged, unemployed, and poor emerge as essentially six manpower planning tasks: (1) Out of the population eligible for service (always many times greater than the number who can be served with available resources) establish priorities among and within target groups; (2) identify present and potential job openings accessible to the client groups after receiving program services; (3) identify the barriers that currently impede access of the target groups to those jobs; (4) design a mix of manpower services capable of removing or overcoming those barriers for the service group and for individuals; (5) choose an agency or combination of agencies and organizations capable of delivering the needed mix of services; (6) monitor the performance of the service delivery agencies, evaluate their results, and feed back learnings from the evaluation step to improve this and other programs. Each of these tasks deserves brief comment.

Universe-of-need methodology

The most widely used technique for calculating the demand for manpower services is the Department of Labor's universe-of-need (UON) method. The basic intent of the UON approach is to make an unduplicated estimate of the total number of individuals who could benefit from manpower services sometime during a given year. It classifies persons in need on three basic dimensions: labor force status, income, and disadvantagement. Labor force status is indicated in estimates of the unemployed and the underutilized. The underutilized estimate is subdivided into three additional sub-categories: (1) those employed part time for economic reasons, (2) those employed full time but with family income at or below poverty level, and (3) those not in the labor force but who should be. The poverty classifications used in the UON estimates are the poor, the near poor, and the nonpoor. The poverty classifications are based on the Social Security Administration's poverty index. The disadvantaged are defined as members of poor households who lack adequate employment and who additionally fall into one of the following groups: (1) school dropouts, (2) minority group members, (3) persons under 22 years of age, (4) persons 45 years of age or over, and (5) handicapped persons.

The UON is best seen as a stacked target group structure. Figure 13-1 illustrates the major elements of this structure with data for a large urban labor market area with a work force of approximately 220,000. The example assumes a total universe of need of 59,740 comprised of unemployed and underutilized individuals who will be potential recipients of manpower services sometime during fiscal year 1974. The total is then divided and subdivided on the basis of the poverty index, disadvantagement (as previously defined), and employment status. The major breakouts are designed to provide a fix on the estimated size of groups in a manner that suggests the relative need for manpower services.

Very little detailed data are systematically collected specifically concerning the unemployed, the underemployed poor, and disadvantaged persons on a subnational basis. To compensate for this lack the UON makes use of proportions derived from national surveys in computing several of the basic breakouts. For example, the methodology for calculating the number of persons who are unemployed and also poor uses a multiplication factor that varies with the area's unemployment rates. Similar factors of proportionality are used to account for low-income full-time workers, underrepresentation of specific groups in the labor force, the census undercount, near-poverty unemployment, and several other key components employed in building the UON estimates.

Figure 13-1   Illustrative universe of need for fiscal year 1974 (number of different individuals needing manpower services at some time during the year).

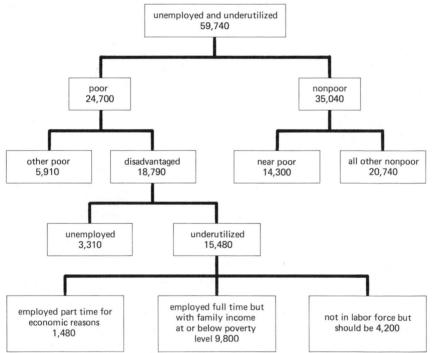

Source: Garth Mangum and David Snedeker, *Manpower Planning for Labor Markets* (Salt Lake City, Utah: Olympus Publishing Co., 1974), p. 119.

The chief criticism of the UON has centered on its narrow target group orientation, the use of national relationships in the methodology, and the lack of estimates of sufficient specificity to enable planners to use it as a basis for mix-of-service prescriptions at the local labor market level. The use of national factors of proportionality is especially serious when estimates must be prepared for smaller cities and areas. Questions also have been raised as to the applicability of the same factors to inner-city and rural planning areas.

In preparing the CAMPS activity for transition to CETA, Manpower Administration guidelines suggested analyses beyond the simple UON tables. The revised approach suggested attempts to classify the planning area population by race, sex, age, specific labor force status, educational attainment, income levels, and several specific target group indicators drawn from 1970 census data. The objective of this approach was to develop estimates that were more useful in designing an appropriate mix of service than was the UON methodology. While census data rapidly become dated and are limited in a number of other ways, the effort has helped to standardize the base data available to state and local manpower planners. Efforts are continuing to update the census materials and develop additional data on the assessment of the need for manpower services.

Despite the greater availability of census data in more usable form and the recent updating of the UON methodology, little real impact has yet been made on the actual operation of manpower programs. The present manpower planning process still largely ignores decisions about whom to enroll and why. Age, race, and income guidelines are used to screen in and screen out applicants who, within those broad categories of eligibility, are enrolled basically on a first-come, first-served basis. The result has been a nightmare for operational planners and precluded any kind of rational or efficient job development effort. Program operators are faced with the problem of serving an almost endless variety of enrollee interests, aptitudes, and needs. Rational planning is most difficult under these circumstances.

Planning tools are needed that group prospective clients by the specific types and degrees of service needs they have in common. The incidence of barriers to employment for these homogeneous groups must be identified, and the barriers must be related to specific employment requirements. The planner should identify which barriers are amenable to modification by what services. Resources can then be allocated to services in proportion to the incidence of the relevant barriers in the group to be served. These tasks require an overall construct that relates the population to the labor market and allows the use of static measures in what is actually a very dynamic environment.

A great deal of research and experimentation will be required before this essential first task of labor market manpower planning can be accomplished satisfactorily. Even then, since needs always exceed resources, choice of whom to serve must be made largely on political grounds among the groups needing manpower services, but the decisions could be made more rationally with relative costs and effectiveness in mind.

Accessible job openings

The ultimate payoff for manpower planning, as long as it has a social welfare orientation, is a better job and a higher and more stable income for members of the target groups chosen from among the UON. A first principle for any labor market manpower planner to remember is that the demand for labor is a derived demand. No one buys labor for its own sake. Jobs come into existence only when someone spends (or is expected to spend) money for the purchase of a good or service and an employer hires someone to produce what is demanded. The only exception to that market orientation is when a public agency charged with responsibility for employment opportunities spends public funds directly for the hiring of a target individual with the job as the product and the production as a byproduct.

Therefore, the first concern of the manpower planner employed under the CETA system is the availability of jobs. But that is not sufficient. The planner must assure that (1) a job is available and (2) his client has realistic access to that job. Also, since planning is a future-oriented activity, the planner must be sure not that the job is there now but that it must be accessible at the end of whatever preparation process is involved. This requires a knowledge of the current employment structure and the relations of supply and demand, an ability to project that relationship, and a knowledge of the entrance requirements and access routes to jobs and an ability to manipulate them.

The primary tool for planning job access is (1) an industry-occupation employment matrix, current and projected for the future and (2) some indicator of the relative accessibility of available jobs to particular clients. National data may not be much help to the planner for a local labor market. Therefore, the Department of Labor and the state employment security agencies are cooperating to produce a State Industrial Occupational Matrix System, which is already available in some states. As a measure and a base for projections, it will become an invaluable tool for the manpower planner.

Given the number of jobs that do now and will exist, the next question is the relation of demand to supply. At a moment in time, the concept of job vacancy would provide the answer. Just as a person without a job and actively seeking one is unemployed, a job vacancy would be a situation signaled by active efforts of an employer to fill a position. Unfortunately, there is no such measure generally available among U.S. labor statistics. The next best measure is one of relative tightness: For which occupations is unemployment low? And for which occupations is it high?

Over a longer period, net growth in employment in an occupation plus replacement needs resulting from quits, retirements, and deaths measures the accessible demand. Accessible supply is more difficult. For jobs requiring specific skills the output of the training system—academic education, vocational education, apprenticeship, OJT, and so on—provides an indicator. However, relatively few jobs have very specific skill requirements. Many jobs can be satisfactorily held without previous training, and skills learned on the job are often easily transferable to another job. However, manpower planning can never be an exact science. The planner deals in probabilities. Data, though weak, can provide guidance to the alert planner knowledgeable in the workings of the labor market, in identifying those occupations in which a client is more likely to be able to find jobs than in other occupations.

Finally, the planner must be knowledgeable about employer recruitment, selection and hiring practices, and the objective requirements of jobs. Vital concepts are the relationship between the external labor market and the internal labor market and the ports of entry through which persons are hired from outside the establishment and then move through transfer and promotion within the internal labor market. Only then can the planner judge which jobs might be accessible under what conditions to which job seekers and then prescribe measures to prepare people for the jobs or aid them to remove or surmount barriers to job access.

Barriers assessment

Having established priorities among the target population and identified accessible jobs, the labor market manpower planner must next assess the barriers confronting particular groups or individuals among the chosen clientele. That task in turn is followed by prescriptions of a mix of services to surmount the barriers. Barriers assessment is at a very rudimentary stage, however. The disadvantaged designation is a useful evaluative measure to judge to what extent a particular program or agency is attempting to serve those most in need of help. It has little value as a diagnostic tool; people are not unemployed because they are black or young or old but perhaps because employers discriminate against people having those characteristics. They may be unemployed because they lack particular skills and knowledge or because employers require high school graduation certificates regardless of their relevance to job performance but not because they are dropouts.

In general, barriers can be divided into two groups: (1) those that are inherent in the individuals themselves—lack of skill, experience, motivation, and so on—requiring some change in the individual and (2) those incorporated into the institutions of the labor market and the society—discrimination is an example—and requiring institutional change.

Little is known currently about the relative incidence of barriers to stable employability within population subgroups. The individual assessment of manpower clients requires gathering accurate information about the aptitudes, skills, attitudes, personality traits, life and work histories of manpower enrollees. The potential exists for the use of such individual assessment data in making estimations of handicaps or barriers within entire population groups, but substantial effort is still required to develop usable techniques.

The most serious problem encountered in the projection of such data is the fact that traditional methods of assessment are quite inappropriate for use with the seriously disadvantaged. Newer, specially designed methods are coming into use, but they have yet to be tested adequately for validity. Some methods of assessment have been designed for specific local purposes such as the assignment of individuals to training programs geared to specific labor market opportunities, but their data may lack flexibility for more general estimating purposes. Nevertheless, some form of individualized assessment of service needs is inescapable, whether done by some formalized system or casual judgment. To identify or develop an orderly and consistent system for making such assessments the planner must be aware of the various methods under use or experimentation, the rationale behind their usages, and their limitations.

Assessment tools need to be validated under varying circumstances in various types of labor markets with different subgroups of the disadvantaged if they are to be useful in the planning and administration of decentralized manpower programs. At present, the state of the art permits few well-supported generalizations based upon assessment data. As promising assessment tools are administered to larger groups of manpower clients, a data base for improved understanding should emerge. Until that time, however, it is at least possible at present to categorize particular groups in relationship to particular jobs as being job ready and immediately placeable, subject to modest employment barriers, or faced by high barriers to placement and to identify for each of those groups generally the most persistent and serious barriers to their employment.

The mix of services

Given identification of the barriers faced by target groups in assessing available jobs, prescription of the type of service or services needed to avoid or surmount those barriers is a logical next step and is usually indicated by the barrier itself. Twelve years of manpower program experience have identified a long list of different manpower services useful for some people under some conditions. The challenges are (1) to identify who needs what and (2) to deliver that "what" effectively. Essentially, these services can be categorized under six headings:

1. Employability improvement—improves the basic employability of individuals.
2. Job access—removes obstacles that impede access to available jobs.
3. Job creation—creates jobs for the target individuals.
4. Income maintenance—provides income through transfer payment sometimes attached to some work activity short of a recognizable job.
5. Entry services—recruit and enroll manpower clients and assess their needs.
6. Supportive services—nonmanpower services that facilitate participants in manpower programs or jobs.

A critical task of the manpower planner is adjusting the mix of services to changing labor market conditions. Changes in local economic conditions have two basic impacts on the mix of services. First, changes can alter the UON. For example, the characteristics of the unemployed change as the unemployment rate changes. A rising unemployment rate will generally decrease the proportion but not the numbers of the unemployed having serious barriers to employment. The second major impact of rising unemployment on the appropriateness of the service mix is the obvious decrease in accessible jobs. Not only does the absolute number of job openings decrease, but the selection criteria of employers is likely to rise. Competition for available jobs increases, and workers are generally willing to settle for lower wages than their skills and education would warrant at other times. Placement rates from skill training programs fall off. Opportunities for OJT are harder to obtain. Referrals tend to become less and less disadvantaged. Job creation begins to look more attractive. The program operator and the planner begin to question the appropriateness of the service strategies.

There has been need throughout the manpower experience for a set of criteria to determine which mix of services is likely to be most effective and efficient for which people, for which jobs, under what conditions. In developing such criteria, the manpower planner needs reliable estimates of the relative incidence of specific barriers to stable employability within the subgroups included in the UON. Those barriers, once identified, can become the basis for prescription: What mix of manpower services are most likely to be successful in removing or superseding those barriers?

The problem, of course, is that present methods for predicting the existence of barriers within population subgroups are inadequate for the purpose of prescription. Until techniques are available for identifying the barriers faced by individuals and aggregating them into proportions among groups, manpower planners and practitioners will be left with only the most general notions of barriers and how they relate to particular occupations and service strategies. Nevertheless, decisions must be made, and the planner will make them on the basis of the best information and judgment available.

Choosing among alternative service deliverers

The freedom implied by the decentralized and decategorized manpower planning model would allow the manpower planner working for a governor, mayor, or county executive to choose, with the advice of a manpower planning council, which of the available public and private agencies should have the assignment of delivering to the chosen clients which components of the service mix. Available in every community are the public schools and, in most communities, the public employment service. There are also public welfare agencies, vocational rehabilitation agencies, private schools, community action agencies, community-based organizations representing various minority groups, private organizations, both profit and nonprofit, and other alternatives. The choice is a mix of response to political forces and objective judgment concerning the relative effectiveness of various agencies for various tasks. The planning unit may either contract separately with each agent for performance of a particular task or may choose one as prime contractor to subcontract to others. Whatever the choice, the planner under this new system is in a politically sensitive but potentially powerful position to influence both the relative welfare of agencies and their staffs and the effectiveness with which services are delivered.

Monitoring and evaluation

Whether or not the plan accomplishes its objectives depends in part on its appropriateness under prevailing circumstances and in part on the efficiency and effectiveness with which it is carried out.[4] Therefore, to test his plan, the planner, must be able to monitor performance to assure efficiency on the part of the service deliverers and evaluate the results to determine whether the prescriptions worked—that is, did an improvement in the employment and income of the clients result that would not have happened in absence of the services? The evaluator at the national level asks: Was the effort worthwhile? Could the funds have been better spent on something other than manpower services? The labor market planner asks: Could a more effective mix of services have been provided, or could they have been delivered more efficiently? As the only purpose of monitoring and evaluation at this level is service improvement, it is followed by feedback and modification in subsequent planning cycles.

The political environment

Planning, like nearly everything else encompassed by the manpower field, is a means, not an end. The goals are clear and relatively uncluttered: (1) a successful and satisfying working career for the individual and (2) efficient use of available manpower resources for the economy. This chapter has concentrated on planning for the needs of those individuals facing various disadvantages in obtaining satisfactory employment, and, therefore, the job is the thing. With the goal of a satisfactory working career clearly in longer-range focus, an immediate job or preparation for it is the beginning objective. The planner must assess the strengths and weaknesses of his position in pursuing that objective and perceive realistically roles to be played within the prevailing environment that will maximize influence over the manpower system.[5]

Sources of influence

The manpower planner for a state or local prime sponsor operates in an amorphous political environment. He has no political power of his own but must depend for influence and clout upon the power of the governor, mayor, or county executive to whom he is ultimately responsible. However, his distance from, contact with, and influence upon that elected official will differ widely by circumstance and issue. In some cases, the distance will be great; yet little can be accomplished without at least the appearance of power. Power, in politics, is counted in votes, dollars, patronage jobs, and public services. The manpower planner has direct control over none but can have some impact upon each and from that must garner whatever influence he is to exercise.

An anomaly of the decentralized manpower concept is the negative political reward system. It is assumed that local politicians have a better fix on the needs of people and labor markets within their jurisdictions than is possible from a national or even a state level. That is undoubtedly true but with two reservations: Does the politician have (1) the incentive to care and (2) the expertise to do anything about it? As noted earlier, the customers for manpower services to date are a group not large enough or cohesive enough to reward significantly political officials who serve them particularly well. At the same time, they may be able to do the officials damage if the officials do not serve the customers well enough. Yet doing a good job for the disadvantaged is as likely to bring negative as positive marks from the remainder of the populace. Serving the unemployed in general and such special groups as veterans can be more politically rewarding. There will be fewer people receiving manpower services in the future than in the past, but to whom they owe any gratitude for service will become more clear.

The manpower budget is a significant amount of money when focused upon a limited target group in a particular jurisdiction. Planners, of course, influence the distribution of funds among agencies first and citizens thereafter. However, the service delivery agencies are what planners are most interested in being able to influence. The planner's power to reallocate funds and, therefore, to exercise clout through the budget again reflects back to relationships with the political executive. The planning councils upon which both agency and target group representatives normally sit are customarily advisory in nature, with the staff reporting ultimately to the executive rather than to the council as such. The planner's ability to direct the allocation of funds among agencies is measured by his or her influence, relative to theirs, over his or her principal.

The planner's impact upon staff slots in the planning office is a strength, but these are few compared to the staff jobs in the service delivery agencies. This influence over the ultimate jobs in the labor market toward which the clients are being directed is limited to those that subsidization can provide. Employers are jealous of their hiring prerogatives, and only the unions (by labor market power) and governments (by regulation) have been able to wrest away any job control. Manpower planners have no market power to win job control. They can only plan to prepare people to compete successfully for available jobs, to persuade employers to accept a civic duty, or "bribe" them by subsidizing private or public employment. Yet, eventually, the manpower clientele must learn to face labor market forces and compete successfully with other claimants for the same jobs.

The planner cannot exercise influence in the labor market by expertise in the provision of labor market services. His expertise is to plan, review, and evaluate, not to deliver. Delivery of services is the expertise of service agencies, which the planner must involve by alliance. The manpower planner surveys a product considered substandard and passed over by the potential customer—the employer. He deals in the economics of misery and wrestles daily with residual problems, left over from a long line of attempts to solve the same set of problems.

Yet the manpower planner, like most others in the manpower field, is driven essentially by compassion. Why else operate in a field of uncertain tenure, deep-seated and complex problems, and limited public praise? The only explanation is a desire to make life better for one's disadvantaged, unemployed, or ill-paid fellows. The motive is the personal welfare of others. The stock in trade is to perceive need and then parlay limited resources and limited influence into effective programs of employability and employment. The politics of that assignment is at least as important as the planning.

A unique aspect of the CETA legislation, noted in Chapter 12, is that it gives the state and local manpower planner (or, more accurately, his principal) some control over no more than two-fifths of the funds available for employability and employment programs and expects him to plan for the whole of it. Coordinated planning encompassing the full range of available services and resources for the disadvantaged is essential to success. Yet the only incentive for participation by controllers of non-CETA resources is conviction that the results can be better for all.

Non-CETA manpower programs avoid some painful decisions by tending to be limited by law to a narrowly prescribed service population—for instance, the physically and mentally retarded or welfare recipients. CETA, on the other hand, focuses on the disadvantaged, the unemployed, and "those most in need of manpower services." But these are very inexact terms, applicable to populations many times larger than the available budget can serve, and offering no clue as to the reasons for unemployment and poverty.

Moreover, CETA may prove to be detrimental to the disadvantaged, or, more accurately, to minority groups. The CAAs and racially and ethnically oriented service organizations emerged from the conviction that old-line agencies could not and would not serve the poor, particularly the minority poor. These new community-based organizations, by and large, never became particularly effective as deliverers of services, but they had a major impact on local and even national politics by giving control of budgets to the formerly powerless. The older agencies profited from the experience by changing to meet the unfamiliar competition. Under CETA the power will rest with elected officials.

It remains to be seen what relative attention they will give to the disadvantaged in allocation of resources and how they will choose between public agencies and community-based or minority organizations as deliverers of the services. It will be a major planning, monitoring, and evaluative responsibility to assure that the commitment to equal employment (and other) opportunity is not weakened. The planning staff through its distribution of service delivery assignments and contracting authority can manipulate requirement or policy. Fiscal and delivery systems and the compliance of the most obdurate agencies can be radically modified if the anxiety of agencies to win in the competitive contracting environment is exploited fully—and if the elected official will back the planner.

As noted in Chapter 12, CETA is a fruition of ten years of groping toward a system combining federal resources and enforcement of accountability with delivery of manpower services adapted to local labor market needs and realities. But there are no unmixed blessings. Decentralized planning and delivery of manpower services, combined with decategorization among manpower services, offer new opportunities but include inherent threats. It is important to review the strengths and weaknesses in order to build upon the former and avoid the latter.

Potential contributions

The key element, of course, is the possibility of identifying local needs, setting local goals, and designing programs that are realistic and desirable within the realities of local labor market conditions. There is no guarantee that it will be so. Local planners can still ignore or never discover those needs and realities. Programs can be designed in prejudice, inertia, or in accord with political pressures more easily than by knowledgeable and objective analysis. The best-conceived plans can fail in delivery and vice versa. One can only be certain that such adaptation was impossible with nationally uniform manpower services. Whether the change will be an improvement is, at this point, a matter of faith.

A possible consequence and corollary of adaptability is responsiveness. The locally planned system does have the potential capability of responding to changing or newly recognized needs, which is almost impossible to do with nationally directed programs. But the potential is not necessarily the actuality. It remains the path of least resistance to do this year what was done last year and to follow this year's plan to the end regardless of changes that may occur during the period.

Accountability also becomes a possibility but may never

achieve reality. It requires that objectives be clear and progress measurable, that some force monitor progress and reward or punish good or bad performance. In the past primarily a contractual relationship existed between federal agencies and state and local public and private institutions. But there were never the resources and the energy to monitor and evaluate performance in a meaningful fashion. Overall, national program evaluations could assess whether a program had been useful on the average. Each program's total impact on the social and economic system was too small to be measurable, but it was possible to judge whether or not the average enrollee was better off for having participated. It was not possible to hold local service deliverers accountable for their stewardship, or at least it was not done.

The basic notion of CETA is that state and local politicians will be held accountable by their voters for their stewardships. The flaw in this argument is the low level of visibility of manpower concerns among the many pressures impinging on a local political executive and the usually weak organization of the manpower constituency. The manpower planner is in a key position to act as the conscience of the program in a local community to see that the appropriate people are served. It is not realistic to expect the federal agencies to monitor and evaluate any significant number of individual programs. In fact, it has been the painful experience that federal plan approval and monitoring tend to enforce the wrong measures. It is relatively easy to determine whether prescribed procedures are being followed but nearly impossible to determine whether a plan or program fits current need or has the elements of success. Success can be determined after the fact, if objectives are measurable, but retroactive reward and punishment is a politically difficult concept. The tendency of such monitoring is to limit flexibility rather than enforce responsiveness. Monitoring and evaluating, too, must be a planner's responsibilities. They will not get done unless he does them. He can be objective about the evaluation of individual service deliverers, but can he be impartial about the planning function or the overall manpower activity?

A promising potential advantage of decentralized and decategorized planning is the coupling of both services and service deliverers in ways that were rare under national programming. It was not only because of legislated categorization that clients were required to fit programs rather than vice versa. With each agency often responsible for only a particular category of service, interagency cooperation was necessary for an appropriate mix of services. With a functional hierarchy extending from the national level through regional state, and local levels, there was little incentive and considerable disinclination for such cooperation. MDTA training is an example. Even within one piece of legislation institutional training was an educational responsibility, with the U.S. Employment Service primarily responsible for OJT. The latter agency had capability for employer contracts, and OJT contracts were written. It had none for designing, recognizing, or enforcing training quality, and there was always a question regarding how much actual training occurred. A stereotype of OJT evaluations was the trainee interviewed in a follow-up survey responding: "What training program? I've never been a trainee." An attractive training format would have been an initial period of general skills training in a classroom or lab followed by OJT for practice and gaining more specific skill, perhaps followed by another institutional stint and a return to OJT. Programs coupling classroom and on-the-job training were always rare because of the bilateral requirements.

The local labor market planner, however, could solve the problem of this example. The plan could call for the Employment Service to solicit and vocational education to monitor OJT. The plan could direct alternate periods of institutional and on-the-job training with the relevant employment service and schools responding as subcontractors. The prime sponsor can now marshall by contractual assignment and through council participation the varied expertise and resources of private and public education, Employment Service, vocational rehabilitation, minority and community organizations, day-care facilities, welfare and family services, employers, unions, housing and transportation agencies, and others. There is, of course, no guarantee that this will be done; there is only the possibility that it can be done.

Also related is the end of agency monopoly on particular services. The planning arm has the authority, if politically able to exercise it, to assign a task to the most competent provider of that service, regardless of past history. In all probability the traditional agency for that service will be the one most capable of delivering it. But potential competition may sharpen public enterprises' awareness of consumer needs. Actual competition may invoke duplication of capacity; potential competition is a relatively costless good.

The dangers

The dangers of decentralization are equally serious. Perhaps the most threatening is the slackening of the emphasis on equal employment opportunity. It was certainly easier for a minority group to marshall sufficient national power to influence legislation and administrative fiat than to impact upon all local political scenes across the land. The locations where minorities are majorities are usually resource- and opportunity-starved locations. Mayors in many large cities may be vulnerable to minority political power. Governors, county commissioners, and mayors of modest-sized cities almost never are. When prime sponsors continue to emphasize service to minorities and to the most disadvantaged, it will be more likely because they believe it to be right than because they feel pressured. Political power is a more dependable currency than moral commitment. It is reassuring to have both on the same side. The manpower planner is in a unique position to keep them parallel.

Whether or not it is a likely consequence of decentralization, CETA has been the occasion for a substantial cut in manpower funding. Including both dollar cuts and inflation, available resources dropped about 30 percent in the transition from MDTA and EOA to CETA. There is no tradition of local funding for manpower services. Not until continuing and recurrent education for adults is recognized to be as much an educational responsibility as education for youth will there be any significant state or local investment. There is no likelihood for other manpower services. There is undoubtedly a tendency to make larger aggregate appropriations to several programs than to one consolidated one. These threats were clear to decentralization advocates. They thought the prize worth the cost but hoped to avoid the latter.

A program of labor market manpower planning should be able to encompass and influence the total flow of resources on behalf of determined objectives. It is not a criterion of decentralization but only a fact of political life earlier noted that CETA encompasses only two-fifths of the federal manpower budget allocated to employability and employment problems. The three-fifths remain outside the CETA planning requirement. However, by their nature, the non-CETA manpower programs are not categorized regarding the services they are allowed to deliver. Programs like WIN and vocational rehabilitation are categorized by service groups but are at least as free as CETA in the choice of mix of services. The problem is to bring them under the labor market planning umbrella. Mingled in planning though kept separate in financial control, they serve an overlapping clientele and add to total resources.

Excessive decentralization also threatens CETA. Under political pressure from local governments, sublabor market areas became potential prime sponsors. The financial incentives for consortia are weak relative to the political advantages of independent prime sponsorship. Yet consortia were formed which will hopefully serve total labor markets rather than fragmented areas. The net result remains to be seen.

The lack of staff competence for manpower planning is obvious. Yet the assumption that federal staffs are more competent than their local or state counterparts is not justified. There may be an upward selection process, but there is also a growing desire for a life style that cannot be offered in the national capital. The fact is that there was no similar function or skill as labor market manpower planning ever required at the national level. The demand for manpower planners is a new one, and the competence would have to be developed anew, whether in Washington, D.C., in regional offices, or at the state and local levels. It might as well be developed where the action is.

Problems of political influence and patronage are aggravated by decentralization, though these problems are not absent in the federal system. Politics is involved and will continue to influence the legislating, appropriating, and administering processes. State and local politics too will be added to the total. However, one cannot simultaneously argue for local adaptation and local political responsibility while decrying local political maneuverings.

Whether the advantages of decentralized planning and administration outweigh the disadvantages remains to be seen. It took 12 years to bring federal manpower policy competence to its present relatively satisfactory level. There is as much to learn at the local level, but there is a base of experience in most sizable communities, federal capability to draw upon, and a body of technical assistance and training competence in and out of government. The long learning process can be short-cut, but only if the lessons of past experience are identified, codified, disseminated, and heeded and if the available talent is marshaled and magnified through development of technique and staff trained in its use. Those techniques and that staff competence will emerge if there is aggressiveness from both suppliers and demanders of manpower planning competence.

Notes

1. This chapter is adapted from Garth L. Mangum and David Snedeker, *Manpower Planning for Local Labor Markets* (Salt Lake City, Utah: Olympus Publishing Co., 1974).
2. Sar A. Levitan and Joyce Zickler, *The Quest for a Federal Manpower Partnership* (Cambridge, Mass.: Harvard University Press, 1974).
3. *Manpower Planning and Forecasting in the Future: An Explora-*

tory Probe (Minneapolis, Minn.: Industrial Relations Centers, University of Minnesota, 1968).

4. Joseph S. Wholey et al. *Federal Evaluation Policy, Analyzing the Effects of Public Programs* (Washington, D.C.: The Urban Institute, 1970).

5. James E. Sawyer, *Crucial Elements in Manpower Planning* (Salt Lake City, Utah: Human Resources Institute, University of Utah, 1974).

14

the role of the public employment service

At the beginning of the 1960s, only two public institutions existed at the local level for administration of manpower programs: the public schools and the federally funded, state-operated employment services. Schools were involved only in the basic education and skill-training aspects of the manpower effort. The federal-state employment service, the only nationally available local manpower agency, offered a wider, but still limited, range of services. During the dozen years in which the federal government has worked to impart salable skills to the less competitive members of the labor force, other institutions—vocational rehabilitation agencies, welfare departments, community action agencies, organizations representing racial and ethnic groups, the school systems, manpower planning agencies, private employment agencies, among others— have entered the manpower field. Yet the public employment service remains the most pervasive source of manpower services in most communities. This chapter reviews its continuing and changing role.

Changing objectives and functions

Few institutions have been asked to change so much in so brief a period as the employment service system during recent years. New functions have been assigned, new and often inconsistent goals have been set, and major shifts have occurred in the distribution of power within the system. Often, these new assignments have not been related to existing employment service responsibilities, competence, or objectives.

The employment service's primary goal has been defined suc-

301

cessively as, first, to administer the work test for unemployment insurance claimants; then to act as a labor exchange providing employers with qualified workers; subsequently, to serve the entire community as a manpower center providing diverse information and services for present and prospective employers and employees; more recently, to give special priority to the employability and employment problems of the disadvantaged; and now back to emphasis on the labor exchange function. With its policies and practices rooted in legislation and fixed by tradition, its leaders' willingness to adjust to new goals and perform new tasks would be a major determinant of the system's success or failure. In shifting gears to accomplish each new objective while meeting current demands, some parts of the system invariably have lagged several stages behind. Inevitably, these attempts to bring rapid changes in such a large institution have engendered frustration and ambiguity in regard to goals and functions.

A nationwide public employment service created during World War I all but died out during the 1920s. It was reestablished at the low point of the Great Depression with the previously mentioned Wagner-Peyser Act of 1933, whose broad charter provided states with federal matching funds as an incentive to establish employment services. The federal funds were drawn from general revenues. Twenty-four states picked up this option during the first two years. Whether more would have done so is not known because Title III of the Social Security Act of 1935 created a trust fund financed by a payroll tax for the payment of unemployment compensation. Because it was considered essential to ensure that a claimant was ready, willing, and able to work, the employment service was assigned this work-test responsibility, and funds were made available for its support from the proceeds of the payroll tax. The states could either establish and administer an employment service with 100 percent federal financing or lose the proceeds of the tax to other states.

During the 1930s, with few jobs available in private industry, the employment service was mainly an instrument for screening applicants for welfare and work-relief projects. The system was barely operative when it was challenged by the manpower problems of the imminent war. Shortly after American entry into World War II, the state employment services were federalized and placed under the direction of the War Manpower Commission, under which they became a mechanism for allocation of scarce manpower. The prewar status was restored with the termination of hostilities, and the employment service became intimately involved in demobilization. To ease the adjustment of returning veterans the employment service developed a six-point program—

an effective placement service, employment counseling, special services to veterans, personnel management services, labor market analysis and information, and cooperation with community organizations and government agencies in community employment planning—which provided the goals that prevailed through the 1950s. It was also involved in the Korean War mobilization and adjustments.

Following those years of intensive activity, the employment service subsided into the doldrums that, in spite of the 1946 Employment Act, characterized domestic manpower policy during the 1950s. Periodic recessions kept the loads of unemployment insurance claims high and resulted in the diversion of employment service staff and attention to the administration of unemployment insurance. With no other specific assignment, it was not surprising that many local offices were content to process UI claims and match passively a limited number of employer job orders with available workers. Because unemployment insurance overshadowed other employment service activities, the growth of an unemployment-office image was also to be expected. Economy drives were so successful that the 1960 budget was smaller than that for 1948. As budgets declined and staffing was cut back, a minimum staff was maintained in small-town offices, imposing relatively greater cuts on metropolitan offices and amplifying an already existing small-town and rural bias.

This moribund state was noted in 1958 by Secretary of Labor James P. Mitchell in a speech to the Interstate Conference of Employment Security Agencies, an organization of state administrators. In a strong statement he accused the employment service of failing adequately to maintain its role as a placement agency. He pointed out that not only had the employment service's volume of placements not kept pace with the nation's expanding labor force but also that its regular nonagricultural placements had actually declined. His feeling that "the employment service stands or falls upon its main purpose, placement, and that all subsidiary activities fail when placement fails" led him to conclude that there had been "a steady decline in the activities of the employment service." Mitchell and those providing the staff work upon which his criticisms were based were disturbed not only by the limited extent of employment service involvement in the labor market but by its nature as well. They wanted to move from concentration on lower-level skills to involvement in the technical and professional fields, which were being emphasized by the schools.

The Mitchell speech was followed by plans for a resurgence of employment service activity but not by additional budgets to implement them. In addition to greater emphasis on white-collar and professional manpower, plans included enlarged staffs and better facilities, an improved public image, and a sharper separation between unemployment insurance and employment functions to remove the unemployment-office stigma. However, new funds came only with a new administration—and after policy emphasis had shifted. Thus funds were provided to serve employers by finding them highly educated manpower and avoiding labor shortages for them at a time when public concern was shifting to the unemployed.

Presidential candidate Senator John F. Kennedy promised in a West Virginia campaign speech to improve the employment service. In his first economic message as President in February 1961 he directed the "Secretary of Labor to take the necessary steps to provide better service for unemployment insurance claimants and other job applicants registered with the United States Employment Service." The report of the Special Committee on Unemployment Problems and the discussions surrounding passage of the MDTA both appeared to assume that the unemployed were mostly recipients of unemployment compensation. Subsequent experience was to identify target groups needing employment assistance for whom the unemployment assistance system was totally irrelevant.

The efforts to implement the President's declaration were quite successful as the result of planning in the Labor Department after the Mitchell speech and work by several of President Kennedy's task forces. Funds were provided in fiscal 1962 for a substantial addition to employment service staff positions, allocated primarily to major metropolitan areas. In that sense, it put the money where it was needed; but having no performance measures, it permitted some variance in volume and quality of service rather than set a standard. Previously, a workload and performance budget had encouraged employment service staff to minimize the time spent with each client. Nevertheless, the response to this infusion of funds and the recovery from the 1961 recession was immediate—nonagricultural placements jumped more than 800,000 between 1961 and 1962 to a 6.7 million level never since duplicated.

Outside of its wartime activities the employment service had, until 1962, been completely at the mercy of employers who listed job openings and demanded the best-qualified applicants. Lacking any substantial leverage, the employment service catered to the employers and administered the work test. Practices varied by states and local offices; but, in general, unemployment insurance claims were processed, and the recipients and other applicants were referred to fill whatever employer job orders were listed. Only limited attempts were made to attract job applicants.

The 1962 reorganization included a promise to cease operating "merely as a system of labor exchanges but to take on expanded responsibilities as a manpower agency concerned with all aspects of manpower." It stipulated further that "each local office must serve as the local community manpower center and beyond that, must also function in a strongly linked nationwide network of offices operating to meet national manpower purposes and goals." The goal was more efficient labor market operations, and to achieve it the employment service had to be deeply involved with employers, schools, unions, community development efforts, and almost every aspect of the local economy.

The philosophy was compatible with the placement focus in emphasizing employer contacts and in establishing separate white-collar and professional placement offices to move the employment service into the most rapidly growing occupational fields; but it went further in encouraging the outstationing of employment service personnel on college campuses to offer counseling and placement services and in revitalizing the Cooperative School Program, which sends employment service personnel into high schools for the testing and counseling of noncollege-bound seniors. Considering that criticisms of its apathy had goaded the employment service into a more activist stance, it is ironic that its moderate responses created for the first time some bitter political opposition. Private, fee-charging employment agencies resented the competition in the more lucrative professional and white-collar field, and the College Placement Council was disturbed by campus activities.

New tools for the employment service

The most notable change in the public employment service from the manpower experience was the addition of a number of new services for those who found it difficult to compete successfully for jobs. At the beginning of the 1960s services were limited to counseling, testing, referral in response to employer job orders, and, for those eligible, payment of unemployment compensation. The first fundamental change occurred when MDTA added the goal of improving the qualifications of those not meeting employers' standards. The employment service was to identify occupations with "reasonable expectation of employment," recruit and screen eligible unemployed and underemployed as trainees, work with vocational educators in setting up training courses, and place graduate trainees. To carry out this new mandate, the employment service had to adopt some new techniques.

The 1963 MDTA amendments provided for pilot projects to test the potential of relocation assistance as a solution to unemployment. These labor mobility demonstration projects, which functioned from 1965 to 1969 and relocated 14,000 people, were largely administered by the state employment services. The projects were dropped as decentralization became a watchword, assuming that state and local jurisdictions could use their decategorized moneys for that purpose where appropriate without a national program. However, while it lasted, a number of state employment services did gain experience with a new and useful tool.

The employment service responded to the growing awareness of minority youth employment problems by involving itself in new youth-oriented activities. In 1964 a national network of Youth Opportunity Centers (YOCs)—to be located near but not in central-city ghettoes—was established within the employment service. Shortages of personnel for the YOCs led to crash training programs for 3300 new youth counselors, two-thirds of whom were offered jobs they accepted within the state agencies. The development of the YOCs led to employment service involvement in other training and referral activities: referrals to and limited job creation activities for the Neighborhood Youth Corps, referrals to the Job Corps, and assistance to certain Selective Service rejectees through referral to jobs or training programs. These are only a few of the new experiences that have made significant changes in employment service attitude and capabilities.

New objectives and new directions

The Civil Rights Act of 1964 was destined to have a major impact on employment service policies and practices. Under the labor exchange emphasis the employment service typified the local mores and employee attitudes. Typically, employment service staff knew which jobs employers in that community felt to be appropriate for which race and which applicants the employer was likely to accept. Usually, the staff functioned in accordance with those presumptions. But after 1964 it was illegal to discriminate on grounds of race and sex. The employment service became a civil rights enforcer in the employer's eyes when it referred without regard to race or sex as the law required. Later, age was added to the prohibitions. Many observers and the staffs of the public employment service find in this development the primary explanation of the exploding growth of private fee-charging agencies over the same years. Whereas the public employment service cannot respond to the employer's prejudices, not only because of law but because of policy as well, the private agency can.

In addition to these new responsibilities, the Economic Opportunity Act brought a competitive challenge to the employment service in the form of the new community action agencies (CAAs) whose funds come directly from Washington, bypassing the states. Initially, some CAAs viewed their role as one of making existing services available and responsive to their clientele, the poor. Not infrequently, they took belligerent positions vis-à-vis established institutions such as welfare departments, schools, and the employment service. Other CAAs felt the best route was to organize one-stop neighborhood centers within target areas where all services could be offered, eliminating the need to shuffle the poor from one place to another. In some cases the CAAs attempted to establish competing institutions, particularly for employment-related functions—for example, outreach to locate the out-of-work poor and job development to sell employers on hiring now and training later.

The makeshift outreach services drew many slum residents who would have been reluctant to approach the more formidable employment service offices, although their inability to provide jobs often created disappointment. In some cases the CAAs successfully sought to have employment service personnel outstationed in their neighborhood centers. Administrative control over the personnel generally remained with the employment service, but the funding agreement varied from city to city.

The employment service and the disadvantaged

The poverty emphasis proved to have great staying power. The original target of MDTA had been the displaced family head of long labor force attachment. Rising employment levels helped many of the unemployed, but it soon became clear that regardless of the level of economic activity some people would require special assistance in order to find a satisfactory place in the world of work. Increased sensitivity to human distress and long, hot summers of ghetto riots kept their problems from being ignored. Thus just as the notion of a community manpower service center had begun to supplant that of a labor exchange at the state and local levels, the Labor Department sharply shifted emphasis toward serving the poor and disadvantaged—sending another shock wave through the employment system.

In 1965 Secretary of Labor W. Willard Wirtz announced the creation of a human resources development program that would combine the resources of a number of agencies in an intensive effort to solve the employment problems of ghetto residents. Frank Cassell, a new U.S. Employment Service director brought in to direct the reorientation, stated the new priority: "To serve the disadvantaged in whatever ways were deemed necessary, in cooperation with other agencies, so that the greatest needs are met first, and that those who were last in everything else would receive the services of USES first."[1]

The national office moved to have the human resources development concept adopted as operating policy at all levels of the employment service. The goal was to screen in rather than screen out the disadvantaged; it was to be implemented through outreach into urban slums and rural pockets of poverty, referral to supportive services to improve the employability of those not ready for training or a job, counseling and interviewing, training, job development, and placement geared to the special needs of the disadvantaged. The new policy was fostered by shifts in funding, by the push for local plans of service, and by adoption of a new budget system designed to abandon the transaction orientation of the past and concentrate on achievement of the new objectives. Not all personnel were convinced of the desirability of these moves. Many feared that the new emphasis would hamper their ability to service other groups and damage their image in the eyes of employers and communities. Nevertheless, the national leadership was determined to redirect the federal-state system.

In 1968 the employment service was awarded responsibility as "presumptive provider of manpower services" in the Concentrated Employment Program after it protested assignment to the CAAs of the role of "presumptive sponsor." Later that year, the new Work Incentive program made the employment service responsible for the training and placement of welfare recipients, and soon thereafter it was directed to recruit disadvantaged applicants for JOBS.

In the same 12-month period CEP, WIN, JOBS, and CAMPS were introduced. New budgets and reporting systems were undertaken, as were experiments in computerized recordkeeping and placement. All of these changes occurred before the human resources concept had been clarified and relations with the CAAs defined. In 1969 computerized job banks, a more dominant role in CEP, and an excursion into the realms of vocational rehabilitation with experimentation in work evaluation and work adjustment followed closely upon a major reorganization of the federal-state structure. Thus new tools had accompanied new objectives and responsibilities in such rapid succession as to give the system an acute case of administrative indigestion.

A special 1965 task force to review the operations of the federal-state employment service—appointed by the Secretary of

Labor and chaired, as it turned out, by his successor—recommended that the institution be reoriented to become a Comprehensive Manpower Services Center in each community. Emphasis was given in the report to specialized efforts on behalf of those with special needs, including: (1) identifying these persons and providing special counseling services in order to determine their rehabilitative needs; (2) developing plans commensurate with individual needs, such as referral to another agency for remedial education, institutional training, or on-the-job-training; (3) seeking employment opportunities of a special kind to accommodate the capabilities of persons in this group; and (4) providing supportive follow-up services while they are on the job until they develop self-confidence in the employment relationship.

An electronic employment service

With new approaches the watchword, the federal-state system became rife with experimental programs. Efforts were made to automate all traditional aspects of the employment service, of which the most significant were job bank, computerized job-matching, and the Employment Security Automated Reporting System (ESARS).

In essence, the job bank is a computerized system for the accumulation and display of current job-order information. The job orders submitted to the employment service in a particular city or metropolitan area are accumulated for display the following day in a job bank book, or microfiche, or on film and are distributed daily to public agencies that can effectively utilize this information in the placement process. This system has been effective in providing current job-order information for all applicants, especially those in areas outside the operational scope of a particular local office. Now, for the first time, welfare agencies, CEP, CAA, high schools, and other public agencies that provide services to the disadvantaged have current, complete, and systematic access to all job orders in employment service files. The system does not include applications for jobs and does not match applicants and job orders. Its advantage is widespread circulation of knowledge concerning the nature and extent of current job openings, generally to those who have reason to represent jobseekers, rather than to the jobseeker himself.

As a successor to the job bank, some state and federal planners had advocated a nationwide network of computerized job-matching installations. The concept differs from the job bank in that it would describe the characteristics of workers and the requirements of jobs and instantaneously match them.

There were four pioneering computer-assisted job-matching systems in the United States. The first, LINCS (Labor Inventory Communications System), is now defunct, but its vocabulary, relying entirely upon descriptors, has been refined into one appropriate for use elsewhere, called DECAL (Detailed Experimental Computer-Assisted Language). The second system, the Utah Job-Matching System, is the only operational system which is both occupationally and geographically comprehensive.[2] In operation since 1968, it has seven automated and five nonautomated offices and serves about 93 percent of the state's population.

The third system, ESOPS (Employment Service On-Line Placement System) operating in Wisconsin, is occupationally comprehensive. A unique feature is the use of an "open-ended" vocabulary for the descriptor system. This method utilizes *all* the words commonly included in both applicant and job description, rather than relying on a DOT code as some systems do.

The fourth system, operating in New York City, was formerly designated AMDS (Area Manpower Data System) and is now called JBSS (Job Bank and Screening System). It utilizes a DOT descriptor system to carry out an on-line search of its computerized file of appropriate job openings for the applicant. With this system, applicant interest determines the number of times the file is matched to his qualifications. This system is now operative throughout New York City offices.

These experimental matching systems are all part of a larger federal scheme, a Phased Implementation Progression (PIP), moving from the installation of job banks to the eventual establishment of a national system of computer-assisted job-matching. In addition to the pioneer programs described above, the Manpower Administration has been sponsoring a test of alternative job-matching vocabularies and modes of operation in scattered sites across the country. DECAL, the offshoot of LINCS, is being tested in Corpus Christi, New Haven, Topeka, and Southwestern Missouri. The Job Analysis Vocabulary (JAV), which utilizes the DOT supplemented by 600 descriptors, is in experimental use in Las Vegas, Portland, and central Pennsylvania. All these efforts to implement computerized job-matching have aspired to the same objective: to increase placement efficiency by substituting machine for staff in matching applicant characteristics with job order specifications.

Since the Comprehensive Employment and Training Act of 1973 directs the Secretary of Labor to "establish and carry out a nationwide computerized job bank and matching program ...," further efforts to attain this objective can be expected. Since the job bank was much cheaper to install and required less sophisticated staff for its operation, it served as a starting point. The computerized job-matching systems have further advantages, however. Every applicant can be matched against every job rather than the interviewer merely selecting the first reasonable match. Information can be circulated and matches made over a broader geographical area. The job-matching systems will provide no solution, however, to the basic imbalance between applicant supply and number of job openings frustrating employment service staff job-matching manually.

The employment service has traditionally accumulated statistics on activities performed—that is, placements, referrals, counseling interviews, and the like. But the individual applicant could not be identified, and hence there was no way of determing what applicant was receiving what services. With the emphasis on serving all applicants, but primarily the less fortunate, a method of identifying the applicant was required; ESARS was developed to fill this need. In effect, each applicant is identified in the system, and the services provided him are recorded as they occur. No longer is one referral or placement the same kind of datum as any other. For instance, if three counseling interviews are necessary to prepare an applicant for work, all three are directly attributed to his case.

In 1973 the employment service adopted a balanced placement formula for allocating funds among the state agencies. The formula assigned varying weight to placements of applicants who are veterans, poor, minorities, handicapped, or unemployment insurance claimants, who are priority groups demanding more attention, and who are, therefore, more costly to serve. Transactions, not individuals served, as well as services provided that do not necessarily culminate in job placement are counted rather than placements alone. The allocation formula was based on quantifiable services and, therefore, improved the equity of the funding process but ignored quality. Moreover, reporting procedures before 1969 produced little information on who was served or how well. In 1969, for the first time, the Labor Department initiated regular reports on the target groups being served and, thereby, has filled in much of the gap in the knowledge of who uses the employment service successfully and unsuccessfully. The expanded application of data-processing techniques in the state agencies, coupled with the introduction of ESARS and POSARS, has accelerated the flow of data from local offices to state agencies and the national office. But how can one tell whether the presence of the employment service makes any significant difference in the labor markets? Does the employment service effectively serve the disadvantaged? Unless some measures are developed for answering such important questions, the employment service can only operate on hunches.

Table 14-1   Employment Service Activities, Selected Years 1960–1973 (thousands)

Years	Nonfarm Placements	Referrals	Job Openings Received	Employer Visits
1960	5,818	10,224	7,124	1,117
1965	6,473	13,348	8,690	1,095
1970	3,845	11,969	6,146	614
1973	4,513	n.a.	8,102	1,519

Source: Edward J. Giblin and Louis Levine, *Achieving Manpower Goals Through More Effective Employer Services Programs,* Final Report to the Office of Research and Development, Manpower Administration, U.S. Department of Labor, February 1973, Table 1-1, p. 4 (updated by the U.S. Employment Service).

The employment service might have been more reluctant to give up placements as the appropriate measure of its performance had the number of nonagricultural placements not declined since the mid-1960s (Table 14-1), despite combined increases in the size of the labor force and employment. The employment service attributes the drop to the amount of time invested administering the manpower programs and the loss of good relations with employers. The fact that there was also a considerable drop in the total number of applications suggests that other factors were involved—whether it is because employment is shifting in the direction of occupations and industries not accustomed to using the employment service or because the service is becoming less attractive to the nondisadvantaged is still not clear.

Labor exchange experimentation

One of the most important changes in employment service policy brought on by falling placement activity was the decision to upgrade the ability of local offices to serve employers. Beginning in 1973, the employment service began to emphasize steps that would benefit employers seeking job-ready workers. Promotional activities and involvement of local offices in local business planning were encouraged. The employment service began to overhaul its management system—introducing a so-called closed-loop management system with cost performance standards—in hopes of showing employers a modern, efficient operation. Work continued on the computerization of job placement activities. A 1971 executive order requiring all employers with federal contracts to list their openings with the employment service was first invoked to aid in placing Vietnam veterans, but it is now hoped that this requirement will open the personnel offices of employers to employment service representatives.

With the return to the labor-exchange emphasis, the focus of employment service experimentation was shifted from improving service to the disadvantaged to increasing the visibility of the employment service to the employer community and improving its service to it.

In 1972, the Department of Labor set up the National Employers' Committee for Improvement of State Employment Services and asked it to analyze what could be done "to improve the quality and relevance of employment service performance to employers."[3] In reviewing employment service operations, the committee noted that employment service offices were given so many priorities that in effect there were no priorities at all. They recommended a strengthening of federal leadership and, expressing amazement at the multiplicity of manpower programs and funding patterns, suggested a streamlining of federal operations. In addition, they recommended that the federal employment service structure be stabilized and local employment service offices given more latitude locally to handle their assignments.

During the same period, the Department of Labor sponsored a research and demonstration project to develop a model for improvement of the employer services program.[4] The major hypothesis of the project was that, if impediments to employers' use of the employment service could be identified, then it might be possible to utilize the cooperative efforts of employers and employment service to remove them. In the initial survey of employers, the study noted that employer objections to using the employment service related to operations beyond the employer services unit: the employment service did not adequately screen applicants; its staff lacked an adequate understanding of employer requirements and needed training; it needed to develop a more effective communications program with employers as well as a more aggressive public relations stance. Consequently, the survey suggested that its model would have to encompass changes in employment service functions beyond the employer services operation if the model was to be viable.

The demonstration survey for implementing change was a process model for developing solutions to problems at the local level rather than a set of remedies imposed from above. The key elements were:

> an ad hoc committee of employers representative of those in
> the community to identify problems affecting employer

relationships, to provide feedback from the employer community, and to generate community support for changes in employment service operations;

a task force of local employment service staff to develop workable solutions to the problems presented by the employer committee;

an objective catalytic agent to initiate the problem-solving process and provide technical assistance to both the representative employer group and the employment service task force;

an effective and supportive local employment service manager to implement the changes recommended by the ES task force; and

a system of support for such change emanating from the top of the employment service structure.

All areas in which the project was operated showed tangible improvement in employer relations except for a rural area with a small employment service office for which all parties agreed the project was inappropriate. Since the process model developed by a consulting firm appeared to have widespread applicability, it was followed by a one-year crash effort to implement such change in twenty other communities which trained state staff to operate as change agents.

The "public communications project," initiated by the Virginia employment service, has been an effort to develop wider public visibility. To obtain better quality openings and a larger applicant supply, the Virginia employment service has invested in a multi-media public relations campaign, including an award-winning television commercial, newspaper advertising, and colorful brochures on the wide range of services it offers. Since the project has produced a substantial increase in applicants as well as better-quality orders, it has been adopted by the employment service in Maryland and other areas.

Closing the circle

The same reexamination that brought criticism and antagonism to the Great Society programs was focused on the employment service in the early 1970s. While applications, job orders, and placements had been falling steadily, many within the system had complained continually that an employment service could not be a welfare agency. Its lifeblood was employer job orders. If employers were not convinced that employment service could best meet their manpower needs, there were other competitive sources of supply.

The hypothesis that the emphasis on serving the disadvantaged and minorities was "turning off" the employers was in accord with prevailing sentiments about the social welfare emphasis of the 1960s. The new policy was to return to the labor exchange emphasis and seek out and serve the employers, and, whether causally or coincidentally, placements began to turn upward for the first time in a decade.

Reexamination also questioned the central-city emphasis of the 1960s. The riots had quieted. The 1970 census showed that the poor, like everyone else, were now primarily living outside of the central cities. The rural areas that had suffered from inattention were in the process of being rediscovered, and rural services needed reemphasis.

Then as a final shock came the decentralization policy. Governors, mayors, and county officials were to decide not only who to serve and what services to provide but also who was to provide the service. The employment service would have to compete for its formerly guaranteed role in administration of manpower programs. It already had numerous competitors for its placement role.

If declining applications and placements were not enough to encourage redirections in employment service policy, continuing monetary constraints and realignments in local office responsibilities under CETA have demanded the attention of policy makers. The employment service trust fund allocations are not expected to be altered significantly in the next several years in spite of anticipated increases in unemployment accompanying anti-inflation policies. Moreover, nontrust fund moneys from manpower programs purchasing local office services are no longer a certain source of continued support. In fiscal 1973, 25 to 30 percent of state agency budgets—or 14,500 jobs out of 46,000—came from these funds. Although it is likely that most state and local CETA sponsors will continue to subcontract with the employment service, local offices are no longer the presumptive providers of counseling, placement, and job development services.

Lessons from the experience

Relief seems to be the general response of employment service personnel to the return to emphasis on employer services. But nagging questions remain: What difference does the public employment service make? If it served those most in need of service, though it might not be successful, at least it was filling a role left otherwise vacant. But if there are private agencies willing to provide a service for a fee and people willing to pay a fee for the services received, why support a public service at taxpayers' expense? And if the employer is to be served and prefers the best employee available, is the service doing more than aiding those who would "make it" anyway? The schools were being accused of selecting those with the most promise and taking credit for their success. Would the employment service operate any differently? How could the employment service prove its worth?

Then it is argued that emphasis on employer services maximizes job orders and leads to more placements for all, including the disadvantaged. But will employment service staff take the line of least resistance, serving the job-ready, experienced worker and ignoring the new entrant and the disadvantaged? The manpower programs provided new tools to the employment service so that there existed alternatives to serving only the job ready. But if CETA prime sponsors choose other service deliverers, and particularly if at some point the proposed welfare reforms discussed in Chapter 15 take away the WIN emphasis on placing welfare recipients, will the employment service again be left without employability services?

And, finally, was the 1962–1972 decade a net loss except for learning that priority must go to the employer? What about other lessons learned from that experience? Every observer may read different lessons from the same text, but we find three worthy of note.

The employment service as labor market intermediary[5]

An important change has occurred in American labor markets since the Wagner-Peyser Act established the federal-state employment service in 1933. A high proportion of the labor force was still engaged in agriculture. Unionism was relatively weak. There were no significant intermediaries to function between employer and worker in the placement process. Now agriculture represents only 4 percent. Over a quarter of the labor force (and a much higher proportion of nonprofessional employed labor) is unionized, and many unions operate hiring halls, while private fee-charging employment agencies abound. Most large employers have their own personnel departments and do their own recruitment and selection. Schools and colleges often have their own placement services. Many trade associations and professional associations have a placement role. The CAAs and community-based organizations provide some of the same services. To be one intermediary among many, though the only public intermediary among many private ones, is substantially different from being the only organized reliance of the job seeker. The need for a free, public employment service is almost certain to be questioned.

However, the public employment service is the only one of these intermediaries whose primary objective is to serve the public at large. The others have as their primary objectives their own needs and purposes or those of a restricted clientele.

Certainly, the public employment service is the most ubiquitous of the available intermediaries. It is undoubtedly the most criticized, but that is probably more a function of its visibility than its incompetence. There is no evidence that any of the alternative intermediaries do a better job. The proportion of the total hiring transactions in the labor market that involves the employment service is small, but no alternative comes close to its coverage. The newspaper want ad is the only other generally available low-cost source of labor market information. Preliminary data from a recent study indicate that the employment service is a far superior information source to the want ad. When nationwide boiler-plate ads, the "come-on" ads often used by private agencies, and those that are fronts for door-to-door commission sales are removed, the employment service appears to have far more extensive coverage, even at the professional level.[6]

However, the presence of the alternative, self-supporting intermediaries does raise the question of the employment service's role. Should the taxpayer-supported service attempt to be all things to all people, or should it try to identify and fill the gaps among the services provided by the others? If it followed that path, would its organization and services be uniform everywhere, or would the gaps differ radically among communities? Does the analytical capability exist to identify those gaps and design structure and services to fill them?

Reexamination of the employment service role as labor market intermediary lays bare the single great structural weakness of the public employment service: It has no job control. It can place workers only in those jobs employers choose to list. As mentioned previously, an executive order requiring federal contractors to list their openings has added significantly to the supply of job orders, but federal, state, and local governments rarely use the employment service for their own recruitment. The employment service is also bound by public policy. It cannot discriminate in placement just because an employer has preferences by race, ethnic origin, sex, or age. Alternative intermediaries can discriminate— not legally, but there is little means for policing. Only the private fee-charging agencies, like the public employment service, have no job control, and they have the edge when departures from public policy are preferred.

Yet the public employment service offices persist in acting as though they did have jobs to purvey. Since the reward system constructed for it gives credit primarily for placements, the incentive is to act as *the* intermediary rather than facilitating the job-matching process without worrying about credits. An important innovation of the model employment service offices mentioned earlier was a walk-in cafeteria-style, self-service approach. Job orders were displayed in an attractive lounge. Job-ready persons could walk in, read the descriptions, and choose a job order of interest. (Staff were left free to serve the disadvantaged.) However, the name and location of the employer was kept secret until the applicant approached the counter to seek a referral order. The innovation is an attractive one, but it raises a broader question. Why not, where other intermediaries are available, concentrate on coaching applicants in the job search process? Then why not provide them with information on the employers in the labor market who have the jobs and who hire the workers most likely to meet the needs of the applicant? Finally, why not then encourage self-search?

Service to the disadvantaged

It was charged at the beginning of the manpower experience that the employment service would not and could not serve the poor and the disadvantaged. Though the data prove to the contrary, the refrain has never ceased. Other institutions may be more committed, but none is more competent. The task is simply a difficult one for the employment service lacks control over the job supply while attempting to serve the least job ready.

Nevertheless, experience does indicate that the more employment service staffs are directly and intimately involved in serving the disadvantaged, the more they become committed to that task. If that is their assignment and the source of their rewards, they can be as "simpatico" as anyone else. California carried the commitment to serving the disadvantaged so far that it set up two separate employment services: human resource development offices for the disadvantaged and traditional offices for the rest. The effectiveness of the former was limited, but not for lack of commitment. Central to the concept was the job agent who was to be assigned a caseload of individuals modeled after the individualized vocational rehabilitation approach. However, the vocational rehabilitation counselor can choose a clientele and then buy for them the services they need. The job agent had to accept all applicants and had available as services only the existing slots in manpower programs and whatever job orders employers offered.

It was higher-level policy makers, not the human resource development staff, who gave up on the bifocal approach and returned to the traditional single service. Whether or not the earlier or the later decision was a mistake may never be known. The point is that employment service staff can and did serve the disadvantaged. The primary limitation is job control and resources for employability services. Commitment is not inherent but can be promoted.

The computer in job matching

The job bank, computer job matching, and ESARS (along with POSARS) represent a commitment to modernize the public employment service through use of the latest data-processing equipment. The experience to date suggests that the computerization is useful but has its own dangers. A job bank does print out and circulate data on job openings, but it may also perpetuate the myth that the demand side of the labor market has been described by those print-outs. The public employment service is the best *single* source of current demand data. Nevertheless, its job orders are only a small proportion of the total universe of hiring transactions. Who is to teach the job seeker how to tap other sources and to best use those provided by the employment service?

At present no computer can adequately describe an employer's requirements, the advantages and disadvantages of a job, and the characteristics and qualifications of a worker. It can never replace the judgments of a knowledgeable interviewer and counselor, though it may be preferred to uninformed incumbents in those positions. A computerized job match is a high-cost approach to low-volume operations. It can serve as a useful screening device for high-volume matching by sorting out the possible matches from the unlikely ones. But human judgment must enter there. The tremendous volume of employment service data must, for economy, be electronically processed. But once programmed, the entire system and its judgments may be locked into a narrow frame. If the computer records only certain kinds of transactions and if that record determines the reward system, then only those transactions are rewarded. If all placements carry equal weight, the premium will be on easy placements. If only hirings that follow a specific employment service referral of a job applicant are recorded and rewarded, those are all the staff can afford to participate in. If teaching job search techniques, if giving a job seeker information on employers who hire his skills but have placed no current job orders, if mining job bank data, operating statistics, and so forth for more thorough knowledge of the labor market—if none of these are programmed as credited contributions, they are unlikely to be performed. The point is not to blame the computers but to note that they can only do what they are programmed to do; if they record the wrong things or not enough, they may seriously limit the incentives and contributions of employment service staff.

Summary

The public employment service is the most ubiquitous and public service oriented of the many intermediaries between employer and job seeker that inhabit the labor markets of the United States. Simply because this is true—because it is everywhere seeking to serve everyone, it cannot but be a constant target of criticism, and it is unlikely ever to have a stable, consistent set of assignments, objectives and policies. The years in which its emphasis was on the disadvantaged were productive ones in the development of techniques. Yet it was unlikely to be able to maintain that stance as long as a broader range of taxpayers sought service. It was probably inevitable that its pendulum swung to employer services and the broader universe of job applicants. It is to be hoped that in that reversal of policy those at the labor market's lower margins will not disappear from view. So far, WIN is one defense against that neglect. The public employment service can defend its existence only if it can demonstrate that it supplies services that are not available elsewhere at a price the recipients of service can afford to pay—in short, that its social contributions exceed its social costs.

Notes

1. Frank H. Cassell, *The Public Employment Service: Organization in Change* (Ann Arbor, Mich.: Academic Publications, 1968), p. 184.
2. Willis Nordlund, *Computer-Assisted Placement Systems* (Salt Lake City, Utah: Human Resources Institute, University of Utah, 1973).
3. *Report of the National Employers' Committee for Improvement of the State Employment Services*, prepared for the U.S. Department of Labor, Manpower Administration, July 1972 (mimeo.).
4. Greenleigh Associates, Inc., *The Employer Services Improvement Program: A Year of Action*, prepared for the U.S. Department of Labor, Manpower Administration, June 1974 (mimeo.).
5. Miriam Johnson, *Counterpoint: The Changing Employment Service* (Salt Lake City, Utah: Olympus Publishing Co., 1973).
6. John Walsh and Miriam Johnson, "Want Ads and the Job Market," *Manpower* (October 1974), pp. 15–22.

15
work and welfare

Traditional welfare policy assumed a clear-cut dichotomy between those who could not or should not work (the disabled, aged, and widows) and were, therefore, deserving of public support and persons who were able-bodied and should make their own way. To discourage the employable from seeking aid assistance payments were generally kept at rock-bottom levels.

More recently, as an affluent society has provided rising support to the poor, the sharp distinction has blurred between those who should work and persons for whom society should provide. It has become ever more difficult to define and identify employability and employable persons or, for that matter, productive employment. As the boundaries between work and welfare have become increasingly vague, public policy has recognized a new obligation— to assist the working poor to receive a decent income.

The growth of welfare

The Social Security Act of 1935, passed in the depths of the Great Depression, was the federal government's first general attempt at income maintenance on a sustained basis. The act established two groups of programs. First, social insurance programs—including old age, survivors, disability, and unemployment insurance—distribute income payments on the basis of prior earnings and tax contributions. Because benefits under the social insurance programs depend on past work and level of earnings, those most in need may be excluded. Second, public assistance programs—for the elderly, the blind, the disabled, and families with dependent children—provide income support on the basis of need alone. Public assistance payments, however, depend on need alone and were initially designed to help the unemployable.

When the Social Security Act was passed, female household heads with small children were usually considered to be unemployable. The prevailing assumption was that they should remain in the home to take care of their children instead of entering the labor force. Because of a persistant job shortage, few women had the choice between gainful employment and support at home. But even when jobs became more plentiful, the structure of the law discouraged work by some who might have been able to earn at least partial support. Benefits were often deducted dollar for dollar from any earnings, and this "100 percent tax" discouraged any work effort.

Moreover, because the only jobs most welfare recipients could find offered little stability, income from employment was uncertain. A mother on relief who succeeded in finding a job and achieving economic independence was likely to experience difficulty in returning to the welfare rolls if her income fell or even if she lost her employment. There was often no financial gain in working, and frequently the efforts to achieve self-support could be undertaken only at a risk of losing even the meager sustenance provided by public assistance. Not until 1969—more than three decades after the beginning of federal public assistance—were incentives offered generally to recipients who sought partial or complete self-support.

The problem of persons preferring welfare to work was small in the first years of the act because relatively few individuals qualified and the majority on public assistance rolls were disabled or too old to work. In the three decades since 1945, however, profound changes have occurred in Aid to Families with Dependent Children (AFDC), which became the major public assistance component. The number of AFDC recipients approximately doubled each decade between 1936 and 1966, and again by 1970. Since then, however, there has been relatively little growth in the welfare rolls, and there was even a small decline during 1973 (Table 15-1).

Table 15-1   Number and Benefits of AFDC Recipients, Selected Years 1936–1973

December of Year	Number of Recipients (thousands)	Benefit Payments (millions)
1936	546	$22.9
1946	1,190	173.1
1956	2,270	616.4
1966	4,666	1,719.7
1970	9,657	4,065.5
1973	10,980	6,954.6

Source: Department of Health, Education, and Welfare, National Center for Social Statistics.

The rise of AFDC during the 1960s was puzzling because it was not congruent with other trends of that decade. Between 1960 and 1969 the number of Americans below the poverty level dropped steadily from 40 million (or 22 percent of the population) to 24 million (or 12 percent); the unemployment rate, after a spurt up to 6.7 percent in 1961, fell to 3.5 percent in 1969. But the number of AFDC recipients rose from 3.1 million in 1960 to 8.3 million in 1969.

Originally planned as a transitional program that would wither away as the contributory insurance components were broadened, AFDC grew for many reasons. First, population growth could be expected to expand the welfare rolls over time, other things being equal. Between 1940 and 1973 total population increased by 59 percent, and the population aged 14 years and under grew by more than 69 percent.

Second, federal legislation extended coverage to groups not previously eligible. In 1961 children who were dependent because of the unemployment of an employable parent were included in the unemployed-father component (AFDC-UF), in mid-1969 a a foster-care component was added, and most states also have adopted a provision that permits children to receive assistance after age 18 if attending school.

Third, the Supreme Court struck down two typical state provisions that prevented many persons from receiving AFDC. In 1968 the Court ruled unconstitutional the "man-in-the-house" rule, which made a man living in an AFDC home responsible for the children's support; the decision precluded cutting off aid because the mother lived with a man not obligated by law to support the children. The following year, the Court invalidated residence requirements for public assistance, then in effect in more than 40 states. Also a 1970 Court ruling specified that a stepfather is obligated to support his wife but not her children by another marriage who remain eligible for benefits.

Fourth, at least as important as the foregoing have been alterations in family structure. Divorces, desertion, and illegitimacy have risen sharply since the mid-1930s. All such changes, which leave a mother as head of household, increase the number of potential AFDC clients. The incidence of poverty is six times as high in families headed by females as in families where both parents are present. While the rate of marriage per 1000 population has been virtually unchanged since 1935, the divorce rate has more than doubled. Illegitimacy has increased even faster. Between 1940 and 1971 the proportion of all births that were illegitimate rose from 1 in 25 to 1 in 9. The structure of AFDC itself has been criticized for encouraging female-headed families. For example, an able-bodied man who cannot earn enough to support his family may not qualify for AFDC-UF. To provide income for them he may desert and thus enable them to qualify for assistance. Similarly, the father of an unborn child may not marry the mother so that she may qualify for AFDC.

The foregoing developments substantially expanded the number of persons who qualified for AFDC benefits. But at least as important was the greater availability and attractiveness of AFDC relative to earnings—which induced those eligible to apply for aid. As the federal government assumed a larger share of the costs, states became less reluctant to qualify individuals for aid; as the level of aid grew, participation in the program became increasingly preferable for those eligible. Between 1963 and 1970 AFDC became increasingly attractive as welfare payments rose faster than spendable earnings and the AFDC rolls grew about 20 percent annually. Since 1970, however, earnings have increased faster than welfare payments, and the AFDC rolls have grown by 2 percent annually. Increased administrative curbs on overpayments or inappropriate payments, plus the fact that there are more AFDC adults per family and more are working, have kept payments per recipient relatively stable.

In 1973 a mother with one child had to make a considerable work effort in many states to equal AFDC benefits. A mother with three children generally had to work one and one-half times as much. To equal California's AFDC benefits a mother with one child had to work over 11 full days out of an average of 22 work days per month at $2.20 an hour—before taxes; a mother with three children, 16.5 days. In New York a mother with one child had to work nearly 14 days; a mother with three children, 20 days. In Ohio a mother with one child had to work 8 days; a mother with three children, more than 11 days. Any income or Social Security taxes and work expenses would require additional days of work.

In many cases a mother can benefit not only from AFDC but also from food stamps—which increase her purchasing power at the supermarket. Taking into account both AFDC and food stamp benefits, federal income and Social Security taxes, and modest work expenses, it has been estimated that a family of four had to earn over $5000—$2.50 for 40 hours a week for 50 weeks a year —in a number of states to equal welfare benefits (Figure 15-1).[1]

Additional benefits would further increase the level of wages needed to equal welfare benefits. It should be noted that many welfare families also benefit from Medicaid—which pays doctor and hospital bills. Some also live in public housing—which reduces their rent. An increase in family size would act similarly to boost welfare benefits and the level of earnings needed to equal them.

Figure 15-1   Earnings needed to equal AFDC and food stamp payments in selected states, 1974.

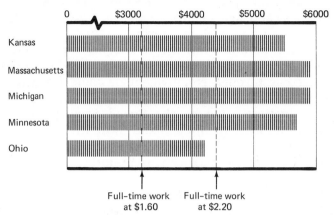

Note: Benefits are for a family of four; earnings are net of federal income and Social Security taxes and modest work expenses.

Source: U. S. Congress, Joint Economic Committee.

To determine eligibility for AFDC states specify "standards of need" for various family sizes. As the standard is increased, more families fall short of it and hence are eligible for assistance. However, states are not required to pay in full what they designate as the full standard. In July 1973, for example, only 17 states paid 100 percent of needs and 5 states paid less than 50 percent.

The amount of income disregarded in calculating assistance payments has become increasingly important. Since mid-1969 states have been required to exempt earnings of $30 each month, plus one-third of all additional income and work expenses, in determining an AFDC family's needs. States that pay benefits below the standard of need may elect to disregard part or all earned income up to the needs level. States are also required to exempt full earnings of a child who is a full-time student or a part-time student not working at a full-time job. In addition, several states have adopted a provision that permits monthly earnings of up to $50 per child or $150 for the children in any family to be disregarded in determining eligibility. Because the disregards now in effect apply only to families already receiving AFDC, they will not add more persons to the rolls; however, they do allow many recipients to remain who otherwise would have been disqualified.

The revolving door

There is little opposition to paying public assistance to the disabled, blind, and aged. Few of these people could work even if jobs were available. By contrast, most heads of AFDC households are of working age and without physical handicaps, including women with school-age children and unemployed male family heads eligible under provisions offering assistance to such families in 25 states. As the number of AFDC recipients has increased, so has the proportion of those on welfare who could be supplementing their income through employment or could leave relief rolls altogether.

The distinction made by the Social Security Act between those who can support themselves and those who cannot has been challenged, as work and welfare are closely intertwined. AFDC family heads need not make an all-or-nothing choice but may select the best combination of the two.

Contrary to common misconceptions, welfare recipients are not unable or unwilling to work, nor do they languish on the rolls forever. AFDC turnover is high as many families join and leave the AFDC rolls. In recent years approximately 30 percent left within a year; half within two years; and three-fifths within three years.[2] Changes in the earnings of family members are prominent among the reasons for opening and closing cases. Families headed by men tend to go on welfare because of loss of jobs; women tend to join welfare rolls because of loss of support due to divorce, desertion, or husband's illness and leave because of remarriage. Moreover, about one current welfare family in three had previously received assistance, some more than once. It is probably not an overstatement to suggest that for certain socioeconomic groups receipt of public assistance at some time is a normal occurrence.

Nor is it true that AFDC recipients avoid work. In recent years a substantial and increasing proportion of welfare mothers were consistently in the labor force; moreover, the proportion in full-time work increased:

	1961	1969	1973
Total in labor force	19%	20%	28%
Employed full time	5	8	10
Employed part time	9	6	6
Unemployed	5	6	12

A closer examination of these data reveals wide variation among states. A 1973 survey reported 14 percent of AFDC families had some income from the mothers' earnings; state rates ranged from 5 percent in Nevada to 33 percent in Iowa. An estimated 40 percent of AFDC mothers worked at least part of the year.

Not until the 1960s was there any significant change in the structure of the AFDC program. But, as the burden of the rolls rose, as the welfare population became less "deserving," and as the AFDC-UF component allowed relief for the first time for employable men, public assistance for dependent children came under increasing criticism. Moreover, few married women, and especially mothers, were in the labor force when the Social Security Act was passed. But in the succeeding four decades AFDC outlays continued to rise while a growing proportion of wives and mothers in all income levels were entering the labor force, as discussed in Chapter 5. The work force participation rate for mothers jumped from 9 percent in 1940 to 44 percent in 1973, including one of every three mothers with children under six. Exempting welfare mothers from employment when two-fifths of all married mothers were working no longer seemed justified.

The employability of welfare mothers

The public debate dealing with AFDC frequently has been concerned more with rhetoric than reality. The issue of whether they *should* work. And because of the failure to recognize that work and welfare are not mutually exclusive, the ability of welfare mothers to enter the labor market and earn some money has been confused with their ability to achieve economic self-support.

Employability is a complex balance of economic, social, and psychological factors. The presence of young children is the most obvious barrier to the employment of most welfare mothers and one that normally figures prominently in surveys of barriers to their employment. Even though it is increasingly acceptable for mothers to leave their children in another's care while they work, the limited supply of day-care facilities may be a severe constraint.

Almost two of every five welfare mothers in 1971 had a child under 3; another 22 percent had no child under 3 but one under 6; one-third had only 6-to-17-year-old children. This means that 60 percent of the mothers probably needed full-time, year-round day care if they were to find steady employment.

According to Department of Health, Education, and Welfare estimates, the total capacity of licensed day-care centers and family day-care homes in 1971 was about 912,000. In the same year there were 1.6 million AFDC children under 6 (who presumably required full-time care if their mothers worked) and another 2.1 million between 6 and 12 (who presumably needed part-time care). Licensed facilities fall far short of being able to accommodate the children of welfare mothers. And, of course, nearly 5 million working mothers with children below age six are competing for existing facilities.

Largely because the potential demand is far greater than the available supply, child care has been hailed as the panacea for the employment problems of welfare mothers. Emphasizing the scarcity of licensed child-care facilities, however, may divert attention from the ability of these mothers to locate such services on their own. A woman's willingness to bear the costs of leaving her child(ren) depends largely on the expected benefits of doing so, especially on the potential earnings. A survey of mothers in ten cities found that seven in ten mothers "said they could make 'arrangements' to work if a good job were available."[3]

The problem of dependency is less one of the lack of jobs or of child-care services than the lack of *good* jobs. Even if welfare mothers were not limited in their labor force activity by child care, health, and other problems, their earnings ability would be quite limited.

By virtually every available criterion, welfare mothers are concentrated in the most unfavorable occupations, and their job status is likely to deteriorate in the future. About a quarter of all AFDC mothers had never been employed. Only 2 percent of those who were ever employed were professional, technical, or managerial workers, and only a quarter were clerks, salespersons, craftsmen, or operatives. About half had worked in private households, in other services, or in unskilled work. The unfavorable occupational mix of AFDC mothers is due in large part to deficient education. In 1973 over two-thirds of welfare mothers had not completed high school, compared with one-fourth of all female adults.

In addition to the difficulties of child care, poor health, unfavorable occupations, and lack of education, nearly half of the welfare mothers must contend also with economic discrimination because of race. Although the AFDC rolls were predominantly white during the program's early days, by 1961 nonwhites comprised nearly half of the caseload. This proportion changed little over the next dozen years:

	1961	1969	1973
White	51.9%	50.5%	48.7%
Nonwhite	48.1	49.6	51.3
Black	43.2	47.5	47.6
Indian	1.6	1.4	1.1
Other	3.2	0.7	2.6

A final consideration is the structure of work incentives. The treatment of income earned by AFDC recipients is a crucial variable in the choice between, or combination of, work and welfare.

The factors just reviewed provide an indication of the extent to which welfare recipients *can* compete for employment and earnings in the labor market. But in the absence of a work requirement, their decision to enter the labor force—whether they *will* compete—hinges on the incentives offered for work effort. The employability of AFDC recipients depends frequently upon the incentives offered for work.

Work and training for relief recipients

Beginning in the early 1960s, the federal government implemented a series of work and training programs for AFDC recipients. These schemes alternately promised economic independence for those on welfare and relief from the welfare burden for the nation's taxpayers.

"Working-off" public assistance

The presumption that AFDC recipients were "unemployable" and outside the work force became untenable in 1961 when the federal government extended coverage to families headed by an unemployed parent. The need for the new law was clear: Because the original Social Security Act denied assistance to families headed by an able-bodied male, the whole family was penalized if the father could not find employment. The presence of employable parents on relief prompted Congress, in 1962, to amend the Social Security Act to subsidize employment programs for relief recipients; until 1962 all AFDC recipients were presumed to be outside the work force, and public assistance funds could not be used to provide work. States were encouraged to adopt Community Work and Training (CWT) programs designed to offer work relief rather than handouts and hopefully also to help recipients to achieve economic independence.

The purpose of this amendment was twofold: to allay public criticism of relief payments to persons able to work and to create work-relief projects that would train and "rehabilitate" recipients. "Working-off" relief was justified as being better for the recipients' morale and providing useful public services under safeguards to prevent exploitation or the displacement of regular workers. The formal emphasis of CWT on training and rehabilitation reflected the nascent movement in the early 1960s toward more organized manpower and training programs for the disadvantaged.

Although the 1962 amendments were hailed as a vehicle for encouraging work and training for persons on relief, the provisions of the law tended to reinforce the more traditional social services associated with public assistance. Only 50–50 federal matching funds were provided for the administration of CWT projects, compared with the 3–1 ratio (75 percent federal–25 percent state) to cover the costs of social services. Project sponsors also had to contribute all of the costs of supervision, materials, and training on CWT projects in addition to their regular matching share of public assistance. It was, therefore, not surprising that, in order to obtain the maximum federal contribution, most states and localities chose to expand "social services" rather than set up CWT projects.

Projects in CWT provided little training that would improve the employability of participants. It was estimated that about 90 percent of the funds were disbursed for work payments, leaving very little for rehabilitative services. Nor did recipients have any monetary incentive for participating in CWT. A consistent feature of all projects, which varied considerably otherwise, was a prohibition on additional income for participants in return for work performed (other than work-connected expenses). Instead, participants were required to work-off the amount of assistance they received, usually at the prevailing wage for comparable work performed in the community.

Antipoverty work and training

The Economic Opportunity Act of 1964 expanded the CWT program. Under Title V of the act grants were to be given to state and local welfare agencies to pay the full costs of demonstration projects so that the states could establish Work Experience and Training (WET) programs and provide for the expansion of CWT projects. In addition to unemployed parents on relief, other needy persons, including single adults, were declared eligible. The program reached its peak enrollment of 71,000 in 1967.

The additional funds allocated to this effort and the broadening of eligibility reflected an increasing realization that low national unemployment rates might not be sufficient to assure a job for everyone who wanted work. Even though unemployment dropped throughout the 1960s, certain groups continued to experience considerable joblessness. A basic tenet of the antipoverty effort was an attempt to reach out, even beyond the welfare rolls, to help persons who could not compete in the labor market—to remove the structural barriers to their employment.

The challenge to the sponsors of the work and training programs was to provide useful training and work for participants.

This proved to be a formidable task; most enrollees had multiple handicaps and little attachment to regular work. While the enrollees' work assignments featured a certain amount of informal vocational instruction, the bulk of these assignments was limited to low-paying, unskilled occupations. This phenomenon was understandable in light of the trainees' limited skills and educational attainment. Furthermore, work experience assignments were limited almost exclusively to government agencies and nonprofit organizations, and few trainees were assigned to private employers. This reluctance to become involved with the private sector hindered efforts to promote economic independence through employment for a significant number of persons.

There is little evidence that Title V administrators made adequate use of the flexibility they had in utilizing funds. While the basic combination of vocational training, work experience, education, and day care as part of the individual employability plan was certainly needed, the flexibility existed more in the rhetoric of WET officials than in project implementation. Similarly, transitional supportive services—for example, helping individuals during the early stages of regular employment—might have been provided with Title V funds. But only in isolated instances were these services offered.

The welfare agencies responsible for the administration of Title V projects found it difficult to expand their activities beyond traditional income-support efforts. With little or no prior experience with training or placement or awareness of labor market operations, the state and local welfare agencies were hard pressed to design work-experience projects that would enhance the employability and earning potential of enrollees.

Despite laudable goals of rehabilitation and uplift, WET remained primarily a work-relief and income maintenance program. Expenditure patterns show this clearly: In fiscal 1968, for example, well over one-half of the funds were spent for income maintenance, but only one-sixth each for work-experience activities and vocational education.

The major failing of WET was that few participants moved on to become self-supporting through private sector employment. The limitations of the program's training and rehabilitative services were partly to blame, but perhaps of greater importance was the lack of incentives and the failure of participants to find jobs that paid above the poverty income level. There were some rewards for participation, however, because enrollees could receive the full amount of the state's minimum standard welfare payment and allowances for work-related expenses; but neither of these was available for former participants with private jobs. Without any "sticks" or "carrots," few chose to leave welfare rolls.

The work incentive program

In an attempt to induce public assistance recipients to seek "worthwhile" employment, Congress enacted the Work Incentive (WIN) program, as part of the 1967 amendments to the Social Security Act. By providing work and training incentives, Congress affirmed again the interdependence of work and public assistance, even though the incentives left much to be desired.

Rather than including persons not on AFDC, WIN consolidated its target population by aiming only at public assistance recipients in order to stem the burgeoning welfare rolls. This strategy also assisted WIN administrators. Because clients already received income maintenance, there was less pressure to place them quickly; instead, more thorough training could be provided. Moreover, funds did not have to be siphoned off for maintenance payments but could be concentrated to increase employability.

During training, participants received $30 per month along with continued welfare payments and the social services needed for successful completion of training. Along with the inducements for participation to entice welfare recipients to enter training or to find work, WIN also featured a work requirement. Most adults in AFDC families were required to register with a local welfare agency for referral. But because registrations far exceeded available positions, a list of priorities was used to ration the flow in decreasing order of job readiness.

To make these persons employable WIN offered a wide range of services, presumably adapted to each individual's needs. These could include orientation, job tryouts, basic education and other prevocational training, institutional training, OJT, referral to other manpower programs, follow-up, and day care for children. In theory an employability development plan was to be developed for each participant, detailing the package of services appropriate to his needs. The intent of WIN was that participants would receive more intensive and more individualized services than they had under WET.

An ostensibly more ambitious program than its predecessors, WIN emphasized institutional training, including basic education and day care. But at an average cost of $1000 per enrollee for nine months of training (exclusive of work incentives once jobs were found), WIN could not offer much more extensive services than WET. Most WIN enrollees received either nominal instruction or no instruction at all, and many were provided little besides orientation and placement counseling.

Day care is a necessary ingredient to increase the employability of AFDC mothers. In many ways, it is the most critical component of WIN. Meager day-care expenditures have limited program performance, although WIN has made more extensive provision for day care than earlier programs.

Through its first four years WIN suffered considerable attrition, as fewer participants remained at each successive stage. The initial stage in the funnel—determining who was appropriate for referral—was necessary to weed out persons with obvious problems: only one quarter of the 2.8 million persons assessed were found appropriate. But weeding out at later stages continued to whittle down the number of potential participants. Whatever the reasons for these leaks—that those referred were deemed unsuitable, failed to cooperate, or could not be accommodated—a great deal of wasted motion was involved. Of those persons found appropriate, only about four of every five actually enrolled. Of nearly 400,000 persons enrolled through May 1972 about 267,000 had left the program—55 percent because of pregnancy, required family care, or withdrawal from public assistance rolls; 21 percent dropped out for other causes; and the remaining 24 percent completed their courses of training.

Despite WIN's training and other services, the earnings of employed graduates were usually modest—a median hourly wage of $2.42 in 1972. Clerical, sales, and service occupations, which attracted a disproportionate number of women, paid relatively low wages; semiskilled and skilled manufacturing jobs, in which men were overrepresented, paid higher wages. These levels were generally sufficient to reduce welfare payments, but in a number of states even employed WIN completers were still entitled to partial benefits.

WIN underwent a major policy change after Congress enacted in December 1971 a series of amendments introduced by Senator Herman E. Talmadge of Georgia. The objective of the Talmadge amendments was to induce welfare recipients to seek gainful employment. Seeking to correct the many problems encountered in WIN's first four years, Congress specified more precisely not only who would enter the program but also what services would be available and authorized funding for a limited number of jobs.

Originally, local welfare agencies had wide latitude in determining who would be found appropriate for referral to training and related activities. This produced wide variation among states in the proportion of adults who were screened for employability, found appropriate for referral, and actually referred. Moreover, lack of coordination between the referring welfare agencies and the receiving manpower agencies led, in some areas, to mass "paper referrals" to nonexistent training slots and, in other areas, to a paucity of referrals so that training opportunities were wasted.

The Talmadge amendments were designed to avoid such problems. They continued to exempt from participation any person who was under 16 or attending school; ill, incapacitated, or aged; too remote to participate effectively; caring for another household member; caring for a child under six; or a mother in a family in which the father has registered. All other adults were required to register for work or training as a condition of receiving assistance. The amendments, too, specified that unemployed fathers be referred first; next in line were mothers who volunteered (regardless of whether required to register); they were followed by other mothers and pregnant women under age 19; and, finally, came youths age 16 and over who were not in school, at work, or in training.

In addition to requiring individuals to participate or lose benefits, Congress required that by mid-1973 states had to certify to the local employment office as ready for employment or training at least 15 percent of the number of individuals who are required to register. For every 1 percent under this quota a state was supposed to lose 1 percent of its federal assistance payments.

Dissatisfied with progress in moving welfare recipients into jobs, Congress mandated that the training components focus even more on job placement. The financial burden on states was eased as their share of training costs was halved from 20 percent to 10 percent. The Labor Department also decided to shift emphasis from training to direct placement. At least one-third of manpower expenditures were to be used for on-the-job training and public service employment, but the Labor Department experienced difficulty in arranging on-site training.

Recognizing also the importance of child care by requiring that local welfare agencies certify individuals to manpower units only when child care and other supportive services were available, the Talmadge amendments increased federal matching funds for such services from 75 to 90 percent. In addition, the new amendments gave the Labor Department authority to provide allowances for transportation and other costs.

The complexion of WIN was drastically altered by these amendments (Figure 15-2). Funds for institutional training were cut considerably, while expenditures for on-the-job training and public service jobs increased. The largest component, however, was for labor market services—to place WIN enrollees in jobs,

Figure 15-2 WIN expenditures emphasize on-the-job training and job placement instead of institutional training.

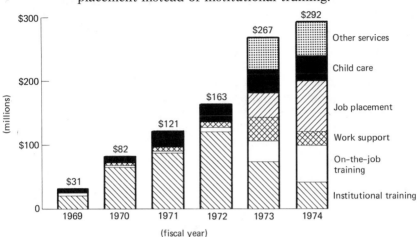

Source: U. S. Department of Labor.

especially unsubsidized employment, and to provide follow-up services for 90 days.

To distinguish the expanded WIN from the initial effort the post-Talmadge amendment program became known as WIN II. In four years of the older program about 80,000 persons graduated by being placed in jobs and keeping them for at least 90 days. Under WIN II the Department of Labor announced that in the first 21 months 155,000 persons were placed in unsubsidized jobs for more than 90 days—half of them were no longer receiving AFDC. In addition, almost 42,000 persons were working in unsubsidized jobs but had not completed their follow-up period. Another 69,000 persons were in subsidized public service employment or on-the-job training.

As under the original WIN design, men fared better than women, largely because men had better work histories and fewer work impediments. Those participating in WIN were far more likely to complete job entry and command higher wages than women. Almost one in four male participants landed an unsubsidized job in 1973, compared with one in ten female participants. Women who were placed in jobs earned an average of $1.87, compared with $2.58 for men. The fact that half of female participants were in orientation, training, or simply waiting for services, compared with 7 percent of men, is indicative of the fact that women were harder to place and the jobs they found tended to pay insufficient wages for economic independence. Women's comparative lack of success in finding employment through WIN stems from several reasons—including inadequate job skills and work experience, job discrimination, and a generally soft labor market for unskilled women workers. Because WIN personnel realized from past experience that women with many service needs have low potential for steady employment, they concentrated efforts on likelier candidates.

A woman's mandatory registration status was apt to change due to pregnancy or collapse of child-care arrangements, and female volunteers could terminate participation in WIN at any time without fear of sanctions. Consequently, about one in eight female participants returned to welfare.

A continuing problem confronting women in WIN was the lack of adequate child-care facilities. In 1973 approximately 81,000 WIN participants received child-care services for about 126,000 children. Nearly half of these children were under six years old. Only about one-fourth of these arrangements were made in licensed day-care facilities. Most arrangements were informal and involved relatives.

Child care is costly. In 1973 the estimated annual cost of group day care meeting federal standards for three- to five-year-olds was $1670. After-school and summer-care centers for children ages 6 to 13 cost an estimated $862 per year.[4] These standards of acceptability and estimates of cost may be high; in many cases cheaper arrangements could be made with relatives or friends— but the price tag would still have been substantial.

In order to sweeten the prospects of employing welfare recipients, the 1971 Revenue Act provided a special tax credit to employers equaling 20 percent of wages paid to former WIN perticipants during the first 12 months. Employers in 1973 collected in tax-credit for 25,000 hires, but utilization of the program remained low for several reasons. Employers do not like the red tape, some harbor fears that the government will interfere with business operations, and some are prejudiced against welfare clients. Also, some welfare recipients do not want to be identified as such to employers because of the associated stigma.

Even before WIN II had completed its second year, Labor Department officials announced in mid-1974 its successor—WIN III. Once again, the content of the program was streamlined, or gutted, to get actual and potential welfare recipients into jobs quickly, with little pretense remaining that their employability was being upgraded.

Persons were required to register for WIN job placement services from a manpower agency at the same time they applied for AFDC benefits from a welfare agency, with WIN registration becoming a condition for AFDC eligibility. Previously, WIN registration was required only of persons already receiving welfare payments, except for adult males.

This earlier exposure to the manpower agency was coupled with a more intensive requirement for job search. The announced reason for requiring concurrent registration for welfare assistance and manpower services was to eliminate the costly lapse of up to 90 days between these stages under WIN II.

With the advent of WIN III public policy has virtually abandoned earlier rhetoric about helping welfare recipients to achieve financial independence, opting instead to move beneficiaries into any job as soon as possible. By reaching deeper into the barrel of welfare recipients and providing them less substantive services, the Labor Department denies enrollees the opportunity to acquire skills that would contribute to long-run employability.

An assessment

Whether inducements and training will prove effective depends on how easily the obstacles impeding those with higher employment potential can be overcome. Given the limited earnings potential of most AFDC mothers, the obvious strategy is to concentrate on those who are most employable and face the fewest obstacles to work. This means that male family heads, female heads with access to free or low-cost child-care facilities, or those whose children no longer need day care would be served first.

This has been the strategy of WIN. But even in serving such a select clientele, performance has been meager. It is doubtful that the investment in WIN would show positive returns on the basis of a cost-benefit study.

Some would argue that efficiency of performance should be considered secondary to substituting "workfare for welfare." This argument is based on the assumption that jobs are available for everyone who wants to work and that dependence upon welfare robs children of self-esteem and breeds future generations of welfare recipients. Few would deny that a working family head sets a better example than one who lives on the dole, and it is probable that welfare begets welfare, but there is much debate about the degree of such effect. It has been demonstrated, however, that lack of education, poor diet, and crowded housing also generate dependency. There is a need, therefore, to balance the impact of WIN with income-maintenance expeditures. The money used to create work, if a positive cost is involved, could be applied to other ends that might reduce future welfare rolls to a greater or lesser extent. Little is known about intergenerational effects of receiving welfare, or the impact of putting the family head to work and the children in day care. Without evidence those arguing for jobs at any cost cannot be proved wrong, and the price to be paid in substituting welfare for workfare must be resolved politically.

Alternatives for the future

The CWT, WET, and WIN programs tried with scant success to solve the welfare problem by rehabilitating AFDC recipients. Despite these efforts, relief rolls—and criticism of the public assistance system—continued to grow.

One of the thorniest problems that all welfare reform proposals must confront is the overlap of cash and in-kind assistance. This overlap is inevitable under the current welfare structure with a large number of separate categorical programs, and in many cases it is desirable to the extent that it results in increased well-being for welfare recipients. Virtually all AFDC families nationwide are eligible for some medical benefits; two of every three receive food stamps or commodities; three of every five benefit from free or reduced-price lunches; and one in eight lives in public housing.

This multiplicity of benefits tends to discourage AFDC families from seeking economic independence. First of all, as an AFDC family's earnings rise, it is confronted with a decrease in assistance of 67 cents for each dollar earned above $30 plus work expenses, a Social Security tax of 5.85 percent on all covered earnings, federal income tax of 14 percent or more on income above $4300 for a family of four, and possible state income tax—all of which severely limit the net cash rewards for working. Moreover, a family that also receives food stamps loses another 30 cents for each dollar of earnings after certain deductions are made. And most perverse is the structure of Medicaid, whereby a family qualifies either for full benefits or for none—and can lose several hundred dollars' worth of benefits when its earnings exceed the eligibility level.

Because of the multiplicity of benefits and cumulative tax rates, earnings were not always profitable to households receiving several benefits. In 70 percent of a sample of urban households, a dollar of earnings yielded no more than 32 cents in additional economic welfare.[5]

During the past decade, several schemes for reforming the welfare system have been proposed. Three broad criteria can be used to compare the wide variety of proposals: the extent of coverage and the levels of assistance; provisions made to enhance the employability of recipients (including work incentives and work requirements, provisions for training, and supportive services); and the costs involved. And the proposals can be grouped into three basic categories: guaranteed income, or negative income tax; family allowances; and employment guarantees, including wage subsidies.

Income-maintenance strategies

The simplest and yet most comprehensive welfare proposal is the guaranteed income, or negative income tax. This would maintain an income floor for all persons by granting cash assistance to those whose earnings fall below that level. To encourage low-income workers not to drop out of the labor force a percentage of earnings would not be considered in calculating subsidies. Out of each dollar earned, the low-income family could keep some fixed amount without an equal reduction in its guaranteed minimum income.

Proposals vary widely as to the minimum floor and the percentage of income that could be retained. The lower the floor and the proportion of income retained as a work incentive, the lower the cost of the program. If the guaranteed income was higher and incentives were lower, costs would multiply and more people would be likely to drop out of the labor force and live off the dole. However, a lower floor would be injurious to those families whose head could not work and for whom incentives are meaningless. The basic problem of the guaranteed income is that it leaves such families at a minimum level of subsistence because their subsidity could not be raised without increasing payments to all those who work and supplement their subsidies.

Another method of providing cash assistance for the poor would be to pay all families with children a regular allowance to supplement their own income and meet some portion of the costs of child rearing. This proposal recognizes that the wage system distributes income inadequately because wages are based on productivity or on tradition rather than on need. While the principle of equal pay for equal work is desirable as a protection against discrimination based on color or sex, it ignores the differing needs of families and tends to deprive children in large families of basic necessities. The underlying justification for family allowances is that a child's well-being should concern society at large. Family allowances are now paid in one form or another in over 60 countries, including most industrial nations. But despite this wide acceptance elsewhere and its frequent proposal here, the idea has never received active consideration in the United States.

Family allowance programs are not a complete alternative to

a guaranteed income because many poor do not have children; but because family size is so closely correlated with poverty, such allowances would lift many adults out of poverty along with their children. As with the guaranteed income, family allowances make no distinction based on labor force status. But the family allowance has several advantages. Because an income (or means) test is not needed, the plan would greatly reduce administrative costs and would interfere relatively little with work incentives. Because the program gives benefits to all children, it would probably find broader political support than any other alternative.

Less heralded than the guaranteed income were proposals to guarantee employment and to subsidize wages. Immediate drawbacks were that only employable persons would benefit and that the government's role in the economy would be much increased. If the federal government became employer of last resort, for example, it would expand greatly both as an employer and as a provider of goods and services. Furthermore, unless wage levels in the public-sector jobs were low, workers might be induced to leave private employment for them. But low wages would not lift many, especially large families, from poverty. Similarly, wage subsidies would assist only the employed and might result in serious distortions of the market mechanism.

Combining work and welfare

In August 1969 President Nixon proposed the Family Assistance Plan (FAP), which would have established a guaranteed minimum income for all families with children throughout the nation. In addition to the traditional clients of public assistance, FAP would have included almost 1.3 million families whose head worked full time, year round and another 650,000 families whose head worked substantially during 1969 but remained in poverty.

The plan would have doubled the number of persons eligible to receive assistance and income supplements—at an estimated annual price tag of $8 billion. These added initial costs were intended to help avoid greater outlays in the future. The purpose of boosting work incentives, expanding training, and providing day care was to replace welfare with workfare, to move all those able to work off welfare rolls and onto payrolls, and to stop the growth of relief.

FAP included several improvements over AFDC. Extension of coverage to the working poor eliminated the anomaly of welfare recipients' receiving higher incomes than those who work regularly at low wages or intermittently. By establishing minimum standards on a nationwide basis, FAP would have significantly decreased the fragmented provision of public assistance. Similarly, by reducing interstate differentials, it would have diminished incentives to move to areas offering higher levels of assistance.

Despite these many potential improvements, the FAP approach had drawbacks. In attempting to put more welfare recipients to work, the issues raised under WIN become more critical. Are private-sector jobs available? If not, is it worthwhile to subsidize employment? Are the high costs of day care, training, and subsidies justified? The answers to these questions are not clear-cut.

Many people feel that jobs are available for those who really want to work. They point, for instance, to the unfilled needs for domestic workers in most upper-class neighborhoods or to openings for dishwashers. In fact, however, such jobs are limited in number, pay, and accessibility. Graduates of WIN who find jobs usually earn little more than the minimum wage, and frequently these jobs offer little opportunity for upward mobility. But even dead-end jobs are in limited supply, and if those welfare recipients who are not now seeking work were to find jobs, the job shortage would become even more acute.

The various proposals for welfare reform pose the additional problem of determining the minimum income floor and appropriate incentive formulas. These are critical because all low-income families, not just those on welfare, would be eligible. If the income floor was raised or the work incentives were increased, the cost of the program would be significantly magnified as those with a higher income became eligible for assistance and they retained a larger share of the guaranteed minimum. Payments to those who cannot or do not work could be raised only by increasing the subsidies to those who do work. Thus the welfare of those at the bottom would probably suffer because they could not be helped without vast increases in costs. But if the income floor was raised and work incentives were kept low, it is likely that persons able to work would be willing to remain in dependency.

Notes

1. Joint Economic Committee, Subcommittee on Fiscal Policy, *Studies in Public Welfare*, Paper No. 14, "Public Theory and Work Incentives: Theory and Practice" (Washington, D.C.: GPO, 1974).
2. Sar A. Levitan, Martin Rein, and David Marwick, *Work and Welfare Go Together* (Baltimore, Md.: Johns Hopkins Press, 1973), Chap. 1.
3. Andrew K. Solarz, "Effects of Earnings Exemption Provision on

AFDC Recipients," *Welfare in Review* (January–February 1971), p. 19.

4. Donald G. Ogilvie, *Estimated Cost of the Federal Day Care Requirements* (Washington, D.C.: The Inner City Fund, 1972), p. 8.

5. Joint Economic Committee, Subcommittee on Fiscal Policy, *Studies on Public Welfare*, "Additional Materials for Paper No. 6: How Public Welfare Benefits Are Distributed in Low-Income Areas" (Washington, D.C.: GPO, 1973), p. 109.

16
lessons from manpower programs

Under CETA a major change took place in manpower programs. A system of flexible locally planned combinations of service replaced MDTA, Neighborhood Youth Corps, Operation Mainstream, New Careers, and all the other antipoverty manpower programs except for the Job Corps. However, vocational education, adult basic education, vocational rehabilitation, the Work Incentive program, the health manpower program, special programs for veterans, and the basic support for the employment service and accompanying unemployment compensation were not directly affected by that act. All that was done under MDTA and EOA can still be done under CETA; yet both are losses to be lamented. More than an antipoverty program, as important as manpower programs with that orientation were and are, MDTA was the charter for long-term concern for the development of the nation's manpower resources at all levels. While CETA's Title III authorizes research and development at the discretion of the Secretary of Labor, it does not have the same mandate included in MDTA's Title I. The demise of the Office of Economic Opportunity is also a loss. It was the conscience of government on behalf of the poor, but that conscience, to use a scriptural phrase, was already being "seared by the hot iron" of budget costs and unsympathetic appointments.

However, history is not halted by the exchange of legislation. All of the known types of manpower services were encompassed somewhere within the bevy of manpower programs. Though CETA can affect their mix, it cannot change their nature. Current manpower administrators earned their spurs under MDTA and EOA and will pass forward into CETA patterns already set. Change will come, but it should not come so rapidly as to forget the lessons of 12 years of manpower experience. Thus it is well to record some of the most important lessons of that era. These can be divided between insights into the way labor markets work at their lower margins and more specific lessons for the design and delivery of manpower services.

Probing the labor market's lower margins

Probably the most vital of the lessons of the 12-year experience is that manpower programs work or do not work depending upon the expectations and social philosophy of the observer. There is considerable evidence that most enrollees left those programs better off in some way, usually in employment stability and earnings, than when they entered. There is no evidence that the programs reduced overall unemployment rates (other than by the number temporarily enrolled in the programs) nor that they reduced the total quantity of poverty. Unemployment is reduced only by (1) expanding the total number of jobs, (2) reducing the size of the labor force, or (3) ending mismatches between job seekers and job vacancies. The first step was beyond the reach of all programs except the job creation programs. The second step could only be a temporary phenomenon during enrollment. The last step would have been possible except that job vacancies in desirable jobs requiring skills within the reach of manpower programs are rare in U.S. labor markets. There is probably less poverty because of the programs, but there is no way to prove it.

The structure of unemployment

The early arguments concerning the structure of unemployment and its relation to the rate of economic growth are now well resolved in principle if not in exact measurement, with few caring to continue the debate. Certainly, neither unemployment nor poverty can be solved without jobs. And jobs are created only by the expenditure of money for the purchase of goods and services. Unemployment can be reduced at almost any time by increasing the spending rate, but the economic costs may be high. The key concept of labor market economics is that the demand for labor is derived from the demand for the goods and services it produces. No one buys labor for its own sake. Since the labor force tends to grow and output per unit of labor tends to rise, the purchase of goods and services must expand at a pace equal to the sum of labor force growth and productivity increase or unemployment must rise. If unemployment is to fall, the rate of purchase must exceed that sum. It is not simply the flow of spending but the actual purchase and consequent production of real goods and services that determines the rate of job creation. Inflation does not create jobs. Therefore, it is the constant dollar GNP rather than the current dollar GNP that must expand at least as fast as labor force growth and productivity, both of which are also real. Public service employment can supplement the normal process of job creation only because it is another way of financing the purchase of services.

The U.S. labor force is relatively mobile, and its employers are resourceful, but there are limits. If employment expands too rapidly and the market fails to adjust, spending is siphoned off into empty inflation. Where barriers exist, either in the capabilities of the labor force or in the biases of the employers, the spending pressures needed to force adjustment may be excessive. Where the available work force departs too far from the employers' preferences, the employers may simply bid against each other for those already employed. Where the jobs are substandard, they may be ignored by those who would seek and accept better employment, or they may be accepted only temporarily with consequent high turnover. There is some point at which the leftover personnel and the equipment or management with which they would be combined is too marginal for reasonable productivity. Where demand is intense, either employers in the product market or employees through their labor organizations or individually may seek to exploit the situation to their narrow advantage.

An important factor in the unemployment-inflation trade-off in the early 1970s was the age and sex mix of the work force. Teenagers and women move in and out of the labor force with greater alacrity than adult men. The larger those components of the labor force are, the more difficult it is to reach and maintain any given level of unemployment. The manpower experience has demonstrated that (1) no meaningful reduction of unemployment can occur without speeding the rate of economic growth; (2) the economic growth will speed the rate of job creation but at increasing cost in inflationary pressures; (3) a trade-off between unemployment and inflation does exist, and no action to date has demonstrated a proved ability to make that trade-off less costly; (4) the exact levels of that trade-off will depend, among other things, upon the composition of the labor force and the efficiency of the labor markets; and, (5) a great many sources of inflation exist that have nothing to do with that trade-off or even with the labor market at all. Reduction of the unemployment-inflation trade-off remains the great frontier of employment and manpower policies.

The need for manpower services

At any known level of unemployment there remain potentially employable people in need of manpower services, and they number in the millions. That universe of need, or UON, as it was learned earlier, consists of at least the unemployed who seek jobs and those who have become discouraged with the job search, and those employed but at wages so low they could not earn their way out of poverty.

The term "disadvantaged," as it was also learned, came to be used to categorize the target populations of these programs. It was evaluative rather than prescriptive in its origin and use. Being disadvantaged was not an explanation for unemployment or poverty and provided no prescription for curing them. Its use was to identify the particular categories among which those with the highest incidence of unemployment and poverty were most likely to be found as evidence that a program was in fact seeking to help those most in need of help. One is not unemployed because he is too young but because he is inexperienced, because he is between school and a job, or because employers prefer not to hire persons of that age regardless of competence. It is not blackness *per se* but the discrimination factor present that accounts for the high incidence of black unemployment, and so on. There exists as yet no test that will identify the particular barriers between an individual or groups and available jobs, providing the basis for a directly relevant prescription.

The great dichotomy

There continues, whether explicitly or by implication, a debate that underlies the whole manpower experience: when an individual or group suffers more than its proportionate share of unemployment and poverty, does the shortcoming reside in the individual or group—that is, does the individual or group lack skill or experience or motivation or some other prerequisite of employability—or are the labor market and its institutions biased against that individual or group? The policy implications are clear—if personal behavior is at fault, take action to change the people and if institutions are biased or ineffective, reform the institutions. The answer, obviously, is varying combinations of both. But what combination for whom and when, and how is it to be achieved? Earlier programs—MDTA and the Job Corps, for instance—opted for changing individuals. The Civil Rights Act of 1964 and job creation programs argued that institutions needed reform. These considerations raise another key question for manpower research that may open new vistas for manpower policy.

Therein also lies a promise of CETA. Perhaps at the local level and without categorization, an examination, a diagnosis, and a tailored prescription can emerge.

The dual labor market

The demand side for that dichotomy introduces the concept of the dual labor market, discussed earlier in Chapters 3 and 7. Clearly, some people are stranded in locations where there are no satisfactory jobs. Less frequently, there may be people unwilling to accept permanent employment. Whereas earlier it had been assumed enough to ensure a sufficient supply of jobs, attending to the quality of jobs available is now recognized as being necessary. Evidence does not support the dual labor market hypothesis that those programs and services that attempt to change people can have little effect, though the institutions are probably more at fault than the people. Institutions often impose unnecessary barriers to employment through discrimination by age, sex, race, and more subtle factors and through recruitment, selection, and hiring practices unrelated to potential to perform the job. It is a rare person who does not want to be self-supporting and who cannot be used effectively in some kind of job. Nevertheless, people and systems are not as inflexible as suggested by the dual market thesis. Except for perhaps the Native Americans on reservations, more members of demographic groups designated as difficult to employ "make it" than those who do not. For instance, twice as many blacks as whites suffer unemployment, but nine out of ten of the former who are in the labor force are working as are seven out of eight of the teenagers, who suffer triple the average unemployment. Even though institutions may pose the basic obstacles, most people can be prepared and supported to surmount those obstacles. Even though some people may be difficult to employ, a committed institution can absorb and use them productively. It is more efficient to attack directly the basic cause, but it is not the only way.

The usefulness of the manpower tools

The types of services provided by manpower programs may have been fewer than the number of programs themselves. They can be categorized and reviewed as (1) outreach, assessment, and intake services, (2) classroom education and training, (3) on-the-job training, including apprenticeship, (4) work-experience training, (5) subsidized public and private employment, (6) supportive services, and (7) placement-related services.

Outreach and assessment

Experience has demonstrated that there are those who are so isolated and alienated from the existing social and labor market institutions that they must be sought out and offered or convinced to accept manpower services. But at most times and places the eligible persons who sought out the programs and applied for their services have exceeded the capacity of those programs. Outreach would have required rejecting eager applicants to seek out, at some expense, those not anxious to be served and this was rarely done. The exceptions to the general rule of applicants exceeding slots have been (1) programs offering no long-term gains beyond minimal income support (the news of who got what out of a program spreads quickly), (2) situations of overallocations of funds to the wrong programs in rapidly expanding local economies, and (3) services so encumbered by red tape and deliberate hurdles that only those least in need can find their way through the maze.

Assessment, as already noted, is a relatively unplowed field. Culture biases built into many assessment tests have been amply demonstrated, and progress has been made in remedying that problem, in part by modifying or replacing the tests and in part by abandoning them in favor of interviewer judgment. The extent to which factors such as arrest records, with no demonstrated relevance to job performance have been serious barriers, has been probed. But remedy remains largely in the hands of the individual employer and civil service boards. Devices designed to identify more objective employment barriers, as a prerequisite to prescribing cures, are under experimentation. They have exotic names such as Biographical Inventory Blanks and Job Readiness Postures, but even more is required to do the job.

Classroom education and training[1]

Strangely, the first resort of the manpower effort has proved the most controversial. Beginning in a small way under the Area Redevelopment Act in 1961, and then through MDTA in 1962, providing skills to the unemployed seemed the obvious answer. As soon as training effort began, it became apparent that remedial basic education was a need for many. Even general education for youth is a subject of disillusionment, as discussed in Chapter 8. The real issue is the relation of supply to demand. Education and training operate only on the supply side and can only affect whom the employer hires and not how many. They can only have impact upon the total demand for labor if, by improving productivity, they encourage employers to expand their total production and sales. To train without indication that jobs are or will be available is a doubtful investment. At best there should be a direct linkage between training and job such as has been provided in the limited cases of cooperative education in the public schools and coupled institutional and on-the-job training programs under MDTA.

Nevertheless, the evidence is clear for MDTA and reasonably strong for the Job Corps that the average enrollee has experienced a substantial improvement in employment stability and earnings as a result of participation in those programs. Both have been justly criticized for concentrating on training for occupations characterized by high turnover rather than expansion and stability. Yet these same occupations could guarantee high placement rates following training at low per capita cost. More ambitious occupational choices would have resulted in fewer enrollees at any given level of budget, but they might have proved more cost effective.

Training in institutional settings has been provided for occupations that are ordinarily learned on the job. Justification has been that disadvantaged workers needed the extra edge to compete with others who are available to the employer. In fact, vocational education in this country is usually designed to provide primarily entry-level training. Everyone at every level must ultimately learn his job on the job. Only for a few can the work atmosphere and the full range of required tasks be simulated in the classroom or lab. Yet a good guide would seem to be to consider what employers do when left to their own devices. For which occupations do they appear to consider OJT appropriate or preferable? For which do they customarily look to the schools? Every training style has its advantages and disadvantages, its benefits and costs. More careful study is needed of what works best for whom.

On the more positive side, much has been learned of training methods and learning styles. That those with cultural and educational disadvantages could not be successfully trained by the same institutions with the same methods as the more general population was the first lesson. Some institutions did change, and where they did not, skills centers were developed to specialize in the training of the disadvantaged. The latter did an impressive job of training but created another problem. The facilities were too often substandard in relation to the available postsecondary vocational-technical institutions, tending to stigmatize their enrollees and isolate them from the training mainstream. Better results seemed to occur when special services to the disadvantaged were provided within a more general training institution.

Those special services contributed as much to postsecondary vocational-technical training as those institutions did to the disadvantaged. Though not unique to or invented for manpower training programs, a number of important innovations were developed and advanced through the programs: (1) prevocational orientation to help with personal problems and occupational choice; (2) on-site counseling, which involved intervention and client advocacy as well as self-discovery; (3) open-entry–open-exit training, which allowed a trainee to enter without prerequisite, move at his own speed, train in a modular fashion, and leave with a salable skill if he did not complete the full course; (4) the use as instructors of people with proved job and teaching skills but without necessarily having formal teacher education and teacher certification; (5) basic education integrated with skill training; (6) coupled institutional and on-the-job training; (7) on-site placement services; and (8) follow-up job coaching. It was also made clear that many needed only job skills accompanied by training stipends and could be referred individually and enrolled directly in regular vocational-technical courses.

The lessons learned from the training experience are summarized as follows: (1) Basic literacy is almost essential as a prerequisite to employment in the United States, and techniques for teaching it to adults in conjunction with skill training had to be and have been developed. (2) Training is also useful and often essential to those whose work experience is unusually limited and for jobs for which employers expect some experience or exposure before hiring. (3) A variety of supportive services and a sympathetic but challenging atmosphere are necessary to train the really disadvantaged. (4) Training will be taken seriously when it is evident that it leads to attractive jobs but is a frustrating waste when it does not. A direct linkage to employment or a demonstrated high placement rate in desirable jobs is essential.

OJT and apprenticeship

Chapter 10 has explored OJT and apprenticeships as techniques of manpower development. However, it is worth some extra space to identify what was learned about them through manpower programs. It is difficult to analyze OJT in manpower programs separately from subsidized employment. The job placement rather than the training has been the objective, and there has been little attention paid to the latter by manpower administrators as long as the former occurred. Nevertheless, most jobs are learned on site, whether formally or informally, and either formal OJT or informal learning under the direction of a supervisor or a fellow employee must occur. Manpower programs have underwritten preapprentice training and coaching to prepare minorities for apprentice tests. But in most cases the target has been entry to apprenticeship rather than the content of training.

Work-experience training

Enrollment on work crews or in work stations such as Neighborhood Youth Corps and Operation Mainstream, ostensibly justified as a route to employability, is primarily income maintenance accompanied by a minimum of useful activity. This does not mean that it is not desirable, only that it should be approached more honestly. Poor youth need income and something at which to keep busy as a bridge between school enrollment and work or to help them at a vulnerable age when employment opportunities may be scarce. Adults for whom training is inappropriate because of age or location need the income and can collect it with more dignity. Both can provide useful services. The tendency over the years has been for the quality of the work experience to improve and the accompaniment of basic education to grow. There is evidence that the Neighborhood Youth Corps makes a positive contribution to employability. This was not to be expected for Operation Mainstream, which focused on immediate, short-term useful employment for older workers with limited years of employability ahead of them.

Subsidized private and public employment[2]

Experience with JOBS and public employment programs indicates that employers, when properly motivated, will hire the unemployed and disadvantaged. In the short run, appeal to public duty may be effective; for the longer run, the public must be prepared to pay for what it asks employers to do. Modest subsidization of the private sector is not likely to bring a significant expansion of total employment. Only stimulating the demands of consumers can do that. Public-sector employment is a product of government budgets anyway, and it does not matter much whether additional funds flow through either agency budgets or manpower program budgets. Public agencies will hire all of the employees for whom the taxpayers will pay. That is how the incentive system is structured.

Most, but not all, employers, public or private, will prefer to hire the most competent employees (and those having similar ethnic and socioeconomic backgrounds to their present work forces) they are allowed within the subsidy rules. However, a significant number of private employers, but few public ones, accept as a special challenge the hiring of the truly disadvantaged. The experience of NAB-JOBS has taught many an employer valuable lessons about his recruiting, selection, hiring, training, and other personnel practices. The result has been significant, though not extensive, improvement in these practices. However, subtle pressure and technical assistance from public manpower agencies are necessary to maintain and extend those gains. A great deal of civil service reform will be needed before government can demonstrate that it is doing its share in employing the disadvantaged.

It has also been learned that the output from the jobs is not a serious problem. Private employers place the subsidized employees in the same jobs they would have given to others. Public employers can always expand public services. The uncertainties in the public sector are twofold: (1) Will the employing agency use the subsidy as an offset and reduce its own budget accordingly? (2) Will the system be permanently opened up to the disadvantaged? For the private sector there is only one uncertainty: Do the characteristics of the subsidized employee differ significantly from those of the employee who would otherwise have been hired?

Supportive services

An important lesson of the Great Society social welfare effort is that everything is related to everything else. The worker must get to work, and that fact depends upon the transportation system and the availability and location of housing. Poor health can be a serious limitation. Child care can be an almost absolute bar to employment of female family heads. Even where any of these may not be a complete bar to employment, they may cause absenteeism sufficient to make it difficult to keep or advance in a job.

Some are in such condition in their personal finances that even the acceptance of a training stipend brings an influx of creditors upon them. Many have legal trouble but cannot afford professional advice. The incidence of drug addiction and alcoholism may be high in manpower target groups. Manpower programs are often used as therapy in alcohol and drug rehabilitation programs, which is all right if it works; but those manpower programs should not be held to the same placement and retention standards as others. Recently and about-to-be released prison inmates are especially in need of help.

Each and all of these supportive services, it has been demonstrated, are essential for some of those needing services as prerequisites and accompaniment for program enrollment and for successful employment. Contrary to the traditions of the counseling field, which advocates primarily nondirective counseling and client self-discovery, the counselor in the manpower program tends to perform as the "hustler" of these services, most of which cannot be purchased with manpower funds.

Placement services[3]

Chapter 13 deals at length with placement and other services provided by the public employment service. That chapter emphasizes that the employment service, though the most ubiquitous and complete in its services, is only one labor market intermediary among many. It has no power over the supply of jobs, or workers but can play an important facilitative role that will differ according to the structure and needs of labor markets. The manpower programs have demonstrated the usefulness of job development— that is, an advocate of the job seeker works to find jobs that fit a particular individual or group and convinces the employer to accept the individual or group. By the same token, the programs have demonstrated the need for placement officers assigned to a particular program and representing its enrollees. From an overall economic viewpoint one might argue for more global judgments in the allocation of the work force. But if the disadvantaged are to have their needs redressed, they must have special advantages. The manpower planner's role is to consider the entire labor force and labor market in recommending policy and priorities within that scope. The manpower administrator should administer according to the priorities set.

Equal employment opportunity[4]

Inasmuch as they seek to redress the disadvantages of the disadvantaged, all manpower programs can be viewed as equal employment opportunity programs. How have those programs fared that had the explicit assignment to prevent discrimination on the basis of race, sex, or age? Chapter 21 addresses itself to efforts to end social discrimination in employment, and Chapter 5 discusses sex discrimination. It is obvious that discriminaton has lessened and the economic position of most racial minorities and of women has improved. But it is equally obvious that there is a long way to go. Antidiscriminatory measures are especially difficult to administer, but aggressive administration can demonstrate that the public policy is meant to be taken seriously. Equal employment opportunity efforts represent more than a paper tiger. Many have had a significant impact on employer practices. Continued progress could combine holding employers "feet to the fire" and continually chipping away at all of the objective shortcomings that might be used as an excuse for discrimination.

Welfare recipients[5]

One group of manpower services deserves further comment, even though it is treated fully in Chapter 15. The public maintains an antipathy toward public assistance recipients. It refuses to recognize that the beneficiaries are in reality largely dependent children, that welfare is not an economic problem but a social one, primarily caused by family breakup in the urban society. Not only child-care problems but the wage structure of those jobs available to women, particularly those without education, militates against self-support. The evidence is that welfare recipients and their children have the same ambitions as most everyone else but less opportunity to fulfill them. For example, WIN has no difficulty in enrolling welfare recipients for training and other services, and it can even place them. Retention is the problem, and that problem has its roots in work expectations and the family.

Research, demonstration, and staff development[6]

Throughout the dozen years since MDTA was passed, a small but exceedingly fruitful research and demonstration program has been sponsored from within the U.S. Department of Labor. Administrators and staff in the Office of Research and Development have been aggressive and innovative. They have identified areas of needed research and asked for help in that identification from the manpower profession. They have then sought out those most competent to do the research, have jointly worked out the projects, and contracted for them to be done. There has been hard-headed analysis of, choice among, and adherence to research priorities and no distribution of contracts and grants according to political influence. Knowledge has been advanced. Experimental and demonstration projects have broken new ground. The annual *Manpower Report of the President* has popularized the subject and spread knowledge of manpower problems. A particularly fruitful dissertation support program has won at small cost the allegiances of emerging academics to careers in manpower research.

There has been little staff training for the administrators of manpower programs, not even OJT. They have had to pick up the trade by experience. The U.S. Employment Service had had internal training programs. The Area Manpower Institutes for Development of Staff (AMIDS) sponsored by the U.S. Office of Education has provided a substantial in-service staff-training effort for MDTA staff and has now shifted attention to the staff of CETA prime sponsors. The new state and local manpower planners and administrators have had no available training. A few universities are now beginning to supply professional staff training, and the Labor Department is investing in expansion of that effort through its institutional grant program. The Labor Department has also launched an extensive program of in-service training in the policy and procedures necessary to the implementation of CETA.

How much should be spent on research, on demonstration, on evaluation is subject for debate. However, little progress can be made without a constant flow of new knowledge and experiment and without competent staff.

State and local manpower planning[7]

As Chapters 12 and 14 indicate, the prime sponsors of manpower programs under CETA do not start from zero in developing the techniques and experience upon which to base state and local manpower activities.

From the Cooperative Area Manpower Planning System and the Comprehensive Manpower Program experiences and from those jurisdictions that have undertaken manpower planning on their own without CMP designation can be drawn a set of crucial variables that seems to have determined relative success and failure and that offers lessons to new participants on the manpower scene.

Executive involvement. It is the basic premise of the decentralization concept that manpower policy and program will be both better attuned and more responsive to the needs of the local labor market and those with labor market disadvantages if responsibility rests with the chief elected executive of the relevant governmental jurisdiction. Whether this will prove to be true will be read from experience. Pilot experience is supportive; but then those jurisdictions that entered manpower planning at their own volition are likely to have been the most responsive, as well as the most aggressive and innovative, insofar as manpower activities are concerned.

When is an elected executive—governor, mayor, county commissioner, or county supervisor—likely to be responsive to manpower needs, and how important is this factor? Responsiveness can be expected when the potential beneficiaries of manpower efforts are politically organized and vocal. Many politicians will be responsive to manpower needs out of sheer concern for the victims of labor market pathologies. Political responsiveness is a universal motivation, and it is the force most to be relied upon. Yet those state and local political bodies that led in decentralized manpower planning appear to have been sensitive to manpower needs often because their chief executives or influential members of their staffs were convinced that it was the right thing to do. There was rarely political pressure or political reward for them. In general, the political risks were greater than the potential political gains. This picture probably changes when decentralization is the order of the day and when it is known that the political executive who seeks to avoid manpower responsibilities has turned down control over substantial federal funds. Nevertheless, to assure political responsiveness manpower target groups or those concerned for the welfare of those groups will have to look to their own organization and political potency.

Experience with CMP and other pilot experiments indicates that involvement of key staff of the chief elected executive and access to him by that staff are crucial variables in successful state and local manpower planning. These two variables were vital for the innovators in the field who led rather than followed federal initiative. Typically, initiative came from staff who convinced the executive and used his influence to overcome local agency opposition and persuade federal officialdom. Manpower programs as originally structured bypassed established state and local political processes. Funds from MDTA flowed directly to state employment services and state boards of vocational education without involving governors. Programs under the EOA were more deliberately designed to bypass not only local political structures but state and local governmental agencies. The assumption was that established institutions were disinterested or incapable of serving the poor, and a new set of institutions by, of, and for the poor was needed. Also, WIN relied upon state bureaucracies rather than elected officials. The Public Employment Program arrived after decentralization commitments had been made and was the first manpower program deliberately placed in the hands of elected officials.

With that history, state and local agencies, answerable primarily to themselves and the federal government for manpower program funds and activities, were often reluctant to become answerable to the more direct presence of governors, mayors, and their staffs. Nevertheless, governors generally had enough avenues of clout that they could not be ignored by state agencies, and mayors had the EOA amendment prerogative to intervene with the CAAs.

Typically, pre-CETA manpower initiatives were the undertaking of key staff assistants to a governor or mayor. The only requisite was their personal persuasiveness and influence upon their principals. Where manpower planning has emerged at the level of a county or a council of governments, there were more decision makers to persuade. How deeply chief elected officials needed to be involved has been a function of how aggressive the planning effort was. Where no more has been attempted than the CAMPS-type interagency communication, such involvement was not important. But equals cannot coordinate equals. Ultimate differences not resolvable by negotiation can only be settled by a superior power or through advance agreement on some form of binding arbitration. Planning that is likely to challenge vested interests or make substantial changes in established patterns will require access to a higher power.

It is not realistic to expect an elected executive to involve himself on a day-to-day basis with manpower policy or planning decisions. The politician's first concern, as anyone else's, is survival. After setting his first priority—to avoid serious political trouble—he asks how he can do good and get credit for it. With the multitude of issues of concern to a jurisdiction and its constituency, manpower issues will seldom have high visibility and priority. However, so long as the manpower staff can use the chief executive's name and authority and then can deliver his direct intervention when the "crunch" comes, executive involvement is real and adequate. This has been the case in every pilot state and local manpower planning effort that has attempted meaningful change and has been successful in it.

Agency administrators. In some cases the heads of state and local manpower-related agencies—such as the state employment service, state boards of vocational education, the Office of Rehabilitation Services, the state Office of Economic Opportunity, welfare departments, community action agencies, and so forth—have been members of manpower bodies. In other situations they have not been members, but the manpower planning councils have been advisory to them or vice versa. As in the case of executive involvement, the decisive factor determining whether such membership is appropriate and needed seems to be the ambition and aggressiveness of the manpower planning body. Regardless of the extent of executive involvement and the degree of clout available to the planning council, the heads of established agencies, especially those of long standing, generally have an extensive array of politically potent supporters with vested interests in the status quo. Achieving policy changes on issues central to the interests of such agencies without their acquiescence is difficult. This is particularly true over a long period of time, since a characteristic of any bureaucracy is durability. The more politically oriented executive with pluralistic responsibilities soon must turn his attention to other matters, and unwelcome change is stifled in the day-to-day operation of a public agency. Experience seems to be that if major change is desired in the assignment of an agency or in its *modus operandi*, its agreement or acquiescence in those changes will be required. Therefore, it must be party to the decisions that direct such change.

An additional advantage of involving agency heads in the manpower planning process is that it forces their attention to the manpower program practices of their own agencies. Particularly when manpower is only a part of an agency's responsibilities, that part may be delegated to lower-level staff and may rarely be reviewed. Having to respond to the queries of other planning council members concerning an agency's action has forced many an administrator to be aware as never before of the performance of his or her own staff.

Clout. Planning without implementation is a meaningless exercise. The history of city planning, for instance, is littered with beautiful multicolored maps representing the fruitful imaginings of planners who knew what would be good for a city but who had no influence on its decision makers. The need for involvement by the executive and agency administrator is primarily a source of clout to turn plans into realities.

Sources of clout used by successful manpower planning organizations have varied in structure and by circumstance. The Office of Management and Budget's A-95 directive giving governors the right to review and clear all proposals passing from state to federal agencies has been an especially effective one when used for that purpose. Other executives have used various forms of budget control. Prior to the passage of CETA some governors' and mayors' offices had managed to get themselves designated as the officials responsible for a number of the programs, then subcontracted them to the agencies for delivery of services. In the latter case competitive contracting, generating competition among public and private agencies, has been a rarely used possibility. Under CETA the elected chief administrator of an office and the manpower staff representing that office have the ultimate source of clout—the power to reallocate moneys and change service delivery assignments. The only limits are the political repercussions that may result. The degree to which this clout is exercised with state manpower services councils and prime-sponsor planning councils under CETA remains to be seen. Experience only dictates that for planning to be meaningful and effective, there be some such potent source. Clout is unnecessary only when there is no intent to disturb the status quo.

Separating planning and administration. It has become abundantly clear through the limited experience to date that any organization confronts difficulty when it attempts to combine responsibility for broad strategic planning with day-to-day operation of programs and the delivery of services. The myriads of day-to-day decisions absorb immense amounts of time and energy. Since agencies represented on the planning council have various administrative responsibilities, defensiveness arises when tactical, as opposed to strategic, types of decisions are under consideration. An organization can rarely be objective in monitoring and evaluating its own activities. Even when it does achieve objectivity, its impartiality is always suspect. To specify a course of action, assign it to a subordinate entity, and then require effective service delivery is a more comfortable approach and seemingly the only tenable position over the long run. It has been suggested that one of the major advantages in the decentralization of manpower responsibility is that it removes federal agents from direct responsibility for the effectiveness of manpower programs and places them in a position to monitor, evaluate, and direct improvements in the quality of services. The same principle is no less important between planners and administrators at state and local levels.

Labor market planning scope. Once a jurisdiction seriously undertakes manpower planning, it soon becomes apparent that it is concerned with far more than the administration of a discrete array of federally funded programs known as manpower. A wide range of social and economic institutions impinges upon the employment process. A whole variety of social, educational, and other services over a lifetime determines employability. The manpower function itself forms an interface between social welfare problems and economic development interests. Those who have been employed long in manpower planning soon recognize the need to encompass in the planning process the geographical scope over which most of the community's work force live and are employed —the employing establishments, the full range of service agencies, and all resources available that can contribute to the solution of manpower problems.

Staff competence. Staff competence clearly separates the successful from the unsuccessful in manpower planning. Unfortunately, that factor appears to be largely accidental at this point. The need for preservice and in-service professional staff-training programs is gaining increasing attention, as noted previously. A tremendous training task lies ahead.

Experience suggests that staffs need independence as well as competence. Those manpower planning bodies have been most effective that have protected their staffs from the pressures of particular agencies.

Other variables. Other crucial variables emerged in some jurisdictions but have not become generalized, usually because they require sophistication that develops only with time and experience. These can be briefly summarized:

Management through the budget denotes an emphasis upon cost effectiveness, upon measuring client success according to the increase in employability and incomes derived from manpower services, and upon measuring manpower program success according to the economy with which specific increases in client employability and incomes are obtained. Viewing the budget as the primary manpower planning document requires support information that has not been available, to this point, in most jurisdictions. Prime sponsorship will allow budget analysis to proceed with the availability of information from contractors to planning bodies on the characteristics of those serviced, services provided, and costs per unit of services.

A process orientation focuses upon comprehending manpower development as a series of discrete processes. Four staff competencies are derived from analytic skills and are suggested as critically important elements in the planner's bag of tools. These are: (1) occupational accessibility, (2) allocation modeling, (3) production scheduling and evaluation, and (4) program information and monitoring. A few jurisdictions have begun to develop expertise in occupational accessibility and geographical allocation models, but the latter skills are more rare.

Public-member advocacy entails the active support, particularly of client members, to ensure their full participation in the planning dialogue. The concept that recipients of programs should plan for having their own needs met is attractive, but experience shows that client members are generally appointed in token acknowledgment of federal guidelines or political necessity. Little is effectively done to solicit their involvement, and they ordinarily lack the sophistication to make their presence felt politically. Only where minority organizations are forcefully militant does there seem to be a meaningful influence on policy decisions.

Query

Are these lessons worth the $30 billion spent in manpower programs over the past dozen years? Who can measure and say? The lessons are best viewed as bonuses over and above the primary gains in employment stability and income of target groups that were the program objectives. Nevertheless, it is important to document and transmit to new entrants to the manpower field the useful lessons from the past. This is particularly true now that under decentralization state and local officials and planners must decide who gets what services to prepare for successful participation in local labor markets. Theirs must be the determination of local need and the reshaping of services to meet it. But decentralization, decategorization, and local addressing of local needs are not a complete policy but only one piece. There is still the necessity of a national manpower policy to determine what can best be handled locally and what nationally, to evaluate both local and national efforts, to assure that some localities and groups are not left out, and to foresee and respond to national needs and national problems. That need is no less than in 1962, and the machinery for accomplishing it is still not fully developed.

Notes

1. Garth L. Mangum and John Walsh, *A Decade of Manpower Development and Training* (Salt Lake City, Utah: Olympus Publishing Co., 1973); *Manpower Policy and Progress: A Look Ahead; 1973* (Washington, D.C., National Manpower Policy Task Force, 1972).
2. Sar A. Levitan and Robert Taggart, eds., *The Emergency Employment Act; The PEP Generation* (Salt Lake City, Utah: Olympus Publishing Co., 1974); Sar A. Levitan, Garth L. Mangum, and Robert Taggart, *Economic Opportunity in the Ghetto* (Baltimore, Md.: Johns Hopkins Press, 1970).
3. Miriam Johnson, *Counterpoint: The Changing Employment Service* (Salt Lake City, Utah: Olympus Publishing Co., 1974).
4. Benjamin W. Wolkinson, *Blacks, Unions and the EEOC: A Study*

    of Administrative Futility (Lexington, Mass.: Heath, 1973); Sar A. Levitan, William B. Johnston, and Robert Taggart, *Still a Dream* (Cambridge, Mass.: Harvard University Press, 1975).

5. Sar A. Levitan, Martin Rein, and David Marwick, *Work and Welfare Go Together* (Baltimore, Md.: Johns Hopkins Press, 1973).

6. Garth L. Mangum, "A Review of Manpower Research," in Benjamin Aaron et al., *A Review of Industrial Relations Research*, Vol. 2 (Madison, Wis.: Industrial Relations Research Association, 1971).

7. James E. Sawyer, *Crucial Elements in Manpower Planning* (Salt Lake City, Utah: Human Resources Institute, University of Utah, 1974); Sar A. Levitan and Joyce Zickler, *The Quest for a Federal Manpower Partnership* (Cambridge, Mass.: Harvard University Press, 1974).

four
minority income and employ-ment

17

economic theory of racial discrimination[1]

The theory of discrimination is important for human resource development because discrimination has been a basic cause of labor market segmentation and low incomes. A major objective of manpower policy has been to improve the conditions of minorities. An adequate theory would promote this objective by facilitating our understanding of the causes and effects of discrimination.

An analysis of the economics of discrimination also makes it possible to examine the usefulness of labor market theories—especially the neoclassical theory—in dealing with this problem.[2]

According to Becker, "If an individual has a 'taste for discrimination,' he must act as if he were willing to pay something, either directly or in the form of reduced income, to be associated with some persons instead of others."[3] Becker makes the usual assumptions of neoclassical wage theory, especially perfect competition, homogeneous factors of production, and fixed institutional arrangements.

Becker defines a coefficient of discrimination in monetary terms for different factors of production, employers, and consumers, where it is assumed that the factors of production are equally productive. If an employer pays a money wage rate of W for workers, then $W(1 + d_i)$ defines a *net wage* rate, where d_i is the discrimination coefficient against this factor. If the employer has a preference for this factor, d_i will be positive; if he has a taste for discrimination against it, d_i will be negative.

The *market* discrimination coefficient *(MDC)* is defined as

$$MDC = \frac{W_W - W_B}{W_B}$$

where W_W is the equilibrium wage rate of white workers and W_B is the equilibrium wage rate of black workers.

The obvious implication of the discrimination coefficient is that the employer is willing to pay the favored workers $(W + d_i)$ and the ones discriminated against $(W - d_i)$, so that if W_W is the wage of white workers and W_B the wage of black workers and the employer prefers W's to B's, then $W_W > W_B$.

Neoclassical theory of discrimination

Besides the difficulties in making the model square with reality and the problems with the neoclassical model to be discussed next, the Becker-type model has other limitations for those interested in using the theory of discrimination to explain reality. For example, the long-run implication of the model is that employers with no discrimination coefficients would hire blacks because $W_B < W_W$, forcing their competitors to do the same, in which case the long-run equilibrium would be where the wages of minorities equaled the wages of whites either in integrated or completely segregated situations. If $W_W - W_B > d_i$, where d_i is the money value of the discrimination coefficient, employers would hire only B's; if $W_W - W_B < d_i$, employers would hire only W's; and if $W_W - W_B = d_i$, work forces would be integrated. This implies that employers would change their work forces in response to changes in wage rates. The implication of this analysis is that economic discrimination is mainly a reflection of market imperfections and monopoly power; otherwise, discrimination should tend to disappear in the long run.

Economists writing in the neoclassical tradition have attempted to modify Becker's model to make it conform with a reality in which racial wage differentials and employment patterns are perceived to be relatively stable. Barbara R. Bergmann utilized a Becker-type model to show how discrimination can cause wage differentials among equally skilled occupations.[4] Bergmann assumes two occupations requiring equal skills, one menial *(M)* and the other prestigious *(P)*.[5] Her analysis suggests that discrimination can cause wage differentials among equally skilled occupations and that racial wage differentials may be maintained by occupational segregation rather than by overt wage discrimination. Her analysis also is useful in indicating that the discrimination coefficient differs among occupations because of status considerations. This is better than assuming that discrimination is a taste or distaste for physical association. Occupational segregation, or the crowding of blacks into a limited number of occupations, seems clearly to be a more realistic assumption than that equally qualified blacks and whites doing identical jobs in the same firms are paid different wages. However, the use of wage differentials and discrimination coefficients to explain how crowding occurs and how jobs get integrated seems unsatisfactory, a point soon to be developed at greater length.

Welch uses a model similar to Becker's to demonstrate that discrimination is caused more by employee preferences for working with members of their own race than by employers' taste for discrimination.[6] If a worker's wage is a decreasing function of the proportion of that worker's race in the firm's work force, it is possible to show that cost minimization in competitive equilibrium requires total segregation within a work force rather than combinations of black and white workers' receiving different wages, as implied by Becker's model.

Much of the work on the economics of discrimination assumes blacks and whites to be perfect substitutes. However, Welch and others point out that blacks might be complementary to white workers, making segregation impossible.[7] This would be the case, for example, if white foremen worked with all-black work forces and required a premium to do so equal to a coefficient of discrimination. This would increase the employer's cost of hiring blacks, who could, therefore, only be hired if $W_B < W_W$.

Arrow has developed the most complete statement of the neoclassical theory of discrimination.[8] His main objective was to explain racial wage differentials not based on productivity. He specifically sought "to develop Becker's models and to relate them more closely to the theory of general competitive equilibrium, though frequently by way of contrast rather than agreement.[9]

According to Arrow, the usual neoclassical assumptions would call for smooth rapid adjustments in employment to changes in relative wages. However, in the real world these changes do not occur, partly because of adjustment or personnel costs associated with hiring and firing workers. These costs are of training for specific jobs and administration costs associated with turnover. Personnel investments thus provide a cushion to prevent changes in employment with small changes in the relative wages of blacks and whites.

Arrow also prepared an alternative model to employer discrimination; in this case the employer's actions are based not on tastes but on perceptions of reality. If employers believe B workers are less productive than W workers, they will hire B's only if $W_B < W_W$, an idea also developed by Edmund S. Phelps.[10] This finding was based on three assumptions: (1) The employer can distinguish between B workers and W workers; (2) the employer must incur some cost before it is possible to determine the employee's true productivity; and (3) the employer has some conception of the distribution of productivities within the B and W groups of workers.

Arrow assumed two kinds of complementary jobs, skilled and unskilled. Some workers are known to be able to perform skilled jobs, while all are able to perform unskilled jobs. The employer does not know if any given worker is qualified but believes that the probability of a random W worker's being qualified is p_W, while p_B is the probability that a random B worker is qualified. If $p_B < p_W$, it follows that $W_W > W_B$. Arrow also noted that the wage rigidities that prevented W_B from falling much below W_W would lead to B's being excluded entirely.

Arrow recognized, however, that shifting from Becker's taste for discrimination (which is exogenous to the system and, therefore, not analyzed) to *beliefs* required some explanation for the beliefs. He considered one possible explanation to be the theory of cognitive dissonance, which argues that "beliefs and actions should come into some sort of equilibrium; in particular, if individuals act in a discriminatory manner, they will tend to develop or acquire beliefs which justify such actions."[11] Clearly, however, these beliefs would not persist if they were based merely on perceptions of reality that experience demonstrated to be erroneous, an argument made by John J. McCall.[12]

Critique of the neoclassical theory

There is no commonly accepted standard for evaluating a theory of discrimination. For example, if Arrow's objectives to make the theory of discrimination compatible with competitive equilibrium theory and explain racial wage differentials are accepted, it can be concluded that he succeeded in achieving both objectives. But in accomplishing this he failed either to provide a satisfactory explanation of the basic causal forces at work in the real world or a guide to policy. On the other hand, a particular theory of discrimination designed to support policy might not adequately fit a general equilibrium model.

Conception of discrimination

In order to make it fit the wage theory mold, neoclassical economists define discrimination as a taste prompting an economic agent to act as if he were willing to pay something to be associated with some persons rather than others. This definition creates a number of conceptual problems. First, if it assumes discrimination to be a physical phenomenon—a desire by whites, for example, not to associate with blacks—it scarcely conforms with reality, because whites have been in close physical association with blacks. Clearly, discrimination is more a status or caste phenomenon, a concept that makes the theory more general because the physical phenomenon surely cannot be applied to sexual discrimination. Discriminators object to discriminatees partly because the latter are generally regarded to be inferior people who would lower the status of the discriminators.

Motives of the economic agents

But an economic theory of discrimination should show how discrimination interacts with the motives of certain economic actors. The neoclassical model does this, in part, by assuming that actors with discrimination coefficients modify the usual motives specified in the neoclassical utility functions. The model assumes that employers are motivated mainly by profits, but this motive is modified by a taste for discrimination or a perception of reality. If the model assumes physical association to be a problem, it is difficult to understand why employers, especially in large firms, would discriminate against blue-collar workers with whom top management would not be associating, at least in large firms. As noted earlier, Krueger attempts to overcome this difficulty by assuming that employees are motivated by desires to maximize the incomes of white workers, which is perhaps a bit far-fetched. However, it is possible that the discrimination coefficients of employees could be transmitted to the employer, as Arrow specifies, causing behavior *as if* the employer had a discrimination coefficient. If the employer has a status motive for discrimination, there would be no objection to hiring discriminatees for inferior jobs, but employers would object to hiring them for higher-status jobs.

It cannot be proved that status motives are more realistic than benevolence toward white workers or the desire not to associate with blacks, but the empirical evidence seems to support this conclusion. Whites clearly have been more strongly motivated to bar blacks from status jobs such as mechanical craftworkers in the construction industry, railroad conductors and engineers, and managers and supervisors of integrated work forces than they have from jobs such as carriers (not a low-wage job), foundry work (also not low wage), cement masons, service workers, and laborers—all of which are considered to have lower status. This analysis of the empirical evidence is complicated by the fact that occupants of higher-status jobs also usually have more power to bar blacks, making it difficult to isolate motive from power.

It might be noted in passing that the neoclassical assumption of physical discrimination does not fit comfortably with the conclusion that competitive firms (which are likely to be smaller and have closer relations between employees and employers) are less likely to discriminate than those firms operating under conditions of imperfect competition; the latter type of firm is presumably larger and characterized by more impersonal employer-employee relations.

The model also proffers unrealistic assumptions about the motives of white workers, who probably are more responsible than employers for discrimination in blue-collar jobs. The neoclassicals assume that white workers with discrimination coefficients are motivated mainly by wage rates. This assumption leads to some curious results. First, white workers are presumed to demand higher wages to work with blacks who are perfect substitutes. This is curious in view of the usual neoclassical assumption that people act rationally, because surely white workers could see that such demands would be self-defeating, since blacks would displace whites, as the neoclassical model stipulates. White workers are more likely to demand that blacks be excluded entirely from status jobs than to demand racial wage differentials. As noted later, however, whether white workers succeed in barring blacks depends on the power relations between the parties. If employers are firm in hiring blacks and if adequate supplies of black workers are available, whites are not likely to quit good jobs because blacks are hired.

Moreover, the white workers' basic motivation is likely to be job control rather than wage rates. The wage rate is an important part of the job, but the job's status, working conditions, stability, opportunity for advancement, and the extent to which workers participate in the formulation of job rules also are important considerations. Discriminators are likely to desire to practice job control by monopolizing the better jobs for themselves, and they capitalize on race, sex, and other biases to achieve their ends.

Power relations among the agents

However, a theory of discrimination should be able to say something about what gives discriminators the power to exclude discriminatees. The neoclassical model fails to do this because it does not deal with bargaining among groups and assumes wages to be the only objectives and wage differentials and wage changes to be basic causal forces. The neoclassical model also is silent with respect to the motives of black workers and the determinants of their power to overcome discrimination by white workers and employers.

Institutional discrimination

The neoclassical model also fails to distinguish between specific overt acts of discrimination, when, for example, a worker is not hired or promoted because of race, and institutionalized discrimination, which pervades social and economic institutions. When discrimination becomes institutionalized, as it has for blacks, overt discrimination becomes a relatively less important cause of the disadvantages of discriminatees, because inadequate education, segregated labor market institutions, and other forces that deny equal access to jobs, training, or information greatly reduce the probability that those discriminated against will aspire to, prepare for, or seek to enter the status occupations. In neoclassical language institutional discrimination makes it less likely that black and white workers will be homogeneous substitutes.

While the distinction between overt and institutional discrimination is useful, discriminators can practice overt discrimination while appearing to be objective. An example is the use of recruiting sources or screening devices that strongly reflect institutional discrimination.

The neoclassical theory does not deal with institutional discrimination because the model mistakenly assumes that institutions are fixed and do not interact, therefore, with the basic variables in the model. However, since the discrimination coefficient is itself considered exogenous to the system, the neoclassicals can hardly claim to have a *theory of discrimination*. A theory of discrimination should be able to explain the causes of discrimination and show how the economic variables in the model interact with the central phenomenon to be explained. The neoclassicists, because of the way they specify the model, must rely on competition operating through wage differentials to produce equilibrium. This probably requires that discriminators either be eliminated in the long run or change their tastes. But there is no indication of a relationship between competitive market forces and discrimination itself. It is unknown whether the taste for discrimination is irreversible and the persons of discriminatory persuasion are merely eliminated from the market in the long run or whether economic pressures cause discriminators to change their behavior and thus cause discrimination to be reduced or eliminated over time. These alternatives, while perhaps producing the same results in the model in the long run, are in fact substantively quite different.

Arrow realizes the need to deal with this problem in his alternative specification of the model, but his treatment raises questions for the model. To assume that the employer's discrimination is based on a perception of reality is a vastly different matter from assuming a taste for discrimination. This alternative formulation also raises the question of what happens when the employer's perception of reality is proved false by accurate information. It might be assumed in this case that the perception would conform with reality and that discrimination based on misinformation would disappear. Moreover, in this formulation, if the factors are really homogeneous, as the neoclassical theory ordinarily assumes, the congruence of perception and reality would reduce discrimination to zero, which would mean that there is no racial discrimination at all because the resulting discrimination would be due to reality and not to race.

A more realistic specification of the process of change would appear to be when some pressures (from government, the black community, or market forces) provide employers or employees with some motive to change black employment patterns with no necessary change in racial attitudes. Once the actors are required to cease discriminating, that part of their action based on inaccurate perceptions of reality changes immediately, but negative racial attitudes persist. The latter probably are eroded by a tendency for people to rationalize actions that their economic or other motives require them to take. Gradually, as discrimination declines, those discriminated against cease being regarded as inferior people, and status considerations for excluding them are reduced. Thus the line of causation probably is this: Overt discrimination is changed, attitudes change, and institutions change.

Wages and competition

The assumptions that wage differentials and wage and price competition are basic causal forces are necessary to make the neoclassical model compatible with competitive equilibrium theory, but these assumptions also cause some problems for the theory. We have noted this problem as it relates to the behavior of white workers. But the assumption that racial wage differentials are important facts to be explained also creates some question of the model's congruence with reality. If it is correct to assume that job control and status are the workers' main objectives and that profits and status are the main objectives of employers, then discriminatory wage differentials for homogeneous labor in the same firms are not likely to be very significant forces in the real world.[13] There is indeed no evidence that such differentials exist for workers who are perfect substitutes. Because of the importance of job specificity and OJT, it would almost be necessary to show that blacks and whites in the same firms and occupations were paid different wages, and this seems to be a highly unlikely occurrence.

There is, however, considerable evidence of job segregation and the concentration of blacks in certain kinds of jobs. The larger supplies of blacks in these traditional jobs undoubtedly tend to cause wages in these jobs to be lower than otherwise, but there is at least a partial compensation on the demand side because the dependable supplies of blacks cause employers to prefer blacks for these jobs. The neoclassical model does not ordinarily deal with this problem because of its questionable assumption that demand is independent of supply.

To be sure, there are racial income differentials. But this is not the same as showing racial wage differentials for homogeneous units of labor, even though neoclassical analysts sometimes use incomes and wages as if they were interchangeable concepts. Incomes are influenced by factors such as nonwage income, occupation, hours worked, and method of wage payment, as well as by wage rates.

Neoclassical analysts could argue, of course, that hiring blacks who are more productive than whites would have the same effect as paying racial wage differentials, but this requires the homogeneous factor assumption to be relaxed. This in turn would disrupt the marginal productivity theory because it would not be possible to say whether productivity changes were caused by changing units of labor or by the addition of more or less productive workers.

The neoclassical formulation, therefore, approximates a theory of wages with an extra term, the discrimination coefficient, where the specification of the model predetermines the outcome, rather than a theory explaining the basic causal forces of discrimination. The results of this formulation are true by definition—blacks must accept lower wages than whites in order to get jobs.

The neoclassical competitive assumptions also ignore the importance of bargaining and group activity, which seem important in changing racial employment patterns. The usual neoclassical assumption is that decisions are made on the basis of individual motivations and that in the long run these will erode group rules that are incompatible with individual marginal productivities and wage- and profit-maximizing motives. However, there may be no way to test this assumption, for an employer may not be able to determine the productivity of an individual worker, especially when adding a black worker to a group of whites. He must calculate the costs of reactions of the whites as well as the gain from hiring a qualified black. This often will become a bargaining problem among groups of blacks and their supporters (black community, government agencies, etc.), white workers and their organizations, and employers. The power relations will determine whether or not blacks get hired. Within the institutional framework (including laws and prevailing race relations in the larger society) black power to gain access to jobs ordinarily will be determined by the ability to inflict losses on (or convey profits to) employers and their control of supplies of labor qualified to satisfy the employer's demands if whites boycott or strike to protest the hiring of blacks. Employers are motivated by net profits resulting from the racial employment bargain.

Black or white workers' power will not come from the marginal productivities of individual workers, therefore, but from the productivities of groups of workers. Moreover, the effect of change on the net productivity of work groups will determine the extent to which employers are likely to make new racial rules.

Employers will not only be influenced by the net effect of the employment decision but also by the impact of such external pressures as government, general employment conditions, and the nature of product markets. Product markets are important in bargaining situations because they influence the employer's vulnerability to consumer pressures—generally, consumer-oriented companies are more vulnerable to prevailing racial attitudes (negative or positive) than those whose main output is producers' goods.

A model of employment discrimination that ignores the power of unions is incomplete, but unions are generally ignored by the neoclassical model. A union's racial practices are determined mainly by the influence of race on the union's control mechanisms.[14] These control mechanisms are the procedures used by the labor organization to protect and promote its basic objectives, which vary with the type of organization; and they will be explored at greater length in the outline of a bargaining model that follows.

On balance, a labor organization is not a basic force creating discrimination; it is a force to be used by its members to carry out their objectives whether one such objective is discrimination by whites or the eradication of discrimination. Orley Ashenfelter shows that craft unions have caused black wages to be lower than they would have been otherwise, while industrial unions have caused them to be higher.[15]

This suggests another major problem with the neoclassical model, namely, the assumption that competition necessarily erodes discrimination and group interests. Showing that competition does not play this role would cause considerable difficulty for the neoclassical model. Whereas the primary motivation for discrimination at the blue-collar level comes from white workers—which is a more realistic assumption than pointing to employers—oligopolistic firms might hire black workers faster than competitive firms in order, for example, to weaken the bargaining power of white-controlled unions. There is considerable historical evidence that blacks broke into nontraditional jobs in oligopolies like the steel and auto industries as strikebreakers long before they ever were hired outside menial classifications in more competitive industries like textiles, which avoided black areas in the South and has been known as a white man's industry.

It is true that blacks are concentrated more in industries with low product-market concentration ratios, but this does not prove that competitive industries are less discriminatory or that competition tends to erode discrimination. Blacks tend to be concentrated in competitive industries because these are low-wage jobs that hire mainly unskilled and semiskilled workers, consistent with black skill levels. Industries with higher product-market concentration ratios tend to have fewer blacks at least partly because they also have higher skill requirements than competitive firms and blacks generally have lower skill levels than whites.

There is no evidence showing—and considerable evidence to the contrary—that blacks have good employment opportunities in the white-collar and skilled jobs within competitive industries.[16] A major reason the neoclassical model can ignore the case in which blacks do not compete with whites in terms of wages is its assumption of full employment, which makes it difficult for employers to meet their labor requirements exclusively from one race. In reality, competitive firms have tended to locate in labor surplus areas, where their labor requirements were small relative to available labor pools.[17]

The neoclassical emphasis on competition also ignores the possible effects of bargaining on the racial employment practices of the large employer. Because of their low skills white or black workers in small competitive firms have very limited bargaining power, but, by the same token, the competitive employer has less slack with which to respond to black demands for better jobs. These employers are more likely to be consumer oriented and concerned that unpopular racial policies will reduce their sales and profits. Black consumer boycotts can be more effective against these firms than against the intermediate goods-producing oligopolists, who are less vulnerable to consumer boycotts but might be more responsive to threats of lawsuits or the loss of government contracts.

There is an important distinction between arguing, as neo-classical economists do, that competitive market forces tend to erode discrimination and that *industrialization* and the efficiency requirements of enterprises do so, as argued, for example, by Kerr, Dunlop, Harbison, and Myers.[18] These scholars rely on evidence from international studies to conclude that the logic of industrialism tends to erode discrimination. Industrial societies, in their view, tend to be open socities "inconsistent with the assignment of managers or workers to occupations or to jobs by traditional caste, racial groups, by sex or by family status."[19] This formulation emphasizes the interactions of employers' decisions with major institutions in the larger society, so that industrialization, rather than the neoclassical competitive market, causes changes that erode discrimination. Industrial societies not only tend to be open, but they also tend to produce urbanization and to be pluralistic, both of which increase the political and economic power of blacks to combat discrimination. Industrial societies also tend to give greater roles to governments and put a premium on using the political process to achieve economic ends.

The form in which the neoclassical model of discrimination is expressed impedes—if not precludes—empirical testing or use for policy purposes. As already noted, the model offers few suggestions for ways blacks might improve their employment patterns other than by accepting lower wage rates, improving their productivity, getting whites to change their attitudes, or enforcing antitrust laws. Because OJT is such an important method of acquiring skills, blacks also must find some way of gaining access to those jobs having skill development potential.

A number of features of the neoclassical model make it difficult to derive meaningful policy prescriptions from it. For one thing, the model is too simple and abstract to include enough relevant variables that can be tested empirically. Moreover, the model's assumption that institutions are given causes it to pay very little attention to specific measures to improve simultaneously black economic positions in the short run *and* initiate long-run reforms to eliminate institutionalized discrimination.

An alternative formulation

This critique of the economics of discrimination suggests at least the outlines of an alternative formulation that incorporates features of the neoclassical and other models but specifies the motives of the various actors and the contexts within which they operate on the basis of empirical evidence rather than a priori deductive reasoning. This alternative formulation could be called an industrial relations or bargaining model and is similar to that developed for industrial relations by John Dunlop in his *Industrial Relations Systems.*[20] However, it is not possible to present a definitive comparison of this alternative formulation with the neoclassical model because each model has different objectives and is formulated in different terms and at different levels of abstractions. The alternative formulation is less designed to be compatible with a general equilibrium model and, therefore, is less rigorous, but, hopefully, it can be tested empirically, is more relevant for understanding the basic forces causing and perpetuating discrimination, and affords more insight into appropriate antidiscrimination policies. Each group of actors in the racial employment process develops mechanisms to improve its power relative to other groups. In this formulation wages merely constitute one aspect of the job.

Also, a bargaining model assumes racial employment patterns in any given situation to be products of the power relationship between the actors and the specific environmental contexts within which they operate. These relationships and contexts can be empirically determined to some extent, and while relatively stable in the short run, they change through time and involve dynamic mutual causation rather than one-way causal relationships.

The actors

The main actors involved in the determination of racial employment patterns are managers, white workers, black workers, unions, and government agencies responsible for the implementation of antidiscrimination and industrial relations policies. The main environmental features influencing racial employment patterns include: economic and labor market conditions, community race relations, the distribution of power in the larger community, industry structure and growth potential, the labor market skills and education of black and white populations relative to the labor requirements of various companies and industries, and the operation of labor market institutions.

Employers

It has been argued that the employer's main motivation is profit maximization and status. However, profit maximization must be considered in a much broader context than the effect of individual marginal productivities on wages.

Management hiring decisions also historically have been influenced by firm size, industry structure, and the nature of labor supplies. Assuming employer motives to hire blacks because of profit considerations, the strongest factor influencing the black workers' ability to combat discrimination is not marginal productivity of each worker but total labor supplies to meet management's requirements if whites strike or boycott. In the bargaining model the control of larger supplies of labor increases bargaining power. Although many other factors influence this relationship, whites will rarely be able to exclude large supplies of blacks qualified to take their place. Moreover, where there are adequate total labor supplies, employers frequently prefer minority workers for certain kinds of jobs because the limited job options available to blacks and their traditional employment in those occupations cause them to be crowded into these occupations and make them dependable sources of labor. Because blacks traditionally have been hired in certain occupations, employers have developed stereotypes that blacks are best suited for those jobs. Blacks have been preferred mainly for menial and disagreeable occupations but also for some higher-paying jobs such as musicians, athletes, trowel trades in the construction industry, waiters, and longshoremen. In short, unless their own status is threatened by hiring blacks, employers' profit motives will cause them to hire blacks when all-black work forces can be employed in particular occupations for less than all-white work forces and when dependable supplies of labor are available to perform particular tasks. The employers' demand for black workers may be influenced by pressures from governments or black communities.

However, employers maintain status motives for discrimination. Top management's status probably will not be adversely affected by integrating blue-collar work forces, but if members of management have racial biases, resistance to integration will increase as the integrated jobs come closer to their own in the occupational structure. This at least partly explains the lower representation of blacks in white-collar and managerial positions. Of course, partly because of institutional discrimination fewer blacks have the education, training, and skill requirements for managerial and white-collar jobs.

White workers

This conceptual model assumes that white workers are primarily motivated by status and job-control considerations in excluding blacks from "their" jobs. However, whether or not whites succeed in excluding blacks depends on whites' ability to bring pressure to bear on the employer. If whites are in sufficient supply to fill particular occupations, in the absence of countervailing powers, employers will find it profitable to hire only whites. However, if blacks are in sufficient supply to meet employers' labor requirements, employers might turn to blacks to weaken white unions. They will not necessarily pay the black workers a different wage, but their presence tends to moderate wage pressures unless blacks and whites form a united bargaining front. Similarly, the white workers' bargaining power would be weakened even if blacks are in helper or other mislabeled occupational categories while really performing the same jobs as whites. If they have inadequate bargaining power to prevent the entry of blacks into "their" jobs, bigoted whites are not likely to quit good jobs because of their racist attitudes, nor are they likely to demand wage differentials to compensate for their prejudices. Even assuming they have adequate knowledge of alternatives, prejudiced whites are likely to stay on their jobs if moving is costly in terms of loss of seniority, good wages, and the advantages of specialized nontransferable job skills in places where they have worked.

Unions

White workers will use the unions they control to preserve and ration job opportunities. On the other hand, black workers might use labor organizations to preserve or enlarge their own opportunities.

The race issues enters union operating procedures in a variety of ways. Different kinds of unions have different motives, procedures, and control mechanisms and, therefore, will react differently to the presence of black workers in an industry or trade. If there are few or no blacks in an industry or trade, craft unions have been motivated by job control and status considerations to keep them out. Whether or not these unions are able to bar blacks depends mainly on their control of entry into the occupation. Craft unions, for example, ordinarily have considerable control of the supply of labor. The main job-control instruments of craft unions are control of training, entry into the trade and union, and job referrals. In order to penetrate these crafts and unions blacks must ordinarily either threaten the unions' control instruments or inflict monetary losses on those organizations.

Because they confront different situations, industrial unions generally have adopted different procedures. Their members are not any more or less racially prejudiced than craftsmen, but job-status considerations seem to be weaker in the case of industrial unions. The main difference between craft and industrial unions is that the latter have little direct influence over hiring. In order to organize their jurisdictions, therefore, industrial unions must appeal to the workers hired by the employer. Thus if blacks have been hired in competition with white workers, the union's ability to organize and its bargaining strength will depend on its ability to attract blacks.

Union racial practices also are influenced by union structure. Since federations and national unions have broader political objectives than the locals, the motive for racial equality increases as we move from the local to the national level. Moreover, national craft unions also have stronger motives to take in blacks than their locals because the national unions' power depends to some extent upon the size of the membership, whereas the local often perceives its power to depend more narrowly on control of labor supplies in local labor markets.

Blacks

The blacks outside craft unions derive their power mainly from the strength of employer motives to hire them and the extent to which they can threaten wage rates and job-control procedures of discriminating white union members and their leaders; this in turn depends, primarily, on the number of blacks in a labor market who possess the necessary skills to compete with white union members and, secondarily, on the extent to which the black community and antidiscrimination forces are organized to overcome white resistance to the admission of blacks. Even if civil rights forces are well organized to achieve this objective, they will have limited impact unless they produce black applicants for employment, upgrading, apprenticeship, and/or journeyman status who meet the qualifications imposed by unions and employers or unless they successfully challenge the standards and specifications themselves. These considerations make it obvious that an effective strategy to overcome local union resistance ordinarily will require considerable attention to local labor market conditions and the control mechanisms used by the local union to regulate labor supplies and control jobs.

Environmental factors

These specific and immediate forces affecting black employment patterns are influenced by environmental factors such as the relative amount and quality of education available to blacks, race relations in the larger community, the age and sex composition of the black work force, alternative income sources available to black workers and their families, housing patterns and transportation costs relative to the location of jobs, the physical and emotional health of blacks relative to whites, whether an industry is growing or declining in terms of employment, black and white migration patterns, the structure of industry in terms of its customers (blacks, whites, other employees, or government), general business conditions, skill requirements and job structures within industry, the black community's relative accessibility to job information, and the process through which employers and unions recruit and train workers for jobs.

While all of these factors are important determinants of black employment patterns, some are more important and measurable than others. General business conditions are very important because tight labor markets facilitate the employment and upgrading of blacks. However, this view must be qualified because experience makes it clear that tight labor markets are not sufficient causes of change. Many cities in the South have had low official unemployment rates, but they also had stable racial employment patterns between 1920 and the 1960s. Moreover, there is a difference between a labor market in which unemployment is declining and one in which unemployment is low and stable. Similarly, the overall unemployment rate obscures particular labor market conditions where blacks are able to get jobs. Finally, concerted efforts to change institutional arrangements can make it possible for black employment to increase in a particular category even when white employment is falling.

The bargaining model has some policy implications that are similar to those of the neoclassical model. The neoclassicals are correct in stressing measures to increase black productivity as a means of improving their economic positions. But they are wrong in assuming that market forces alone will gain blacks access to the jobs for which they qualify themselves. Policies must be taken to overcome employer and community opposition and white workers' control of jobs. Indeed, if blacks are unable to gain access to jobs, there is no effective way they can acquire the OJT so essential for access to many better jobs. Black workers certainly are not going to be able to gain access to many of these jobs and OJT opportunities by agreeing to work for lower wages than white incumbents.

The neoclassical model gives no place to group activities in changing employment opportunities, whereas the bargaining model stresses the need for group action to initiate changes in rules and laws to which individuals adapt. The bargaining model also stresses the need to build public policy (as well as group strategy and tactics) on an understanding of the responses of organizations and groups to various kinds of pressures, not merely on an understanding of market forces. However, there is an overlap between these formulations in the sense that market forces influence the power relations among groups.

The industrial relations model also stresses the need to explore the relationships among atttitudes, overt and institutional discrimination, and market forces in order to determine how discrimination can be reduced or eliminated.

The policy implications of Arrow's formulations depend in part on whether we accept either the taste-for-discrimination or perception-of-reality formulation. The former would imply measures to reduce discriminatory tastes directly or indirectly through competitive forces. The latter would require more accurate labor market information to cause the probabilities of selecting qualified whites and blacks to converge.

Conclusions

This chapter outlines theoretical conceptions of racial discrimination advanced by neoclassical, radical, and dual labor market economists. It emphasizes these theories or hypotheses, especially the lack of agreement among the various proponents of the various systems and the formative nature of the dual labor market and radical approaches. These formulations also differ in their purposes. In general, discrimination does not occupy a central place in any of these formulations but is part of a broader conceptual framework. The neoclassical theory has been developed more systematically than the others, but, except in terms of compatability with competitive neoclassical general equilibrium theory, it seems to be inadequate in its definition and conception of discrimination, in treating discrimination as "given" and not to be explained by the model, in not taking into consideration the influence of groups and bargaining, in using deductive, rather than empirically derived, concepts that are difficult to test, in producing mechanical results that add little information about the forces increasing or reducing discrimination, in omitting significant factors impinging on discrimination, and in leading to inadequate policy recommendations.

For the purposes of understanding racial discrimination in employment and producing strategies, tactics, and policies for changing discrimination, a broader bargaining model is recommended. This model should distinguish between overt and institutional discrimination, call for an analysis of the motives of various actors impinging on the employment decision, emphasize the need to examine the power relations among these actors, and stress the need to examine the broader social and economic context within which the actors establish formal, informal, and institutionalized rules governing racial employment relations. There are clear overlaps among the neoclassical, radical, dual labor market, and bargaining formulations, but it appears that the last provides a better conceptual framework both for understanding the dynamics of racial employment relations and for formulating policies to improve black opportunities.

Notes

1. This chapter relies heavily on Ray Marshall, "The Economic Theory of Racial Discrimination in Employment," *Journal of Economic Literature* (September 1974), pp. 849–871.
2. For a review of empirical research see Dale Hiestand, *Discrimination in Employment: An Appraisal of the Research* (Ann Arbor, Mich.: Institute of Labor and Industrial Relations, University of Michigan and National Manpower Policy Task Force, 1970).
3. Gary Becker, *The Economics of Discrimination*, 2nd ed. (Chicago: University of Chicago Press, 1971).
4. Barbara R. Bergmann, *Occupation Segregation, Wages, and Profits When Employers Discriminate by Race and Sex* (College Park, Md.: Project on the Economics of Discrimination, mimeograph, 1970); "The Effect on White Incomes of Discrimination in Employment," *Journal of Political Economy*, Vol. 79, No. 2 (March/April 1971), pp. 294–313.
5. This is our notation, not Bergmann's.
6. Finis Welch, "Labor Market Discrimination: An Interpretation of Income Differences in the Rural South," *Journal of Political Economy*, Vol. 75, No. 3 (June 1967), pp. 225–240.
7. Ibid.
8. Kenneth J. Arrow, "Models of Job Discrimination" and "Some Models of Race in the Labor Market," in A. H. Pascal, ed., *Racial Discrimination in Economic Life* (Lexington, Mass.: Heath, 1972); "The Theory of Discrimination," in Orley Ashenfelter and Albert Rees, eds., *Discrimination in Labor Markets* (Princeton, N.J.: Princeton University Press, 1974).
9. Arrow, "Theory of Discrimination," op. cit.
10. Edmund S. Phelps, "Statistical Theory of Racism and Sexism," *American Economic Review*, Vol. 62, No. 4 (September 1974), pp. 659–661.
11. Orley Ashenfelter, "Discrimination and Trade Unions" in Ashenfelter and Rees, op. cit., p. 26.
12. John J. McCall, *Racial Discrimination in the Job Market: The Role of Information and Search* (Santa Monica, Calif.: Rand Corporation, 1971).

13. Lester Thurow, *Economics of Poverty and Discrimination,* (Washington, D.C.: Brookings Institution, 1969).
14. Ray Marshall, *The Negro and Organized Labor* (New York: Wiley, 1965); Ray Marshall and Virgil Christian, eds., *The Employment of Southern Blacks* (Salt Lake City, Utah: Olympus Publishing Co., 1974).
15. Ashenfelter, "Discrimination and Trade Unions," op. cit.
16. Marshall and Christian, op. cit.
17. Welch, "Labor Market Discrimination," op. cit.
18. Clark Kerr et al., *Industrialism and Industrial Man* (Cambridge, Mass.: Harvard University Press, 1960).
19. Ibid.
20. John Dunlop, *Industrial Relations Systems* (New York: Holt, Rinehart & Winston, 1958).

18
black employment and income

Low income and inadequate employment opportunities were among the most important human resource development problems for blacks and other minorities in the 1960s. Underutilization and underdevelopment not only deprive blacks of opportunities to improve their material welfare but also cost the nation the economic contribution they could make if they had better employment and income-earning opportunities, to say nothing of the costs of social instability.

Minority groups, particularly blacks, did much to stimulate human resource development programs during the 1960s. The civil rights movement's concentration on political rights during the 1950s gave way to greater demands for economic equality during the 1960s, when it became abundantly clear that abstract rights without economic opportunity had little meaning. Moreover, the real nature of racial discrimination came into sharper focus as the adoption of programs to overcome specific overt acts of discrimination produced limited results. It became increasingly apparent that institutionalized racism was more deeply rooted and pervasive than more overt forms of discrimination and, therefore, that vigorous and comprehensive education, manpower, and welfare measures would be required to combat it. Institutionalized racism affects all aspects of life—education, housing, jobs, social affairs—and causes the persons discriminated against not to aspire to or prepare for the kinds of jobs from which they are barred.

Population shifts

Some of the nation's most significant race problems have come about in large measure because of the migration of blacks out of the rural South. Until roughly the time of World War I, almost all

385

blacks were in the South and most of them were concentrated in the so-called black belt, a crescent of counties extending from Washington, D.C., through east Texas, each of which had a majority black population until the 1940s. Indeed, as late as 1940, over three-fourths of the nation's black population resided in the South. Because of the great outmigration since around the time of World War I, today only about one-half of the nation's blacks remain in the South. Until the 1960s, black outmigration appears to have been largely in response to job opportunities, which opened up initially because of the cessation of immigration from Europe into Northern labor markets with the outbreak of World War I.

In the South most blacks had been employed in agriculture or in certain black nonfarm jobs. In agriculture the sharecropping system predominated; it provided little incentive for blacks or whites to improve either themselves or the soil. The sharecropping system required very little education or training. Indeed, even the managerial experience that many farmers acquire on the job was denied the sharecropper because landlords made most of the major decisions.

Nonagricultural jobs available to blacks were, for the most part, hot, dirty, or otherwise disagreeable, except for jobs in the black community, where segregation protected black craftsmen and technical and professional workers from white encroachment. Outside their own communities, blacks were concentrated in labor and service jobs with very few exceptions, and these were mainly cases in which blacks were too numerous to be excluded from an occupation or trade. For example, many blacks were trained as bricklayers and carpenters before the Civil War. After emancipation, whites had considerable difficulty excluding blacks from these jobs because there were sufficient numbers of black craftsmen to protect their share of the market. As a consequence, black bricklayers were admitted to white unions or were organized into segregated locals; on the whole, black bricklayers have suffered relatively little discrimination in employment.

Crafts (for example, electrical workers and plumbers) that flourished mainly after the Civil War had very few blacks in them. Thus whites were able to freeze blacks out of these occupations except for limited work in the black community or in residential construction. Whites refused to permit blacks to work in commercial and industrial construction. If it had not been for the black colleges, which trained black craftsmen, there would have been very little opportunity for blacks to learn crafts that required considerable technical and on-the-job training. Blacks were generally barred from apprenticeship programs that supplied many skilled workers and could not work in the higher-paying sectors of many industries except as laborers; hence they had very limited opportunity to acquire skills on the job.

In manufacturing industries blacks usually were restricted to jobs as laborers regardless of their qualifications. Whites, of course, were hired into lines of progression that made it possible for them to move up into a wide range of jobs from which blacks were barred. Moreover, this pattern did not change significantly until the 1960s in the South.

As will be noted at greater length when we look at the statistics on racial employment patterns, very few blacks have held white-collar jobs and these have been restricted almost exclusively to Southern black communities. Racial segregation is partly a caste system, so that the prevailing sentiment in the South made it unthinkable before the 1960s that blacks would seek better white-collar jobs, especially those jobs whose occupants had supervisory authority over whites.

The ample supply of black labor and the workers' lack of permanent attachment to employers made it difficult for some jobs to be structured in such a way as to exclude blacks. In these cases racial quota systems were adopted. General longshoreman's work, for example, has been divided along racial lines in many Southern ports since the Civil War. It should be observed, however, that the quota system usually gave blacks inferior job opportunities. In New Orleans, for instance, the general longshoreman's work was divided, although blacks greatly outnumbered whites in this labor market. This meant that each black received less employment than each white worker attached to the market. In addition, whites reserved the better clerical jobs for themselves.

Black migration out of the South, which was accelerated by World War I, continued during the 1920s, slowed down some during the depression of the 1930s, speeded up again during World War II, and has continued since then. In 1940, 77 percent of the nation's blacks were in the South, compared with 60 percent in 1960 and about 50 percent in 1970. This black outmigration from the rural South has been one of the most significant developments of the past half century. In a relatively short time the black population has been transformed from predominantly rural and Southern to predominantly urban and equally divided between the North and the South. Although segregation was not as institutionalized outside the South, racism was a problem for blacks in the North as well as in the South. Moreover, because they were not very well prepared by training or experience for nonfarm jobs, blacks held mainly menial jobs in Northern as well as Southern cities. Indeed, in some ways the black's lot was worse outside the South. Blacks did not even hold the better jobs in black neighborhoods and were concentrated in central cities outside the South. In addition, those blacks who moved North during and after World War II found declining job opportunities in many of the industries that traditionally had absorbed large numbers of semi-skilled and unskilled workers. Moreover, ghetto labor markets had characteristics that made it difficult for many young blacks to move into the mainstream even when discriminatory barriers were lowered. (See Chapter 21.) The ghetto labor market syndrome probably explains why blacks recently arrived from the South have better income and employment experience than blacks with similar characteristics who were born in Northern cities. The submarginal or marginal labor markets, which predominate in ghettos, have many job openings that ghetto dwellers find unattractive or occupy only for short periods. Blacks fresh from the South probably find these submarginal or marginal jobs more attractive than the opportunities that had been available to them.

Other problems confronted blacks outside the South. Indeed, although greater political power was available to them than had been the case in the South and they confronted less formal segregation imposed by law, nevertheless, blacks encountered discrimination and hostility from whites in other areas. The influx of Southern blacks with different values and limited education or job training caused many Northern whites to move out of central cities, leaving behind areas with larger black majorities, especially in the schools, and working-class or retired whites who had insufficient income to move out or who had such large investments in their homes that they were reluctant to move. These developments created racial tensions between black and white workers. Indeed, some observers believe that these tensions will upset the New Deal coalition, which included blacks and white ethnics, who had been concentrated in many of the neighborhoods into which blacks have moved.

Migration created problems for the South as well as the North. Those Southerners who thought they could export their black welfare problems to the North were very short-sighted indeed. By not taking measures to retain blacks, the South aggravated its human resource development problem because the most productive part of its black population moved out, leaving behind the older, less well-educated blacks who have limited productive potential and, therefore, are not attractive even to the marginal industries that predominate in the region's economy. These industries have moved out of the non-South into the South in search of workers with higher qualifications who will work at lower wages. Because of the rapid displacement of Southerners from agriculture (discussed later) and the lower level of industrialization, labor markets have been more attractive to marginal enterprises in the South than they have been in the North. In addition, lower welfare payments in the South have forced more secondary workers in a family to work than is true in those areas where welfare payments are higher.

Employment changes

The evidence reveals perceptible economic progress made by blacks during the 1960s, but it also shows uneven progress and the continuation of wide economic gaps between blacks and whites. Moreover, the economic gains of blacks relative to whites slowed down and in some cases was reversed during the 1970s. Discrimination and racial inequality remain very serious problems requiring the strengthening of antidiscrimination and other human resource development activities. Moreover, the causes of racial inequality are deeply imbedded in American society; therefore, progress will require sustained efforts and programs on numerous fronts. Also, experience with various techniques in improving black employment patterns provides a useful base upon which to build more effective public policies to enhance black employment opportunities and patterns.

For the nation as a whole there were some perceptible changes in black employment patterns during the last half of the 1960s, although these employment changes slowed during the 1970s. Nonwhites (who are over 90 percent black) have increased their proportions of higher-status and better-paying white-collar jobs while they reduced their proportions in the service and laborer categories. (Table 18-1)

Black women's relative employment gains were particularly striking, especially in professional, technical, managerial, clerical, and sales categories. Blacks, males and females, in the 25-to-34-year-old group improved their employment patterns relative to whites and relative to blacks in other age groups.

Despite these gains, however, blacks have a long way to go to gain employment equality with whites. Blacks account for over half of all private household workers and over a fifth of all laundry and dry-cleaning operatives, laborers, hospital attendants, janitors and sextons, maids and cleaners, and practical nurses. At the other end of the employment scale blacks represent only 2.6 percent of managers, administrators, and proprietors; 3.1 percent of sales workers; and very low proportions of many professional and technical workers.

Indeed, blacks experienced dramatic percentage increases in

Table 18-1 Relative Occupational Distribution of Whites and Non-whites, 1958 and 1972

	Nonwhites		Whites		% Non-whites to Whites in Occupations	
	1958	1972	1958	1972	1958	1972
Total	100.0%	100.0%	100.0%	100.0%	1.00	1.00
Managers and administrators	2.4	3.7	11.7	10.6	0.21	0.35
Professional and technical	4.1	9.5	11.8	14.6	0.35	0.65
Craftsmen	5.9	8.7	14.3	13.8	0.41	0.63
Clerical	6.1	14.4	15.4	17.8	0.40	0.81
Operatives	20.1	21.3	17.9	16.0	1.12	1.33
Sales	1.2	2.2	6.9	7.1	0.17	0.31
Farmers and farm managers	3.7	0.6	5.0	2.2	0.74	0.27
Service	33.0	27.2	9.5	11.8	3.47	2.31
Nonfarm laborers	14.7	9.9	4.5	4.6	3.27	2.15
Farm laborers	8.8	2.4	3.0	1.6	2.93	1.50

Source: Manpower Report of the President (Washington, D.C.: GPO, 1973), Table A-12.

some professional-technical jobs, but within these occupations they are heavily concentrated among jobs such as social and recreation workers, registered nurses, medical and dental technicians, and elementary and high school teachers. Blacks traditionally have been concentrated in professional jobs serving black communities. When jobs are integrated, blacks appear mainly to get "new traditional" jobs, in which they replace whites who previously served black clients. Similarly, in the craft occupations blacks are underrepresented in the electrical, pipe, and printing crafts and overrepresented, as noted earlier, among brick masons, cement and concrete finishers, cranemen, derrick operators, painters, and roofers and slaters.

Black males earn less than whites even after adjusting for years of schooling, regularity of work, and occupational differentials. For adult black males the unexplained variation after adjusting for these factors was 25 percent. After adjusting their incomes for education, intermittent work, and occupation, black males in the 25-to-34-year-old age group still earn only 82 percent as much as whites. On the other hand, adjusting relative female incomes for education, regularity of work, and occupation causes black females to earn 108 percent as much as white females. Nevertheless, 25-to-34-year-old black women earn less than white women and less than half as much as black males at the same age. It also should be emphasized that black women's employment gains were impressive because they were relative to those of white women, which are low, at least partly, because white women also face discrimination. Moreover, black women have experienced employment gains in a narrow range of industries compared with black men.

Blacks also suffer more from unemployment than whites. Only slightly over 50 percent of adult nonwhite males worked a full year in 1970, compared with 60 percent for whites. Over 20 percent of nonwhite males had no work experience, compared with 16 percent for whites; among those who found some employment, 38 percent of nonwhites, but only 29 percent of whites, experienced work interruptions during the year.

Because of these interruptions and the fact that they have more recently entered many nonagricultural jobs, blacks tend to have less tenure on the job than whites. In 1968, for example, employed nonwhite males had been on the job an average of 3.3 years as compared with 5 years for white males. Since seniority is an important determinant of job security, occupational upgrading, and other benefits, work interruptions and relatively short job tenure have long-run consequences beyond the immediate problems they cause.

Because blacks are attempting to improve their occupational positions, labor market conditions are very important for blacks, whose unemployment tends to fluctuate more than that of whites in every phase of the business cycle. Indeed, tight labor markets tend to be the most significant factors promoting improvements in black employment patterns. Nonwhites of all ages, especially males, benefited more than whites from tight labor markets in the mid-1960s. Even black teenagers, who as it was noted earlier suffer very high relative unemployment rates, were helped by these tight labor market conditions, although this only briefly offset the disturbing long-run trend of rising unemployment for this age group.

Unemployment

It would be a mistake, however, to conclude that tight labor markets alone will solve black employment problems, because there are numerous examples of places where average unemployment problems are very low and black employment patterns remain virtually unchanged.

The higher unemployment rates of nonwhites are due largely to the fact that blacks are concentrated in occupations and industries such as nonfarm laborers, operatives, and service workers, in which unemployment tends to be high. Although education tends to be correlated with unemployment, blacks of all ages and educational levels are more frequently unemployed than whites. As large a proportion of nonwhites with some college were unemployed in March 1972, as of whites with only a high school diploma.

Nonwhites also suffer relatively high unemployment rates because they are more likely than whites to be concentrated in secondary labor markets, in which seniority means very little and in which wages and working conditions are barely preferable to street life and welfare. On the average, in 1972, nonwhite workers were two-thirds more likely than whites to have lost and quit their jobs and 2.2 times more likely to be experiencing reentry or first-entry problems.

Unemployment rates are imperfect indicators of nonwhite labor market disadvantages, however, because these rates only reflect those who are willing and able to work and actively seeking jobs—they do not reflect those working part time who would like full-time jobs, those working but not earning enough to raise them above the poverty level, or those who have become discouraged and ceased looking for jobs. There is some reason, therefore, to be concerned about the fact that, relative to whites, the labor force participation rates for nonwhite males over 16 years of age declined from 86 percent in 1950 to 83 percent in 1960 and to 74 percent in 1972 (when the white rate was 80 percent). Among nonwhite females there was a slight increase in participation from 47 percent in 1950 to 49 percent in 1972, but over the same period the white female rate rose substantially, from 33 percent to 43 percent.

The most significant labor force factor to be explained was the decline in participation by young blacks between 1967 and 1972, when the annual average proportion of nonwhite males aged 16 to 24 outside the labor force increased from 32.5 percent to 36.8 percent. Fortunately, however, rising school attendance accounted for about three-fifths of the decline in young nonwhite male participation.

Nevertheless, many blacks not counted in the labor force are discouraged workers who would like to work but have given up looking for jobs. Among nonwhites in 1972, 14 percent of males and 17 percent of females said they wanted to work but were not looking for work. There were 188,000 of these discouraged nonwhites, accounting for a fourth of all discouraged workers.[1]

It is sometimes argued that blacks have withdrawn from the work force, even though jobs are available, because of unrealistic wage expectations or because of a preference for illegal activities. While it cannot be denied that these considerations are partly responsible for labor force withdrawal, the existence of some unknown number of blacks who do not want to work should not obscure the fact that many nonwhites are looking for but cannot find jobs. The evidence is clear that most blacks will take jobs if they are available. Between 1961 and 1969, for example, when the average unemployment rate dropped from 6.7 percent to 3.5 percent, the number of employed black adult males rose by 11 percent, as compared with only 9 percent for adult white males.

Another indication of black economic disadvantage is the employment and earnings inadequacy index (which counts persons aged 16 to 64—except students aged 16 to 21—who are unemployed, discouraged, involuntarily employed part time for economic reasons, household heads working full time at poverty-level wages, and household heads working intermittently and earning too little to raise their families above the poverty thresholds), which was 25 percent for blacks and 10 percent for whites in March 1972. Blacks in nonmetropolitan areas were particularly disadvantaged—nearly a third of them having indequate employment and earnings campared with 24 percent of those in central cities and 20 percent in the suburbs.[2]

Blacks continued to be displaced from Southern agriculture and rural areas at a very rapid rate during the 1960s. Many of these displaced blacks were unprepared by background and experience for nonfarm employment. Indeed, the black population of the rural South declined by 5 percent during the 1960s, while the white population in those areas grew by 9 percent. The net outmovement of blacks and other races from the metropolitan South was 1,346,000 during the 1960s, down only slightly from 1,568,000 during the 1950s.

To a very large extent, the continued outmigration of blacks from the rural South is due to inadequate employment opportunities for blacks in those areas. Agricultural policy and discrimination in U.S. agricultural programs have long been major problems facing blacks in the South, but there is also evidence that blacks have not shared proportionately in the rapid growth of nonfarm jobs in the rural South during the 1960s. As a consequence, there continues to be heavy white migration into many counties from which blacks are forced to move because of inadequate employment opportunities.

Despite heavy black outmigration from agriculture, however, more blacks remain employed in this sector than in any four manufacturing industries in the South. Therefore, any strategy to improve the economic conditions of rural blacks must give some attention to improving the opportunities for small farmers and agricultural workers.

Problems of the central cities

Outside the rural South blacks are increasingly locating in large metropolitan areas, especially in the North and West. In 1970 slightly over half of the nation's blacks lived outside the South. (Table 18-2) In the South the black population was about evenly divided between metropolitan and nonmetropolitan areas, but almost all blacks outside the South lived in urban areas, especially in the central cities of several large metropolitan areas. As a consequence of these population shifts, poverty—black and white— is mainly a rural phenomenon in the South, but outside the South it is mainly urban. Moreover, in 1973 the black population was more metropolitanized (76 percent) than was true of whites (67 percent).

The concentration of blacks in central cities creates a number of serious social and economic problems. For one thing, the flight of whites from central cities as blacks move in leads to increasing racial segregation in housing and schools. Moreover, the flight of higher-income whites and the decentralization of industry to suburban rings create serious financial problems for the cities, making it difficult for them to render much-needed human resource development services to their populations. The decentralization of jobs creates special problems for blacks because of the transportation costs in money and time to reach jobs in outlying areas. The slum areas of many central cities are characterized by poor housing, crowding, high incidence of crime, poverty, and inadequate public services.

Because of the heavy concentration of blacks in the central city slums, there is a strong tendency to conclude that many problems associated with these areas have racial origins; this is no doubt true, but many also are due to the nature of the slum itself. For example, although much has been made of the disintegration of black ghetto families, presumably because of the legacy of slavery, the incidence of broken homes among Mexican Americans and Puerto Ricans closely resembles that of blacks today, and the incidence of broken families in Irish slums of westside Manhattan at the time of World War I was actually higher than the present black rate.[3] This and other problems of low-income slum dwellers are clearly more related to factors associated with ghettos than with race.

Table 18-2 Population Distribution and Change, Inside and Outside Metropolitan Areas: 1960, 1970, and 1973 (thousands)

Area	Black			White		
	1960	1970	1973[a]	1960	1970	1973[a]
United States	18,872	22,580	23,189	158,832	177,749	179,574
Metropolitan areas	12,741	16,771	17,619	105,829	120,579	120,631
Inside central cities	9,874	13,140	13,868	49,415	49,430	47,206
Outside central cities	2,866	3,630	3,751	56,414	71,148	73,425
Nonmetropolitan areas	6,131	5,810	5,570	53,003	57,170	58,943
Percent Distribution						
United States	100	100	100	100	100	100
Metropolitan areas	68	74	76	67	68	67
Inside central cities	52	58	60	31	28	26
Outside central cities	15	16	16	36	40	41
Nonmetropolitan areas	32	26	24	33	32	33

[a]Five quarter average centered on April 1973. Quarterly estimates for the months of October 1972, and January, April, July, and October 1973 were used. These figures do not include annexations since 1970.

Source: U.S. Department of Commerce, Social and Economic Statistics Administration, Bureau of the Census.

Nevertheless, there are important racial aspects to ghettos because discrimination in housing and employment contributes to the inability of many blacks to leave the ghetto, restricting them to employment within these areas, to "hustling" and other forms of illicit activity, or to welfare dependency. Discrimination in employment combines with inadequate education and other human resource development programs to trap many ghetto residents to lives of poverty and low incomes.

With respect to employment many central-city jobs are characterized by low incomes, limited upward occupational mobility, and high turnover rates. Unions in these occupations tend to be weak, so that workers have very limited job protection. Many employers and workers apparently adapt to these conditions, causing black concentration in these jobs to become self-perpetuating. Marginal jobs require limited skills or education, so that employers need only make limited investments in training and thus are not overly concerned about turnover. Many of the workers in these jobs are not motivated to discipline themselves to perform well and to avoid absenteeism and high quit rates. Surprisingly, however, many ghetto workers in these low-wage jobs have long job tenure and exemplary job performance.

There have been, in recent years, heated debates about how to solve the problems of the ghetto. Some observers argue for ghetto development, or "gilding the ghetto," while others argue for dispersing the ghetto through vigorous housing and employment antidiscrimination programs, increased job training, and improved transportation. However, these are not alternative solutions—both approaches should be used to increase the options available to ghetto residents—to either stay in the ghettos if they choose and improve their economic conditions or to work and live outside these areas. Currently, too many ghetto residents have no choice because they are trapped by low incomes and discrimination. It is particularly important to adopt measures to combat discrimination in housing as well as employment and public accommodations. There also is a pressing need to improve housing within ghetto areas.

It is also doubted very seriously that the concentration of blacks in ghettos will give them adequate political power to solve their problems. Despite the heavy concentration of blacks in central cities, whites still constitute the overwhelming majority of the populations of these places—78 percent in 1970; in 1970 blacks constituted 21.8 percent of central cities, 4.9 percent of suburbs, and 9.5 percent of nonmetropolitan areas. Therefore, black separatist politics is very unlikely to be sufficient to solve black economic problems. Solutions must be based mainly on interracial cooperation.

Causes of black employment disadvantages

Black income and employment problems are caused by a deeply entrenched constellation of forces that are difficult to overcome and that will require intensified and concerted remedies on a variety of fronts. Because these causal forces are so interrelated, it is difficult to assign weights to each of them. Our understanding of this problem is also complicated by the fact that many causal factors cannot be quantified, making it difficult for us to measure their intensity. Nevertheless, some consistencies are discernible.

Discrimination

While it might be argued that overt discrimination has declined, there is little doubt that institutional discrimination and statistical discrimination continue to be major problems. Nor is it a valid conclusion to say that enforcement of the Civil Rights Act of 1964 caused even overt discrimination to collapse. Direct studies of the impact of the act uniformly minimize its direct effect in changing black employment patterns.[4] For one thing, until 1972, the Equal Employment Opportunity Commission, the agency charged with enforcing the Civil Rights Act, had very limited enforcement powers. If discrimination collapsed before the relatively weak onslaughts of this agency, it was nowhere near as deeply entrenched as most students of this problem assumed it to be. But we suspect that the dynamics of the process of changing even overt discrimination are much more complex. The Civil Rights Act had limited direct impact on employment patterns because it was mainly aimed at combating overt discrimination, which could be proved in the courts, whereas institutional discrimination is a much more serious cause of black job disadvantage. Moreover, antidiscrimination laws operate mainly on the demand side of the employment process and do very little to change the supplies of blacks qualified to move into jobs when race bars are lowered.

Those who attribute the black employment changes of the 1960s to legislation probably confuse cause and effect and misread the processes involved in changing racial employment patterns. More probably, both the antidiscrimination legislation of the 1960s *and* the changes in black employment patterns were responses to the urban riots and other manifestations of black dissatisfaction with their rate of economic progress. It would be easy, therefore, to attribute to formal antidiscrimination measures the consequences of pressures for change from blacks.

Similarly, many of the changes apparently were due more to the indirect effects of laws than to their enforcement. As noted earlier, many employers were motivated by profit considerations to hire blacks but were reluctant to do so for fear of adverse reactions from white employees or, probably, to a lesser degree, white customers. One of the most significant aspects of legislation is that it carries considerable moral force as representing the attitudes of a majority of voters. Thus many employers who faced limited opposition to change probably responded to legislation by adopting antidiscrimination policies. Even those employers who faced opposition from white communities and employees used the law to neutralize this opposition when they were inclined for profit or moral reasons to hire or upgrade blacks.

We suspect, for example, that the hiring or upgrading of blacks in many relatively low-wage industries in the South can be attributed to the fact that these employers were having trouble locating an adequate supply of whites who met their hiring standards, whereas qualified blacks, whose employment opportunities have been more narrowly restricted because of discrimination, formed more dependable supplies of labor for these jobs.

Thus the indirect effects of antidiscrimination laws clearly are most effective when they are compatible with employers' economic motives. Indirect effects will have less impact in higher-level jobs for a number of reasons. One is the limited supplies of blacks who meet the skill, experience, or education standards for these jobs. Second, whites in these occupations have more power to resist change because of their higher level of skills, their organizations, and their control of supplies of skilled manpower. These skilled craftworkers have stronger status and job control motives for resisting the entry of blacks. Gaining greater entry for blacks into these occupations will require more direct measures to overcome white resistance, increase the supplies of qualified blacks, and overcome institutionalized barriers to entry.

Public policy also requires attention to the dynamics of the relationship between race bias and discrimination. The authors believe that race prejudice is changed mainly by reducing discrimination directly rather than the reverse. By changing discriminatory procedures, many of the myths influencing black-white relations are exploded. Moreover, people tend to modify their racist views as they are forced to rationalize their attitudes to make them conform with their nondiscriminating behavior. Thus it is more important to eradicate discrimination than to exhort people to change their attitudes, although both should be done.

Labor market conditions

There is almost universal agreement that tight labor markets—such as existed during World War II—generate powerful forces to improve black employment patterns. During such times, employers have stronger motives to hire, train, and upgrade black workers. At the same time, opposition by white employees to the hiring of blacks diminishes.

Nevertheless, tight labor markets alone will not guarantee improvements in black economic conditions, as seen from the fact that many occupations and skills remained closed to blacks despite tight labor markets during World War II. Similarly, many Southern cities have had very low levels of unemployment for years with no perceptible impact on black employment in particular trades or occupations. Clearly, therefore, tight labor markets must be supplemented by antidiscrimination, education, and manpower programs in order to produce changes in particular employment patterns. In the construction industry outreach programs have proved particularly effective in recruiting, tutoring, and placing blacks in apprenticeship and journeyman programs. Current demonstration projects to extend the outreach concept to other areas seem highly promising.

Transportation

The impact of transportation on black employment varies according to the characteristics of a place. In some cities the availability of housing is such that blacks live near job opportunities. In these places transportation is only a minor barrier to black employment. Similarly, transportation is less important as a barrier if blacks are able to get relatively high-paying jobs, even if these jobs are some distance from their homes. As noted earlier, however, transportation is much more important as a barrier to black employment in low-wage jobs because the net returns (wages less transportation) would be lower. Studies in major Southern cities show transportation to be a much more important determinant of black female than black male employment, probably because black females are more heavily concentrated in low-wage service occupations.

Labor market procedures

Blacks have more limited access than whites to labor market information about higher-paying jobs. Since blacks have tended to live in segregated housing, attend segregated schools, and work in segregated jobs, they are unable to acquire job information through informal means. Moreover, the widespread tendency for jobs to be filled through existing employees or relatives and friends perpetuates the exclusion of blacks from many jobs.

Blacks tend to rely more heavily than whites on formal information sources like the employment service, although many employers do not use the employment service for skilled professional and technical jobs. Similarly, many employers have recruited professional, technical, and managerial employees primarily from predominantly white colleges and universities. Because these job search and industry hiring practices tend to be deeply entrenched, special efforts are needed to enlarge the labor market information available to blacks and others that tend to be disadvantaged by these procedures. Special consideration should be given to changing the employment service's image in black communities and making that agency a more effective instrument for improving black employment opportunities.

Industry structure and skill requirements

A problem of considerable importance for black employment opportunities is the tendency for black employment to be inversely related to industry skill requirements and growth rates. Black employment is an increasing proportion of marginal, low-wage industries and a declining proportion of the high-wage, growth industries. In the South rapidly growing rural industries are avoiding areas with high black population densities and are not providing equal job opportunities for blacks even in those areas with heavy black population concentration. As noted earlier, much high-wage industry also is avoiding black population areas in the central cities. The inability of blacks to gain equal access to higher-paying jobs and employment in growth industries clearly limits their prospective economic opportunities relative to whites.

The causes of these black employment patterns are difficult to disentangle. Since blacks have lower levels of skills and education than whites, many employers practice statistical discrimination by recruiting from labor pools where the probabilities of recruiting employees who meet their standards are higher. Nevertheless, we cannot avoid the conclusion that some overt and much institutionalized discrimination is responsible for the low participation of blacks in growth industries and skilled jobs.

Improvements will require continued upgrading of black education and training, but other measures are also necessary. Antidiscrimination agencies must vigorously challenge discriminatory and unfair employment and selection procedures that deny blacks an opportunity to enter jobs having growth potential. Greater penetration of blacks into growth jobs would also be greatly facilitated by outreach efforts to recruit, train, and place blacks in specific growth jobs.

Manpower programs

Studies of manpower programs adopted during the 1960s generally show that disadvantaged people as a group derived measurable benefits from participating in those programs. In general, blacks have benefited relatively more than whites from MDTA programs, but whites have made greater absolute gains and there is considerable variation among programs.[5]

The participation of blacks in manpower programs has changed through time. Between 1963, when three-fourths of enrollees were white, and 1969, when only slightly over half of the participants were white, there was a steady decrease in the proportion of whites in these programs. Since 1968 the relative participation of nonwhites has declined, so that by 1973 two-thirds of all participants were nonwhite. Moreover, in 1970 blacks represented 92 to 94 percent of minority employees, but by 1973 the proportion of blacks within the minority group dropped to 83 percent. The impact of manpower programs on black employment opportunities and the implications of declining proportions of blacks in these programs should be given careful consideration. However, a detailed study of black employment in the South concluded that, despite considerable potential, manpower programs had had relatively little impact on black employment patterns.[6]

Income and occupational structures

Andrew Brimmer, a black and a former member of the Board of Governors of the Federal Reserve System, reviewed the extent of economic progress blacks made in the 1960s and projected these trends into the future.[7] His main theme was that blacks benefited more than whites from economic expansion during the 1960s, although the greatest gains have been made by blacks with the highest levels of education, and the disadvantaged in the black community are lagging behind. Brimmer expected the black community to benefit more than whites in the 1970s, primarily because of expansion in the national economy but also because of improvements in education. But he was concerned that black separatist programs would impede the economic progress of blacks by diverting them from the achievement of technical competence.

Nevertheless, blacks still lag considerably behind whites in these indicators, and there are some disturbing trends. Although black men gained in income relative to white men during the 1959–1967 period, the income gap widened within the black community because the greatest black gains were at the higher educational and income levels.

The absolute median family incomes for blacks continued to rise after 1970, but not as fast as the white median, causing the black median to decline from 61 percent of that of whites in 1970 to 58 percent in 1973 (Table 18-3). The major reasons for the relative decline in black median incomes were: (1) a decrease in the proportion of multiple earners within black families; (2) a significant decrease in the proportion of black working wives (60 percent in 1969, 54 percent in 1972); (3) an increase in the proportion of black families headed by women (who generally have lower incomes than men); and (4) a slowdown in the number of blacks moving into higher-paying jobs. These relative declines in black median family incomes between 1970 and 1973 were associated with very limited gains in the proportion of blacks earning $10,000 a year and over, after perceptible *gains* during the last half of the 1960s, and almost no change in the percentage of blacks earning less than $3,000, after significant *declines* during the last half of the 1960s.

If blacks continue to improve their occupational distribution at the rate they experienced during the 1960s, nonwhites will fill 12 percent of all jobs by 1985, distributed as follows:

Professional and technical	10.6%
Clerical	8.4
Sales	6.0
Skilled craftsmen	8.8
Nonfarm laborers	24.0
Private household workers	38.4
Farm laborers	24.6

Thus blacks and other minorities will have to change their occupational positions even faster during the last half of the 1970s than they did during the 1960s if they are to attain occupational parity with whites by 1985.

A more extensive examination of black-white income and occupational structures shows that because women have lower incomes than men, regardless of race, the income disadvantages of nonwhites can be accounted for, in part, by differences in family structure. For example, a larger proportion of nonwhite families are headed by females (34.6 percent of black and 9.6 percent of whites in 1973), and a lower proportion are husband-wife families (61.8 percent of nonwhites and 87.7 percent of whites in 1974). If we contrast family income changes by race for craftsmen and operatives only, controlling in a rough way for differences in oc-

Table 18-3 Changes in Black Income Relative to Whites', 1964–1973

	Median Family Income		Black as Percent of White
	Blacks	Whites	
1964	$3,724	$6,858	50%
1965	3,886	7,251	50
1966	4,507	7,792	58
1967	4,875	8,234	59
1968	5,360	8,937	60
1969	5,999	9,794	61
1970	6,279	10,236	61
1971	6,440	10,672	60
1972	6,864	11,549	59
1973	7,269	12,595	58

Source: Bureau of the Census, *Social and Economic Status of the Black Population in the United States in 1973,* Series P-23, No. 48, Table 16.

cupation and family structure, the relative income picture improves considerably. In 1966, for example, census figures show that median nonwhite family incomes were 60 percent of those of whites in the United States, ranging from 51 percent in the South to 74 percent in the North Central region. However, if we compare craftsmen and operative families having husband and wife present, the nonwhite-white ratio rises to 72 percent in 1966 and 75 percent in 1970 for the United States and 63 percent in the South and 82 percent in the non-South.

Between 1960 and 1970 nonwhite craftsmen and operative husbands clearly had greater income gains in the South than in the non-South (56 percent and 30 percent), and their incomes increased faster than whites' incomes in both the South (where whites gained 58 percent) and the non-South (where whites gained 27 percent). The relatively large gains for nonwhites might be explained, in part, by the lower base from which they started in 1960, but Southern nonwhites gained more than whites in *absolute* as well as relative terms. And Southern nonwhites gained more absolutely than Northern nonwhites. In the South white husbands who were heads of families gained $1524 in median family incomes compared with $1704 for nonwhites. Outside the South whites gained $1786 and nonwhites $1677.

Nonwhite husbands in craftsman and operative families made considerably more relative income progress in 1966–1970 than in 1960–1966. Indeed, median incomes of nonwhite husbands actually *declined* from 84 percent of whites' in the non-South in 1960 to 82 percent in 1966. The relative income decline was particularly noticeable in the metropolitan non-South, where it went from 81 percent of whites' in 1960 to 77 percent in 1966. In the South, however, the nonwhite median income of husbands in craftsman and operative families increased more between 1960 and 1966 (26 percent) than between 1966 and 1970 (24 percent), due in part to the relatively better position of nonwhites in the rural South in 1960–1966 than in 1966–1970. In the metropolitan South nonwhites made more progress in 1966–1970 than in 1960–1966. These differences undoubtedly reflect the displacement of blacks from Southern agriculture during the late 1960s at a time of relative prosperity in metropolitan areas.

The income gap between whites and nonwhites is attributable, in part, to educational differentials. Although the median educational attainment of blacks and other races rose from 8.6 years in 1959 to 11.3 years in 1969, it still lagged over a year behind that of whites, which rose from 12.1 years in 1959 to 12.4 years in 1969. The median educational levels of white males equaled those of white females in the work force in 1970, but black males lagged 1.1 years behind black females (11.9 to 10.8). Black males thus lagged 1.6 years behind white males, whereas black females lagged only half a year behind white females. Of course, allowances also must be made for the differences in the quality of education of whites and blacks.

Bureau of the Census data for 1970 show the relationship between the median earnings of craftsman and operative husbands by years of school completed by race for 1960, 1966, and 1970. Nonwhite husbands who had completed high school lost in the 1960–1966 period but gained relative to whites between 1966 and 1970. Relative to whites, nonwhites with elementary educations gained in both periods. For husbands who had completed elementary school, the nonwhite/white median income ratio was 0.63 in 1960, 0.72 in 1966, and 0.71 in 1970. For those who had completed high school, the ratios were 0.75, 0.73, and 0.79. However, in 1970 whites who had completed elementary school had higher median incomes ($7064) than nonwhites with one to three years of college ($6909). This differential can hardly be explained by differences in the quality of education.

Part of the white-nonwhite income differentials also might be due to the age composition of the work force because incomes ordinarily increase with age, reach a peak, and then decline. Although the median age of white and nonwhite husbands who were craftsmen and operatives in 1960 was 42, ten years later the nonwhite median was two years lower (40) than that of whites.

Conclusions

Despite perceptible black economic progress since 1960, the racial gaps remain very large. Overt and institutional discrimination remain important problems, and antidiscrimination measures should be expanded and strengthened. Nevertheless, antidiscrimination measures alone will not do the job. Also needed are improved human resource development activities, including job creation, education, manpower, and health, welfare, and income-maintenance programs. The causes of black disadvantage are deeply entrenched; therefore, they will be overcome only through concerted action on a variety of fronts.

Notes

1. *Employment and Earnings,* Vol. 19, No. 7 (January 1973), Tables 30–31.
2. Sar A. Levitan and Robert Taggart, *Employment and Earnings Inadequacy: A New Social Indicator* (Baltimore, Md.: Johns Hopkins Press, 1974), Chap. 3.
3. Thomas Sowell, "Minorities and the City," paper prepared for the conference on Manpower and the Metropolis (Tarrytown, N.Y.: November 29–30, 1973).
4. Arvil V. Adams, *Toward Fair Employment and the EEOC: A Study of Compliance Procedures Under Title VII of the Civil Rights Act of 1964,* prepared for the U.S. Equal Employment Opportunity Commission (August 31, 1972).
5. Sar A. Levitan, William B. Johnston, and Robert Taggart, *Still a Dream* (Cambridge, Mass.: Harvard University Press, 1975), Chap. 12.
6. Ray Marshall and Virgil L. Christian, Jr., eds., *The Employment of Southern Blacks* (Salt Lake City, Utah: Olympus Publishing Co., 1974).
7. Andrew Brimmer, "The Black Revolution and the Economic Future of Negroes in the United States," an address at Tennessee A & I University (June 8, 1968).

19

americans of spanish origin

Next to blacks, the largest minority group in this country is that of Spanish origin (referred to hereafter as Spanish Americans). Spanish Americans live all over the United States but are concentrated primarily in the Southwest.[1] Although they have serious employment and income difficulties, the problems of this group have not been as pervasive or intractable as those of blacks.

Overt discrimination against the Spanish speaking has declined in intensity since World War II and never was as rigidly institutionalized as discrimination against blacks. Moreover, relatively few legal cases have been filed alleging discrimination against Spanish Americans. This undoubtedly is due, in part, to the fact that these groups have not been as vocal as blacks in demanding equality of employment opportunities. But this situation is likely to change as Spanish Americans become quantitatively more important (at present rates of growth, Spanish Americans might be more numerous than blacks by the year 2000) and follow the example of blacks in demanding economic equality with whites.

Spanish Americans are a very difficult group to define. They do not all speak Spanish—some speak Spanish and English, some only Spanish, and some English. Racially, this group may be black, brown, or white. They live in every state in the United States; the 1970 census indicated at least 20,000 Spanish-speaking people in 31 states. Almost 60 percent of the Spanish speaking are of Mexican origin; over 14 percent are Puerto Ricans (not counting the 2.7 million in Puerto Rico), and another 26 percent come from Cuba, South America, and other countries (Table 19-1). About the only thing the Spanish speaking have in common is their Spanish language heritage.

Table 19-1 Total and Spanish-Origin Population by the Type of Spanish Origin, for the United States, March 1974 (thousands)

| | | Percent Distribution | |
| | | Total Popula-tion | Spanish-Origin Popula-tion |
Origin	Total	Total Popula-tion	Spanish-Origin Popula-tion
All Persons	207,945	100.0	n.a.
Persons of Spanish origin	10,795	5.2	100.0
Mexican	6,455	3.1	59.8
Puerto Rican	1,548	0.7	14.3
Cuban	689	0.3	6.4
Central or South American	705	0.3	6.5
Other Spanish	1,398	0.7	13.0
Persons not of Spanish origin[a]	197,150	94.8	n.a.

[a]Includes persons who did not know or did not report on origin.

Source: U.S. Bureau of the Census, *Current Population Reports*, Population Characteristics, "Persons of Spanish Origin in the United States: March 1974," Series P-20, No. 267 (Washington, D.C.: GPO, July 1974), Table 1.

Demography, income, and education

Despite the census statistics that show the Spanish speaking number almost 11 million people, or 5.2 percent of the population of the United States, there is considerable controversy over the actual number. Unofficial estimates based on local census studies, migrant studies, public school enrollments, the Cuban resettlement program, and other data indicate that the actual total might be as high as 16 million.

According to the 1970 census figures, the largest concentrations of Spanish Americans are as follows:

1. The Southwest (Arizona, California, Colorado, New Mexico, and Texas) has about 60 percent of the Spanish speaking, and the overwhelming majority of Mexican Americans are located there.
2. Eighty percent of the Puerto Ricans in the continental United States are located in New York City.
3. Over 600,000 people of Cuban descent and many others from Central and South America live in Florida.

A major problem for Spanish Americans has been their rural background, which partly explains their ethnic isolation. Although discussions of ethnic values always run the risk of stereotyping, the chairman of the Cabinet Committee on Opportunities for Spanish-Speaking People suggests that cultural attributes identify most of the Spanish speaking:

1. Relations between individuals are more important than competitive, materialistic, or achievement norms.
2. Strong family ties.
3. A sense of solidarity and pride in a unique heritage (a feeling sometimes referred to as La Raza).
4. Machismo, meaning male dominance, patriarchy, emphasis of man's masculinity.
5. Aspirations for professional rather than business or managerial occupations.[2]

The income levels of Spanish Americans in 1974 were higher than those of blacks (who had higher education levels than Spanish Americans), but they were substantially below those of whites. In some categories Mexican Americans were better off than Puerto Ricans, while Cubans and persons from Central and South America were better off than other Spanish Americans.

The median income of a Spanish-speaking family of four was $8,759, or 75.8 percent of the $11,549 median for a white family that size in 1972; the median for black families was $6,864, or 55.9 percent of the white median. The Spanish family tended to be larger than the white family, so that the median income for all Spanish-speaking people was $8,180, or 70.8 percent of the median for whites.

Those percentage distributions for various groups in 1972 were:

	Percent Under $7,000	Percent Over $10,000
Spanish		
Males	60.7	18.1
Females	91.0	2.2
Blacks	52.0	30.0

There is considerable variation in income among Spanish-American groups (Table 19-2). In general, Mexican Americans had lower median levels of earnings, but this seems to be due in part to their lower levels of education, because comparisons by levels of education show Mexican Americans to have higher median incomes than the average for all Spanish-origin groups (Table 19-3). However, Puerto Ricans who have completed high school have higher earnings, perhaps because they are more concentrated in relatively high-wage Eastern states.

Table 19-2 Median Income in 1973 of Persons 25 Years Old and over by Years of School Completed and Type of Spanish Origin, for the United States, March 1974

Years of School Completed	Total, 25 Years Old and Over	Spanish Origin				
		Total	Mexican	Puerto Rican	Cuban	Other Spanish[a]
Total, 25 years Old and Over	$6289	$5369	$4982	$5432	$5471	$6204
Elementary School						
0 to 4 years	2378	3378	3388	4085	(B)	(B)
5 to 7 years	3313	4440	4303	4778	(B)	5319
8 years	3878	4916	4958	4975	(B)	(B)
High School						
1 to 3 years	5156	5789	6422	5160	(B)	5463
4 years	7055	6611	6620	7172	6306	6427
College						
1 year or more	9989	8636	8786	(B)	8267	8542

(B) Base less than 75,000.

[a] Comprises persons of Central or South American and other Spanish origin.

Source: U.S. Bureau of the Census, *Current Population Reports*, Population Characteristics, "Persons of Spanish Origin in the United States: March 1974," Series P-20, No. 267 (Washington, D.C.: GPO, July 1974), Table 8.

Table 19-3 Percent Completed Less than Five Years of School and Percent Completed Four Years of High School or More for All Persons and Persons of Spanish Origin 25 Years Old and over by Type of Spanish Origin, for the United States, March 1974

Years of School Completed and Age	Total	Spanish Origin				
		Total	Mexican	Puerto Rican	Cuban	Other Spanish[a]
Percent Completed Less than 5 Years of School						
Total, 25 years and over	4.4	19.4	26.5	17.6	8.9	6.0
25 to 29 years	1.2	9.1	12.6	7.5	(B)	2.8
30 to 34 years	1.3	9.6	14.6	9.0	(B)	1.6
35 to 44 years	2.2	16.3	22.3	18.0	3.8	2.8
45 to 54 years	3.4	23.1	32.0	23.0	9.3	6.1
55 to 64 years	5.3	29.8	39.9	(B)	16.1	11.0
65 years and over	11.9	47.4	63.6	(B)	(B)	(B)
Percent Completed 4 Years of High School or More						
Total, 25 years and over	61.2	36.4	29.1	29.6	47.7	55.9
25 to 29 years	81.9	52.5	46.7	39.6	(B)	73.7
30 to 34 years	77.9	48.2	41.9	40.3	(B)	64.0
35 to 44 years	70.4	38.3	31.0	29.5	52.0	60.1
45 to 54 years	63.0	30.2	20.6	18.8	49.0	54.0
55 to 64 years	50.0	17.4	9.6	(B)	30.2	31.2
65 years and over	33.1	13.3	5.2	(B)	(B)	(B)

(B) Base less than 75,000.

[a]Comprises persons of Central or South American and other Spanish origin.

Source: U.S. Bureau of the Census, *Current Population Reports*, Population Characteristics, "Persons of Spanish Origin in the United States: March 1974", Series P-20, No. 267 (Washington, D.C.: GPO, July 1974), Table 5.

Puerto Ricans had a relatively high incidence of people below the poverty level in 1973, as indicated by the following percentages:

	Percent Below Poverty Level
All persons	11.1
Persons of Spanish origin	21.9
Mexican	23.5
Puerto Rican	34.1
Cuban	7.5
Central or South American	13.5
Other Spanish	12.5

Cubans were the only Spanish-origin group with lower percentages of people below the poverty line than the average for all people. Cubans have higher earnings in part because they were older and had higher levels of education. Cubans also have benefited from special aid from the federal government to help them settle in the United States. Many of those aided as refugees were persons with more wealth than other Spanish-origin people. In Miami Cubans have entered a broader spectrum of industries and occupations than blacks, except for the construction industry, in which there are more blacks than Cubans. In general, however, Cubans in Miami tended to have higher incomes and better employment opportunities than blacks.[3]

Puerto Ricans in New York generally have not fared as well relatively as Cubans in Miami. This is due in part to the better work experiences and higher educations and incomes of Cubans. A detailed study of poverty groups in New York concluded that "Puerto Rican workers were the most deprived of all workers residing in the city's major poverty neighborhoods. They were far more likely than others to be unemployed or to hold lower paying jobs. Typically, they held blue-collar or service jobs requiring relatively little skill."[4] Puerto Ricans in New York were concentrated in industries with unstable employment and suffered unemployment rates almost three times those of whites and twice those of blacks.

The median family incomes for Spanish-speaking people in 1973 were:

		Percent Under $2000
Male-headed families	$6321	14.9
Female-headed families	$2760	37.6

Except for Cubans consisting predominantly of adult immigrants, the Spanish population is considerably younger than the rest of the U.S. population. In March 1973 the median ages were:

	Years
Spanish	20.1
Cuban	35.3
Mexican and Puerto Rican	18.8
Total U.S. population	28.4

With respect to education Spanish Americans were far behind blacks and whites. For example, the percentages of each group completing four years of high school in 1972 were:

	Percent Completing Four Years of High School
Whites	90
Blacks	65
Spanish	35
Mexican American	27
Puerto Rican	26
Cuban	53
Other Spanish	54

Thus education gaps were particularly serious for all Spanish Americans relative to other groups, but the gaps for Mexican and Puerto Rican Americans were especially wide. Some indication of the relative intensity of discrimination is suggested by the fact that Spanish Americans have relatively higher median incomes even though their education levels are lower.

However, as the figures in Tables 19-3 and 19-4 show, the education of various Spanish-origin groups and blacks is converging with that of whites at lower age groups. For black males between 20 and 29 years of age the median levels of education have converged with blacks and lag behind those of whites by only 0.6 of a year. Older Spanish groups fall further behind whites. It will be observed, however, that the main reason Spanish Americans lag behind blacks is because of the relatively low education levels of Spanish-American females. The male levels are closer together.

Chicanos

Chicanos, or people of Mexican descent, constitute by far the largest group among the Spanish speaking—they total over 6.4

Table 19-4 Median Years of School Completed by Persons 20–69, by Age and Sex, 1970

Sex and Age	All Spanish	White	Black
Males			
20–24	12.2	12.8	12.2
25–29	12.1	12.7	12.1
30–34	11.5	12.6	11.7
35–39	10.6	12.5	11.0
40–44	9.7	12.3	10.1
45–49	9.4	12.3	9.3
50–54	8.9	12.1	8.5
55–59	8.2	11.0	7.6
60–64	7.0	10.0	6.9
65–69	6.1	8.9	6.0
Females			
20–24	12.2	12.7	12.3
25–29	11.8	12.6	12.2
30–34	10.8	12.5	11.9
35–39	10.0	12.4	11.4
40–44	9.4	12.3	10.8
45–49	8.9	12.3	10.0
50–54	8.4	12.1	9.0
55–59	7.8	11.6	8.4
60–64	6.7	10.7	7.9
65–69	6.2	9.5	7.0

Source: U.S. Bureau of the Census, 1970.

million people, or almost 60 percent of all Spanish Americans (see Table 19-1). In fact, those of Mexican descent exceed in number the combined total of all minority groups other than blacks (i.e., Puerto Ricans, Cubans, Native American, Chinese Americans, and Japanese Americans).

Despite their numerical importance, however, the definition, identification, and measurement of Chicanos have caused considerable debate. Many Mexican Americans are more American Indian in origin than Spanish. Most other terms commonly used to describe them are equally misleading.

Although there is some disagreement over its use, "Chicano," derived from the word *Mexicano,* is the term increasingly used by Mexican Americans to identify themselves. Younger Mexican Americans seem particularly to favor being called Chicanos, while some of their elders resist its use. The terms "Chicano" and "Mexican American" will be used interchangeably here.

The Mexican-American population is both a racial and a

cultural minority; 95 percent of the Chicano population is part American Indian.[5] The Chicano concept of *la raza* (the race), however, does not refer to a set of racial characteristics, because Chicanos are a blending of Spanish colonists, American Indians, Anglos, and blacks. Moreover, the Mexican-American culture is significantly different from that of the majority of Anglos in language, religion, music, food, and literature.[6]

Almost all Chicanos live in the five Southwestern states—Arizona, California, Colorado, New Mexico, and Texas. Thus they contribute to and are affected by the Southwest's unique features. The Southwestern population is more urbanized than the nation as a whole, and the region's urban percentage is approximately the same for Anglos, nonwhites, and Chicanos. The urbanization of all racial groups has resulted from water shortages over much of the region, which cause people to group together in an "oasis society."[7] There are, however, significant differences in population patterns in the five states. In Texas, Colorado, and New Mexico Chicanos are highly concentrated in the poorest and least developed areas. In California and Arizona they are relatively more dispersed. In 1972, 83 percent of all Spanish-American families lived in metropolitan areas; there was, however, considerable difference in residential patterns according to country of origin—81 percent of Puerto Ricans but only 43 percent of Mexican-American families lived in central cities.

Although current and accurate statistics are not available, the Mexican-American population apparently is growing both relatively and absolutely. The factors responsible for this growth include continued immigration (unrestricted until 1968, at which time a maximum of 120,000 from the Western Hemisphere was imposed), inordinately high fertility rates (fertility rates for Chicanos are 70 percent higher than those of Anglos in the Southwest), and uncounted numbers of illegal entrants across the 1800-mile common border between Mexico and the United States. Most of the Chicano population is native-born of native-born parentage; less than 15 percent of Mexican Americans were born in Mexico.

As noted previously, poverty and low education are serious problems for Chicanos. In 1970, 1.2 million Chicano family members (26.8 percent of the population) and 83,000 unrelated individuals (43.2 percent of the total) were officially classified as in poverty. There is a heavy incidence of poverty and lower levels of education than for nonwhites, and their functional illiteracy rate is twice that of blacks and over six times that of Anglos. The 1966 Coleman Report on the equality of educational opportunity revealed that Chicanos also are further behind Anglos on standardized achievement test scores in the higher grades; by the 12th grade, for example, Chicanos were 3.5 years behind their Anglo classmates in verbal ability, 3.3 years in reading comprehension, and 4.1 years in mathematical achievement.[8] Although these tests made no pretense of being culturally fair, it was alleged that their content measured knowledge that is "increasingly important for success in our society."[9] Nonetheless, it is significant that one of the most characteristic aspects of Chicano labor market experience is their higher earnings than other minority groups when earnings are adjusted for differences in educational attainment.

Chicano Labor Markets

Although Chicanos have long been identified with the Southwest, numerically they have become a sizable population only in the twentieth century and thus have had less time to be assimilated. Immigration came in two major spurts: the first in the mid-1920s and the second from 1955 to 1964. Since 1900 over 1.4 million people from Mexico have been legally admitted, and many more have probably come into the United States illegally.

Because of statistical complications, however, we must interpret the data on Chicanos with care. For example, data on Chicano urbanization are likely to be overstated because a large number of Chicanos with urban addresses work in agriculture. This is particularly true of migrant workers, who often use cities as home bases. A more serious data problem arises because Mexican nationals employed in the United States at the time of the census are included in the head count.

As compared with other Spanish-origin groups, Mexican-American men are more likely to be farm laborers and blue-collar workers and less likely to be white-collar workers (Table 19-5). We do not have separate figures for Cubans, but it is known that this group has a relatively high proportion of professional, technical and managerial workers, which probably accounts for the relative size of these groups in the "Other Spanish" category in Table 19-5.

The Southwestern economy

Control of the land has played a major part in ethnic relations in the Southwest. The early Spanish settlers fought the Indians; the Mexicans fought the Anglos; the Anglos fought the remaining Indians and each other. There also was violent conflict between

Table 19-5 Employed Men 16 Years Old and over by Major Occupation Group and Type of Spanish Origin, for the United States, March 1974

Occupation	Total Men 16 Years Old and Over	Spanish Origin			
		Total	Mexican	Puerto Rican	Other Spanish[a]
Total Employed (thousands)	51,678	2,236	1,344	271	621
Percent	100.0	100.0	100.0	100.0	100.0
White-Collar Workers:					
Professional and technical	14.1	6.7	5.2	4.5	11.0
Managers and administrators excluding farm	14.1	7.3	5.7	9.7	9.8
Sales workers	6.1	3.0	2.7	4.1	3.4
Clerical workers	6.6	7.0	5.0	13.8	8.4
Blue-Collar Workers:					
Craft and kindred workers	20.9	17.6	19.2	10.8	17.4
Operatives, including trans.	17.9	27.0	26.8	31.6	25.3
Laborers, except farm	7.3	11.5	14.2	7.8	7.1
Farm Workers:					
Farmers and farm managers	3.0	0.4	0.4	—	0.3
Farm laborers and supervisors	1.8	7.4	11.4	1.1	1.5
Service Workers	8.2	12.0	9.3	16.7	15.8

— Represents zero.

[a]Comprises men 16 years old and over of Cuban, Central or South American, and other Spanish origin.

Source: U.S. Bureau of the Census, *Current Population Reports*, Population Characteristics, "Persons of Spanish Origin in the United States: March 1974," Series P-20, No. 267 (Washington, D.C.: GPO, July 1974), Table 6.

farmers and ranchers, sheepherders and cattlemen, and management and labor in the mining industries. Many conflicts over the
legal ownership of land remain unsettled. For example, *la alianza*
movement in northern New Mexico, led by Reies Lopez Tijerina,
centers on the validity of Spanish land grants supposedly guaranteed under the 1848 Treaty of Guadalupe Hidalgo. At the same
time, the Indians have filed counterclaims challenging the Spanish
king's right to give title to this land to the Spanish settlers.

However, economics probably was as much a cause of conflict
as greed or bigotry. Agriculture, ranching, and mining have dominated the region's economy. These industries initially were very
labor intensive and relied heavily on migrant labor. They also required considerable capital and attracted Eastern money and absentee ownership.[10] Moreover, the sheer scale of operations in
the Southwest meant that few immigrants could have the opportunity to become farm or ranch owners themselves. The only
exceptions were the settlements in northern New Mexico, which
date back to the seventeenth century and which were largely
isolated from regional development until the 1940s. For this group
a major cause of discontent has been the incorporation of their
communal grazing lands into the national forest system.[11] But
Leo Grebler and associates demonstrate this fact: "Most of Southwest agriculture was always the province of big business and
vast financing that people with modest means could not enter or
even influence."[12] The scope of agribusiness of the Southwest has
been described as follows:

> It has been said that the strings of California's $3.6 billion-a-
> year agribusiness are pulled from the redwood-paneled offices on
> San Francisco's Montgomery Street, the Wall Street of the West.
> In addition to growers, packers, processors, middlemen, and dis-
> tributors, agribusiness embraces allied enterprises such as banks
> (the Bank of America, the world's largest, is the prime financer of
> California farms), shipping and transportation companies, land
> companies (Kern County Land Company for all practical purposes
> *is* Kern County), and utilities, plus other large corporations which
> have a stake in the prosperity of the field-to-table process.
> The anatomy of this "giant octopus," as one packing company
> executive put it, can be seen by studying the interlocking director-
> ships of the agribusiness corporations. Packing executives sit on
> the boards of directors of banks and land companies. Bankers
> who trade in farm loans proliferate on the boards of packing and
> land companies. Realty executives who deal in farm acreage sit on
> the boards of shipping and packing companies. The labyrinth goes
> on and on.
> As a group, agribusiness executives are hardheaded and dol-
> lar-oriented, which is by way of saying they are not much different

from executives in other fields. The tremendous technological advances of agriculture are all to their credit, but where they differ from executives in other fields is in their archaic concept of their responsibility to human beings.[13]

For Chicanos this means that it is "almost impossible to convert hard work into a stable base for gain."[14] Scant opportunities exist for advancement because most agricultural jobs are dead-end, low-paying jobs. As noted in Table 19-1 earlier, Chicanos have a much larger percentage of their numbers below the poverty level than any other Spanish-American group except Puerto Ricans.

The border

The 1800-mile common border with Mexico has had a profound effect on the economic conditions of Chicanos. Immigration from Mexico since the 1920s has centered on agriculture, and Chicanos have been an important factor in the Southwest's agricultural labor supply (see Table 19-5). According to a 1964 report from California, for example, 41.9 percent of farm laborers were Spanish speaking.[15] The original impetus to immigration from rural Mexico was the push of the Mexican revolution and the simultaneous pull of labor shortages in the United States during World War I. These shortages not only were caused by the diversion of American workers into the armed forces but also because immigration from Europe was stopped. After the war the demand for Mexicans remained, and because they were not covered in the quotas imposed by the National Origins Act of 1924, the supply was forthcoming to meet the demand. When the depression hit and displaced "Okies" and "Arkies" became the cheap labor supply, many Chicanos were forceably repatriated to Mexico.

There was another influx of Mexican farm workers during World War II, when an agreement between the United States and Mexico provided guarantees on working conditions and employment for short periods of seasonal farm work. This Mexican labor program was better known as the bracero program. It remained in effect until the end of 1964. The program was strengthened in 1951 with the passage of Public Law 78, which was strongly supported by growers as a means of meeting labor shortages induced by the Korean conflict.

This controversial program displaced many native Chicanos from the rural labor market. The proportion of Chicanos living in urban areas increased from 66.4 percent in 1950 to 79.1 percent in 1960.[16] In 1974, 75.1 percent of Chicano families lived in metropolitan areas as compared with 94.2 percent of Puerto Ricans and 91.4 percent of other Spanish Americans.

The bracero program is a good example of how public policy affects rural labor markets. The wages of agricultural workers relative to manufacturing workers declined sharply during the bracero period, forcing native Chicanos to migrate in search of jobs that paid them enough to meet living costs in the United States. Although growers complained of shortages of domestic workers during the bracero period, the labor market experience since the end of that program has clearly shown that domestic labor is available at competitive wages. The bracero program also exemplified the indifference of public policy to the welfare of the native Chicano population; Chicanos had little to say about that program, which had a profound impact on their economic welfare.

Although the bracero program no longer exists, the problem of illegal entrants (or wetbacks) remains. In 1968 it was estimated that 300,000 illegal entrants came from Mexico to the United States (a figure that is two-and-half times the official quota that year for the entire Western Hemisphere).[17] The number of illegal entrants has increased dramatically since the bracero program was terminated. In 1967, the last year braceros worked in the United States, 107,695 illegal entrants were returned to Mexico; in 1973, 609,673 illegal entrants were returned to Mexico, and their number exceeded 800,000 in 1974. It is estimated that between one-fourth and one-third of illegal aliens are apprehended, making the estimated total about 2 million.

There is considerable controversy over the relative merits of employing illegal aliens, braceros or domestics. Those who advocate the importation of Mexican nationals argue that domestic workers cannot be found to do the kind of work performed by nationals. To some extent this is correct because domestic workers apparently avoid jobs in which many illegal aliens are employed because conditions there are likely to be undesirable. Illegal aliens have almost no protection from exploitation. Moreover, the aliens are likely to be more willing to work very hard for short periods of time because even low wages in the United States are much higher than those that they can earn in Mexico. Therefore, domestic workers consider it undesirable to compete for sustained periods with workers who are "working scared" for short periods of time and limited objectives. However, apparently little difficulty was encountered in reverting to the use of domestic workers in many California industries after the bracero program was terminated.

Legislation has been proposed to make it illegal for employers to hire illegal aliens. The Immigration and Nationality Act of 1952 made it a felony "to import and harbor" illegal aliens but exempted employment and related services to employees (i.e., transportation, housing, and feeding).

There also are very weak penalties imposed on the illegal aliens who are apprehended. Almost all such illegal aliens are simply deported to their native countries at federal expense. They are rarely subjected to formal deportation proceedings that would make their future entry a felony. Apparently, the failure to utilize formal deportation proceedings more often is due mainly to the limited number of hearing offices.[18]

Commuters

Commuters who live in Mexico and work in the United States also depress wages and working conditions for native Chicanos. Commuters may be Mexican nationals or U.S. citizens. If they are aliens, they are either "green carders" (i.e., those who have been legally admitted as immigrants and are free to live and work in the United States) or "white carders" (i.e., legal visitors who can supposedly stay in the United States for only 72 hours at a time). White carders are technically not supposed to be employed, but that law apparently is not very well enforced.[19] Similarly, it is an amiable fiction that many green carders reside in the United States, because many actually live in Mexico. Green carders must obtain labor certification specifying that a shortage of workers exists in their particular occupations in the United States and that their employment will not adversely affect wages and working conditions. The certification is made only once—at the time of the initial application as an immigrant. Once the green card is obtained, the holder is free to come and go as long as no absence from the United States exceeds one year or the holder becomes unemployed for longer than six months.

The exact number of green- or white-card commuters is unknown. A 1969 report claimed that "approximately 70,000 persons cross the Mexico border *daily* to work in the United States."[20] It was estimated that in 1972 there were 735,018 Mexican green-carders in the entire United States.[21] The latest estimate of the number of white carders, which was made in 1968, placed their number at 1,250,000.[22]

A 1967 restriction bars green carders from employment as strikebreakers in places where the Secretary of Labor certifies that a labor dispute exists. However, the effect of this antistrikebreaker restriction apparently is nullified by the fact that employers usually have ample time to employ green carders before a dispute is officially certified.

After Congress permitted the bracero program to expire, the Secretary of Labor issued new regulations that made it clear that braceros would not be admitted under various subterfuges. These regulations specify wages and other conditions that employers must offer to domestic workers before foreign labor can be imported, and apparently they reduced the flow of Mexican nationals who applied for green cards after January 1, 1965. However, opinion differs as to the extent to which these rules really are enforced. Chicano and labor spokesmen still think too many commuters are permitted to enter, and thus they advocate tighter restrictions on entry, while employers complain of labor shortages.

The commuter system rests on administrative interpretation rather than statute. In 1927 the status of commuters was changed from alien visitors to immigrants by the Immigration and Naturalization Service. The justification for the perpetuaton of this system is derived from a Board of Immigration Appeals decision in 1958: "The commuter situation does not fit into any precise category found in the immigration statutes. The status is an artificial one, predicated upon good international relations maintained and cherished between friendly neighbors."[23] Consequently, the U.S. worker who competes with Mexican commuters pays a substantial part of what the Secretary of State regards as foreign aid.

Although many commuters work in low-wage garment industries and retail shops on the U.S. side of the border, according to one estimate 60 percent or more of all commuters entering California and Arizona are farm workers; in Texas the figure is 18 percent. According to the U.S. Civil Rights Commission:

> The impact of the commuter is particularly acute in agriculture where mechanization is rapidly reducing job opportunities. Due to the high concentration of farms along the border and the fact that commuters often work in the lowest skilled, lowest paid jobs, farm workers, who are already underpaid, are the first to suffer competition from the commuter. Furthermore, the use of commuters as strikebreakers is especially damaging to this group's organizational struggles.[24]

Moreover, according to the Civil Rights Commission 88,700 South Texas farm workers were forced to migrate elsewhere in 1968 in search of employment, while commuters easily found jobs in the local economy. A VISTA (Volunteers in Service to America) worker summarized the difficult and ambiguous relationship of the commuter problem to migratory workers as follows:

> These people see the problem of the commuter as a very major one. They see that the people from Mexico, which are our brothers, come over on this side to work because the living conditions in Mexico are far worse than ours, they are poor. It is not their fault that they come and take our jobs, it is the fault of the

U.S. government which exploits our brother because they pay lower wages and at the same time the Mexican Americans on this side are left without jobs and they have to travel up North.[25]

Numerous proposals have been offered to terminate or to lessen the effects of the commuter system.[26] Among these are its immediate termination; regularization of the labor certification process to require periodic reviews rather than simply the initial determination of the impact of the green carder; establishment of a nonresident work permit with regular review decisions; installation of a commuter tax on employers; purchase of tickets by those who cross the border for employment; a drive to give preference in employment to U.S. residents; the imposition of sanctions against U.S. employers who knowingly employ white carders; and specific limitations on the time a green carder can be employed in the United States before making it mandatory that he become a U.S. citizen. Moreover, Fred Schmidt contends that the current border employment practices violate Title VII of the Civil Rights Act of 1964,[27] which bans discrimination on the basis of national origin, by favoring Mexican nationals. The view one takes of the movement of people across the border depends on the perspective taken. The State Department favors rather free movement of Mexicans into the United States. Chicanos have mixed feelings. Some of them resent the competition from people whose living costs in Mexico are lower and who are forced to work very hard under fear of deportation.

Agricultural employment and public policy

Because so many of them are farm workers, no discussion of Chicanos would be complete without looking at the special problems of agricultural workers. Regardless of race or national origin, many agricultural workers are disadvantaged. For although large farm owners have been among the most privileged group in American corporate society (with import quota protection; exemptions from antitrust laws; price supports; soil bank purchases; subsidized research, irrigation, land reclamation, and erosion projects; and special property tax rates), farm laborers have few legal protections and very little economic or political power.

Farm workers receive very limited coverage under state labor laws. No state minimum wage law would bring the worker up to the minimum poverty level even if it was possible to secure year-round employment. Only California provides workmen's compensation, despite the fact that agriculture is one of the nation's most hazardous industries. And the hazards of agricultural employment have become greater because of the increasing use of herbicides and pesticides—with their yet unknown effects on farm workers. No state provides unemployment protection.

Agricultural workers also have inadequate coverage under federal as well as state statutes. They are not covered by such laws as the National Labor Relations Act and do not receive unemployment compensation, mainly because the political power of agribusiness has been sufficient to prevent their coverage.

Several special enactments during the 1960s affected Chicanos. Among these are the Bilingual Education Act (passed as Title VII of the Elementary and Secondary School Act Amendments in 1967) and amendments to Title I of the same act, which, for the first time, provided compensatory education funds for migratory workers. The earlier Migrant Children Educational Assistance Act of 1960 and the Migrant Health Act of 1962 represented the initial breakthroughs in federal legislation pertaining to the welfare of migratory workers. These programs, however, were based upon matching funds to state-initiated projects. In addition, the Farm Labor Contractor Registration Act of 1963 was enacted in response to abuses by unscrupulous crew leaders. However, this regulation apparently has very little effect because of weak penalties. The Interstate Commerce Commission has imposed regulations affecting the transportation of three or more farm workers for a distance of 75 miles or more across state boundaries. The regulations pertain to equipment safety, required rest stops, seats for passengers, and regular driver changes. As for intrastate transportation of farm workers, only one Southwestern state—California— has provided state regulations.

Chicanos and manpower policy

The impact of the "manpower revolution" of the 1960s upon Chicanos has been negligible. The nationwide thrust of manpower policy has been upon improving the employment potential of urban workers. It is generally conceded by manpower officials that rural areas have not received a proportionate share of manpower funds.

There are several reasons why rural workers tend to be ignored. First there is the political weaknesses of rural workers. Training slots represent patronage. Urban areas have had more power in securing these funds. The competition for supporting funds usually combines the vested interests of public schools, vocational schools, community action agencies, and junior colleges with the lobbying strength of city governments, organized community pressure groups, unions, and corporate interests. As one official of the Rural Manpower Service of the U.S. Department of Labor put it, "when the state politics divvy up the MDTA money, the rural areas don't get anything." Second, many rural areas fear that the formal training afforded under these programs is designed to prepare young people for jobs that can only be had if they migrate to the city. Hence older people and employers tend to oppose them. The result, of course, is that the young leave anyway, suffering severely from inadequate academic and vocational preparation in anything other than agriculturally related subjects. Third, the rural poor have a severe audibility gap. In urban areas public officials have responded to civil disorder and collective action. Because population is diffused in rural areas opportunities for organized protest are limited. Finally, there are few people in rural areas who have the expertise to formulate manpower plans, make application for funds, or administer programs. The lack of manpower expertise is particularly serious in those declining areas where local governments have been weakened by heavy outmigration.

Chicanos who live in rural poverty also suffer because their concentration in the Southwest leaves them virtually unknown to most Americans. Thus they have been neglected in the formulation of program designs and in the staffing of program operations. Because the civil rights movement of the 1960s did not focus public attention on Chicanos, the impetus given by this movement to the development of manpower policies has included Chicanos only as an afterthought.

As indicated earlier, most of legislation affecting Chicanos has been designed for migratory workers—especially their health, transportation, treatment, and education. Little has pertained to occupational training, although the National Migrant Workers Program inaugurated in 1972 is designed to settle workers out of the migrant stream.

Of course, individual manpower projects are also scattered throughout rural areas having heavy Chicano populations. No careful study of Mexican-American participation in these programs is available, but limited observations suggest that very little occupational training is being provided to Chicanos in these areas.

Conclusion

This chapter has explored the conditions of the Spanish speaking, especially Chicanos, who are one of the most economically disadvantaged groups in the United States. Chicanos have worked primarily in agriculture and as migrants. Their concentration in the Southwest, where large-scale agricultural operations predominate, has limited the Chicanos' ability to become farm owners and operators. Moreover, large families, inadequate education, cultural isolation from the dominant Anglo groups, language barriers, discrimination, poor health conditions, and political powerlessness have caused the Chicanos' conditions to be self-perpetuating. Besides all of these disadvantages, Chicanos face the added problems of competition from Mexican nationals. Ironically under the bracero program these Mexican nationals had even better working conditions, guaranteed by the federal government, than were available to many native Chicanos. Their proximity to the border not only causes Chicanos to face competition with Mexican nationals, but successive waves of immigrants have made it difficult for Mexican Americans to be assimilated into American society as other groups have been.

The Chicanos' conditions clearly will not be improved very much by the continuation of present policies. Improvement would require that human resource development measures be enlarged and intensified. One of the most urgent needs is job creation in areas where Chicanos are concentrated. However, many of these areas have few economic advantages other than a supply of cheap labor and, therefore, are not very attractive to private employers. Although some private employers might be attracted to these areas, there is little prospect that many unemployed or underemployed Chicanos will find private nonfarm employment in rural areas. Many of the employers who come into these areas are able to attract workers with higher levels of education and training, doing little for the more disadvantaged Chicanos. The obvious answers to these problems—training, public service employment, programs to move workers from labor-surplus to labor-shortage areas, education improvements, antidiscrimination measures, improved care, and an income-maintenance programs for people who cannot or should not work—are easy to specify but difficult to implement; it is even more difficult to muster sufficient political support to ensure that these programs are adequately funded. The poor in general, and Chicanos in particular, have been relatively powerless. However, a number of Chicano leaders are emerging who might change this situation. Significantly, all of the Chicano leaders who have attracted national attention—Cesar Chavez (whose *la causa* movement is based on organizing agricultural workers), the previously mentioned Reies Lopez Tijerina (whose *la alianza* movement is built around land claims of rural families in northern New Mexico), and Jose Angel Gutierrez (leader of *la raza* movement) to secure educational and community reforms in rural areas of South Texas—are associated with rural life.

However, human resource development measures are not likely to be very effective unless labor competition from Mexico is limited. Serious consideration should, therefore, be given to measures that further reduce the flow of Mexican nationals into U.S. labor markets. That this has not been done is a further reflection of the powerlessness of Chicanos, who have had little impact on public policies in these matters.

The exclusion of agricultural workers from workmen's compensation, unemployment compensation, minimum wages, and the right to collective bargaining cannot be justified on objective grounds. The only reasons for these exclusions is the powerlessness of agricultural workers relative to their employers. Hopefully, public policy will change as Chicanos become better organized and as public attention is drawn to their problems.

Notes

1. This chapter relies heavily on Vernon M. Briggs, Jr., *Chicanos and Rural Poverty* (Baltimore, Md.: Johns Hopkins Press, 1973).
2. Henry M. Ramirez, "America's Spanish-Speaking: A Profile," *Manpower* (September 1972), p. 34.
3. Dale Truett, "Black Employment in Miami," in Ray Marshall and Virgil Christian, eds., *The Employment of Southern Blacks* (Salt Lake City, Utah: Olympus Publishing Co., 1974).
4. U.S. Department of Labor, Bureau of Labor Statistics, *The New York Puerto Rican* (New York: Middle Atlantic Regional Office of the Bureau of Labor Statistics), Regional Report No. 19, May 1971, p. 1.
5. Jack D. Forbes, *Mexican Americans: A Handbook for Educators* (Berkeley, Calif.: Far West Laboratory for Educational Research and Development, 1970).
6. Leo Grebler et al., *The Mexican-American People* (New York: Free Press, 1970), Chaps. 13–20.
7. Fred H. Schmidt, *Spanish-Surnamed American Employment in Southwest*, prepared for the Colorado Civil Rights Commission, under the auspices of the EEOC (Washington, D.C.: GPO, 1970), p. 50.
8. James S. Coleman et al., *Equality of Educational Opportunity*, U.S. Department of Health, Education, and Welfare, Office of Education (Washington, D.C.: GPO, 1966), pp. 274–275.
9. Ibid., p. 273.
10. Steve Allen, *The Ground Is Our Table* (Garden City, N.Y.:

Doubleday, 1966); see the discussion entitled "Agribusiness: The Corporate Sector," in Chap. 4.

11. Stan Steiner, *La Raza: The Mexican Americans* (New York: Harper & Row, 1968), Chaps. 3–7.

12. Grebler et al., op. cit., p. 90.

13. Allen, op. cit., p. 46.

14. Grebler et al., op. cit., p. 90.

15. Rev. William E. Scholes, "The Migrant Workers" in Julian Samora, ed., *La Raza: Forgotten Americans* (Notre Dame: University of Notre Dame Press, 1966), p. 74. The figure includes a small number of Filipinos.

16. Donald N. Barrett, "Demographic Characteristics," in Julian Samora, op. cit., p. 163. The figures are from the U.S. census for the respective years.

17. John H. Burma, ed., "Economics," in *Mexican Americans in the United States* (Cambridge, Mass.: Schenkman, 1970), p. 144.

18. Vernon M. Briggs, Jr., *The Mexican-United States Border: Public Policy and Chicano Economic Welfare* (Austin, Tex.: Center for the Study of Human Resources and the Bureau of Business Research, 1974).

19. "The Commuter on the United States-Mexico Border," staff paper presented in *Hearings* before the U.S. Commission on Civil Rights, San Antonio, Tex. (December 9–14, 1968), p. 983.

20. Anna-Stina Ericson, "The Impact of Commuters on the Mexican-American Border Area," *Monthly Labor Review*, Vol. 93, August 1970), p. 18. Emphasis supplied.

21. U.S. Congress, House of Representatives, Committee on the Judiciary, Subcommittee No. 1, *Hearings on Illegal Aliens*, pt. 5 (Washington, D.C.: GPO, March 22, 1972), p. 1328.

22. The Commuter on the United States-Mexico Border," op. cit., pp. 985, 1000.

23. Ibid., p. 987. The original citation is Matter of M.D.S. & Immigration and Naturalization, p. 209 (1958).

24. Ibid., p. 998.

25. Ibid., p. 461.

26. Ibid., p. 1001.

27. Schmidt, op. cit., p. 46.

20
the isolated indians

There is no universally accepted legal definition of an American Indian, or Native Americans as many prefer to call themselves. Government agencies, depending upon their assigned functions, have used different measures of identification. The Bureau of the Census relies upon the individual respondent to decide his own race. Other government agencies cannot accept self-definition because eligibility to participate in their programs and services is normally determined by statutes or treaties. Eligibility under federal Indian law was made dependent upon being half-Indian or quarter-Indian or being listed on a tribal roll. These statutes are typically designed to fulfill obligations assumed by the United States when the Indians were forced to accept reservations of land in return for their "safety." These various definitions make it easier to understand why estimates of the total American Indian population range from one-half million to more than twice that number.

Population and demography

It is important to stress that Indians are American citizens, free to move within the 50 states. Many have done so: Next to the Navajo reservation, the largest concentrations of Indians are found in Los Angeles, Oklahoma City, and other large cities. Like other Americans living in central cities, Indians have their share of problems, and, like other migrants, they face problems of adjustment. But the urban Indians have unique difficulties as well. In 1970 the Bureau of the Census counted a total of 792,000 Indians in the United States. By counting only reservation Indians living on or adjacent to reservations, the Bureau of Indian Affairs (BIA) estimated in 1973 the total Indian population entitled to its services to be 543,000; but, this number included all Alaskan natives because the term "adjacent" in this case encompasses all of Alaska.

Table 20-1 Estimates of Indian Population on or Adjacent to Federal Reservations, Total and Selected States, March 1973

State	Population (thousands)
Total	543
Arizona	114
New Mexico	93
Oklahoma*a*	85
Alaska*b*	61
California	38
South Dakota	32
Montana	26
Washington	18
North Dakota	15
Minnesota	11
All other states	50

*a*Includes former reservation areas in Oklahoma.
*b*Includes all Indians and Alaskan natives.
Source: Bureau of Indian Affairs, *Indian Reservation Population, Labor Force, Unemployment, and Rate of Underemployment—March 1973* (Washington, D.C.: The Bureau, 1973), p. 2.

The BIA also counts Oklahoma Indians who live on former reservations as its clients. Nearly nine of every ten Indians that the BIA considers in its jurisdiction live in ten states (Table 20-1).

According to one BIA official, there are 270 reservations, 24 other scattered land areas maintained in federal trusteeship for Indians, Eskimos, and Aleuts, and over 100 government-owned areas used by Indians and native people in Alaska.[1]

American Indians exhibit no single typical residential pattern: Some tribes group into small villages; other tribes scatter themselves with miles among neighbors; and others live in towns or familial groups or tribal enclaves of greatly varying populations. By far the largest and most highly populated reservation is the Navajo, which spans part of Arizona, New Mexico, and Utah and covers an area the size of West Virginia. About 137,000 Navajos live on this reservation. At the other extreme are more than 70 tribes with fewer than 100 persons each (Table 20-2). Some tribes are located near large cities, but more are located in isolated rural regions where there is no easily accessible transportation to urban areas. The 300 separate languages spoken by American Indians are evidence that these communities contain members whose traditions, values, and cultures vary as much among them-

Table 20-2 Number of Indian Reservations by Size of Population, 1973

Population Size	Total Population	Number of Reservations
Total[a]	452,565	245
Less than 100	2,179	71
100–499	21,014	79
500–999	20,272	28
1,000–1,999	42,649	26
2,000–4,999	80,815	23
5,000–9,999	89,512	13
10,000–19,999	38,024	3
20,000–99,999	21,414	1
100,000 and over	136,686	1

[a]Does not include Indians administratively grouped together in Alaska and California.

Source: U.S. Bureau of Indian Affairs, Indian Reservation Labor Force and Unemployment—1973 (Washington, D.C.: The Bureau, 1973), pp. 3–12.

selves as they do from other ethnic groups and the dominant white society.

Indians are a comparatively young and growing population. Despite a mortality rate higher than the national average, an unusually high birth rate is causing the Indian population to increase by 3 percent annually—twice the national rate of natural increase. And it is a comparatively young population. The median age of Indians living on or adjacent to reservations is only 17 years, compared with a median age of about 29 for the rest of the nation.

From all indications the Indian population will continue to increase substantially in the near future. If current preventive health- and medical-care programs reduce Indian death rates, especially in the younger age groups, the immediate effect will be to lower the death rate at all ages. While an increase in persons in older age cohorts will tend to level the death rate and eventually decrease the birth rate, it will contribute to the rapid net growth in population.

Socioeconomic conditions

With the exception of blacks living in rural areas, Indians on reservations suffer the worst economic conditions of any group in the United States. Median family income for all rural Indians in 1969 was barely half that for rural whites (Table 20-3). More than half of rural Indian families received less than $5000 income in

Table 20-3 Median per Capita Family Income of Minorities by Residence, 1969

	Total		Urban		Rural Nonfarm		Rural Farm	
	Family	Per Capita	Family	Per Capita	Family	Per Capita	Family	Per Capita
Indian	$5,832	$1,573	$7,323	$2,108	$4,691	$1,147	$4,319	$1,104
Black	6,067	1,818	6,581	1,989	4,035	1,094	3,445	964
Chicano	6,962	1,716	7,256	1,797	5,329	1,236	5,020	1,267
White	9,961	3,314	10,629	3,567	8,542	2,673	7,534	2,560

Source: U.S. Bureau of the Census, *U.S. Census of the Population 1970, American Indians,* PC(2)1F, Table 9; *General Economic and Social Characteristics,* PC(1)C1, Table 94; and *Persons of Spanish Origin,* PC(2)1C, Table 10.

1969, compared with three-fifths of black families but only one-fifth of whites. Among Indians residing within reservation boundaries median family income was only $4088.

When the effects of large Indian families are added, per capita income comparisons are even more bleak. Even after adjustments for residence Indian per capita income is only half that of whites (though it is about 6 percent higher than that of blacks). Since more Indians live in rural areas, the overall Indian average is below $1600 per year, the lowest among any ethnic group. Among Indians on the 115 largest reservations surveyed by the census in 1970, per capita income was only $962, less than a third of the national average for all whites and only three-fifths of the levels for blacks and Chicanos. Even this figure disguises the depths of Indian poverty in some areas. For example, on the Papago reservation in Arizona per capita income in 1969 was $588 and for the Navajo reservation it was $776—levels not far above those in underdeveloped countries

The obvious explanation for this poverty is the lack of employment opportunities on reservations. Most Indian reservations contain few natural resources, are remote from large markets, have inadequate transportation systems, and lack trained and educated labor forces. As a result, the economic base on and near reservations is usually small or nonexistent, and the critical problem is joblessness. In the 1970 census little more than half of Indian men over 16 years of age living in rural areas were in the labor force compared with more than three-fifths of blacks and three-fourths of whites. (Table 20-4). With so few jobs available many of the nonparticipants in the labor force have evidently given up hope of finding a job. Yet the census found rural unemployment rates (which include only those actively seeking work) to be more than double black rates and nearly quadruple white totals. More recent BIA estimates, which count all those able to work but not working as unemployed, found that more than a third of all Indians were without jobs in March 1973. On some reservations half of all Indians were out of work.

	Percent Without Jobs
Hopi	49
Pine Ridge	39
Blackfeet	37
Navajo	35
Papago	29
Rosebud	22
Cherokee	22
Gila River	18

Table 20-4 Male Labor Force Participation and Unemployment, 1970

	Number Employed (thousands)			% Participation Rate			% Unemployment Rate		
	Indian	Black	White	Indian	Black	White	Indian	Black	White
Total	116	6,449	43,030	63.4	69.8	77.4	11.6	6.3	3.6
Urban	62	5,220	31,365	72.0	71.9	78.3	9.4	6.6	3.6
Rural	55	1,229	11,665	55.8	61.0	75.8	14.0	5.9	3.7
115 Largest Reservations	(22)	—	—	(50.3)	—	—	(18.6)	—	—

Source: U.S. Bureau of the Census, *General Economic and Social Characteristics*, PC(1)C1, Table 90, and *American Indians*, PC(2)1F, Tables 4 and 12.

The jobs that are available in reservation economies reflect the dominant influence of government. Forty-six percent of all jobs on Indian reservations are state, local, and federal positions, delivering the services provided by the BIA, the Health Service, and other agencies. This percentage is three times the national average for government employment. By contrast, employment rates in wholesale and retail trade and in manufacturing are far below proportions common in the rest of the economy.

In terms of occupational status Indians are predictably concentrated on the lowest rungs. Surprisingly, however, the occupational status of Indian men is considerably better than that of blacks, with higher proportions of professionals, managers, salesworkers, and craftsmen, and with fewer operatives, laborers, and service workers. Another important but little-noticed aspect of reservation economies deserves attention: the limited and declining importance of agriculture and forestry. Though Indian lands comprise the chief natural resource on reservations, farming and forestry employ only one-tenth of Indian men. Since 1940 the decline in farm employment among Indian men has been dramatic:

| | Percent of Those Employed | | | |
	1940	1950	1960	1970
Farmers and farm managers	46.7	24.2	9.5	2.3
Farm laborers and foremen	21.7	22.4	14.0	5.7

Though these figures are for all Indians, even on reservations only 12 percent of Indians were employed in farm occupations by 1970.

The job deficit and low incomes are further reflected in deplorable housing conditions. While three-fifths of Indian families live in unsanitary or dilapidated housing, only 8 percent of all American families live in inadequate houses. Though federally funded public housing was initiated during the 1930s, a quarter-century elapsed before the federal government began to take steps to alleviate the poor housing on Indian reservations.

Moreover, poverty and substandard housing conditions are reflected in the serious health deficiencies suffered by American Indians. The average infant mortality rate among Indians is 22 percent higher than that for the rest of the population, and the life expectancy of those who do survive is much lower than that of either the white or black populations. The average life span for an Indian is six years shorter than for the average American. Poverty and its symptoms—poor diets and unsanitary living conditions—have contributed to a widespread incidence of disease caused by malnutrition.

Education

If Indians are to share in the high standard of living that surrounds their reservations, they must improve their educational attainment. Ever since the white man settled on this continent, he has made attempts at, or at least paid lip service to, "civilizing" the native "savages." Nearly three centuries ago, the Virginia House of Burgesses established a "college for the children of the infidels." Concern with educating Indian children has been sustained ever since and, some would add, with possibly too little change in attitude. Compulsory education applies equally to Indian as to all other American children.

In recent years responsibility for the education of Indian children on reservations has tended to shift from the federal government to the states and communities. But because Indians living on reservations are exempt from property taxes and contribute little to state or local taxes, the law provides for federal reimbursement to states and localities enrolling Indian children in their schools. More than two-thirds of the 204,000 Indian children and youths attending school are registered in public schools. Mission schools, some dating to the colonial period, still enroll about 6 of every 100 children attending school. The balance, 25 percent, attend BIA schools. Enrollment in these schools ranges from a few children in an isolated Indian reservation to several thousand in a modern boarding school. In 1973 the BIA operated 76 boarding schools enrolling some 34,000 Indian children and 117 day schools for another 17,000.

Whether an Indian child attends an integrated public school or a federal school for Indians depends primarily upon locational access. The policy of BIA is to encourage the child to attend public schools whenever possible. If there is no public facility within a reachable distance of the child's home, the bureau makes every attempt to allow him to attend a federal day school. In isolated areas where existing transportation is inadequate to allow school-age children to live at home, they are sent to federal boarding schools. A child may also be referred to a boarding school by the BIA Division of Social Services or the Public Health Service. Many students who are placed in boarding schools away from their homes are delinquent, overage for their grade achievement, orphans, or children of imprisoned, hospitalized or separated parents. Students who have been unable or unwilling to adapt to a day school are transferred to boarding schools as a last resort with the mutual agreement of the youths and their parents.

Running the boarding schools for 34,000 Indian children is an expensive proposition—averaging more than $4000 per child during the school year, or more than three times as high as the cost per child in public schools. These schools have been subjected to a great deal of criticism, and the news media have played up frequently unverified incidents of cruel discipline and the meager achievements that the BIA can show for the high costs. In response to public criticisms and to avoid high costs the BIA has attempted to place Indian children in regular public schools or reservation day schools. But completely viable alternatives to the BIA boarding schools have not been devised. It is not economically feasible to deliver educational services to the thousands of Indian families that live in utter isolation; the boarding schools will remain the only means for providing these Indian children with any education.

The schools responsible for the education of the nation's Indians are plagued by all of the problems confronting American education in general, but compounding the situation are conditions unique to Indian education. Like other school systems, especially those located in areas inhabited by other minority groups, they are troubled by the lack of continuity between teacher training and the actual school setting, language barriers, the lack of empathy of teachers and administrators for the children with whom they are entrusted, a shortage of qualified personnel and instructional materials, and the limited community involvement in scholastic affairs. Peculiar to schools serving Indian children are problems caused by the unique relationship of the tribes with the federal government and the distinct cultural heritage of the American Indian. Two-thirds of the students entering school have little or no skill in the English language, and even more are totally unfamiliar with the ways of the white people that are perpetuated through the school system.

The effects of these problems can be seen in the statistics concerning Indian education. According to the 1970 census, the average educational attainment for American Indians was only slightly less than ten years of schooling. The high school dropout rate among reservation youths is considerably higher than for the rest of the nation. In 1970, 57 percent of Indian males aged 20 to 24 years had graduated from high school, a smaller proportion than the 63 percent of blacks and far below the 85 percent rate for whites. On reservations the dropout rate was even more severe, with less than half of rural Indian men ages 20 to 24 years having finished high school.

Increasing numbers of Indians who graduate from high school are going on to college. According to the Bureau of the Census, 14,200 Indians were enrolled in college in March 1970, 2,000 more than the total number of Indian college graduates. A survey of colleges by the federal Office for Civil Rights in the fall of 1970 produced even more encouraging results.[2] According to the school administrators (who may have had an incentive to inflate the totals, since the schools were under pressure from the Office for Civil Rights to raise their minority enrollment ratios), 28,500 American Indians were on their rolls, including 60 medical and dental students, 190 law students, and 1,300 other postgraduates. Based on the census figures, approximately 12 percent of Indians age 18 to 24 years were in college in 1970, compared with 15 percent of blacks and 27 percent of whites.

Once in college, the evidence indicates that Indians are about as likely to stay on until graduation as other students. Among students receiving BIA college scholarship grants (which includes most Indian college students), the dropout rate was about 48 percent, compared to a national average of about 47 percent who left school before graduation.[3]

Labor force participation and employment

Even though reservations are endowed with valuable mineral resources and Indians receive substantial transfer payments from the government and from their tribes, the bulk of their income is earned through employment, much of it related to developing natural resources. In the United States as a whole about 70 percent of personal income is derived from wages and salaries, and the proportion of Indian income is very nearly the same. But because their earnings are meager, 55 percent of Indians live in poverty. They work intermittently if at all, and typically their jobs are low paying, unskilled, and unattractive. There is a critical and chronic job shortage in and around most reservations, and Indians are usually ill prepared for the few available jobs and are frequently discriminated against when they apply for work. The government accounts for almost half of Indian employment, with private industrial and commercial enterprises providing jobs for a small fraction of the labor force on a man-year basis.

These severe employment problems can be measured in many ways. Perhaps most striking is the fact that only 47 percent of rural Indian men aged 16 or over are employed, compared with 73 percent of rural whites. Because far fewer adults have jobs and much more of the Indian population is under 16, on the average only 18 persons out of each 100 on reservations work to support themselves and their dependents, compared with 38 for each 100 throughout the United States.

Unemployment is extremely high on the reservations, though technical problems make it difficult to apply the normal unemployment measures. Because jobs are scarce on or near reservations, many Indians are not seeking work even if they would welcome employment and are, therefore, not counted as unemployed under conventional government practices. To secure more realistic estimates the BIA began to compile its own statistics in 1963. Its measure of the labor force excludes only those who cannot work because of health problems, child-care responsibilities, or school attendance; those who can work but are not seeking jobs are included among the unemployed. According to this definition, 37 percent of reservation Indians were unemployed in 1973. This rate overstates the problem if it is compared with national rates, which averaged 4.9 percent in 1973 according to the census definition. If the census measure were used, unemployment would be 19 percent among Indian males on reservations, still much higher than the national rate.

Underemployment and seasonal employment are also high. In a study prepared for the Joint Economic Committee, Alan Sorkin found that peak unemployment during the winter months is 70 percent higher than during the summer months when jobs are more plentiful because of agricultural work.[4] In a survey of five Indian reservations Benjamin J. Taylor and Dennis J. O'Connor found that the proportion of Indians aged 16 and over who worked for more than ten months during the year ranged from a low of 12 percent on one reservation to a high of 36 percent on another reservation.[5] Farming and related rural occupations, which involve a variety of chores, generally do not afford much opportunity for complete idleness even on small or marginal farming units. For example, while the Navajo sheepherder is not completely unemployed, neither can it be claimed that he is gainfully employed or that the income from his occupation is sufficient to support himself and his family.

Working Indians are also concentrated at the lower end of the employment totem, in part reflecting their rural residence. Over 8 percent of the male Indians employed in 1970 were farmers and laborers, compared with 4 percent nationally. Few rural Indians held skilled positions: Only about 9 percent of all males were professional, technical, and kindred workers, compared with 15 percent nationally. Similarly, few were in entrepreneurial and managerial jobs, with less than 5 percent of male Indians being nonfarm managers, officials, and proprietors; the national rate was 12 percent.

The federal government is the source of an inordinate proportion of full-time jobs held by Indians. The BIA employed an estimated 8500 Indians full time as of December 1973, the Indian Health Service, an additional 3,900, and the Department of Health, Education, and Welfare, the Economic Development Administration, and other federal agencies, hundreds more. This accounts for a large share of total nonagricultural employment. Industrial and commercial enterprises located on or near reservations provided only an estimated 7500 man-years of employment in fiscal 1973, compared with the 13,500 in the Indian Health Service (IHS) and BIA alone.

Indians are concentrated in low-level jobs even when the government is their employer. Though Indians fill more than one-half of the jobs within BIA, they hold less than one-fifth of the executive jobs. In the IHS, although more than half of all employees are Indians, less than 1 percent of doctors or nurses are Indians.

The employment problems of Indians on reservations are severe. Though they cannot be attacked apart from the other Indian problems, two basic approaches must be taken. Efforts are obviously needed to increase the number of jobs available to Indians on or near reservations. More private firms must be attracted to the environs, and tribes and individuals should be assisted in initiating their own industrial and commercial enterprises. At the same time, efforts must also be expanded to improve the productivity of the Indian work force through manpower training and to provide whatever other labor market services may be needed to put Indians to work. Manpower and economic development programs must work hand in hand to strengthen the economies and human resources of the reservations.

Obstacles to economic development

There are some very good reasons why more businesses are not located on reservations or near enough to hire substantial numbers of Indians. Most reservations are geographically inaccessible to product markets. With their low average income and typically widespread settlement, they provide only a limited market themselves for any products. The Indian labor force is generally unskilled; and because of their poor education Indians may be expensive to train. Though many on a reservation may be unemployed, only a limited number are available for work at a single geographical point because of the dispersion of population. With differing cultural attitudes Indians find it difficult to adapt to sustained employment and job discipline, and the result is higher labor costs due to absenteeism and seasonal turnover, at least in the early stages of operation.

Capital for public and private investment is also in short supply. Financial institutions are unfamiliar with reservations and unwilling to take the high risks often involved in lending to Indians—especially because lands, which are the Indians' major asset, cannot be taken as collateral on loans. Public funds are equally limited, and the few tribes with substantial resources are sometimes reluctant to use them for commercial and industrial purposes.

Reservations generally lack the social overhead capital such as adequate transportation systems and sewerage and electrical facilities needed to attract businesses. In competing with many other localities for the limited number of new and relocating firms, they are usually at a disadvantage because they cannot offer the amenities available elsewhere.

To complicate matters, knowledge about conditions on reservations is scarce. Businessmen do not know what to expect because little information is usually available on labor forces, prevailing wage rates, skill levels, worker attitudes, and overhead capital. All of these factors can vitally affect the profitability of any operation. There is an equally severe shortage of trained personnel on the reservations to coordinate industrial development efforts; tribal leaders, who are often elderly, are sometimes unqualified or uninterested in planning and administering such programs. Faced with these uncertainties, businessmen understandably turn their attention to more predictable locations.

Improvement of reservation economies also depends on the health of the national economy. Even with special incentives, businessmen may not flock to out-of-the-way reservations if labor is more readily available elsewhere. The Area Redevelopment Act of 1961 attempted to cope with the problem. Although unemployment was more chronic on Indian reservations than in other areas in the country, Congress found it necessary to provide specifically for reservations to ensure that Indians would not be excluded. The program, however, was of little help to reservations while the labor market was slack generally. Tightening labor market conditions through the second half of the 1960s made reservations, with their abundant labor supply, increasingly attractive for expanding new companies, and carrots offered by the federally supported depressed-area programs added incentives to locate on reservations. Hardly any factories were located on reservations in 1960; 12 years later there were more than 200 factories employing over 7000 Indians. The trend was likely to continue only if tight labor markets were sustained in the rest of the country and if adequate incentives continued to attract new industries to reservations. An overall increase in unemployment and a reduced demand for labor would no doubt reduce the attractiveness of reservations for the location of new or expanding plants.

Federal manpower programs

Unless more jobs are provided on or near the reservations, Indians will continue to have low employment rates; but Indians could hold many existing jobs if they were qualified. Without improvements in the labor force it is unlikely that industrial and commercial development can proceed; hence manpower programs must be coordinated with economic development efforts.

Many cultural factors can impair Indian labor force participation. A major obstacle is that Indians often have a limited command of English and especially of the industrial lexicon. Another obstacle is that few Indians adjust their activities by the clock, which makes it difficult for them to adjust to factory discipline. Many Indians do not carefully plan for the future. For instance, they may abandon full-time, year-round jobs for attractive summer employment even though this means losing stable employment. Usually, Indians value landholdings and open spaces, preferring to live in isolated units rather than in congested areas. As a result, they are often scattered around the countryside and, with the poor transportation system, are unable to get to a place of work.

Such cultural factors are significant and can add both to the costs of hiring Indians and to their difficulty in finding and holding jobs. Yet these obstacles are relatively easy to overcome. At the Fairchild semiconductor plant in Shiprock, New Mexico, for instance, instructions, procedures, and expectations have been adjusted fairly successfully to these cultural differences. Industrial terms were added to the Indian language or approximate translations were used; "aluminum" was converted to the Navajo phrase for "shiny metal" and "oscillator" became "tunnel." Time schedules were adjusted, with the clocks in the plant being divided into ten sections, painted red and white alternately and numbered consecutively. Thus a six-minute "section" was used as the basic unit of time rather than minutes and hours. Problems in attracting workers to the area and retaining them at their jobs were solved by offering adequate wages and opportunities for upgrading. The lesson has been that many Indians are willing to modify their own life styles to obtain jobs that are dependable and reasonably well paying and that offer opportunities for advancement.

What is much more basic and much more difficult to overcome is the fact that Indians generally lack the skills and the knowledge to be productive workers. Their educational attainment, as noted earlier, is substantially below national norms, and the education they receive is often inferior. Because they have lacked job opportunities in the past and because outside training opportunities are limited, they have acquired few skills. As education improves, so will the abilities of the labor force, but more direct steps need to be taken through remedial training and basic education, along with the other manpower services Indians may require to find employment and to improve their productivity and earnings.

BIA manpower programs

The BIA has provided manpower services for Indians on reservations for more than two decades. Until recently, these were almost the only efforts made on behalf of Indians, and they still are of great significance despite the extension of Labor Department programs to the reservations. More than 16,000 entered BIA's employment assistance or manpower programs in fiscal 1973, and they received services costing more than $42 million, or over $2,600 per person. Though BIA's efforts may be less extensive than those of the Labor Department, they are much more intensive.

These programs are grouped administratively into two categories: direct employment and adult vocational training programs. Under the first (and older) program Indians can be placed in jobs on or near the reservations or may be helped in finding urban jobs. Assistance is provided in the form of relocation allowances, temporary subsidies, medical services, placement, and counseling. Also direct employment program funds are used to operate two experimental residential training centers; they provide basic education and vocational training for entire Indian families who are so seriously disadvantaged that they cannot benefit from other training opportunities. The adult vocational training program, which accounts for the bulk of training, offers institutional courses both near reservations and at vocational centers in larger urban areas that serve a number of reservations. This program also provides funds for OJT, which in turn can provide placement, counseling, health, and other services for participants, but usually it only pays wage subsidies to employers covering up to one-half of the minimum hourly wage for some training period. This subsidy has been used to attract employers to reservations and to induce them to hire Indians.

Under the direct employment program the BIA attempts to

assist Indians living on or near reservations to find jobs either within commuting distance or farther away where they may be relocated. Although there is no training component, some individuals who have received assistance may have participated in adult vocational training. Direct employment is designed to assist individuals who have a salable vocational skill for which there is no outlet in the nearby Indian community. Based on individual needs, a wide variety of services—including interviewing, testing, counseling, and health care—is available. Perhaps most important are subsistence grants until placement. Rates depend on family size and whether the individual being assisted can commute to his job or must relocate. Arrangements can be made for an individual interested in being placed within commuting distance within two weeks, while relocation may take two months or perhaps longer if the individual has some significant problem. However, more than 40 percent of the relocatees are placed in jobs within one week, and nearly 30 percent more are placed by the end of the second week. Total costs for individuals and families provided direct employment services in fiscal 1973 averaged about $2900 per person.

The critical issue underlying the direct employment program is whether assistance should be used to relocate Indians to urban areas where jobs are more readily available or to help them find jobs on or near reservations. Fluctuations in the funding levels reflect a shift in national policy concerning the most appropriate method of serving reservation Indians. Direct employment—and termination—were obvious tactics of the dominant philosophy of the early 1950s, which favored integrating Indians into the economic mainstream. A change of emphasis, however, grew from such factors as disappointment with the effectiveness of such efforts, opposition from Indian groups lamenting the loss of their best human resources, and increasing job opportunities resulting from industrial and commercial development on reservations.

Almost all studies of the relocation effort have agreed that Indians working in urban areas can earn substantially more than those placed on or near reservations but that very few successfully adapt to urban life. For instance, a 1968 BIA follow-up of 1963 placements in urban areas found that almost three-fourths had moved back to or near the reservation. Records of the BIA from 1953 to 1957 indicate that about one-half of the relocatees had returned within the first year. Others have estimated that between one-half and two-thirds of all relocatees eventually return to the reservation.[6]

Whatever success relocation may have in raising wage rates and income, the costs are not justified if clients return without

Table 20-5 Direct Employment Placements, Selected Years, 1952–1970

Fiscal Year	Total	Employment Training Centers	Percent	On or Near Reservations	Percent	Urban Areas	Percent
1952	442	—	—	—	—	442	100.0
1958	2373	—	—	63	2.7	2310	97.3
1964	1985	—	—	254	12.8	1731	87.2
1968	2928	718	24.5	1136	38.8	1074	36.7
1969	2975	612	20.6	1614	54.2	749	25.2
1970	3757	904	24.1	2000	53.2	853	22.7

Source: U.S. Bureau of Indian Affairs, *Annual Statistical Summary, 1970* (Washington, D.C.: The Bureau, 1970).

gaining skills or saving money. However, those who want to leave the reservation should be helped because urban areas still offer greater opportunities. The BIA has, therefore, reversed its earlier preference for relocation and is trying to walk the tightrope of assisting without advocating relocation. Current policy thus seeks to make the reservations themselves viable economic units, and there is far more accent on locating jobs on or near reservations (Table 20-5).

Intensive services costing around $5000 per trainee are provided in two residential centers funded under the direct employment program; they operate in Madera, California, and Bismarck, North Dakota. To be eligible a single individual or family head must lack a skill, have the equivalent of fewer than nine years of education, and be unqualified for institutional training. These centers care for the participant's whole family and offer adults a wide range of assistance, including intensive and innovative basic education, skill training, and home economics instruction, as well as job placement. Day care is provided for younger children. Most of those connected with the program are enthusiastic, but effectiveness cannot yet be measured.

Institutional training is provided on a much larger scale under adult vocational training and is intended primarily for those 18- to 35-years old. In fiscal 1973, 7600 persons entered training, most at institutions in Chicago, Cleveland, Dallas, Denver, Los Angeles, Oakland, or San Jose—with only a minority receiving training on or near their reservations. Enrollees receive the same types of health and counseling services plus grants as those in the direct employment program, plus subsistence payments throughout the training period. In addition, however, they receive tuition and related expenses for vocational training, so that costs run over $5000 per enrollee. Institutional courses typically last about ten months, but some trainees remain in school for two years. About 1800 courses in nearly 600 public and private schools have been accredited by BIA.

The BIA's institutional training program has demonstrated its effectiveness in increasing the employability and earnings of participants. The five-year follow-up of 1963 enrollees established that their earnings had increased several times over preenrollment levels. Those who went to urban training centers and then found jobs in these areas received much higher wages, but, as under the direct employment program, many gradually drifted back to the reservation. Again the question arises of whether it is wise to transport reservation Indians to urban training centers where they will be prepared for existing jobs within the area. And again the answer is uncertain, but there is little evidence that those who receive training are any more likely to remain in the cities than those who are simply relocated. Accordingly, training opportunities are being increased near the reservation, and the portion of participants who are sent off to urban institutes is being reduced.

The OJT segment of adult vocational training is becoming increasingly important as industrial and commercial development efforts progress and in 1973, 1975 Indians participated. Employers receiving subsidies provide only nominal training in some cases; in others it is extensive. Although average cost per individual served in fiscal 1973 was about $1000, most contracts specified a training period longer than one year. Hence average costs per placement are higher. Whatever the manpower services provided, those enrolled benefit from jobs that might not otherwise be available, almost all of which are close to or on the reservations. Given the demonstrated preference for such locations, OJT subsidies should be increased, which will, in turn, require that they be larger on a per enrollee basis. Few firms can be expected to locate near reservations to receive a $1000 BIA subsidy when they can receive more than $3000 per enrollee to locate near a ghetto.

Recipients of employment assistance services in fiscal 1970 were generally young and well educated; males and single individuals predominated, and families were relatively small. However, nearly nine of every ten were unemployed when they applied for services. And the few who were employed held low-paying jobs.

An evaluation of BIA institutional and OJT programs in Oklahoma concluded that both programs resulted in significant increases in participants' annual earnings. Institutional trainees increased their pretraining earnings by slightly more than did on-the-job trainees; however, the significantly higher costs of institutional training suggest that OJT may be a more effective method to upgrade the skills of American Indians.[7]

Labor department efforts

Public concern about this country's disadvantaged mounted during the 1960s and was enunciated in a series of antipoverty programs, most notably MDTA and EOA. A number of regular manpower programs operate on or near reservations, providing services to reservation Indians as well as those who have moved to urban areas. About 68,000 participated in fiscal 1972, though a substantial number were students receiving supplementary income with only nominal work and training under the Neighborhood Youth Corps (NYC).

Expenditures for Indians cannot be separated from the totals. However, extrapolations based on the percentage of Indians in the various Labor Department programs suggest that about $50 million is spent for Indians; of this probably about two-thirds, or $35 million, is spent for reservation Indians. In addition, state employment security agencies placed a number of Indians in jobs.

The most important manpower program in terms of enrollments is NYC. In-school and summer projects sponsored by the Indian tribal councils are designed to provide students with some work experience and training, but mainly with a source of income during their school years. And the summer employment program has provided employment for 10,000 students. These NYC programs have enjoyed widespread support among Indians. The income provided, usually at the minimum wage, is large relative to the low average family income, and NYC tasks are not demanding. The problems are those that apply to the program nationally. Counseling and supervision are inadequate, and the jobs are often "make work." Little preparation for later employment is offered, but few challenge the value, on balance, of NYC programs.

Out-of-school NYC employs a much smaller number of Indian youth—on a year-round basis, less than 1000 in fiscal 1973. This program would have to be expanded drastically to serve the critical needs of young Indians who have dropped out of school and for whom jobs are almost nonexistent. But this segment of NYC is not popular among the tribes. For one thing, the minimum wage paid often exceeds what is available elsewhere, and older tribal members resent the fact that dropouts can earn more than they; the high wage could conceivably encourage dropouts. The program also has been plagued by alcoholism, absenteeism, and high dropout rates. Despite these shortcomings, some assistance is needed for Indians who have dropped out of school; they constitute perhaps the most serious problem group on the reservations.

Operation Mainstream is a highly popular program where it has been implemented, but through fiscal 1973 only 16 projects had been started because too little effort had been exerted by Labor Department field personnel. Mainstream is ideally suited to the needs of the reservations. It employs mostly older Indians, whose capabilities and prospects elsewhere are meager. They are put to work in road maintenance, planting, beautification, and conservation jobs that require little training and in which the older Indians usually have some experience. Little emphasis is placed on education and training, so that the program has a low cost and high payoff in terms of useful work done. Mainstream has had problems with alcoholism among its older enrollees and high dropout rates among females who leave for family reasons. A major difficulty has been transporting participants from their homes to work sites, a matter that usually must be worked out before a project can get underway. Despite these problems, Mainstream is undoubtedly worthwhile and should be organized more actively on other reservations.

The other major manpower program operated on or near reservations includes projects initiated under MDTA before the federal funds were allocated directly to Indian tribes under the Comprehensive Employment and Training Act. Although enrollment under these projects has been substantial, most tribes prefer to work with similar BIA programs because they are more familiar with BIA activities.

Participants in OJT have jobs upon completion, but there is a serious question about the jobs for which institutional trainees should be prepared. If skill training is to be coordinated with economic development efforts, its policies must be made more flexible. The alternative of providing training courses for job shortages in other areas is a debatable strategy. Where training courses have been offered off reservations, participants have had serious financial and social problems leading to high dropout rates. If those trained on reservations are relocated to cities, these problems are likely to occur again.

The employment service is playing an increasing role on the reservations, but much more needs to be done. In 1970 local public employment offices employed 200 persons, 119 of them Indians, to work directly with the tribes. In some states these personnel have played an active role; for instance, more than 14,000 Indians were placed in nontemporary jobs during fiscal 1969 in Arizona, New Mexico, and Wyoming alone. In most states, however, the employment services ignore the needs of Indians because they are not sure what they are supposed to be doing where job opportunities and training slots are few. Their active efforts are required as manpower programs for Indians grow and as economic development proceeds.

Increasing attention has been given to Indians under the manpower programs administered by the Labor Department; and based on the relative size of their population, Indians receive a disproportionate amount of funds. For instance, Indian enrollment in fiscal 1972 accounted for 2.6 percent of all manpower program participants, well above the proportion of Indians in the population. But considering the concentration of need on the reservations, these shares still are inadequate; greater efforts must be directed toward making Indians employable, helping them to find work, and creating jobs.

Two recent federal manpower initiatives have authorized direct contracts with Indian tribes, thus providing for increased Indian participation in program planning and administration. Under the Emergency Employment Act of 1971 Indian tribes were allocated special funds to hire Indians on public payrolls on the reservations. During the first two-and-one-half years of operation, about $10 million per year was set aside for Indian hiring. In 1974 approximately $12.2 million was available, which paid for the employment of about 1800 Indians from more than 200 tribes in 30 states. Although the program was criticized in some areas for providing only make-work jobs, and for not allowing sufficient expenditures for career development, counseling, and training, there was no question that these supplemental jobs had a positive effect on chronically depressed reservation labor markets and that they provided an important new measure of program control to tribal governments.

The public employment program and other categorical manpower programs operated by the Labor Department were slated to end by 1975, but Indians have been made eligible for manpower training and public employment funds from the Labor Department under CETA. With an estimated $42 million slated to be distributed directly to the tribes for use in manpower efforts as they see fit, this annual block grant should have a significant impact on orienting manpower programs specifically to Indian needs. All tribes or bands with a governing body and a membership of at least 1,000 that are eligible under the act's formula for an annual grant of at least $50,000 may apply for CETA contracts. The implementation of this act should be an important step to the realization of Indian self-determination.

In increasing the funds allocated for Indians, emphasis should be placed on upgrading, especially in public employment. Because so many Indians are employed by federal agencies efforts to raise the skills and responsibilities of these workers should be encouraged. There is no reason why Indians should continue to hold the lowest positions in government agencies such as BIA and IHS, which are intended to serve them. There is justification for moving Indians upward in these agencies, even at the expense of non-Indian workers, if they are prepared for better positions.

In its manpower efforts the BIA has cordial relationships with state employment services and administrators of the Labor Department's programs. Little conflict has occurred, probably because of the obvious need for all services that can be provided and because operations at the field level rarely overlap. Despite this cordiality, there has been little coordination, and the role of the various approaches has not been spelled out. Coordinated manpower services for Indians must become a reality if Native Americans are ever to become self-sufficient. Most of all, manpower programs must be expanded along with economic development efforts so that Indians can become self-sufficient and still maintain the reservation life that is so important to them.

Treating causes rather than symptoms

To meet all the needs of reservation Indians resources would have to be substantially increased. Some improvement can be accomplished through reallocation of resources, but this is difficult to engineer unless funds are increasing. The key, as in the solution of most social problems, is more money and more intelligent use of existing money.

The resources committed to solving Indian problems will probably increase as the public becomes more aware of their plight. But it is improbable that the forthcoming funds will be adequate to meet all demands. It will be necessary to make difficult choices among competing claimants and to determine priorities on the basis of rational analysis.

A significant proportion of disease and premature death among Indians is a direct result of poverty, dilapidated housing, unsanitary water, and inadequate diets. A sound economy would mean that the necessary resources would be available to both the tribal community and individual families to build adequate housing, purchase nutritional foods, and construct sanitation facilities. Schools and communities could offer health education programs and individuals would have the financial ability to follow their recommendations for better health care.

With economic development the number of Indians dependent upon welfare would also decrease. For those not benefiting from increased economic opportunities, more intensive services and substantial assistance could be provided. Another potential benefit is that as Indians take on more responsibilities and are trained for meaningful jobs, they will become increasingly qualified for technical, managerial, and supervisory positions.

The primary goals of Indian programs are to increase Indian control over their own destinies and to improve their standard of living. Developing reservation economies is the *sine qua non* for achieving both of these goals. Past experience has indicated that a growing and productive economy is the single most important factor in the betterment of a population's social institutions. While this is not the only approach that can be taken to improve the conditions on Indian reservations, it does seem to be the most promising. And the right combination of Indian participation with federal assistance is the key to the development of Indian self-reliance and independence.

Notes

1. Bill King, "Some Thoughts on Reservation Economic Development," in U.S. Congress, Joint Economic Committee, *Toward Economic Development for Native American Communities,* 91st Cong., 1st Sess. (Washington, D.C.: GPO, 1969), p. 68.
2. U.S. Department of Health, Education, and Welfare, Office for Civil Rights, *Racial and Ethnic Enrollment Data from Institutions of Higher Learning, Fall 1970* (Washington, D.C.: GPO, 1972), pp. 116, 177, 185, 190, 200.
3. U.S. Congress, House, *Department of Interior and Related Agencies for 1974,* Part 4, *Hearings* before Subcommittee of the Committee on Appropriations, 93rd Cong., 1st Sess. (Washington, D.C.: GPO, 1973), p. 664.
4. Alan Sorkin, "Trends in Employment and Earnings of American Indians," in U.S. Congress, Joint Economic Committee, *Toward Economic Development for Native American Communities,* op. cit., pp. 107–108.
5. Benjamin J. Taylor and Dennis J. O'Connor, *Indian Manpower Resources in the Southwest* (Tempe, Ariz.: Arizona State University, 1969).
6. Joan Ablon, "American Indian Relocation: Problems of Dependency and Management in the City," *Phylon* (Winter 1965).
7. Loren C. Scott and Paul R. Blume, "Some Evidence on the Economic Effectiveness of Institutional Versus On-the-Job Training," paper presented to the Forty-fifth Annual Conference of the Western Economics Association (Davis, Calif.: University of California, August 1970).

21

combating discrimination in employment

We have seen that black, Chicano, and Indian workers are situated in lower occupational positions and earn lower incomes than whites. They also incur higher unemployment rates and have lower labor force participation rates than whites. Moreover, they suffer disproportionately from from long periods of unemployment. The causes of minority economic disadvantages clearly are deeply rooted in social and economic institutions that cause them to be at the end of the line when it comes to obtaining jobs.[1]

Overcoming the complex constellation of forces causing blacks to be economically disadvantaged will require a variety of programs, the most obvious of which are measures to combat overt discrimination. The chapter will analyze the effectiveness of these measures.

Legal and administrative remedies

Since World War II, enforceable laws against discrimination have been passed in over half of the states and in many municipalities. These laws cover virtually the entire nonwhite population outside the South, but only Kentucky had adopted such a statute by 1974. Generally, these laws are administered by part-time commissioners who ordinarily have powers to (1) receive, investigate, and pass on complaints; (2) use conferences, conciliation, and persuasion in an effort to resolve complaints; (3) conduct public hearings, subpoena witnesses, and compel their attendance under oath as well as requiring the production of records relating to matters before the hearings; (4) seek court orders enforcing subpoenas and cease-and-desist orders; and (5) undertake and publish studies of discrimination.

Before the Civil Rights Act of 1964 blacks also used the courts to overcome discrimination in employment, although most court cases dealt with unions because, in the absence of statutes or nondiscrimination clauses in collective bargaining contracts, employers had no legal obligation not to discriminate. However, unions acquired legal rights and duties as a result of the National Labor Relations and Railway Labor Acts. Specifically, the Supreme Court ruled that the Constitution imposed upon unions, which acquired the privilege of exclusive bargaining rights, the duty to represent all members of the bargaining unit fairly. Aggrieved minorities have, therefore, brought legal action for injunctions and damages against discriminating unions. Moreover, in the 1964 Hughes Tool case the National Labor Relations Board (NLRB) held violation of the duty of fair representation to be an unfair labor practice, giving aggrieved minorities a measure of administrative relief because they can file charges with the NLRB instead of with the courts.

The Civil Rights Act

Title VII of the 1964 Civil Rights Act outlawed discrimination on the basis of race, color, religion, sex, or national origin in hiring, compensation, and promotion. The law applied to all private employers, employment agencies, and labor organizations employing or serving 25 or more persons; an Equal Employment Opportunity Commission (EEOC) was created to enforce its provisions. Initially, this commission's role was limited to information gathering, mediation to encourage voluntary compliance, and "friend-of-the-court" legal support in antidiscrimination suits brought by others. Amendments in 1972 extended coverage to smaller organizations (15 or more people) and to state and local governments, government organizations, and educational institutions. More significantly, the EEOC was empowered to act as a plaintiff bringing civil actions in federal court seeking remedies on behalf of those who had suffered from discrimination. The 1972 amendments also shifted functions from the civil rights division of the Justice Department to the EEOC. Title VII initially had authorized the Attorney General to bring suit against respondents referred by EEOC after it had been unable to obtain voluntary compliance.

The number of charges of discrimination flowing into the EEOC nearly tripled between 1970 and 1972, when it reached over 47,000. Approximately six of every ten alleged racial discrimination. Over 85 percent of the complaints were against employers, with the rest against unions, employment agencies, and, in a few cases, against other parties. Complaints of racial discrimination usually involved a refusal of employment, a discharge, or an inferior job classification. Charges of exclusion from unions on the basis of race were relatively rare, accounting for only 4 percent of the racial discrimination charges against unions; complaints about unequal referral practices were more common.

Despite this rising caseload, the EEOC did not have a major impact in its first six years. Unable to use the courts actively, it relied on the conciliation process, seeking written voluntary agreements complying with the legal standards of Title VII; formal decisions were less frequently rendered. The procedures were time consuming, and the results were meager. In fiscal 1972 the commission completed action on over 2800 cases without a formal decision, and in only 412 of them was a written agreement achieved; of the 970 cases closed after a decision was issued, 314 ended with agreements.

Even when conciliation agreements were reached, they had no legal force and thus often produced marginal changes in the marketplace. A typical example involved the complaint of two black women who were twice refused sales jobs in a small Southern general merchandise store in 1966. After an initial investigation established reasonable cause to suspect discrimination, the EEOC negotiated an agreement with the home office of the parent company, which offered the two women jobs and $1300 in back pay. In addition, the company agreed to treat the job applications of blacks and whites equally and to develop policies to recruit and promote blacks. By 1971, however, no substantial changes had occurred. The women had ultimately refused the jobs they were offered, blacks had not filled the two positions, and only one black had been promoted. The EEOC had not checked back to monitor the terms of the agreement. Instead, the home office of the store had issued several policy statements on equal employment opportunities. The overall impact of the conciliation was to benefit the two complaining parties without any continuing influence on black employment or any specific change in company policy.

Such ineffectiveness was not uncommon. On the one hand, conciliations often dealt with less severe discrimination problems. A study comparing firms charged with discrimination by the EEOC with other firms not involved in such actions found that one in four of the respondents had better minority employment records than other similar firms. And the overall effects of the EEOC activities were usually not discernible. In Memphis, Tennessee, where 16 successful conciliations were negotiated in 1967 and 1968, minority employment among employers subject to the law increased from only 29.1 to 29.7 percent for men between 1966 and 1969. In Atlanta, Georgia, where 8 conciliations were successful during 1967 and 1968, minority employment among males dropped from 16.5 to 16 percent.[2] Apparently, there were too few successful conciliations to have a direct impact on total employment in the community, and too few uninvolved employers felt threatened enough to reduce discrimination.

The basic compliance procedure remained unchanged throughout the period prior to March 1972, when the expanded powers became law. However, as court decisions broadened the definition of discrimination and the employers' liability for such acts, the EEOC gained leverage. In 1971 the Supreme Court ruled (*Griggs* v. *Duke Power Co.*) that Title VII "proscribes not only overt discrimination but also practices that are fair in form, but discriminatory in operation." Preemployment tests that were not job related were ruled illegal, since arbitrary achievement tests were more likely to exclude blacks and other minorities. The precedent was expanded to include other job requirements that were not business necessities. The Court ruled (*Gregory* v. *Litton Systems, Inc.*) that a company's policy of refusing to employ people with a number of arrests, but no convictions, was discriminatory because blacks are statistically more likely to be arrested than whites. Perhaps most significantly, a landmark case in 1971 (*Robinson* v. *Lorillard Co.*) established the principle of monetary relief in class action cases and raised the spectre of substantial settlement costs.[3]

The commission's new potential for filing civil court class actions with large settlements caused considerable concern among employers. Many who feared conciliation activities might be abandoned in favor of litigation became much more amenable to the former. In 1973 the American Telephone and Telegraph Company (AT & T) signed a consent decree providing $15 million in restitution and back pay for several classes of female employees and a $23 million promotion package for women and minorities.[4] This agreement was apparently the first shot in a stepped-up campaign, and it was based on a novel approach whereby the company's right to a rate increase by the Federal Power Commission was challenged because of racial discrimination. The EEOC's staff of lawyers was increased more than fivefold in the first six months of 1973, and the goal was to file 600 suits during the succeeding year. Priority was placed on cases involving major companies and unions with large numbers of outstanding charges against them, with the aim of benefiting the maximum number of people with each settlement. In all likelihood, then, the impact of the EEOC will increase in the 1970s, forcing large employers to respond out of fear of reprisal.

Even without strict enforcement actions, the Office of Federal Contract Compliance (OFCC) exerted strong pressure on many contractors, particularly those in aerospace and construction. In 1969 the Department of Labor issued the Philadelphia Plan for affirmative action by federal construction contractors in that city, to be discussed shortly.

Exerting leverage in the marketplace

Another way to pursue equal employment opportunity is to use the market leverage of the government. The OFCC in the Department of Labor is responsible for administering equal employment regulations affecting government contractors. The OFCC was created in 1965 by Executive Order 11246, which forbade discrimination by government contractors on the basis of race, creed, color, sex, or national origin. In February 1970 the OFCC issued orders requiring contractors to examine their utilization of minority workers, to establish affirmative action goals and timetables for filling the goals, and to collect data to demonstrate their progress.

Unlike the EEOC, the OFCC from its beginning has had specific enforcement powers. It could cancel, terminate, or suspend current contracts, and it could blacklist offenders from future participation in government contracts. These enforcement powers applied to companies employing an estimated one-third of the labor force. But the OFCC did not fully utilize these powers, limiting its enforcement thrust to delaying contract negotiations while establishing affirmative action plans with contractors and unions. In only a few cases were contractors blacklisted, and in only one case, that of Edgeley Air Products, Incorporated, in 1971, was a contractor barred.[5]

Despite this power, the OFCC has not had great success in significantly altering extreme or long standing practices of employment discrimination. The major reason is that the problems involve an interrelated system of institutions and interests that supports employment patterns. The OFCC is particularly limited because of its inability to bring action directly against labor organizations, because the latter are not parties to federal contracts. As an example, in 1967 the OFCC found that at the Sparrows Point, Maryland, plant of the Bethlehem Steel Company eight of every ten black employees were working in 14 of the plant's dirtiest and hottest departments, storing coal and manning the furnaces. Each of the company's departments had its own lines of progression, and within the black departments there were few highly skilled jobs. To transfer to a department with better job progression, blacks were required to start at the bottom, frequently losing pay as well as seniority.

In 1968 the Department of Labor ordered the company to give the plant's 5400 black employees the opportunity to transfer to better jobs without loss of seniority. But this settlement violated the terms of the union agreement and threatened the cornerstone of union organization—the seniority system. Whites in other departments felt their advancement opportunities were being threatened, and the complained bitterly. Five years after the original decision, the Department of Labor reviewed the case, reversed itself, and no transfers were affected. The case illustrates inherent difficulties of ignoring existing institutional arrangements and the dangers of failing to consider the potential damages to the interests of the whites involved.[6]

Even where plans are clearly articulated and enforced, changes may not be sweeping. As a result of a Justice Department suit decided in 1971, 1600 black employees in Bethlehem's Lackawanna plant were granted the right to transfer. Given four months to sign up, only 430 did so, and only 70 actually changed jobs. Some were unqualified for the new positions; others with lengthy service saw no advantage in moving as they drew close to retirement; some preferred to stay in departments where they were familiar with the job and with co-workers. Clearly, a longstanding status quo of institutional discrimination cannot be easily erased, even by judicial decree.

This was again especially well illustrated by the meager success of the OFCC efforts to overcome discrimination in the construction trades in Washington, D.C. In 1971 central-city blacks were overrepresented among the 70,000 construction workers in the metropolitan area but grossly underrepresented in the skilled trade segments paying the highest wages. They made up over 90 percent of union laborers, 85 percent of roofers, 87 percent of teamsters, and 71 percent of cement workers but less than 1 percent of electricians and less than 5 percent of glaziers, ironworkers, pipefitters, plumbers, and painters—occupations paying above-average wages.[7]

To combat this discrimination the Labor Department in 1971 initiated the Washington Plan which, like its predecessor in Philadelphia, established goals and timetables for the hiring of minority workers, with the aim of getting the black employment share of skilled workers up to its proportion in the metropolitan population (26 percent).

By May 1972 aggregate data revealed that hiring was already lagging behind the targets for asbestos workers, elevator constructors, glaziers, lathers, painters, and sheet-metal workers. Some contractors were shifting minority employees from nonfederal to federal sites and from one federal site to another to satisfy inspectors. Unskilled minority workers had been hired at the last minute and had been given titles and wages as skilled craftsmen, although in fact they were doing other work. A large proportion were neither apprentices nor union journeymen; rather they were trainees or workers who had been given temporary work permits by the unions. Between June 1968 and May 1971 a hundred extra minority apprenticeships, at most, could be attributed to the Washington Plan, and less than half of those entering could be expected to become journeymen if the usual dropout rate occurred. At best, the impacts of the Washington Plan were marginal.[8]

This modest success was typical of that experienced in other areas. Some attempts were made to meet quotas, and lip service was paid to the regulations, but there was little institutional change. A few blacks were hired in better-paying jobs, certainly justifying the effort, but institutional discrimination will not evaporate in the face of government pressure unless that pressure is more consistent and more forceful than in the past.

In 1974 in an action some observers feel, along with the already mentioned AT & T settlement, might greatly improve employment opportunities for women and minorities, nine major companies and the United Steelworkers of America entered into a consent decree to end a lawsuit filed by the Justice Department on behalf of Peter J. Brennan, Secretary of Labor, and the EEOC. In the settlement, the union and the companies agreed to pay 40,000 minority and women workers $30.9 million in back pay and to set up goals and timetables to increase the number of women and minority workers in areas in which they had been underrepresented. Meeting these goals is expected to cost the companies millions of dollars in higher wages for women and minority workers, who are given preference in moving into previously white male jobs until the goals are reached. A tripartite (union-industry-government) audit and review committee will monitor compliance with the program for five years. Company-union-minority implementation committees are established at each plant to ensure compliance with goals and timetables.

The union and the companies entered into the consent decree in order to avoid what they considered to be the danger that the industry-wide lawsuit would lead to widespread disruptions of seniority rules and the substitution of unworkable regulations written by judges, threatened bankruptcy of many locals, and a possible severe crippling of the international union. The negotiated settlement minimized these dangers. (The only major company refusing to accept the consent decree was Inland Steel, which objected to the implication that it had practiced discrimination in employment.)

The construction industry

The civil rights movement's assault on racial employment practices in the construction industry increased in intensity during the 1950s and 1960s, when black employment opportunities were declining in major Northern metropolitan areas. In a number of cities coalitions of black organizations, formed especially for that purpose, closed construction projects through demonstrations in order to press their demands for more jobs for black workers.

The campaign also was pressed by the National Association for the Advancement of Colored People (NAACP). In announcing new legal attacks, Roy Wilkins, the NAACP's executive secretary, charged that the building trades were the "last bastion against employment of Negro workers as a policy" and said that blacks wanted their just share of the $80 billion budgeted for construction.[9] The NAACP filed suits to enjoin federal, state, and local officials from spending money and proceeding with construction until the job demands of black workers were met. Herbert Hill, the NAACP's labor secretary, said that the association's new thrust would be to develop through law a public policy that would prevent the expenditure of public funds to subsidize racial discrimination.

Simultaneous programs were launched to increase the supply of black construction workers to fill jobs once they opened up. One of these efforts was a program to provide assistance for black contractors, who have traditionally been unable to acquire sufficient labor and capital resources and technical competence to perform large-scale commercial and industrial projects.[10] Organizations of black construction workers also were formed in a number of cities to challenge the building trades unions.

The apprenticeship problem

Civil rights leaders have concentrated on apprenticeship programs because they lead to good jobs in the skilled trades and because there have been very few blacks in them, in part because few black youngsters attempted to enter apprenticeship programs before the 1960s. Moreover, the craft unions' recruitment patterns excluded most black youngsters from any opportunity to enter the system. Blacks also have been disadvantaged in meeting the qualifications for entry into apprenticeship programs. Many programs require high school, and not only does the education level of nonwhites still lag behind that of whites, but many blacks have been handicapped by what Kenneth Clark calls "the massive inefficiency of the public schools where the masses of Negroes go."[11]

In 1963 Secretary of Labor Willard Wirtz approved new federal apprenticeship standards designed to "provide full and fair opportunity for application." These regulations had limited impact for a variety of reasons, but basically it was because few blacks applied for or could meet the qualifications and testing procedures.

In addition to the federal regulations apprenticeship programs are subject to Title VII of the Civil Rights Act of 1964, the National Labor Relations Act, government contract clauses (which require observance of BAT's apprenticeship regulations as a condition of compliance with the executive orders), and various state apprenticeship regulations and equal employment opportunity laws.[12]

Legal sanctions have not been especially successful, although they have perhaps had the effect of creating among apprenticeship sponsors a climate conducive to change; apprentice standards and programs have raised their qualifications. The possibility of sanctions also seems to have strengthened "voluntary" compliance programs. Although sanctions have been used very rarely (because relatively few formal written complaints have been lodged against discrimination in apprenticeship training and because discrimination is difficult to prove), antidiscrimination agencies have succeeded in making investigations that have clarified the extent of black participation in apprenticeship programs and have focused attention on some of the problems involved in increasing the number of black apprentices.

The limitations of legal sanctions led to the creation of apprenticeship information centers to give information about apprenticeship programs and outreach programs to recruit, tutor, and place apprentices. These programs were discussed in Chapter 10, so that one need only note here that they were fairly successful in increasing the number and proportion of minority apprentices. Successful outreach programs have been operated primarily by the Recruitment and Training Program (the RTP was formerly the Workers Defense League), the National Urban League, Building Trades Councils of the AFL-CIO, the AFL-CIO Human Resource Development Institute, and other local organizations in some places. Largely as a result of these outreach programs, the proportion of all apprentices who are members of minority groups has increased steadily since 1960 from only 2.5 percent to 4.4 percent in 1966, 8 percent in 1969, and other 14 percent in 1973. Minorities accounted for only 6 percent of all new apprentices in 1967 but for 17 percent in 1973–1974. In July 1974, when Secretary of Labor Peter J. Brennan reactivated the Federal Committee on Apprenticeship (which had not met for five years), he announced that outreach programs had recruited and registered 30,000 apprentices since 1968.

Although apprenticeship outreach programs have been more successful than any other approach to this problem, it remains to be seen whether they can cause the kinds of changes throughout the country that will replace institutionalized discrimination with institutionalized equal opportunity. So far, however, they have demonstrated the importance of a comprehensive approach to recruiting and preparing black youngsters for apprenticeship programs. Moreover, this approach has demonstrated its effectiveness in getting blacks into other jobs more effectively and at lower costs.

Model Cities

The controversial Model Cities construction programs raised hopes for more jobs for black construction workers, but, by the summer of 1971, these programs were marked more by controversy than by their success in providing jobs for minorities. Much of the controversy centered on the provisions of the Model Cities Act that required maximum participation by residents of areas where housing was being constructed or rehabilitated. The AFL-CIO Building and Construction Trades Department (BCTD) agreed to the employment of residents of these areas in special residential construction classifications, but black militants insist that the programs be controlled by people from the areas. For example, a Model Cities agreement worked out in Boston and based upon the BCTD's guidelines was challenged as tokenism by militant blacks and the NAACP. The NAACP labor secretary called a plan (similar to the one proposed by the BCTD) worked out by the Construction Industry Joint Conference (CIJC) a fraud because it did not assure union membership or preferential treatment of ghetto residents in construction projects.[13] Moreover, according to the NAACP official, jobs would not be controlled by residents of the areas but by "discriminating building trades unions." The unions argue that membership will be available to all who are qualified and to trainees as they qualify. Of course, determination of qualifications is likely to be a continuing source of conflict under the Better Communities Act, which replaced the Model Cities Act in 1974.

Patterns of discrimination

The Justice Department's power under Title VII of the Civil Rights Act to move against patterns of discrimination has raised a number of difficult issues, especially that of the weight to be given to discriminatory procedures adopted before July 2, 1965, the effective date of Title VII. In a suit filed in February 1966 the Justice Department alleged that the St. Louis Building and Construction Trades Council and several of its affiliates had violated Title VII and were tortiously interfering with a nondiscrimination agreement between the United States and a contractor. Action was brought against the unions after their members walked off the job to protest the hiring of a black plumbing contractor and his employees who were represented by an integrated union not affiliated with the AFL-CIO. The unions offered to admit all who were qualified and argued that the strike had been called because substandard workers had been hired not because of race. Although the unions admitted discriminating against blacks before the Civil Rights Act became effective, they argued that they had discontinued their practices and were willing to take blacks who met their qualifications and paid initiation fees and dues required of all new members.

The U.S. Court of Appeals at St. Louis found that Local 36 of the Sheet Metal Workers and Local 1 of the International Brotherhood of Electrical Workers were not guilty of discrimination after the Civil Rights Act became effective but were guilty of a pattern or practice of discrimination in violation of Title VII. The court of appeals ordered modification in the unions' referral systems to require them to place blacks who were "reasonably qualified" in the highest groups for which they were eligible. The court also required one union to modify its journeyman's examination so that tests were objective, relevant to the applicant's ability to do the work, and given and graded in such a way as to permit review.[14] The main impact of the St. Louis case was to uphold the Justice Department's contention that in pattern or practice cases the government does not have to prove specific practices of discrimination after the effective date of the Civil Rights Act. However, unions cannot be held guilty of discrimination committed before the effective date of the act if they ceased their discrimination after that date, although the weight to be given past practices is far from settled. Another area of conflict involves the employment of building tradesmen on state government construction projects when the unions have no black members. In a 1965 New York case[15] plaintiffs brought suit to desegregate all state construction projects in which labor was recruited by nine defendant unions accused of discrimination. The New York Court of Appeals decided the case for the unions, on the grounds that when they worked on public projects, the labor organizations were not state agents and that their actions, therefore, were not "state action" under the equal protection clause of the Fourteenth Amendment to the Constitution.

The NAACP was more successful in a case decided in 1967.[16] A federal district court in Ohio enjoined the state of Ohio from contracting to build a $12.8 million medical science building at Ohio State University until it was assured that the contractor obtained his labor supply from a nondiscriminatory source. The unions did not appeal this case, and the NAACP hailed it as a significant breakthrough in getting blacks into the building trades. The association increased its legal staff from four to eight and planned a series of suits throughout the country relying on the Ohio ruling. The NAACP labor secretary said, "no Negroes, no work." The NAACP executive director said that his organization was calling for "absolute cancellation of building contracts if they do not observe Title VII or the Ohio ruling."[17]

Quotas and preferential treatment

Various programs to increase black employment opportunities in the construction and other industries have raised the highly controversial legal and moral issue of quotas and preferential treatment. Policies proposed by some civil rights leaders and government agencies are based upon the belief that progress in eliminating patterns of inequality requires compensation for past discrimination against blacks. However, unions and employers have resisted these efforts on the grounds that they discriminate against white workers and cause inefficiency.

Affirmative action plans

One of the most important recent controversies over quotas in the building trades came in the summer of 1969, when Assistant Secretary of Labor Arthur Fletcher issued an affirmative action plan for government contractors in the Philadelphia construction industry. The order, designed to implement the provisions of Executive Order 11246, was a revision of a plan initially introduced by Secretary of Labor Wirtz in November 1967 but withdrawn after the Comptroller General Elmer B. Staats ruled that the plan violated the principle of competitive bidding.

However, subsequent investigations, later disputed by the

president of the AFL-CIO, George Meany, revealed that the crafts in question had only about 1.6 percent minority group membership and adhered to practices that resulted in few blacks being referred to jobs. As a result, the Labor Department issued the revised Philadelphia Plan. The revised plan required bidders on government contracts of over $500,000 to "commit themselves to specific goals of minority manpower utilization." Contractors and subcontractors were required to submit affirmative action plans that provided employment goals for six specified trades (ironworkers, plumbers and pipefitters, steamfitters, sheet-metal workers, and elevator constructors) ranging between 4 percent and 9 percent to 26 percent the fourth year. The criteria announced by OFCC in arriving at its standards included the extent of minority participation in the trade, the availability of minority tradesmen for employment, and the need for training programs and the impact of the program upon the existing labor force. The specific goals were "not intended and shall not be used to discriminate against any qualified applicant or employee." Moreover, in the absence of positive evidence of discrimination, if a post-award compliance review found that the successful bidder's goals were being met, the OFCC would assume that the contractor was in compliance with the executive order. Even if the goals were not being met, "the contractor shall be given an opportunity to demonstrate that he made every good faith effort to meet his commitment." But "it is no excuse that the union with which the contractor has a collective bargaining agreement failed to refer minority employees."

The Philadelphia Plan produced strong opposition from some members of Congress, the construction industry, and Comptroller General Elmer B. Staats, who said that the plan imposed racial quotas in violation of Title VII. But the plan also gained some impressive support from influential newspapers, members of Congress, and the Nixon administration and caused a rift in the civil rights and labor forces in December 1969, when the U.S. Senate added a rider to an appropriations bill that would have invalidated the plan. The AFL-CIO lined up in favor of the rider, while many civil rights leaders opposed it. After considerable pressure from the administration, the rider was defeated.

A court challenge of the Philadelphia Plan was initiated by the Contractors Association of Eastern Pennsylvania, which charged that the plan violated the Constitution and laws of the United States and the laws of Pennsylvania. However, in 1970, a federal district court in Pennsylvania upheld the plan as valid under Title VII and the Constitution. The court pointed out that the concept of affirmative action had been upheld as a valid exercise of presidential powers in a number of cases and added:

> The heartbeat of "affirmative action" is the policy of develop-
> ing programs which shall provide in detail for specific steps to
> guarantee equal employment opportunity keyed to the problems
> and needs of minority groups, including, when there are deficien-
> cies, the development of specific goals and timetables for the
> prompt achievement of full and equal employment opportunity.
> The Philadelphia Plan is no more or less than a means for imple-
> mentation of the affirmative action obligations of Executive Order
> 11246.[18]

Moreover, according to the court:

> The plan does not require the contractor to hire a definite per-
> centage of a minority group. To the contrary, it merely requires
> that he make every good faith effort to meet his commitment to
> attain certain goals. If a contractor is unable to meet the goal, but
> has exhibited good faith, then the imposition of sanctions, in our
> opinion, would be subject to judicial review.[19]

Thus the court argued, in effect, that the establishment of goals is
legal but that an attempt to force an employer to meet those goals
might be illegal. Because much turns on the definition of "good
faith" and the procedures to determine qualifications and standards, the issues involved in the Philadelphia Plan obviously have
not been settled. In October 1971 the Supreme Court refused to
review this case, letting the lower court's ruling stand.

In contrast with the Philadelphia Plan, which was imposed
on the industry, the Chicago Plan—signed January 14, 1970, after
months of conflict and negotiation—is very much in the collective
bargaining tradition of attempting to negotiate a settlement among
unions, employers, and minority communities.

The Chicago Plan was an agreement among the Coalition for
United Community Action (comprising of ten civil rights organizations), the Chicago and Cook County Building Trades Council,
and the Building Construction Employers Association of Chicago,
Incorporated. It provided for the recruiting or training of 4,000
black construction workers. Black leaders originally demanded
training and admittance of 10,000 blacks to skilled positions in
90 days and the right to supervise the program, but they scaled
down their demands in order to reach an agreement. At least 1,000
who could qualify for journeyman status were to be recruited by
the coalition and put to work immediately. A second thousand
with 2 or more years' experience in particular crafts, after a 30-
day probationary period, were to be slotted into apprenticeship

programs at a level based upon their experience. Another thousand were to be recruited through an apprenticeship program of outreach and prepared for apprenticeship examinations. For those who failed apprenticeship tests or who did not wish to take them, the Chicago Plan provided for an OJT program, with wages geared to apprenticeship rates, and supplementary schooling through evening classes. These recommendations applied to persons who had lived in Chicago for at least one year, and the plan established a goal of minority participation in the building trades equal to their percentage in the community at large. It was reported at the time of the agreement that there were 90,000 skilled construction workers in Chicago, 3 percent of who were from minority groups.[20]

The Chicago Plan provided for an administrative committee representing Mayor Richard Daley, the coalition, the building trades, and the employers association. Operations committees were established for each craft with four representatives from the coalition and two each from the unions and employers "to formulate and determine particular plans for each craft and industry." However, in spite of the high hopes of those who believed negotiated plans might succeed, the Chicago Plan was in trouble in 1971 because an administrator misappropriated funds. Even before this was discovered, however, the Chicago Plan had encountered difficulties because the Building Trades Council could not bind its local union affiliate and the coalition could not bind the black community. By 1974 several attempts to form a new Chicago Plan had failed because of an inability to reach agreements by all of the groups involved.

While pushing the variations of the Philadelphia Plan, the Nixon administration also attempted a new procedure to resolve these problems in the Seattle area. As indicated earlier, Executive Order 11246 did not give the OFCC authority to apply direct pressure on labor unions, but rather it insisted that the employers were responsible for implementing equal employment opportunity provisions. In 1969 the Justice Department filed a suit asking that five labor unions in the Seattle area be enjoined from practicing racial discrimination.[21] Several settlements with contractors and unions had been negotiated during the preceding months in the Seattle area, but whites walked off when blacks came onto the job. Simultaneously, efforts were made by the black workers, aided by the American Friends Service Committee, to get workers into the construction industry. The black workers' organization —the United Construction Workers Association (UCWA)—apparently played a major role in getting blacks admitted to construction unions in Seattle by bringing direct pressure to close construction sites and by recruiting applicants for the construction industry after a March 1970 federal court order required the hiring and training of blacks.

The Seattle court order restructured the membership and referral procedures of four construction unions—to make it possible for blacks to enter these trades and unions more easily. As a consequence of all of these measures—the law suit, organization of black construction workers, and outreach activities to recruit and place black workers—over 400 blacks obtained jobs in the Seattle construction industry between July 1970 and August 1971.

In the Seattle case the judge, largely due to continued pressures from the UCWA, initiated a new and potentially useful procedure—the establishment of a court-ordered advisory committee comprising representatives from employer, union, minority, and public groups. This advisory committee served as a forum to bring the parties together and to open communications among them and thereby diffuse hostility.

In July 1974, after dissatisfaction with the results of the "hometown" plans, of which the Philadelphia and Chicago plans were examples, the Department of Labor imposed mandatory hiring goals on 101 local building trades unions involved in 21 hometown plans. These goals were imposed after the OFCC determined that the participants in these places were not making an effort in good faith to meet voluntary standards for increasing minority participation. The OFCC did not release statistics showing the extent to which the hometown plans had failed, but a 1973 survey of 31 of 70 government-approved plans showed that less than a third of the local unions had met their goals.

At about the time the OFCC imposed the mandatory goals, the EEOC released figures showing that minority membership in building trades unions reporting to that agency increased by 2.4 percent between 1969 and 1972. Minority membership was relatively much greater in the laborers, painters, roofers, and trowel and miscellaneous trades than it was in the more highly skilled mechanical crafts (Table 21-1). These patterns are not unlike those of other industries in which minorities are heavily concentrated among the lower-paying occupations. If anything, few other industries offer minorities relatively as many high-paying opportunities as the building trades.

Conclusions on hometown plans

The main conclusion about areawide agreements is that they show considerable promise when efforts to make them work are made in good faith. However, they are not likely to be very effective when unions and employers continue to resist the employment of minorities. But insistence by community leaders that they have

Table 21-1 Minority Membership in Building Trades, 1972

	Total Union Membership	Minority %
Mechanical Trades	600,049	6.9
Boilermakers	32,804	11.4
Electrical workers	237,719	7.5
Elevator constructors	9,066	5.5
Ironworkers	84,931	9.3
Plumbers, pipefitters	189,814	4.2
Sheet-metal workers	45,715	6.9
Trowel and Miscellaneous Trades	626,609	10.7
Asbestos workers	9,569	3.7
Bricklayers	32,646	13.1
Carpenters	366,215	11.4
Lathers	2,978	14.2
Marble polishers	3,125	15.2
Operating engineers	183,207	6.2
Plasterers and masons	28,869	32.5
Laborers, Painters, Roofers	377,793	37.5
Laborers	295,563	43.4
Painters	67,446	14.8
Roofers	14,784	23.4
Total Building Trades	1,604,451	15.6

Source: Equal Employment Opportunity Commission-based on 1972 reports from 2615 local unions.

complete control over the programs ordinarily will encounter opposition from unions that fear a dilution of standards and increased competition for jobs and from employers who are concerned about efficiency and costs. Industries with strong apprenticeship programs are particularly likely to encounter disagreement over taking workers into the skilled trades through means other than apprenticeship. Unions also are likely to continue to resist programs based on quota systems and preferential treatment. In the South, however, where there is a history of racial quotas on government contracts, some union leaders accept negotiated quota systems as a way to protect the interests of whites and blacks. In the South quota systems have had the appeal of simplicity because they do not concern themselves with the mechanism whereby the quotas are met. If the quotas are compatible with labor supplies, they also ensure results in terms of minority employment. However, the quotas merely transfer racial conflict to negotiations rather than solving it altogether.

The debate over the Philadelphia Plan did not resolve the issues, in part because the protagonists addressed themselves to different questions. The defenders of the programs argued for the legality of the executive order and affirmative action, not whether quotas or goals could legally be imposed; opponents of the plan argued that it required quotas—which was not the case, at least in the sense that employers would lose the contracts for failing to hire a fixed number of black craftsmen.

Although the Philadelphia Plan may have stimulated areawide agreements, the latter have the advantages of goals without the emotional conflict accompanying the preferential treatment problem, even though at this writing, neither the Philadelphia Plan or the hometown solution has produced significant results. Nevertheless, the outreach concept has demonstrated its efficacy wherever its essential components are present. Administrators of outreach programs set their own achievement goals in consultation with the Labor Department or the appropriate funding agency or in negotiations with the parties involved. (It is significant that both Chicago and Philadelphia adopted goals.) Disadvantaged persons are given special help to meet entry requirements but are expected to meet the same performance criteria as anyone else. Unlike the Philadelphia Plan, which attaches goals to government contracts because of the limitations of the executive order, the outreach program can attach goals to a labor market and leave recruitment to the agency administering the plan. The agency also can render supporting services to help applicants meet objective industry criteria. Under the outreach concept the costs of helping the disadvantaged are borne directly by the government rather than by contractors, who are not likely to be as effective at recruiting the disadvantaged and rendering supportive services as a specialized agency can be. Of course, the outreach concept has the advantages and disadvantages of voluntarism, although the disadvantages are offset by other antidiscrimination pressures on unions and employers.

Although it is a key factor in minority participation in the building trades, inadequate attention has been given to the qualifications question during conflicts with the construction industry over black employment. The question is important because, in the absence of some agreement over the definition of a particular craft, it is difficult to see how black workers in those crafts are to be identified and put to work. Although the technical difficulties involved probably account for the inadequate attention given to this question, other factors undoubtedly are at work. For one thing, a prevailing assumption seems to be that there are many fully qualified black construction workers who are ready to be put to work but who are unemployed or underemployed because of union discrimination. To some extent, this idea rests on the belief that the construction industry has exaggerated its qualifications for discriminatory reasons. There also seems to be a middle-class bias that qualifications and standards really are not too important for manual crafts—an assumption that *all* manual jobs are of low status and, therefore, do not really require mathematics or a four-year apprenticeship.

Public representation in determining qualifications is more important than attempting to agree on specific qualifications and standards for each craft. However, the standards and qualifications established for journeymen should be applied to whites who have worked in unionized sectors of the construction industry as well as to blacks who have been excluded from those sectors for racial reasons.

Of course, what many people fear is that quotas and preferential treatment will cause blacks with less-than-minimum qualifications to be hired ahead of more-qualified whites in order to compensate blacks for past discrimination. Regardless of its short-run consequences, this kind of preferential treatment has serious long-run implications. No better statement of this point can be made than the following comment by the noted psychologist Clark:

> I cannot express vehemently enough my abhorrence of senti-mentalistic, seemingly compassionate programs of employment of Negroes which employ them on Jim Crow double standards or special standards for the Negro which are lower than those for whites.
>
> This is a perpetuation of racism—it is interpreted by the Negro as condescension, and it will be exploited by them. Those who have been neglected and deprived must understand that they are being taken seriously as human beings. They must not be re-garded as peculiar human beings who cannot meet the demands more privileged human beings can meet. . . . I suspect that the significant breakdown in the efficiency of American public educa-tion came not primarily from flagrant racial bigotry and the delib-erate desire to create casualties but from the good intentions, namely, the sloppy sentimentalistic good intentions of educators to reduce standards of low-income and minority group young-sters. . . .[22]

Segregated seniority rosters

Efforts to desegregate or integrate seniority rosters have involved many issues similar to those raised in the construction industry, as well as some that are unique. Indeed, in many ways the seniority question is more complex than the issues raised by minority participation in the construction industry. This is an important area because of the prevalence of job segregation, especially in the South, where institutionalized discrimination confined blacks to agriculture and the most menial or undesirable nonagricultural jobs, and because desegregation is essential to significant improvements in black employment patterns. The main issues raised by this question relate to whether blacks are to be compensated for past discrimination when seniority rosters are merged; whether company or plant seniority will be used for blacks alone or for blacks and whites; and whether such impediments as wage reductions, time limitations, and loss of pay will be permitted to deter integration.

Considerable attention was devoted to the segregated seniority issue by various government contracting committees during and after World War II. However, the impact of the contracting committees was limited by their inherent weaknesses and the fact that they concentrated on industries in which blue-collar employment was declining.

By the time of the Civil Rights Act, only token integration of blacks had taken place in major Southern manufacturing plants. In addition to the factors previously mentioned, seniority integration was impeded by the fact that many blacks hired as laborers lacked the education and experience to move up. Conversely, many senior blacks would have been forced to accept lower wages and lose job seniority in order to enter the bottom jobs in previously all-white lines of progression. Because seniority is a jealously guarded right and influences the profitability of industrial plants, it is not surprising that the terms under which seniority rosters are desegregated are such a controversial and complex issue.

An important pre–Civil Rights Act decision came in the 1959 Whitfield case, in which the U.S. Court of Appeals for the Fifth Circuit ruled that it was legal for unions to permit blacks to transfer to the bottom of the formerly all-white line of progression.[23] However, the Whitfield decision has not been followed in a series of post–Civil Rights Act cases.

In the 1968 Quarles case departmental seniority at the Philip Morris plant in Richmond, Virginia, was held not to have been illegal per se. However, a system based on previous discriminatory practices was not legal, if employers "maintain differences in employee operations which were the result of discrimination before the Act went into effect."[24] In this case "the restrictive departmental transfer and seniority provisions . . . are intentional, unlawful employment practices because they are imposed on a departmental structure that was organized on a racially segregated basis." The court also concluded that Title VII of the Civil Rights Act "does not require that Negroes be preferred over white employees who possess employment seniority. It is also apparent that the Congress did not intend to freeze an entire generation of Negro employees into discriminatory patterns that existed before the Act." The court required the company to permit permanent black employees who had been discriminated against to transfer into formerly all-white departments on the basis of company seniority. However, the Quarles decision, which has been relied on in other cases,[25] reduced the seniority rights of temporary black employees and did not disturb the departmental seniority system.[26]

Partly because the Supreme Court refused to review it, the Crown Zellerbach case has been regarded as a landmark decision by many civil rights leaders.[27] In this case, brought by the Justice Department under Title VII and Executive Order 11246, a U.S. court ruled that a departmental seniority arrangement at the company's plant in Bogalusa, Louisiana, violated the Civil Rights Act. As in Quarles, the court held that blacks who had been discriminated against could be promoted to jobs that they were qualified to perform on the basis of company and not departmental seniority. Moreover, the court held that "institutional systems or procedures which deny to Negroes advancement to jobs held by whites with comparable mill seniority and ability consistent with [the] employer's interest in maintaining [the] skill and efficiency of [his] labor force . . . must be removed." These institutional arrangements included prohibitions on promotions of more than one job slot at a time in instances when intermediate jobs did not afford training necessary for the next higher jobs or when employees had acquired the necessary training through temporary assignments; requiring black employees to enter the previously all-white lines of progressions below those steps necessary to provide training for the next higher jobs; limiting time intervals for promotion to periods longer than necessary to learn the job before promotion; and "deterring Negro employees from transferring to formerly all-white lines of progression by requiring these employees to suffer a reduction in wages and a loss of promotional security as a condition of transfer."

In the 1970 Bethlehem Steel pattern or practice case, a U.S. district court in New York found that a multiple-unit seniority did not itself violate Title VII if that system "was not and is not designed or motivated by racial discrimination." However, because of the company's discriminatory hiring and assignment practices, the seniority system "operates in such a way as to tend to lock an employee into the department to which he is assigned."[28]

Although the courts' rulings on the question of the remedies for discrimination might appear confusing and many of the issues remain to be resolved by the Supreme Court, some consistent threads seem to be emerging. With respect to imposition of affirmative action programs to correct pre–Civil Rights Act discrimination, the courts seem clearly to have held that no penalties can be imposed for preact discrimination, but that procedures adopted prior to the act cannot be continued where the procedure was clearly adopted for discriminatory purposes, as was the case in Quarles and Crown Zellerbach. However, both of these cases, and Griggs[29] and Bethlehem, recognized that there might be legitimate business reasons for the practice of job seniority if it is not designed to perpetuate discrimination.

These and other rulings in the building trades raise the question of the effectiveness of the pattern or practice suits. The Justice Department has been attempting to establish some general principles in this area in order to avoid a case-by-case approach, but a U.S. district court observed in a leading case:

> . . . while recognizing the desirability for enforcement purposes of having general propositions answered by the judiciary in categorical terms one way or the other, the court is convinced that both the proper administration of the statute and the goal of equality in employment opportunity will best be served by the essentially pragmatic approach of judging each case in the light of its own facts and the actual problems to be resolved.[30]

Conclusions on legal remedies

Obviously, the direct impact of state, federal, or local civil rights legislation and court decisions on black employment has been very limited. In part, the limitations of legal procedure are due to correctable defects such as inadequate funding and the EEOC's limited enforcement power. Moreover, the agencies themselves should be encouraged to coordinate their activities, although some differences among them are inevitable because of their different missions, constituencies, and powers. It is also possible to observe a trend toward strengthening legal remedies—from the relatively weak NLRB decisions before the Hughes Tool case in 1964 and the even weaker wartime FEPC and government contracting committees to the strong affirmative action requirements of OFCC and EEOC and the Justice Department under Title VII.

Even with all foreseeable improvements, however, legal procedures are incomplete tools in the fight for equality for a number of reasons. For one thing, under our system the evolution of the law and legal principles is a slow process. Experience to date suggests that there is little hope of avoiding a case-by-case approach, especially in the seniority cases, in which different racial histories, technologies, and skill requirements make it very difficult to generalize.

Legal sanctions, moreover, can do more to strike at overt forms of discrimination than they can to change the paterns that permeate social, political, and economic institutions. Hopefully, of course, measures that curtail overt discrimination also will initiate changes in the institutionalized patterns; but by generating conflict, legal approaches also cause a hardening of racial positions, thus stiffening resistance to change.

Legal approaches also are limited because, in the economist's language, they operate only on the demand side of the problem and do little to change supply. Lowering the racial barriers does not ensure a supply of qualified people to take advantage of new opportunities. Positive approaches such as the outreach programs are required for this. Affirmative action programs, which tacitly recognize this, can change supplies where they are established by consent decrees or by voluntary programs. However, under Title VII, employers and unions can be compelled to stop discriminating against blacks, but they apparently cannot be compelled to recruit actively and to train them.

Experience with antidiscrimination programs seems to support the following conclusions:

1. Antidiscrimination measures are necessary but not sufficient to eliminate institutionalized discrimination in employment. These measures must be supplemented on the supply side by outreach programs.

2. While there is considerable apprehension by the collective bargaining establishment about the detrimental effects of the civil rights challenge, government agencies and courts seem, in general, to have strained to preserve traditional collective bargaining procedures. However, federal courts apparently are in no mood to permit subterfuges that perpetuate discrimination under the guise of legitimate business practices. In Seattle, Columbus (Ohio), Cincinnati, and other places courts have ordered unions and employers to adopt measures to cure racial discrimination through reducing the unions' control of apprenticeship, referrals, and the determination of standards and qualifications.

3. The hometown plans, outreach programs, and the Model Cities agreements suggest that collective bargaining can yield, however reluctantly, to demands for greater participation by minorities in rule making. Indeed, the Chicago Plan was negotiated in the collective bargaining tradition of settling a dispute. How-

ever, the hometown plans still have not proved themselves, and the impact of the civil rights challenge will depend upon the collective bargaining establishment's willingness and ability to take steps to ensure equal opportunities for employment. The parties will lose control of hiring, promotion, training, and referral systems that perpetuate discrimination. Just as federal controls were imposed on voter registration procedures when the states attempted to adopt seemingly neutral qualifications that nevertheless barred blacks, federal controls will be imposed on collective bargaining institutions that attempt to hide behind qualifications that, although seemingly fair and neutral, perpetuate discrimination.

4. The imposition of affirmative action requirements raises some difficult questions. The parties to collective bargaining should actively encourage programs such as apprenticeship outreach and plans to recruit and train minorities. Programs should help minorities meet entry and job performance standards, but they should not permit lower performance standards for minorities than for whites. Outreach programs should establish agreed-upon goals, but they should resist the establishment of rigid quotas. If apprenticeship outreach goals had been quotas, there would be fewer minority apprentices because the programs have almost uniformly exceeded their goals. Quotas, especially when imposed by the government, will generate unnecessary friction and ordinarily involve racial discrimination against either minorities or whites.

5. The establishment of fair and relevant qualifications and standards is essential to the resolution of many conflict areas in collective bargaining. Fair procedures for establishing standards and qualifications, with outside participation, would go a long way toward closing the credibility gap between the collective bargaining establishment and minorities and others outside the system.

6. The segregated seniority question is complicated by considerable diversity in technology and local realities. However, it will be difficult to continue practices that were designed to discriminate because of race and that deter job integration. Federal courts have preserved employers' rights to demand that upgraded workers be qualified and have not eliminated job or departmental seniority per se.

7. In spite of differences in priorities and conflict over the speed of employment integration, which have strained black relations with unions, the mutual benefits of collective bargaining and the civil rights–labor political coalition make it unlikely that most minority leaders will seek drastic changes in the collective bar-

gaining system, especially if credible efforts are made to include minorities in the benefits of that system.

Conclusions on minority employment

The causes of unequal employment opportunities and patterns are very complex and, therefore, will require that remedies be taken on many fronts. Antidiscrimination measures have an important role to play, but they are not sufficient to cause changes to take place. A tight labor market and adequate job vacancies also are important, but tight labor markets alone will not solve the problem if discrimination and unequal access to education and training bar blacks from meeting job requirements. In the final analysis, all of these conditions coupled with special remedial programs such as the apprenticeship outreach programs seem to offer some chance for success.

Statistics on actions, successful settlements, and policies of the EEOC and OFCC provide only some of the clues to their real impact. There may be, for instance, important spillover effects as employers change their practices in fear of government sanctions. Voluntary affirmative action efforts may also result from appeals to corporate consciences. If even small marginal changes are widespread, the impacts can be very beneficial for minorities. In 1972 there were over 3 million nonagricultural business establishments with payrolls, and if only one in six hired another black, the unemployment rates of whites and blacks could have been equalized. On the other hand, there may be many institutional impediments that remain obdurate. Court orders and government mandates may receive only nominal support from employers.

One way to estimate the net impact of OFCC, EEOC, and federal court actions is to compare the experience of firms that have government contracts with those that do not. The assumption is that the former would be more responsive to governmental affirmative action policies. Data for a sample of over 40,000 establishments filing EEOC reports on minority employment in both 1966 and 1970 showed that, after controlling for firm size and region, firms with government contracts increased their employment of black men by 3.3 percent more than those not doing business with the federal government. In firms having no black employees in 1966, those with government contracts were 10 percent more likely to have hired at least one black male than those without. The employment effect was largest in firms having more than 500 employees. But the occupational upgrading of blacks was only slightly greater in government contracting firms. Overall, the wage share of black workers in the average firm with government controls increased by 28 percent between 1966 and 1970, compared with 25 percent in other firms.[31]

While such gains are modest in terms of changing discriminatory practices, it may be that none would have occurred either in contracting or noncontracting firms had no governmental efforts been exerted on behalf of blacks. In general, the marginal changes in the behavior of a number of firms may have had a substantial impact for blacks. On the other hand, evidence suggests that progress has been meager in overcoming more serious impediments to equal opportunity.

Notes

1. Lester C. Thurow, *Poverty and Discrimination* (Washington, D.C.: Brookings Institution, 1969), Chap. 12.
2. Arvil V. Adams, *Toward Fair Employment and the EEOC: A Study of Compliance Procedures Under Title VII of the Civil Rights Act of 1964* (Washington, D.C.: U.S. Equal Employment Opportunity Commission, August 31, 1972), pp. 117–122.
3. U.S. Equal Employment Opportunity Commission, *Sixth Annual Report* (Washington, D.C.: GPO, March 30, 1972), pp. 23–24.
4. Karen E. DeWitt, "Labor Report/Strengthened EEOC Accelerates Action Against Business, Labor Employee Discrimination," *National Journal* (June 23, 1973), pp. 913–923.
5. Adams, op. cit., p. 101.
6. Maia Licker, "Bringing Equality to the Nation's Steel Mess Is a Long and Bitter Task," *Wall Street Journal* (August 8, 1973), pp. 1, 21.
7. Robert Taggart, *The Manpower System in the District of Columbia: At a Critical Juncture* (Washington, D.C.: National League of Cities–U.S. Conference of Mayors, March 1973), pp. 80–87.
8. Sar A. Levitan, William B. Johnson, and Robert Taggart, *Still a Dream*, (Cambridge, Mass.: Harvard University Press, 1975) Chap. 13.
9. *New York Times*, September 3, 1969, p. 43.
10. G. Douglas Pugh, "Bonding Minority Contractors," in William F. Haddad and G. Douglas Pugh, eds., *Black Economic Development* (Englewood Cliffs, N.J.: Prentice-Hall, 1969).
11. *Social and Economic Implications of Integration in the Public Schools*, seminar on manpower policy and program, U.S. Department of Labor, Manpower Administration, Office of Manpower, Automation, and Training (Washington, D.C.: GPO, 1964), p. 6.
12. F. Ray Marshall and Vernon M. Briggs, Jr., *The Negro and Apprenticeship* (Baltimore, Md.: Johns Hopkins Press, 1967).

13. *Wall Street Journal*, March 29, 1968, pp. 1, 26.
14. *U.S.* v. *Sheet Metal Workers, Local 36, and IBEW, Local 1*, 416 S 2d 123 (1969), 2 FEP 128. No. 68-C-58 (2), 1968. *U.S.* v. *SMW*, two FEP cases, 128.
15. *Gaynor* v. *Rockefeller*, 15 N.Y. 2d 120, 204 N.E. 2d 627, 256 N.Y.S. 2d 584 (1965).
16. *Ethridge* v. *Rhodes*, 268 F. Supp. 83.
17. *New York Times*, June 28, 1969, p. 61.
18. *Contractors Association of Eastern Pennsylvania* v. *Shultz*, D.C.E. Pa. (1970).
19. Ibid.
20. Seth S. King, "Chicago Negroes Win Accord on Construction Jobs," *New York Times*, January 13, 1970, p. 28.
21. *U.S.* v. *Local 86, International Association of Iron Workers, et al.*, 315 F. Supp. 1202 (W.D. Washington 1970); 443 F. 2d (9th Cir. 1971).
22. Kenneth B. Clark, "Efficiency as a Prod to Social Action," *Monthly Labor Review* (August 1969), pp. 55–56.
23. *Whitfield* v. *United Steelworkers*, 263 F. 2nd 546; cert. denied, 360 U.S. 902.
24. *Quarles* v. *Philip Morris, Inc.*, D.C.E. Va. (January 4, 1968).
25. *Irvin* v. *Mohawk Rubber Co.*, 380 S. Supp. 152 (1970), two FEP cases (1970).
26. Herbert R. Northrup, *The Negro in the Tobacco Industry* (Philadelphia: University of Pennsylvania, 1970), pp. 78–80.
27. *U.S.* v. *United Paper Makers*, Local 189, 71 LRRM 3070 (1969); cf. *Hicks* v. *Crown Zellerbach, Corp.*, 69 LRRM 2005 (1968).
28. *Daily Labor Report*, April 24, 1970, p. A-1.
29. *U.S.* v. *Duke Power Company*, 91 S. Ct. 849 (1971), 3 FEP, 175.
30. *U.S.* v. *H. K. Porter*, 296 F. Supp. 40.
31. Orley Ashenfelter and James Heckman, "Changes in Minority Employment Patterns, 1966 to 1970" (Washington, D.C.: Equal Employment Opportunity Commission, January 1973), mimeo., pp. ii–vii.

five

---

labor
markets
and
eco-
nomic
policy

22

manpower and economic policies

The goals of manpower programs fall into three general categories. First, the programs seek to help match the supply of and demand for labor, increasing the efficiency of the labor market mechanism. Second, they are aimed at helping workers who suffer particular disadvantages in competing for available jobs. And finally, in the broadest sense, they are designed to provide every worker the vocational preparation needed for the occupation of his choice, while at the same time ensuring that societal labor requirements will be met.[1]

Given currently limited public and private manpower resources, only marginal progress can be expected in the realization of these goals. Some frictional unemployment will always remain—when workers search and prepare for new jobs and are temporarily unemployed or when employers relocate or close their businesses. Seasonal and cyclical trends in employment continue. Some structural unemployment will exist as long as technology continues to make some skills obsolete, as long as many entrants to the labor force are ill prepared, and as long as the supply and demand for labor do not match perfectly. Workers will never have complete freedom of choice nor will industry's needs be exactly met when the future is uncertain, and particularly when those needs are not the same as workers' preferences.

Nonetheless, a persuasive case can be made that manpower programs can minimize these labor market imperfections. Through improved labor market services—such as better reporting of job vacancies, testing, outreach, and counseling—the duration of unemployment and the number of unfilled jobs may be markedly reduced. Through special rehabilitation and training programs for disadvantaged workers, combined with increased efforts to break down discrimination and restructure jobs for those with few skills, workers with deep-seated and long-lasting employment problems can become more productive and self-sufficient. With increased education and training for work, with better vocational guidance, and with firmer projections of occupational demands, workers can increasingly be placed in occupations of their choice in which their skills will be used productively.

Measures to increase the productivity, reward, satisfaction, and availability of employment are potentially far-reaching. Such improvements would affect all those who are in, can be drawn into, or will eventually enter the labor force, especially those who would encounter the most problems in their work lives. Because of this potential impact manpower programs must be recognized as an increasingly important economic factor. To be fully effective manpower efforts must be put to work in concert with other government economic policies. Therefore, the relationship between manpower policy and the other economic policies of the government should be carefully examined and articulated.

Monetary and fiscal policies

The major objective of government economic policy is to regulate the aggregate demand for goods and services, which, in turn, affects the level of total output. Monetary and fiscal measures are the major tools. By changing the quantity of money in circulation (monetary policy), the government can stimulate or cool down business and consumer spending. As more money is made available, consumption increases, profits rise, interest rates fall, and investment is stimulated. Conversely, as the quantity of money is reduced, money incomes rise less quickly, so that consumers spend less and funds for investment are more difficult to acquire, decreasing aggregate investment. By changing its taxing and spending (fiscal policies), the government can change the amounts of cash in the hands of consumers and adjust its own demands for goods and services. Tax increases and reduced government spending will lead to a decline in aggregate demand, while tax cuts and increased government spending will add to demand.

One of the major reasons for regulating demand is to balance the economy's production of goods and services with consumption and, in turn, to generate an economic climate in which the labor needed to produce these goods and services will be fully employed. This was articulated in the Employment Act of 1946, which exhorted the federal government to assume a continuing policy to promote maximum employment, production, and purchasing power. Monetary and fiscal policies can be used to alter the level of unemployment by affecting the demand for final products, which, in turn, changes the demand for labor. Arthur Okun, one-time chairman of the President's Council of Economic Advisers, estimated in 1962 that for every 1 percent increase in real GNP, unemployment is reduced by 0.3 percent. Though the exact figure has been modified by subsequent experience, "Okun's Law" suggests a rather straightforward relationship between monetary and fiscal measures regulating aggregate demand and the level of unemployment.[2]

Monetary and fiscal policies also affect the level of prices. When the economy is running near or at full capacity, a sudden increase in spending can pull prices upward; demand-pull inflation is the result. A policy contracting the money supply is one way to attempt to control this type of inflation. But a more disturbing and more difficult type of inflation to treat is the cost-push variety because it may occur while unemployment is above full employment and while production is below capacity. It arises largely from imperfections in the market that allow unions and corporations to push costs and, therefore, prices up. A special case of these inflationary forces is the ability of business and labor to prevent wages from falling in declining sectors of the economy as demand shifts to growth areas. Aggregate demand controls are not likely to cure cost-push inflationary ills, and policy makers may be forced to consider some form of market intervention.[3]

Attempts to regulate prices may have significant side effects throughout the economy. Maintenance of full employment is, of course, not the only goal of monetary and fiscal policy. By affecting the domestic price level, these policies change the relative attractiveness of exports and imports, altering the balance of trade and the balance of payments. By regulating the pattern of business, consumer, and government spending and by changing aggregate economic conditions, these measures affect the level of investment in the short run and the rate of economic growth in the longer run.

Structural versus demand-deficient unemployment

The relationship of manpower policy to monetary and fiscal measures has been a source of controversy in recent years. Some economists claim that structural unemployment has increased markedly, as more and more workers have become obsolete because of technological change. According to this theory, there has occurred a twist in the demand for labor, so that educated and skilled workers are in short supply while large numbers of unskilled and poorly educated workers are no longer needed. If this is the case, an increased demand for goods and services will lead to wage increases in the occupations with a deficient supply of labor and to subsequent price rises. Though less skilled workers will be hired, a high level of inflation may also result, rendering impractical the necessary monetary and fiscal policies. Manpower programs, it is argued, are needed to train and retrain disadvantaged workers for available jobs and to employ those who cannot be trained.

There is continuing debate over the magnitude of such structural changes in the economy—and, consequently, over the policy implications. In the early 1960s argument raged openly between structuralists and those who urged a cut in taxes to increase aggregate demand and thereby reduce unemployment.[4] A tax cut, combined with the Vietnam build-up, did cut unemployment sharply. The 4 percent unemployment rate reached by the end of 1966 temporarily weakened the case of the structuralists, who had argued that such expansionary fiscal policies would have unacceptable inflationary consequences.

Low unemployment after 1965 postponed debate for some time, but with rising unemployment in 1970, the arguments resurfaced over proposals for an enlarged public employment program. Structuralists claimed that such a measure was needed to provide for an ever-increasing number of workers whose skills were no longer required by the industrial system. Reviewing past experience, they asserted that much of the decline in unemployment after 1964 was due to (1) the induction within three years of an additional 800,000 men into the armed forces, many of whom have either been unemployed or would have filled jobs opened to disadvantaged workers; and (2) counting manpower program enrollees as employed, an accounting practice that reduced reported unemployment by about 0.5 percent.[5]

Economist R. A. Gordon has suggested that part of what was previously thought to be structural—unemployment among teenagers and blacks, for example—was due to high turnover rates among those workers rather than prolonged periods of unemployment.[6] Although vacancies may exist in a low-wage sector, workers displaced in the high-wage sector may choose not to switch due to the potential high wages or other attractions of the high-unemployment sector; in this case unemployment may more accurately be called "differentially high frictional unemployment." True structural unemployment only exists when workers wish to, but cannot, move to fill job openings in other sectors. This type of structural unemployment calls for a breakdown of discrimination based on age, sex, and race, which segments labor markets. Efforts leading to the reduction of labor turnover and improvement in job search techniques would decrease long-term frictional unemployment.

A review of the labor market experience of disadvantaged workers during the sustained prosperity of the 1960s tends to bolster the structuralists' arguments. Unemployment rates for those with poor education declined, for example, but their labor force participation rates went down even more.[7] These developments highlight the fact that monetary and fiscal measures must work along with manpower programs and antidiscrimination policies to train, retrain, and give the structurally unemployed greater mobility in the labor market.

Manpower programs as a countercyclical tool

While manpower policy is an increasingly important adjunct to monetary and fiscal policies over the long haul, it has only recently been applied to the short-run goal of controlling business cycle fluctuations. Monetary and fiscal measures have been reasonably successful in limiting the more pronounced fluctuations in economic activity, which once seemed inevitable, and they have proved their ability to maintain sustained growth; nevertheless, minor business cycles still exist. In recent years real growth rates varied from 0.5 percent in 1970 and 1.9 percent in 1960 to 4.8 percent in 1962 and 6.5 percent in 1972. The business downturn in 1974 clearly indicated, if any proof was needed, that postmortems for the business cycle were premature or at least that periodically engineered slowdowns may be necessary to reverse the upward spiral of inflation. Until the implementation of the Emergency Employment Act in 1971 manpower policy played little or no role in efforts to control economic fluctuations. Manpower expenditures and programs expanded continuously throughout the 1960s but were applied without any countercyclical intent. With the passage of the act, however, and the subsequent success of this program, public employment was added to the manpower arsenal as a new tool for countering business downturns. From this and other manpower efforts a number of lessons have been learned concerning the effectiveness of different strategies during periods of varying economic conditions. (An overall review of lessons learned from manpower programs was presented in Chapter 16.)

First, regular manpower programs oriented toward the private sector are most effective in tight labor market conditions. Subsidies to hire and train disadvantaged workers, to induce business to locate in depressed areas, or to eliminate discrimination will have their greatest impact when qualified workers are in short supply and when firms are expanding and opening new plants. Conversely, when firms are forced to lay off employees because of declining demand, when they have excess capacity and are trying to eliminate all but their most efficient plants, and when fears of unemployment lead to employee antipathy toward newly hired disadvantaged workers, OJT or locational subsidies will be less effective.

Second, public employment is perhaps the most effective manpower strategy for holding down unemployment during cyclical troughs. Analyses have indicated that public service jobs offer the greatest "bang for the buck" in terms of lowering unemployment with a given amount of federal investment. Simulations by the Federal Reserve Board estimated that a billion-dollar expenditure for public employment would reduce the unemployment rate 0.2 percentage points—more than an equal increase in federal government procurement or other grants-in-aid. A substantial proportion of the workers hired came from the disadvantaged segments of the labor force, thus providing help to those who were hurt worst by the business cycle.

Apparently, public employment can be expanded or contracted with little difficulty, if funds are available. Many thousands of public service jobs require little or no training and only a small capital investment, and people can be put to work on these jobs as a temporary measure with little prior notice. Within six months of the passage of the Emergency Employment Act, over 140,000 workers had been placed on state and local payrolls, and according to subsequent evaluations, they were performing real rather than make-work jobs.

Third, public-sector training becomes more important and effective in slack times, if for no other reason than to fill the gap left by declining private-sector participation. Institutional training provides at least income maintenance and perhaps useful training and basic education. Loose labor markets reduce trainees' chances of opting for jobs instead of training and diminish pressures by employers on training institutions to speed the delivery of trainees. Under these circumstances trainees are more likely to complete manpower training courses. Since placements and employment rates are closely correlated with duration of training, institutional training programs probably become relatively more effective during slack times.

Fourth, manpower programs serve a different clientele when unemployment is high than when jobs are plentiful. Increasingly during the 1960s, the more seriously disadvantaged workers were helped—to a large extent because of expanding employment opportunities generally. The labor queue moved forward rapidly, and the disadvantaged became next in line for employment and hence were most in need of manpower services. The fact that the manpower programs emphasized the needs of the unskilled, poorly educated, and members of minority groups subject to discrimination does not mean that the process is irreversible. In all programs there is a tendency to "cream" the available and intended clientele for those most likely to benefit from assistance. When demand slackens, less disadvantaged workers seek out and are selected for manpower programs, so that those with more severe problems receive less attention. For instance, as unemployment increased after 1969, the average family income of participants under the program subsidizing employers for hiring disadvantaged workers rose, indicating the selection of a less disadvantaged group.

Fifth, labor market services should be adjusted to changing economic conditions. When jobs are plentiful, the employment service can not only function as a labor exchange, but also reach out to disadvantaged persons to provide them with needed counseling and services and induce them to seek and find employment. However, when unemployment is high, fewer employers turn to the employment service, and those that do can choose among recently employed and less disadvantaged workers. This is the time when job development and placement efforts should be increased, even though they will be less successful in terms of placement. While the recently unemployed should be aided in their return to the labor force, the hard-core unemployed should not be ignored. If private jobs cannot be found, they must be directed to manpower programs or to public employment.

These five lessons suggest that, if manpower programs are to be administered in a countercyclical way, there must be flexibility to shift among different programs and approaches as economic conditions change. Since control over most manpower funds has been shifted more to the states and localities under CETA (1973), this goal can only be met by concerted and coordinated efforts of local manpower administrators, coupled with an incentive system of federal payments geared to business conditions. This could be accomplished either by appropriating additional funds to local manpower programs during economic declines or by establishing a standby federal public employment program that might be implemented when unemployment passed a certain level. This trigger mechanism might provide that manpower funds or public employment moneys be released when unemployment reached a predetermined level, say, 4.5 percent. Public employment funds could be added if unemployment continued to climb. For example, for each 0.5 percent increase in unemployment above 4.5 percent, an additional 10 percent increase in manpower funds might be provided. Thus if unemployment rose to 6 percent, manpower funds would rise by 30 percent. Alternatively, the public employment program might be designed to soak up a percent of total excess unemployment above a predetermined acceptable level. Under this approach it may be decided that sufficient government funds would be released to hire 25 percent of the excess unemployment. This would mean that when unemployment reaches the 6 percent level, it would require federal funds to hire about 425,000 unemployed workers. The formula might also be applied in determining allocations for each state and locality, to help depressed areas that are especially hard hit by rising aggregate unemployment.

While conceptually appealing and justified on humanitarian grounds, there are a number of formidable obstacles to the use of manpower training as a countercyclical tool. Difficulties exist not only in forecasting manpower needs in local labor markets but also in estimating current conditions. Manpower planners often cannot estimate skill shortages, and since skill training takes some time, manpower programs face a timing problem. Training programs could aggravate unemployment by increasing the supply of labor and could contribute to inflation if their costs are not kept relatively low.

There are problems, too, in expanding and contracting public employment in a countercyclical fashion. Economic contractions since World War II have averaged less than a year in length, barely enough time to initiate large-scale public employment efforts. The best that could occur in such periods is for existing programs to be expanded. Still, any reasonable expansion in manpower programs would absorb only a small proportion of recession victims. At its peak the Emergency Employment Act employed only 3 percent of the nation's unemployed. Enrollments in all the manpower programs funded by the Labor Department in 1973, exclusive of short-term summer youth programs, equaled about one-tenth of all those unemployed during the year. Manpower policy is hardly a substitute for monetary and fiscal measures in controlling economic fluctuations.

Nevertheless, manpower programs have a vital if limited role to play. While aggregate-demand management can change the level of unemployment, the effects must filter down through the economy. For instance, an increase in spending to reduce unemployment will lead to increased profits and increased earnings for those already employed as well as to the hiring of some additional workers. Manpower expenditures, however, are directed specifically to those who are most in need of help. For any dollar of expenditure, manpower programs probably have more impact on unemployment than other types of spending, and expansion of such programs may be the best way to help the unemployed when demand slackens.

The trade-off between inflation and unemployment

It is a fact of life that as unemployment is reduced and the pool of employable labor is diminished, firms must pay higher wages and salaries and/or accept workers of lower productivity. This increases the labor cost per unit of output, and in order to maintain their profit margins firms must increase their prices. The ultimate cost of goods and services to the consumer is raised, with the inflationary pressures intensifying as the supply of idle manpower decreases. The accepted strategy for achieving greater price stability is to reduce aggregate demand—which will lead to the termination of less productive workers, some reduction in wage and salary demands, and thus to falling labor costs per unit of output. Price stability, therefore, is facilitated by a higher level of unemployment.

Although the relationship between price changes and the level of unemployment is not exact—as the rising inflation and rising unemployment of the early 1970s regrettably demonstrated—it has tended to be inverse as shown in Figure 22-1 by plotting the changes in the cost of living and level of unemployment. In determining the thrust of its monetary and fiscal policies, the government must balance the harm caused by inflation with the bitter consequences of unemployment—though the latter may be reduced by unemployment insurance payments and other forms of income transfers. The trade-off is not made explicitly, but pressures mount for more inflationary monetary and fiscal policies when unemployment grows, and policy makers are more ready to accept the consequences of additional unemployment when wages and prices accelerate too fast. At any given time, there is some preferred point on the curve toward which monetary and fiscal policies are directed. This is suggested in Figure 22-2 by a series of indifference curves, I_1, I_2, and I_3. All combinations of unemployment and inflation rates represented by a single curve are equally acceptable to the formulators of public policy. The curves are concave because at lower rates of unemployment policy makers will be more willing to trade off increased unemployment in order to reduce hyperinflation and vice versa. They would prefer both a lower rate of unemployment and inflation—that is, any point on I_1, to any point on I_3, but they are indifferent to the combinations represented by any one curve.

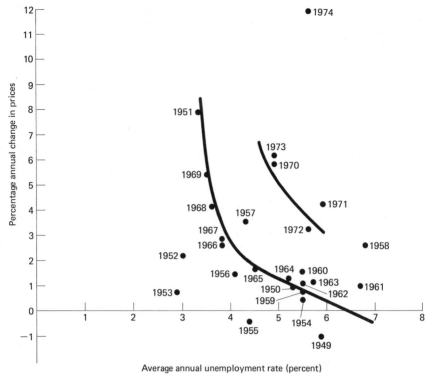

Figure 22-1   Annual changes in consumer price index and level of unemployment, 1949–1973.
Source: U. S. Department of Labor.

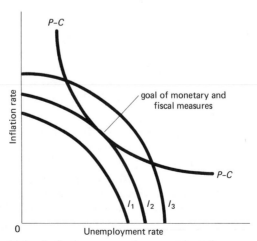

Figure 22-2   Inflation-unemployment indifference curves.

The attainable combinations are represented by the Phillips curve, the *P-C* line drawn in the chart. In choosing the goal of monetary and fiscal measures, policy makers will try to move to the lowest possible indifference curve. This is the one that is tangent to the Phillips curve, or I_2 in the diagram.

Although the correlation of higher rates of unemployment and lower rates of inflation appears to have broken down in recent years, some still argue that in the long run the continuation of high unemployment will bring prices down. To explain the persistence of inflationary pressures in a relatively high unemployment economy, it is argued that it takes the economy longer to change its inflationary expectations than it used to. To ameliorate the dire consequences of high unemployment and inflation policy makers have attempted to develop strategies that would shift the Phillips curve to the left, bringing both unemployment and prices down.

Shifting the Phillips curve

One hope for manpower policies is that they might alter the structure of the economy so that the terms of trade-off between unemployment and price changes is improved, or, in technical terms, the Phillips curve is shifted leftward and any given level of unemployment can be achieved with less effect on prices—or, in terms of Figure 22-2, society can move to a preferred indifference curve. Rehabilitation and training programs, for instance, might reduce structural unemployment by preparing technologically displaced or educationally disadvantaged workers for useful work. Unemployment will be reduced and prices will be lowered to the degree that the social benefits of the training programs exceed their cost. Improved labor market services that increase the rate of placement reduce the waiting time between jobs and thus the level of unemployment. If the mobility of workers can be improved, jobs will be filled that would otherwise have remained vacant and would have raised prices in the tight labor market areas. Thus improved placement, counseling, outreach, and mobility-inducing measures could reduce frictional unemployment, resulting in a decline in both prices and unemployment. Finally, manpower efforts to improve vocational training and counseling for all workers and to ensure a supply of skilled laborers where they are needed may increase productivity to the degree that preparation for employment is improved and output is higher in more personally satisfying employment; and such efforts may reduce the pressure on prices from labor bottlenecks. Helping those with the most severe labor market problems and the highest rates of unemployment will reduce the disparities among the unemployment rates of various groups in the labor force and, in turn, lower the pressure on wages so that there will be less price rise at any level of unemployment.[8]

The impact of past manpower programs on the trade-off between unemployment and the rate of price change cannot be measured. Claims that manpower training efforts have shifted the Phillips curve to the left (or at least slowed its shift to the right) are based on faith rather than empirical evidence. The effects of increasing manpower expenditures are undoubtedly dwarfed by other changes in the structure of the economy. Also, their impact will probably be felt only in the longer run because the payoff on manpower expenditures comes in increased earnings and productivity of assisted workers over many years. If increased manpower expenditures should result in a large positive effect, manpower policy should have an important role alongside the monetary and fiscal measures, making possible a more favorable trade-off between inflation and unemployment.

The policy mix

The fluctuations in price change and unemployment rates in the post–World War II period resulted not only from exogenous economic factors but also from misapplication of monetary and fiscal tools and changing notions about the proper trade-off between inflation and unemployment. During the Eisenhower years, more emphasis was given to fighting inflation than to lowering unemployment. The government's tight monetary and fiscal policies were blamed for the recession of 1958 and 1959. The Democratic victory in 1960 is frequently attributed to the high level of unemployment, which reached 6.8 percent in December 1960. Promising to "get this country moving again," President Kennedy emphasized the need for full employment, proclaiming an interim goal of 4 percent unemployment. To this end he proposed an income tax cut, which was not initiated until 1964, after President Johnson assumed office. During the Johnson administration, increasing employment was still given priority over fighting inflation. Budget expenditures increased markedly without adequate monetary restraint or taxation, with the result that prices began to rise too fast and a surtax had to be implemented to cool the economy.

In 1968 the Republicans were voted into office pledging to stop the rise of prices. Tacitly, GOP economic advisers acknowledged that this would probably be accompanied by a rise in unemployment to a level estimated at 4.3 to 5 percent; the rate actually rose to 6.2 percent, reviving charges of Republican insensitivity to unemployment. In the early 1970s administration planners reverted to expansionary monetary and fiscal policies, which stimulated renewed economic growth and trimmed unemployment. Again the inflationary push became severe, but half-hearted wage-and-price controls resorted to in 1971 did little to arrest inflation. While the shifts in policy were not always explicit —because both parties gave lip service to the incompatible goals of unemployment *and* price stability—it is clear that there have been some major swings in public preferences over the past two decades.

The fact remains, however, that monetary and fiscal policies can only move the economy toward a more preferred position on the Phillips curve, or at least in a preferred direction. Measures affecting aggregate demand can reduce unemployment only at the expense of accelerated price rises, though the trade-off may not be exact.

Incomes policies

The progression from monetary and fiscal measures to increase aggregate demand to a derived demand for more labor, an increase in wages, and a resulting increase in prices is far more complex in reality. As a result, monetary and fiscal measures to expand or contract the economy do not always have the desired impact on the levels of unemployment and/or prices. For instance, in 1958 restrictive monetary and fiscal policies were applied to brake the rise in prices. While wholesale prices took another year to stabilize, unemployment remained high, averaging 6.1 percent of the labor force for the 1958–1961 period. In 1970 this same phenomenon occurred but at different levels. Consumer prices rose twice as fast as in 1958 despite restrictive monetary and fiscal policies; unemployment continued to climb, though not reaching the peaks of the earlier years.

The explanation for these aberrations is that our economy is not perfectly competitive. Most goods are produced by firms having some degree of control over prices, while labor unions and other associations of working people, such as professional associations, have some power to maintain or raise their wages or money incomes. There is a consequent rigidity in prices and wages because large firms are reluctant to lower prices and union bargainers will rarely accept wage reductions, even when sales and employment are slack. Perhaps even more serious, some firms with excess capacity and declining sales will raise their prices to bolster falling profit margins, labor unions will sometimes press for wage increases despite rising unemployment, and service industries will take advantage of shortages that may persist even in a recession. Concentrations of market power can thus lead to rising prices, wages, salaries, and fees despite reductions in aggregate demand.

The measured empirical relationship between unemployment and price changes reflects these structural characteristics of the economy. To the degree that corporations and labor unions have market power that they use to maintain or raise prices and wages where aggregate demand is falling, the trade-off between unemployment and price rises will have worsened. And because market power implies discretionary behavior, the reaction of the economy to any monetary and fiscal measure has become less predictable. One method of attempting to gain greater control over the economy is to enforce some type of regulation over wage-and-price changes, instituting what is called an incomes policy.

Wartime controls

Because the regulation of wages and prices involves the transfer of power from the private to the public sector, wage-and-price controls were historically a wartime phenomena prior to 1971. They have been used to allocate goods to military needs and to ensure that lower-income families get a fair share of scarce commodities, which otherwise would be available only to those able to pay inflated market prices.

During World War II, the National War Labor Board, made up of business, labor, and other public representatives, was established to administer wages, while the earlier mentioned Office of Price Administration was set up to stabilize prices and rents and to regulate the rationing of scarce goods. The mechanisms for controlling prices and wages were generally rated as successful. From 1914 to 1920, with only the very limited controls of World War I, average hourly earnings rose 142 percent and the cost of living 100 percent. From 1941 to 1945, when controls were in full effect, wages rose 40 percent and prices 22 percent despite more severe labor shortages and a more prolonged war.

Controls were also instituted during the Korean hostilities, which lasted from June 1950 until February 1953. Despite relatively mild inflationary war pressures, prices rose much more rapidly during the control period of the Korean War than during World War II. By the time wage-and-price controls were instituted, about eight months after the outbreak of hostilities, most of the inflationary pressures generated by the military action had run their course; and the wage-and-price controls administered by the Wage Stabilization Board and Office of Price Stabilization remained a holding action, providing insurance and standby machinery in case the limited Korean action spread into a full-blown war.

Though experience with these wartime controls is not directly transferable to peacetime conditions, it highlights several issues that are relevant under any circumstances. Most obviously, the almost universal rejection of controls after both wars raises questions about their effectiveness and the difficulties of substituting regulation for the allocative efficiency of the free market in the long run. For instance, the pent-up postwar consumer demands and the expressions of serious labor unrest after World War II suggest that distortions had occurred in the rationing process and that resumption of market functions was necessary to relieve them. There is also the basic issue of how to allow wages to adjust to the cost of living. The National War Labor Board rejected arbitrary freezing of wages and permitted wages to catch up to the increases in cost of living prior to the imposition of controls in October 1942. After that period the wage-and-price controls were maintained, and no general wage increases were permitted until the war was won. Despite the inflationary pressures, President Franklin D. Roosevelt insisted that no increases in prices and wages could be tolerated. "The only way to hold the line," he declared, "is to stop trying to find justification for not holding it here and not holding [it] there."[9] This meant that wages could not be adjusted to increases in cost of living and that values in consumer products deteriorated. The policy was effective as long as the support of the war remained universal. Such widespread support was lacking during the Korean period, and the inflationary pressures were milder; therefore, wage-and-price controls were much less stringent than in World War II.

Even though there was little change in money wages, wage controls raised problems concerning changes in hours of work, pensions, fringe benefits, shift premiums, vacations, upgrading, and merit or length of service increases. During both wars, these forms of remuneration increased markedly, frequently in lieu of general wage increases. Some of these resulted in deferred increases that were reflected in increased labor costs after controls were removed, and others raised unit labor costs immediately but did not show up in average hourly wage or salary schedules and, therefore, could be glossed over by the regulatory officials. Finally, there is the issue of raising the wages of workers receiving substandard earnings. Equity dictates that such increases should not be controlled, and even the rigid regulations of World War II permitted such increases. But raising wages of low-paid workers reduces wage differentials and encourages higher-paid workers and their unions to press for wage increases in order to maintain historical advantages.

The guideposts

The problems inherent in wage-and-price controls argue persuasively against peacetime controls. However, when inflation combines with high levels of unemployment, the public becomes amenable to some degree of control. This was the case in 1962, when President Kennedy, through his Council of Economic Advisers, announced a set of voluntary guidelines for price and wage changes. They carried no penalty for violation and were intended to show business and labor the limits of good behavior compatible with price stability. The guideposts set forth by the Council of Economic Advisers coupled wage-and-price increases to overall productivity growth, suggesting that the rate of wage gain or price adjustment should follow output per manhour and unit labor costs.[10]

Many complications were concealed by these simple rules, and some exceptions were recognized explicitly by the council. Wage increases could exceed the guidepost rate in industries or areas that attracted insufficient numbers of workers. Prices could rise, or at least fall more slowly, in industries unable to attract capital to finance expansion, but they should rise at a lower rate where profits were being earned because of market power. Because almost every firm or industry could claim an exemption on one of these grounds, the guideposts were far from clear cut. Nevertheless, the central idea was that wage and price changes would depend on productivity changes.

From 1962 to 1964 these guideposts were enforced with varying enthusiasm and success. Though there were no sanctions imposed on industries or unions violating the rules, the government applied a variety of pressures from "jawboning" to market retaliation. Whether the guideposts had any impact outside the few cases of active intervention is debatable. Studies comparing wage and price changes during guidepost years with those of earlier years suggest that annual wholesale price changes were between 0.5 and 1.5 percent less than expected and that annual consumer price increases were reduced, on the average, by 0.5 percent. These reductions were probably due to the guideposts, though their significance has been questioned, since in the long run suppressed wage and price increases are likely to exert themselves. At most, the impact of the guideposts was not large, and it could not check the price increases that resulted from increased war spending.[11]

Peacetime wage and price controls

The prolonged economic expansion of the 1960s, stimulated by government spending without tax increases, built up severe inflationary pressures in the economy that spilled over into the 1970s. The rate of inflation reached 5 percent in 1970 even though business conditions had deteriorated, with unemployment topping 6 percent in December. When consumer prices continued to rise during the first half of 1971, despite continued 6 percent unemployment, the administration elected to institute a 90-day wage-price freeze followed by nationwide wage-and-price controls.

Congressional sentiment for the adoption of an incomes policy had been building for some time. Indeed, the freeze action taken by President Nixon was based on legislative authority passed earlier by Congress—over the President's protest. Though the move was distasteful to the President and his economic advisers, there seemed to be few alternatives that would convince the public that the government was committed to combating inflation. Moreover, inflation aggravated the balance-of-payments situation. Fiscal and monetary policy alone no longer seemed capable of tuning the economy to a politically acceptable combination of inflation and unemployment necessary for both foreign and domestic confidence in American business.

From the initial freeze through four successive phases of wage and price controls, the impacts of controls were disputed. Some argued that controls were political window dressing that had little effect independent of business and credit conditions—Milton Friedman referred to the controls as cosmetics, at best. Others felt controls were too successful, creating distortions in the allocation of resources and hurting wage earners worse than employers. There was support for both sides. When controls were finally ended in 1974 with inflation racing ahead at more than 10 percent annually, there was a general consensus that, though controls might have accomplished some specific goals for a limited time, over the long run they were both ineffective in regulating powerful market forces and disruptive of the economic system.

The three-year experiment with regulated wages and prices did not produce unequivocal evidence about the impacts (or lack of them) of controls. It did, however, establish more clearly the parameters and limitations of incomes policies. Several conclusions stand out:

1. Controls are of little use in curbing the inflation caused by

excess demand in an overheated economy. When controls are imposed under such conditions, they tend to create shortages and dislocations in the economy, frequently exacerbating rather than curing the problem.

2. Wage and price controls and/or freezes may have had some impact in limiting the inflation caused by expectations or by the market power of large economic units. The initial freeze and the first period of controls apparently did temper inflationary expectations. When controls were lifted, the surge in consumer spending indicated that expectations of rising prices had been revived. The evidence indicates that controls can be of use in holding down prices and wages in sectors that are temporarily subject to excess demand. The rapid increase in subsidized medical care, the shortage of gasoline, and the rapidly rising contruction wages in the surging housing market were three situations in which controls curbed what probably would have been excessive increases. For this purpose stand-by monitoring and stick-in-the-closet control mechanisms appear to be warranted.

3. The life of any control system is limited. If controls are not to be administered by a large enforcement agency, they must depend largely on voluntary cooperation. Public willingness to abide by the regulations quickly evaporates if controls are viewed as unfair. Less quickly, but just as surely, the usefulness of controls will diminish in time, even though the public accepts their equity. If controls are successful, there will be calls for their abandonment as unnecessary. If they fail, the arguments will be that they should be ended because they are useless. In a freely competitive economic system, all factions seldom agree that they are receiving their due; when the government is the arbiter, everyone soon feels cheated.

This was crtainly the course of events under economic stabilization. Initially, bipartisan congressional sentiment, business, labor, and academic groups supported or at least were willing to try controls. Once controls were implemented, however, defections began quickly. By the time controls were ended in 1974, there was hardly a voice raised in their defense. Business claimed its profit margins had been unfairly crimped and its investments thereby curtailed. Labor claimed it had been the "patsy" accepting wage hikes within the guidelines while prices climbed far faster.

4. The imposition or retention of controls during periods of excess demand harms labor's interests more than those of business. Overall, the control period did not dramatically help or hurt anyone, despite the complaints from all sides. The share of national income going to employees in the private economy remained relatively stable from 1970 to 1974. But during 1973, with the

economy expanding and corporate profits booming, real hourly earnings leveled off and then declined. Part of this trend was due to the sudden acceleration of the inflation rate in 1973. Few were prepared for the sharp increase in prices, and even the labor contracts with cost-of-living escalator clauses seldom fully protected workers. This unexpected erosion of wages should prove temporary as the price rise slows or as labor negotiates catch-up increases and more adequate cost-of-living adjustments.

It appears, however, that controls aimed at curbing the market leverage of large economic units are more effective in holding down wages than prices during cycles of business expansion. With unemployment remaining over 5 percent throughout most of the control period, there was never any generalized labor shortage such as might be experienced in wartime and thus no natural demand pull on wages. At the same time, union bargaining power was compromised by the 5.5 percent guideline, and non-union employee leverage was no doubt also hurt, as employers could claim a legal and moral right to limit salary raises. But controls were unable to check demand-induced inflation of prices. Under pressure, prices rose rapidly, while wages, in the absence of excess demand for labor, could not rise as easily. Initially, perhaps, during the slack, economy controls on those with market power may have been equally effective against both large corporations and large unions. The experience during the crest of the business cycle, however, indicated that labor was squeezed between continued wage guidelines and inadequate price controls.

Wage and price controls remain controversial. Apparently, the rising costs of raw materials, the changing mix of the labor force, the increasing skill requirements of the job market, and rising inflationary expectations are continuing to shift the Phillips curve to the right, with ever higher levels of inflation associated with given levels of unemployment. Though wage-price controls have been discarded, President Ford was apparently persuaded by the potential salutory impact of the monitoring device, and he prevailed upon the Congress to revive this tool when he ascended to the presidency. Clearly, however, neither incomes policies nor manpower programs can be relied upon to solve the problem of the unemployment-inflation trade-off. Monetary and fiscal policies are still the prime levers controlling the trade-off between unemployment and inflation. Controlling wages and prices, improving the workings of the labor market, retraining workers, and employing workers on public payrolls can be helpful in tuning the economy to the best possible point on the Phillips curve, but they cannot be relied on to solve the chronic problems associated with rising levels of unemployment and inflation.

Notes

1. William G. Bowen, "What Are Our Manpower Goals," in R. A. Gordon, ed., *Toward a Manpower Policy* (New York: Wiley, 1967), p. 59.
2. Arthur Okun, "Potential GNP: Its Measurement and Significance," *Proceedings of the Business and Economic Statistics Section of the American Statistical Association* (1962), pp. 98–104.
3. Jerry Pohlman, *Economics of Wage and Price Controls* (Columbus, Ohio: Grid, 1972), pp. 44–52.
4. The opposing views are presented by Walter Heller and Charles C. Killingsworth in Garth L. Mangum, ed., *The Manpower Revolution* (Garden City, N.Y.: Doubleday, 1965), pp. 97–146.
5. Charles C. Killingsworth, "Rising Unemployment: A 'Transitional' Problem?" in U.S. Congress, Senate Committee on Labor and Public Welfare, Subcommittee on Employment, Manpower, and Poverty, *Hearings on Manpower Development and Training Legislation* (Washington, D.C.: GPO, 1970), Part 3, pp. 1254–1267.
6. Robert A. Gordon, "Some Macroeconomic Aspects of Manpower Policy," in Lloyd Ulman, ed., *Manpower Programs in the Policy Mix* (Baltimore, Md.: Johns Hopkins Press, 1973), pp. 14–50.
7. Karen Schwab, "Early Labor Force Withdrawal of Men," *Social Security Bulletin* (August 1974), pp. 24–38.
8. George L. Perry, *Inflation and Unemployment* (Washington, D.C.: Brookings Institution, 1970), p. 42.
9. Executive Order 9328, April 8, 1943.
10. *Economic Report of the President, 1962* (Washington, D.C.: GPO, 1962), p. 189.
11. John Sheahan, *The Wage-Price Guideposts* (Washington, D.C.: Brookings Institution, 1967), pp. 79–95.

23

the role of unions and collective bargaining

Labor organizations have become important labor market institutions in all industrialized economies. It is important, therefore, to understand their role in labor markets. In order to do this, however, it is necessary first to outline the origin, development, and structure of unions. This will be followed by a discussion of the role of collective bargaining in labor markets. We conclude with an assessment of the impact of unions on manpower and training programs.

The nature of labor movements

The term "labor movement" means different things in different countries. In most it refers to trade unions, political parties, and other cultural or educational organizations that represent workers. However, in the United States, "labor movement" refers almost exclusively to trade unions.

The differences between the labor movements in the United States and other countries are rooted in political, social, and economic institutions. The main reason American unions have not formed a labor party relates to our political and economic conditions, which have fostered less class consciousness than conditions in European countries. In Europe workers had to form political parties in order to gain the right to vote. The franchise became particularly important with industrialization and the growing importance of government in the lives of individuals. In the United States, however, workers were born free in the sense that they had the right to vote at an early date. It was not necessary, therefore, for the working class to organize itself in order to gain the right to vote. Moreover, unlike European workers, Americans did not conceive of themselves as a permanent working class. In part, this was because no political stigma attached to them by denial of the right to vote. Moreover, the United States did not have feudal traditions as did European countries. Feudalism was a class system whose impact on social relations remained long after the system itself ceased to be important. No titles or other formal class distinctions existed in the New World.

Although American workers had serious problems—which they sought to alleviate through collective bargaining and the political process—they were comparatively better off than their European counterparts. Their economic well-being was due, in large part, to relative labor shortages as the United States was being developed. Economic mobility made it difficult for socialists, who were active in the United States at a very early date, to organize workers on a class basis. As the twentieth-century American socialist leader Norman Thomas put it, socialists had difficulty gaining labor support in the United States because American workers found it easier to rise out of their class than to rise with it.

The American political system also has worked against the formation of a labor party. Because of the vast power of the Presidency, a political party must have some chance to elect a President in order to become significant nationally. However, the manner in which the American President is elected gives great advantage to major national political parties and makes it very difficult for third parties to become established. In European parliamentary systems the chief executive is elected by parliament and not from geographic areas. Moreover, those systems sometimes have proportional representation, which gives urban workers more equal representation. As a consequence, minority labor parties can exercise political influence in selecting prime ministers by participating in coalitions within the parliament and gradually building their political strength to become majority parties.

Another aspect of the two-party tradition in the United States that makes it difficult for third parties to get started is the ability of the major parties to incorporate popular features of third-party platforms, thus co-opting popular issues with workers and other voters. As a consequence of lack of class consciousness, relative economic mobility, and the American political system, the American labor movement was organized mainly around the job.

Although American workers were relatively better off economically than their European counterparts, they had serious problems that they sought to redress within the political system and through collective bargaining. Moreover, American unions had to overcome stiff opposition from employers and governments in order to achieve their status as generally accepted institutions. Before the 1930s employers generally were free to oppose unions by a variety of tactics, including discharging workers for union activity; requiring employees to sign yellow-dog contracts (agreeing, as a condition of employment, not to join unions); planting company spies in union ranks; blacklisting union members; making it difficult for those discharged for union activity to find new jobs in their localities, crafts, or industries; and intimidating union members and organizers with armed guards and physical violence.

Governments not only permitted use of these antiunion tactics, but actively opposed unions by a variety of tactics of their own. The courts interpreted many union tactics as being illegal and often nullified legislative attempts to outlaw yellow-dog contracts and other antiunion tactics. The Sherman Antitrust Act of 1890 was used against union activities and courts issued injunctions against strikes, picketing, and boycotts. Injunctions were particularly onerous to unions because they could be issued by proemployer judges without a hearing and be sweeping in their prohibitions. Union leaders and members were subject to fines and imprisonment for defying these injunctions, however unfair their restrictions. Therefore, labor leaders had to spend considerable amounts of money and time defending themselves against hostile judges.

Also at the state and local levels, courts were hostile to unions as were legislatures and governors. Union organizing, strikes, picketing, and boycotts were actively counteracted by state officials, who used state and local police to curtail union activity.

Unions also suffered from periodic recessions and depressions before the 1930s. Even without government opposition rising unemployment made it very difficult for workers to win strikes. Recessions and the hostile legal environment made it difficult for any other than the strong craft unions in the transportation, printing, and construction trades to become very well established before the 1930s.

The social ferment of the 1930s created an environment much more favorable to union growth, though workers with limited skill—like those in agriculture, Southern textiles, food processing, sawmills, and other low-wage industries—continued to have great difficulty getting organized. The main factors facilitating union growth in the 1930s were:

1. The depression, which was blamed in part on the private enterprise system, resulted in mass unemployment and economic hardship. Sentiment grew that it was good social policy to pro-

mote collective bargaining in order to make it possible for workers to protect themselves from arbitrary employer decision and to combat future depressions by sustaining wages and, therefore, purchasing power.

2. As a consequence of growing acceptance of collective bargaining, new legislation curtailed some traditional antiunion tactics of governments and employers. Courts, which had been particularly hostile to such union tactics as strikes, boycotts, and pickets, became much less hostile. The main favorable laws were the Norris-La Guardia Act of 1932, which limited the use of court injunctions against unions and outlawed the yellow-dog contract, and the National Labor Relations Act of 1935 (Wagner Act) which curtailed employers' antiunion activity, created the National Labor Relations Board (NLRB) as an enforcement agency, and provided for representative elections supervised by the NLRB.

3. Organizing activity was stepped up by intense rivalry between the American Federation of Labor (AFL), organized in 1886, and the Congress of Industrial Organizations (CIO), formed in 1935. The CIO challenged the AFL for leadership mainly around the question of organizing workers along industrial lines (e.g., steelworkers, rubber workers, auto workers, etc.) instead of around particular crafts (electricians, plumbers, sheet-metal workers, etc.). In general, the CIO adopted broader social objectives than the more conservative AFL. The CIO was actively supported by many intellectuals who saw the new federation as a vehicle to reform society. There can be little question that the CIO spurred the AFL to action, but both organizations agreed that rivalry ultimately caused more harm than good. They merged to form the AFL-CIO in 1956.

4. World War II greatly encouraged the growth of union organization, particularly among semiskilled workers. Organization was facilitated by tight labor markets, which made it easy for unions to exhibit gains for the members; a favorable government attitube because the government wanted union cooperation in the war effort; and the activities of the National War Labor Board, which had the power to compel employers—under threat of seizure by the armed forces—to sign collective bargaining contracts.

Despite changes in the political, social, and economic environment within which they operate, the basic character of the American labor movement—its emphasis on collective bargaining and disinclination to form a labor party—remains.

The origin of labor movements

The role of unions and collective bargaining in American labor markets will be illuminated by looking at some of the major forces causing labor movements to start and to develop. Although they disagree over the roles and objectives of labor organizations, most authorities agree that labor movements originated with industrialism. Industrialism invariably creates a number of problems for workers. Chief among these is the fact that the workers depend on employers for jobs in a market often characterized by unemployment. It might be argued that demand and supply will protect workers, but these impersonal forces have little regard for workers' welfare. Industrial societies are characterized by economic instability because of difficulties in maintaining a balance between the production and the sale of goods. Because industrialization causes workers to be dependent on wages, workers have considerable insecurity unless they acquire some means to protect themselves from competitive market pressures.

Producing units in industrial societies also tend to be larger and more impersonal than under preindustrial conditions. Impersonalization makes it necessary for workers to create machinery through which they can express their grievances to management.

Workers in industrial societies may also be deprived of income by factors such as industrial accidents, early superannuation, and illness. Economic security was much less of a problem in preindustrial societies because the family was the basic producing unit. The family took care of its own in time of distress, and in any event was much less dependent on the market than the industrial society family. Industrialization created needs for new social security procedures as the family ceased to be the basic producing unit.

The industrial society, therefore, created a need for workers to have some means of protecting themselves from market forces and of participating in the formulation of rules governing wages, hours, and working conditions. Every industrial society, therefore, has produced the same kind of labor movement. In some cases, the movement is dominated by revolutionaries who believe that the workers' problems are inextricably bound up with the capitalist system and that that system must be eliminated if the workers' problems are to be solved. Other labor movements are socialist-dominated and hold that destruction of the system by revolution might not be necessary, but that solutions to the workers' problems will require considerable modification of capitalist institutions. Specifically, the socialists advocate the public ownership and/or control of all large-scale man-made and material means of production. Socialists believe that control of the socially necessary industries and considerable economic planning will be required to eliminate economic insecurity while maintaining individual freedom and initiative.

American unions have believed they can solve the workers' problems through collective bargaining and political action within the framework of the existing economic political system. Although the movement's ideology is not necessarily immutably fixed, the forces that shaped it for the most part remain—the standard of living, the rate of economic growth, the absence of class consciousness, the nature of the American political system, and the relative success of collective bargaining.

However, it should be noted that the American and Western European labor movements have drawn closer together ideologically since World War II. European socialist labor movements have de-emphasized radicalism and given greater emphasis to collective bargaining, while the American labor movement has become much more active politically since the depression of the 1930s. Indeed, American unions have actively backed much of the social legislation adopted in the United States since the 1930s and have participated in every national campaign.

Labor movements in the developing countries

The labor movements of the developing countries are quite different from those of the United States and Europe. Indeed, when examined from a Latin American or African perspective, the European and American movements appear to resemble each other closely. In Western industrial countries trade unions are likely to be more independent of political leaders and place more emphasis on collective bargaining and economic gains for their members. The labor movements of the developing countries, however, face unique pressures. They have greater difficulty establishing collective bargaining relations with employers, partly because their leaders are likely to be intellectuals whose talents and interests incline them toward political activities rather than collective bargaining. In some countries—for example, India, Indonesia, Ghana, and Israel—the labor movements were used to establish political independence. Collective bargaining also is impeded by the workers' weak bargaining power, caused by labor surpluses and limited skills. A major obstacle in the developing countries is opposition from political leaders who consider collective bargaining to be incompatible with industrialization. The basic argument is that unions increase consumption at the expense of production, promote economic instability, and divert resources from capital formation. Political leaders in these countries, therefore, are likely to insist that unions play a productionist role until the economy is developed, when they can become more consumptionist.

The insistence on a productionist role for trade unions has been advanced by leaders with a wide variety of political persuasions. Countries led by dictatorships have greater power to hold down consumption through centralized planning and the military power of the state. Countries that try to follow democratic procedures have greater difficulty, but their industrializing elites also ordinarily insist on a productionist role for unions. It might also be noted in passing that where labor movements have been used to help countries achieve independence, political leaders have encouraged consumptionist roles for the labor movement before independence and productionist roles after independence.[1]

Factors shaping the American labor movement

An examination of some of the factors shaping the growth of unions in this country will help to explain their current role in the labor market. One of the most important influences has been the spread of markets. Although some labor unions existed in preindustrial times, there was nothing that could really be called a labor movement because these local unions were isolated and rarely came in contact with each other. However, with industrialization and the widening of product markets, workers in formerly isolated labor markets came in direct competition with each other and, therefore, organized in order to protect their wages and working conditions. The spread of the market influenced wages by causing workers as well as goods to compete directly over wider areas. For example, before industrialization, shoemakers in Philadelphia could operate on the basis of the demand-and-supply conditions within the Philadelphia labor market; but with the spread of the market they had to be concerned with competition from shoemakers throughout the United States. Transportation and communications improvements made it possible for merchants to buy in the cheapest market and undermine the wages and working conditions of workers throughout wide geographic areas. In order to prevent wage competition indirectly through the flow of goods or directly through the flow of workers, local unions in various parts of the country formed national unions and federations. The national unions were concerned mainly with the activities of a particular trade or industry, whereas the federations organized different local unions at the city or state level and different national unions (made up of affiliated locals) into national federations. The federations were concerned more with political and interunion matters than with collective bargaining directly. In other words, the spread of the market gave workers all over the United States common interests that they organized to protect and promote.

Another factor influencing the growth of unions in the United States has been the size of firms. In the manufacturing sector, particularly, unionism is directly related to the size of the firms. There are a number of reasons for this. For one thing, large firms are more easily organized by unions because the cost of organizing is less than it would be to organize the same number of workers in many smaller firms. But, more important, employers and employees in large firms rarely have close working relationships. Consequently, rules must be adopted to govern wages, hours, and working conditions. Workers, therefore, are likely to organize either into informal groups or formal trade unions in order to have some influence on the formulation of working rules and some means of redressing their grievances. Grievance adjustment is particularly important in a large firm because of the difficulties involved in communicating directly with management.

Skill levels are also important in determining union growth. The earliest unions to be organized usually were among the skilled workers in the printing and building trades or on the railroads. In such industries, the workers' investment in their skills gives them a common interest to protect. Moreover, a union of skilled workers has more bargaining power than one of unskilled workers because the skilled workers are much more difficult to replace in the event of strike. The ability to inflict damage on an employer during a strike is an extremely important aid to the growth of unions that emphasize collective bargaining. Unions of skilled workers perpetuated their power by controlling the supplies of workers in particular crafts through control of entry into their unions and crafts.

Not all of the unions that have been able to acquire strength in American labor markets have had great skill. Unions of workers located at strategic points in the production or distribution process hold a strategic advantage. For example, teamsters and longshoremen have had very strong unions, mainly because of their strategic location rather than the amount of skill they possess. Their ability to win strikes has been due to the damage they cause by refusing either to move goods or to load or unload ships.

Business cycles have played an important role in the fluctuation of union strength in the United States. As a general rule, unions have gained membership and power during periods of prosperity and lost ground during periods of recession or depression. The reason for this is not difficult to find. During prosperity, the unions' power to win a strike is considerably enhanced because there are likely to be labor shortages and employers are likely to offer less resistance because they can usually pass wage increases to consumers in the form of higher prices. Moreover, employers are likely to lose sales if strikes occur when there are backlogs of unfilled orders. Conversely, during recessions and depressions, employers are under much less pressure to give in to union demands and are more likely, therefore, to offer more resistance. Moreover, employers might be able to win strikes when rising unemployment gives them a plentiful supply of strikebreakers. It should be observed, however, that unions sometimes have gained considerable membership during recoveries immediately following prolonged depressions. At such times workers have accumulated dissatisfactions stemming from the depression period but that could not be translated into union organizing because of their inability to win strikes. As noted earlier, depressions also cause public sentiment, and hence government policy, to become more sympathetic to workers and their organizations. When recovery starts, the workers' power increases relative to that of employers', and union membership thus grows very rapidly.

Wars also have played an important role in the growth of union membership. Indeed, many of the same forces influencing the growth of unions during periods of prosperity are present during war—particularly tight labor markets. Moreover, during wars the government is likely to adopt a more favorable attitude toward unions in order to gain cooperation with war production. Therefore, governments are likely to enhance the prestige of union leaders by appointing them to important positions in the war effort and to assent to other measures that will encourage union growth. Thus a combination of the government's favorable attitude and tight labor markets often causes union membership to increase considerably during and immediately after wars.

These great spurts in union membership are, however, ordinarily followed in the postwar period by counterattacks from antiunion forces that make it difficult for the unions to hold their wartime gains. For example, in the aftermath of World War I came the so-called open-shop movement of the 1920s in which employers all over the United States joined in a concerted effort to reduce union strength. The movement was so successful that this was one of the few prosperity periods when union membership actually declined after reaching a peak in 1920. By the 1930s only the strongest unions had survived.

Public opinion also has an important influence on the growth of unions. Public opinion influences legislation and government attitudes toward unions, as well as the workers' willingness to associate with them as organizations. Ironically, there seems to be some inverse relationship between the unions' public image and their economic power. During the Great Depression of the 1930s, when the unions' economic power declined, their public image benefited from public sympathy for the underdog. Other factors were at work, then, too, of course. Similarly, during World War II and the immediate postwar period, when unions grew greatly and increased their economic power, public support of them apparently declined because they were no longer considered to be the underdog.

Laws and court action also have influenced union growth. As noted earlier, before the 1930s governments—especially the judiciary—were generally hostile to unions and collective bargaining. The legislation and court decisions of the 1930s and 1940s created a more favorable environment. But the tide turned again after World War II. Congress passed the Taft-Hartley Act of 1947 and the Landrum-Griffin Act of 1959 (both of which restricted union activity and made organizing more difficult); many states, particularly in the South, passed antiunion right-to-work laws, which sought to prevent unions and employers from entering into contracts making union membership a condition of employment. Although courts restricted union activities more than during the late 1930s and early 1940, neither they nor other branches of government have returned to the antiunion stances they took before the 1930s.

It is very difficult to gauge the importance of these laws and court decisions for the growth of unions. There seems to be little question that early court hostility hurt unions, particularly those of semiskilled and unskilled workers who were not strong enough to withstand the employers' antiunion tactics. Discharging and blacklisting workers for union activity made it difficult for unions to organize. Moreover, the need to defend themselves in time-consuming and expensive litigation often sapped the strength of unions.

The more favorable legal environment of the 1930s made most of the employers' antiunion activities illegal and greatly reduced the use of injunctions against unions, but it did not necessarily make it easy for unions to organize. The Norris-La Guardia and National Labor Relations acts reduced union-management relations more to a purely economic (instead of physical, economic, and legal) struggle but did not necessarily allow unions to win those economic struggles by striking or boycotting employers. As a consequence, unions in many industries—textiles, food processing, and work clothes, for example—have not been able to organize very extensively. Moreover, in spite of numerous organizing campaigns, unions remain relatively weak in the South. On balance, therefore, the evidence suggests that legislation is only a marginal factor in union growth and that the basic determinants are the economic, strategic, and skill factors influencing a union's ability to induce employers to bargain. A major effect of legislation is the moral climate it creates by crystallizing majority opinion.

Of course, to argue that labor laws have had limited impact on union growth does not mean that governments *could not* influence union growth. The activities of the National War Labor Board clearly stimulated membership in the weaker unions. Moreover, Presidents Kennedy and Johnson stimulated union membership among federal employees by encouraging collective bargaining between federal agencies and unions. The federal government *could* encourage union membership in countless other ways, especially by giving preference in contracts to employers who engage in collective bargaining.

Another factor influencing the growth of unions has been product market concentrations. Since the 1930s concentration of product markets controlled by a few firms has been directly correlated with union strength, as measured by contract coverage. To a very large extent, this relationship obtains because the larger firms tend to have the highest concentration ratios and, as noted earlier, are more likely to be unionized. However, the concentration ratio is a measure of market control as well as size, and those firms that have the greatest ability to control their destinies in the market can tolerate unions more successfully than highly competitive firms such as those in the textile industry that resist unions for fear that collective bargaining will undermine their competitive positions. Also, the change in public opinion during the 1930s apparently influenced the organizability of large firms with high concentration ratios. Before that time large and powerful firms were able to use their political, economic, and physical power to prevent unions from unionizing. With the change in public opinion during the 1930s, however, it became much more difficult for these companies to employ antiunion tactics. Under these conditions it was much easier for the unions to organize large companies.

Public support of collective bargaining

Another force influencing the growth of unions in the United States has been the emergence of general public support for the concept of collective bargaining. When their employees were first organized, many companies dealt with unions as necessary evils, but as these relationships became established, a rationale for collective bargaining emerged that has become widely accepted among unions, employers, and the general public. Some of the main ideas supporting collective bargaining were embodied in the National Labor Relations Act of 1935 and reaffirmed in the Taft-Hartley Act of 1947. One of the reasons for passage of the former act was the belief that collective bargaining was a good anticyclical measure. The depression of the 1930s, it was argued, was caused in part by the workers' inability to organize and bargain collectively and thus maintain their wage levels.

Another rationale for collective bargaining is the assumption that rules governing wages, hours, and working conditions are best made jointly by workers and employers. Indeed, collective bargaining has been considered an extension of democracy to the work place. Rules based on participation, it is argued, are much better than those unilaterally imposed by employers on unions or by unions on employers. Moreover, this form of rule making is considered superior to government-imposed rules because it can be more flexible. The argument continues that the people who experience the problems are in a better position than anyone else to make the rules governing those problems. Collective bargaining, therefore, permits greater flexibility because the rules can be made to fit the circumstances. And collectively bargained rules can be changed more rapidly to fit changing circumstances than would be possible with government regulations.

The idea of participatory democracy, therefore, has been accepted by many employers as a force for social stability. This concept is based on the belief that by participating in the formulation of working rules and joining political organizations workers gain a stake in the system. For this reason many employers support efforts to extend the so-called free labor movements to the developing countries. They feel that collective bargaining will buffer the spread of revolutionary unionism in those countries. Supporters of this idea are impressed by the fact that revolutionaries never seem to make much progress in countries with advanced collective bargaining systems.

Another rationale for collective bargaining is equity. The National Labor Relations Act declared that governments had helped employers gain power by permitting them to form corporate and other forms of business activities but that the power of the state had been used to impede union growth before the 1930s. Thus it was only equitable to protect workers in their right to organize and bargain collectively. This reflected the belief that individual workers had unequal bargaining power when dealing with individual employers and that it was unjust to enforce the freedom of contract between parties who were not of substantially equal bargaining power.

Problems of collective bargaining

Collective bargaining generates many problems. First, there is the problem of strikes, which become increasingly important as the economy becomes more interdependent. The strike creates a dilemma for those who have accepted the institution of collective bargaining without the right to strike. At the same time, strikes can inflict considerable inconvenience, if not damage, on the public. Therefore, much attention has been given to the problem of how to maintain collective bargaining while preventing the damage that might be inflicted by strikes. To date, no effective solution has been found, but a number of remedies have been attempted, including prohibition of strikes by certain workers, mediation and conciliation by outside government or private experts, fact finding by outsiders to narrow the range of disputes and influence public opinion, and labor court systems to settle disputes by judges. The problem with all of these approaches is the fact that they inject an outside opinion and power source into the collective bargaining relationship and thus nullify some of the benefits of participatory democracy discussed previously. In this as in many other matters there is no ideal or unique solution.

Another drawback of collective bargaining is that because it is based on power and conflict it does the most for the people who need it least. The stronger workers in the labor market such as skilled electricians could protect their incomes because of their skills; the weakest workers in the work force, like agricultural or textile workers, those in marginal and submarginal labor markets, have very limited ability to form unions because they have great difficulty winning strikes. However, there is some evidence that unions might be adopting different strategies to organize submarginal and marginal workers. Weapons other than strikes—including consumer boycotts—are being used to bring pressure on employers.

A third problem is the ability of an entrenched labor organization to exclude outsiders for reasons like race, sex, or national origin in order to monopolize labor markets. Moreover, the public interest might be ignored by collusion between strong unions and employers to fix prices. This is a particularly important problem with respect to discrimination against blacks and other minorities. If a union effectively controls the labor market, it can exclude blacks from operating in that market by refusing them admission to the union. This problem is discussed at greater length in Chapter 17 on the economics of discrimination.

Union structure

Union structure tends to define the power relationships among different levels of a labor organization. In the United States the basic labor organization is the local union, which is typically restricted to workers in a particular craft in a local area or a particular industry or group of related industries in a local area. For example, the carpenters in a local construction labor market might be members of a local carpenters union, whereas the workers in an automobile assembly plant might be members of the United Automobile Workers (UAW) local union, regardless of their particular craft or occupation.

Craft and industrial locals differ in several fundamental ways. Craft unions are ordinarily made up of workers who have very limited attachments to particular employers. In the building trades, for example, the craftsmen change employers quite frequently and, therefore, rely on unions for jobs, which gives the union considerable power in the labor market. If the union can control the supply of skilled craftsmen, employers must hire workers through the union. Moreover, labor organizations may have considerable control over training through their control, jointly with employers, of the apprenticeship system. Finally, some craft unions enhance their power in a labor market by influencing licensing arrangements.

The industrial union, however, has very limited control over hiring. Most of its power comes from control over the internal labor market in a particular firm. Its main impact ordinarily is to formalize arrangements that were already in existence. For example, the lines of progression, which determine promotion priorities within the internal labor market, are determined to a significant degree by the logical relationships among jobs, which reflect the technology of a particular process. The industrial union can formalize this relationship, help establish seniority as the main factor determining progression, establish grievance procedures, and exert some influence on wage rates, but these unions ordinarily have much less control of the labor market than craft unions.

Local unions are affiliated with national unions or, if they have locals outside the United States, with international unions. The internationals are combinations of locals within an industry or group of related industries or crafts or groups of related crafts. To follow up our early example with the locals, the local auto workers' union would be affiliated with the UAW nationally, and the local carpenters union would be affiliated with the United Brotherhood of Carpenters and Joiners of America (UBCJ). The UBCJ is an international based mainly on the craft principle, and the UAW is an international composed mainly of local industrial officials. A union is an international when it has affiliates outside the United States—in Canada, for instance—but the terms "national" and "international" are used interchangeably.

Power relationships between local and national unions depend largely on the scope of the market. If the market is mainly local, as in the building trades, the local union has more influence vis-à-vis international unions than would be true if the market were national in scope, as with the automobile industry. But relationships between the local and national unions also are influenced by factors such as the national union constitutions, the political power of the particular local leaders, the power and personality of the national leaders, and the collective bargaining alternatives available to the local if it secedes from the national union. If, for example, the local union can secede and affiliate with another national union, its power in dealing with a particular national union is enhanced. However, the local's ability to continue its collective bargaining relationships depends upon whether the scope of bargaining is national or local. It might be very difficult for a local to pull out and affiliate with another union if all other local unions in the same company in other areas are affiliated with another national union and if all deal with the same company.

The next level in the union structure is the federation. Federations might be city, state, or national. These organizations are comprised of groups of local unions at the city or state levels and groups of national unions and nonaffiliated local unions at the national level. Although their power is probably increasing somewhat, the federations are the weakest link in the American union structure. A city or state federation has very limited power over local unions because locals can continue to operate independently of the federation. Similarly, national unions can and have withdrawn from the AFL-CIO, which has been the main national federation in the United States since 1956, without seriously impairing their collective bargaining position. The United Mine Workers never joined the AFL-CIO, the UAW withdrew in 1967, and the International Brotherhood of Teamsters (IBT) were expelled from the AFL before that organization merged with the CIO in 1956. The federations' main functions are political and mediatory; that is, they represent the labor movement in dealing with public agencies and help settle disputes among the unions affiliated with them. Because the federations are the keepers of the labor movement's conscience, they ordinarily take broader positions on public issues than the national and local unions, which are mainly economic collective bargaining organizations. If the federation were a bargaining agency, as it is in many countries where federations deal on a more centralized basis with employers, its power over the local unions would be strengthened considerably, because expulsion from the federation would cause the national or local to lose bargaining rights. Similarly, the power of federations increases as the importance of the political and mediatory functions becomes more significant.

The impact of unions on wages

Economists have differed sharply over the extent of the union's power to influence wages. Not surprisingly, this topic has received considerable public attention: The impact of unions on wages has significant implications for economic growth and stability as well as for the distribution of income between union and nonunion workers and between labor and other factors of production.

The layman may be surprised to learn that economists have questioned whether unions have much impact on wages. The role of unions generally has been exaggerated by employers, newspaper editors, and even unions leaders, who take credit for wage increases that might have been caused by increasing productivity and rising general price levels. Because wages rise when unions negotiate contracts, many assume that unions cause the wages to rise; actually, some wages increase might have occurred in the absence of unions.

Economists, and particularly economic theorists, tend to minimize policy decisions, especially in the long run, and to emphasize market forces as determinants of wages and employment.[2] The classical view has it that market forces are the only determinants of wages in the long run; but after the depression of the 1930s revealed such obvious "imperfections" in the market mechanism and spurred the growth of unionism and government regulation of wages and employment, few economists could deny the importance of nonmarket forces in wage determination. Nevertheless, most economists continue to give major emphasis to markets in wage determination, even if laymen give greater emphasis to bargaining and policy.

If one compares wages under union and nonunion conditions, economic theory would lead him to expect that the elasticity of demand for union labor would be an important determinant of the unions' impact on wages. If the demand is relatively inelastic, unions will be able to raise wages without greatly increasing unemployment. Elasticity of demand, however, is determined by derived demand, which means that the demand for labor is derived from the demand for the final product and the demand for other factors of production. Economic theory would also lead us to expect that the demand for labor would be more inelastic (1) the more essential union labor is to the production of the final product, (2) the more inelastic the demand for the final product, (3) the smaller the ratio of the cost of union labor to the cost of the product, and (4) the more inelastic the supply of other factors of production.

Although this economic analysis is fairly straightforward, measuring the impact of unions on wages is much more difficult because it is not easy to isolate the unions' influence because this is a problem of multiple causation. For example, unions are influenced by factors such as the ratio of labor cost to total cost and economic conditions, which also influences wage levels. There is consequently a strong positive correlation between the percentage of workers organized in a given industry and wage rates in that industry. However, it is difficult to determine whether unions are strong because of the factors that make wages high or whether wages are high because of the unions. An empirical investigation also might find very little difference between union and nonunion wages because employers in nonunion sectors raise wages in order to avoid unions. If a union established a pattern that was followed by the nonunion sector, measurement of the differences between union and nonunion wages would fail to detect the impact of the union.

In spite of the measurement difficulties, a large number of empirical investigations have produced some consensus among economists concerning the relative extent of union influence. These investigations have been primarily of two types: (1) cross-sectional analyses at a given time to determine the difference between union and nonunion wages and (2) time-series analyses which attempt to study union and nonunion conditions through time.

These studies indicate that the unions' relative impact is strongly influenced by business conditions. Unions seem to exert their greatest influence relative to nonunion control groups during the early stages of a recession or depression, in part by producing a downward rigidity in wage movements. If the depression is prolonged, however, the union influence tends to disappear because not even the strongest unions can withstand the adverse effects of a severe depression. Unions also seem to have an advantage during periods of high employment and stable prices, but the extent of the advantage depends upon the strength of the union. Strong unions raise wages by as much as 15 to 25 percent above what they would have been in the absence of unions. The strongest union influence seems to have come from unions of skilled craftsmen and organizations such as the United Mine Workers, which have been able to organize large sections of their labor markets. Strong industrial unions such as the United Steelworkers probably have an impact in the range of 10 to 15 percent when employment is high and prices are stable. But even during periods of high employment and stable prices, some unions have very limited impact on relative wages because of adverse economic conditions that make it very difficult for nonunion sectors to organize or for unions to raise wages without generating substantial unemployment.

Albert Rees, a careful student of the impact of unions on wages, concluded in the early 1960s that "my own best guess of the average effect of all American unions on wages of their members in recent years would lie somewhere between 10 and 15 percent."[3] Rees also concludes that because unions enter into contracts for fixed time periods, their relative impact on wages is least during periods of rapid and unexpected inflation because union wages lag behind those in nonunion sectors and because employers, knowing that unions will resist wage cuts when labor markets slacken, resist union wage pressures during inflated periods.

In a detailed review of 20 empirical studies of the impact of unions on relative wages, Harold G. Lewis found some uniformity in the evidence concerning the union's advantage. The ratio of union to nonunion wages seems to have been greatest during the bottom of the Great Depression, when the union advantage might have reached 25 percent. With recovery from the depression the union advantage declined to between 10 and 20 percent by the end of the 1930s and almost disappeared during the 1940s. Lewis concluded: "I estimate that in recent years the average union/nonunion relative wage was approximately 10 percent to 15 percent higher than it would have in the absence of unions."[4] Lewis thus agrees with Rees' estimate of the unions' relative impact.

As for the unions' impact on labor's share of the national income, empirical studies are highly inconclusive, although (as with relative wages) there are a number of measurement difficulties. It is not inconsistent to argue that unions influence relative wages but not labor's share, because it is possible for unions to redistribute income from the nonunion to the union sector.

With respect to the size distribution of income, the evidence suggests that unions have raised incomes of more highly paid blue-collar workers, narrowed the income gap between the best-paid manual workers and more highly paid white-collar workers, and widened the gap between the best-paid blue-collar workers and the very poor. This is largely due to the fact that unions have had their greatest influence in mainstream labor markets and have done very little in marginal and submarginal markets.

One reason for the unions' concentration in the mainstream is that they are likely to have greater success in raising wages in the less competitive firms that predominate in that labor market. The unions' success in mainstream markets is due, in part, either to the fact that they have helped employers control their product markets or to the fact that they occupy strategic positions in the labor and product markets, as is the case with the teamsters. In assessing the significance of product market structure, it also is important to emphasize the multiplicity of causes influencing the determination of both wages and union structures. Of course to say that there is a strong correlation between market structures and wages is not to deny that other factors are at work.

The prevailing institutional arrangements must also be considered in assessing the importance of market structures on union strength. For example, as noted earlier, before the 1930s, unions undoubtedly had much less influence on wage determination in oligopolistic industries than they did after that time. In the institutional setting of the 1920s large employers were freely able to use their economic and political (and, in some cases, physical) power to prevent unions from organizing their employees, but this changed during the social ferment of the 1930s.

This is not to argue that in dealing with unions oligopolistic employers conceded larger wage increases than if workers had not been organized, even though a number of factors might have caused higher wage increases in unionized oligopolistic firms. Because many of these companies had considerable monopsonistic power in the labor markets, traditional economic theory would hold that wages might be raised without reducing employment. However, if the monopsonists are making only normal profits (sufficient to keep firms in this industry) before unionization, raising wages might reduce employment in the long run because the firms could not continue to operate. The sudden reduction of monopsony power in the short run may explain the phenomenon commonly found in empirical studies. Unions have a sizable wage advantage over nonunion firms during the early stages of unionization, but the discrepancy disappears through time. Obviously, a continuing advantage to firms operating under oligopolistic conditions would require changes in the extent of the monopoly powers through time, which is hardly realistic.

Similarly, in oligopolistic firms whose product and labor demand curves are kinked at prevailing prices, increasing costs will not necessarily reduce employment. The kink is as indicated in Figure 23-1a, which assumes that employers will not gain much

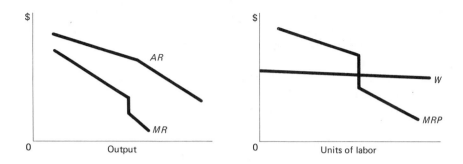

Figure 23-1

business if they lower prices (because their rivals are likely to follow suit) and will lose if they try to raise prices (because their rivals are not likely to follow). Since the demand for labor is a derived demand, it, too, will be kinked, as indicated in Figure 23-1b. Prices are likely to be inflexible under this condition because employers lose total revenue when they lower or raise prices. In such cases unions might be able to raise wages within the limits of the discontinuity of the marginal revenue product curve without creating unemployment, as depicted in Figure 23-1b. Indeed, oligopolistic employers might offer less resistance to wage increases that they could shift to consumers in the form of higher prices. It is even conceivable that oligopolies that raise prices by some percentage amounts as they increase wages could actually profit from wage increases, depending on the ratio of labor cost to total cost and the elasticity of the demand for the final product.

Other conditions exist in which wage increases will not necessarily lead to unemployment. One of these is the so-called shock effect, in which rising wage pressures cause employers to become more efficient and, therefore, able to absorb the wage increases without reducing employment.

The argument that union wage policies distort resource allocation does not necessarily assume that the labor market would be perfect without union influence; there are many market imperfections besides the operation of unions. Moreover, some unions perform functions—such as providing better job information and training—that improve the operation of some labor markets. Furthermore, the judgment that unions make for a worse allocation of labor implies that a higher GNP is better than things such as greater worker participation in the formulation of work rules. Finally, a large GNP is not necessarily better for all groups in the economy.

Other authorities doubt that the impact of unions on wages can be ascertained through the uses of traditional economic theory. Reynolds, for example, has advanced the proposition that "the effects of trade unionism cannot be deduced from first principles and that on the contrary, simple economic models of union behavior are likely to be quite misleading." Reynolds' survey led him to the following hypotheses:

1. Collective bargaining has reduced occupational differences within particular industries and has probably brought them closer to what they would have been under perfect competition.
2. Collective bargaining has reduced interplant differentials, on a national scale in industries characterized by regional or national competition and on a local basis in local industries. In this respect, also, collective bargaining has probably produced a closer approximation to the competitive wage structure.
3. Collective bargaining has probably widened interindustry differentials and in an anticompetitive fashion. Unionism has penetrated most effectively into the relatively high-wage industries and has tended to make the rich richer.
4. Collective bargaining has probably reduced geographical differentials, but this effect has been weaker than the first three effects and largely incidental to the reduction of interplant differentials. The reductions of geographical differentials have probably brought the wage structure closer to competitive standards than unions in a few industries that have overshot the mark.[5]

Conclusion on union's impact on wages

In conclusion, therefore, there is a consensus among those who have studied the problem that unions have had considerable influence on relative wages in the labor markets where they have gained strength. But their relative impact varies with business conditions, being greatest during recessions and least during inflation. The unions also tend to have a relative advantage immediately after becoming organized that declines with time. In general, the unions' ability to raise wages depends upon the elasticity of demand for labor, which is, in turn, influenced by the nature of competition in the product market. Unions have had their greatest impact in mainstream labor markets and thus probably have narrowed the income gap between the higher-paid blue-collar workers and white-collar workers, but they probably have widened the income gap between the well-organized blue-collar workers and those working in marginal and submarginal labor markets, who tend to be less well-off.

Unions, education, and manpower

Trade unions vary widely in the interest they show in education and training. Craft unions such as those in the construction trades are interested in apprenticeship and other training programs as a means of maintaining wages (by limiting the supply of labor as well as improving its quality) and craft identity (by instilling pride in a particular craft). (See Chapter 11.)

Industrial or noncraft unions, however, have a different stake in education and training, which reflects their collective bargaining concern over maintaining wage rates, protecting wage rates from being undercut by trainees, gaining educational and training benefits for their members through collective bargaining, and using training programs to protect such vital collective bargaining interests as seniority. This last objective may be achieved by giving senior employees the right to be trained for jobs for which their seniority makes them eligible. Industrial unions might also use training as a means of protecting their members' jobs from technological changes or merging or relocating plants.[6]

Because of their special interests and functions, state, local, and national federations are likely to take a broader view of education and training. For example, they are apt to favor general education that enables workers to participate in the political process. They have also been major supporters of free education for workers and programs to help the disadvantaged. Federations also are interested in education and training as a part of manpower programs and other policies designed to reduce unemployment. The federations' broader interests derive in some measure from their political role, which requires them to work actively with civil rights and other groups to achieve common economic, social, and political objectives. Still, federations are likely to see social objectives in terms of their effect on the institution of collective bargaining. They tend, therefore, to insist that education, manpower, and training programs be compatible with such established collective bargaining procedures as union wage scales, the apprenticeship system, job referral procedures, and seniority. But more often than most national or local unions, federations attempt to promote the interests of blacks and other minorities who sometimes are barred from union benefits by racial discrimination.[7]

American unions played an important role in establishing universal free education in the United States in the nineteenth century. The labor movement realized that workers were not likely to make very much progress in an industrial society without education, which in the early 1800s was too costly for workers' children. Workers' demands for free public education were met with vigorous opposition from the conservative classes who feared that educated workers would turn to radical politics and who simply balked at paying taxes to educate the children of the working class. Selig Perlman explains the situation in the following terms:

> That the education situation was deplorable much proof is unnecessary. Pennsylvania had some public schools, but parents had to declare themselves too poor to send their children to a private school before they were allowed the privilege of sending them there. In fact, so much odium was attached to these schools that they were practically useless, and the state became distinguished for the number of children not attending school. . . .
>
> To meet these conditions, the working men outlined a comprehensive educational program. It was not merely a literary education that the working men desired. The idea of industrial education, or training for a vocation, which is even now young in this country, was undoubtedly first introduced by the leaders of this early labor movement. They demanded a system of public education which would "combine the knowledge of the practical arts with that of the useful sciences."[8]

Although the labor movement supported academic training in order to prepare workers for citizenship, they were more interested in vocational training. But their attitude toward vocational education was somewhat ambivalent. Unions were strongly committed to the apprenticeship system as a means of preparing workers for the skilled trades, in part because apprenticeship systems usually were products of collective bargaining and thus were controlled to a significant degree by unions, and also because apprenticeship training combined academic with on-the-job training— which workers always seem to have favored. Hence even though unions endorsed vocational education very early—Samuel Gompers supported both the Smith-Hughes and George-Deen acts, which established the vocational educational system in the United States—they have rarely deviated from a traditional belief that most trades cannot be learned in classrooms and that vocational education by itself does not provide adequate preparation for the skilled trades. Unions have, therefore, favored vocational schools that provide instruction in academic subjects and otherwise prepare students for the apprenticeship programs.[9]

Union concerns: manpower and education

The unions' attitudes toward education and manpower programs can be understood by considering their fundamental concerns.

First, the American labor movement has always given top priority to collective bargaining as an institution. Unions, therefore, have strongly favored those forms of education and training that were most directly related to the collective bargaining system.

Second, the skilled trades derive their power in large measure from their control of labor supplies. They have, therefore, been very much interested in controlling the means of training skilled nonunion workers who might compete with them, and they have always taken a dim view of skill training outside the collective bargaining system.

Third, unions are very much concerned with the productivity of union members. Union leaders realize that they will not be able to maintain high wages unless unionized workers are more productive than the alternatives available to their employers—unproductive union workers give employers an incentive to substitute machinery for labor or to operate under nonunion conditions. In order to police their jurisdictions then unions have found it necessary to have an adequate supply of well-trained labor. Thus craft unions strongly favor the apprenticeship system not only because it is controlled by collective bargaining but also because they are convinced that it gives the worker practical on-the-job experience as well as some understanding of the theory of his trade. The unions believe that workers trained in both the theory and the practice of their trades will be much more flexible and able to perform a greater variety of jobs than would be the case if training were narrow and specialized. General training, they feel, makes workers less vulnerable to unemployment than specialized training, which employers are more likely to favor. Employers tend to retain the best-trained workers when demand for labor declines.

Although unions prefer training through apprenticeship, they admit members who are trained by other means. Indeed, a majority of craftsmen have not served apprenticeship. Unions are likely to admit such workers in order to maintain control of the labor market: They would clearly weaken their position if there were many workers the employers considered to be craftsmen who were outside union jurisdiction.

Unions have recently become interested in education, manpower, and training programs because of the pressures to admit more blacks and other minorities to the skilled trades. Historically, craft unions on the railroads and in the printing and construction trades barred blacks from membership. In part, this practice stemmed from a monopoly instinct that caused local unions to exclude all except certain favored groups from their unions and thus from union-controlled crafts. But the civil rights movements of the 1950s and 1960s generated considerable pressure on unions to admit minorities to membership. The unions responded by insisting that blacks and other minorities come into the crafts primarily through the apprenticeship system. They realized that not many blacks could get into their crafts this way because apprenticeship programs graduate very few workers each year. But they argued that blacks who entered unions through apprenticeship would be well trained and, therefore, the markets would not be flooded with unqualified craftsmen.

Union training programs

A number of unions participate in joint union-management programs for training apprentices and journeymen. Journeyman training programs are necessitated in some crafts by rapid changes in technology and work procedures. For example, the International Typographical Union (ITU), which has long had an interest in education, has established a training center in Colorado Springs that specializes in short courses to teach journeymen new techniques in the printing and publishing trades. The ITU has attempted to ensure that members whose jobs are destroyed by technological changes are given first claim to jobs utilizing the new techniques.

The International Brotherhood of Electrical Workers (IBEW) and the United Association of Journeymen and Apprentices of the Plumbing and Pipe Fitting Industry of the U.S. and Canada (UA) also have maintained strong apprenticeship and journeyman-upgrading programs. As early as 1944, the IBEW established an electronics school at Marquette University to train instructors who in turn trained journeymen at the local level. The IBEW and the National Electrical Contractors Association established a national Joint Apprenticeship Committee in 1941; in 1947, when other training became more important, the name was changed to the National Joint Apprenticeship and Training Committee for the Electrical Industry. The national committee has adopted national standards for training programs administered by local joint commitees. Programs are jointly financed, but a percentage of payroll contributions by employers was becoming the most widely used plan for financing during the late 1960s.

In 1956 the UA and the Mechanical Contractors Association of America, Inc. established a national retraining program for steamfitters and plumbers. In order to finance this program the union and employers established a national training fund to which the contractors contribute on the basis of the number of hours worked. The program is administered by a joint union-management committee that assists local joint training committees and provides equipment and national guidelines for journeyman-upgrading training. The UA has a staff of training coordinators and a program for training superintendents and instructors at Purdue University. The plumbing industry feels that training is necessary in order to keep journeymen abreast of new materials and methods. In 1956 the plumbers had 32 training programs for about 1,000 journeymen; by 1967 there were 397 training programs, which trained 18,000 journeymen. Between 1956 and 1967 the plumbers program trained over 80,000 journeymen. Grants from the national fund for training average about $1.2 million a year and are supplemented by much larger funds from local union and contractors.[10]

Union interest in education and training has not been restricted to the crafts; many industrial organizations also have established programs to educate and upgrade their members. The industrial unions are mainly interested in preparing their members to advance in the internal labor market. Some interest in education and training programs has been stimulated by federal manpower training programs, which seek to help the disadvantaged, and by civil rights movement insistence that lines of progression be desegregated. Many older workers, already on the job but unable to obtain upgrading because of limited education, are apt to resent these efforts to help blacks and other minorities. Moreover, many black workers lack the necessary qualifications for upgrading. Finally, industrial workers face the threat of technological displacement and have attempted to use retraining programs to help them adjust to new jobs.

One of the most widely known cases of an effort to retrain workers who have lost their jobs because of technological change is the Armour and Company experience. In 1959 Armour permanently closed six plants, thus losing about 20 percent of its total capacity and displacing 5000 production employees. In order to soften the shock of unemployment, Armour and United Packinghouse Workers and the Amalgamated Meat Cutters agreed to establish an automation committee, which had a $500,000 fund to carry out its program. The program screened workers on the basis of aptitude tests, but its placement rate was not very satisfactory, and many of those who were retrained were offered jobs that paid lower wages than they had earned at Armour. As a result of this experience, the committee concluded that retraining on a crash basis would be of little help to displaced workers who were middle-aged and had limited education. Moreover, the retraining program clearly required jobs that many of the workers could not find.[11]

Unions and manpower programs

It is difficult to generalize about the labor movement's attitude toward remedial manpower. Reactions have varied widely according to the multiplicity of motives and interests within the movement. The federations, which are mainly public relations and political organizations, viewed the new training activities more favorably than did national unions, which, in turn, viewed them more favorably than did their local affiliates. Many local craft unions feared that the manpower programs would flood the labor market with partially trained craftsmen who would depress wages and generally undermine working conditions. They also saw the new training programs competing with the established apprenticeship activities. Union fears were aggravated by those who oversold the manpower programs as a solution to the social and economic problems of the disadvantaged. It was understandable, for example, that a construction union in a labor market that ordinarily admitted no more than 100 new craftsmen a year would be alarmed by claims that 2000 or 3000 disadvantaged people were to be trained in these crafts. Fears were intensified by the civil rights advocates' attack on the all-white policies of many local unions. These unions, therefore, were persuaded that manpower programs would be used to channel blacks into union training programs from which they had been excluded.

The steel program. Labor opposition to the new programs was not restricted to the craft unions. Many members of industrial unions feared that the new programs would give preferential treatment to the disadvantaged and advance them ahead of workers already in factory jobs. A frequent complaint of union members was that the disadvantaged were being given opportunities that older workers had never enjoyed, even though these older workers also had limited qualifications for advancement. In the steel industry—as in many other basic industries—a large number of workers with very limited education were recruited during World War II (many workers with very low levels of education had been hired even before that time). At the Inland Steel Company, for example, more than 1000 Mexican Americans who could not speak English were hired during the war.

In response to the problems of old as well as new workers some unions simply adopted programs that would help all of the workers similarly situated and not just the disadvantaged. For example, in 1965 the United Steelworkers and ten major steel companies agreed to establish an education and training program to increase workers' educational levels and make them eligible for promotion. The program was to be administered by a non-profit organization called the Board of Fundamental Education. The contract negotiated that year by union and management included the following clause:

> In order to serve the basic educational need of the employees and thereby enhance their qualifications for job opportunities on new and improved facilities and enable employees, including those on layoff, to improve their capacities for advancement or re-employment with the Company, the Company and the Union, together with various agencies of the United States government, have been and will continue to actively explore the development of certain training programs under the Manpower Development and Training Act of 1962 (MDTA) and other applicable laws.

At the same time, the Departments of Labor and Health, Education, and Welfare were concerned about the limited educational levels of many American workers and were planning a pilot program for in-plant remedial education. Representatives from the federal government and the steel industry adopted the Cooperative Steel Industry Education Plan. The curriculum included two levels of instruction:

I. A basic level for individuals performing below the 4.5 grade levels.
II. An advanced level designed for individuals performing between the 4.5 and 8.0 grade levels in both work meaning and arithmetic computation.[12]

Labor-management participation was stressed at every step in the program. Special efforts were made to brief supervisors, workers, and union leaders. The classes were conducted in a very informal manner, and every effort was made to have the students encourage each other. To the maximum extent possible, the program's administrators sought to avoid the schoolroom atmosphere.

The steel industry program is considered to be a success by unions, employers, and government representatives. John S. Mc-Cauley reported that 4100 steelworkers have attended classes in basic elementary education; of the 2762 workers who attended at least one class the first year, 1726 (62 percent) graduated. Union-management satisfaction with the program was reflected in the 1968 collective bargaining agreement that stated that "these efforts have been sufficiently beneficial to warrant the continuation of this type of program for further exploratory development under MDTA, other applicable laws, and through other mutually agreed-upon means."

Extent of union participation. The AFL-CIO and its affiliates also have supported the new manpower programs and have actively participated in a number of them. In August 1969, for example, it was reported that there were 13 national contracts with 7 unions, providing for 15,000 training slots under the MDTA-OJT program. The largest contract with any union was with the United Brotherhood of Carpenters (UBC), which was training almost 5000 persons. The previously mentioned IBEW, the Laborers International Union, the International Union of Operating Engineers (IUOE), and the AFL-CIO Appalachian Council also held OJT contracts. Indeed, the IUOE has been particularly active in the manpower field. It was reported in 1966, for example, that the IUOE had received over half of all OJT money going to building trades unions. A number of regional labor councils and state federations and local unions had an additional 3300 training slots for MDTA-OJT programs in August 1969.

Job Corps. Organized labor also has supported the Job Corps concept of residential training for hard-core disadvantaged youths. The first union to become involved with this program was the IUOE, which ran training programs for heavy-equipment workers at the Jacobs Creek Center in Tennessee. The instructors were journeymen IUOE members; the union agreed to place the trainees who completed the training course. Trainees were allowed to enter the IUOE apprenticeship program and ultimately to become regular journeymen. The IUOE subsequently entered into an agreement for two Job Corps conservation centers to train 130 disadvantaged workers in equipment repair, maintenance, and operation. The previously mentioned also trained several hundred Job Corpsmen to be slotted into the union's regular apprenticeship program.

The Appalachian Council. Some of the OJT programs provide greater insight into the nature of the labor movement's involvement with this kind of training. One of the largest of these programs is Operation Manpower, which is sponsored by the AFL-CIO Appalachian Council in cooperation with the Departments of Labor and Health, Education, and Welfare. The Appalachian Council, which was formed in 1964, works closely with the Institute for Labor Studies at West Virginia University and covers an 11-state area (Alabama, Kentucky, North Carolina, Virginia, Georgia, Maryland, Ohio, Pennsylvania, Tennessee, West Virginia, and South

Carolina). Operation Manpower began in June 1967 with the award of two federal job development contracts. The Appalachian Council was awarded a number of additional job training contracts in subsequent years. The council's basic approach is to work through affiliated local unions or their employers. It has emphasized OJT as well as coupled programs that combine OJT with vocational and basic education. Although it has worked with such large employers as Kaiser Aluminum, Goodyear, and Hayes International, most of the jobs developed by the council have been with small firms, many of which are located in rural areas. By November 1970 Operation Manpower had developed 13,361 jobs and placed 7,817 trainees, at an average actual cost of $445.08 for each trainee placed.

The Human Resource Development Institute. As a result of the apprenticeship outreach and other programs in which unions participated, it became apparent that a joint effort between the U.S. Department of Labor and the whole labor movement could produce beneficial results for manpower programs. Such a cooperative arrangement, it was felt, not only would take advantage of the labor movement's network of affiliated organizations but also would overcome worker resistance to helping the disadvantaged. It was also considered to be important for the labor movement to (1) convince field-level government officials and employers that unions could participate effectively in manpower programs and (2) establish its credibility with the hard-core unemployed—especially minority groups, which were assuming an increasingly antiunion stance because of publicity given to discrimination against blacks and other minorities by various unions.

In order to accomplish these objectives, the AFL-CIO executive council created the Human Resource Development Institute (HRDI) in September 1968. The institute received about $4.2 million from the U.S. Department of Labor for a "nationwide program to recruit, train, employ, and upgrade the unemployed and underemployed."[13] The 100 people from 27 different unions who comprise HRDI's staff also seek to promote better coordination of manpower programs. Staffers come from a wide range of backgrounds and involvements in civic and community organizations. The institute is particularly active in apprenticeship outreach programs—which it encourages and provides with local liaison and follow-up—and in preapprenticeship training programs.

One of HRDI's major activities has been to develop, in cooperation with the National Alliance of Businessmen (NAB), the Job Opportunities in the Business Sector (JOBS) program—a "buddy system" to ease the transition of the disadvantaged into plants where unions have contracts. By December 1970 more than

200 companies in 50 cities had developed systems in which 1000 members of 47 national unions had served as buddies to give assistance on and off the job to the newly hired during their probationary periods.

During 1973 and 1974, HRDI expanded its activities into a variety of areas. One of the most significant of its new activities was to take over the coordination of apprenticeship outreach programs operated by local building trades councils in 21 cities. These programs are designed to recruit, tutor, and place minorities in unionized apprenticeship programs. Under subcontracts with HRDI the 21 local building trades councils remain responsible for central coordination, direction, evaluation, and program performance.

The HRDI continued its job development and placement programs in 1973 and 1974. Its staff cooperated with union officials in placing disadvantaged workers in jobs not ordinarily listed with the employment services. Since these jobs were covered by union contracts, they usually provided better wages and working conditions for the disadvantaged than ordinarily were available to them from other sources. During 1973, for example, HRDI developed 31,649 jobs and made 11,375 placements; of these 986 were people on welfare, 979 were ex-prisoners, and 2,286 were veterans.

In the prisoner program, the institute works with local unions and correctional institutions to develop training programs for prisoners and helps released prisoners find job opportunities in unionized plants. In its veterans' assistance programs the HRDI helps returning Vietnam veterans find jobs and training to facilitate their return to civilian life. Finally, the HRDI actively promotes adequate union representation on state and local manpower planning councils. Although unions generally were not too enthusiastic about manpower revenue sharing, HRDI has a technical assistance program to help organized labor understand and participate in the Comprehensive Employment and Training Act of 1973. Indeed, the CETA guidelines stipulate that, where appropriate, labor organizations should be consulted in the design and conduct of OJT programs whenever there are collective bargaining agreements. In order to facilitate organized labor's participation in manpower programs, the HRDI urges the creation of manpower committees by local central labor councils.

Conclusions on unions and labor markets

Although unions represent only about 28 percent of all nonagricultural employees in the United Sates, their influence extends far and wide in American labor markets because collective bargaining covers most of the blue-collar workers in the mainstream transportation, construction, high-wage manufacturing, printing and publishing, and other industries. The unions' overall impact on wages might be debated, but it is generally agreed that they have influenced wage structures and have a significant impact on the wages of their members—although the specific impact varies with the particular labor market and general economic conditions. Therefore, unions are major labor institutions in both the external and internal labor markets. As noted in Chapter 7, they also contribute to labor market segmentation.

It should also be noted that unions and collective bargaining have played an important role in education and manpower programs. Historically, the labor movement was a major influence for universal free public education. Unions have been particularly interested in vocational education, although union leaders generally consider it inferior to apprenticeship training. Reflecting the workers' preference for practical OJT, unions feel that few crafts can be learned in the classroom. They also prefer job training that is established under collective bargaining to that provided unilaterally by employers. Labor leaders point out that collective bargaining makes it possible for training to reflect the interests and needs of employers and workers and also ties the costs of training to those who are to benefit most from it. They argue, for example, that employers by themselves would not provide broad, general training to make employees more "unemployment-proof" and adaptable to diverse job situations. Rather, they argue, employers are more interested in minimizing training costs and maximizing profits, which often dictates narrow, specialized job assignments. Moreover, employers tend to desire excessive supplies of workers in order to meet peak labor requirements and minimize upward pressures on wages. In contrast, the unions attempt to see that workers are well trained and that supplies of labor are no greater than necessary to meet the demand for workers at negotiated wage rates. Unions have used training programs not only to provide general training but also to train members for the new jobs generated by technological changes that render older skills obsolete. Moreover, some unions—especially those in casual occupations in the transportation and construction industries—maintain job information and referral systems for their members.

The labor movement's manpower functions create problems for those who advocate comprehensive national manpower programs. For one thing, some unions attempt to use their control of training and referral systems to monopolize job opportunities for their members. They are, therefore, very suspicious of government or other training programs that are not at least partly controlled by unions or that compete with union programs. Where unions are strong enough to impose closed-shop conditions (whereby workers must join unions *before* they come to work), they can prevent the employment of the workers trained in public programs by refusing to accept the trainees as union members. Although the closed shop is outlawed by the National Labor Relations Act, strong unions have been able to enforce de facto closed-shop conditions because of their control of labor supplies.

The AFL-CIO generally gave strong support to the manpower legislation of the 1960s, even when some of its affiliates and their members were unenthusiastic. With few exceptions unions participated only in manpower programs that were compatible with collective bargaining. Unions can be expected to resist programs that are incompatible with that system—if they threaten to undermine union control of training or referral systems.

In view of the growing importance of public and private manpower programs, education and training will undoubtedly become an increasingly important subject of collective bargaining in the future. Moreover, it can be expected that agencies such as the AFL-CIO's HRDI will be strengthened to link manpower programs to collective bargaining and that machinery will be established to resolve conflicts between union-controlled programs and public policy. Conflicts are particularly likely because of continued pressure to enlarge the employment opportunities of blacks and other minorities who have not had adequate access to many training, upgrading, and referral programs controlled by unions. Government agencies probably will become increasingly concerned about the implications of control of labor supplies for price stability. To whatever extent these pressures threaten the sanctity of collective bargaining, they undoubtedly will elicit continuing and increasing resistance from labor unions.

Notes

1. Good discussions of labor in the developing countries can be found in Walter Galenson, ed., *Labor in Developing Countries* (Berkeley, Calif.: University of California Press, 1962), and idem., *Labor and Economic Development* (New York: Wiley, 1959). See also Everett M. Kassalow, *Trade Unions and Industrialization: An International Comparison* (New York: Random House, 1969), Part II.
2. For example, the statements of eight leading economic theorists in David McCord Wright, ed., *The Impact of the Union* (New York: Harcourt Brace Jovanovich, 1951).

3. Albert Rees, *The Economics of Trade Unions* (Chicago: University of Chicago Press, 1962), p. 79.

4. Harold G. Lewis, *Unionism and Relative Wages in the United States* (Chicago: University of Chicago Press, 1963), p. 5.

5. Lloyd G. Reynolds, "The Impact of Collective Bargaining on the Wage Structure of the United States," in John T. Dunlop, ed., *The Theory of Wage Determination* (New York: St. Martin, 1957), p. 220.

6. Jack Barbash, "Union Interests in Apprenticeship and Other Training Forms," *Journal of Human Resources* (Winter 1968), pp. 63–83.

7. Ray Marshall, *The Negro and Organized Labor* (New York: Wiley, 1965).

8. Selig Perlman, *History of Trade Unionism* (New York: Augustus M. Kelly, 1950; reprint of the original 1922 edition), pp. 14–15.

9. Sumner H. Slichter, James J. Healy, and E. Robert Livernash, *The Impact of Collective Bargaining on Management* (Washington, D.C.: Brookings Institution, 1960), p. 70.

10. Derek C. Bok and John T. Dunlop, *Labor and the American Community* (New York: Simon & Schuster, 1970), p. 347.

11. Ibid. See also Arnold Weber, "Experiment in Retraining," in Gerald G. Somers, ed., *Retraining the Unemployed* (Madison, Wis.: University of Wisconsin Press, 1968), p. 257, and George P. Shultz and Arnold L. Weber, *Strategies for the Displaced Worker* (New York: Harper & Row, 1966).

12. John S. McCauley, "A Cooperative Steel Industry Education Program," in Peter B. Doeringer, ed., *Programs to Employ the Disadvantaged* (Englewood Cliffs, N.J.: Prentice-Hall, 1969), p. 134.

13. Kenneth Fiester, "Putting Labor in Work Training," *Manpower* (December 1970), p. 24.

24

industrialization and rural development

Economists have attempted to explain the causes of the wealth and income of individuals and nations since long before the time of Adam Smith. That economic productivity has been due to the joint efforts of capital, human and natural resources, and entrepreneurs is well established, but the weights to be given each factor of production and the precise causal relationships among them are not as clear.

In recent years economists have devoted considerable attention to the economic development process. Some of this work has attempted to explain the role of human capital investments in economic development, especially in the developing countries. Others have been concerned with the differential rates of growth among regions, individuals, and sectors of the economy. Although the issues are far from settled, as this chapter makes clear, experience with the industrialization of either underdeveloped countries or lagging regions and sectors leaves little doubt that the development of human resources plays an important role in raising incomes.

An overview

Industrialization and human resource development (HRD) are closely linked because industrialization shapes people to its own requirements. Economic development, or the growth of income-earning opportunities, influences education and training by providing the resources to support educational activities as well as means of acquiring OJT experiences. The interaction among economic output and education and training is similar to the formation of nonhuman capital: HRD requires prior production to support education and training activities until those in whom these investments are being made can become productive.

However, the interactions between HRD and income-generating activities make it very difficult to establish with precision causal relationships between national incomes and investments in human resources. As noted in Chapter 8, such investments are unquestionably closely related to the growth of per capita income, but we do not know whether the HRD investments cause the incomes to grow or whether incomes cause HRD investments to grow. Moreover, there is some question over the extent to which joint returns to all factors of production can be attributed to human and nonhuman capital.

Similar linkages exist among manpower programs, economic development, and education. Manpower programs that match people and jobs increase individual and national productivity by helping people to be more productive. For example, mobility or training programs to move people from labor-surplus to labor-shortage areas increase national income if the costs of making these moves are less than the incomes gained. However, measures to influence the supplies of workers assume that there are jobs available for them. Moreover, jobs are an important part of the training process because most of the skills and attitudes needed for modern industry are learned either on the job or by being exposed to economic activities.

However, our problem is complicated by the fact that HRD is not entirely economic. Education, for example, has consumption characteristics because it involves processes through which education improves noneconomic as well as economic aspects of life. Similarly, education and training might have social benefits in improving political processes and facilitating social order. Therefore, efforts to determine the economic returns to education and training encounter the problem of how to factor out these consumption and social benefits, all of which undoubtedly facilitate economic development.

An HRD strategy must also concern itself with programs to eliminate barriers to personal improvement that are not related to productivity. The major factor here is discrimination because of race, sex, age, or national origin (discussed at length in Part Four).

Similarly, while industrial societies must provide for the maintenance of those who cannot or should not work, many health and welfare activities have no direct measurable relationship to productivity, even though they play important roles in shaping economic development. The manner in which these health and welfare services are rendered also has important implications for economic development. Ill-fed children suffer psychophysical damage that permanently affects their ability to be educated and trained for productive work. Moreover, income maintenance clearly is necessary if workers are to support themselves and their families while they are being trained. The interaction of education, income, health, and jobs is nowhere more evident than in the well-known vicious cycle that makes it difficult for many poor nations and individuals to improve their positions.

Institutions, human resource development, and industrialization

Not only are there close causal interactions between the various components of HRD (jobs, education, manpower, antidiscrimination, and welfare) and industrialization, but industrialization itself interacts in a very significant way with political, social, and economic institutions. The nature of HRD programs is closely related to levels of economic development, national objectives, and the nature of the society in which industrialization takes place. Kerr, Dunlop, Harbison, and Myers, for example, demonstrate that HRD programs are closely related to the logic of industrialization.

As these same authors show, industrialization requires increasing levels of technology, which have significant manpower implications. These levels of technology necessitate the development of a science and technology based upon a variety of research organizations, particularly in the advanced stages of industrialization. Moreover, industrial systems require wide ranges of skills and professional competence, which must be widely distributed throughout the working population. As a consequence, it is their view that the creation of a highly skilled professional and technical labor force is as important for industrializing societies as the accumulation of capital goods: "The professional, technical, and managerial component of the labor force, private and public, is particularly strategic since it largely carries the responsibility of developing and ordering the manual and clerical labor force."[1]

Because of the centrality of science and technology in the industrial society, technical competence tends to replace traditional ways of assigning people to jobs. Industrial societies tend to become meritocracies in which people are assigned to jobs primarily on the basis of their abilities, not on the basis of caste, racial groups, sex, or family status. Moreover, the industrialization process has a profound impact on the family. In preindustrial societies the family is likely to be the producing unit, whereas industrialism tends to disintegrate the family and to make the business firm the primary production unit.

A nation or a region adopting HRD strategies must decide (1) which people within the population are to be educated and trained and (2) at what level of education. Moreover, decisions must be made about the kinds of education and training to be undertaken: Are resources to be devoted to scientific and technical training or to the arts and humanities? To some extent, these decisions might be made by the market because activities that are in greatest demand will provide for the largest rewards and, therefore, induce people to enter them. But choices about HRD cannot be left entirely to the market.

Harbison and Myers have shown that the HRD strategies adopted clearly depend on the level of economic development, among many other things.[2] These authors identify various levels of economic development with corresponding HRD strategies. In underdeveloped countries, for example, the main national objectives tend to be national sovereignty and independence, and the rapid development of primary industries is likely to be considered an important means for achieving these national objectives. Because educational levels tend to be quite low in the underdeveloped countries, the development of primary education is usually an important HRD goal.

As societies become partially developed, they concentrate upon building the base for industrialization while increasing productivity in agriculture. During this stage, there are likely to be shortages of skilled and technical manpower. As a consequence, these manpower needs are met by importing personnel from more advanced countries. The important HRD objective during this stage of economic development is likely to be extension of universal primary education, which becomes attainable because of the resources made available by economic development. Secondary education, especially in science and mathematics, must also be expanded in order to meet the need for subprofessionals and technicians. Because of the shortages of skilled and educated manpower, the extension of education and training requires improvements in educational technology in order to overcome critical shortages of teachers.

As the society reaches the third, or semiadvanced, stage, the national economic objective is likely to be rapid and massive industrialization. During this stage, large-scale unemployment of unskilled workers is likely to be coupled with continuing shortages of those with higher levels of education and skill. As a consequence of this imbalance, institutions of higher education, as well as those providing job training and adult education, are subjected to considerable pressures. It becomes particularly important for higher education to emphasize science and technology and for vocational and adult education to meet more closely the requirements of employers.

In advanced countries HRD needs tend to emphasize innovations in order to maintain a rapid rate of economic development. Full employment will be elusive in advanced industrial societies because of the difficulty of distributing the output of a highly productive economy. As productivity rises and the same output can be produced with fewer people, it becomes necessary to adopt specific measures to prevent rising unemployment. During this stage—when science and technology play an important role in continuing innovation—higher education, particularly at the post-graduate level, is given priority. At the same time, however, advanced societies experience strong pressures for universal secondary education in order to place higher education within the easy reach of all people. Measures also are necessary in advanced economies to eliminate inequalities among various segments of the population because these inequalities become increasingly apparent as incomes rise, and rising national incomes make it possible to reduce inequalities. Moreover, dynamic changes make skills obsolete and lead to knowledge explosions, all of which require perfection of education and training in order to prevent maladjustments and to promote equality of economic opportunity.

Attitudes of political leaders

Strategies for HRD are influenced not only by the stage of economic growth but also by the nature of the institutions and the attitudes of the political leaders in the areas undergoing industrialization. For example, revolutionary intellectuals tend to harbor quite different attitudes about the role of education and training than political leaders with middle-class values. The revolutionaries are likely to conceive of education as a primary means of achieving national objectives—as a means of developing man for the state and not for his own enjoyment. Moreover, the educational system is likely to be more specialized and functional, with a high priority on science and technology. In the Soviet Union, for example, science and education have become important instruments for state power. Max Lerner has explained:

> For the Russians, science has become mainly an instrument of state power, part of their Grand Design for world domination,

indeed part of their political religion. This is something that we need to understand; for the Russians there is a political mystique of science. There is a belief that nothing is impossible for man once he has the weapons of science.[3]

Pluralistic societies such as the United States, however, are less likely to have unified educational objectives. Education, like other institutions, is apt to reflect the divergent interests and influences of different groups within the society. However, the society as a whole tends to emphasize widespread public education as a means of making political democracy more effective. Education in the United States also tends to stress human development, not the establishment of functional relationships to the economic system. Scientific, technical, and vocational education are likely to become increasingly important in such a society, but not at the expense of training in law, art, and the humanities.

Regardless of the political persuasions of the national leaders, education is clearly regarded as "the key that unlocks the door to modernization." Not only does education have a direct impact upon development, but also it has an indirect effect through its influence on factors such as natural resources, markets, the ratio between people and human resources, political stability, social and cultural institutions, and leadership. Moreover, although education is likely to play an important role in the growth of national income, it is important to recognize that the particular type of education and training system is probably as important as the amount of education. In other words, at a given stage in economic development some kinds of education and training are likely to be more important than other kinds. For example, increasing expenditures on art, humanities, and law when a country needs more scientists and technicians is not likely to promote economic development, and as countries develop, the percentage of national income for HRD is likely to rise everywhere.

Building an industrial labor force

Kerr and his colleagues identify four interrelated processes in building an industrial labor force. The first of these processes is *recruitment*, either through compulsory or voluntary means. Examples of compulsory recruitment are slavery and peonage. In modern times, however, only the communist countries have relied extensively on compulsory recruitment of labor—partly because "compulsory methods generally have proved to be unreliable as a permanent means of building an industrial labor force."[4] Fortunately, as industrialization proceeds and the amenities of industrial jobs become clearer to workers, the recruitment process is relatively easy. This is not due entirely to the attractiveness of industrial jobs but to the benefits that are much greater than those available to the workers in agriculture. Because the recruitment process tends to be relatively easy, manpower shortages are likely to be mitigated fairly rapidly during the process of industrialization.

The second process, *commitment*, tends to be much more difficult. The "committed worker is one who stays on the job and who has severed all his major connections with the land." The process of commitment takes place in four stages—the uncommitted worker, the partially committed worker, the generally committed worker, and the specifically committed worker—the degree of commitment varying with the stage of economic development. The uncommitted worker takes an industrial job for a particular purpose with the intention of returning to the land when this limited purpose or objective is achieved. The partially committed worker takes an industrial job but maintains his rural connections. The generally committed worker has completely severed his rural connections and has become committed to employment with a particular firm. Specific commitment is particularly important in Japan, where workers have strong commitments to particular employers and where employers are likely to view some workers as lifetime employees. It is also significant in Italy, France, and England and is becoming more important in the United States as a result of seniority systems and employers' heavy investment in the education and training of their employees.

Environmental factors, of course, may speed or retard the process of commitment. In large urban areas commitment is more easily achieved than in more isolated communities. Cultural factors such as religious and ethical valuations, the family system, class, and race all have a bearing on commitment, but, in one way or another, workers are uprooted from the old order and relatively soon become generally or specifically committed to the new.

The third process is *advancement*, which means developing the skills and attitudes necessary for industrial production. This is a most critical process in building industrial work forces. Advancement may be carried out by workers themselves, by company training programs, or by governmental or community programs. However, in modern times, increasing education and skill requirements make it difficult for workers to train themselves. As a consequence, a very large part of industrial training must take place on the job. Besides, OJT imparts to workers not only skills but also attitudes conducive to industrial efficiency.

Because skill acquisition requires formal education as well as OJT, however, formal schools have an important role to play in the advancement process. As noted earlier, during the early stages of industrialization, schools are not likely to be particularly well suited to turning out efficient work forces. Hence developing nations must draw their skilled manpower from other countries. But as the country develops, education becomes more closely related to economic institutions. In advanced industrial societies workers are required to have considerable formal education; and because education is likely to have social as well as individual benefits, governments tend to expand their role in education and training.

The fourth process is *maintenance*, which involves providing for the general welfare and security of the population. Industrialization invariably gives rise to the need for unemployment insurance, compensation for accidents, maintenance of people during their old age, and other forms of social security. Public maintenance increases in importance because the family ceases to be the primary producing unit and workers become dependent on their work for a livelihood. Provisions must be made, therefore, for people who either cannot or should not work. However, maintenance systems frequently are closely related to the other steps in the development of an industrial work force—because the level of maintenance depends upon the productivity of the whole work force and because various incentive systems might be developed to facilitate the entry of people into productive work rather than relying on welfare for maintenance.

In commenting on the problems involved in developing an industrial work force, Galenson admits that there is considerable evidence that difficulties are involved in commitment, but he warns that the difficulties appear to have been exaggerated. During the early stages of industrialization, there tend to be such problems as absenteeism, tardiness, high turnover, and high absentee or desertion rates during harvest times, but Galenson concludes that these problems appear to be more a function of poor management, which uses labor wastefully because it is cheap, than of any inherent characteristics of the labor force.[5] Galenson also concludes that, during early stages of industrialization, workers seem to be quite as responsive to monetary incentives as are their counterparts in the advanced societies. In some African countries, for example, employers have justified low wages on the grounds that the labor supply function is backward bending, so that as wages rise, workers are willing to offer less labor because they have a greater preference for leisure than for high incomes. But others have found that the absence of worker economic motivation does not appear anywhere as a serious consideration.

The lack of worker commitment during early stages of industrialization might have positive as well as negative effects. The tensions generated by the industrial routine probably are relieved by occasional visits to a worker's village. Low labor productivity is an important deterrent to economic development during the initial stages of industrialization, but it is not a very serious problem once industrialization gets under way. As Galenson emphasizes, the extent to which low productivity is overcome seems to be largely a function of the degree to which management assumes responsibility for training: ". . . the essential ingredient for rapid skill formation is the recognition by management that creating an efficient labor force may be every bit as demanding from a technical point of view as installing and operating machinery." Moreover, the developing countries often have shortages of high-level managerial talent.

The relationship of education and training to economic growth

The relationship between the amount of educated manpower and economic growth has not been clearly established. For example, countries such as Great Britain and the United States have spent large sums on research, development, and scientific manpower yet have lagged behind Japan in economic growth—at least during the 1950s and early 1960s. No one is as yet able to assert that a large pool of scientific manpower has a positive and direct impact on output and growth—even though theoretically such expenditures are considered as investment in educational capital and should raise productivity and output per person.

Harbison and Myers constructed an index of HRD consisting of (1) the number of teachers at the elementary and secondary levels as per 10,000 population, (2) the number of engineers and scientists per 10,000 population, (3) the number of pupils enrolled in elementary school as a percentage of total possible enrollment, and (4) several other measures of development in education. They finally arrived at a composite index—the total of

> enrollment at second level of education (secondary equivalent) as a percentage of the age group 15–19, adjusted for length of schooling and enrollment at the third level of education (higher education) as a percentage of the age group, multiplied by a weight of 5 (reflecting a greater weight for the influence of higher education).[6]

Using per capita GNP in U.S. dollars and percentage of population engaged in agriculture as indexes of economic output,

Harbison and Myers found a significant correlation (+ 0.89) between their index and GNP per capita. There was negative correlation between the index and the percentage of population engaged in farming occupations (− 0.81). But these quantitative relationships, the authors caution, do not establish causal relationships. In some cases (such as Japan), however, a claim of causality between an educated labor force and economic growth seems to be supported by the evidence. Japan made an initial heavy investment in its educational system, which certainly contributed to later rapid economic growth.

Although Harbison and Myers are cautious about assigning causal relationships between education and economic growth (see Chapter 7), other economists have not been as reluctant. There is, however, increasing skepticism about the large role some economists have assigned education as a factor in economic growth. Clearly, these relationships are not linear and homogeneous. At early stages of development general literacy is important in modernization. Moreover, the development of technicians and skilled workers also is important as the economy develops and becomes more technical. However, the relationship becomes more difficult to determine at later stages of economic development. Nevertheless, a relationship between education and individual incomes can be established because employers use education as a screening device.

Manpower programs and regional development

Economic development is significant for regions and smaller economic subdivisions as well as for nations. The development problem of regions derives from the fact that many areas are characterized by unemployment, underemployment, and incomes far below national averages. In the United States, government and private agencies have been anxious to develop these areas. A basic question is whether this approach is more sound, in the sense of improving per capita real income, than moving the people in those areas to jobs in places with greater economic potential.

The development of places is not necessarily incompatible with the development of people, but it can be. For example, creating marginal jobs might not be in the best interest of the younger, adaptable, better-educated people for whom the jobs were created. Subsidizing industry to locate in a depressed area could be particularly disadvantageous because a town's costs for public services are likely to rise faster than its revenue, thus depriving the town of funds to improve education, training, health, and other necessary investments in its people. Policies to improve mobility from such places into others might be in the people's best interest. (But marginal jobs might be in the best interest of *some* of the people in the depressed area.)

Even when successful, such efforts are likely to attract low-wage, labor-intensive enterprises with dead-end jobs that will make a very limited improvement of real incomes. High-wage firms are not as likely to be attracted by the blandishments of cheap labor and tax incentives as they are by skilled workers, markets, resources, or external economies found in growing cities and towns. Because industry adapts to the kinds of resources available, higher-paying extramarginal industries might be attracted if a region upgraded its resources through education and training.

Indeed, the need for HRD programs in lagging areas is suggested by the fact that many former residents, whose education and skills enabled them to migrate, often return when jobs open up—leaving those without education and training still unemployed. Lagging regions might, therefore, attract better industry by making investments in manpower than by giving direct subsidies to firms to locate there.

Regional development policy in the United States

The basic U.S. policy for assisting lagging areas was established by the Public Works and Economic Development Act of 1965. This act is administered by the Economic Development Administration (EDA), which has attempted to aid development districts (defined largely in terms of high levels of unemployment and low income) by providing job opportunities in nearby growth centers to which migrants can be channeled through job information, resettlement assistance, and training.

Although this program has made some important contributions, it has several limitations. First, the EDA has not had adequate funds to produce significant economic development in many areas. Second, the cities selected were generally too small to provide significant growth prospects. A 1974 report to the Congress by the Office of Management and Budget was critical of EDA's past performance:

> The policy of dispersing assistance rather than focusing on those with the greatest potential for self-sustaining growth has resulted in much of EDA's funds going to very small communities. Over a third of its public works funds have gone to towns with less than 5,000 population. There are relatively few kinds of economic activities which can operate efficiently in such small com-

munities, so the potential for economic development in the communities is relatively small.[7]

Third, the development centers selected by the EDA also ignored cities outside the lagging areas, which might have had greater growth potential. According to Niles Hansen,

> . . . if a federal subsidy can accelerate growth in a center which is already rapidly growing, and if this subsidy is made conditional on providing employment opportunities for residents of lagging areas, then it might well be more efficient for EDA to tie into the growing environment than to attempt to create growth in a relatively stagnant area by putting in water or sewer lines.[8]

Finally, greater attention to investment in health, education, and training of the labor forces in lagging areas probably would be more effective than investing in sewer and water lines. Hansen argues:

> . . . it is not clear that public works projects in which EDA is primarily involved, chiefly infrastructure in the narrow sense, will really lead to rational migration policy. If the unemployment and welfare difficulties of rural migrants in large metropolitan areas are largely a function of lack of job skills and education, as EDA correctly maintains, why should the migration of these people to smaller growth centers not pose similar problems?[9]

Another regional development program was the Appalachian Regional Commission (ARC) created by the Appalachian Regional Development Act of 1965. By the end of 1971 ARC had allocated about $1.3 billion to the development of Appalachia. Approximately 60 percent of this amount went for highway construction, and the remaining 40 percent went for vocational and technical education, higher education, health facilities and components, water pollution control, and land reclamation.

Although it is difficult to evaluate ARC's impact on Appalachia, some observations seem to be supported by the experience to the end of 1974. It is clear, in the first place, that the scope of ARC's funding levels is not adequate to do much about many of the problems it seeks to redress. Although ARC has allocated $1 billion in the region for all purposes, it is estimated that $6 billion would have to be invested just to change substandard housing. Secondly, ARC has attempted to influence the development policies of the states in the region. In this it has had some successes and some failures. On the positive side, ARC was sufficiently successful in developing and implementing a coordinated child development program so that the Department of Health, Education, and Welfare has requested the commission to coordinate technical assistance in child development for all 50 states. Also ARC apparently has been successful in strengthening the often weak executive branches in the Appalachian states.

In other areas the commission has been less successful. It has encouraged the development of multicounty local development districts, but these organizations have not done very much to facilitate intercounty or county-state cooperation, mainly because these districts serve mainly in an advisory capacity. Perhaps the greatest problem with ARC—a problem that perhaps is compounded by inadequate resources—has been the commission's tendency to become more preoccupied with bureaucratic matters than with substantive programs.

Marginal economic activities

While the long-run desirability of capital-intensive industry and manpower-upgrading programs for lagging regions is generally conceded, there are cogent reasons for arguing the HRD programs should also include a strategy for developing labor-intensive activities, at least in the short run. For one thing, labor-intensive jobs, especially in rural areas, are needed for people whose educations and experience have not prepared them for high-wage occupations. Many of these people are likely to work in marginal enterprises or receive welfare wherever they live. The limited welfare resources might be more effectively utilized in subsidizing marginal enterprises in the rural areas than in income maintenance alone. Measures are especially needed to improve the position of small farmers by making it possible for many of those who wish to remain in agriculture to do so. With adequate technical assistance and loan programs many small farmers could switch from capital-intensive crops to such labor-intensive ones as vegetables and livestock production. It is possible that the ascendancy of large farms has resulted, in part, from federal agricultural policies, which favor large-scale activities, as well as from economies of size or comparative economic advantages that large farmers enjoy. The long overdue reform of American agricultural policies might slow down the displacement of small farmers.

Although cooperatives and other labor-intensive activities might be marginal economic enterprises, they could have significant noneconomic advantages that would have long-run beneficial implications for HRD. For example, significant actions against discrimination, poor education, unwise agricultural policies, and inadequate health and welfare services are unlikely without political pressures. Marginal economic enterprises might, therefore, form bases to generate pressures for improving the productivity of the rural poor and their children as well as providing minimum income bases for those who wish to remain in rural areas. Marginal enterprises also make it possible to slow the deterioration of many rural communities. In addition to marginal enterprises, public service employment programs could be launched in lagging regions to give jobs to persons with limited education or non-agricultural work experience.

Rural development

Rural HRD is an important national problem because of the continuing rural-to-urban migration of people who are not prepared by education or work experience for many urban jobs. In many cases people who could work in rural areas, and prefer to do so, are forced to migrate and, therefore, contribute to urban congestion because of inadequate rural job opportunities. In addition, this is an important national problem because rural people suffer from some very serious HRD problems that cannot always be solved with the approaches adapted to urban environments.

Despite its importance for domestic policy, a number of factors have caused neglect of rural HRD:

1. Perhaps most important is the invisibility of rural areas in a society in which the news media are mainly urban and, therefore, concentrate on urban problems.
2. Except for agribusiness, many rural groups have been disorganized and powerless, a condition aggravated by the declining financial bases of many small towns and the outmigration of people in the more productive age and education groups.
3. Many people have minimized rural problems because of the mistaken belief that rural populations were declining. This error was caused by equating *agricultural* with *rural* populations. It is true that the agricultural population has been declining rapidly, but between 1960 and 1970 the total rural population has remained fairly constant. Thus the size of the rural population and its higher birth rate will cause rural development and rural-to-urban migration to be national problems for a long time.
4. Finally, HRD activities have been severely restricted in rural areas for a variety of reasons, including lack of interest in this topic by agribusiness, the absence of organizations to represent

workers and small farmers, and the special problems involved in serving sparse populations.

Changes in rural America

The wholesale displacement of farm populations has been one of the most dramatic developments since World War II and has created some serious HRD problems. The proportion of farm residents to the total population declined from about 25 percent in 1940 to about 5 percent in 1970, and the farm population declined from 30.5 million to 10.3 million during this period. The displacement of the rural black population was particularly dramatic. In 1950 blacks and other minorities constituted 16 percent of the farm population as compared with only 10 percent in 1969.

Labor requirements in agriculture have declined mainly because of rising productivity. Between 1947 and 1973 farm output per manhour increased three times as fast as nonfarm output. Although some crops, such as cotton, have been fairly thoroughly mechanized, many technological breakthroughs in the production of tobacco, fruits, and vegetables have not been thoroughly exploited and are causing considerable displacement of labor during the 1970s.

These technological developments have increased the nation's agricultural output, but they have also created many problems for those displaced because these workers have inadequate education and training for nonagricultural jobs. Additional problems for rural development are created because the best-educated and most adaptable part of the rural population tends to move to urban areas, leaving behind many people who are unable to compete either with larger agribusiness or for rural jobs. In 1970, 45 percent of the rural population aged 25 years and older had 8 years or less of education; only 25 percent of the people in metropolitan areas aged 25 years and older had 8 years or less of education. Moreover, about three-fourths of all black farm residents had education of 8 years or less. Rural populations also have relatively fewer people of working age. In 1969, 25 percent of the rural and 33 percent of the metropolitan population fell in the prime working-age group of 20- to 44-year-olds.

These factors have caused some significant changes in rural employment patterns. For one thing, large numbers of small farmers and tenants became agricultural laborers. The distinctions between farm and nonfarm workers also are diminishing. Improved roads and better communication made it possible for farm residents to commute to nonfarm jobs and for urban residents to commute to farm jobs.

Rural problems

The main problems for HRD in rural areas are widespread under-employment and poverty. In 1972 the poor constituted one-fifth of rural, one-tenth of city, and one-fourteenth of metropolitan populations. Unemployment rates are very poor measures of the looseness or tightness of rural labor markets because these rates do not count part-time employment or those who are not actively seeking jobs. In other words, hidden unemployment would be a much more significant measure, although there are no precise measures of this condition. However, a rough measure of the extent of hidden unemployment in Southern agriculture is the fact that in 1950 there were about seven full-time jobs for every ten workers, whereas in 1969 there were only about five full-time jobs for every ten workers.

The pattern that emerged in American agriculture by the early 1970s was considerable mechanization, growing farm sizes, and rising incomes for some rural residents but low incomes and underemployment for many others. Moreover, the people remaining in rural areas seemed to have many disadvantages for HRD purposes: They were old or very young, had larger families, had less and inferior education, or were minorities. In addition, they tended to be economically and politically disorganized and powerless, causing public policies that vitally affect them to ignore their interests. Finally, rural people suffer because their geographic dispersion makes it difficult to deliver manpower services to them with traditional approaches, which often were developed for urban populations.

The problems of rural areas are not solving themselves by natural developments. The following rough statistics for 1971 indicate the dimensions of various rural groups:

	Millions
Rural population	54.0
Rural work force	30.0
Agricultural work force	3.9
Self-employed farmers	1.84
Wage and salary agricultural workers	1.44
Unpaid family farm workers	0.64
Seasonal farm workers	0.82
Migrant farm workers	0.18

Thus agricultural employment is a small part of the total rural work force, and hired farm labor is less than half the agricultural work force.

Rural manpower programs

Traditionally, the employment service concentrated mainly on meeting the seasonal farm needs of employers and did very little to help farm workers acquire nonagricultural jobs. In order to become more effective in rural areas the Department of Labor created the Rural Manpower Service (RMS) in 1971. The immediate aim of RMS was to use existing staff more effectively in providing equity of access to manpower services for all groups in rural areas. However, even after the creation of the RMS, the delivery of rural manpower services was limited by inadequate funds, the frequent isolation of the former farm labor specialist from the mainstream of rural manpower activities, and the inflexible organizational structure of the local employment office. The RMS attempted to solve these problems with a number of experimental projects to improve the delivery of rural manpower services.

Although training programs have not been very effective in rural areas, primarily because of inadequate training facilities, rural workers have participated in a number of regular manpower programs. In fiscal 1972, for example, 14,350 people in rural counties were enrolled in the Work Incentive Program. The largest enrollments in rural areas were in the Neighborhood Youth Corps programs, which an independent study suggests should be a major vehicle for easing the rural-to-urban transition, since the majority of the rural youth will be migrating and in need of assistance. Institutional and OJT programs enrolled only about 35,800 rural people in 1972, and very few of these were trained for expanding skilled farm jobs.

Rural workers have participated in a number of other manpower programs. About 17,400 were enrolled in Operation Mainstream, which was designed to give meaningful work experience in public works to unemployed older workers. As of March 1972, Operation Mainstream programs operated in every state except Delaware. Because it concentrated on meaningful work in community power structures, Operation Mainstream seems to have been a fairly successful work program, although it provided very limited skill training and upgrading opportunities and did very little to get its participants absorbed into private employment.

Rural governments have also participated in the Public Service Careers (PSC) and Emergency Employment Act (EEA) programs, designed to open government jobs to the unemployed and disadvantaged. Since many government programs operate in rural areas, public employment offers considerable promise as a means of providing employment. However, these programs have been limited because so few rural governments have merit systems (which are required for PSC participation) or personnel to administer the programs. Rural participation in EEA programs has been limited because the allocation formula used by the EEA (unemployment) discriminates against rural areas and because the EEA's framers were not sufficiently sensitive to the unique problems of rural areas. Rural areas have benefited from provisions that provide funds to Indians on reservations and migrant workers. Nevertheless, the restructuring of public employment programs and an expansion of Operation Mainstream-type programs could do much to provide employment to the unemployed and underemployed in rural areas, many of who are not likely to be absorbed by private enterprise unless economic expansion is much greater than it is likely to be in the absence of intense inflation.

The adequacy of manpower outlays in rural areas

Manpower expenditures, like most other social outlays, have had an urban bias. Rural areas receive a less-than-proportional share of human resource program funds, except for elementary and secondary education. In part, this is because the problems of urban areas are more conspicuous and because the cities have more proposal-writing and administrative expertise. As a consequence, most rural residents apparently know nothing about manpower services.

There are a number of obstacles to effective manpower planning for rural areas, including: program inflexibility, which causes (1) the unique needs of rural people to be ignored; (2) a preoccupation with perpetuating a bureaucracy rather than encouraging innovation, which often produces inappropriate attempts to fit urban models to rural situations; and (3) poor coordination, which causes interagency coordination often to be characterized by lip service instead of meaningful action.

Moreover, the Comprehensive Employment and Training Act of 1973 perpetuates the disadvantages of rural areas in the allocation of manpower funds. This is done both through the allocation formula, which gives heavy weight to unemployment in the allocation of funds to the states, and through "hold-harmless" clauses, which guarantee prime sponsors that their funds will not be reduced too much below past allocations. Unemployment statistics discriminate against rural areas because they do not reflect the larger rural needs—needs that arise from the large proportion of the rural population not working because of the relatively few jobs available, the relatively large numbers of people working parttime, and the higher incidence of poverty. Formulas that gave greater weight to these factors rather than to unemployment would be better for rural areas. However, an equitable formula would be difficult to devise, and it would probably be too complex to be readily understood. Perhaps then it would be better practice to simply have separate parts of major legislation deal with the unique manpower, health, and other human resource problems of rural areas.

The role of manpower programs for rural development

As noted earlier, essential economic problems of rural areas are how to provide income or employment for the unemployed or underemployed and how to facilitate the movement of people from labor-surplus areas to areas where jobs are more plentiful. Manpower programs could play an important role in both the process of industrialization and the movement of people to where job opportunities exist. Manpower programs could facilitate industrialization by providing potential employers with information about local labor markets, helping employers train their work forces, and providing training for unemployed workers or upgrading training for those who are employed.

If private industrialization does not soak up that part of the potential work force that is unemployed or underemployed, full employment can only be achieved through outmigration, public employment, or welfare payments to those who cannot work. Therefore, it might be good to use public funds to subsidize marginal firms partially, many of which might have considerable growth potential. Agricultural as well as nonagricultural enterprises might be encouraged. These activities are not likely to produce high incomes, but they could provide supplementary family incomes that might significantly improve the conditions of the rural poor.

Migration and relocation

Many economic development experts believe that migration is the most effective remedy for the problems of labor surplus in many rural areas. Migration is necessary, according to this view, because continuing technological change in agriculture reduces jobs faster than industrialization creates them. Consequently, there has been substantial outmigration from rural areas, especially during periods of full employment in the national economy. Migration varies inversely with age, and the potential gains of the typical mover who remains in urban areas apparently outweigh the pecuniary costs of moving. However some migrants suffer income losses when they move, causing many of them to return to rural areas. Most important is the finding that natural massive outmigration from rural areas since 1940 has not by itself improved significantly the relative labor incomes of farm workers or reduced the income inequality within agriculture.

Because natural migration patterns have not been sufficient to reduce surplus populations in many rural areas, many consider relocation programs as superior alternatives to fruitless attempts to attract industry to rural areas with little economic potential, to transfer payments, or to a continuation of the economically irrational migation patterns based mainly on friends, relatives, and other not necessarily knowledgeable contacts. Those who favor growth center strategies advocate programs to rationalize the labor market by moving people to these growth centers rather than leaving workers free to migrate to congested urban areas.[10]

Most rural income and employment problems have come about because of the displacement of people from agriculture who have not always been prepared for nonfarm jobs. Although nonfarm employment has been growing, it has not been sufficient to close rural-urban income gaps or to provide jobs for all of those who have been displaced from farms and have not migrated to urban areas. Manpower programs could play a larger role in helping find solutions to all of these activities. However, if this is to be done, some governmental entity—preferably the states with the assistance of the federal government—must adopt rural manpower policies, develop innovative programs geared to local realities, and provide support for more adequate manpower resources in rural areas. More specifically, rural manpower could promote a rural HRD strategy by:

1. Facilitating rural industrialization by providing better labor market information and helping to upgrade available work forces.
2. Helping people relocate from labor-surplus to labor-shortage areas.
3. Providing better job information and job training to rural youth through schools (schools could also be used as manpower delivery systems to provide information to and help upgrade adults who are in the labor force).
4. Providing outreach programs to deliver manpower services to groups who have not had equal access to these services (the extension service, private organizations, or other entities could be used for this purpose).
5. Providing public employment in a variety of public service

areas that could simultaneously provide jobs and training while supplying important needs such as improved health and recreation facilities, nursing homes, nutrition and food supply, and day-care programs.
6. Encouraging cooperative and other organizations to represent disorganized rural groups.

Conclusion

The strong presumptive relationship among education and manpower programs and economic development has been explained. It is presumptive because many aspects of the causal relationships between these activities and economic development remain to be established. For example, no clear relationship has been discovered among expenditures on education, economic productivity, and incomes. Lack of precision in establishing these relationships is attributable both to the complexity of our problem and to the fact that education has noneconomic as well as economic objectives, and its effects are difficult to measure.

Nonetheless, considerable support exists for several conclusions. Fundamental is the realization that the development (recruiting, commitment, advancement, and maintenance) of industrial work forces is a prerequisite to economic development.

Second, the particular HRD strategy depends to some extent on the stage of economic development; for example, the emphasis on science and technology varies directly with the level of economic activity. However, at advanced stages, noneconomic objectives become relatively more important because economic problems are less acute and people are concerned with the quality of life rather than with the struggle for survival. During this stage, the consumption aspects of education assume greater importance. Education in the arts and humanities again becomes important, as it was during the preindustrial period—with the difference that it is now available to the masses, not only the elite.

Before this stage is reached, however, there are likely to be urgent demands for equalizing the incomes of different groups and regions that have lagged during the industrial process. Minority groups are apt to demand that discrimination be ended and economic opportunities be enlarged, and people in low-income areas are apt to demand programs to reduce the gap between their incomes and those of more affluent regions. Programs HRD can play important roles in all of these objectives. Measures will be demanded to provide jobs in lagging geographic and industrial areas and reduce the pressures on large metropolitan areas. This will

require programs to create public or private employment opportunities in underdeveloped areas. Moreover, it will be necessary to
prepare people for expanding job opportunities and redirect the
flows of people to growth centers. Proper mixes of private and
public programs also will be needed to facilitate the retraining and
upgrading of people who already are in the labor force but whose
skills have been made obsolete or those who want to acquire the
necessary skills and education to upgrade themselves.

Notes

1. Clark Kerr et al., *Industrialism and Industrial Man* (Cambridge, Mass.: Harvard University Press, 1960), p. 35.
2. Frederick Harbison and Charles A. Myers, *Education, Manpower, and Economic Growth* (New York: McGraw-Hill, 1964).
3. Max Lerner, "Humanistic Goals," in Paul R. Hannah, ed., *Education: An Instrument of National Goals* (New York: McGraw-
   Hill, 1962), p. 103.
4. Kerr et al., op. cit., p. 167.
5. Walter Galenson, *Labor and Economic Development* (New
   York: Wiley, 1959), p. 3.
6. Harbison and Myers, op. cit., pp. 31–32.
7. *Report to the Congress on the Proposal for an Economic Adjustment Program* (Washington, D.C.: Department of Commerce and the Office of Management and Budget, February
   1974), p. 25.
8. Niles Hansen, "Growth Centers, Human Resources, and Rural
   Development," a paper written for the Rural Labor Market
   Strategies Project, the University of Texas (1971).
9. Ibid.
10. For further discussion of rural labor markets see Ray Mar-
    shall, *Rural Workers in Rural Labor Markets* (Salt Lake City,
    Utah: Olympus Publishing Co., 1974).

25
comparative
manpower policies

Explicit policies for the development and use of manpower resources have been a worldwide phenomenon since World War II.
Useful perspective on U.S. manpower policies can be gleaned by
comparing them with the approaches of other nations to related
problems. Whether the practices can be found applicable to the
United States is another question. The democratic industrialized
countries of Western Europe and Canada have the most similar
environments, yet they provide sharp contrasts in policy and program. At the beginning of the 1960s designers of the emerging
U.S. manpower policies made pilgrimages to Europe in search of
inspiration. There is now probably more to learn about manpower
programs through a reverse flow, but the United States still has
much to learn about employment policy. Third-world developing
nations represent the greatest economic distance from the world's
wealthiest nation; their manpower policies and practices have
relevance to the United States only for our most rural and underdeveloped areas. In between the Western industrial nations and the
primitive economies are a number of nations with manpower
policies that illustrate how various peoples have made the transition from ancient systems to modern ones.[1]

For purposes of illustration, Great Britain has been chosen as
an orthodox representation of an advanced industrialized and
capitalistic society; Norway represents the more intense manpower orientation of the Scandinavian countries; Japan is included as an example of a nation emerging from feudalism into a
westernized democratic capitalism; the Soviet Union is the leading
socialistic industrial nation. Because of the similarites of conditions in developing countries, three (India, Egypt, and Colombia)
were selected and treated as a group.

United Kingdom[2]

The population of the United Kingdom* amounted to 55.3 million in 1968 with 25.8 million in the labor force; about 65 percent of the labor force were males, and 35 percent were females. Over 72 percent of the labor force were engaged in the manufacturing industries, mining, and services. The forecasts indicate that the working population of the United Kingdom will reach 27 million by 1981, an increase over the period 1967–1981 of about 825,000 or 0.2 percent per annum, while population has been growing by 0.7 percent per annum. The factors making for the slower growth of the working population during the forecast period are:

1. The structure of the population is changing. Fewer women are remaining single, women are marrying earlier, and the number of elderly people is increasing.
2. The numbers remaining in full-time education after the age of 15 are also increasing.
3. Workers are retiring earlier.
4. Net population losses from migration are expected.

Manpower problems

As in all Western European countries, the United Kingdom has been pursuing an elusive economic formula that would allow its people to achieve full employment and simultaneously maintain price stability and a favorable balance of payments. To find an appropriate solution to this complicated formula labor productivity must rise as rapidly as wages, exports must be promoted, and labor supply must respond to labor demand in terms of skill requirements and location. The solution to this formula, which is universally sought among Western democracies, has been particularly elusive in the United Kingdom.

For a quarter-century after 1945, unemployment in Great Britain rose only twice around the 3 percent level, on both occasions—in 1947 and 1963—for short periods of a few months during exceptionally hard winters; and for over two-thirds of the time it has been under 2 percent. By 1972 unemployment had risen to 3.6 percent and persisted around that level into 1974. One basic problem is that unemployment rates vary widely internally. For example, when unemployment reached 2.3 percent in Great Britain at one point, it was as low as 1.6 percent in London and the south-

*Whenever possible, data in this report relate to the whole of the United Kingdom (i.e., England, Wales, Scotland, and Northern Ireland).

eastern region and as high as 4.5 percent in the northern region (Ireland), 3.9 percent in Wales, and 3.7 percent in Scotland. Therefore, a key policy approach has been to bring down the rates in some regions while maintaining a low level in others. In general, the areas with high unemployment rates—Ireland, Scotland, and Wales—are areas with old and declining industries. To meet these structural problems the emphasis has been placed on attracting new industries and encouraging labor mobility.

In the United Kingdom collective bargaining has traditionally been considered a private matter neither supported, opposed, nor controlled by law. The parties are expected to enter into negotiations and conclude gentlemen's agreements without any interference from the government. Officials usually intervene as fact finders or conciliators if they are asked to. Labor disputes have led the British economy in certain instances near to economic catastrophe. For example, in 1968 the dock workers' strike almost paralyzed the whole economy and brought the balance of payments into such disarray that the British government was forced to devalue the pound sterling by 17 percent. In 1974 a coal miners' strike was sufficiently potent to defeat the Conservative party and bring the Labor party into power. Thus the strength and the impact of the British trade unions have been a major obstacle preventing policy makers from curbing inflation and achieving full employment. The power of the trade unions appears to rise unabated. In 1962 about 4.4 million workers were involved in disputes, with 5.8 million working days lost; these figures jumped in 1971 to 11.8 million workers and 13.6 working days lost. The trade unions have succeeded in improving the wage levels of workers without corresponding improvement in productivity. For example, while the wages of nonfarm workers doubled between 1962 and 1971, labor productivity increased by only 25 percent, contributing to a 48 percent increase in prices during those periods and accelerating since. All these factors have negative impacts on the international competitiveness of the British economy and consequently contribute to deficits in the balance of payments, followed by more inflation and increasing unemployment.

Manpower programs and policy

The British government has adopted various manpower policies to deal with these problems. They can be examined under five main categories.

The first policy is employment promotion in development areas. The main objectives of regional economic policy are to achieve a more even balance between supply and demand for labor throughout the country, in order to avoid waste of manpower in the less prosperous areas, and wage inflation in those where demand is too high. Development areas (DA) have been selected in accordance with employment, unemployment, population changes, and migration. About one-fifth of all employment in Great Britain is considered to be in these DAs. The policy tools that have been used to support and encourage employment in DAs are as follows:

1. *Financial and training assistance.* To encourage investment and employment in DAs, the Board of Trade through the Industrial Development Act of 1966 is entitled to extend investment grants up to 45 percent on new plants and machinery in the manufacturing, extractive, and construction industries, compared with the national rate of 25 percent. In addition to that, the Board of Trade is also entitled to provide financial assistance up to 25 percent to any project likely to create employment within the DAs. To encourage employment in DAs further, financial assistance has been extended to employers in DAs for training and retraining their own workers.

2. *Regional employment premium (REP).* The intention of the REP, which came into effect in September 1967, was both to draw business away from the areas with inflationary pressure and to stimulate expansion in DAs by reducing wages. Industrial employers in DAs receive a small weekly subsidy for each employee.

3. *Industrial development certificate (IDC).* In accordance with the Town and Country Planning acts, no building development can take place without planning permission from the local planning authority. Any valid application for industrial building involving more than a specified area must be accompanied by an IDC from the Board of Trade. To encourage investment expansion in DAs, the board refuses IDCs outside DAs unless they are satisfied that the project could not reasonably be undertaken in a DA.

4. *New and expanding towns.* To alleviate the congestion of population in certain areas such as London, Glasgow, and Birmingham and to encourage workers to move from such areas, new towns are created and some existing ones are expanded. In 1968 there were in Great Britain 23 new towns accommodating 1.5 percent of the population and the further development of these towns is expected to bring their total population to 1.5 million, or about 2.5 percent of the population by the middle of the 1980s.

A second major manpower policy of the British government is industrial training and occupational guidance service. During the 1950s and 1960s, it was concluded that a lack of required skills was more serious than a lack of labor demand as a cause of unemployment in Great Britain; for example, in 1955 unemployment was equal to only 80 percent of the unfilled vacancies. Prior to the passage of the Industrial Training Act of 1964 (ITA), too many firms relied on other firms for training, and training methods were too unimaginative and ill adapted to meet the need. Under ITA industrial training boards were formed covering 30 different branches of industry. The boards have the authority to raise levies from all employers in their branches and use these funds to pay grants to those who undertake training of a certain quality. In addition to these boards, a Central Training Council was formed on the national level to forecast the occupational structure and provide the branch boards with guidelines on future skill requirements. Whatever the long-run result, the number of trainees of various age levels has increased as has the number and variety of courses provided.

Pursuing the same goal of better manpower utilization, a national corps of guidance officers has been introduced to give vocational advice to workers and to investigate the possibilities of better labor utilization among employed workers and those seeking employment.

A third manpower policy of the British government worthy of note is the public employment service. To facilitate matching workers and jobs, 900 employment offices are spread over the country. Although the primary objective of these offices is placement for job seekers, most of these register primarily to receive unemployment benefits. To penetrate more effectively in the labor market, these offices have expanded their functions and become more involved in vocational guidance for adults and in promoting mobility in the labor market. The British public employment service is unique in that there is a separate youth employment service (YES) whose duties include occupational guidance for the young. The validity of having a separate YES has become questionable, however, and there is a tendency to merge the youth services with the public employment offices.

A fourth manpower policy consists of redundancy payments. A scheme of redundancy pay was introduced in 1965, with the objective of compensating redundant workers for loss of jobs and encouraging mobility and acceptance of technological change. The idea of a redundancy payment, paid partly by the state and partly by the individual employer, is twofold: (1) to discourage dismissal of employees, since the employer must pay 50 percent of their wages for up to ten weeks, and (2) to ease the social costs for those who are dismissed because of technological changes. The redundancy payment scheme is also thought to promote labor mobility by tying the continuity of payments to the readiness of the beneficiaries to accept jobs in other geographical areas.

A fifth major manpower policy involves an antidiscrimination act. The policy of the U.K. government is to promote equal opportunity in employment for all citizens irrespective of color, race, national or ethnic origins and to encourage racial harmony. As Commonwealth immigrants have settled in large numbers in the main industrial areas in recent years, discrimination in employment by race, language, education, and religion has risen seriously. To overcome such discriminatory attitudes, a Race Relations Act was passed in 1968 to outlaw discrimination on grounds of race, color, or ethnic origin. Since then, all employment complaints have been investigated by suitable voluntary industry machinery or, where no such machinery exists, by the Race Relations Board.

Norway[3]

Norway is a small country, with a population of 3.9 million in 1972, growing at a slow rate of less than 1 percent per year. Labor shortage is a major constraint on its economic growth. In 1969 its civilian labor force of 1.5 million included only 14,600 unemployed people (less than 1 percent of the labor force). Its unemployment was totally frictional or a consequence of inadequate skills; there were far more jobs looking for people than there were people looking for jobs. Although it is classified as one of the advanced countries, about 13.8 percent of Norway's civilian labor force was still engaged in agriculture in 1972, compared with 1.6 percent in the United Kingdom, and 3.5 percent in the United States. On the other hand, about 49 percent of the Norwegian labor force were engaged in services, commerce, and transport and about 27.3 percent in manufacturing in 1970. Norwegian per capita income reached $3699 in 1972, but this high level was being eaten into by inflation, which reached an annual rate of 11 percent in 1972 and 1973.

Manpower problems

Suffering from widespread physical destruction caused by World War II and German occupation, the Norwegian economy depended heavily on capital-intensive industry to reconstruct its postwar economy and continued this high rate of investment into the 1960s. The estimated gross fixed capital per employed person in Norway in 1964 compared with other countries was: Norway $12,500; France, $9,900; Belgium, $7000; West Germany, $5900; and the United Kingdom $4,800.

In the mid-1960s economic growth began to decline to a

slower rate than most other European countries; for example, the Norwegian GNP grew by 5.1 percent yearly between 1965 and 1967 and by 4.3 percent yearly between 1965 and 1970; meanwhile the GNP in the European Economic Community (EEC) countries as a whole grew at rates of 3.4 and 4.6 percent during the same periods. The cause of the decline in the economic growth rate was not lack of demand or investment; it was largely failure of the labor force to expand in accord with demand. Early in the 1970s, the Norwegian authorities realized that given the law of diminishing returns, any further expansion in investment must be accompanied by further expansion in the labor force if economic growth was to be sustained. Building the labor force has become the manpower authorities' most pressing responsibility, and the low population growth and low labor force participation rate are their more pressing problems. The low Norwegian labor participation rates are largely due to low female participation rates (23.6 percent in 1969), rising required years of compulsory schooling (from 7 to 9 years), early marriages, and the reduction in the age of retirement (from 70 to 67 years). In addition, reducing the weekly working hours to 40 hours has added to the labor shortage.

These are quantitative problems, however. The really challenging problems facing the Norwegian manpower planners are those dealing with the qualitative aspects of the labor force. Industries and services are becoming more diversified and production processes more sophisticated. Manpower resources are too limited and the potential production losses are too great for Norway to bear restricted mobility and inadequate skills.

Manpower policy and programs

Full employment, price stability, and economic growth are the main goals of economic policy in Norway, as in all other Western countries, and manpower policy is integrated into that overall economic and social policy. Manpower planners are aware of the labor shortage and the skill requirements for the future, and the manpower policy objectives are broadly defined in the national objectives. The manpower policy agencies—the Minister of Local Government and Labor and the Directorate of Labor—are directly involved in the process of formulating national economic and social policy.

Manpower policy goals are designed to meet the manpower needs of the Norwegian economy in quantitative and qualitative terms and to ensure social justice and equal income distribution for the employed as well as the unemployed. Three objectives in accomplishing these goals are as follows.

1. Participation rates must rise to avoid overall labor force shortages.
2. On-the-job and institutional training must be promoted to raise productivity and to avoid any skill bottlenecks.
3. Forecasting and research tools must be refined to adjust manpower demand and supply.

Three additional sources of labor force recruitment are available: women, older workers, and foreigners. At present there are two sources, internal and external. The former includes raising the female participation rates, especially among married women. Married women, whose participation rate was 13.8 percent in 1968, represent the largest single reserve for an expanding work force. To encourage women to enter the labor market the government provides one-third of the building costs of both private and public nurseries and also extends help for their administration and operation. Furthermore, induction and training programs in plants are being increasingly adapted to the special needs of women with family responsibilities, in terms of physical accessibility, time schedules, occupations, training courses, and allowances. Technical and financial assistance is provided for employers who are willing to retrain their older workers for new jobs. To encourage those who are over 65 years old and who intend to reenter the labor market, the Labor Ministry continues to pay unemployment benefits for unlimited periods even when these persons are reemployed. Attempts are made to increase participation rates by providing rehabilitation programs for the handicapped and extending vocational guidance for the youth.

Despite the labor market stringencies, Norway has not actively encouraged the recruitment of foreign labor, though it has provided education and training for those foreigners already available in the labor market. The maritime industry has over 15,000 foreign employees. According to the terms of the 1954 Nordic Labor Market Convention, Danes, Finns, and Swedes can enter the country without residence or work permits, but since the wage levels in Norway are relatively lower than those neighboring countries, the 1954 agreement has not boosted the Norwegian labor supply.

In pursuit of qualitative improvement in their labor force, the Norwegian authorities have reorganized their educational system. Seven years of elementary education have been compulsory since 1829. As new demands for longer and more adequate training systems became urgent, in 1959 Norway introduced as an experiment nine years of compulsory education, which became mandatory in 1969 for the whole country. According to the new nine-year compulsory education system, students in the first seven years are instructed in the basic academic skills and in English as the first foreign language; in the last two years education is vocationally oriented, and guidance is provided. Beyond the ninth year the upper secondary schools are sharply divided between the vocational schools and the academic ones, which prepare young students for the universities or higher technical schools. The latter are projected to grow from 30,000 students in 1960 to 90,000 in 1990. To answer these demands, the country organized in 1969 a new tertiary educational institution, the district college.

The secondary vocational training system is also being revised in response to the extension to nine-year compulsory education. The traditional apprenticeship system is now often supplemented by workshop schools. Locally, these schools are supervised by national trade councils and an apprenticeship council in the Ministry of Church and Education. Secondary-level vocational training is designed for four years, though the term has been reduced to three years in some cases. Apprentices are required to complete 304 classroom hours for each of the three years. The training for some special crafts is conducted in three-year in-school programs, some of which are government operated and others that are run by enterprises. There were about 8000 apprentices in the manual trades and about 2000 in office occupations in 1972.

To increase the productivity and competence of skilled workers and middle management and to keep their knowledge up to date, the government established in 1967 a Department of Adult Education in the Ministry of Church and Education to supervise all adult education in the country. In the more technical fields the State Technological Institute offers extension courses in technical subjects and programs in general business and economic subjects. The Ministry of Manufacturing Industries is sponsoring the further expansion of this work. The Labor Directorate is also arranging additional extension courses where needs are not being met.

To help unemployed adults—those who move from rural to urban sectors, women, the handicapped, and youths over 20 years old—to become more employable, public vocational training programs of three to six months are available.

The national insurance system embraces old-age benefits, disability benefits, rehabilitation assistance, and widows' and mothers' benefits. In January 1971, the scope was extended to include health insurance, workmen's compensation, and unemployment insurance. These benefits were integrated into one scheme in the national insurance law of 1966, which became effective in

1967. The national insurance system is oriented toward preparing and guiding the unemployed to active employment. Cash benefits are considered payments of last resort, reflecting the temporary inability of the employment offices to find employment for individuals, though they hold themselves available for suitable jobs.

Japan[4]

Japan is a unique case in which growth and development have been achieved primarily by its own people without any significant assistance from abroad. The average annual rate of increase in GNP between 1953 and 1968 was 9.7 percent, and an annual rate of 11 percent was expected between 1968 and 1975 until the oil crisis of 1974 struck the Japanese economy. The unusually high growth rate was explained by a high investment rate. Although private and public consumption were expected to increase by 16 percent annually from 1968 through 1975, private and public gross fiscal capital formation was expected to increase by 27 percent annually during the same period.

Japan is a country with poor natural resources; raw materials are provided by Southeast Asian and African countries, oil comes from the Middle East, and coal from the United States and Western European countries. Japan's industrial products have been competing in almost all the world markets. Accordingly, the strength of the Japanese economy rests on three main factors: the growth of its export sector, the growth of its import sector, and the productivity of the Japanese labor force. Some economists call the Japanese economy a bicycle economy because it must maintain its growth momentum if it is to survive.

The economic miracle achieved by the Japanese people is reflected in the rapid increase of per capita income from $222 in 1955 to $2724 in 1972. Aware of their space limitations, the Japanese took stringent measures following World War II to control population, which consequently grew at an average annual rate of about 1 percent per year between 1950 and 1975.

In view of the relatively slow population growth and the increasing rates of economic growth, high labor force participation rates are necessary. The 1972 population of 107 million produced a labor force of 52 million. The rates for those 15 years old and over reached 65.9 percent in that year, with 60 percent males and 40 percent females. This 49 percent labor force participation rate compared with 40 percent in Norway and 47 percent in the United Kingdom. With further increases in the participation rate unlikely, the Japanese labor force will likely grow no more than the population. According to the latest five-year plan, the age structure of the labor force is expected to change, for example, while 22 percent of the labor force in 1968 were between 15 and 24 years old, this percentage is expected to decline to 15.5 percent in 1975. That decline is expected primarily because of longer years of schooling. On the other hand, while 36.4 percent of the labor force were between 40 and 64 years old in 1968, this percentage is expected to rise up to 42.7 percent in 1975 because of better health facilities, safety precautions, and better training programs for the middle-aged and the older workers.

As everywhere else in the world, the proportion of workers in agriculture and mining is declining (from 19.1 percent in 1969 to 12.8 percent in 1975). However, the Japanese economy is sufficiently industrialized that its manufacturing sector (27 percent of the labor force) and its commerce and service sectors (40 percent of the labor force) are expected to change little. Construction and public utilities workers are expected to achieve the highest rate of increase; while those workers accounted for 14.2 percent in 1969, they are expected to constitute 17.5 percent of the labor force in 1975.

Meantime, if education is a measure of labor force quality, the new entrants to the Japanese labor market show a marked improvement. In Japan compulsory education comprises primary education (six years) and lower secondary education (three years). The Japanese government provides free education up to that point. After completing this cycle, students may proceed for another three years to complete the upper secondary education. There are three kinds of upper secondary schools: those providing general education only, those providing vocational education only, and those providing both. Upon graduation from the upper secondary schools, students are then qualified for entrance examinations to a university or a junior college. As a result of this educational system, literacy in Japan exceeds 99 percent. The school enrollment rate of Japanese children receiving nine years of compulsory education is almost 100 percent; those who proceed to upper secondary levels accounted for 82.1 percent in 1970, and about 24.3 percent of those proceeded into higher education. In 1955, 68 percent of the new entrants to the labor market had completed secondary school. However, this proportion is falling as it becomes the norm to continue to upper secondary school. The percentage has dropped to 21 percent and is expected to fall to 13 percent in 1975. The percentage of new entrants who hold upper secondary school diplomas rose from 25 percent in 1955 to 57 percent in 1970, and it is expected to reach 60 percent in 1975. Rates of new entrants from universities and high technical schools rose from 7 percent in 1955 to 22 percent in 1970, and they are expected to reach 27 percent in 1975.

Manpower problems

During the period of economic recovery and up to the mid-1950s, job opportunities were not sufficient to absorb the available labor force. Unemployment was the main concern of the manpower authorities in Japan. By the late 1950s the whole manpower situation was reversed. Along with the high economic growth rate, employment opportunities improved and shortages began to appear for the first time, and although the number of job openings exceeded the number of job applicants all through the 1960s, unemployment remained relatively high among those of middle age and older. To understand the tightness of the Japanese labor market, it is necessary to have more than unemployment rates. Although that rate reached 1.4 percent (about 750,000 workers) in 1970, and remained there in 1973, job openings exceeded job applicants by 2.4 million openings. Excluding new school graduates, in 1970 there were 16 job openings for every 10 job applications. In addition, the number of job openings for school graduates had exceeded the number of job applications of school graduates by 5 million openings, a ratio of job openings to job applications of 6.8 to 1.

These labor shortages eventually created serious bottlenecks in an economy enjoying an annual 10 percent growth rate. The seriousness of the labor shortages, while 1.4 percent of the labor force remained unemployed, led many to the conviction that the privately run training system was inadequate.

Japanese experience has been that labor participation rates, at certain levels of incomes, begin to decline. A larger proportion of students remain in school for longer periods, and greater numbers of married women leave the labor force. In addition, the rigidity of labor mobility together with the increasing dissatisfaction of the young labor force have aggravated the labor shortages.

The low unemployment rate and the labor shortages do not necessarily mean that those who are employed are fully utilized. In Japan there has been a great difference in labor productivity between those engaged in the modern sectors and those in the backward sectors. The choice facing the Japanese policy makers is whether to replace the backward sectors with modern ones of higher value added or to improve the labor productivity of the older sectors.

The Japanese labor market has been under cultural and traditional pressures. The lifelong commitment of workers and employers to each other and the seniority wage system have been its main characteristics. Labor security and protection have always been provided by the private sector, and market forces have rarely intervened in management-labor relations. Now, with the opportunities offered by the labor shortage, the paternal system is breaking down, labor mobility is rising, and unions are becoming more active and demanding; yet improvement in labor productivity is the only available source of economic growth.

Manpower policy and programs

Manpower policy has reflected this economic and social situation. During the recovery period, unemployment was the main concern of the Japanese government. Immediately after the war, the Ministry of Labor was established under the pressure of the war-generated inflation and the acute unemployment situation. In 1947 the Employment Security Law was passed restricting private employment agencies and expanding the role of the state employment offices. In 1956 more than 70 percent of hiring transactions occurred through public employment security offices. In 1949 legislation was enacted empowering the government to launch work-relief projects for the unemployed. However, by the mid-1950s, when the country's growth rate began to exceed its target levels, the labor surplus had disappeared and the country began to face increasing labor shortages, especially in skilled manual occupations in all sectors of the economy and in the construction sector in particular.

Unlike the United States and most of the Western European countries, Japan, with its cultural and traditional pressures, rejected immigration as a solution to labor shortages. Instead of importing labor to Japan, the government exported capital to countries with low labor costs. By doing so, the forward momentum of economic growth was maintained without involving the country in social conflicts. Within the country, the productivity of the existing labor force was increased by transferring from labor-intensive industries to capital-intensive industries and by replacing low-value-added industries with higher-value-added ones. Mechanization of agriculture and transfer of its surplus labor to industry was a major factor in that achievement.

Japanese manpower policies had to confront the three traditional elements of the manpower system: (1) lifetime commitment, (2) the seniority wage system, and (3) the enterprise union. Traditionally, the worker committed himself to lifetime employment with a single employer who, in turn, provided protection and security to the worker until compulsory retirement, usually at age

55. In principle, any expansion of a firm was done by hiring new school graduates with no previous experience and by providing within the firm over the working lifetime training and retraining to meet the changing needs of the firm. Wage levels and promotion depended upon the length of service more than on job content. Educational background and individual family responsibilities were also considered in determining wage levels.

Collective bargaining, particularly concerning wages, is between the individual enterprise and its regular employees organized in an enterprise union. Part-time and temporary employees are not entitled to receive the same benefits as regular workers, but due to the labor shortages all employees regardless of status are treated equally. This system has helped to stabilize the labor market and acted as a countermeasure against cost-push inflation. The traditional Japanese employment system now faces collapse because of labor shortages and an increasing imbalance between the supply and demand for young school graduates. Employees feel they have more to gain from shopping for better jobs than from remaining in the firm. Unions grow more powerful and more restless. Wages reflect the market and relative bargaining power rather than the traditional noneconomic considerations.

With labor shortages, vocational education is receiving more emphasis, after having been formerly provided by employers with some financial assistance from the government. In view of the growing imbalances between the demand and the supply of skilled labor, the government through the 1969 Vocational Training Law has taken the full responsibility for vocational training with the aim of trebling the volume of training for the young and doubling it for adults (both in public institutions and supported private activities) as a target for 1975. As a long-term goal, the government is also aiming to adjust the vocational training system to become lifelong training for those whose earlier training was inadequate, who become displaced, or who seek upgrading.

Up to 1970 there were 700 employment security offices and branches all through Japan. These offices are highly computerized and closely coordinated. Placement is their main function, and because of the labor shortages they are in a relatively privileged position to be able to advise employers on personnel policies and recruitment practices. These offices also handle the unemployment insurance system. Unlike other countries, employment offices in Japan pay lump sum bonus payments to the insured unemployed so as to encourage them to find new jobs quickly. This system has shortened the job search period drastically and acted as an incentive for the unemployed to look seriously and willingly for new jobs. In addition to these services, employment offices provide vocational guidance for young, middle-aged, and aged workers. The latter are helped through separate centers called talent banks. The purpose of these banks is to provide placement services and some kind of vocational training, especially for the old and the retired workers.

Japan is unique in its pension system. Although retirement age is 55, pensioners do not receive public pensions until they reach age 60. The five-year gap is used to prepare old workers gradually for their new life. After age 55 employers begin to reduce the responsibilities of the old workers by transferring them to less important jobs, and they continue doing so until the age of 60, when they start receiving public pensions.

Soviet Union[5]

In a capitalist economy such as that of the United States, supply and demand play the major role in determining price levels. Economic planning plays a supplementary role, taking the form of government efforts to sustain economic growth, to achieve full employment, to maintain price stability and to modify income distribution. Broad instruments such as monetary and fiscal policies are the major tools, and planning tends to be partial and indirect. In contrast, in the Soviet Union planning is comprehensive and direct. The government owns the means of production and controls nearly all aspects of economic activity. The government achieves its goals through administrative commands such as output quotas, input norms, and allocation orders. Prices and markets play important but supplementary roles in the implementation of the government economic and social plans.

In 1972 the population of the USSR was 247.5 million, out of which 106.7 million were in the civilian labor force, or about 43.1 percent of the total population. Manufacturing and mining industries accounted for 27.4 percent of the labor force, followed by the agricultural sector, which accounted for 24.6 percent, and the service sector, which accounted for 21.8 percent. Although the Soviet economy is considered one of the advanced economies, its per capita income is still far behind the per capita income of the United States. In 1972 the USSR per capita income reached $1708 or about one-third of the U.S. level.

Up to 1952 the economic resources of the USSR were mobilized to achieve a high rate of industrial growth, planning was highly centralized, and training and reallocation of labor were geared to achieve that goal. Although unemployment was and still is theoretically nonexistent, there were serious manpower bottlenecks and underutilization of the labor force. Following the death of Joseph Stalin, economic and social policy became more liberalized. Various combinations of planning and reliance on market forces have emerged, including central and decentralized planning. Wage levels were used in manipulating the labor market, and incentive systems were applied to raise productivity. Manpower policies changed to give individuals increased freedom to respond to market forces.

Manpower problems

Soviet manpower planning starts from the bottom up. Each enterprise submits its labor requirements to the regional economic council. The council works out a balance to meet the needs of all its establishment for all types of labor, and administrative and government agencies work out the combined balance for the cities, regions, and republics. Theoretically, a command economy is expected to work smoothly, but, practically, the Soviet labor market has been facing serious problems.

Soviet officials insist that their system ensures full employment by organizing the distribution of labor through planned recruitment and preparation. In accordance with Soviet theory, work is obligatory for all able population (men ages 16 to 59, women ages 16 to 54) with the exception of students and women occupied at home in household work and caring for children. Work is the only source of income in the Soviet Union; unearned income from private profit or speculation is forbidden. Accordingly, work is obligatory, and the right to work is guaranteed by the state. However, rules and regulations are not enough to achieve full employment or full utilization of labor. Despite the definitional abolition of unemployment, complaints occasionally creep into Soviet journals of surplus labor reserves in various parts of the country and of the failure of labor statistics to identify those in need of placement; there are also references to unoccupied people and to citizens needing labor placements. Although the concept of frictional and seasonal unemployment is not recognized, Soviet authorities are concerned over loss of time between jobs. They consider this problem to be one of labor force instability or defects in the organized distribution of manpower, which needs improved planning.

Underemployment is a greater problem facing the Soviet economy. Although officials state that jobs are always available for qualified labor, management is asked to keep workers, even if their services are not needed. Some plants have unnecessary workers because of poor organization and lack of mechanization, especially in materials and product handling. Underutilization of workers also results when mechanization has not been accompanied by adequate shifting and retraining of workers.

A related problem is low labor productivity, often due to the rigidity of the wage system. Wage standards are determined by the government for each occupation, regardless of differences in productivity, and since workers have no fear of layoffs, the wage system provides no incentive for increasing productivity. Such rhetorical approaches as the Stakahnovite movement, which glorified the worker who exceeded production goals, are dramatic but of little long-term influence. Since union leaders are government employees, they have no influence in improving the living standard of the workers. Their role is only to provide social and recreational facilities to the labor force and to make sure that the government labor policy is adequately enforced.

There are no coordinated job information and placement services. Local employment exchanges went out of existence early in the 1930s, since there was no longer to be any unemployment. Following this concept, Soviet officials say that the question is one of choosing jobs not finding jobs. People generally find jobs for themselves through notices at factory gates, street bulletin boards, and newspaper and radio ads and through the spread of job information by friends and fellow workers. This unrealistic system has led to improper placements and to increasing frictional unemployment.

Unlike local placements, recruitment needs for distant areas have been coordinated. A special agency is responsible for handling the huge flow of the labor force from villages to cities and from one region to another. Although this administration has succeeded in moving labor from regions with labor surplus to regions suffering from labor shortages, the inadequacy of skills required and the lack of housing facilities have led to dissatisfaction among the workers.

At the party congress in 1961, concern was expressed over the costs of unnecessary turnover, and the problem continues to receive considerable concern. Unnecessary turnover results not only in loss of work time but also in lower initial productivity on new jobs, and it adds to the cost of retraining the many workers who change occupations when they shift jobs. For all industry and construction the annual loss from turnover is estimated at almost $4 billion. Turnover varies among regions with high rates in the east and north.

Manpower policy and programs

Wage policy in the Soviet labor market has been the backbone of manpower policy. Unlike free economies, wages in the Soviet

Union have been used as an instrument to manipulate the movement, allocation, and distribution of the labor force. The structure of wage rates consists of the base rates for the lower wage grade and the schedules of percentage increase for the higher grades for each occupation. The structure of differentials is designed to compensate for differences in training and for difficulties or dangers in working or living conditions. In addition, differentials are used to promote employment in occupations, industries, and regions of special national significance. Although the Soviet worker is free to choose his or her occupation, industry, and region, this freedom is undermined by the fact that, if one wants to increase earnings and acquire a claim to a larger share of the still scarce consumers' goods, one must work where the government wants one to work. To ensure conformity all over the country, the wage systems established in the plants are expected to conform to central standards.

To induce entrance into specific occupations of high demand, especially during the takeoff period of the Soviet economy, wage differentials between skilled and unskilled occupations were intended to be large. Actual earnings of skilled workers were sometimes 4 to 8 times the base rates of the unskilled. However, as education and skills improved, such extreme differentiation became unnecessary. Minimum wages were raised and the lower base rates were adjusted. After 1956 the differential dropped drastically, giving the most skilled group only 1.8 to 2 times the lowest rate.

Industrial and regional differentials have persisted in order to attract workers to priority areas. In 1960 the ranking of a group of 17 industries by average wages showed coal at the top, followed by iron ore, iron and steel, oil, paper and pulp, chemical, and machinery and electric power production. Further down were textiles, woodworking, printing, footwear, and at the bottom were food processing and garment manufacture. Those who accept work in the far north receive the highest benefits, such as cash supplements to monthly pay (depending on the length of service), extra vacations, and more disability pay. In addition, starting from 1960, one year of work in these regions is counted as a year and a half for the record of service that determines pension rights.

The Soviet planned wage system is not entirely different in its operation from a free labor market. Though wage levels are not determined by demand and supply, those forces do signal needs that are responded to by centralized wage setting. However, the rigidity of the Soviet wage system limits the freedom of managers to adjust wages when they feel necessary. Any such adjustment must await the action of government officials.

Placement and recruitment within regions are still disorganized. However, because of the rising incidence of unoccupied people, especially among the youth, commissions on labor placement have been created to see that jobs are available for youths, along with opportunities to continue their studies. Since 1957 these commissions have had the power to assign 3 to 5 percent of the workers of any enterprise. A youth is not required to take an assigned job, but the enterprise must accept any worker sent with the commission's order of placement. In addition to helping young people find jobs, the commissions make sure that these jobs are in accordance with the worker's qualifications. By doing so, they have improved job satisfaction, and productivity has increased and youth turnover rates have dropped. On the other hand, the arbitrary approach has created some dissatisfaction on management's side, and there are reports of instances when managers have rejected some persons who came with the commission's orders.

Although Soviet authorities are aware of the turnover problem, they have taken little action to reduce it. Proposals were made to limit the freedom of workers to change jobs, but these were not taken seriously because authorities were concernd about the reaction of workers to any such limitation. Instead, authorities have used a combination of social pressure and the attachment of physical benefits such as preferences in housing, additional vacations, pensions, disability benefits, and shorter working hours to the length of continuous service. Continuous efforts are made through the press, the unions, the party, and older workers in the plants to promote habits of stability. That policy has succeeded to some extent in maintaining stability among workers in general, but it does not have the same effect on youth stability.

Education is another important factor in manpower policy and programs. To meet the labor requirements of a planned economy, education at almost all levels is tied to the skills required in the labor market. Education and training are centrally planned. The number of students and number of educational institutions are determined by the USSR Council of Ministers. Plans for technical training in schools or universities are the responsibility of the Ministry of Higher and Specialized Secondary Education; state committees are responsible for planning and organizing state vocational training, while on the local levels enterprises together with educational and planning authorities work to relate education to the needs of the local economy.

Education is free at all levels. Education is compulsory through the eighth grade, after which three years are required to finish high academic school or to complete courses in a polytechnic institute. Completers of the eighth grade are encouraged to enter the labor market and to finish high school at night courses. High school completers are also encouraged to spend at least two years in productive work before applying for university education. To encourage work experience before university education, universities tend to give preferences to those who apply having work experience. The main purpose for combining work with education is to tailor the education to the establishment's needs. This policy has been hindered by a lack of teaching facilities and qualified teachers and the reluctance of young workers to attend night courses. To encourage further education the requirements for high school and university education have been reduced to ten years. Education is highly specialized and vocationally oriented.

Although institutional training is growing, OJT is still the predominant means of preparing skilled workers. Apprenticeship usually requires six months. Short-term courses provide training to meet the needs of changing technology; they are thought useful for their close relation to current needs but are criticized as tending to be too narrow.

Recent labor developments in the U.S.S.R. have been influenced by the economic reforms undertaken during the 1960s. Industrial growth has been rapid, and the industrial labor force has been growing faster than the rate of the working population by drawing workers from nonindustrial sectors. Early in 1970 the economic structure was shifted in favor of the service sector. Between 1966 and 1970 the industrial labor force grew by 14.6 percent, then slowed to 6.3 percent for 1971–1975. More than half of the projected total growth of employment under the 1971–1975 five-year plan was to be diverted to the service sector and other nonmaterial production sectors (trade, education, medicine, science, etc.). However, this does not mean that the industrial sector was ignored in the five-year plan. Future industrial growth will be based primarily on the more intensive utilization of existing labor resources. Increased output will have to be achieved essentially through improving labor productivity rather than through increasing the number of workers. The desire to improve productivity and to link it more closely with wages was mentioned in the 1971–1975 plan. While the plan called for an increase of 36 to 40 percent over the five years, it also mentioned increases in wages and salaries amounting to 20 to 22 percent for production and office workers and 30 to 36 percent for farmers. To achieve the productivity rates of the current plan, incentive systems are to be used on a group basis rather than on an individual basis and to shift from a time-rate wage system to a piece-rate wage system. Already, 60 percent of all industrial wages are now based on piece rates, compared with the 40 percent on time-rate systems.

Relating productivity to wages and using incentives to increase productivity are the main characteristics of the labor market reforms manifested in the current five-year plan. To ensure flexibility in implementation more authority has been given to plant managers, and the tendency toward decentralization in planning and decision making has been growing.

Selected developing countries[6]

Unlike the developed countries, in which manpower problems and policies differ by demographic, geographic, political, and cultural characteristics, the manpower situations of the developing countries bear great similarities to each other. Though the manpower problems are similar, this similarity does not carry over to the specific policies that the developing countries use in solving their problems. Some of them attempt to copy the policies applied in advanced countries without regard to the relevance of such policies. Others apply policies dictated by the culture of their people, whereas others apply manpower policies only to serve the interest of those who are in power. For example, to convince the people that the ruling party is concerned for their welfare some governments expand the educational institutions to increase the quantity of educational output, with no concern for the quality of education. Others begin to invest in higher education, thinking that such policy will bring them close to the technological level of the developed countries; they often end up with an overinvestment in higher education and high levels of unemployment among the highly educated.

Three countries have been selected as examples representing Africa, Asia, and South America—Egypt, India, and Colombia.

Manpower characteristics

Characteristic of most of the developing countries is the low labor force participation, especially of women. For example, rates for women were 33.5 percent in India, 26.4 percent in Egypt, and 29.4 percent in Colombia, compared with 42 percent in the United States. Along with the low participation of women, the young age profile of the population in these countries is an important factor. In India about 42 percent of its population in 1971 were under 15 years of age, and in Colombia that rate was as high as 46 percent in 1964. In most developed countries the rate ranges from 30 to 35 percent.

Population growth rates in developing countries are also typically very high. Some of these countries have zero rates of per capita economic growth and even negative rates because the growth of the economies fails to catch up with the population growth. The main purpose of the construction of the Aswan Dam in Egypt was to increase agricultural production to keep up with the population growth, not to improve the per capita agricultural production. The average population growth rate between 1960 and 1970 was 2.7 percent in India, 2.5 percent in Egypt, and 2.3 percent in Colombia, compared with 1.2 percent in the United States. The high population growth has inversely affected the per capita income for those countries. For example, the 1970 per capita income measured by 1963 prices was $194 in Egypt, $186 in Colombia, and $49 in India, compared with $3751 in the United States.

Most of those who are economically active in developing countries are still engaged in the agricultural sector, 35 percent or more in most countries. In India this rate was 72.9 percent in 1961; it was 53.3 percent in Egypt in 1966 and 47.2 percent in Colombia in 1964, compared with 4.2 percent in the United States in 1971. Those involved in the service sectors still constitute low percentages of the total labor forces; for example, in the same years just mentioned these rates were 18 percent, 14.9 percent, and 8.8 percent in Colombia, Egypt, and India respectively compared with 30.2 percent in the United States. In addition to that, the labor market in these countries is still dealing with relatively small enterprises. In the same years mentioned previously, 46 percent and 41 percent of those employed in Egypt and Colombia respectively were either family workers or self-employed, compared with only 9.5 percent in the United States. On the other hand, while 57 percent, 54 percent, and 25 percent were salary and wage earners in Colombia, Egypt, and India respectively, that rate reached 90 percent in the United States.

With the majority of the labor force engaged in agriculture, the wage levels in this sector are extremely low and sometimes below the subsistence levels. For instance, in 1971 the weekly wages in agriculture in India and Colombia were 2.5 percent and 5 percent respectively of those of the United States. The wage levels in the nonagricultural sectors are still very low compared with those of the advanced countries.

As far as education and training are concerned, the quantity rather than the quality is the main concern of educational planners in the developing countries. Almost all of these countries provide at least nine years of free and compulsory education; the last three years of secondary education are usually provided free but are not compulsory. Emphasis in education is still academic rather than vocational, but, due to shortages in technical skills, some of these countries have been shifting their emphasis to vocational education. Investment in higher education has been growing without checking the validity of such investment. Higher education is still motivated by prestige rather than economic need. The shortage of blue-collar jobs and the surplus of white-collar jobs result from the way these jobs are perceived by society in general and by the workers in particular.

Manpower problems

In accordance with the demographic characteristics of the populations in general and the labor forces in particular, the major manpower problems facing the developing countries are unemployment and underemployment. Although the official figures of the unemployment rates are relatively low (for example, 3.1 percent in Egypt in 1968), the actual rates are much higher. Scarce job opportunities coupled with low pay cause high percentages of the labor force to become discouraged and leave the labor market, leading to an undercount of unemployment. Even if the official unemployment rates are accepted, there is still the problem of underemployment. In certain sectors such as agriculture, construction, and government, a high percentage of those who are supposedly fully employed are in fact underemployed. That is, employment could fall without reducing output. With scarce job opportunities compared to the high values attached to university graduation, many more seek higher education than the job markets can absorb. Furthermore, when more and better education is tied together with the increasingly youthful age composition of the population, labor force participation rates increase more rapidly than job opportunities, thus increasing unemployment in the early stages of development.

In developed countries wages are usually directly related to productivity; in developing countries this is rare. In Egypt, for example, the government is the largest single employer. The government is responsible for finding employment for each job seeker, and since wages are determined by seniority and educational certificates regardless of performance, productivity deteriorates and prices increase. Factors other than employment policy also lead to low rates of productivity. The majority of the labor force in the developing countries are engaged in agriculture, and since agricultural output depends mainly on rainfall and weather, agricultural output and the productivity of the agricultural labor force become unpredictable. Any decline in agricultural productivity will decrease the average labor productivity in the whole economy. The high percentage of underemployment in nonfarm sectors has also contributed to low labor productivity. Lack of training is another factor. Enterprises in these countries are relatively small, and most of them operate at a marginal level. Any increase in costs will force them out of business. Since OJT will definitely add to the immediate costs of these enterprises, whether or not it raises long-run productivity, most of the enterprises are reluctant to undertake training. Institutional training programs are very limited and are carried out on a small scale; expansion of such programs is hindered by the lack of qualified trainers. Even those who graduate from such institutions are not easily absorbed by the labor market, since the training quality acquired is still low and often irrelevant to the skills required by the labor market.

Labor market information is almost nonexistent in these markets and, if available, is often unreliable and sometimes misleading. The process of matching individuals and jobs is still carried out in very primitive ways. Vocational guidance and counseling are rare.

Manpower policies for developing countries

Manpower policies in developing countries are so rudimentary that it is more useful to discuss what is needed than what exists. A major obstacle to manpower policy making in every developing country is the lack of data for manpower planning. Starting from rudimentary levels, data are needed on the stock of manpower, including age structure, sex composition, educational attainment, labor force participation rates, types of workers, the distribution of labor force by economic activities, unemployment, productivity, and the wage levels. On the supply side, manpower data needed include: the expected rate of population growth, the expected rate of labor force growth, the expected educational output, and the expected replacement rates. Manpower projections by economic activity, occupation, and sex become the next step. In accordance with estimates of shortages and surpluses, vocational guidance and counseling are needed to guide students to the occupations in which shortages are expected and away from surplus occupations.

Population control takes top priority among policy needs in such countries but is rarely successful. As for the immediate problem of unemployment and underemployment, labor-intensive projects should be emphasized by extending financial and technical assistance to them. Since average productivity largely depends upon agricultural productivity, special emphasis should be given to improving productivity in this sector through agricultural extension services for farmers, irrigation projects, and so on. Yet the temptation is always to undertake more impressive, intensive capital industrial projects.

Educational policies are needed that can be adjusted to meet the labor market requirements and to emphasize quality rather than quantity. Some small enterprises could be subsidized through tax reductions or direct payments and encouraged to run their own training programs. Vocational training institutions in nearly every developing country need to expand in accordance with the labor demand. Yet the emphasis has traditionally been on a more classical academic education. The necessary staff is generally not available but could be imported free through bilateral or multi-lateral agreements with developed countries. Experts who come to serve in developing countries should be utilized fully to train local employees rather than to do the work by themselves and leave. Counterparts are needed to work with these experts all through their service periods.

To ensure flexibility in training programs there is need for institutions capable of providing training programs adapted to market needs. Colombia has launched one of the largest, most extensive, and best-financed training organizations in all Latin America. It develops and operates a vast array of training services for workers in commerce, industry, agriculture, animal husbandry, hotel management, and catering as well as medical services (nurses) and even vocational training for the military. Financial support for training is drawn from a tax of 2 percent on salaries and wages paid by both public and private enterprises with capital exceeding $21,000 or employing at least ten workers and from a tax of 0.5 percent on salaries and wages paid by the central government and the territorial departments and municipalities. Programs are developed in response to requests by enterprises and government agencies, guided by regional manpower surveys. The training programs are thus constantly changing. In general, the entire training activity is geared to the needs of the modern sector. In effect, the training organization is the servant of its constituency, the public and private enterprises whose payrolls are taxed to support its activities. But all of this depends upon some basic cultural changes. Probably the single greatest manpower need of the developing countries is the concept of career education discussed in Chapter 11, particularly that directed at the development of work values, the changing of cultural commitments, and the spreading understanding of the economy and the labor market and the individual's role in them.

Conclusion

In the early 1960s it was customary to lament the failure of the United States to develop manpower policies and programs equivalent to those in Western Europe. Indeed, many lessons were learned that were helpful in the design of U.S. programs. No direct transfer was possible; social, political, and economic systems differed too greatly in tradition and structure. Now the shoe appears to be on the other foot. The United States made rapid manpower progress during the 1960s. Whereas pilgrimages were once made by Americans to Europe and elsewhere to import manpower ideas, now, increasingly, the United States is the exporter of manpower strategies. For the developed nations such transfers of knowledge are possible and profitable.

Bringing economic development to an underdeveloped land has proved to be a frustrating task. Despite unprecedented effort and foreign assistance, no developing nation has been launched into the modern industrial world in two generations. A destroyed Europe was rebuilt within a decade after World War II, utilizing the availability of well-educated manpower with industrial traditions. The Soviet Union and other nations of Eastern Europe seem to be moving successfully over the boundary between primitive agrarianism and modern industrialism. After 30 years of post–World War II effort it seemed that those nations that had passed through the agrarian age into the industrial economy and on to relative abundance had found no way to export the path they trod. A few nations in Latin America, notably Mexico, appear to be experiencing some progress on the same path. China seems to have promise as a strong economy as well as a world power. But for the rest of Asia, Latin America, Africa (except for South Africa) and the Middle East (but for Israel and the oil exporters) the path to industrialization and abundance seems blocked. Perhaps we of the developed nations need to be reminded that our progress was a matter of centuries, not just decades.

A few significant points for comparing and contrasting the manpower policies of different countries appear to be justified and useful:

1. The process of rural-to-urban migration has been and will be painful everywhere. The life styles of the cities and the rural areas are too divergent for the transition to be made easily. The development of industrial commitment, including the willingness to accept and the ability to cope with the complexities and interdependence of life, is a process of generations. The United States and the Western European nations invested more than a century in their transition from agrarian to industrial social institutions. The newly developing nations are trying to traverse the route in one or two decades. The road cannot but be bumpy.

2. No country has discovered a satisfactory way to mesh education and training activities with its manpower needs. In

part, this reflects the difficulties of forecasting the future. More profoundly, it is probably inherent in the nature of education and of occupational choice and skill acquirement. Education has so many objectives—imparting culture, teaching citizenship and the use of leisure time, providing intellectual stimulation—that it is difficult to separate or coordinate its manpower development function. As long as there are relatively free occupational choices, there will be uncertainties, missteps, and second thoughts. Yet the alternative is a slave labor system. No one has yet satisfactorily traced the pattern by which skills are acquired in order to orchestrate native ability, nonwork experience, work experience, informal and formal OJT, academic and general education, and classroom skill training.

3. Whatever the political and social setting, there is a tendency for workers to seek some means of participation in the process by which the rules are made that govern their working lives. That participation—whether through collective bargaining, worker self-management, or workers' councils—is integral to the manpower policy process. Wherever workers' organizations exist, they will pursue workers' benefits more avidly than they do productivity; hence there is an inherent inflationary bias in organized labor markets. Similarly, the pursuit of workers' welfare will conflict with the free market allocation process, which requires differentials in earnings and employment opportunities to direct the flow of labor to socially optimum uses.

4. No one has successfully isolated the role of human resources and human capital investments in economic viability and growth. Can deliberate investments in human resources comprise an independent factor in economic development? Rather than attributing an otherwise unclaimed residual of economic growth as a return to investment in human capital, can a nation deliberately invest in human capital with reasonable assurance that the investment will pay off? The answer seems to be that no one knows.

5. Everywhere the basic relationship among birth rates, age-sex structure of the population, labor force participation rates, productivity increases, and growth of economic output is the ultimate limitation of both economic policy and manpower policy; yet it is also the source of success or failure. How to conceptualize the relationship and manage it is another relative unknown.

6. The work place is a society in miniature. As long as there are tendencies for people to structure their social relationships according to generalized myths, there will be discrimination in the work place. No country is free from ethnic, social, sex, age, or class discrimination in its labor markets.

But despite these essentially negative conclusions, viable manpower policies and programs do emerge and improve conditions that would otherwise be even more chaotic. A prominent practitioner of the manpower arts stated: "In the labor market the invisible hand is all thumbs." Typical of manpower planners throughout the world is a modesty of ambition. Given the complexities of the labor market, few expect to solve manpower problems. They are satisfied to tinker sufficiently with the system to make marginal improvements. To promise any more is unrealistic hope or political rhetoric.

Notes

1. Frederick H. Harbison and Charles A. Myers, *Management in the Industrial World* (New York: McGraw-Hill, 1969); Frederick H. Harbison, *Human Resources as the Wealth of Nations* (New York: Oxford University Press, 1973).
2. "Organization for Economic Development," *Manpower in the United Kingdom*, OECD (1970).
3. "Organization for Economic Development," *Manpower in Norway*, OECD (1972).
4. *New Economic and Social Development Plan*, 1970–1975, Economic Planning Agency, Government of Japan, May 1970; *Manpower Policy in Japan*, OECD (1973).
5. V. Jalrina, *Some Recent Developments in the Labor Field in the USSR*, (ILR) Vol. 106, Nos. 2 and 3 (August and September 1972); Morris Bernstein and D. R. Fusfeld, *The Soviet Economy*, 3rd ed. (Homewood, Ill.: Irwin, 1970).
6. International Labor Office, *International Labor Statistics* (1972); *Monthly Bulletin of Statistics*, U.N. (February 1974); *Yearbook of National Account Statistics*, U.N. (1972); *Demographic Yearbook*, U.N. (1972); *Statistical Yearbook*, U.N. (1972); Pamphlet-World Bank Atlas, *Population Per Capita Product and Growth Rates*, published by the International Bank for Reconstruction and Development (1972).

epilogue

26

issues for the next decade

What will be the critical human resource issues in the forseeable future? Crystal-ball gazing is a hazardous pursuit. For example, few foresaw the increasing importance of female workers over the past three decades, the population explosion that followed World War II, and the more abrupt decline in birth rates that occurred during the past decade. Nonetheless, social institutions and trends are to a large extent shaped by past events. This review provides at least a tentative basis for pinpointing some of the major issues and indicating future directions of human resource development in the United States.

Scarcity and the Malthusian specter

From a broad perspective human resources and labor markets are influenced by world population growth and movements. Of concern is the absolute size of the population, its characteristics, and its geographic distribution. The need to provide the knowledge and means to limit population growth has become a worldwide necessity because of the pressure of population on resources and living space. Experts estimate that the world's food supply must double during the next generation just to maintain present nutrition levels. Present levels are far from adequate for most of the world's people, and given existing technology, it is not at all clear that food production can be expanded to meet projected population growth. High-energy and capital-consuming techniques used in the United States are being limited by environmental concerns as well as energy shortages.

Our perspective must and will be modified during the 1970s and 1980s to deal with the economic realities the world faces. The major long-run problem of the 1970s and 1980s is likely to be eco-

nomic shortages, not surpluses. Moreover, national economic policy must pay more attention to measures to overcome scarcities
and increase productivity. We must be concerned with developing
adequate technologies to deal with the food, energy, and environmental problems.

Moreover, a major theme of this book has been that economic
policy can no longer assume homogeneous labor markets. Monetary and fiscal policies must be supplemented by labor market
policies geared to the unique characteristics and problems of particular labor markets. For example, the Phillips curve analysis
appears to be valid only as a long-run approximation; in the short
run, though, inflation can arise outside labor markets (as with
shortages of food and energy), and unemployment can be the
product of structural changes not necessarily related to prices and
the general level of economic activity.

Traditional microeconomic theory must be reexamined in the
light of the problems of the 1970s and 1980s. Much human resource policy has been based on neoclassical economic reasoning,
which has serious limitations when applied to social problems.
The neoclassical framework is useful when examining *individual*
behavior, but it offers less guidance for group and community
activity. We have noted the theoretical and practical limitations in
applying the human capital concept (which grows directly out of
the marginal productivity theory) to human resource development. Moreover, reliance on profit- or utility-maximizing concepts
provides inadequate guides to public policy. For example, preoccupation with individual profit maximizing in farming has
tended to maximize the profits and incomes of those farmers who
survive, but it pays no attention to those who are displaced in the
process and has not counted the direct public costs involved in
promoting agribusiness interests through direct subsidies and the
land grant college system. A preoccupation with *private* benefits
may exaggerate the efficiency of the system and ignore social costs.

Preparing for work

In regard to the United States alone, the declining rate of population growth is likely to be sustained. Concern with ecological balance, improved birth-control technology, the desire of mothers to
opt for careers outside their homes, and the erosion of mores that
hindered effective family planning will continue to reduce birth
rates, conceivably to the point of stabilizing the population. With
an increasing proportion of the voting population beyond the
childbearing and child-rearing age and a large proportion of child-

less couples, there will be less political pressure to pour money into education. Nevertheless, it will remain true that those who gain their high incomes from their personal knowledge and talents will be concerned about gaining for their children the credentials and skills for similar earnings. These two trends will likely combine for a slowed growth rate for total educational expenditures but a rising per capita investment in education. More resources will be available for the development of each child, and radical changes are likely in the way this smaller number of American children are reared and educated.

Educational facilities have been hard pressed during this century to expand as rapidly as population and the demand for higher education. Consequently, institutional arrangements for children until they reach the normal school-entry age of six have been delayed, and many communities still lack organized provisions for children under age five. Despite the continuing and almost exclusive reliance upon home and mother to take care of children prior to their entering kindergarten, the number of working mothers continues to grow. They are likely to demand that society provide day care for their children. The experience of other countries that have grown to rely upon female labor has been to expand preschool child-care facilities, as the United States did during World War II. The government already provides some facilities, particularly for the poor under the antipoverty programs, and the more affluent purchase nursery care for their children; but expanded coverage is needed. Child-care arrangements also might include educational and training components. This would involve the expansion of government-supported educational facilities to age three or possibly earlier. In all likelihood, child care, whether in school facilities or in specially designed institutions, will expand in the years ahead.

At the other end of the school-age spectrum the continued growth of higher education during the past century is likely to be arrested. Already, three of every four young Americans continue their schooling until their 18th birthdays, and almost one of five continues for four or more years. The need, wisdom, and practicality of prolonging school attendance is being increasingly questioned; too frequently, the added school years have little relation to preparation for work or for life. Education throughout one's work life will probably emerge rather than further prolongation of the exclusively preparatory period during one's childhood, youth, and early adulthood. Changing technology and skill needs are likely to induce an increasing number of persons to undergo specific training periodically throughout their lifetimes.

While mature and committed workers may occasionally turn

to the educational system to recharge their intellectual batteries or their manual skills, youths and young adults may combine experience beyond their school walls with educational pursuits. This may lead to a restructuring of both educational facilities and labor market institutions to provide flexibility for the student-worker to enter and leave school and work. As greater specialization is required and more of one's lifetime is spent in school, greater attention to counseling and exposure to work options will be necessary to facilitate successive occupational choices during the work career. Too often, career decisions are now being made on the basis of scholastic aptitude alone. Combining work experience with school attendance may lead to sounder career choices.

Career education is a significant development in preparation for the job market. It signals the recognition that work values and attitudes with an impact on the entire career have more basic importance than immediate job skills. The conceptual challenge is to fit all phases of education and training that are relevant to preparation for employment into a work-career framework. With the voting weight and political attention shifting to people in the older age brackets, it may be concluded that education is too important to be wasted on the young—that is, the preparation for employment that begins in childhood must be available throughout a lifetime as sought and needed. Europeans call this periodic career upgrading "recurrent education."

Work attitudes

Less tangible than the changing institutional arrangements for job preparation, but potentially of no less significance, will be the continued transformation of attitudes toward work. Much has been made of the alleged loss of pride in craftsmanship and the deterioration of the quality of services. These developments presumably reflect not only widespread job dissatisfaction but also a general antipathy to work, forsaking the traditional work ethic. Among youth, in particular, there is claimed to be a widespread rejection of the work ethic as the incentive of material rewards are becoming less important. To a large extent, these may be only youthful manifestations, and exaggerated at that. It is likely that the addiction to creature comforts that "hooked" their elders is also going to take hold of the current young as the responsibilities of family life induce them to maximize their incomes.

Nonetheless, real changes are taking place in work attitudes, and they will have a pervasive influence in the future. Workers are becoming increasingly concerned with the qualitative aspects of work—not only with wages, hours, and benefits but also with opportunities, responsibilities, and freedom on the job. As wages increase, income may become a less potent incentive and other motivating forces will be needed to ensure discipline in the work place. If economic prosperity and growth are sustained, the work ethic is likely to weaken as a generation of workers that has experienced nothing but relative affluence and job security takes its place.

Adequacy of employment

Other changes have been occurring in the labor market. The growth of income-supported programs has provided many workers with more than one basic source of income. One-ninth of total personal income is the product of transfer payments, and a significant proportion of the population experience periods of idleness cushioned by government programs. Nonetheless, the availability of jobs, as measured by the unemployment rate, is not a true indication of the *adequacy* of employment.

Low wages are a serious and persisting problem deserving at least as much attention as forced idleness. Raising the minimum wage is one possible policy, but the income gains for some may result in increased unemployment at the end of the labor queue. An alternative is a wage subsidy for low-income family heads. A reevaluation of employment and earnings inadequacy also might turn policy makers' attention to nonmetropolitan areas, where at least one-third of the needy are located but who have been short-changed by federal employment programs.

Work and welfare

The inevitable growth of public income-support efforts will continue to erode the distinction between work and welfare. As the welfare floor is raised to help those nominally unable to work because of old age, infirmity, child-care responsibilities, or lack of jobs and as supplements are extended to those who work but earn less than a socially acceptable minimum income, increasing numbers may opt for welfare instead of workfare, to borrow from well-publicized rhetoric.

The challenge is to develop adequate work incentive schemes to ensure that those who can support themselves will do so. But work incentives are of no help to the millions of poor who are unable to find or hold jobs. Thus maintaining a low guaranteed income and expecting the poor to supplement their welfare by earnings is not realistic.

Manpower programs

As the overlap between welfare and work increases, manpower programs will have an expanded role. Opportunities must be provided for all individuals who will work but are unable to earn an adequate income. Artificial credential barriers can be broken down through subsidies, employer education, and governmental fiat; upgrading can be assisted through supplemental education and training; the employability of participants can be improved by training, counseling, education, and related services. However, those who believe that manpower programs can substitute employment for welfare are likely to be disappointed. Only a minority of all welfare recipients can become self-supporting; manpower programs may have to maintain the more modest aim of helping some recipients to supplement their welfare income.

In many cases, however, manpower programs offer a second chance to those who failed in, or were failed by, the educational system and for those whose skills have been eroded by technological change. As more knowledge is gained about the needs of particular individuals and about the effectiveness of particular services or combinations of services in meeting these needs, the manpower programs may become an alternative for those who do not succeed in the regular school system. The experience gained from the manpower programs may also help the regular school system to avoid many mistakes.

Manpower programs have been consistently treated as a separate remedial system for a separate clientele. They have never been viewed as a component of a broader human resource development system. Their resources have always been minor in the total scheme of public and private efforts to prepare and maintain human resources. In fact, most such preparation is private, occurring in the homes and the employing establishments. Schools, churches, neighborhoods, and the entire community are involved in the process. Certainly, manpower programs are marginal efforts that can make sense only in a broader labor market/human resource context, but there is hope that the emergence of local labor market planning may encourage the integration of manpower and other human resources programs.

Equal Employment Opportunity

Manpower programs are closely related to combating discrimination in employment. On the one hand, manpower programs are frequently needed to help train the victims of discrimination in order to help them compete for available employment opportunities. On the other hand, manpower programs can be effective only if discrimination in employment is eliminated. Civil rights legislation and manpower programs have contributed to the substantial gains of blacks; pressures from women's liberation groups and action under civil rights legislation opened some doors for women; the problems of Chicanos, Indians, and other minorities also have been documented, and some efforts have been made to alleviate them. Nevertheless, discrimination remains a persistent and festering disease in the American economy.

It is naïve to assume that progress toward equal employment opportunity is guaranteed or that freedoms achieved in the past will necessarily persist. Other labor market problems may demand priority, or opposition may increase from those who are challenged by the gains of minorities. Also, if positive steps are not taken, the situation may deteriorate because of adverse developments in the labor market. An increasing number of educated blacks will demand entrance into better-paying or more responsible positions, while the value of a college education is declining as a guarantee of choice jobs. Constant vigil must be kept, therefore to ensure that progress continues to be made.

It is the prime goal of manpower policy to ensure that all human resources are fully developed and utilized. As long as discrimination exists and certain minorities are given fewer opportunities, assistance must be concentrated among these minorities. Therefore, manpower policy must continue to focus on the victims of discrimination. Education must be improved, occupational training provided, and discriminatory barriers broken down. Both a push and a pull are required if those who are discriminated against are to get an equal chance in the work force.

The role of government

To achieve the expanded goals of human resource development, the government will have to assume an ever-increasing responsibility. In recent years the government's role in education, manpower programs, and related efforts expanded drastically. At the same time, there is a heightened awareness of the effect that a wide range of government actions has upon the development and utilization of our human resources. No longer viewed separately and in isolation, these actions more and more are being examined for their manpower implications.

One example has been military manpower policies. During

wartime, youths who were more likely to be unemployed were siphoned off, thereby easing unemployment pressure. And as the troops came home, the reverse situation became painfully evident. Another example is the role of government as a civilian employer. In the past neither the federal government nor the many state and local governments have acted as model employers. Pressures to eliminate discriminatory practices, to remove arbitrary credential barriers, and to expand training and advancement opportunities for the disadvantaged have resulted in some changes in governmental manpower practices. Yet much remains to be done, especially at the state and local levels, to make governments equal opportunity employers.

The government also plays a major role through such regulatory functions as the enforcement of antidiscrimination laws and wage-and-hours regulations. Perhaps most significantly, the federal government has assumed responsibility for the maintenance of a favorable economic climate. But because high employment is not the only goal, the Employment Act of 1946, which made it the policy of the federal government to sustain maximum employment, remains largely an exhortation. The consensus among economists, politicians, and informed citizens is that the unemployment rate can be lowered or raised almost at the public will. The problem is to achieve high employment without undue inflation, and thus the key issue is the trade-off between unemployment and inflation. At least in the short run we can choose whatever employment level or price stability we are willing to pay for, but we cannot have both high employment and stable prices. In time manpower programs and other structural measures such as aid to depressed areas may help to improve the terms of trade-off, but there is no indication that both full employment and stable prices can be achieved in the immediate future. Given this dilemma, experience dictates measures that will cushion the negative effects of inflation in order to sustain a high-employment economy. The progress made during the past three or four decades justifies optimism that increasingly sophisticated designs will ease the choice between inflation and unemployment.

The emergence of human resource policy

According to dictionary definitions, no policy for human resources now exists. At the federal level most efforts have been a reaction to the special problems—real or imaginary—that caught public attention. Federal aid to elementary and secondary schools was initiated to help financially troubled areas, with little emphasis on educational innovations. Grants and loans to students were largely motivated by the Sputnik-induced fears of a technology gap. Manpower programs were funded in a haphazard fashion, in response to perceived needs. Military policies were promulgated to fight an unexpectedly difficult and unpopular war at what was thought to be the least political cost. Monetary and fiscal policies were geared to affect normal economic activity with little consideration of their impact on special groups or their relation to programs that focused on special needs.

It is not at all clear, however, that the impact of human resource programs would be more salutary if a definite policy was selected to guide decision. What would be the nature and scope of such a policy? From our examination of past and present developments, we cannot answer this vital question, but we can define the ingredients and objectives of a human resources policy. Such a policy must be capable of identifying problems, setting goals, designing programs, marshaling resources, and mounting activities encompassing the entire labor market. To achieve the dual objectives of efficient allocation of manpower resources and optimum choice for participants in the work force, a manpower system should allow each individual to plan a working career in full awareness of his own abilities and the alternatives open to him. A high and sustained level of economic activity is necessary to provide opportunities of sufficient number and range. Restrictions unrelated to productivity or equity—such as overcredentialization and discrimination based on age, race, or sex—must not be allowed to interfere with access to, and rewards for, these opportunities. The distribution of jobs must be open and flexible: Only the lack of potential competence should restrain preparation and access to individual occupational choice; lateral and upward mobility should be maintained; help in adapting to economic and technological change should be available. The reward structure— income, status, and job satisfaction—should be similarly unencumbered. All those able and willing to work should thus find both opportunities and rewards in the production of goods and services favored by society as reflected in the marketplace and the ballot box.

To what degree should policy be directed toward the achievement of these objectives? The supply of social energy is always limited and should be conserved for high-priority efforts. Interrelated with the development of human resources, as we have noted, are fiscal, monetary, education, housing, transportation, welfare, health, defense, and myriad other economic and social problems. Such linkages should be noted, and policy makers in each arena should act consistently, but no single policy can comprehend all the others. Indeed, experience suggests the wisdom of leaving to unguided individual choice all those decisions that will cause no serious problems in the aggregate, for centralized decisions are not necessarily wiser; and if they are short-sighted, they may cause more damage than a series of unwise individual decisions.

Public intervention is, in some cases, appropriate, but its limits must be understood. First, programs concerned with development of human resources can hope to solve only problems related to unemployment and earnings. A manpower program can contribute to the solution of poverty only for those families with present or potential workers; it can solve social discontent only for those whose problems relate to the lack of meaningful employment. Manpower policies are likely to affect only marginally problems connected with family breakups, pollution, congestion, and other ills of a complex urban society. Second, public policy has only two sources of leverage; dollars and votes. Policies that do not affect the distribution of either are only pious declarations and have little influence.

Finding appropriate techniques to evaluate social programs is a pervasive constraint. Benefit-cost techniques provide very limited bases for a program evaluation. Aside from conceptual shortcomings, cost-benefit analysis may fail to raise the right questions. For example, in connection with welfare programs, we should be more concerned about our ability to redistribute available resources rather than whether a dollar spent on the poor adds a dollar to GNP. Evaluation is elusive because value judgments cannot be avoided.

Despite these limitations, important strides have been made toward more conscious and comprehensive action in human resource development. Insights have been gained by improved data and measurement techniques; one result has been a "cross-fertilization" showing the interdependence of problems and programs that had previously been dealt with independently. Educators are growing more aware of the need to prepare students for work, while manpower policy makers realize the difficulty and high cost of providing remedial attention where the schools have failed the first time around. The need to maintain full employment has been stressed by manpower analysts and the possibility of making monetary and fiscal policies more effective through manpower programs has received increasing scrutiny. Interdependence of equal employment opportunity for minorities with education and manpower policies is clearly recognized; the relation of all these policies to overall economic growth is also being examined

Recognizing the interdependence of various aspects of human resource development is a far cry from articulating a comprehensive human resources policy. But it is not clear that such a policy is necessary or even desirable. The importance of various problems fluctuates as priorities change; public policy is hammered out step by step; the full consequences of existing programs and newly discovered concerns unfold slowly. Hence the trial-and-error approach may, in the long run, prove as effective as the most elaborate planning, possibly even more so. A comprehensive human resource policy may not be compatible with a pluralistic society such as ours, and perhaps the best that we can hope for is fragmented approaches to complex problems. The judgment of history may be that the search for a comprehensive manpower human resources policy is in line with the search for the Holy Grail.

Responding to change

Some of the probable directions of change have been outlined and their implications identified. But there is no certainty that these will bear out or that, even if they do, they will be the most significant developments of the coming years, for the only certain prediction about the future is that it will be different from the past. Clearly, changes lie ahead, and our policies and practices must be able to adapt.

Several steps can be taken to increase adaptability. Perhaps the most important is to expand the flow of information. Data and evaluative techniques must be improved, and the knowledge that is gained must be widely disseminated. This will facilitate the recognition of changing circumstances and the rapid replication of successful techniques for dealing with them.

Another ingredient of adaptability is experimentation. Research and development have been important components of the manpower programs. Old approaches must be reexamined in the light of changing circumstances and improved accordingly; new ideas must be generated and tested; the future must be projected and its implications incorporated as plans are developed. In the evolution of policy one of the most difficult tasks is developing more orderly means of eliminating programs and practices that are no longer effective and of weeding out ideas and theories that have lost their relevance. But change for change's sake must be discouraged, and constant attention must be given to retaining what is useful from the past.

Finally, one of the most critical prerequisites to adaptability is an understanding of the historical context of change. Problems may gain sudden visibility, though they usually emerge gradually and are long undetected. To understand the present and to be able to cope with the future we need to know what has gone before. In this sense, the knowledge contained in this volume will, hopefully, serve as a basis for more comprehensive analysis and action so that we can make more effective and rewarding use of our human resources.

man-
power
bibliog-
raphy

Ashenfelter, Orley, and Albert Rees, eds. *Discrimination in Labor Markets*. Princeton, N.J.: Princeton University Press, 1973.

A collection of papers on discrimination in wages based on race and sex. Following a general economic theory of discrimination are papers devoted to consideration of education and trade unions. A final topic is an examination of public policy and discrimination.

Becker, Gary. *Human Capital*. New York: National Bureau of Economic Research, 1964.

The author first constructs a general theoretical framework within which investment in human capital can be analyzed and then illustrates the effect of human capital upon economic variables such as earnings and employment by a systematic analysis of on-the-job training. The second half of the book examines the empirical relationship between productivity and investment in human capital. Emphasis is on rates of return from investment in high school and college education in the United States.

Berg, Ivar. *Education and Jobs: The Great Training Robbery*. New York: Praeger, 1970.

Berg, a sociologist, argues that education in the United States is becoming a formalized credentialing procedure that acts as a barrier to the advancement of the poor. He analyzes the educational requirements for thousands of jobs along with Census Bureau reports on educational levels of the work force by occupation. His study examines the relationship between educational achievement and workers' performance and promotion expectations.

Blau, Peter M., and Otis Dudley Duncan. *The American Occupational Structure*. New York: Wiley, 1967.

An empirical analysis of the determinants of the occupational position and mobility of American workers, using the tools of modern sociology. Of special interest is the readable summary of quantitative methodology and the special attention given to the effects of race, region, migration, and farm background on occupational status.

Bok, Derek Curtis, and John T. Dunlop. *Labor and the American Community*. New York: Simon & Schuster, 1970.

A comprehensive overview of the present state of the American labor movement, which explores the public attitude toward labor, reviews the growth of trade unions and assesses their internal government, and discusses the changing nature of collective bargaining and the political impact of labor.

Bowen, William G., and T. Aldrich Finegan. *The Economics of Labor Force Participation.* Princeton, N.J.: Princeton University Press, 1969.

A comprehensive and detailed analysis of the factors determining who is in the labor market and who is not working or seeking work. The effects on labor force participation of many individual characteristics and labor market conditions are analyzed for specific population groups. Also analyzed is the sensitivity of participation rates to the tightness of labor markets. Extensive appendixes.

Doeringer, Peter, and Michael Piore. *Internal Labor Markets and Manpower Analysis.* Lexington, Mass.: Heath, 1971.

Examines the nature of labor markets within which the pricing and allocation of labor are governed by administrative rules and procedures. Part I develops theoretical concepts of the internal labor market. In Part II these concepts are applied to a number of topics that are often of interest to manpower policy makers: manpower adjustment to labor market imbalances, technological change, racial discrimination, and the relationship of low-income employment to the disadvantaged labor force.

Folger, John, Helen Astin, and Alan Bayer. *Human Resources and Higher Education.* New York: Russell Sage Foundation, 1970.

A study of the processes involved in developing and utilizing professional workers. After analyzing the market for college graduates, the authors discuss the problems faced by women, persons from the lower socioeconomic levels, and immigrants in obtaining access to higher education and to professional and specialized fields. The final section evaluates the effectiveness of manpower policies and suggests areas requiring additional research.

Grebler, Leo, Joan W. Moore, and Ralph C. Guzman. *The Mexican American People.* New York: Free Press, 1970.

During the 1960s, Grebler and his colleagues conducted an interdisciplinary study of the socioeconomic position of Mexican Americans in selected Southwestern urban areas. Utilizing research materials drawn from census data, household surveys, interviews, and direct observation, the study team constructs an accurate picture of Mexican Americans as a national minority. The minority's interaction with the dominant system is emphasized.

Ginzberg, Eli. *Manpower Agenda for America*. New York: McGraw-Hill, 1968.

The papers in this volume identify the many barriers blocking the escape of people from poverty and unemployment, which must be considered in the formulation of public policy. Ginzberg concludes that the "final challenge to manpower policy . . . is to reduce waste in the acquisition and utilization of skill without jeopardizing other important values."

Ginzberg, Eli. *Career Guidance: Who Needs It, Who Provides for It, Who Can Improve It*. New York: McGraw-Hill, 1971.

A broad study of the role of both occupational and educational guidance in enhancing the ability of people to make optimum use of their options in acquiring an education and in pursuing a career. After establishing the social dimensions of career guidance, the author examines the institutions through which it operates. Recommendations are offered for the guidance profession and the public, and likely developments during the 1970s are discussed.

Gordon, R. A. *The Goal of Full Employment*. New York: Wiley, 1967.

This monograph deals with full employment as a goal of national economic policy. The relationship of full employment to other, often conflicting, economic goals is discussed. In order to ascertain patterns of unemployment the labor force is analyzed in terms of age, sex, color, education, industry, and occupation. The author concludes that with expanded and more effective manpower and public employment programs, along with a modified incomes policy, the United States could achieve a level of unemployment of around 3 percent.

Harbison, Frederick H. *Human Resources as the Wealth of Nations*. New York: Oxford University Press, 1973.

In contrast to the traditional view of development, which relies on the growth of GNP as the sole measure of progress, the author argues for human resources as a measure of a nation's wealth. He analyzes problems in developing the fullest utilization of the skills and capacities of the labor force. The human resources problems of developing countries are emphasized.

Harbison, Frederick, and Charles A. Myers. *Education, Manpower, and Economic Growth*. New York: McGraw-Hill, 1969.

The authors, both economists, argue that human resource development is the most important determinant of economic growth. Seventy-five countries are ranked on the basis of a composite human resource development index and then grouped into four levels of development ranging from underdeveloped to advanced. Each level is analyzed qualitatively, and appropriate development strategies are suggested.

Harrison, Bennett. *Education, Training, and the Urban Ghetto.* Baltimore, Md.: Johns Hopkins Press, 1972.

The book analyzes the returns to investment in the human capital of nonwhites by ghetto and nonghetto residence. Using measures of weekly earnings, unemployment, and occupational status, the author found slight payoffs for education and training for nonwhites and suggests that nonwhite urban dwellers are trapped in an unstable secondary labor market. He concludes that strategies to upgrade the secondary labor market must be combined with human capital investment in order to achieve full employment and commensurate returns to workers.

Hoyt, Kenneth, Rupert Evans, Edward Mackin, and Garth Mangum. *Career Education: What It Is and How to Do It,* 2nd ed. Salt Lake City, Utah: Olympus Publishing Co., 1974.

The bible of career education. Explores the need and reasons for the development of the concept, sets forth definitions, outlines the components that career education comprises, and explores the pros and cons of this emerging new approach to preparation for employment.

Johnson, Miriam. *Counterpoint: The Changing Employment Service.* Salt Lake City, Utah: Olympus Publishing Co., 1973.

A veteran of 15 years at the front lines of the employment service reflects upon the impact of the manpower and antipoverty programs on that institution. The author points up the contrast between the labor markets of 1933, when the public employment service was created, and the needs of more complex labor markets 40 years later.

Kalachek, Edward. *Labor Markets and Unemployment.* Belmont, Calif.: Wadsworth, 1973.

A study of the functioning of modern labor markets. The author combines a review of labor market theory with a discussion of empirical research on mobility and unemployment problems. The effects of education on the quality of labor and the impact of technological change on the labor market receive special emphasis.

Kreps, Juanita. *Sex in the Marketplace: American Women at Work,* Policy Studies in Employment and Welfare No. 11. Baltimore, Md.: Johns Hopkins Press, 1971.

After reviewing the literature on women's labor force activity—when women work, at what jobs, and under what arrangements—

the author concludes that women are overeducated for most of the jobs they do.

Lecht, Leonard A. *Manpower Needs for National Goals in the 1970's.* New York: Praeger, 1969.

An analysis of future manpower requirements from the perspective of an illustrative set of national goals to be achieved by 1975. The author warns that if we follow present patterns of employment, discrimination, training, and education, we will face serious labor shortages in the future. The potential impact on the labor market of pursuing alternative goals is also discussed.

Levitan, Sar A. *Programs in Aid of the Poor for the 1970s,* rev. ed., Policy Studies in Employment and Welfare No. 1. Baltimore, Md.: Johns Hopkins Press, 1973.

A concise review of the nation's antipoverty programs. The author appraises income-maintenance programs, efforts to supply goods and services to the poor, programs to prevent youth from falling into poverty, and aid to the working poor. He concludes with an exploration of feasible approaches for future attacks on poverty.

Levitan, Sar A., and Barbara Hetrick. *Big Brother's Indian Programs —with Reservations.* New York: McGraw-Hill, 1971.

A general review and critical evaluation of federal programs for the half-million American Indians living on or near reservations. Programs in education, health, human and natural resources, and community structure are appraised. Problems in public policy and implications for the future are considered.

Levitan, Sar A., and William B. Johnston. *Work Is Here to Stay, Alas.* Salt Lake City, Utah: Olympus Publishing Co., 1973.

The authors discuss the meaning of work, the work ethic, work reform, and the future of work. Disputing the dreams of Utopian theorists, they find that take-home pay is still the key to motivation on the job. Turning to the future, they conclude that the range of work opportunities will expand leading to more fully chosen work.

Levitan, Sar A., William B. Johnston, and Robert Taggart. *Still a Dream: Changing Status of Blacks During the Past Decade.* Cambridge, Mass.: Harvard University Press, 1975.

An analysis of the changes in the socioeconomic status of blacks in the United States. Separate chapters are devoted to income, occupations, education, family status, health, housing, and political power. In addition, the volume assesses the federal programs with the greatest impacts on blacks, including income support, in-kind assistance, education and training, and equal employment opportunity efforts.

Levitan, Sar A., and Garth L. Mangum. *Federal Training and Work Programs in the Sixties.* Ann Arbor, Mich.: University of Michigan Press, 1968.

The authors trace the development of programs for training the unemployed and the disadvantaged: the Manpower Development and Training Act, the Job Corps, the Neighborhood Youth Corps, the vocational education and rehabilitation programs, and the federal-state employment service. They describe and evaluate the major programs and recommend improvements in administration for more effective delivery of services.

Levitan, Sar A., Martin Rein, and David Marwick. *Work and Welfare Go Together,* Policy Studies in Employment and Welfare No. 13. Baltimore, Md.: Johns Hopkins Press, 1972.

The authors trace the growth and change in composition of the AFDC program and development of strategies to promote self-help, emphasizing the Work Incentive Program and social services. Analysis of WIN's initial impacts reveals limited success in curtailing the growth of welfare or removing enrollees from welfare rolls but suggests some benefits in increased earnings and reduced dependency of the participants. They conclude that future policies should recognize the growing interdependence of work and welfare.

Levitan, Sar A., and Robert Taggart. *Employment and Earnings Inadequacy: A New Social Indicator.* Policy Studies in Employment and Welfare No. 19. Baltimore, Md.: Johns Hopkins Press, 1974.

The authors formulate and analyze an employment and earnings inadequacy index that considers individual and family income levels as well as employment status to measure the extent of labor market pathologies. Data from the 1968–1972 Current Population Survey are used to compare and contrast the new index with government unemployment statistics. Cross-sectional and longitudinal analyses indicate how the components of the new index vary by race, sex, family status, and area of residence.

Levitan, Sar A., and Joyce K. Zickler. *The Quest for a Federal Manpower Partnership.* Cambridge, Mass.: Harvard University Press, 1974.

Drawing largely on the experiences of six cities for illustration, the authors trace the development of manpower planning and comprehensive manpower programs, which preceded the passage of the Comprehensive Employment and Training Act of 1973. The preparation of state and local sponsors for their expanded responsibilities under the nation's first New Federalism effort is evaluated, and the strengths and weaknesses of the new law are discussed.

Mangum, Garth. *The Emergence of Manpower Policy.* New York: Holt, Rinehart & Winston, 1969.

A brief history of U.S. manpower policies to 1960 and a summary of the changing goals and methods of government manpower policies in the 1960s. Mangum discusses the relative success of the Job Corps, Neighborhood Youth Corps, and other training programs. The final chapters recommend changes in the administration and structure of federal manpower programs.

Mangum, Garth, and David Snedeker. *Manpower Planning for Local Labor Markets.* Salt Lake City, Utah: Olympus Publishing Co., 1974.

A how-to-do-it manual devoted to manpower planners serving the state and local prime sponsors under the Comprehensive Employment and Training Act of 1973. It traces the legislative background of CETA, describes the role and functions of labor markets, provides a basic planning model, and follows through the steps in the development of a manpower plan.

Mangum, Garth, and John Walsh. *A Decade of Manpower Development and Training.* Salt Lake City, Utah: Olympus Publishing Co., 1973.

Traces the accomplishments, problems, and limitations of the first ten years of the Manpower Development and Training Act of 1972. Identifies lessons that can be used to improve the quality of all adult occupational education.

Marshall, Ray, and Vernon Briggs. *The Negro and Apprenticeship.* Baltimore, Md.: Johns Hopkins Press, 1967.

An analysis of the factors influencing the low participation rates of blacks in apprenticeship programs and an evaluation of the measures being taken to promote equal apprenticeship opportunity. The authors examine black participation in apprenticeship programs in ten major cities and make recommendations for increasing the number of black apprentices. Problems such as discrimination by unions and employers, the limited number of available apprenticeships, and low educational levels of black applicants are discussed.

Marshall, Ray, and Richard Perlman, eds. *An Anthology of Labor Economics: Readings and Commentary.* New York: Wiley, 1972.

A selection of articles covering both the theory and practice of labor economics. It also includes many of the classical articles in labor market theory, changes in the labor force, unemployment, and wage structure as well as readings that discuss collective bargaining, human resource development, poverty, and income. The editors provide commentary on each article and suggest related readings on the various topics.

Miller, Herman P. *Rich Man, Poor Man.* New York: T. Y. Crowell, 1971.

The author, former Chief of the Population Division of the U.S. Bureau of the Census, analyzes the social and economic aspects of income distribution. He demonstrates how personal income is correlated with such personal characteristics as race, sex, and educational attainment.

Patten, Thomas H. *Manpower and the Development of Human Resources.* New York: Wiley, 1971.

The author, previously an industrial relations executive with the Ford Motor Company, examines, in nonmathematical terms, manpower planning and development within businesses and organizations. Separate chapters are devoted to particular types of training apprentices, salesmen, foremen, and executives. Other chapters deal in general terms with the objectives and organization of manpower planning.

Pohlman, Jerry E. *Economics of Wage and Price Controls.* Columbus, Ohio: Grid, Inc., 1972.

Discussion and analysis of the dual problems of unemployment and inflation. It first provides reviews of the rationale for free markets, theories of unemployment, the extent of market power, and attempts to reach full employment without inflation. The second half of the book provides a thorough discussion of the pros and cons of wage-and-price controls and examines the U.S. experience from World War II through 1972.

Reubens, Beatrice G. *The Hard-to-Employ: European Programs.* New York: Columbia University Press, 1970.

A detailed examination and evaluation of nine Western European countries' programs and policies, including attempts to rehabilitate and place the hard-to-employ in the competitive labor market, efforts to create special jobs, subsidies for employers, and government intervention in the economies of depressed areas.

Sheppard, Harold L., Bennett Harrison, and William J. Spring, eds. *The Political Economy of Public Service Employment.* Lexington, Mass.: Heath, 1972.

A collection of articles dealing with public employment, with special attention given to programs for the disadvantaged. Historical perspectives, measurement of unemployment, manpower planning and financing rural public employment and broad policy issues are treated in separate sections.

Somers, Gerald G., and J. Kenneth Little, eds. *Vocational Education: Today and Tomorrow.* Madison, Wis.: Center for Studies in Vocational and Technical Education, University of Wisconsin, 1971.

This collection of papers addresses the major issues confronting vocational education, including its relation with general education, training needs, and the disadvantaged. Also explored are the role of counseling and placement activities; staffing; organization and administration; and research, evaluation, and experimentation.

Somers, Gerald G., and W. D. Wood, eds. *Cost-Benefit Analysis of Manpower Policies.* Kingston, Ontario: Industrial Relations Centre, Queen's University, 1969.

This volume offers several papers presented at the North American Conference on Cost-Benefit Analysis. The first section deals with theoretical and methodological aspects of cost-benefit analysis; the final section considers the application of cost-benefit analysis to various types of manpower programs. Occupational training programs for adult workers, programs for disadvantaged workers, and the Canadian Manpower Mobility Program are examined.

Thurow, Lester C. *Poverty and Discrimination.* Washington, D.C.: Brookings Institution, 1969.

Utilizing econometric techniques and defining poverty and discrimination as problems of income distribution, this study examines their severity, the income differentials between whites and blacks, and factors that contribute to the persistence of poverty.

Thurow, Lester. *Investment in Human Capital.* Belmont, Calif.: Wadsworth, 1970.

Emphasizes the need to integrate the concept of human capital into the main body of economic theory. Although much of the analysis is carried out within the framework of traditional investment theory, care is taken to describe the many peculiarities that differentiate human from physical capital. After dealing with the production and measurement of human capital, Thurow discusses investment decisions at the individual, firm, and government levels.

Ulman, Lloyd, ed. *Manpower Programs in the Policy Mix.* Baltimore, Md.: Johns Hopkins Press, 1973.

A symposium of articles that assesses the role of manpower programs in economic stabilization and income distribution. The contributors generally express optimistic views that an active labor market policy can have an impact on the level of unemployment, the unemployment-inflation trade-off, and redistribution of income. Much attention is given to the effects of labor market imperfections that call for manpower programs as a policy tool.

manpower ABCs

AFDC	Aid to Families with Dependent Children
AFDC-UF	Aid to Families with Dependent Children—Unemployed Father segment
AFL-CIO	American Federation of Labor-Congress of Industrial Organizations
AMDS	Area Manpower Data System
AMIDS	Area Manpower Institutes for Development of Staff
ARC	Appalachian Regional Commission
AVA	American Vocational Association
BAT	Bureau of Apprenticeship and Training, U.S. Department of Labor
BCTD	Building and Construction Trades Department, AFL-CIO
BIA	Bureau of Indian Affairs, U.S. Department of Interior
BLS	Bureau of Labor Statistics, U.S. Department of Labor
CAA	Community Action Agency
CAMPS	Cooperative Area Manpower Planning System
CAP	Community Action Program
CEA	Council of Economic Advisers
CEP	Concentrated Employment Program
CETA	Comprehensive Employment and Training Act of 1973
CIJC	Construction Industry Joint Conference
CIO	Congress of Industrial Organizations
CMP	Comprehensive Manpower Program
CPS	Current Population Survey
CWT	Community Work and Training Program
DECAL	Detailed Experimental Computer-Assisted Language
DOT	Dictionary of Occupational Titles

EDA	Economic Development Administration, U.S. Department of Commerce
EEA	Emergency Employment Act
EEC	European Economic Community
EEOC	Equal Employment Opportunity Commission
EOA	Economic Opportunity Act
ES	Employment Service, U.S. Department of Labor
ESARS	Employment Security Automated Reporting System
ESEA	Elementary and Secondary Education Act of 1965
ESOPS	Employment Service On-Line Placement System
FAP	Family Assistance Plan
FEPC	Fair Employment Practices Commission
FLSA	Fair Labor Standards Act of 1938
GNP	Gross national product
GPO	Government Printing Office
HRD	Human resource development
HRDI	Human Resource Development Institute, AFL-CIO
IBEW	International Brotherhood of Electrical Workers
IBT	International Brotherhood of Teamsters
IHS	Indian Health Service, U.S. Department of Health, Education, and Welfare
ITA	Industrial Training Act of 1964 (in Britain)
ITU	International Typographers Union
IUOE	International Union of Operating Engineers
JAC	Joint apprenticeship committee
JAV	Job Analysis Vocabulary
JBSS	Job Bank and Screening System
JOBS	Job Opportunities in the Business Sector Program
LFPR	Labor force participation rate
LINCS	Labor Inventory Communications System
MDTA	Manpower Development and Training Act of 1962
NAACP	National Association for the Advancement of Colored People
NAB	National Alliance of Businessmen
NLRB	National Labor Relations Board
NYC	Neighborhood Youth Corps
OECD	Organisation for European Cooperation and Development
OEO	Office of Economic Opportunity
OFCC	Office of Federal Contract Compliance, U.S. Department of Labor
OIC	Opportunities Industrialization Center
OJT	On-the-job training
OMB	Office of Management and Budget
PEP	Public Employment Program

PIP	Phased Implementation Program
POSARS	Plan of Service Automated Reporting System
PSC	Public Service Careers program
R & D	Research and development
RMS	Rural Manpower Service, U.S. Department of Labor
RTP	Recruitment and Training Program
SAC	State apprenticeship council
SAT	Scholastic Aptitude Test
SER	Service, Employment, Redevelopment Program
SMSA	Standard metropolitan statistical area
UA	United Association of Journeymen and Apprentices of the Plumbing and Pipe Fitting Industry of the U.S. and Canada
UAW	United Auto Workers
UBCJ	United Brotherhood of Carpenters and Joiners of America
UC	Unemployment compensation
UCWA	United Construction Workers Association
UI	Unemployment insurance
USES	Employment Service, U.S. Department of Labor
VISTA	Volunteers in Service to America
WDL	Workers Defense League
WET	Work Experience and Training program
WIN	Work Incentive program
WPA	Work Projects Administration
YOC	Youth Opportunity Center

indexes

index of names

A

Ablon, Joan, 450 n
Adams, Arvil V., 405 n, 476 n
Allen, Steve, 426 n, 427 n
Altman, Jack, 51 n
Arrow, Kenneth J., 189, 198 n, 367, 368, 369, 371, 382, 383 n
Ashenfelter, Orley, 374, 383 n, 384 n, 477 n, 601
Astin, Helen S., 198 n, 602

B

Bakke, E. Wight, 139 n, 198 n
Barbash, Jack, 534 n
Barrett, Donald N., 427 n
Barringer, R., 139 n
Bayer, Alan E., 198 n, 602
Becker, Gary, 120, 124, 139 n, 167, 169 n, 365, 366, 367, 368, 383 n, 601
Beer, S., 139 n
Bell, Daniel, 270 n
Berg, Ivar, 157, 167, 168 n, 169 n, 601
Bergmann, Barbara R., 366, 383 n
Berls, Robert H., 196, 198 n, 199 n
Bernstein, Morris, 584 n
Bixby, Lenore, 75 n
Blank, David M., 189, 198 n
Blau, Peter M., 21, 23, 26 n, 601
Blechman, Barry M., 198 n
Bluestone, Barry, 140 n
Blume, Paul R., 450 n
Bok, Derek C., 534 n, 601
Bolten, Roger E., 198 n
Bowen, William G., 49 n, 51 n, 111 n, 163, 169 n, 500 n, 602
Brackett, Jean, 51 n
Bradshaw, Thomas F., 25 n
Brennan, Peter J., 457, 460

Briggs, Vernon M., Jr., 218 n, 426 n, 427 n, 476 n, 607
Brimmer, Andrew, 401, 405 n
Burma, John H., 427 n

C

Cain, Glen G., 51 n
Capron, William M., 189, 198 n
Cartter, Allan M., 171, 177, 182, 185, 198 n
Cassell, Frank H., 308, 320 n
Chamberlain, Neil W., 167, 169 n, 198 n
Chavez, Cesar, 425
Christian, Virgil, 384 n, 405 n, 426 n
Clark, Kenneth B., 196, 199 n, 459, 469, 477 n
Coleman, James S., 168 n, 199 n, 426 n
Creamer, Daniel, 188, 198 n
Crowley, Michael F., 198 n
Cutright, Phillips, 90 n

D

Daley, Richard, 465
Davis, Karen, 198 n
Denison, Edward F., 171, 198 n
Deutermann, William V., 33, 51 n, 87, 90 n
DeWitt, Karen, 476 n
Doeringer, Peter, 123, 124, 127, 139 n, 214, 218 n, 534 n, 602
Duncan, Otis Dudley, 21, 22, 23, 26 n, 601
Dunlop, John T., 121, 139 n, 376, 377, 384 n, 534 n, 537, 601

E

Easterlin, Richard, 111 n

617

Eisenhower, Dwight D.
  and area redevelopment, 251
  macroeconomic policy, 492
Ericson, Anna-Stina, 427 n
Evans, Rupert N., 159, 168, 604

F

Falk, Charles E., 183, 184, 185, 198 n
Farber, David J., 217 n
Fernbach, Susan, 243 n
Fiester, Richard, 534 n
Filley, Alan C., 218 n
Finegan, T. Aldrich, 49 n, 51 n, 111 n,
  602
Fisher, Lloyd, 121, 126
Fletcher, Arthur, 462
Folger, John K., 198 n, 602
Foltman, Felician F., 218 n
Forbes, Jack D., 426 n
Ford, Gerald R., 499
Franklin, Raymond J., 129, 139 n
Franklin, William S., 217 n, 218 n
Friedman, Milton, 497
Friedmann, Georges, 12, 25 n
Froomkin, Joseph, 197 n
Fuchs, Victor R., 25 n, 73, 76 n, 88,
  90 n
Fusfeld, Daniel R., 584 n

G

Galenson, Walter, 533 n, 542, 543,
  556 n
Gardner, John W., 194, 198 n
Garfinkle, Stuart H., 16, 49 n
Gellner, Christopher, 51 n
Giblin, Edward J., 312
Gilroy, Curtis L., 25 n, 42, 51 n
Ginzberg, Eli, 603
Glover, Robert, 217 n, 218 n
Gompers, Samuel, 523
Gooding, Judson, 25 n
Gordon, David, 139 n
Gordon, Margaret, 51 n
Gordon, Robert Aaron, 51 n, 94 n,
  484, 500 n, 603
Grebler, Leo, 417, 426 n, 427 n, 602
Green, Gloria P., 111 n
Greenberg, Leon, 75 n
Gregory, Peter, 140 n
Gutierrez, Jose Angel, 426
Guzman, Ralph C., 602
Gwartney, James, 51 n

H

Haddad, William F., 476 n
Hannah, Paul R., 556 n
Hansen, Niles M., 546, 556 n
Hansen, W. Lee, 167, 169 n
Harbison, Frederick, 2, 6 n, 169 n,
  270 n, 376, 537, 538, 543, 544,
  556 n, 584 n, 603
Harrison, Bennett, 604, 608
Hayghe, Howard V., 26 n, 51 n, 78, 84
Healy, James J., 534 n
Heckman, James, 477 n
Hedges, Janice Neipert, 25 n
Heller, Walter, 500 n
Henle, Peter, 26 n
Hernstadt, Irwin L., 217 n
Hetrick, Barbara, 605
Hiestand, Dale, 383 n
Hill, Herbert, 458
Horowitz, Morris A., 217 n
Hoyt, Kenneth, 228, 243 n, 604
Hu, Teh-Wei, 243 n

I

Iacobelli, John L., 218 n
Illich, Ivan, 168
Ingerman, Sidney, 218 n

J

Jalrina, V., 584 n
Jencks, Christopher, 161, 168 n, 199 n
Johnson, David B., 23, 26 n
Johnson, Lyndon B.
  and Comprehensive Manpower
    Programs, 266
  and JOBS, 257–258
  and labor unions, 511
  macroeconomic policy, 255, 492
  and vocational education, 232
  and War on Poverty, 253, 260
Johnson, Miriam, 320 n, 361 n, 604
Johnston, Denis F., 111 n
Johnston, William B., 15, 25 n, 49 n,
  75 n, 362 n, 405 n, 476 n, 605

K

Kalachek, Edward, 75 n, 604
Kassalow, Everett M., 533 n
Kaufman, Jacob J., 155, 168
Kendrick, John W., 94
Kennedy, John F.
  antipoverty programs, 250, 253
  and ES, 304
  and labor unions, 511
  macroeconomic policy, 255, 492
  and unemployment statistics, 94
  and wage-price guideposts, 496
Kerr, Clark, 121, 122, 123, 126, 139 n,
  376, 384 n, 537, 540, 556 n
Kershaw, Joseph, 270 n
Killingsworth, Charles C., 126, 139 n,
  500 n
King, Bill, 450 n
King, Seth S., 477 n
Kreps, Juanita, 25 n, 79 n, 90 n, 604
Krueger, Anne, 369

L

Lebergott, Stanley, 111 n
Lecht, Leonard, 111 n, 243 n, 605
Lee, Arthur M., 243 n
Lerner, Max, 539, 556 n
Levine, Louis, 312
Levitan, Sar A., 15, 25 n, 49 n, 50 n, 75 n, 270 n, 299 n, 341 n, 361 n, 362 n, 405 n, 476 n, 605, 606
Lewis, Harold G., 518, 534 n
Licker, Maia, 476 n
Little, J. Kenneth, 609
Livernash, E. Robert, 534 n
Low, Seth, 90 n

M

McCall, John J., 368, 383 n
McCauley, John S., 528, 534 n
McGuire, Joseph W., 22, 26 n
Mackin, Edward, 604
Magnusen, Karl O., 218 n
Mangum, Garth L., 111 n, 168 n, 270 n, 285, 299 n, 361 n, 362 n, 500 n, 604, 606, 607
Mark, Jerome A., 75 n
Marshall, Ray, 217 n, 218 n, 383 n, 384 n, 405 n, 426 n, 476 n, 534 n, 556 n, 607
Marwick, David, 341 n, 362 n, 606
Meany, George, 463
Michelotti, Kopp, 26 n
Miller, Herman P., 89 n, 608
Miller, S. M., 26 n
Mincer, Jacob, 51 n, 75 n
Mitchell, James P., 303, 304
Moore, Geoffrey, 25 n
Moore, Joan W., 602
Morse, Dean, 75
Morton, J. E., 110 n
Mossell, B. F., 169 n
Moy, Joyanna, 46
Myers, Charles A., 169 n, 376, 537, 538, 543, 544, 556 n, 584 n, 603
Myers, Robert J., 51 n

N

Neef, Arthur, 74
Nemore, Arnold L., 111 n
Nixon, Richard M.
    con't. manpower programs, 260
    emergence of manpower programs, 250
    and FAP, 340
    and hometown plans, 463, 465
    macroeconomic policy, 493
    and PEP, 259
    vocational education, 232, 234
    wage-price controls, 497
Nordlund, Willis, 320
Northrup, Herbert R., 477 n

O

O'Boyle, Edward, 75 n
O'Connor, Dennis J., 438, 450 n
Ogilvie, Donald G., 342 n
Oi, Walter Y., 124, 139 n
Okun, Arthur, 39, 51 n, 483, 500 n
Oliver, Richard P., 49 n
Oppenheimer, Valerie Kincade, 90 n

P

Parnes, Herbert, 21, 24, 26 n, 49 n, 75 n
Pascal, Anthony H., 383 n
Patten, Thomas H., 608
Pearl, Arthur, 270 n
Perlman, Richard, 167, 169 n, 607
Perlman, Selig, 523, 534 n
Perrella, Vera C., 26 n, 198 n
Perry, George L., 500 n
Phelps, Edmund S., 367, 383 n
Pichler, Joseph A., 22, 26 n
Piore, Michael J., 123, 124, 127, 139 n, 214, 218 n, 602
Plotkin, Lawrence, 196, 199 n
Pohlman, Jerry, 500 n, 608
Pugh, G. Douglas, 476 n

R

Ramirez, Henry M., 426 n
Rees, Albert, 383 n, 518, 534 n, 601
Rein, Martin, 341 n, 362 n, 606
Resnik, Solomon, 129, 139 n
Reubens, Beatrice G., 608
Reynolds, Lloyd, 21, 26 n, 140 n, 521, 534 n
Rhine, Shirley H., 188, 198 n
Ribich, Thomas I., 167, 169 n
Riesman, David, 199 n
Riessman, Frank, 270 n
Rings, Eleanor, 75 n
Roosevelt, Franklin D., 495
Rosenthal, Neal H., 108, 111 n
Ross, Arthur M., 217 n

S

Samora, Julian, 427 n
Sawyer, James E., 300 n, 362 n
Schmidt, Fred H., 422, 426 n, 427 n
Scholes, William E., 427 n
Schultz, Theodore W., 120, 139 n, 162, 169 n
Schwab, Karen, 500 n
Sconzoni, John, 90 n
Scott, Loren C., 450 n
Shamseddine, Ahmad Hussein, 90 n
Sheahan, John, 500 n
Sheppard, Harold L., 608
Shultz, George P., 265, 534 n
Slichter, Sumner H., 137, 140 n, 534 n
Snedeker, David, 285, 299 n, 607

Solarz, Andrew K., 341 n
Solow, Robert, 169 n
Somers, Gerald G., 243 n, 534 n, 609
Sorkin, Alan, 438, 450 n
Sorrentino, Constance, 46
Southwick, Lawrence, Jr., 198
Sowell, Thomas, 405 n
Spindler, Pearl, 90 n
Spring, William J., 608
Staats, Elmer B., 462, 463
Stein, Robert L., 75 n
Steiner, Stan, 427 n
Stekler, Herman, 111 n
Stern, James L., 23, 26 n
Stigler, George J., 189, 198 n
Strauss, George, 217 n, 218 n
Swerdloff, Sol, 51 n

T

Taggart, Robert, 51 n, 270 n, 361 n,
    362 n, 405 n, 476 n, 605, 606
Talmadge, Herman E., 333, 334
Taylor, Benjamin J., 438, 450 n
Thurow, Lester, 139 n, 167, 169 n,
    384 n, 476 n, 609
Tijerina, Reies Lopez, 417, 425
Truett, Dale, 426 n

U

Ulman, Lloyd, 137, 140 n, 270 n, 500 n,
    609

W

Waldman, Elizabeth, 88, 90 n
Walsh, John, 320 n, 361 n, 607
Weber, Arnold, 534 n
Weisbrod, Burton, 167, 169 n
Welch, Finis, 367, 383 n, 384 n
Wholey, Joseph S., 300 n
Wilkins, Roy, 458
Williams, C. G., 63
Wirtz, W. Willard, 48, 208, 307, 459,
    462
Wolfbein, Seymour, 51 n
Wolkinson, Benjamin W., 361 n
Wood, W. D., 609
Wool, Harold, 150
Woytinsky, W. S., 51 n
Wright, David McCord, 533 n

Y

Young, Anne M., 51 n, 90 n

Z

Zickler, Joyce K., 299 n, 362 n, 606

index of subjects

A

Additional worker hypothesis, 34–35, 118
Adult Basic Education program, 343
Affirmative action plans, 462–466, 473, 474
Africa, 506, 542, 566, 582
Age Discrimination in Employment Act of 1967, 89
Aid to Families with Dependent Children. *See also* CWT; FAP; Guaranteed income; WET; WIN
  alternatives to, 338–341, 591
  benefits, 324–325
  and day care, 327
  employment, 326–329
  growth, 321–324
  turnover, 326
  unemployed father component, 323
  work incentives, 27, 324–325, 328, 338, 354
  work and training programs, 329–338
Aliens in labor force, 419–420
Amalgamated Meat Cutters, 526
American Federation of Labor. *See* AFL-CIO
American Federation of Labor-Congress of Industrial Organizations, 461, 463
  Appalachian Council, 529–530
  Building and Construction Trades Department, 208, 460
  Building Trades Councils, 459
  endorsed apprenticeship outreach, 208
  formation, 504
  Human Resources Development Institute, 459, 530, 533, 536
  and other unions, 515
  Operation Manpower, 529–530
American Friends Service Committee, 465
American Telephone & Telegraph Co., 454, 457
Appalachian Regional Commission, U.S., 546–547
Appalachian Regional Development Act of 1965, 546
Apprenticeship
  adequacy, 205–207
  entrance into, 211–212
  established, 200
  forecasts, 102
  industries and occupations 202–203
  and labor unions, 204
  outreach program, 208
  program diversity, 204–205, 211–213
  racial discrimination, 207–209, 386–387, 458–460, 473
  supply restrictions, 47
  trends, 202
  for women, 87
Area Manpower Data System, 310
Area Manpower Institute for Development of Staff, 355
Area Redevelopment Act of 1961
  appraisal, 256
  enactment, 251
  on Indian reservations, 440
  training provisions, 348
Armour and Co., 526
Australia, 46

B

Balanced Placement Formula, 311
Balkanization of labor markets, 121

Bargaining theory of labor markets, 377, 381
Belgium, 562
Bethelehem Steel Co., 455–456, 471, 472
Better Communities Act of 1974, 460
Bilingual Education Act of 1967, 423
Biographical Inventory Blank, 348
Blacks
  in apprenticeship. *See* Apprenticeship, racial discrimination
  causes of employment disadvantages, 397 ff.
  in central cities, 394–396
  discrimination against, 397–398
  earnings, 23–24, 390–391
  geographical distribution, 385–389
  and higher education, 195–197
  income, 401–404, 431
  labor force participation, 29–30
  occupational mobility, 23–24
  occupations, 389–390, 401–404
  unemployment, 391–394
  and unions, 380
Board of Fundamental Education (steel industry), 528
Braceros, 418–420
Building Construction Employers Association of Chicago, Inc., 464
Bureau of Apprenticeship and Training, U.S. Department of Labor, 200–213 *passim*, 459
Bureau of Indian Affairs, U.S. Department of Interior
  education programs, 435–437
  as employer of Indians, 434, 439
  labor force statistics, 432–434, 438–439
  manpower programs, 442–446
  service population, 428–430
Bureau of Labor Statistics, U.S. Department of Labor
  and CPS, 91
  projections, 102–103, 148, 180, 275
  urban worker budgets, 34
Bureau of the Census, U.S. Department of Commerce
  and CPS, 96–97
  data on geographic mobility, 24

C

Cabinet Committee on Opportunities for Spanish-Speaking People, 408
Canada, 45, 46, 557
Career education, 159
  components, 220–223
  defined, 219
  funding, 224

  issues, 224–230
  phases, 223–224
  and postsecondary education, 228–229
  prospects, 240–243
  scope, 227–228
  and vocational education, 230
Chicago and Cook County Building Trades Council, 464, 465
Chicago Plan, 464, 465, 466, 468, 473
Chicanos. *See* Spanish Americans
Child care. *See* Day care
China, 582
Civilian Conservation Corps, 253
Civil Rights Act of 1964
  apprenticeship, 208, 459
  and Chicanos, 422
  and ES, 306
  higher education, 197
  labor markets, 256
  provisions, 89, 452, 461, 470–471, 473
  results, 397
  and War on Poverty, 254, 261, 346
Coalition for United Community Action, 464
Coefficient of discrimination, 365
Coleman Report, 161, 196, 414
College Entrance Examination Board, 196
College Placement Council, 305
Colombia, manpower policy in, 557, 577–581 *passim*
Commission on Civil Rights, U.S., 421
Commission on Human Resources and Advanced Education, 179
Community action agencies (CAA). *See also* Community Action Program
  and CETA, 294–295
  and ES, 307, 308, 309, 316
  and urban politics, 264, 356–357
Community Action Program, 254, 256, 261. *See also* Community action agencies
Community colleges. *See* Higher education
Community Work and Training program, 329–330, 338
Comprehensive Employment and Training Act of 1973, 266–269
  administration, 358–359
  and apprenticeship, 216
  and CEP, 262
  and community colleges, 160
  and ES, 265, 269, 291, 315, 316
  funding, 270, 298
  and Indians, 447, 448
  and job matching, 310–311
  and labor unions, 531

Comprehensive Employment and Training Act of 1973 (*Continued*)
and manpower planning, 277–291 *passim*, 347, 478
and public employment, 260, 268–269
purpose, 280
replaced EOA, MDTA, 265, 295, 343
research under, 343
and rural areas, 552
Comprehensive Manpower Program, 266–267, 355
Computerized job-matching, 308–310, 319
Concentrated Employment Program
and ES, 308, 309
formation, 257
funding, 252, 262
services, 262–263
Congress of Industrial Organizations. *See* AFL-CIO
Construction Industry Joint Conference, 460
Contractors Association of Eastern Pennsylvania, 463
Contractors Association of Eastern Pennsylvania v. *Shultz*, 477 n.
Cooperative Area Manpower Planning System, 263–264, 278, 285, 355, 357
Cooperative School Program, 305
Cooperative Steel Industry Education Plan, 528
Cooperative work-study program, 154, 222, 237
Council of Economic Advisers, U.S.
fiscal policy in mid-60s, 255–256
forecasting, 275
wage-price guideposts, 496
Craft unions. *See* Labor unions
Crown Zellerbach Corp., 471, 472, 477 n
Cubans, 32
income and education, 409–410
location, 407
number and ages, 406–407, 412
occupations, 415
poverty, 411
Current Population Survey, 95, 96, 97
Cyclical unemployment, 38–39, 41

D
Davis-Bacon Act of 1931, 211
Day care
availability and costs, 352
and CETA, 262, 297
funding, 252, 270
in the 1970s, 589
for welfare mothers, 327

in WIN program, 333, 334, 336
for women workers, 80–82, 589
during World War II, 589
Decategorization of manpower programs, 264–266 ff., 296. *See also* CETA
Decentralization of manpower programs, 264–266 ff., 296. *See also* CETA
dangers of, 297–299
Deficient demand, 483–485
Department of Commerce, U.S., 92. *See also* Bureau of the Census
Department of Defense, U.S., 254
Department of Housing and Urban Development, U.S., 263. *See also* Model Cities program
Department of the Interior, U.S. *See* Bureau of Indian Affairs
Department of Justice, U.S., 456–472 *passim*
Department of Labor, U.S. *See* BAT; BLS; ES; MA; OFCC; RMS
Department of State, U.S., 422
Depressed areas. *See* Appalachian Regional Development Act; Area Redevelopment Act; Public Works and Economic Development Act
Detailed Experimental Computer-Assisted Language, 310
Dictionary of Occupational Titles, 310
Disadvantaged, defined, 256, 284
Discouraged workers, 119
Discrimination. *See also* BAT; Civil Rights Act of 1964; Department of Justice; EEOC; Executive Order 11246; Hometown plans; NLRB; OFCC; Seniority systems
in apprenticeship. *See* Apprenticeship, racial discrimination
Federal laws, 452
institutional, 371–372
patterns, 461–462
quotas and preferential treatment, 462–466
seniority, 469–474, 474
state laws, 451–452
Dual labor market hypothesis, 126–128, 257, 347

E
Economic development. *See also* Labor mobility
and discrimination, 376
education and training, 543–544

Economic Development (*Continued*)
and education, training, and work
ethic, 11–14
human resource development,
535 ff.
regional, 544–548
role of institutions, 537–539
rural development, 548–555
stages of, 540–543
Economic Development Administration, U.S. Department of Commerce
appraisal, 545–546
as employer of Indians, 439
Economic Opportunity Act. *See also*
Community Action Program;
Head Start; Job Corps; Neighborhood Youth Corps; New
Careers program; Operation
Mainstream; Special Impact
program; Work Experience
and Training program
and CETA, 265, 269
1966 Amendments, 257
1967 Amendments, 257, 265
program administration, 356
research under, 343
and War on Poverty, 253, 261
Economics of discrimination, 365 ff.
Edgeley Air Products, 455
Education. *See also* Career education; Higher education; Vocational education
black-white differences, 404
compensatory education, 161
as consumption good, 165
and earnings, 153
and economic growth, 143 ff.
and employment, 149, 151–153
expenditures, 144, 160
future prospects, 148–151
goals, 159
inflated requirements, 157–158
and job-search techniques, 154
in manpower development, 158–162
by occupation, 147, 150, 151
returns on investment in, 162–168
and socioeconomic status, 153–154
and unemployment, 152
as work prerequisite, 144–148
Egypt, manpower policy in, 557, 577–581 *passim*
Elementary and Secondary Education Act of 1965, 160, 256, 423
Emergency Employment Act of 1971.
See Public Employment Program
Employer Services program, 313
Employment. *See also* Peripheral
workers
adequacy, 49–50, 591

concepts and information sources,
94–96
by occupation and industry, 61–69
Employment Act of 1946
and labor force data, 99, 275
provisions, 37, 303, 482, 594
Employment and earnings inadequacy, 49–50
Employment Security Automated Reporting System, 309, 311, 319
Employment Service, U.S. Department of Labor, 301–320, 353.
See also Rural Manpower Service
and CAMPS, 308
and CAP, 307, 308, 309, 316
and CEP, 308, 309
and CETA, 265, 269, 291, 297, 315, 316, 357
and disadvantaged, 307–309, 315, 318–319
establishment, 302, 316
funding, 252, 270, 315
and guidance, 154
and Indians, 447–448
internal training, 355
and Job Corps, 306
and JOBS, 258, 308
as labor exchange, 312–314, 487
labor market data, 287
management, 311–312
and MDTA, 297, 304, 305, 356
1965 review, 308–309
1969 reorganization, 309
and NYC, 306
use by blacks, 400
and veterans, 303, 313
and WIN, 308, 320
and YOCs, 306
Employment Service On-Line Placement System, 310
Equal employment opportunity, 592–593. *See also* Civil Rights Act
of 1964; Department of Justice;
EEOC; OFCC
effectiveness, 353
emergence, 254
and ES, 317
Equal Employment Opportunity
Commission, U.S., 89, 397, 452–476 *passim*
Equal Pay Act of 1963, 88, 89
Equal Rights Amendment, 85, 89
Ethridge v. *Rhodes*, 477 n
European Economic Community, 563
Executive Order 9328, 495, 500 n
Executive Order 11246, 89, 455, 462, 464, 465
Executive Order 11598, 312
External labor markets, 120–125

F

Fair Labor Standards Act
and apprenticeship, 211
provision, 88, 89
and shorter workweek, 18, 20
and youth unemployment, 59
Family allowances, 339–340
Family Assistance Plan, 340–341
Farm Labor Contractor Registration
Act of 1963, 423
Federal Committee on Apprenticeship, 201, 460
Federal Power Commission, U.S., 454
Female family heads. *See* Women, as
family heads
Fiscal policy. *See* Macroeconomic
policies
Fitzgerald Act. *See* National Apprenticeship Act of 1937
Food stamps, 324, 338
Ford Foundation, 254
Forecasts
of labor supply, 100–101, 103–105
methods, 99–100, 109–110
by occupation, 106–109
in planning, 287–288
uses, 101–103
France, 46, 541, 562
Frictional unemployment, 37, 40, 41,
43, 56, 484

G

Gaynor v. *Rockefeller*, 461, 477 n
General Classification Test, 204
Geographical mobility. *See also* Braceros; Immigration
BIA programs, 442–444
blacks, 385–389
extent, 24, 85
under MDTA, 306
Mexican Americans, 422–424
from rural areas, 553–555
George-Barden Vocational Education
Act of 1946, 201
George-Deen Vocational Education
Act, 523
Germany, Federal Republic of, 46,
73, 562
Ghana, 506
G. I. Bill of Rights
apprenticeship, 202
and higher education, 146, 149, 162,
174, 249
Gordon Committee. *See* President's
Committee to Appraise Employment and Unemployment
Statistics
Great Britain, 22, 45, 46, 541, 543, 566
manpower policy, 557, 562
Great Depression

birth rates during, 31, 104, 174
and manpower statistics, 93, 96
reestablishment of ES, 302
rise of unions, 503–504, 510, 518
shorter workweek, 18
Social Security Act passed, 321
unemployment during, 36–37
Green carders, 420–422
Greenleigh Associates, 314, 320 n
Gregory v. *Litton Systems, Inc.*, 454
Griggs v. *Duke Power Co.*, 454
Guaranteed employment, 340
Guaranteed income, 339. *See also*
FAP
Guidance and counseling, 154
Guideposts, wage and price. *See*
Wage and price controls

H

Head Start, 161
Health Manpower Act, 269
Hicks v. *Crown Zellerbach Corp.*, 471,
472, 477 n
Higher education
community colleges, 159–160
costs and benefits, 171–175
enrollments, 172, 175–177
expenditures, 170
of Indians, 436–437
labor market characteristics, 186–
193
occupational mobility, 21
postgraduate supply and demand,
181–185
scope, 170
socioeconomic status of students,
193–197
undergraduate supply and demand,
174, 176–181, 191–193
Hometown plans, 462–469, 473. *See
also* Chicago Plan; Philadelphia Plan; Washington Plan
Hughes Tool case, 452, 472
Human capital theory, 120, 162 ff., 255
Human resource development
in economic development, 535–537
and ES, 307
role of education, 143 ff.
Human Resource Development Institute. *See* AFL-CIO

I

Immigration
and geographical mobility, 24
historical importance, 59–60, 249
Mexican Americans, 418–420
of skilled manpower, 188
and social mobility, 21
Immigration and Nationality Act of
1952, 419

Immigration and Naturalization Service, U.S. Department of Justice, 421
Income maintenance. *See* AFDC; OASDI; Pensions; UI
Incomes policies, 493–499
India, 506
  manpower policy in, 557, 577–581 *passim*
Indian Health Service, U.S. Department of Health, Education, and Welfare, 434, 435, 439, 449
Indians. *See also* BIA; EDA; IHS
  in CAMPS, 264
  under CETA, 268
  definition, 428
  economic development, 439–441, 449–450
  education, 435–437
  geographic distribution, 428–429
  health, 434, 449
  housing, 434, 449
  income, 430–432
  labor force and employment, 347, 432, 434, 437–439
  in manpower programs, 441–449
  occupations, 434, 438
  population and demography, 428–430
  unemployment and underemployment, 432–433, 438
  in vocational-technical education, 235, 237
Indonesia, 506
Industrial Development Act of 1966 (Great Britain), 560
Industrialization. *See* Economic development
Industrial Training Act of 1964 (Great Britain), 561
Industrial unions. *See* Labor unions
Inflation. *See also* Phillips curve
  causation, 345
  and unemployment, 345, 489–498
Inland Steel Co., 458, 527
Institutional discrimination, 371–372
Institutional training. *See also* Job Corps; MDTA; Vocatioanl education
  BIA programs, 444–445
  development, 348–350
Internal labor markets, 120–126
International Brotherhood of Electrical Workers, 461, 525, 529
International Brotherhood of Teamsters, 515
International Typographical Union, 525
International Union of Operating Engineers, 529

Interstate Commerce Commission, U.S., 92, 423
Interstate Conference of Employment Security Agencies, 303
Investment in human capital. *See* Education; Human capital theory
Irvin v. *Mohawk Rubber Co.*, 477 n
Israel, 506, 582
Italy, 45, 46, 541

J
Japan, 22, 46, 73, 541, 544
  manpower policy in, 557, 566–571
Job Analysis Vocabulary, 310
Job Bank and Screening System, 310
Job banks, 308–309, 319
Job Corps
  assessment, 349
  and CETA, 269, 343
  and ES, 306
  establishment and intent, 253, 254, 256, 261, 265, 346
  funding, 252
  and labor unions, 529
Job matching systems. *See* Computerized job-matching; Job banks
Job Opportunities in the Business Sector
  appraisal, 351–352
  and ES, 308
  establishment, intent, 258, 260
  funding, 252, 258
Job Readiness Postures, 348
Jobs Optional program, 252
Job turnover, 58, 60
Joint Apprenticeship Committee. *See* National Joint Apprenticeship and Training Committee for the Electrical Industry
Joint apprenticeship councils
  role, 202
  tests, 208

K
Korean War
  ES during, 303
  labor supply and demand, 32
  Mexican immigration during, 418
  wage-price controls during, 494–496

L
La alianza, 425–426
Laborers International Union, 529
Labor force
  composition, 28–32
  entry age, 14
  immigrants in, 31–32
  information sources, 91 ff.

Labor force (*Continued*)
military, 29, 32
participation
  by age, 28–31, 57, 60
  defined, 27
  by education, 33, 57
  by race and sex, 31
  role in theory, 118–119
projections, 103–105
retirement from, 14
work life, 14–17
Labor Inventory Communications
  System, 310
Labor market. *See also* Dual labor
  market hypothesis; External
  labor markets; Internal labor
  markets; Queue theory; Radical labor market theories; Vacancy model of labor market
definition, 114–115
imperfections, 136–138
planning, 278–280
theories of, 112 ff.
types of
  mainstream, 131–132
  marginal, 132
  professional, 131
  submarginal, 132–133
Labor mobility. *See* Geographical
  mobility
Labor queue. *See* Queue theory
Labor unions
and apprenticeship, 209–211, 522,
  525
attitudes toward education, 522–525
and career education, 222
collective bargaining problems,
  513–514
control over labor markets, 46, 524
in developing countries, 506–507
development, 316, 501–506
effect on wages, 374, 516–521
and federal manpower programs,
  528–531
influences upon, 507–511
and minorities, 374, 379–380, 386,
  513–514, 524–525
own training program, 525–527
public support for, 510–513
structure and types, 514–516
support for public education, 522–
  523
La causa, 425
Landrum-Griffin Act of 1959, 510
La raza, 426
Latin America, 582
Leisure, 10, 17–19, 20

M
Macroeconomic policies, 482–485, 492–
  493, 499

Manpower Administration, U.S. Department of Labor. *See also*
  BAT; ES; Office of Research
  and Development
and CAMPS, 262
and CEPs, 262
and CETA, 267 ff., 287, 343
and CPS, 91
occupational projections, 103
program decategorization, 265, 266
programs for Indians, 446–449
and remedial education, 528
survey of recent college graduates,
  191
universe of need method, 284, 285
use of administrative records, 92
and WIN, 334–336
Manpower Development and Training Act of 1962. *See also* JOBS;
  Jobs Optional program
appraisal, 401
and CETA, 265, 269, 343
enactment, 251, 256, 261, 346
and ES, 297, 304, 305, 307, 356
funding, 252
and Indians, 446–447
institutional training, 348
labor mobility programs, 306
and labor unions, 528, 529
on-the-job training, 215
research under, 160
skills centers, 160
Manpower planning. *See* Planning
Manpower programs
changing individual vs. changing
  institutions, 346–347
countercyclical use, 485–489
and economic policies, 481 ff.
emergence, 247 ff.
need for, 346
for the 1970s, 587 ff.
in other countries, 557 ff.
tools, 347–361
Manpower statistics
current status, 94–98
development, 92–94
gaps, 98
Marginal productivity theory, 119
Marginal revenue product, 116–117
Market discrimination coefficient,
  365–366
Marquette University, 525
Mechanical Contractors Association,
  525
Medicaid, 324, 338
Mexican Americans
family structure, 394
income and education, 409–410, 412,
  431
labor markets, 415–423

Mexican Americans (*Continued*)
location, 414, 418
and manpower policy, 423–426
number and ages, 406–407, 412, 414
occupations, 415–416
poverty, 414–415
Mexico, 582
Migrant Children Educational Assistance Act of 1960, 423
Military and labor force, 29, 32, 145, 593–594
Minimum wages. *See* Fair Labor Standards Act
Mobility. *See* Geographical mobility; Occupational mobility; Social mobility
Model Cities program, 460, 473
Monetary policy. *See* Macroeconomic policies
Moonlighting, 19
Motivation of workers. *See* Work ethic
Multiworker families, 33–34

N
National Alliance of Businessmen. *See also* JOBS
cooperation with AFL-CIO, 530
establishment of JOBS program, 258
National Apprenticeship Act of 1937, 200
National Association for the Advancement of Colored People, 458, 460, 462
National Commission for Manpower Policy, 268, 269
National Commission on Technology, Automation, and Economic Progress, 111 n
National Electrical Contractors Association, 525
National Employers' Committee for Improvement of State Employment Services, 313
National Industrial Recovery Act, 13
National Joint Apprenticeship and Training Committee for the Electrical Industry, 525
National Labor Relations Act of 1935, 208, 423, 452, 459, 504, 510, 512, 533
National Labor Relations Board, 472, 504
National League of Cities–U.S. Conference of Mayors, 265
National Longitudinal Surveys, 239
National Migrant Workers Program, 424
National Origins Act of 1924, 418

National Planning Association, 106, 107, 111 n
National Urban League, 208, 215–216, 459
National War Labor Board, 494, 495, 504, 511
National Youth Administration, 253
Negative income tax. *See* Guaranteed income
Neighborhood Youth Corps
antecedents, 253
appraisal, 351
and CETA, 343
and ES, 306
funding, 252
and Indians, 446
intent, 261, 551
Neoclassical theory of discrimination
critique, 368–376
explained, 366–368
implications, 381
Neoclassical theory of labor markets, 115–119
Netherlands, The, 22
New Careers program
and CETA, 343
concept, 158, 257
New Federalism, 266
Norris-LaGuardia Act of 1932, 504, 510
Northern Arizona State University, 235
Norway, 557, 562–566

O
Occupational mobility, 20–25
Occupational Outlook Handbook, 103
Office of Civil Rights, U.S. Department of Health, Education, and Welfare, 195, 437
Office of Economic Opportunity, U.S.
and CAMPS, 263
and CEPs, 262
demise of, 343
program decategorization, 265
Office of Education, U.S. Department of Health, Education, and Welfare
and higher education, 177
Project Baseline, 235
Project TALENT, 193–194
sponsored AMIDS, 355
and vocational education, 231–236 *passim*
Office of Federal Contract Compliance, U.S. Department of Labor, 456–476 *passim*
Office of Management and Budget, U.S., 232, 266, 267, 358, 545

Office of Price Administration, 494
Office of Price Stabilization, 495
Office of Research and Development, U.S. Department of Labor, 354
Okun's Law, 39, 483
Old Age, Survivors, and Disability Insurance, 14, 16, 27, 60, 133, 276, 321
On-the-job training. *See also* Internal labor markets; MDTA
  advantages and disadvantages, 213–215, 350–351
  BIA programs, 445–446
  and discrimination, 381
  employers views, 214
  extent, 213
  and unions, 524
Operation Mainstream
  appraisal, 257
  and CETA, 343
  funding, 252
  and Indians, 447
Operation Manpower. *See* AFL-CIO
Outreach, 208, 347, 348, 459, 474

P
Part-time work, 48, 50, 53–55
Pensions, 27, 60
Peripheral workers, 52–56
Phased Implementation Progression, 310
Philadelphia Plan, 455, 456, 463–468 *passim*
Phillips curve
  methods of shifting, 491–492
  rationale, 489–493, 588
Planning, manpower
  applications, 283–292
  by federal government, 275–276
  by the firm, 277
  for the labor market, 278–280
  political considerations, 292–299
  reasons for, 271–275
  at the state and local level, 277–278, 355–361
  steps involved, 280–283
  types, 275 ff.
Plan of Service Automated Reporting System, 311, 319
President's Committee to Appraise Employment and Unemployment Statistics, 94, 98, 111 n
Price controls. *See* Wage and price controls
Productivity
  in agriculture, 248
  and increased earnings, 74–75
  and increased leisure, 17, 19
  by industry, 72–73
  and labor force, 249

measurement, 70–71
  in other countries, 73
Project Baseline, 235
Projections of manpower requirements. *See* Forecasts; Planning
Project TALENT, 193
Public assistance. *See* AFDC
Public Employment Program
  administration, 356, 486, 487
  and CETA, 269
  funding, 252, 270
  and Indians, 448
  intent, 259, 485, 551–552
Public Law 78 (1951), 418
Public Service Careers program
  appraisal, 551–552
  funding, 252
Public service employment. *See also* CETA; NYC; Operation Mainstream; PEP
  effectiveness, 351–352
  as manpower strategy, 256–260, 266, 486–489
Public Works and Economic Development Act of 1965, 256. *See also* Economic Development Administration
Puerto Ricans, 32
  family structure, 394
  income and education, 409–410, 412
  location, 407, 418
  number and ages, 406–407, 412
  occupations, 416
  poverty, 411
Purdue University, 526

Q
Quarles v. *Philip Morris, Inc.,* 470, 471, 472, 477 n
Queue theory, 119, 130, 135–136

R
Race Relations Act of 1968 (Great Britain), 562
Radical labor market theories, 128–130
Railway Labor Act, 452
Recruitment and Training Program, 459
Relief. *See* Public assistance
Relocation. *See* Geographical mobility
Research and development in manpower, 354–355
Revenue Act of 1971, 82, 336
Robinson v. *Lorillard Co.,* 454
Rural areas. *See also* Economic development; Geographical mobility

Rural areas (*Continued*)
  development of, 548–549
  manpower programs for, 551–553
  problems, 550
Rural Manpower Service, U.S. Department of Labor, 424, 551

S

St. Louis Building and Construction
  Trades Council, 461
Scholastic Aptitude Test, 196
School-to-work transition, 153–157
Seasonal unemployment, 39–40, 43, 56
Secondary labor market. *See* Dual
  labor market hypothesis
Secondary workers, 33–34, 52–53, 55–56
Seniority systems
  and discrimination, 469–472, 474
  and OJT, 213
Sheet Metal Workers' International
  Association, 461. *See also U.S.
  v. Sheet Metal Workers and
  IBEW*
Sherman Antitrust Act of 1890, 503
Skills centers. *See* MDTA, skills
  centers
Skill shortages, 46, 189
Smith-Hughes Act of 1917, 201, 253,
  523
Social mobility, 21
Social Security Act of 1935. *See* Aid
  to Families with Dependent
  Children; OASDI; Unemployment insurance; WIN
Soviet Union. *See* Union of Soviet
  Socialist Republics
Spanish Americans. *See also* Braceros; Cubans; Mexican Americans; Puerto Ricans
  definition, 406–407, 413
  demography, 407–408, 412
  education, 408, 410, 412, 413
  immigration, 32
  income, 408–409, 411
  poverty, 411
  and vocational education, 235
Special Committe on Unemployment
  Programs, 304
Special Impact program, 257
State apprenticeship councils, 200–201, 210
State Industrial Occupational Matrix
  System, 287
Structural unemployment, 40–41,
  483–485, 491
Subemployment, 48
Supply and demand in labor markets, 114, 117–119

Supportive services, 352–353. *See
  also* Day care
Sweden, 22, 46

T

Taft-Hartley Act of 1947, 510, 512
Teamsters. *See* International Brotherhood of Teamsters
Trade unions. *See* Labor unions

U

Underemployment, 38, 98
Unemployment. *See also* Cyclical
  unemployment; Deficient demand; Employment and earnings inadequacy; Frictional
  unemployment; Okun's Law;
  Phillips curve; Seasonal unemployment; Structural unemployment; Subemployment; Underemployment
  by age, 58
  causes, 38–42
  characteristics, 42–46
  concepts and methods, 96–98
  duration, 41–42
  and education, 43–44
  extent, 35–37, 45, 61
  by family status, 43
  and GNP, 483
  by industry, 44
  and inflation, 345, 489–493
  in 1960s, 255
  by occupation, 44
  and policy-making, 250–269 *passim*
  by region, 44–45
  structure of, 344–345
Unemployment insurance
  administrative records, 97–98
  and CETA, 265, 343
  and ES, 302, 303, 304
  establishment of, 302, 321
  and labor force participation, 27
Unemployment Insurance Service.
  See ES; Unemployment insurance
Union of Soviet Socialist Republics,
  73, 539–540
  manpower policy in, 557, 571–577
Unions. *See* Labor unions
United Association of Journeymen
  and Apprentices of the Plumbing and Pipefitting Trades of
  the U.S. and Canada, 525
United Automobile Workers, 514, 515
United Brotherhood of Carpenters
  and Joiners of America, 515,
  529
United Construction Workers Association, 465, 466

United Kingdom. *See* Great Britain
United Mine Workers, 515, 518
United Packinghouse Workers, 526
U.S. Government. *See* individual departments (for example, Department of Labor, U.S.)
U.S. v. Duke Power Co., 477 n
U.S. v. H. K. Porter, 477 n
U.S. v. International Association of Iron Workers, 477 n
U.S. v. Sheet Metal Workers and IBEW, 477 n
U.S. v. United Papermakers, 477 n
United Steelworkers, 18, 457, 518
Universe of need, 258, 284–286, 290, 346
Upgrading, 23, 25
Urban Employment Survey, 92
Utah Job-Matching System, 310

V
Vacancy model of labor market, 137
Veterans, services for, 303, 313, 531. *See also* G.I. Bill of Rights
Vietnam War, labor markets effects, 32, 37, 259
Vocational education, 230–240, 523

W
Wage and price controls, 494–499
Wage Stabilization Board, 495
Wagner Act. *See* National Labor Relations Act of 1935
Wagner-Peyser Act of 1933. *See* Employment Service
War Manpower Commission, 302
War on Poverty. *See* Economic Opportunity Act
Washington Plan, 456, 457
Welfare. *See* AFDC
West Virginia University, 529
Wetbacks, 419
White carders, 420–422
Whitfield v. United Steelworkers, 470, 477 n
Women. *See also* Day care
    discrimination against, 85–88
    dual roles, 223
    earnings, 192
    as family heads, 79–80
    and higher education, 180–181
    labor force participation, 28, 53–54, 78–85
    nonmarket activities, 88, 95
    occupations, 86
    unemployment, 43, 44
    work-life expectancy, 15–17

Workers Defense League, 208. *See also* Recruitment and Training Program
Work ethic, 10, 93, 225, 590–591
Work Experience and Training Program, 252, 254, 330–332, 338
Work experience programs, 53, 351. *See also* Operation Mainstream
Work Incentive Program. *See also* Aid to Families with Dependent Children
    and CETA, 265, 269, 343
    and ES, 308, 316, 320, 356
    funding, 252, 270
    intent, 260, 338
    1971 amendments, 333–335
    results, 333, 335, 337–338, 354
    services, 332–333, 334–335, 336–337, 551
Working poor, 340
Work life, 14–20
Work Projects Administration, 254, 259
Work relief. *See* Community Work and Training Program; Operation Mainstream; WIN; Work Experience and Training Program
Works Progress Administration, 96
Work-study. *See* Cooperative work-study program
Work time, 17–20
World War I
    black migration during, 386, 388
    ES established, 302
    and labor unions, 509
    Mexican immigration during, 418
World War II
    antidiscrimination activities during, 470
    baby boom after, 28, 31, 104, 174
    birth rates during, 174
    and black migration, 387–388
    day care during, 589
    development of paid holidays, 18
    ES during, 302–303
    labor supply and demand, 32, 37, 145, 248, 398–399
    labor unions during, 504, 510–511
    and Mexican immigration, 418, 527
    spur to education, 145
    wage-price controls during, 494–496
    workweek during, 18

Y
Youth Employment Act of 1963, 253
Youth Opportunity Center, 306